T0299414

Tourism, Transport and Travel Management

The terms travel and tourism are often used interchangeably in tourism literature. This comprehensive textbook provides students with essential knowledge of the intricate relationship existing between travel, transport and tourism.

The book analyses the structure, functions, activities, strategies and practices of each of the sectors in the travel industry, such as airlines, airports, tour operators, travel agencies and cruises. It is structured into six parts, covering all modes of transport (air, land and water), travel intermediation, the tour operation business, and impacts and prospects for the future. International case studies are integrated throughout to showcase practical realities and challenges in the travel industry and to aid students' learning and understanding.

Written in an accessible and engaging style, this is an invaluable resource for students of tourism, hospitality, transport and travel management courses.

M. R. Dileep is a noted tourism academic, author and columnist. His qualifications include M.T.A., MPhil, PhD and IATA diplomas. He has worked for the Ministry of Higher Education, in the Faculty of Tourism, CAS Salalah, Sultanate of Oman; and as Head of Tourism at Kerala Institute of Tourism and Travel Studies (KITTS) and at Pazhassiraja College (Calicut University), Kerala, India.

Tourism, Transport and Travel Management

M. R. Dileep

Routledge
Taylor & Francis Group

LONDON AND NEW YORK

First published 2019
by Routledge
2 Park Square, Milton Park, Abingdon, Oxon OX14 4RN

and by Routledge
52 Vanderbilt Avenue, New York, NY 10017

Routledge is an imprint of the Taylor & Francis Group, an informa business

© 2019 M. R. Dileep

British Library Cataloguing-in-Publication Data
A catalogue record for this book is available from the British Library

Library of Congress Cataloging-in-Publication Data
A catalog record for this book has been requested

ISBN: 978-1-138-55738-3 (hbk)
ISBN: 978-1-138-55744-4 (pbk)
ISBN: 978-1-315-15106-9 (ebk)

Typeset in Frutiger and Sabon
by Apex CoVantage, LLC

Visit the eResources: www.routledge.com/9781138557383

Contents

Contents

Contents

PART IV
Travel intermediation   215

Contents

figures

Tables

Case studies

Preface

Describing tourism as "one of the largest industries in the world" is a cliché, often used in tourism literature of the last two decades or so. Certainly, when combining the travel and tourism industries, it is a massive economic sector that could cater, in varying degrees, to a wide range of socio-economic needs of societies across the world. Though the travel industry is often mentioned within the ambit of the tourism industry, it also serves a large section of travellers other than those categorized as tourists. In spite of the fact that travel is a fundamental component of tourism, a clear distinction can be made between the two. However, both terms are used interchangeably in the parlance of tourism for the sake of convenience. The travel industry itself is an amalgam of industries which includes a wide variety of sub-sectors, such as airlines, airports, tour operators, travel agencies, cruises, luxury tourist trains, automobiles and coaches. In other words, the sector, which offers various products and services that can satisfy the needs and wants of the travelling population, consists not only of the transport industries but also some other sectors that enable easy and convenient access to travel products. Certainly, all these sectors, including tourism, are inextricably linked and depend on one another.

This comprehensive book has been structured in a manner to elucidate in detail the intricate relationship existing between travel, transport and tourism and their functioning. Its focus areas include an introduction of tourism in general; its link with travel; air transport; airline operations and management; airport functioning; the roles played by land and water transportation in tourism; the way the travel industry products are distributed; the value being added during the process of tour operation; functioning and management of tour operation businesses; and the nuances of tour guiding. Utmost care has been taken to include almost all areas of the travel sector connected to both domestic and international tourism. The demand and supply patterns, influencing factors, impact of information technology in travel intermediation, and impacts of mass travel and tourism are also dealt with in detail.

This book is organized into six parts, covering all modes of transport (air, land and water), travel intermediation, the tour operation business, and impacts and prospects for the future. The first part, "Tourism and transport", includes two chapters. The chapter titled "Travel and tourism: An introduction" presents the concept of tourism and its rather intricate and inevitable relationship with travel. It introduces the evolution of tourism and travel motivators. The concept of the tourism industry, along with an explanation of its components, is also discussed in the first chapter. The next chapter begins with an introduction of various aspects of transportation along with its relevance and significance in tourism. It also includes a discussion on the relationship between tourism and transport, the spatial interaction and accessibility aspect of tourism, elements of transport, and the linkages among various modes of transport.

The next part of the book covers air transport and its growing significance from a tourism point of view. The first chapter introduces air transport. After the conceptualization and detailing of air transportation and aviation, the evolution and growth of air transport are described. The focus areas cover the elements of air transport; major regulations related to air transportation; and safety aspects in aviation. The next chapter begins with an explanation of the concept of the airport and is followed by its functions. Also covered in this chapter are: airports as commercial entities and their customers and partners; the structure of an airport; physical and service components of airside, air traffic control, etc.; an introduction of the terminal and processes inside; elements of airside; airport certification and standardization; revenue sources of the airport; organizational structure; privatization; and the airport codes. The successive chapter details airport operations. A brief about various operations that fall under ground handling, such as passenger handling, ramp handling and aircraft turnaround, is provided, along with the equipment, systems and technologies required for those operations. There is also a brief discussion on the functions of passenger terminal operations, passenger handling, flow through the terminal, handling within the terminal and direct passenger services.

The third chapter in this part covers the functioning and management of an airline. At the beginning of the chapter, the airline is conceptualized as an industry. This is followed by a discussion of its characteristics and the products offered. Various aspects of passenger transportation, including handling passengers, customer service in airlines, in-flight services and classes of service, are detailed. Customer relationship management practices of airlines are introduced with the help of frequent flyer programmes. Route development and flight scheduling are also introduced in this chapter, while there is further elaboration on fleet planning, together with fleet assignment and the relevant methods. Crew scheduling is described along with crew pairing and crew rostering. This is followed by descriptions of other functions, such as passenger processing, revenue management and maintenance activities. While discussing the international operation of airlines, the concepts of "hub and spoke systems" and "code sharing" are provided in detail. A brief about airline marketing is also part of this chapter.

The next part looks at surface transportation. Its first chapter introduces all land-based transport forms, especially from a tourism point of view. Once road transportation is introduced, the relationship between road transport and tourism is explored in detail. A brief on each of the various forms of bus services as well as the automotive services in tourism is then provided. It is followed by a description of rail transport and its role in tourism. Major rail transport systems in the world and luxury tourist trains, particularly in Europe, Africa and Asia, are discussed in this chapter. The chapter on cruise tourism is a highlight of the book. As a prelude, water transportation is introduced at the beginning of the chapter and followed by a discussion on its role in tourism. After an introduction on cruises, we cover their history and growth, benefits, types, facilities and services on board, and major routes. The demand and market segments of cruise tourism are also described. Apart from cruise tourism, other forms of water transport (from a tourism point of view) are also introduced.

Travel intermediation is the focus of the next part of the book. The chapter entitled "Travel intermediaries" discusses the nature and type of distribution in the travel and tourism sectors. After the introduction, the structure of the distribution system and the functions of the channels are discussed. A description of travel and tourism intermediaries and the levels of tourism distribution follow, along with their significance and benefits. All types of tourism intermediaries are briefly introduced. The factors associated with disintermediation are then explained in the context of the Internet's increasing significance. The next chapter begins with an explanation of the business of a travel agency. We then discuss the functions and activities of travel agents and various types of travel agencies, along with the impact of the Internet on travel agency business and the challenges faced by travel agencies today. In the next chapter we look at electronic distribution. A detailed discussion of global distribution systems (GDSs) is then provided, along with their evolution. Various information-based strategies of GDSs such as display bias, the halo effect and commission overrides are revealed for understanding the strategies of GDSs on a practical level. Airline reservation systems, online travel agents, mobile travel agent, destination information systems and other online intermediaries are also detailed.

Another highlight in the book is the part on tour operation, which is very comprehensive and informative for students pursuing a career in tourism. The first chapter in this part illustrates the concept of tour operation. A description of the evolution of tour operation and the current status are also provided. An attempt is made to conceptualize the product, supplier and consumer of this industry. Various types of tour operators are featured along with examples. Contributions and benefits of tour operation for various stakeholders of the industry are explained in detail. The business environments of tour operators and the risks associated with running a tour operation business are also described. Next, we look at the complex decision-making and buying behaviour of customers of this business. The next chapter covers the package tour, which is defined and conceptualized. This is followed by a discussion of the importance of package tours in tourism. Characteristics of package tours are elucidated along with a detailed discussion of the benefits of package tours. The chapter also covers the elements of package tours after introducing their various types. As part of the discussion of a package tour's planning and designing process, we look at activities such as research, destination selection, planning, identification of suppliers and negotiation with suppliers, itinerary preparation, and costing and pricing. The concept of tour itinerary and the principles/guidelines of itinerary design, difference in tour costing and pricing, cost elements (variable and fixed) and pricing strategies are also elaborated on.

Marketing is a vital function of the tour operation business, especially due to the unique characteristics of the package tour. Various aspects of marketing a package tour are detailed in the third chapter of this part, and different market segments are introduced. Tangible representation of the intangible holiday product is crucial in the marketing of holidays. And from that perspective, the role of brochures is discussed. We then describe the marketing mix and the common product mix in the tour operation business.

The next chapter details all the necessary activities that follow a brochure launch and the commencement of marketing. The major activities explained in this chapter include administration activities, booking, documentation, pre-tour activities, transfer, pre-departure meeting, tour execution, overseas operations, post-tour activities and follow-up. This is followed by the role played by the tour manager/tour leader, the documents to be arranged prior to international travel, and how to handle accidents and emergencies. The significance of customer satisfaction and the causes of dissatisfaction in the context of tour operation are also discussed. The concept of tour guiding is also well covered in this chapter.

The last part identifies the consequences of mass travel and tourism and the possible measures to ameliorate the adverse effects. We look at the various consequences of travel and tourism, particularly those associated with mass travel and tourism, and the haphazard development of facilities, attractions and infrastructure to lure tourists. This chapter discusses the benefits and costs of tourism, and the specific impacts on each sphere of life – economic, social, cultural and environment. Additionally, the link between climate change and tourism is introduced. The part ends with a discussion of the possible measures to ensure the progress of sustainable development of travel and tourism. It includes concepts like sustainable development, visitor management, carrying capacity, environmental impact assessment and environmental management practices. Ongoing carbon emissions reduction practices in aviation are also introduced.

Written in an engaging style and at the appropriate level for students of tourism, hospitality, transport and/or travel management, this book covers in sufficient detail the above-mentioned topics. International case studies are integrated throughout the book to showcase practical realities and challenges in the travel industry and to aid students' learning and understanding. These will provide the reader with a thorough understanding of the intricate relationships in the tourism, travel and transport sectors, and their symbiotic and collective functioning, which makes tourism one of the largest industries in the world.

Dr Dileep, M. R.

Acknowledgements

First and foremost, I humbly tender my wholehearted gratitude to God Almighty for the blessings He has bestowed upon me and for giving me the strength and wisdom to achieve this dream.

This book was brought to fruition through hard work, patience and perseverance along with the support I received from a large number of people. It was not just one or two people who helped me at different stages of my academic career and I am indebted to each and every one of them.

I have immense pleasure in acknowledging all my colleagues and friends at Pahas-siraja College (Pulpally, Kerala, India), Kerala Institute of Tourism and Travel Studies (KITTS, Thiruvananthapuram) and the College of Applied Sciences (Ministry of Higher Education), Sultanate of Oman. Also, I am happy to express my thanks to all the office bearers and members of the Indian Tourism and Hospitality Congress (ITHC), which is the highest body of tourism academics in India. Many of my students who are now in different parts of the world in different positions encouraged me to do better and I personally thank all of them. Moreover, my friends always inspired my accomplishments and I am grateful to them.

The work would not have been successful without the support and prayers of my family members and relatives. I am grateful to all of them for their unconditional support and care, especially my wife, Soorya A. N.; son, Gautham Krishna; father, Mr Madhavakurup; mother, Mrs Radhika Devi; father-in-law, Mr V. K. N. Panicker; and mother-in-law, Mrs Ambika Devi.

Dr Dileep, M. R.

Tourism and transport

Part I

Tourism and transport

Chapter 1

Travel and tourism: an introduction

1.1 Introduction

Tourism has inevitably grown from a rather limited aristocratic activity to a common phenomenon in modern society. During this evolution, the phenomenon has passed a number of milestones, transforming itself into a modern form which permeates deep into the social life of almost all societies in the world. This multifaceted phenomenon has already demonstrated its persuasive economic significance, irresistibly luring both private developers and governments to hastily promote it. Certainly, there are many reasons to suggest why the tourism industry is being so hastily developed by many countries. While domestic tourism contributes greatly to wider redistribution of income, international tourism is more important to the industry as it generates foreign currency through transaction of "invisibles" with consumers from abroad. Many millions of jobs are created by tourism every year and the revenue being generated from the expenditure made by tourists in different stages of their journey is immense. As per the latest figures released by the United Nations World Tourism Organization (UNWTO), receipts from international tourists' spending on accommodation, food and drink, entertainment, shopping, other services and goods reached an estimated US $1,220 billion in 2016 (UNWTO, 2017).

Table 1.1 International tourist arrivals

Region	Sub-regions	1990	2000	2005	2010	2015	2016
World		435	683	803	949	1,189	1,235
Europe		261.5	393.3	438	488.9	603.7	616.2
	Northern Europe	28.7	43.7	51.0	62.8	75.4	80.2
	Western Europe	108.6	139.7	142.6	154.4	181.4	181.5
	Central/Eastern Europe	33.9	69.2	87.8	98.4	121.4	126.0
	South/Med. Europe	90.3	140.8	157.9	173.3	225.5	228.5
Asia and the Pacific		55.8	109.3	155.3	205.4	284.0	308.4
	North-East Asia	26.4	58.3	87.5	111.5	142.1	154.3
	South-East Asia	21.2	35.6	49.3	70.5	104.2	113.2
	Oceania	6.2	9.2	10.5	11.4	14.3	15.6
	South Asia	3.1	6.1	8.0	12	23.4	25.3
Americas		92.8	128.2	133.2	150.1	192.7	199.3
	North America	71.8	91.5	89.9	99.5	127.5	130.5
	Caribbean	11.4	17.1	18.8	19.5	24.1	25.2
	Central America	1.9	4.3	6.3	7.9	10.2	10.7
	South America	7.7	15.3	18.2	23.1	30.8	32.8
Africa		14.7	27.9	37.3	49.5	53.4	57.8
	North Africa	8.4	10.2	13.9	18.8	18.0	18.6
	Sub-Saharan Africa	6.3	17.7	23.4	30.8	35.4	39.2
Middle East		9.6	24.4	38.0	54.7	55.6	53.6

Source: UNWTO (2017)

On the one hand, tourist destinations and governments are engaged in developing and promoting tourism rigorously, while people, on the other hand, are being persuaded to visit and experience tourism. The "travel propensity" has already permeated almost all societies in the world. The surging travel propensity and the consequential growth in the demand for services have invigorated the worldwide expansion of the tourism sector. Of late, tourist destination countries are facing intense competition in attracting tourists, thus increasing the dynamism and innovation in the tourism sector. Tourists therefore get more options, not only in what they see, but also in their experience. As commonly predicted, tourism is poised to grow further, and will remain a very competitive sector, particularly in terms of economic and social contributions.

Though the economic contribution of tourism is getting increasingly crucial, the ramifications of the development do invite some criticism. Environmental, social and cultural consequences of tourism have become a matter of concern, particularly since the end of the 1960s. The increasing rate of anti-tourism propaganda, as well as the growing concerns on the negative impact of tourism, has prompted the search for alternatives and an evolution of a number of development options in the sector. Of these, ecotourism has emerged as a major measure of tourism development, especially in the pristine natural areas; the sustainable development concept has also become a general philosophy of tourism development across the entire sector. Yet tourism, to a large extent, remains a matter of concern socially, culturally and environmentally.

1.2 Travel: the fundamental element of tourism

Movement is one prime reason for the transformation of human beings from the early days of secluded, animal-like beings to the modern social lifestyle humans enjoy today. Movement turns into travel when it is across a certain distance (though there is no accepted *specific* distance for movement to be considered travel). The nature, style, mode, speed, comfort and safety when travelling has transformed over time, surpassing many milestones. In usual contexts, travel is also referred to as a journey from one place to another. A journey can also be made to visit a place. It means that travel can be for various purposes, which include visiting too. Visiting entails travel, and some of those who take part in visiting are called tourists based on certain parameters accepted internationally. This denotes that tourism involves visiting a place of interest, and is essentially a result of travel from one place to another. The following extract from the UNWTO clarifies the relationship:

> *Travel* refers to the activity of travellers. A traveller is someone who moves between different geographic locations, for any purpose and any duration. The visitor is a particular type of traveller and consequently tourism is a subset of travel.
>
> (UNWTO, n.d.)

The above extract makes it clear that there are many types of travel, and with different purposes, but travel for visiting can be considered tourism. All visitors are not considered tourists. The reasons are discussed in the following paragraphs. All tourists are visitors and all visitors are travellers. However, all travellers are not visitors and all travellers are not tourists. Tourism is an activity emanating from visiting of people, and visiting takes place as a result of travel from one place to another. Two geographical locations are involved, primarily in tourism. One is the tourist generating location and the other is the tourist visiting location. There has to be a certain amount of distance between these two locations. The tourist commences travel from the generating location, covers the distance and reaches the destination location. Once the visiting is over in the destination, the tourist returns to the generating location. Travel for visiting, therefore, involves primarily two sets of journeys: onward journey to destination and return. The following elaboration about tourism and its various dimensions will help to explain the concept thoroughly.

1.3 Tourism: the concept and definitions

Tourism is obviously a multidisciplinary subject and should be perceived and learned from a wide range of perspectives. This makes it difficult to conceive of the concept of tourism, not only for a beginner, but also for serious researchers of its nuances and inherent characteristics. Smith (1995) is of the opinion that lack of a consistent and accepted definition is a continuing source of frustration for tourism planners and analysts. Even a limited literature review can identify a wide range of tourism definitions. Some approach tourism from a sociological perspective, while others circle around environment and physical development. The cultural view is common, as is the psychological approach towards tourism movement. A number of definitions can be found from an industry perspective, whereas definitions from an economic perspective are more considered across the world. In order to learn the concept of tourism, it would be of value to look at some definitions propounded by some experts.

Davidson (1989) defines tourism, in the simplest way, as being "about people being away from their own homes, on short term, temporary visits, for particular purposes". Though short, this includes some major fundamental aspects of tourism, such as travel to distant places, limited duration of the travel and the need for a purpose to travel. The World Tourism Organization (WTO), the global agency representing the official/national tourism organizations (currently UNWTO), defines it as "the activities of persons travelling to and staying in places outside their usual environment for not more than one consecutive year for leisure, business and other purposes" (WTO, 1991). This specifies the maximum period of stay as far as a tourist is concerned.

The definition given by Bull (1991) is as follows: "It's a human activity that encompasses human behavior, use of resources, and interaction with other people, economies and environments". This highlights the vital clues about resource consumption as part of tourism, and the social aspects related to interaction that take place between the tourist and the host community, the interface between tourists and economies as well as the environments. A more commonly accepted definition is that it is the "temporary movement of people to destinations outside their normal places of work and residence, the activities undertaken during their stay in those destinations and the facilities created to cater to their needs" (Hunt and Layne, 1991). McIntosh and Goeldner (1990) interpreted tourism from various perspectives by considering different groups that participate in, and are affected by, the tourism industry. According to them, "tourism is the sum of the phenomena and relationship arising from the interaction of tourists, business suppliers, host governments and host community in the process of attracting and hosting those tourists and other visitors". The major groups identified were the tourist, the business providing goods and services to tourists, the host community and the government.

Cooper et al. (2000) define tourism from both the demand side and the supply side perspectives. The demand side definition has evolved by firstly attempting to encapsulate the idea of tourism into conceptual definitions and secondly through the development of technical definitions for measurement of tourism as well as for legal purposes. The conceptual interpretation of their definition involves a number of aspects, including the major factors such as short-term and temporary movement of people. Movement is from the usual environment or normal places of residences and work to a distant place, and staying and engaging in touristic activities in the place visited (Cooper et al., 2000; Burkart and Medlik, 1981). They highlight the technical aspects as well, which include a minimum visiting period of 24 hours, a maximum visiting period of one year, and with the purpose of the visit being one of the internationally recognized categories of purposes. The supply side perspectives focus on the supply of services and products offered by a wide range of businesses involved in the tourism and associated sectors to satisfy the needs of the tourists, and the requisite facilities and amenities.

Here, only a few definitions have been considered, although a number of definitions are available. The above analysis reveals that tourism can be viewed from different perspectives, and certain factors are vital in considering some kind of travel as tourism. Indeed, travel is part and parcel of many people's day-to-day life but is not considered tourism. The necessary aspects for the conceptualization of a tourism framework are listed below:

- Tourism involves movement of people from one place to another.
- The travel takes place due to physical or psychological reasons, or both.
- The movement has to be from the place of residence and/or work to a distant place.

- The visit has to take place in a different environment from the usual, day-to-day life environment.
- A minimum stay of one day (24 hours) in the place visited is required.
- The stay should not extend beyond one year, consecutively.
- The tourist visiting a place may have to take part in certain activities, such as sightseeing.
- The tourist, during the entire process of travel, should not directly take part in any activity that would enable him or her to earn money as remuneration.
- Throughout the travel process (from departure from usual residence until return to the same), the traveller will have a variety of needs, all of which will constitute the elements that contribute to the tourist experiences.
- Different businesses offer services and products that satisfy those various needs.
- The traveller spends money to buy those services and products offered, and this constitutes an economic activity.
- During the travel process, the tourist will interact with different groups of people ranging from service providers to local community members.
- The tourism-related businesses and facilities use a variety of resources, both natural and artificial, in order to cater for the requirements of tourists. Consequently, tourists become the consumers of those resources directly or indirectly.
- During the process of provision of services and products to tourists as well as the consumption by them, a range of benefits as well as consequences will be generated on the environment, society, culture and the economy.
- Tourism takes place in an open environment and the external environment influences it in different ways.

Thus, tourism is a social process that involves short-term movement of people from a place of usual environment to a distant one, staying there for at least 24 hours, and engaging in certain activities that are non-remunerative in nature. During the course of the stay, the traveller interacts with a variety of host communities and consumes a range of services and products offered by different businesses and facilities, which generates an economic activity with positive as well as negative social, cultural and environmental ramifications.

1.4 Traveller, visitor, excursionist and tourist

The tourist and the rest of the travellers are conceptually well distinguished in tourism literature, though the terms traveller and tourist are used interchangeably. A tourist is basically a traveller and is the most crucial element in the process of tourism. The phenomenon called tourism won't be generated in the absence of a tourist. It has already been pointed out that all travellers are not tourists. Some of them travel for the purpose of visiting, whereas others travel for many other purposes. Of those travelling for the purpose of visiting, some will spend less than 24 hours in the place visited, whereas others may stay for more time. This makes the traveller a broad group consisting of a large population with varied purposes of travel, and a visitor is just one segment among them. Visitors include tourists, who are distinguished by staying for a minimum period of 24 hours in the place visited, and others who stay for less than 24 hours can be called **same-day tourists, day visitors** or **excursionists.** Here the terms are traveller, visitor, tourist and excursionist and they are fundamentally distinguished based on the duration of their stay in the place visited along with the nature of the purpose of travelling.

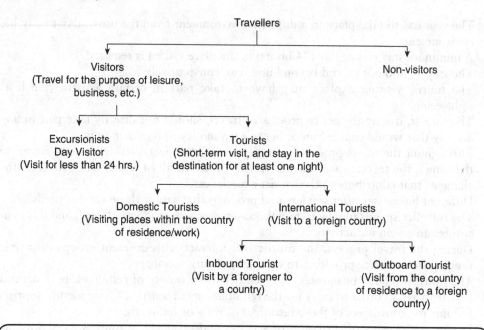

Figure 1.1 Travellers, visitors and tourists

The grouping of travellers into visitor, tourist and excursionist by the WTO makes the concept clearer. According to WTO, a **visitor** is a person who travels with a non-remunerative objective to a foreign country, outside his/her "usual environment", for a period not exceeding one year. The same factors apply in the case of domestic visitor as well, except the maximum duration may be up to six months and the place being visited has to be inside the country of origin. At the same time, an **international tourist** is defined as a visitor who travels to a country other than that in which he/she has his usual residence or work, and stays in the destination visited for at least one night but no more than one year; and whose main purpose of visit is for certain activities that may not be aimed at earning money. On the other hand, a **domestic tourist**'s travel takes place within the country. A **same-day visitor** or **excursionist** is described as a visitor who travels to a destination other than that in which he/she has his/her usual residence, returns within 24 hours without spending the night in the country visited, and whose main purpose of visit is other than the exercise of an activity remunerated from within the place visited (WTO, 1991).

Based on the above discussion, we can identify a range of factors that can be used to distinguish tourists from other types of travellers:

- A tourist is a traveller as well as a visitor.
- The travel has to be to a place away from the usual place of residence and work.
- The minimum period of time spent in the destination visited has to be 24 hours (spend at least one night).
- The stay in a destination visited should not exceed one year.
- The purpose of travel ranges widely, but it has to be one among the international classifications, such as leisure, recreation, rest and relaxation.

- The main purpose of travelling should not be for exercising an activity remunerated from the destination visited.
- Along with staying at the tourist destination, the tourist will engage in a variety of activities which may differ from what he/she engages in while in their usual place of residence and work.
- From the commencement of the travel, until the return, the tourist will spend money so as to consume various services and products as per his/her requirements.
- The tourist ultimately gets a kind of experience from the entire process, usually referred to as the tourist experience.

Considering the gist of all such factors, a tourist can be defined simply as a visitor, travelling to a place away from his/her usual place of work and residence for a minimum period of 24 hours that will not extend beyond a year, who engages in non-remunerated activities at the place visited.

1.5 Basic classifications of tourism

Although tourism can be classified on various bases, the most fundamental classification is based on the origin and destination countries. According to this classification, tourism can be divided into two types: international and domestic. In **international tourism,** both origin and destination are two different countries; the destination is a foreign country to the tourist and the travel involves crossing the borders of countries. The tourist belonging to this category makes an international journey using any mode of transport – by air, sea or land. The destination country is also referred to as the host country, and it would prefer to have more tourist inflows from foreign countries for economic reasons. In the case of international tourism, the travel between the origin country and destination is rather an intricate affair in most of the cases due to the visa requirements and other terms and conditions existing, as well as the travel formalities that must be adhered to while crossing the borders. Yet, there are very liberal conditions that exist between countries in certain regions, for example, international travel is easier among some of the European countries as well as among Gulf Cooperation Council (GCC) countries. On the other hand, **domestic tourism** is the term used to describe tourism activities that take place in the tourist's own country. Here, the countries of origin and destination are the same. There is economic relevance in domestic tourism as well since it helps to redistribute income through expenditures made by tourists inside the country.

Inbound and outbound tourism can be considered two forms of international tourism. **Inbound tourism** refers to visits by foreigners to a country. Here, the use of inbound and outbound tourism is based on the comparison between host and origin countries and their populations. For instance, when a Briton visits France for tourism purposes, then, according to the French, he or she can be called an inbound tourist. This can be further described as the phenomenon arising out of a visit by a foreigner into one's country. Simply put, it involves visits to a country by non-residents. On the other hand, **outbound tourism** is also international tourism, but the term applies to the origin country. For instance, in the above example, as far as Britain is concerned, the British tourist is an outbound tourist, whereas for France, the same tourist is an inbound tourist. Basically, the term "outbound tourist" refers to tourists who leave their country of origin to visit another country, and outbound tourism is concerned with residents of a country visiting other countries.

1.6 Evolution of tourism

Tourism is not something that emerged during a particular period of time in history. Indeed, it would be challenging to specify the evolution in its fullest sense. A glance over tourism literature would give a hint that travel, the bare form of tourism, came about when people began to move from their "usual environment" for certain reasons that can be considered touristic purposes, and such events have been discovered even in the ancient periods. From the stage marked as "Food Gatherers", the phenomenon of travel has been progressing constantly. Travel gained increased momentum at certain times, such as when trade began, the wheel was introduced, rail transport became widespread, the steam engine was invented, and commercial air transport began. The emergence of the accommodation industry also spurred the growth of travel. By the eighteenth century, the term tourism came into use and the formal set-up of tourism from an industrial perspective began to emerge. Trade-related travel was the dominant form of travel during the early periods of history. The invention of the wheel improved the speed of travel: men could now cover greater distances, which stimulated more travel. "Inns", the early form of accommodation, also emerged in order to provide the basic facilities for travellers of those times. Along with transport over land, out of curiosity, man ventured out onto the oceans as well, which led to the "Sailor" stage.

In Greek history, a number of events can be considered early forms of tourism. For instance, Greek tourists, during the third century BC, travelled to visit the healing gods. The same traces can be seen in Egyptian history. Educational and recreational travel was also present during the classical period, and even before that, in Egypt under the Pharaohs. The Greeks had the same travel tendency; for instance they travelled to the Oracle and participated in the ancient Olympic Games. The Roman period also recorded a grand episode in the evolution of travel and tourism. Romans created an excellent network of roads, and transportation and communication systems, in order to manage and maintain the empire. Also, "inns" of some kind were established beside long routes. Some instances of pleasure travel as well as outbound travel were also seen in this era. The "rich and the aristocratic" engaged in recreation activities, travelling to beaches in Egypt and Greece. That period before the Common Era was highlighted as a golden epoch of travel; the later periods recorded a negative trend in travel and tourism growth. The period from the fifth to the fifteenth century is regarded as the "dark era" of tourism.

The centuries that followed the dark era became crucial in the evolution of travel and tourism, as those were associated with the grand inventions and discoveries that changed the world. The social transformation that followed the Renaissance and the emergence of science and technology transformed human life, and consequentially travel increased greatly in all its dimensions and aspects. The **grand tour**, a term used to refer to a special kind of tour of European culture by aristocratic young men, was marked as a great point in the evolution of tourism. Italy, France and other countries in Europe became important hubs. And Paris, Rome, Florence and other cultural centres were visited by scholars eager for education. It is usually distinguished in terms of class, which would determine the places visited and the mode of travel. Towner (1985) points out that the grand tour, which commenced sometime in the seventeenth century and extended until the nineteenth century, was undertaken by the wealthy of Western European society for purposes mainly including culture, education, health and pleasure. The Industrial Revolution is another grand episode in history that also contributed greatly to shaping tourism into its modern form. The Industrial Revolution had a huge impact on travel.

It brought in mechanization of production which tremendously improved productivity, which in turn increased employment opportunities and income levels of people. Also, the continuous work with machines caused monotony in life which forced people to seek out rest and relaxation, away from their working context. Due to advancements in travel technology, the transportation sector experienced huge changes and progress. By then, mechanized companies started to provide "paid holidays". In addition, the lifestyle of people changed over time, and rest and relaxation became inevitable in the life of working employees. All such factors directly and indirectly facilitated the growth of tourism.

Among those factors and events that contributed to the growth of tourism, the development undertaken by Thomas Cook to commence organized tour programmes has been considered revolutionary, especially since it paved the way for a new sector in tourism called tour operation. In 1841, he organized an excursion for 570 members from Leicester to Loughborough, using a train hired exclusively for the trip, at a fare of one shilling. This incident is described in detail later in this book. The accommodation sector was also established and diversified toward the end of the nineteenth century as new forms of accommodation emerged. Hotels had been established in major cities by then and hotel chains began to enter the scene, upgrading the quality of services provided in many locations.

The twentieth century turned out to be crucial in the growth of tourism. The period in which the developments occurred can be clearly divided into two eras, namely the years leading up to the Second World War, and the years after the Second World War. In the first era, growth was at a slow pace and occurred mainly due to the changes that took place in transportation technology. The emergence of the aviation industry as a consequence of the Wright brothers' invention of the aircraft in 1903 was a major milestone, followed by the introduction of the automobile by Henry Ford in 1908. The First World War left a large number of small aircraft used in the war along with experienced technicians and vital crew resources. Later, the aircraft were used for air transport, especially for short distances and for carrying small numbers of passengers. Charter air services began around that time and commercial passenger air transportation had gained prominence by the mid-1930s, with significant progress since then. The Second World War impacted on travel and tourism in different ways, too. The technological breakthroughs which occurred in aircraft design led to the scaling up of air transport as the most viable alternative to shipping for international travel. By the 1950s, air transport had become an important mode of transport across the world.

The post-Second World War era nourished tourism in an astounding manner. A plethora of factors contributed to the growth of tourism during that time. The advent of jet engines and their use for commercial air transport resulted in increased speeds, safety and comfort along with a decrease in the cost of travel due to larger capacity of aircraft. Wide-body jet aircraft came into common use by the 1970s. Enclave tourism in the form of a fully fledged resort came into being during this period. "Club Mediterannee" (1955), the "Club Soleil" (1966) and the "Radisson Club" (1970) are some examples of ideal enclave tourism forms which emerged in the post-war era. The antagonism which had existed among countries lessened considerably, which in turn helped in the gradual improvement of international understanding. This eventually eased movement barriers between countries. Technological advancements in various spheres, especially in transport technology, led to increases in travel tendency. Social changes also facilitated the evolution of tourism. Employment opportunities increased and the level of disposable income of the populations also increased. Lured by the development potential, Third

World countries, especially those in East Asia and Africa, hastily began to develop tourism. This opened up more options for people to visit. The deregulation of air transportation introduced by the US caused the privatization and liberalization in air transport which eventually resulted in increased competition, competitiveness in airfares and international air travel. The advent of and developments in information technology caused revolutionary changes in tourism, which is another key factor. In between, the concept of amusement parks as full-day holiday parks also started spreading. Disneyland, Sun City and Europa-Park are some of the examples that began operations in many countries. Later periods saw the emergence and spread of globalization across the world, and that resulted in the outbreak of international trade. Business travel has turned out to be a major segment in international travel and consequent developments have taken place in the tourism industry as well, like the proliferation of business hotels in almost all the major cities throughout the world.

Tourism had thus grown, transformed and expanded into a huge industry by the end of the twentieth century. A range of events took place in the century thwarting tourism, but the effects were temporary and tourism has shown extraordinary resilience to quickly overcome those challenges. International tourist arrivals have grown consistently since 1950; and 2012 is marked as an important year because the number of international tourist arrivals reached more than one billion.

1.7 Travel motivations

Understanding travel motivators is crucial for all stakeholders in the tourism sector, particularly for marketers. Knowledge of travel motivation is required in all marketing activities; also, it influences the nature of tourism development. Indeed, a number of reasons why people travel and take part in tourism have been expounded in tourism literature, and have exposed different tourist motivational typologies. Some are somewhat similar, whereas others are viewed from different perspectives. Yet it is rather difficult to have a consensus on a single motivational typology. Obviously, it is not just for one or two reasons that people travel, though some common motivating factors can be found across the world. At times, it is very difficult to establish the exact motivation of tourists. There are hundreds of destinations and thousands of attractions. Choosing a particular one to visit is linked to the motivation of the tourist as well. Tourist motivation therefore has many dimensions, mainly deriving from the tourist's personal traits, involving physical and psychological factors, the tourists' socio-cultural and environmental factors, as well as the factors associated with industry and destination. The ultimate base of motivation is something that can be linked to the "inner urge", yet it is linked to the other factors mentioned above in complex ways.

Holloway and Taylor (2006) contend that tourism motivation can be broadly categorized into general and specific motivations. While the general motivation focuses on achieving a broad objective, the specific one is all about achieving the particular objectives of tourists in order to satisfy their specific needs. Here an attempt is made to correlate the objectives in association with the "needs" of the people, as can be seen in Maslow's hierarchy of needs. For example, in beach tourism, relaxation can be a general motivation, whereas snorkelling or diving in the sea can be a specific objective of travel. General motivation is also defined as "why people choose to become tourists" and specific motivator as "why they choose one destination over another" (Kelly and Nankervis, 2009). Attempts have been made to relate Maslow's theory with tourism motivation.

Crompton's list of motivations is also often cited as a typology of tourist motivation. It includes escape from the mundane environment, exploration and evaluation of self, relaxation and rest, prestige, regression (going back to the point of origin), enhancing relationships with kin, facilitation of social interaction, and novelty (Crompton, 1979).

1.7.1 Some typologies of travel motivations

Plog's (1974) psychographic typology

Allocentric motivators
People who have this category of motivators prefer variety and go for adventurous activities, and their self-confidence is very high.

Psychocentric motivators
Self-centred people prefer familiar and safe destinations.

Mid-centric motivators
The majority of travellers fall in between allocentric and psychocentric categories, i.e. neither too allocentric nor too psychocentric. Some may have near-allocentric motivators whereas some others may have near-psychocentric motivators.

Remumbo travel motivators (also suggested by McIntosh and Goeldner, 1990)

Physical motivators
This constitutes physical and mental reasons such as rest, relaxation, refreshment, pleasure and health, e.g. health tourism and sports tourism.

Cultural motivators
These are mainly related to curiosity – a "desire to see and know" more about other cultures, their art, and cultural varieties and features, e.g. cultural tourism and anthropological tourism.

Interpersonal motivators
This constitutes escape from the routine relationships and interest in meeting new people, visiting friends or relatives, and having different experiences, e.g. visiting friends and relatives (VFR). Spiritual tourism also falls within this category.

Status and prestige motivators
This constitutes a desire for ego enhancement, social recognition, grabbing attention from others and personal development.

Gray's (1970) typology of "wanderlust" and "sunlust"

Wanderlust
This motivation relates to curiosity, "to experience the strange and unfamiliar", e.g. cultural and heritage tourism.

Sunlust
"Search for a better set of amenities than are available at home." For example: travelling to a skiing facility at the top of a snow-clad mountain.

There are a number of other typologies and classification of tourist motivations. Tourism encompasses a wide range of human emotions and motivations. A travel or tourist motivation may be considered the fundamental reason for one's decision to go on holiday. Studies also suggest that there may be more than one reason. The above analysis illustrates that there are plenty of reasons why people take part in tourism, and those can be classified under four sets: physical, psychological, social and achievement motivations.

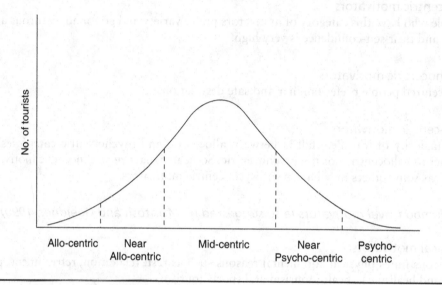

Figure 1.2 Plog's typology of tourists
Source: Plog, 1974

1.8 Why tourism is promoted

Of late, countries are in a race to develop and promote tourism. There is extreme competition between tourist attractions and destination countries, which encourages them to innovate regularly, and provide quality services, facilities and attractions. Destinations develop their tourism industries for its potential economic contribution to their society. Tourism is considered an engine for economic growth. The following description by UNWTO highlights the economic significance of tourism:

> Modern tourism is closely linked to development and encompasses a growing number of new destinations. These dynamics have turned tourism into a key driver for socio-economic progress. Today, the business volume of tourism equals or even surpasses that of oil exports, food products or automobiles. Tourism has become one of the major players in international commerce, and represents at the same time one of the main income sources for many developing countries. This growth goes hand in hand with an increasing diversification and competition among destinations.
>
> (UNWTO, 2015)

Tourism acts as an export form particularly in the case of *international* tourism. While tourists from foreign countries visit, they make expenditures on various items, and through this process foreign currency enters the host country's economy. It means it will have a major influence on a country's balance of payments, which is important for the maintenance of the value of its currency in foreign exchange. While tourists are buying services that are "invisible" in nature, the effect becomes equivalent to "invisible export". The transaction of intangible products happens in the realm of international tourism. Usually, countries try to maximize their travel receipts through promotional and marketing strategies. In the case of domestic tourism, tourism expenditure helps in the redistribution of income and to a certain extent it is treated as an 'export' between the local regions.

Governments also receive revenue through tourism in various forms, particularly from taxes, visa fees, entry fees, and surcharges. Taxes are levied directly through luxury tax in accommodation units, and indirectly through the provision of various imported items. For a government, tourism is a rather easy source of revenue. The employment potential of tourism is another prime reason for tourism development. Regions and countries with higher unemployment rates obviously depend much on tourism for creating employment and income generation opportunities. Tourism involves a wide variety of industrial sectors and therefore the employment opportunities offered are also varied. Due to its inextricable link with other sectors in an economy, tourism generates employment opportunities not only in tourism industries, but a variety of opportunities are created indirectly as well. According to the UNWTO (2014), one out of every 11 jobs is created in the tourism sector. According to a press release of the World Travel and Tourism Council (WTTC), the tourism industry in 2014 supported 277 million jobs (directly and indirectly), which is 9.4 per cent of the world's employment. The direct employment generation includes employment in travel agencies, tour operators, transport undertakings, accommodation establishments and enterprises engaged in marketing destinations. Indirectly, tourism will cause employment generation in other sectors like financial institutions, organizations that supply raw materials to the tourism organization and the like.

Tourism causes the "accelerator effect" as well. It is apparent that the evolution, growth and development of tourism in an area will attract more private and public investments. Direct tourism sectors as well as indirect sectors will be induced to invest more. This will help in general infrastructure as well as in tourism superstructure development. The area will see increased investment and economic development. While tourists spend money on various items, the host community starts earning income in diverse ways. The "multiplier effect" becomes relevant in this context, particularly the income multiplier. Income is generated in the local community directly, indirectly and in induced forms. Tourists spend money to purchase accommodation, food and beverage, transport, communications, entertainment services, goods from retail outlets and other products/services. Due to this, an additional demand in the economy is created. Tourist spending on tourism establishments will pass to other sectors in the economy and that makes more and more rounds of expenditures. Income is created in different forms, such as wages, salaries, rent, interest, commission, profits and the like. This will accrue to the local people. There are also some social and cultural reasons why tourism is promoted. For instance, due to economic development, people in society can have a better lifestyle and social existence. The tourist area will see better infrastructure and facilities for a better way of life for the local people. Many dying art forms may be revived or culturally significant areas preserved as part of tourism, e.g. monuments and historical sites. Overall, tourism is something that countries wish to develop and is now so important that no country can ignore it.

1.9 Tourism industry

As tourism has progressed, so has the industry, which is now one of the largest in the world. It ultimately attempts to satisfy the needs and wants of the tourists during the course of their journey, which includes onward journey, intra- and inter-destination travel, return journey, stay, and the various activities that form part of the visit. Leiper has defined it as "the range of businesses and organizations involved in delivering tourism products" (Leiper, 1990). This also points to the diversity involved in the entity called the tourism industry. The tourism industry is not a single industry or an independent one. Instead it is a combination, an amalgam of diverse industries. This diverse sector with different elements provides different products that can satisfy different needs of the same consumer at different phases of their journey. According to Riley et al. (2002), the tourism industry in general can include the hotel sector, transport, tour operators, travel agencies, tourist attractions, conference businesses, tour guides, tourist information services, souvenir shops, beach vendors, relevant government offices, NGOs, and educational establishments. Moreover, the tourist ultimately has a single need, which can be satisfied only when all the industrial elements concerned provide quality services/products. Although there are industries that produce products of varying nature, the industry in total exists to generate an experience that is on par with or better than the expectations of the tourist. Generating a good "tourist experience" is the ultimate objective of the tourism industry, though each element has similar objectives in accordance with its product. It can be achieved only when all the elements in the industry aim at providing quality services and products. To put it simply, tourist satisfaction is attained only when the tourist gets the expected level of service and products from the entire tourism industry. Most of the industries in it have specific characteristics, though they have a number of similar characteristics as well. The industry has some common characteristics that are unique to some extent, including the following significant characteristics:

- Service orientation
- High fixed costs of service operations
- People orientation
- Heterogeneity
- Geographical fragmentation of the industry
- Dominant role of intermediaries
- Labour-intensive
- Seasonality and fluctuating demand
- Immovability
- High level of interdependence
- Rigidity of supply

The tourism industry predominantly consists of industries with service orientation. Transport services and the hospitality industry, the two major industry elements, are classified as service sectors. Most of the tourism products also possess the characteristics of the service products, which include intangibility, perishability and inseparability. Many are performed rather than manufactured/produced, as in the case of goods. The tourist gains a total experience and each of the services sold contribute to it. Moreover, the product is produced and consumed simultaneously, and the personnel who are with the service firms have some consumer contact and are seen by the customer. The performance of the personnel also matters in the tourist experience. The products have a time span and hence they cannot be stored for future sale. It doesn't mean that all the products are intangible, perishable and inseparable. There are also products with characteristics of "goods". Most of the tourism industries are characterized by high fixed costs and low variable costs. Fixed costs do not vary according to output level or sales revenue, and include rent, buildings, machinery, etc. A firm which has a large proportion of fixed costs in comparison with the total cost is said to have high fixed costs. Hotels, especially upmarket hotels, have high fixed costs. The initial expenses for the buildings and arranging the required facilities are very high. This provides an opportunity to offer flexible pricing. The "break even" point of all these organizations with high fixed costs is usually at a much higher level of output. Also, they require a longer period in order to break even.

CASE STUDY 1.1

Some trends to consider in contemporary tourism

In 2017 the World Travel and Tourism Council (WTTC) (Weissenberg, 2017) highlighted a few trends that define the global travel industry now. The first trend identified is that "the travel brands still aspire to meet high expectations set by non-travel brands". Tourists, mostly, being non-frequent travellers, had relatively limited exposure to travel brands. Everyday brands are increasingly dynamic and are leading on the customer experience front and setting the bar quite high for consumers' brand expectations. Customers expect similar dynamism and high-level customer experience from tourism brands as well. Those who can capitalize on such expectations with novelty, authenticity, personalized experiences, removal of friction and on-demand functionality can earn millions or even billions of dollars in extra revenue. How to deal with the technology paradox is another challenging trend for tourism industries. A variety of innovative and attractive technology options and solutions are entering the market often, so adopting each and every one would be pointless. It's critical to understand what technologies consumers are ready to adopt, and what experiences will drive real value. Envisioning the customer experience they want to deliver is important for the industries, and acquiring the most suited, instead of investing in every innovative technology, is paramount for the industries.

Travel brands prioritizing risk management is another trend seen in the wake of increasing threats that can impact tourism growth negatively. The threats can be varied, like fast-spreading communicable diseases, terrorist activities and natural calamities. According to Adam Weissenberg, "investing in Enterprise Risk Management (ERM) is no longer an option for travel and hospitality companies. Thoughtful awareness of risk should be embedded into the very fabric of the organization – with senior executive and board level support". Moreover, it is important to conceptualize the brand as a platform and to seek new avenues to scale. As tourism is an amalgam of industries, a number of varied businesses can be seen in this sector, like hotels and private accommodations, airlines, cruise ships, multiple modes of ground transportation, destination activities and shopping. Being so dynamic, brands must realize the benefits of scaling across the travel experience – rather than only trying to grow within their vertical by operating in just one (or maybe a few) of these verticals. Certainly the most significant trend to highlight is that the customer experience will drive more loyalty than "points" and "miles". Tourism firms have to leverage an increased awareness of customer expectations, re-imagined technology strategies and differentiated offerings to delight the customers with unmatched experiences.

Source: Weissenberg (2017)

Read the case study carefully and answer the following questions.

- What are the trends that have to be considered seriously by the tourism industries?
- Explain why you cannot invest in every innovative technology introduced in the market.
- Describe the significance of ensuring a high level of customer experience satisfaction for the survival of tourism industries.

The significance of human resources in tourist experience is very high. The tourist, the ultimate consumer of this industry, "purchases total experience, and the experiences include people" (Collier, 2006). The interaction between the employees and the tourist determines the perceived quality. Each and every individual employee who has direct contact with the consumer has a critical role in the successful delivery of the service and in tourist satisfaction. Therefore, in the tourism industry, along with the need for quality product, the need for quality service delivery and quality human resource is very important. Heterogeneity represents the diversity included in the industry as well as the degree of variability of the industry in delivering services and other offerings at different times. According to Gee et al. (1997), there are at least 35 industrial components that serve a traveller in the process of travel and tourism. Hospitality, attractions, transport, travel organizers/intermediaries and public sector agencies are the five fundamental sectors in tourism. Each of these has different products. Moreover, each of these sectors has a number of sub-sectors as well. For instance, hospitality involves two main segments: accommodation; and food and beverage. The accommodation sector consists of several businesses: hotels, motels, rotels, resorts, guesthouses, farm houses, apartment hotels, youth hostels, B&Bs and condominiums. Moreover, the consumers of this industry also have varied attitudes and varied cultural and social backgrounds. This also causes a need for diversity in products and the industrial components.

The tourism industry is spread into different locations to cater to the requirements of tourists wherever they may be. Therefore, it is considered as "fragmented, consisting of companies and other stakeholders with diverse goals and strategies who are responsible for delivering different products and services" (Haugland et al., 2011), and consisting of fragmented and individualistic small businesses (Dredge, 2006). The location of the industry components can be identified in all the "geographical elements" of the entire system, starting from the generating place to the ultimate destination, and still going back to the origin place. Many of the industrial components are located in the tourist destination region that will be away from the source markets. Traditionally, intermediaries have been playing an important role in tourism, more than just that of a wholesaler or a distributor. Many of the tourism industries depend a lot on inter-mediaries. Even in the advanced Internet era intermediaries have a significant role in tourism as they make the product more convenient and accessible, while ensuring additional value. Destinations, particularly the emerging ones, depend considerably on the tour operation sector – an intermediary – for regular inflows of tourists. As the industry is geographically fragmented, there is a need for facilitation and coordination, which can be managed well by tourism intermediaries. Moreover, the relative lack of marketing expertise and capital resources on the part of individual and small and medium destination-based suppliers of tourism products or services makes them depen-dent on travel intermediaries for the distribution and sale of their individual offerings. Currently, as part of "re-intermediation", online travel agents are actively involved in travel product distribution.

The term "labour-intensive" refers to something that needs a large workforce to per-form or a "large amount of work in relation to output". Here, it means that the industry needs a large amount of labour to produce and serve tourists. Most of the industries in tourism, such as hotels and airlines, necessitate large workforces. Tourism industry demand fluctuates greatly across seasons. As a result, the supply side also makes nec-essary adjustments to manage the demand fluctuations. Though there are a variety of reasons behind this phenomenon in tourism, climate remains the principal reason. Insti-tutional causes such as religious, public and school holidays also cause seasonal fluctu-ation in tourist arrivals. Seasonality affects the industry severely in the off seasons when tourist arrivals are much lower. All those factors influence both supply and demand, and consequently the production, distribution and consumption are also affected. Many of the industries in tourism cannot easily and quickly adjust to the increase in demand. This is called "rigidity of supply". Demand variation can occur at different times, but the supply capacity remains the same in the short run. A hotel, for example, cannot add or remove rooms in line with sudden demand variation.

Immovability is perhaps a unique characteristic of the tourism industry. The industries and their products cannot be moved in order to make the consumption easily accessible and possible. Instead the consumer has to travel and consume the product where it is located. According to Collier (2006), "Tourism cannot be taken to consumer; the con-sumer must be taken to it". This denotes that the location of the industry is an important aspect in tourism; the tourist has to reach the location to consume the product. This is quite relevant in most of the tourism sectors, including attractions, hospitality, air transport, etc. Elements of tourist attractions are also immovable. Moreover, most of the industries in the tourism sector depend on each other for their survival, and many are complementary. The dependency and interrelationship may vary, but they all need to be taken into consideration. The supply of one sector depends on the supply of another sector and they complement each other. A change or an issue in one sector can affect the supply and delivery of service in the other sector. For example, when the airline sector suffers due to a sudden increase in fuel prices and the corresponding price hike (resulting in less demand), it can impact a hotel located in a particular destination, because there will be fewer travellers, which will negatively affect the occupancy levels of the hotel.

1.10 Tourism industry: the structure and the components

The structure of the tourism industry is very complex. Despite the fragmentation of the industry, there exists a complex relationship among them. Though each component directly or indirectly aims at satisfying the needs of the tourists, the way they serve, the type of product they offer, the role of each component and the relationship they share with other components will differ. The following list presents the components in this industry:

- Principals/direct providers
- Intermediaries
- Ancillary services
- Attractions and activities
- Developmental organizations
- Support providers

Principals include the producers and suppliers of various services and products which can cater to the requirements of tourists. Major elements in this category include airlines and other tourist transport modes, hotels and other accommodation units, and restaurants. While tourism is the outcome of people's travel and stay, accessibility, a term associated with travel and transportation, plays a critical role in the tourism process. For most forms of tourism, provision of adequate, safe, comfortable, fast, convenient and cheaper public transport is paramount. Quality transportation is seen as a determinant in the success of tourist destinations, especially for the mass market segment. Yet, the relationship between tourism and transportation is symbiotic, as both nurture each other's growth and expansion. The accommodation sector comprises widely differing forms of sleeping and hospitality facilities which can be conveniently categorized as either serviced or self-catering. In the serviced sector, catering and housekeeping are provided. Hotels, motels, rotels, guesthouses, etc. come under the category of serviced accommodation. In the other category, catering facilities are not offered. Apartments, villas and campsites come under the category of self-catering. Many other classifications of the accommodation sector are also there. The hospitality industry is the common term used to refer to the accommodation sector and has expanded widely to include a range of sectors servicing the needs and interests of tourists and as per the trends in the industry. The food and beverage sector is another fundamental component of the tourism industry. Destinations have to provide quality food services to cater to the requirements of tourists. Tourists' needs vary greatly – some may wish to try the local dishes, some may prefer something already familiar to them and some may have special requirements. This difference stimulates the growth of the catering industry worldwide. Though food is an essential item for a tourist "to survive", poor quality food can cause dissatisfaction and lower the level of tourist experience. Moreover, food itself, in many cases, takes up the role of attraction and even culinary tourism is gaining prominence as an alternative tourism and as a special interest tourism (SIT).

Intermediaries include a whole range of wholesalers, distributors, retailers and other players who are present between the final consumer and the principal or suppliers. With any industry, the task of intermediaries is to transform goods or services from a form that consumers may not prefer to a form that they do. The case of tourism is no different. Having a prominent position in the whole tourism system, tourism intermediaries also consist of a variety of intermediaries. However, tour operators and travel agencies, traditionally, have been playing an indomitable role in the distribution and selling of travel and tourism products.

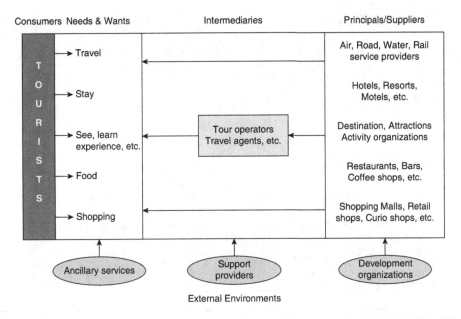

Consumers Needs & Wants | **Intermediaries** | **Principals/Suppliers**

T O U R I S T S

→ Travel

→ Stay

→ See, learn experience, etc.

→ Food

→ Shopping

Tour operators Travel agents, etc.

Air, Road, Water, Rail service providers

Hotels, Resorts, Motels, etc.

Destination, Attractions Activity organizations

Restaurants, Bars, Coffee shops, etc.

Shopping Malls, Retail shops, Curio shops, etc.

Ancillary services

Support providers

Development organizations

External Environments

Figure 1.3 The tourism industry

Attraction, the chief reason for the visit by a tourist, forms the core of the "pull" of a destination. For many destinations, there can be more than one attraction, whereas some destinations may be visited primarily for a single attraction. They tempt people to travel and spend time in a place. However, though attractions are defined as tangible items in most cases, there are intangible elements in them, and at times intangible elements themselves constitute the attraction. For example, a monument is a widely seen attraction which is wholly tangible in nature, whereas a beach gives tangible elements as well as intangible elements, such as the natural beauty that attracts people. For a honeymoon trip to a hill station in winter, the chief attraction can be the climate, which is primarily intangible. Activities are usually seen as part of an attraction and usually difficult to distinguish well. Tourists like to take part in activities when they are in the destination. Those activities vary from destination to destination, based on geographical features as well as the nature and type of attractions. Activity in the area of tourism is something that a tourist can engage in physically while spending time in the destination, other than the routine activities. Activities include a variety of items based on the nature of the destination. For instance, a beach tourism destination can have activities such as diving, snorkelling, surfing, kayaking, fishing, kite flying, boating, playing beach volleyball and sunbathing. It is of interest to note that competing destinations are, of late, trying to expand the range of activities offered in their respective places. Ancillary services complement the tourism sector. Some of them directly contribute to tourist experience whereas in most of the cases, their role is rather facilitative or catalytic. It has also been called auxiliary services and supplementary services.

Tourism development, usually used in the context of destination development or attraction development, is undertaken by public sector agencies. The private sector is also involved, as many attractions are planned and developed by private sector agencies. Considering this, the term developmental organizations can be used to denote the

21

Figure 1.4 Beach resort in Pattaya, Thailand
Courtesy: Wikimedia Commons

government agencies, business firms, associations, voluntary organizations or individuals who are involved in tourism planning and development. Their effort is directly benefiting tourists, and tourism as an overall industry is depending on them. In addition, developmental organizations need to take extra care while planning and developing in order to minimize the negative impacts of tourism. Support providers include the businesses or services that support, aid and give directions to those agencies directly involved in tourism. They can also be considered indirect providers as they do not directly deal with tourists. There are a large number of such agencies whose services are essential for the tourism sector to survive. For instance, the construction industry makes infrastructure and superstructure in the tourism industry. Though they have a considerable role in tourism development, they do not offer services directly to tourists.

1.11 Summary

Tourism, one of the largest industries and fastest growing economic activities, has evolved through centuries to become a common social phenomenon that can be accessed by a large section of the societies around the world. In fact, all the social, cultural, technological and economic developments which occurred after the end of the Second World War spurred the growth of tourism into its modern form. People engage in tourism with a wide variety of purposes.

Tourism is conceptualized as a social process that involves the short-term movement of people from their usual environment to a distant one, where they stay for at least 24 hours and engage in certain activities that are non-remunerative in nature. During the course of their stay, the traveller interacts with a variety of host communities and consumes a range of services and products offered by different businesses and facilities, which themselves generate economic activity with positive and negative social, cultural and environmental ramifications. The tourist is the main actor in the system of tourism. A tourist can be defined simply as a visitor, travelling to a place away from his/her usual place of work or residence for a minimum period of 24 hours which will not extend beyond a year, who engages in non-remunerated activities at the place visited.

The primary classifications of tourism are international and domestic tourism – based on the country of origin and destination country. When a traveller moves to a foreign country, international tourism occurs and when the travel takes place within the country, it will be considered domestic tourism. Inbound and outbound tourism are usually categories of international tourism; the incoming tourist to a country is an inbound tourist, while the outgoing tourist from a country to another is an outbound tourist. Tourists travel for a number of reasons and different classifications of tourist motivations can be seen in tourism literature. Simply, a travel or tourist motivation can be considered the fundamental reason for a tourist to go on holiday. Studies also suggest that there can be more than one reason. All those can be classified under four sets: physical, psychological, social and achievement motivations.

Generally, tourism is something that countries wish to develop and is now becoming so important that no country can ignore its development and promotion. The economic contributions of tourism are the main reasons why countries are interested in tourism development. Tourism is considered neither a single industry nor an independent one. Instead, it is a combination, an amalgam of diverse industries. This diverse sector with different elements provides different products that can satisfy different needs of the same consumer at different phases of their journey. Mostly, tourism industries are service industries that have unique characteristics – they are heterogenous, geographically fragmented, labour-intensive, seasonal, etc. Though each component directly or indirectly aims at satisfying the needs of tourists, the way they serve, the type of the product they offer, the role of each component and the relationship they share with other components vary from one to another.

Review questions

Short/medium answer type questions

- Define tourism and distinguish tourist from other travellers.
- Write down the major conditions that make a traveller a tourist.
- Distinguish between inbound and outbound tourism, citing examples.
- Discuss how industrialization helps in the evolution of tourism.
- What is the grand tour?
- Explain the reasons why people engage in tourism.
- Explain why tourism is considered a prime developmental priority for countries.
- How would you conceptualize the tourism industry?
- What are the characteristics of tourism?

Essay type questions

- Discuss the evolution of tourism in the world.
- Explain the elements of the tourism industry using suitable examples.

References

Bull, A. (1991) *The Economics of Travel and Tourism*. London: Longman Cheshire.

Burkart, A. J. and Medlik, S. (1981) *Tourism: Past, Present and Future*. Oxford: Butterworth-Heinemann.

Collier, A. (1994) *Principles of Tourism*. 3rd edn. Auckland: Longman Paul.

Collier, A. (2006) *Principles of Tourism: A New Zealand Perspective*. Auckland: Pearson Education.

Cooper, C., Fletcher, J., Gilbert, D. and Wanhill, S. (2000) *Tourism: Principles and Practices*. London: Prentice Hall.

Crompton, J. L. (1979) An Assessment of the Image of Mexico as a Vacation Destination and the Influence of Geographical Location Upon That Image, *Journal of Travel Research* 17(4): 18–23.

Davidson, R. (1989) *Tourism*. London: Pitman.

Dredge, D. (2006) Networks, Conflicts and Collaborative Communities, *Journal of Sustainable Tourism* 14: 562–581.

Gee, Y. C., Makens, C. J. and Choy, J. L. D. (1997) *The Travel Industry*. 3rd edn. New York: Van Nostrand Reinhold.

Gray, H. P. (1970) *International Travel – International Trade*. Lexington: Heath Lexington Books.

Haugland, S. A., Ness, H., Gronseth, B. O. and Aarstad, J. (2011) Development of Tourism Destination – An Integrated Multilevel Perspective, *Annals of Tourism Research* 38(1): 268–290.

Holloway, C. J. and Taylor, N. (2006) *The Business of Tourism*. Upper Saddle River, NJ: Prentice Hall.

Hunt, J. D. and Layne, D. (1991) Evolution of Travel and Tourism Terminology and Definitions, *Journal of Travel Research* 29(4): 7–11.

Kelly, I. and Nankervis, T. (2009) *Visitor Destinations*. Milton: John Wiley & Sons.

Leiper, N. (1990) *Tourism Systems*, Department of Management Systems, Occasional Paper 2, Auckland: Massey University.

McIntosh, R. and Goeldner, C. (1990) *Tourism Principles, Practices and Philosophies*. New York: John Wiley & Sons.

Plog, S. C. (1974) Why Destination Areas Rise in Popularity and Fall in Popularity, *Cornell Hall and Restaurant Quarterly* 14(4): 55–58.

Riley, M., Ladkin, A. and Szivas, E. (2002) *Tourism Employment: Analysis and Planning*. Clevedon: Channel View Publications.

Smith, S. L. J. (1995) *Tourism Analysis: A Handbook*. Harlow: Longman Group Ltd.

Towner, J. (1985) The Grand Tour: A Key Phase in the History of Tourism, *Annals of Tourism Research* 12(3): 297–333.

UNWTO, Glossary of Tourism Terms by United Nations World Tourism Organizations, available at http://cf.cdn.unwto.org/sites/all/files/docpdf/glossaryenrev.pdf (accessed 15 June 2015).

UNWTO (2014) Tourism Highlights. Madrid: United Nations World Tourism Organization.

UNWTO (2015) Exports from International Tourism Rise to US$ 1.5 Trillion in 2014, Press release of United Nations World Tourism Association, 15 April.

UNWTO (2017) UNWTO Tourism Highlights 2017, available at https://www.e-unwto.org/doi/pdf/10.18111/9789284419029 (accessed 25 September 2017).

Weissenberg, A. (2017) Trends Defining the Global Travel Industry in 2017, *Travel & Tourism Global Economic Impact & Issues 2017*, World Travel and Tourism Council (WTTC), available at https://www.wttc.org/-/media/files/reports/economic-impact-research/2017-documents/global-economic-impact-and-issues-2017.pdf.

WTO (1991) International Conference on Travel and Tourism Statistics: Resolutions. Madrid: WTO.

Chapter 2

Transport and tourism

After reading this chapter, you will be able to:

- Identify the elements and types of tourism transport.
- Understand the relationship between transport and tourism.
- Describe the diverse roles of transport in tourism.
- Explore the geographical perspective of tourism transport.
- Explain the significance of transport in the accessibility of a destination.
- Understand multimodal transport in the context of tourism.
- Present the characteristics and types of tourism transport.
- Understand the factors that influence tourist transport selection.

2.1 Introduction

Transportation, the act of transporting, enables the movement of people or goods from one location to another. It needs an efficient system with necessary facilities, means and equipment to transport people and/or cargo. Transportation is certainly the prime means and facilitator of growing spatial interaction the world over. The very purpose of efficient transport is to ensure the smooth, safe and rapid movement of people and goods from place to place for various reasons. Economic development of a region necessitates having an efficient transport system and the same is true of tourism and its development. The evolution and growth of tourism in a destination has indispensable dependence on transport. Moreover, transport plays other key roles. The Organisation for Economic Cooperation and Development (OECD) policy document on transport and tourism summarizes the role of transport with regard to tourism in the following way:

> Transport is a key enabler of tourism and plays a vital role in moving tourists from their place of residence to their final destination and on to various attractions. Transport connects the markets in tourism generating regions to destinations and facilitates the internal movement of visitors between components of the tourist experience

(e.g. attractions, accommodation, commercial services, etc.), and can be a major element of the attraction or an experience in their own right (e.g. Queen Mary II, the Orient Express, world heritage listed Semmering Railway). The location, capacity, efficiency and connectivity of transport can therefore play an important role in how a destination physically develops, and significantly influence the mobility of visitors and the connectivity of tourist experiences within destinations.

(OECD, 2016)

Before going deep into the nuances of transport and its inextricable link with tourism, let's take a look at the evolution of modern transport. Travel was one of the earliest human activities; even in the ancient era people used to travel using different modes of transport. Evolution of modern transport began sometime towards the end of eighteenth century when mechanized forms of transport options started to emerge. Before then, animals and wind power were used for long journeys. Public transport was limited and to a certain extent transport wasn't comfortable, safe or smooth. However, international travel occurred over land and sea, mainly for the purpose of trade. Once industrialization began, the stage was set for transformation in transport technology as well. The emergence of mechanized forms of transport was an after-effect of industrialization and it continued into the following centuries. Transportation then began only by providing necessary transport services for people and goods to move to other places. Advancements in transport technology were made and roads were then improved. Railway-, canal- and steamship-based transport began in this era. More common carriers emerged and more scheduled services began. The overall development in society led to more motivation and more money to travel. By the nineteenth century, rail travel had become the backbone of transport in Europe; in America it was sooner. Organized tourism also began in this era when Thomas Cook organized a trip using rail services from Leicester to Loughborough in 1841. The technology advanced further, which resulted in faster, safer and more comfortable travel.

The twentieth century has witnessed dramatic changes in transport. Modern aviation began in its early years, and towards the end of the century it became a huge sector transporting more than a billion passengers and employing millions of people. The automobile sector was also born and grew during this same era. The introduction of the Model T car by Henry Ford in 1908 marked one of the most important milestones in the history of travel. Within a couple of decades, the automobile sector had set a tremendous pace. In between, rail transport lost its prominence, particularly in the West, and ship-based passenger transport, especially in the second half of twentieth century, lost ground. The introduction of jet engines in aircraft was another milestone in the history of travel: aircraft could carry more passengers and cargo at greatly improved speeds. Wide-body jet aircraft were commercially used from 1970, and thus mass tourism philosophy began. After the formation of OPEC and the rise in oil prices in the 1970s, land and air transport was set back for a short period. The introduction of deregulation in the US changed the fate of air transport. Within a decade, air transport became a popular transport mode. Air transport continued to grow and is still in a growth trajectory as its influence spreads to more communities across the world.

2.2 Transport: elements, types and linkages

Transport represents not just the means of reaching places; it is a combination of different elements. The movement of people and goods can be possible with the involvement of all of them. All elements are interlinked. Each element has different sub-elements as well. Cooper et al. (2000) identified four basic physical elements:

1. The way
2. The terminal
3. The carrying unit
4. The motive power

This is one of the simplest representations of transport elements. "The way", the medium of transport, can be both natural and artificial. Roads and railways are examples of artificial media on which transport is undertaken. Sea routes and airways are natural media. In this modern era of transportation, privatization has been used in the construction and management of artificial ways as well, due to the increasing requirement of heavy investment. Once, road and railway investment was done solely by public sector agencies. The "build operate transfer" (BOT) arrangement is common in this sector across the world. "The terminal" provides the access for the passengers. It is usually a built structure with varied facilities and services provided as part of the terminal. Terminals are places where the mode of transport can also be changed. For instance, a passenger arriving in a car can change their mode of transport into air transport at an airport. Bus stations, railway stations, seaports and airports are examples of terminals. Earlier, terminals were simple structures that provided access to another mode of transport. Now, the scope and functions of terminals are being expanded. For instance, airports are now turning into mini cities with almost all the facilities and services of a city available within them. Privatization is in vogue in the airport sector as well. The "carrying unit", simply the vehicle that is being used for the transport, is the most crucial element in the transport system. This is the most diverse element, with a large variety of options available for passengers – from a single-seater bicycle to huge aircraft and ships available for passengers to travel. The carrying unit is seen in all the above elements and its presence is inevitable for the function of all those elements. The "motive power" enables the carrying units to move and it is fundamental to ensuring the speed, range and capacity of vehicles. Over the last two centuries, revolutionary advancements have taken place in the area of motive power, which has resulted in much smoother, speedier and safer transport in short and long distance travels. Since industrialization, motive power has advanced regularly and consistently.

On the basis of the medium in which the transportation activities take place, transportation is classified into three groups: land-based, air-based and water-based. Each form has its own relevance and importance in the tourism sector. A large variety of land-based transport forms are found in the tourism sector. Road transportation is one of the most important forms of tourism transportation, and in the last century it has grown tremendously. A wide variety of modes are involved in road transportation. Buses (including coaches), cars, rental cars, taxi services, etc. are the major road transportation modes. The advent of the automobile in 1920s and the motor car revolutionized the holiday and recreational habits. Road transportation became the primary mode of transport during that period and it is still one of the most attractive modes of transport today. The advent of cars provided families in particular with a new freedom of movement, providing a huge increase in opportunities to take day excursions as well as longer trips. Accessibility to interior resorts also improved. Car ferry services flourished in Europe. Camping and caravan holidays boomed. Many tourism destinations in the world still depend on private motor vehicles. Tour operators offered self-drive car packages. Trains, a mass transportation medium, are perceived to be safe, inexpensive and offer the convenience of movement within the carrying unit. Technological developments have also impacted rail transportation, providing luxury, safety and speed with "green" (i.e. environmentally friendly) credentials. Independent/free tourists rely on railways more than others. Passenger rail transportation is a component in travel anywhere in the world and it is the most important transportation mode in countries like France, Germany, India, South Korea, Japan, China, etc. However, in the US, it is one of the most important transportation modes, as in other countries (Goeldner and Ritchie, 2003).

The last 70 years have seen the transformation and growth of air transport from infant to giant. Throughout the twentieth century, air transportation has been experiencing technological advancements and all helped in managing the air transport industry to become a popular and mass transportation mode. Equipment manufacturers, airports, air navigation, air traffic control (ATC) and airlines are the fundamental components of air transport. Transport by water-borne vessels of all kinds continues to play an important role in this industry. Reaching a destination by sailing has been an important method of transport since the first primitive boats were built. Currently tourism transport over sea is restricted to cruises and other water transport forms, such as ferry services, boats, etc. – for both travel and recreation.

Various modes of transport are interlinked and interconnected. This interrelationship that exists among different transport forms makes transportation more accessible and more convenient. The absence of it will generate difficulty for a passenger while he/she travels. Air transport certainly requires the assistance of other forms of transport, e.g. road. Usually airports will be located some distance from the city, so accessing air transport itself would require another form of transport. For example, buses operate regular airport services. Taxi services also operate to and from airports. Often a passenger will have access to rail transport between their home and the city, while other modes of

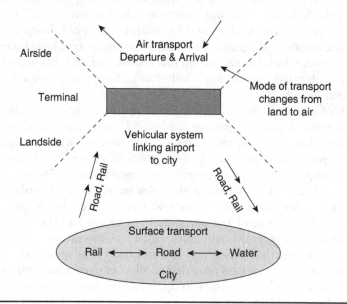

Figure 2.1 Air transport: linkages with other modes of transport

transport can be used for reaching airports from the city. Airports are sometimes linked by rail transport. Air taxis, commuter/feeder services, taxi services, limousine services, scheduled bus services, coach services, etc. are other forms of transport often connected to air transport. In certain cases, passengers can reach a place without the help of other transport forms. For instance, an air taxi can be operated from the office premises to another destination (in the case of business travel) if adequate facilities are available. However, it has to be noted that, within an airport itself, other forms of transport are used to access the aeroplanes.

International travel may involve different forms of transport. If the countries are separated by sea, and if the passenger prefers sea transport, then naturally other modes of transport would be required for him/her to access sea transport. Reaching a seaport would necessitate the passenger using one or more other forms of transport, such as air, rail, bus, coaches, taxis, etc. Here, strong linkages with other forms of transport are essential. If the international travel is by air, similar linkages are involved. If travel also involves road or rail transport, usually a passenger has to depend on some other form(s) of transport for making the primary transport form accessible. The case is also similar for rail transportation. In order to access rail transport, reaching a railway station itself would require using some other vehicles. After reaching the destination, taxis, etc. may be required for the passenger to reach the final destination. Bus journeys may also have to link with other forms of transport. Hence it can be concluded that one mode of transportation generally requires linkages with other modes of transportation or using other types of vehicles. In that case a passenger has to use multi-transport forms to complete their journey.

The dependency relationship varies from one mode of transport to other. For example, air and sea transport necessitate more linkages with other modes of transport since the airports and seaports are usually located away from common places/cities/residential areas. Meanwhile, surface transportation, particularly road transportation, has a greater number of terminals and they are more easily accessible. Hence the dependency on other forms of transport is much less for road transportation, but road transportation is a crucial link for other forms. Road transport facilitates movement of men and material, helps trade and commerce, links industry and agriculture to markets and opens up difficult-to-reach regions of a country. A road system provides last-mile connection for other modes of transport such as railways, air, inland waterways and sea transport.

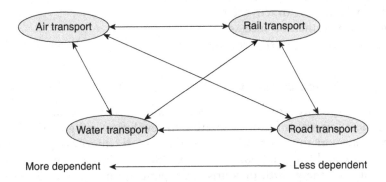

Figure 2.2 Different modes of transport: linkages and dependence

2.3 Tourism and transport: the interrelationship

Thinking of tourism without transport is irrelevant and irrational. Certainly, transport is an inevitable element of tourism. Yet, it is given less significance in tourism. As Predeaux (2000a) points out, travel, from an economic perspective, has been traditionally modelled as a cost, instead of a benefit. Of late, the concept is changing to a lesser cost, and transport is given much more significance due to the increase in comfort, speed and safety as a result of advancements in transport, especially after the deregulation of air travel and the consequent emergence of low-cost carriers, and the advent of high-speed trains and cruises. Tourism and transport are inseparable, i.e. they have a symbiotic relationship, and are also complementary.

2.4 Role of transport in tourism

Transport plays a vital role in tourism. It is not just a means of moving people from their place of origin to their destination to visit places (and then return). The multidimensional roles of transport in tourism need to be discussed from varied perspectives. Collier summarized tourism transport in three forms: transporting the tourists from the generating region to the destination area, transport between host destinations and transport within host destinations (Collier, 1994). In the same manner, Hall (1999) identified four aspects of tourism transport: linking the origin and the destination, providing mobility and access within destinations, providing mobility and access within tourist attractions, and facilitating travel along a recreational route. Tourism transport essentially encompasses the above aspects. Tourism transport also plays other major roles in modern tourism, including the following:

- Facilitator of tourism growth
- Linking the destination with the tourism markets
- Providing mobility and access within a destination
- Providing mobility within tourist attractions
- Providing recreational travel options
- Acting as primary attraction
- Linking host destinations
- Determinant in tourist satisfaction
- Contributor in tourist attractiveness
- Determinant in destination success
- Major contributor in tourism's socio-economic benefits

2.4.1 Facilitator for tourism growth

One of the primary aspects to be noted about transport and tourism is that the former became the most important factor facilitating the evolution and growth of tourism the world over. Transport thus turned into a prerequisite for tourism's growth and development (Boniface and Cooper, 2002; Predeaux, 2000a). The developments in transport certainly stimulated the growth of tourism. As pointed out by Page (2009), "without transport and its associated infrastructure, human mobility for the purpose of tourist travel would not occur, and certainly not on the massive scale. . .". As Robinson (1976) stated decades ago, "transport has been at once a cause and an effect of the growth of tourism. Improved transport facilities have stimulated tourism and the expansion of tourism has stimulated transport". Modern transport is featured with safety, comfort and speed, and is relatively inexpensive (Predeaux, 2004). This was not the case before. Comfort levels were much lower and speed of travel was very low. Advancements in transport technology in the twentieth century dramatically changed transport to evolve modern transport forms. The tremendous developments in transport dramatically reduced the travel time and travel cost, while enhancing the accessibility, mobility and travel experience. Moreover, many inaccessible locations became accessible. Tourism also evolved hand in hand with the developments in transport. While in the nineteenth century tourism progressed mainly due to rail transport, the twentieth century saw remarkable expansion of tourism – initially due to the advent of automobiles but later mainly due to the growth of aviation.

Predeaux (2000b) identified different stages in the process of destination/resort development (referred to as the "resort development spectrum"). According to the process, in the first phase transport options are very limited: road transport is the main mode of transport with little scope for air travel and slight scope for rail if the resort is located close to rail services. As tourism progresses, in the second phase road access is enhanced, other modes of transport begin with the assistance of infrastructure development, and there may be limited scope for air services. In the third phase, scheduled air services may begin; road access continues to increase, along with increases in other modes of transport. While the resort enters into the fourth stage of evolution and becomes international destination, air services commence along with continual expansion of other modes of transport. Air travel, depending on the distance from source markets, will become the dominant mode (Predeaux, 2000a). This reveals two important aspects: road transport is a vital mode of transport in the evolution and growth of a destination in general and air transport is vital to the success of a destination internationally. Also, tourism development demands further developments in transport. As tourism and transportation are inextricably linked and as global tourism increases, additional demand will be placed on the transportation sectors. (Goeldner and Ritchie, 2003; Holloway, 1996).

CASE STUDY 2.1

Long-haul tourism thrived through the rise of wide-body jets

During the 1970s wide-body jets began to be used widely for commercial transportation, which marked the beginning of a new era in international tourism. It was during this period that long-haul holidays became popular among tourists. Long-haul holidays became increasingly affordable for leisure tourists. Wide-body jets could carry more passengers and air travel became cheaper, safer and more comfortable. The first Boeing 747 entered service in January 1970, when Pan American, in collaboration with Boeing, flew the largest aeroplane in those days. The plane could carry 400 passengers, which was a remarkable leap in the history of passenger air transportation. Other wide-body aircraft soon followed, such as the three-engine McDonnell Douglas DC-10 and Lockheed L-1011 TriStar and the twin-engine Airbus A300. Long-range service became a trend that spurred long distance air travel for the purpose of tourism as well as other reasons.

Introduction of wide-body jets gave a fillip to leisure tourism particularly. The augmented affordability and comfort elevated the travel propensity immensely. During those days, major tourism markets were concentrated in the West. Until then, international tourism had been dominated by inter- and intra-regional tourism. Many long-distance destinations were not so accessible for those from the major tourism markets. The trend began to change as long-haul tourism began to prosper. Far Eastern destinations became more accessible for tourists from the West. The increased speed of air travel also enabled explorers to venture out and visit far-flung destinations.

Before the entry of wide-body jets, other jet-engined flights were in use which could also spur the growth of tourism. By the late 1950s, Boeing 707 and DC-8 were in wide use and soon airlines began seeking larger aircraft to meet the rising global demand for air travel. Meanwhile, supersonic flights emerged, but later they were converted into freighters. Indeed, the demand for the wider, quicker and more comfortable flights by the airlines as well as the passenger community pressured the aircraft manufacturers to have more efficient flights and that resulted in wide-body jets. Later, more efficient aircraft entered into service.

All such developments happened in the post-Second World War era. Asian destinations emerged as major tourist destinations in the same era. Air transport growth in these regions has been remarkable in recent times, with phenomenal growth of destinations in the Asia-Pacific region. Now China is the number one tourism market in the world. China, India, Indonesia, etc. have the fastest growing air transport sectors. Air transport growth and the evolution of tourism go hand in hand. Long-haul travel is very common nowadays, a result of the remarkable role played by air transport.

Read the above case study carefully and answer the following questions:

- Explain the major reasons behind the rapid evolution of Asian places as major international tourism destinations and markets.
- Write down the role played by wide-body jets in the growth of international tourism.

2.4.2 Linking the destination with tourism markets

One of the primary features of tourism is that the destinations are away from the markets and the consumers have to travel distances to access the products and consume them. This makes the role of transport so crucial in tourism. As stated in the beginning, transport plays a vital role in moving tourists from their place of residence to their final destination, and connects the markets in tourism generating regions to destinations. Transport provides the means of travel to the destination from the tourist's place of origin and back again. Destinations need to be linked with different tourist markets, as tourists, particularly international tourists, come from different nations located in different parts of the world. For a destination, source markets are different countries. One destination receives tourists from a number of foreign countries. All these market countries, also referred to as tourist generating countries/regions, have to be linked with destinations, and efficient transport systems have to be there to make the destination easily accessible.

2.4.3 Providing mobility and access within a destination

Transport provides the means of travelling in and around the destination after arriving. Once a tourist lands in a destination, he/she has to move within the destination for various reasons. From the airport where a tourist may arrive, transfer is needed to reach the accommodation centre. Sightseeing and visiting various attractions are the most important activities of a tourist when he/she is in the destination. Different attractions may be situated in different locations. Also, for consuming other products, the tourist needs to travel. The mobility of a tourist within a destination is thus crucial, as the primary purpose of the tourist in engaging in tourism is to visit attractions and experience them. It's crucial to ensure suitable infrastructure and adequate means of transportation to facilitate the mobility of tourists.

2.4.4 Providing mobility within tourist attractions

Some of the attractions require travel options within them. For instance, an industrial tourist destination usually requires travel within it so that tourists can visit different parts of the site. In wildlife tourism, exclusive transport is provided in many cases to go into the forest and to see wild animals in their habitat. The type of transport in an attraction may vary based on the type of attraction. Fragile tourist attractions need transport forms suitable for them, e.g. more eco-friendly. Industrial sites may have different types of transport.

2.4.5 Providing recreational travel options

Recreational transport is offered in destinations to enhance the tourism experience. At times, unique transport options are provided along tourist circuits. There are recreational rail services linking a destination with nearby cities. Hop-on, hop-off city tours are common in established destinations around the world. Bicycle tourism and bike tourism are centred on recreational trips using simple transport forms to rural destinations. The Grand Canyon railway in Arizona, the Royal Scotsman, Scotland, Place on Wheels, India, etc. are some examples of rail services which are unique and attractive. They play a key role in attracting tourists. Pleasure boats and dhows are also part of tourism parlance. Different vehicles are used for recreational safaris as well.

2.4.6 Acting as the primary attraction

In certain cases, transport is the primary attraction for visitors. Transport can be a main feature of a tourist trip when the form of transport itself is one of the main reasons for taking the trip. The experience of travel has much more significance than the movement of tourist from the origin to the destination. The vehicle involved in the travel must be unique, with facilities and services for recreation. Cruise voyages and the recreation onboard during the course of the journey constitute the primary attraction for cruise tourists. Here, the role of transport increases and holds the role of travel facilitation as well as attraction. Cruise tourism is becoming more popular, with significant growth recorded. Modern cruise operators are competing with one another on a wide range of onboard services and facilities in the hyper-competitive cruise tourism market.

2.4.7 Linking host destinations

In addition to linking the origin and destination, transport is required to link different destinations as well when a tourist is on a multi-centre tour. In package tours, this is very common (when the package consists of more than one destination). This phenomenon of visiting more than a single destination gained momentum when long-haul tours began to evolve. The distance a tourist has to cover to reach a faraway destination may tempt them to visit neighbouring destination(s) as well. The mode of travel between destinations may vary, unlike the transport between origin and destination which is dominated by air travel. Road and rail travel also have significant roles to play in inter-destination travel.

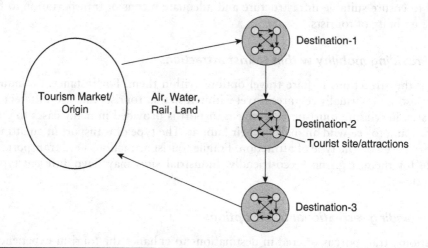

Figure 2.3 Transport linkages in a multi-centre holiday

2.4.7 Determinant in tourist experience

Transport, being an integral element in the tourism system, provides an experience that is also a determinant in the overall tourist experience. Certainly, transport experience is an important element of the tourist experience.

> The nature of tourism transport experience is defined either by a single mode or a combination of transport modes, it still involves movement from one location to another, and a degree of attraction or more precisely a satisfaction of wants associated with the actual process of traveling. The key distinction in transport for tourism tends to offer low intrinsic value within the overall experience and the tourism transport experience a higher intrinsic value.
>
> (Lumsdon and Page, 2004)

Tourists' experience with transport may vary from time to time. Yet, a pleasurable experience adds to the sweet memories of the tour later on. Quality transport makes tourists comfortable and ensures that they return at some point in the future. A bad experience during transport can lead to dissatisfaction and consequently affect the overall tourist experience.

2.4.8 Contributor in tourist attractiveness

A destination with good accessibility and high-quality transport infrastructure can attract tourists. Even if a destination has attractive tourism resources, transport is necessary to draw tourists. However, lack of quality transport can deter the growth of tourism. Moreover, many transport forms themselves can lure tourists. Availability of recreational transport forms, accessibility, etc. certainly contribute in the attractiveness of a destination.

2.4.9 Determinant in destination success

Certainly, quality of transport is a crucial element in the success of a destination. The evolution of the destination is influenced by the growth of transport as well. The accessibility, quality of the transport services, diversity of transport provisions, etc. are factors that determine the success of a destination.

2.4.10 Major contributor in tourism's socio-economic benefits

Transport enables the tourists in spatial interaction, facilitates cultural exchange, paves the way for developing understanding between different cultures and societies, and has other social benefits. Moreover, transport is the major tourism employer and generates other economic and social benefits as well.

2.5 Transport: from a geographical perspective

Transport primarily deals with time and distance. Travel distance is a factor in the accessibility of a destination. Transport facilitates the movement with respect to place and location and provides the essential link. It enables the spatial interaction between different tourist generating regions and destination regions. This flow of people from generating region to destination is almost impossible without transport. From a geographic perspective, travel occurs to satisfy human desire for spatial movement and transport facilitates the process of movement that has economic and budgetary costs. According to Page (1994), "transport results from a desire for mobility and travel, and the provision of different modes of transport aims to facilitate the efficient movement of goods and people". Traditionally, distance has been a bottleneck in the evolution of tourism in many destinations. The proximity of tourist generating countries with high travel propensity has been an advantage for destinations in attracting international tourists. European destinations could enjoy the benefit of proximity to rich tourist markets. The transformation in aviation in the post-Second World War era has eased the difficulties in long-haul travel through speedier and cheaper air transport services. Yet, the cost in covering long-haul destinations is a determinant in tourist buying behaviour. The distance has a geographical perspective. In geography, spatial differentiation is used to indicate spatial interaction between two places, which is the basis of transportation. According to Ullman (1980), there are three major reasons for spatial interaction and, therefore, transport development. They are:

1. Complementarity
2. Intervening opportunities
3. Transferability or friction of distance

In one place (in the case of tourism this would be the generating region), there exists desire to travel, and in the other place there exists the ability to satisfy that desire. A transportation system will link these two and a "complementarity" of demand and supply will produce interaction between these areas. Though complementarity exists between origin and destination regions, intervening opportunities may be possible due to competing attractions. Though one destination has the necessary attractions and facilities to satisfy the needs and wants of tourists from a generating region, other destinations can also offer similar attractions and facilities. Some tourists may visit other destinations as well, even if a particular destination has the needed services and facilities. Hence, intervening opportunities exist in terms of tourist travel. "Transferability" or "friction of distance" does matter in tourism. This refers to the cost of overcoming the distance between those two places. If the time and money costs of reaching a destination are high, then even perfect complementarity and lack of intervening opportunities cannot ensure travel to that destination. Hence, in tourism, spatial interaction has to take place and it should have good complementarity, less intervening opportunities and low friction of distance.

The tourism system concept of Leiper (1990) specifies the geographical aspect of tourism transport. In it, the geographical elements constitute a fundamental component of the system. Geographical elements consist of three different spatial regions based on the movement of tourists. The first sub-element, traveler generating region (TGR), is the area where the tourists are emerging from and is often referred to as the tourism market. The tourist destination region represents the "end" of tourism, which the tourist is ultimately intending to visit. The tourist moves from generating region to destination region via the transit route region (TRR). The tourism destination region (TDR) really attracts the tourists to move there to visit attractions. Leiper says that the "pull" of the destinations energizes the whole tourism system and demand for travel in the generating region. Though the primary focus of tourism transportation is in the TRR, the rest of the parts also have significance in tourism transportation. As stated before, the distance to cover in TRR is important for the tourist in selecting the mode of transport, a determinant in the accessibility of the destination, and consequently in the ability of the destination to attract tourists. Tourism transport commences from TGR and passes through TRR into TDR; transport becomes more complex with a more multimodal transport system. So geographically, tourism transport varies and different modes of transport will be used as part of the process of tourism movement from origin area to destination, visiting within the destination and then returning to the origin area.

2.6 Accessibility and tourism transport

The role of transportation is basically related to accessibility. Transportation renders a tourist destination accessible to their markets in the tourist generating regions. Accessibility is one of the primary elements of tourism and the relationship of tourism with transport is generally conceptualized in terms of accessibility. Good accessibility is an integral characteristic of the overall competitiveness of destinations. Accessibility in respect of destinations involves varied aspects. Distance to reach the destination is an important element of a destination's accessibility. Along with distance, the amount of time needed to reach the destination is another important factor. Accessibility refers to 'how to reach' and the ease in reaching a destination. A destination must be accessible if it is to facilitate visits by tourists. Regions and destinations that are inaccessible or not well served with transport facilities are unlikely to develop as popular tourist locations. Traditionally, destinations that are located near the tourist generating markets and are linked by a network of efficient land transport options receive more tourists. Most of the popular European destinations, coupled with quality attractions, are fortunate to have rich tourist markets nearby with high levels of accessibility. Transport infrastructure within the destination is another important factor of accessibility. Availability of transport services is also a factor. Features of transport services including frequency, convenience, comfort and types are important in determining the touristic accessibility of a destination. The provision of adequate, safe, comfortable, fast, convenient and cheaper public transport is a prerequisite for mass-market tourism. The lack or insufficiency of it will certainly lead to problems for tourism. Both public and private investment is involved in tourism and the transportation industry is a major segment of the tourism industry, particularly in terms of employment and revenue generation. In addition to the accessibility aspect of transport for a destination, there are other aspects to consider. The major roles of transport for a destination include the following:

- Basic requirement
- Catalyst in the growth of tourism
- Determinant in destination success
- Component of tourist attractions
- Value proposition for destination marketing
- Determinant in tourist experience and satisfaction
- Recreational option
- Special interest tourism option (e.g. for safaris and adventure trips)
- Business and economic opportunities

An integrated transport network with convenient transfers between different modes of transport is essential, as are reasonably priced travel options. Within the destinations, tourists need a choice of transport to transfer between port of arrival and their final destination. In most cases, tourism has been developed in areas where extensive transportation networks were in place and the potential for further development was available. Tourism demand has stimulated the rapid development of transportation. Cooper et al. (2000) interpret the tourism product as everything that the visitor consumes, not only at the destination but also en route (to and from the destination). Thus transport consists of some key elements of the product. In certain cases transport itself acts as an attractive tourist product, e.g. Palace on Wheels and the Orient Express.

The transport sector has grown tremendously. But the external environment has forced transport operators to offer more enjoyable and satisfying transport products to tourists. Hence, transport services are particularly relevant and important in the context of tourism experience. And the efficiency of tourism transport services is important in the success of destinations. A wide range of parameters is applied while considering the efficiency of tourism transport. The parameters may include mode of services, efficient intermodal transport system, number of schedules, frequency of services, network, ease

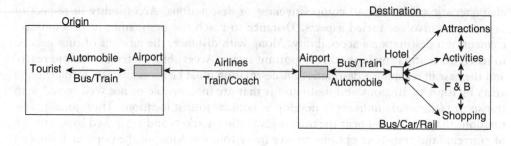

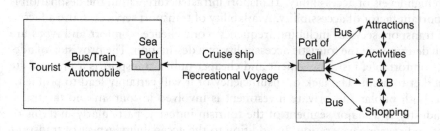

Figure 2.4 Transport connectivity in international tourism and cruise tourism

of booking, availability of information, speed, punctuality, reliability, customer service, customer care, comfort, facilities, ride comfort, safety records and security. In order to optimize the transport potentials, destinations essentially have to ensure the following:

- Quality vehicles
- Provision of an integrated, efficient multimodal transport system
- Safety and security
- Good connectivity
- Quality transport infrastructure
- Proficient travel and tourism information services
- Proper signboards and guidance
- Efficient and quality taxi system
- Efficient drivers/couriers
- Fair rate system
- Provision of experiential and recreational transport
- Provision of efficient online services and GPS systems
- Use of professional vehicle tracking and management systems

2.7 Multimodal transport for tourism

It's always better to ensure a multimodal transport system aimed at tourists is used in destinations. Indeed, every destination will have different transport options. Some have a good road network. Rail transport may also be of a high standard. Airport terminals and seaports may be an option. Public transport as well as dedicated tourist transport mechanisms are found in most tourist destinations. However, these varied transport forms and infrastructure may not have been organized enough to ensure smoother and efficient travel experience for tourists. An integrated approach to transport encompassing all forms or at least more than one form of travel can ensure hassle-free travel around a destination. An integrated transport network can enable a tourist to visit destinations and enjoy tourism with minimum difficulties associated with changing transport and separate bookings for different transport types. Though different forms of transport may be used, a single contract or ticket can often be enough to travel the entire journey – making it more straightforward for the tourist.

According to the OECD (2016), multimodal infrastructure denotes

> the network of airports, seaports, roads, railways, public-transport systems, and human-powered mobility options that are integrated and co-ordinated to form a transport system to move people or freight from one point to another. While a seamless multimodal experience might include, for instance, travelling on two or more forms of transport with a single ticket (e.g. rail and air). . . . In the case of tourism this includes the journey from a tourist's place of residence until arriving at their final or main destination, and then on to supporting attractions in the area.

Many city destinations offer multimodal transport services for visitors. Different types of multimodal tourist transport services are provided in developed countries to enable hassle-free visits for inbound tourists. In many cases, this type of multimodal transport service is provided around a hub airport or city. Efficient transport services are provided at hub cities and rail and road networks are effectively linked to provide better travel experiences. Hub-based integrated network connectivity is seen more in popular tourist destinations. Efficient integration of rail services with air transport is also more beneficial, as they can be complementary. In this modern era of transport, high-speed train services are warranted for such integration. Rail and coach services are also linked together to provide smoother journeys. Air travel and automobile (car) integration is common, particularly in business tourism.

CASE STUDY 2.2

Multimodal transport: Amadeus with a novel initiative for Europe

Linking every transport stakeholder together and ensuring seamless travel across Europe is a dream. With this objective, Amadeus, a leading global travel technology player, initiated a novel idea of multimodal transport in order to make travel across Europe seamless. They are working with the European Union and other travel players to make this dream a reality. Currently, only in very few instances are transport forms really connected, and due to the lack of a unified transport system travellers in Europe cannot see, perhaps, the most efficient travel options that combine different modes of transport. Linking public transport forms together can help to reduce the environmental impacts as well. By having a variety of options, the traveller can choose the most efficient option as per his/her need.

Along with supporting the European Commission in finding good solutions, Amadeus work closely with the rail sector as well, which is one of the most efficient modes of transport with the lowest environmental impacts. Linking air travel and rail travel together with the support of other modes of public transport can help create a seamless and eco-friendly travel experience for travellers. Once realized, it could bring change in travel in Europe: a shift from the use of private cars to public transport.

Amadeus will act as the enabler of multi- and intra-modal travel solutions across the globe and supply the different transport sectors with their technology needs. A well-connected journey can create a good experience for travellers. Those who have faced delays while travelling will have a different experience as this provides seamless connectivity. Those who book such journeys through an intermediary using Amadeus can remain stress-free, even when disruptions occur.

Source: www.amadeus.com

Read the case study carefully and answer the following questions:

- Describe the nature of multimodal transport mentioned in this case study.
- What are the benefits of multimodal transport?
- Describe the role of Amadeus in the above multimodal transport project.

2.8 Tourism transport: nature and types

Tourist transport has certain special characteristics compared to other passenger transport sectors. Seasonality is one factor that influences tourism transport, particularly in respect of variation in transport demand. Destinations that are more affected by seasonality are prone to increased variations in transport demand and supply. Price elasticity is another factor. Some of the transport forms face elasticity of demand. As price increases demand may decrease. For instance, the air transport sector is one in which price elasticity can be seen. Some of the transport sectors are highly capital-intensive. Cruise tourism operation is possible only when the cruise ship is ready to undertake service. Obtaining a ship is a costly affair. The same is true for air transport. Purchasing aircraft necessitates huge investment. Another feature of tourism transport is the presence of too many regulations. This is applicable to some of the transport forms, such as air transport. It makes the sector's "barriers of entry" quite high. Also, "oligopoly" is a feature of a few transport sectors. Cruise tourism is dominated by a few cruise liners. Airline sectors also feature oligopolies. Tourism transport in general possesses the common service characteristics, including intangibility, perishability and inseparability. With regard to tourism, the following types of transport can be identified:

- General passenger transport
- Dedicated tourist transport
- Experiential tourist transport
- Luxury tourist transport
- Recreational transport
- Multipurpose tourist transport (e.g. campervan, rotel)

Though not meant primarily for tourism, general passenger transport is a viable option for tourists in almost all locations. Within the destinations, use of general transport services is very common among tourists, except package tourists. International tourist travel also depends much on regular transport services. The majority of international tourists use scheduled air services for accessing destinations. Dedicated tourism transport services are also present. Charter tour operation is in vogue in many regions. Both long-haul and short-haul tourism rely on charter services for tourist arrival and return. Coaches are also used intensively in tourism in many locations. Dedicated transport is usually part of package tourism services. Experiential tourist transport refers to those transport services that provide unique experience for tourists as part of the tourism offering. Travelling on a vintage train along a hilly rail route can provide a mesmerizing experience. Luxury tourist transport is common in tourism. This aims to offer better comfort and service. Luxury tourist trains are the best examples for this category of transport services. Recreational transport is widely used in tourism. Recreational transport includes, among others: bikes, bicycles, hop-on, hop-off buses, safari vehicles, pleasure boats and dhows. The use of multi-purpose vehicles, such as motor homes, campervans, travel trailers, RV trailers, rotels, etc. is on the increase in tourism.

2.9 Factors influencing tourist transport selection

Tourist choice of transportation can have varied influencing factors. Usually a combination of different factors will come into play during the transport selection process. Different types of tourists have different needs and consequently transport selection determinants will also vary. For instance, as Lubbe (2003) points out:

> the independent traveller requires greater flexibility and freedom of movement while the group traveller generally prefers packaged programmes where travel is restricted to what the group does. . . . Independent business travellers generally need flexibility of movement, but require transport modes that are quick and reliable. The type of tourist also determines the type of fare that will be selected when a transport mode is chosen.

Regarding business tourists, the selection of transport may not be by the traveller, as the travel decision and purchase are made by others. Still, there are some common determinants/factors in the selection of transport by tourists:

- Distance
- Availability

- Schedule
- Frequency
- Route
- Convenience
- Speed
- Price
- Reliability
- Safety and security
- Quality of service
- Type of tour
- Unique experience/recreation

Distance to travel is the prime concern when selecting a mode of transport. For distant locations, tourists usually prefer air transport. For some distant journeys, even rail services are used. Though ships are viable for longer journeys, tourists rarely choose them – except for cruise tourism. While selecting a transport option, another important priority is the availability of different modes of transport. A tourist gets a choice only when the service is available. Tourists from cities have a choice of various modes of transport to travel. Destinations have to have an efficient transport system available, so that tourists can chose the most appropriate for their needs. Service schedules and times are also important to tourists when selecting a transport service. Time of departure and time of arrival are crucial for a tourist. Usually check-in and check-out times of hotels are considered when choosing the mode and type of transport. While some prefer to travel in the night, others may go for daytime travel. For package tours, the schedule of service is considered when using regular transport for international travel. Though schedule is important, the frequency of service is also a matter of concern. The greater the frequency, the easier the decision for the tourists. Again, this aspect is relevant for scheduled services. Charter services operate as per the need.

The route to reach a destination is also a factor of influence for selecting a transport service. Some longer distance journeys have stopovers and flight changes. The time gap in between the two parts of the journey can be a factor while considering the service. Some prefer to have a stopover in between so that they can make a short visit to the city. Some wish to feel refreshed before boarding the next flight to continue their journey, while many others prefer a direct route to their destination. Having a direct route and non-complex travel itinerary is an advantage for destinations. Convenient travel options make the choice easier for tourists. Different convenience-related factors, including the boarding location of a vehicle, time needed to get there and the location of the terminal in the arriving place influence a tourist's choice of transport service. At times, airports are located far away from cities. Reaching the airport itself can make passengers apprehensive.

Speed of the vehicle is also a major concern for passengers. Modern transport often features speed and comfort. Still, some are faster, and this influences tourists to choose them. That is the main reason why the majority of tourists prefer air transport services for international travel. Transport is a price-sensitive sector. Elasticity of demand is often attributed to transport services. Price affects tourism demand. Leisure tourists, particularly, are influenced by price when choosing a transport service. Services chosen should also be reliable; punctuality of service is something that passengers consider. Delays and cancellations of service can lead to disquiet and frustration. Comfort of the transport service is another important factor in the selection of transport service. Even in the same mode of service, different operators provide varied comfort levels. Comfort may also vary according to the price. Also, the distance to travel often correlates with the need for comfort.

Certainly, safety and security are concerns of passengers while travelling. People prefer safer and more secure modes of transport. As part of the decision-making process to buy a transport service, a tourist attempts to understand the level of safety and security. As in any other service sector, the transport sector has to provide quality service to its clients. From coaches to flights, this is certainly relevant. Airlines often try to differentiate their products with quality of service. Type of tour can also be a factor. For example, a group tour can have non-scheduled services more often than independent tourists. An explorer type of tourist may choose different types of transport service compared to a mass tourist, while a leisure tourist may choose different forms of transport to a business tourist. The selection of transport by a VFR (visiting friends and relatives) tourist may also be different. Tourists may often be influenced by the possibility of unique travel experiences or opportunities to engage in a recreational journey. This aspect is more relevant for transport *within* the destinations.

2.10 Tourism demand and transport

Defining tourism demand is a difficult task as there are different approaches pertaining to it. A simple one is a geographers' view. According to this view, tourism demand is the "total number of persons who travel or wish to travel, to use tourist facilities and services at places away from their places of work and residence" (Mathieson and Wall, 1982). The UNWTO's 2017 Tourism Highlights reveals that there were around 1.2 billion international tourist arrivals in 2016 (UNWTO, 2017). Domestic tourist arrivals are much more than the international arrival figures. This shows the quantum of tourism demand as well. These numbers are not the number of tourists, but rather the number of trips, which means that even if one individual makes more than one trip, it will be counted separately. Hence the numbers given are certainly more than the actual number of tourists. According to Tourism Towards 2030, a forecast by UNWTO, the number of international tourist arrivals worldwide is expected to increase by an average of 3.3 per cent per year between 2010 and 2030. By 2030, international tourist arrivals worldwide are expected to reach 1.8 billion (UNWTO, 2017).

UNWTO also reports that air and land (road and rail) are the most widely used means of transport by international tourists. In 2016, 55 per cent of international tourists used air transport, whereas 41 per cent of them used land-based transportation. Some 4 per cent of international tourists used water transport for reaching destinations and for returning. If we analyse the international tourism transport statistics, it is evident that the share of air transport has been increasing for the last few years, while the share of the rest of the modes of transport has been decreasing.

Along with the increase in tourist arrivals, the demand for tourism transport is also steadily increasing, which necessitates an increase in transport supply. Indeed, transport supply in tourism has expanded and now destinations are competing on the basis of transport options to enhance travel experience for tourists and to make tourism transport more attractive. Destinations are essentially enhancing their accessibility to compete internationally. The emergence of low-cost carriers (LCCs) really spurred air transport growth in developing countries as well, which contributed towards the increase in destinations' accessibility. Countries that have good rail networks are increasing the options for luxury tourist trains and rail tour packages to remote tourist destinations. Vintage train services targeted at tourists are also on the increase. Tourist rail passes are common nowadays. Cities are providing recreational transport options. Coaches and hop-on, hop-off bus tours are common in city destinations. Tourist coaches are now provided with the latest amenities and services. Intercity services targeting tourists are also common in cities now. Coach tourism generally is growing significantly, though the automobile is still the primary mode of transport within destinations for tourists. Car rentals are expanding their services and offering competitive products to clients along with expansion of operations into newer regions. Cruise tourism has been diversified and now the trend of offering large ships has changed to providing wider onboard entertainment options instead. Cruises are competing with various recreational and food and beverage (F&B) options. Ferries, too, have significance in tourism in many locations around the world. Other water transport forms are being increasingly used in tourism. Air transport certainly is at the forefront of tourism transport. Both common carriers and LCCs have a strong presence in tourism travel. Charter tourism is in an expansion mode as charter packages are being offered to more regions in the world. Destinations are trying to woo tourists with multimodal transport systems to ensure seamless and hassle-free travel arrangements. Certainly, unlike before, providing quality transport is a major objective of destinations to remain competitive in this hyper-competitive tourism market. Details of tourism transport supply are discussed in the following chapters.

2.11 Summary

Transportation is a crucial sector of any country in the world and plays a critical role in economic development. It is classified on the basis of the medium in which the travel takes place; as air transportation, water transportation and surface transportation. Various modes of transport are interlinked and interconnected. This interrelationship that exists among different transport forms makes transportation more accessible and easier. The absence of it will generate difficulty for a passenger while he/she travels. Each mode of transportation involves a range of carrying units. The experiences reveal that each mode of transport and different types of transport are interrelated and complementary, to some extent. Tourism and transport share a complex relationship and both complement each other in evolution and growth. Transport plays multiple roles in tourism, and is in fact a necessity for tourism to occur. Transport is a facilitator of tourism growth and it links the destination with its tourism markets. Providing mobility and access within a destination and mobility within tourist attractions are some other functions that transport plays in tourism. Transport also provides recreational options for tourists. In a few cases, transport represents the attractions themselves, like cruises. In multi-destination tours, it links the host destinations. Moreover, transport contributes to the attractiveness of destinations. An efficient transport system is a prerequisite for destination success and also a major contributor in tourism's socio-economic benefits.

Transport enables the spatial interaction between different tourist generating regions and destination regions. From a geographic perspective, travel occurs as a response to human desire for spatial movement, and transport facilitates the process of movement, which has economic and budgetary costs. For a destination, it is a basic requirement, a catalyst in the growth of tourism and a component of tourist attractions. It provides a value proposition for destination marketing and is a determinant in tourist experience and satisfaction. Further, it is a recreational option in certain cases and a special interest tourism option as well. It is always better to ensure a multimodal transport system that is aimed at tourists in destinations.

Tourism transport in general possesses the common service characteristics such as intangibility, perishability and inseparability. Tourism transport can be seen in different ways such as general passenger transport, dedicated tourist transport, experiential tourist transport, luxury tourist transport, recreational transport and multipurpose tourist transport. Tourist choice of transportation can have varied influencing factors. Distance, availability, schedule, frequency, route, convenience, speed, price, reliability, safety and security, quality of service, type of tour and the uniqueness of the transport experience do matter in the selection of tourist transport. Along with the increase in tourist arrivals, the demand for tourism transport is also steadily increasing, which necessitates the need for increased transport supply. Indeed, transport supply in tourism has expanded and now destinations are competing on the basis of various transport options to enhance the travel experience for tourists and to make tourism transport more attractive. Destinations are essentially enhancing their accessibility to compete internationally.

Review questions

Short/medium answer type questions

- Define transport and transportation.
- Write in brief the elements of transport.
- Explain the intricate relationship between transport and tourism.
- What are the roles of transport in tourism?
- Discuss how transport aids tourism growth.
- Discuss the role of transport for a destination.
- Write how tourism contributes to tourist experience.
- Describe accessibility of a destination from a transport perspective.
- What do we mean by multimodal transport in tourism?
- What are the factors that influence the transport choice of a tourist?

Essay type questions

- Write an essay on the role of transport in tourism.

References

Boniface, B. and Cooper, C. (2002) *The Geography of Travel and Tourism*. 3rd edn. Oxford: Butterworth-Heinemann.

Collier, A. (1994) *Principles of Tourism*. 3rd edn. Auckland: Longman Paul.

Cooper, C., Fletcher, J., Gilbert, D. and Wanhill, S. (2000) *Tourism: Principles and Practices*. London: Prentice Hall.

Goeldner, R. C. and Ritchie, B. J. R. (2003) *Tourism Principles, Policies and Practices*. New Jersey: John Wiley & Sons.

Hall, D. R. (1999) Conceptualizing tourism transport: Inequality and Externality issues, *Journal of Transport Geography* 7(3): 181–188.

Holloway, J. C. (1996) *The Business of Tourism*. 4th edn. London: Longman.

Leiper, N. (1990) *Tourism Systems*, Department of Management Systems, Occasional Paper 2, Auckland: Massey University.

Lubbe, B. (2003) *Tourism Management in Southern Africa*. Cape Town: Pearson Education.

Lumsdon, L. and Page, J. S. (2004) Progress in Transport and Tourism Research: Reformulating the Transport–Tourism Interface and Future Research Agenda, in L. Lumsdon and S. Page (eds), *Tourism and Transport: Issues and Agendas for the New Millennium*. Oxford: Elsevier.

Mathieson, A. and Wall, G. (1982) Tourism: Economic, Physical and Social Impacts. Harlow: Longman.

OECD (2016) Intermodal Connectivity for Destinations, Organization for Economic Cooperation and Development, OECD Centre for Entrepreneurship, SMEs and Local Development, available at https://www.oecd.org/industry/tourism/2016%20-%20Policy%20paper%20on%20Intermodal%20Connectivity%20for%20Destinations.pdf (accessed 15 January 2017).

Page, J. S. (1994) *Transport of Tourism*. London: Routledge.

Page, J. S. (2009) *Tourism Management: An Introduction*. Burlington: Butterworth-Heinemann/Elsevier Science.

Predeaux, B. (2000a) The Role of Transport in Destination Development, *Tourism Management* 21(1): 53–64.

Predeaux, B. (2000b) Transport and Tourism: Past and Future, in E. Law, B. Faulkner and G. Moscardo (eds), *Tourism in the 21st century: Lessons from Experience*. London: Continuum, pp. 91–109.

Predeaux, B. (2004) Transport and Destination Development, in L. Lumsdon and S. Page (eds), *Tourism and Transport: Issues and Agenda for the New Millennium*. Amsterdam: Elsevier, pp. 79–92.

Robinson, H. (1976) *A Geography of Tourism*. London: Macdonald & Evans.

Ullman, E. (1980) *Geography as Spatial Interaction*. Seattle: University of Washington Press.

UNWTO (2017) UNWTO Tourism Highlights 2017, available at https://www.e-unwto.org/doi/pdf/10.18111/9789284419029 (accessed 15 December 2017).

Website

www.amadeus.com.

Part II

Air transport

Introduction to air transportation

After reading this chapter, you will be able to:

- Understand the categorization of aviation.
- Identify the elements of the air transportation system.
- Understand the evolution of air transport into the modern form.
- Explore the after-effects of deregulation.
- Explain the international regulations in aviation.
- Explain the 'freedoms of the air'.
- Better understand the standardization in air transportation.
- Comprehend the safety and security aspects of air transport.

3.1 Introduction

Aviation is a broad term depicting all of the aspects associated with flying using an aeroplane. To be more precise it consists of a range of businesses and activities involved in building and flying aircraft for various purposes. The design, development and production of aircraft, the use and operation of aircraft, especially heavier-than-air, for various purposes, including for military, and maintenance of aircraft are the essential components of aviation. The term evolved from the Latin word *avis*, which means "bird". As stated before, this is now a huge industry in the world. Aviation enjoys incredible economic significance by way of generating employment opportunities for millions and by generating income in the billions, and other direct and indirect economic benefits. For instance, in the US, according to the Federal Aviation Administration (FAA), "the economic activity attributed to civil aviation-related goods and services totaled $1.5 trillion, generating 11.8 million jobs with $459.4 billion in earnings. Aviation contributed 5.4 percent to GDP, the value-added measure of overall U.S. economic activity" (FAA, 2014). Progress in aviation is often reflective of the progress in the local economy as well. Moreover, it is a facilitator of the long-term growth of a country. A vibrant aviation sector, particularly the general aviation sector, is a prerequisite of economic success.

Air transport, on the other hand, is a segment in the whole gamut of aviation and is the most significant mode of transport, growing at an incredible rate. The significance increases along with the distance covered. Put simply, it is the mode of transport using aerial vehicles for the purpose of moving people, cargo and mail from one place to another. The predominant view of air transport is related to use of the service of "common carriers", which are used in the context of public transport. While analysing air transport from a marketing point of view, it can be seen as an intermediate good, as most people use it as a means to achieve some other purpose (O'Connor, 2001). For example, when tourists fly to a destination, they may have an objective to have a happy vacation; the air strip is largely or entirely a means to this objective.

3.2 Types of aviation

Aviation is an umbrella term covering different aspects of flying. The following are commonly seen categories of aviation for the purpose of transportation.

- Civil aviation
  - o Commercial air transportation
  - o General aviation
- Military aviation

Civil aviation, one of two major categories of flying, represents all non-military flying, including both general aviation and commercial air transport. It consists of all commercial, business and personal transportation using aircraft and flights. General aviation (GA) includes all other civil flights, private or commercial. Although scheduled air transport is the larger operation in terms of passenger numbers, in terms of the number of flights used and the number of airports, general aviation is the largest category in the world.

Commercial air transportation, which is all about the transport of passengers, cargo or mail in a professional manner, is the most prominent one today. Scheduled services (e.g. major airlines) and non-scheduled services (charter airlines) are the two major components of commercial air transportation. Major airlines, regional airlines, low-cost carriers (LCCs) and charter airlines are all components of commercial air transportation. This has turned out to be the most important form of transport, particularly in the international sector, in the post-Second World War era. Furthermore, this sector contributes the largest share of socio-economic benefits of air transportation. A dynamic, strong and fast-growing commercial air transport sector is often considered an indicator of a country's strong economic growth and development.

3.2.1 General aviation

Apart from scheduled and non-scheduled commercial air transport operations, there are a number of other commercial applications, such as air taxi services and aerial application. All of these, which focus mainly on more specialized services that scheduled airline services cannot provide, fall under the general aviation category. ICAO defines general aviation as "all civil aviation operations other than scheduled air services and non-scheduled air transport operations for remuneration or hire" (ICAO, 2009). The flights in general aviation include aerial application planes, land survey flights, air ambulances, holiday vacation flights, air taxi services and special mission flights. A wide variety of services are included in this category. Business aviation, which includes the use of aircraft and helicopters for business purposes, is a dominant category here, serving people who travel for the purpose of attending work-related meetings, visiting clients or expanding and supporting the financial objectives of the businesses concerned.

Air taxi services are common in some developed countries. These are usually small commercial flights by companies holding an air taxi operating certificate, available for hire and used on demand. Usually these services are for short distances. Flights offer limited capacity – 20 people (or fewer). Speed is also lower than other flight operators. Aerial applications of aircraft are diverse, ranging from agricultural use to weather modification purposes. Agricultural aviation, earlier known as crop dusting, is very common.

Table 3.1 ICAO definitions of general aviation

Category	Definition
Instructional flying	This is defined as the use of an aircraft for purposes of formal flight instruction with an instructor. The flights may be performed by aero-clubs, flying schools or commercial operators.
Pleasure flying	This is defined as the use of an aircraft for personal or recreational purposes; not associated with a business or profession.
Business flying	This is defined as the use of an aircraft to carry personnel and/or property to meet the transport needs of officials of a business, firm, company or corporation. These flights may be performed by a commercial pilot or by a private pilot. Corporate aviation is also a part of this, covering the non-commercial operation or use of aircraft by a company for the carriage of passengers or goods as an aid to conducting company business, flown by a professional pilot employed to fly the aircraft.
Aerial work	This is an aircraft operation in which an aircraft is used for specialized services such as agriculture, construction, photography, surveying, observation and patrol, search and rescue, aerial advertisement, etc. Other aerial work includes the use of an aircraft for activities such as aerial photography, patrol and surveillance, prospecting, construction (i.e., aerial work in construction projects), advertising, and medical, relief and rescue work.
Agricultural flying	This is the use of an aircraft for activities such as crop dusting, chemical or fertilizer spraying, seed dissemination, prevention of frost formation, insect fighting and animal herding.
Other flying	This includes all general aviation flights other than glider and free balloon flights that cannot be included in the above four categories. Flights by pilots for maintaining their flying proficiency are also included.

Source: ICAO (2009)

It is used to apply crop protection products, fertilizer and even seed to grow and protect crops. Aerial photography is an interesting one; it's used for locating geographic features and environmental conditions, as a data source for base mapping and the like, or simply for photographing the beauty of the landscape. Aerial firefighting is usually used to combat wildfire. Such aircraft are also referred to as "air tankers" or "water bombers". Aircraft are also used for spotting fish. Usually fishing boats will accompany these aircraft and instructions from the flight will be provided for spotting fish.

Aircraft are also used to spray pesticides to control mosquitoes. Police use aircraft for a variety of purposes. It can be for traffic control, ground support in certain situations, search and rescue operations, etc. Manned or unmanned aircraft are used primarily for pipeline monitoring and safety purposes in the oil and gas industry. Aircraft use for weather modification is a specialized area in which cloud seeding is performed. Here, a seeding agent is spread from the aircraft into the cloud in order to change the nature of the cloud for rain, snow, etc. Wildlife conservation is another major application of aircraft. Nowadays many people take personal flights – among wealthy people, buying small aircraft for their own purposes is in vogue. Pleasure flying has a similar intent, with recreational purposes predominant. Instructional flying is another category; instructional flights are used for learning how to fly an aircraft. Flights are also used for research purposes, marketing purposes and many other purposes that fall under general aviation.

3.2.2 Military aviation

Military aviation denotes the use of aircraft and other flying machines exclusively for military purposes. It is usually part of the defence systems of sovereign nations. Military aviation also has a history spanning more than a century. The first military aeroplane, the 1909 Wright Military Flyer developed by the Wright brothers, was bought by the US Army for $30,000. That paved the way for the evolution of military aviation. Now a range of aircraft are used in military aviation. Usually they are different from those aircraft used in civil aviation. The major types include:

• Fighter aircraft (e.g. MiG-29)
• Ground attack aircraft (e.g. A-10)
• Surveillance aircraft (e.g. U-2 and MiG-25R)
• Common transport and cargo aircraft
• Bombers (e.g. Zeppelin, B-29 and the B-52)
• Helicopters
• Unarmed aerial vehicles

In fact, military aviation was a prime reason for the evolution and growth of modern air transportation. During the First and Second World Wars aviation was extensively (mainly) used for the transportation of arms and ammunition. Some advanced countries spent significant amounts on aviation development to gain the competitive advantage during the wars. The experimental use of aircraft and associated technologies brought rapid growth, greater operational capabilities and status as a reliable transport mode. Thus military aviation gained significance and came into force as a separate category by the end of the First World War. Larger aircraft used in the First World War, mostly single engine or twin-engine bombers, were modified later for civil aviation. Military aviation advanced then and continues to evolve today.

3.3 Air transportation system

The smooth, safe and efficient transportation of people and cargo over air is indeed an arduous task that involves a wide range of complex activities. The system that includes all the elements that ensure the performance of complex tasks and activities associated with air transportation in an efficient and coordinated manner will also be an intricate one. A wide range of physical as well as intangible elements ranging from human elements to the most advanced technological applications make up this air transportation system. All these elements, particularly those associated with civil aviation, can be classified under four headings:

1. Airports
2. Airlines
3. Aircraft
4. Air navigation services

The airport is the hub of air transportation where passengers can board and disembark flights, airlines can process passengers for travel, aircraft can be controlled for smooth flight, and freight forwarders can process cargo/consignments for shipments. Airlines, which provide various types of air-based transportation services, are the businesses that run regular/occasional services for carrying passengers and goods by aircraft. Airlines also make use of the services and facilities provided by the airports. Airports and airlines are described in detail in the following chapters.

3.3.1 Aircraft

An aircraft, a device used for travelling through the air, helps in connecting people and places along with transporting things like cargo. Aeroplanes, another term used instead, is defined by National Aeronautics and Space Administration (NASA) as "transportation devices which are designed to move people and cargo from one place to another. Aeroplanes come in many different shapes and sizes depending on the mission of the aircraft." (NASA, n.d.) Lighter-than-air aircraft are those whose weight is less than the air the aircraft displaces and are supported by their own buoyancy or ability to float. Hot air balloons, gas balloons, and blimps or non-rigid airships are examples of lighter-than-air aircrafts. We are here to discuss heavier-than-air aircraft that are supported by engines to propel and to fly. A variety of heavier-than-air aircraft are in use, and those have advanced significantly since the very beginning of modern air transport way back in the first decade of twentieth century. Commercial aircraft come in different sizes and shapes, with differing purpose, capacity, weight, speed and configuration.

As far as an aircraft is concerned, different parts may be identified. The fuselage, the main body of the aircraft, extends from nose to tail. The passengers and cargo are carried in this portion of the aircraft. The empennage/tail assembly is the rear part of the aeroplane. It consists of a fixed horizontal piece (horizontal stabilizer) and a fixed vertical piece (vertical stabilizer). They help to provide stability for the aircraft, to keep it flying straight. The vertical stabilizer keeps the nose of the plane from swinging from side to side. The horizontal stabilizer prevents the nose from moving up and down. The rudder is the small moving surface installed on the rear of the vertical stabilizer, to deflect the tail to the left and right, as viewed from the front of the fuselage. The elevator is the hinged part of the horizontal stabilizer that is used to move the tail up and down.

A wing has a curved top and nearly flat bottom, to help create the lift that raises an aircraft off the ground and keeps it in the air. Flaps are left, producing additional hinged surfaces. These help while landing and taking off. Slats also help in lifting an aircraft, and are installed on the leading edge of the wing. Spoilers help to reduce the amount of lift generated by the wing once the aircraft has landed. Landing gear (under carriage) consists of wheels (or floats), which move when on ground/water and support the weight of the aircraft. Usually, aircraft have a tricycle landing gear, with 12 wheels under each of the wings, and a nose gear with one or more wheels. It may vary depending upon the type of aircraft. Landing gear is retractable, meaning it moves back into the wings/fuselage after take-off.

The engine provides the power to fly. There are single engine and multi-engine flights. Engines may be attached on the front part of the fuselage, or in the wings, and fuel is usually carried in the wings as well as in the fuselage. In jet engines, the high-velocity jet exhaust from the burning of compressed air provides the power. This powers and spins the turbine wheel; the turbine runs the engine.

Four different forces act in the flight of an aircraft: **gravity, lift, drag** and **thrust**. Gravity is the natural pulling force of earth (pulling things towards it) and lift pushes the aircraft upward. Drag is a force that opposes the forward movement of an aircraft. When speed increases, drag also increases. Thrust, created by engines, helps to oppose drag and moves the plane forward. Wings generate the lift due to their shape. Lift is created only when an aircraft moves in air. Wings are designed to provide an appropriate amount of lift. The movable parts of wings like flaps come into play in speed variations and in landing and take-off. A pilot increases the lift by raising the nose of the plane slightly. To minimize drag created by extra lift, the engine power will also be increased. To descend, engine power will be decreased to reduce thrust. Then the lift will also come down. So the plane will move downward due to increasing gravity. Drag will also come into play and the plane will slow down. To turn a plane, the lift on either of the wing has to be increased.

Aircraft are created by aircraft manufacturers. Aircraft manufacturers develop airframes and the engines used in the aircraft are manufactured by other firms. Major aircraft manufacturers are:

- Airbus
- The Boeing Company
- Bombardier Aerospace Group
- The Embraer – Empresa Brasileira de Aeronautica
- McDonnell Douglas
- Lockheed Martin
- ATR (Avions de Transport Regional)
- Canadair
- Fokker

The world market is dominated by three manufacturers: Boeing, the Airbus Industries consortium of companies in Germany, France, Spain and Britain (British Aerospace), and McDonnell Douglas. The major aircraft engine manufacturers are:

- Rolls-Royce
- Pratt & Whitney (P&W)
- General Electric (GE Aircraft Engines)

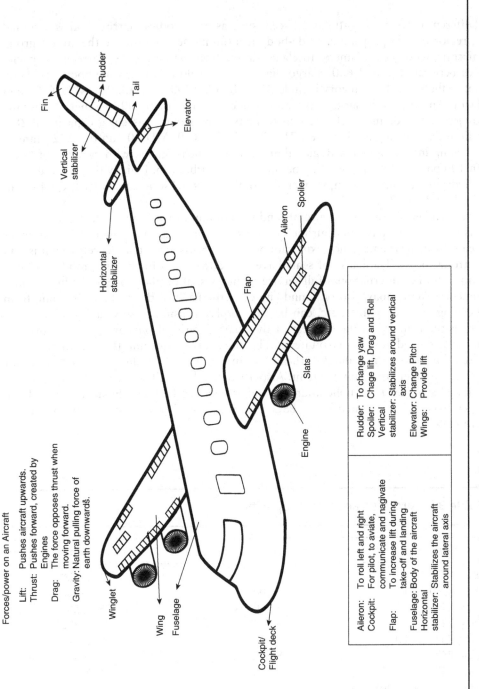

Forces/power on an Aircraft

Lift: Pushes aircraft upwards.
Thrust: Pushes forward, created by
          Engines
Drag: The force opposes thrust when
          moving forward.
Gravity: Natural pulling force of
          earth downwards.

Aileron: To roll left and right
Cockpit: For pilot, to aviate,
           communicate and nagivate
Flap: To increase lift during
           take-off and landing
Fuselage: Body of the aircraft
Horizontal
stabilizer: Stabilizes the aircraft
            around lateral axis

Rudder: To change yaw
Spoiler: Chage lift, Drag and Roll
Vertical
stabilizer: Stabilizes around vertical
            axis
Elevator: Change Pitch
Wings: Provide lift

Figure 3.1 Parts of a wide-body aircraft (jet)

- IAE (International Aero Engines-AG)
- Rolls Smiths Engine Controls

Different types of aircraft can be seen, such as wide bodies, narrow bodies, regional jets, regional turboprops, etc. Wide-body jets (jumbo jets) constitute the largest group of aircraft, with usual diameter fuselage varying from 5 to 6 metres. Passenger capacity varies between 200 and 600. Cargo flights are also flown using wide-body jets. Long distance flights in this category include B747, B767, A300/310, A330/A340, DC-10 and MD-11. An A380 is the largest so far and can carry more than 800 passengers. Narrow-body jets with a diameter of 3 to 4 metres have a maximum passenger capacity of 280. Medium distance flights that use B717, 737, 757, DC-9, MD-80 and the A320 family, etc. belong in this category. Regional aircraft are much smaller, with capacity of fewer than 100 passengers. Engines may be turbofan or turboprop. Usually they operate from small airports to hubs. Examples include Bombardiers, RJ series, Embraer ERJ 145 family, and ATR 42/72.

The number of seats on an aircraft and the amount of legroom given to each passenger is based on the particular airline's decision. Airlines may try to increase the number of seats. Seats near emergency exits cannot recline. Seats are fitted securely to withstand the strong forces. The backs of seats have fold-down trays for holding food, working, writing, etc. For international full-service flights, visual display systems (in-flight entertainment systems) may also be found either on the back of the seat or extending from the ceiling. Movies, games, etc. can be viewed/played using these visual displays, with controls often found in the armrest of the chair. Overhead bins are there for stowing hand luggage and other carry-on items. The passenger service unit (PSU) is found above the seat but below the ceiling/overhead bin and contains a reading light, a "gasper air vent" and a flight attendant call light. Also, there will be small "fasten seat belt" and "no smoking" signage. The public address speaker will also be there. Finally, a drop-down oxygen mask is also located in the PSU. This is activated when a sudden drop in cabin pressure occurs.

Table 3.2 Aircraft: range and capacity

Type of aircraft	Flight range (miles)	Passenger capacity
Airbus A320	4,026	150–180
Airbus A350–1000	7,900	366–440
Airbus A380	8,400–9,445	544–853
Boeing 727	3,060	250–380
Boeing 737 MAX 9	3,515	180–220
Boeing 747	5,500–6,500	430–452
Boeing 747–8	8,900	410–605
de Havilland Twin Otter	745	20
McDonnell Douglas DC-9	2,400–3,000	70–131
Lockheed L-1011 Tristar	2,200	90–139
McDonnell Douglas DC-10	5,998	246–330

3.3.2 Air navigation services

Air travel needs a fine-tuned support system for safe and smooth operation. A range of complexities are involved in air transportation. While flying, an aircraft cannot stop and wait for information. It flies very fast and a sudden change in direction or altitude is very difficult. Air navigation services make air transportation a smooth and safe affair. They include facilities that provide a pilot with information to enable him/her to reach the destination smoothly, safely and on time. This is detailed in another chapter.

3.4 History of air transportation

Air transportation didn't occur all of a sudden; rather, the experimental flight of the Wright brothers which took place in 1903 at Kitty Hawk, North Carolina was the end result of many attempts and developments over several years by a number of people. Many dreamt of flying freely in the sky and to travel to distant places. Many mythological stories mention flying and vehicles used for flying specifically. However, real flight in a controlled way with the help of an engine became possible only in the twentieth century. In fact, even in the eighteenth century people could fly, but it was using hot air balloons. In 1783, the flight became possible in the hot air balloon, which was designed first by the Montgolfier brothers. It had practical difficulties, as the balloon could only travel downwind. In the following year, a steerable balloon was invented by Jean-Pierre Blanchard and that was the first human-powered dirigible air vehicle. In the following year (1785) he crossed the English Channel. Later, in 1799, Sir George Cayley came up with the concept of an aeroplane, a fixed-wing flying machine with separate systems for lift, propulsion and control. A number of similar developments were made prior to the historic event of the experimental flight of the Wright brothers. It was on 17 December 1903, using the "Flyer I", that Orville Wright, with the help of Wilbur Wright, flew a distance of 37 metres (120 ft) for 12 seconds.

Soon, smaller planes were developed with single engines and capacity for 1 or 2 people. Gabriel and Charles Voisin started the world's first aircraft manufacturing company in 1905 in France. Louis Blériot crossed the English Channel in a monoplane in 1909. Pioneering aircraft began transporting items as early as 1910. Earlier military aeroplanes were not all that usable for civil aviation. Experimentation continued and metal-framed aeroplanes were introduced later. During the First World War, the US built 67 airports for military purposes, with only some basic facilities to base, fuel, and maintain aircraft and to provide landing and take-off facilities. The first airline service, in 1914, carried only one passenger, as the plane was a single capacity carrier. The first scheduled passenger air transport, from St Petersburg, Florida in the US, was organized by St Petersburg–Tampa Airboat Line, the first scheduled passenger airline service in the world. The service did not last long; it was wound up within four months.

The first air mail route in the US was established in 1918 between New York City and Washington, DC. In the same year the US Post Office Department took over the entire air mail service. Experimentation continued in using aircraft for transporting things. A regular schedule of freight flying was operated from Chicago. During this period, in order to have a common understanding among air transportation operators, the International Air Traffic Association (IATA) was formed in 1919 in The Hague, Netherlands. Night flying also began in 1924 in the US. After the First World War, European countries such as Germany, France and Britain started almost 20 small airlines using military aircraft from the First World War. National carriers like Imperial Airways (1924), Lufthansa (1926) and Air France (1933) were born over this period. Before that, in Australia, Qantas started operating in 1920. Towards the end of the 1930s, passenger air transportation in the US became a major mode of transport. Japan began airline operations after 1922. The Contract Air Mail Act (called the Kelly Airmail Act) was enacted in 1925 in the US, and it authorized the postmaster general to enter into contracts with private persons or companies for air mail transportation. The Kelly Airmail Act of 1925 provided private airlines with the opportunity to function as mail carriers. They expanded further to transport other forms of cargo; passenger transportation gained importance in US soon after and the US government passed the Air Commerce Act in 1926, which established aids to air navigation, granted authority for traffic rules, created mandatory registration of aircraft, and provided certification for airmen. During the 1920s, scheduled commercial air services started in Africa, Australia, Japan, Mexico, and some South American countries. In the US, passenger service came later, in 1926. Safety issues became a major concern, particularly between 1929 and 1933.

In the 1930s, airports began adding concrete runways (400–900 metres). The first airway traffic control centre was formed in 1935, at Newark, New Jersey, to inform by radio all pilots in the vicinity. In 1935, the British installed a top-secret network of radar transceivers along their coast and equipped their military aircraft with an early transponder known as IFF ("identification, friend or foe"). As transport grew, twin engine aircraft entered, e.g. Douglas DC-3 and Boeing 247. The Boeing 247 was developed in 1933, and was revolutionary as a modern passenger aircraft. The first jet engine aircraft was used by Germany in 1939 for military purposes. The Boeing 247, and Douglas DC-2 and DC-3 also emerged during this period. In the same decade, American Airlines, Eastern Air Lines, TWA and United Airlines were established and Pan American Airways expanded to overseas operations as well. The experimental flight by Charles Lindberg in 1927 across the Atlantic was revolutionary and soon several air transport companies began to set up shop. In 1938, the world's airlines carried almost 3.5 million passengers. Military usage of aircraft and further development took place during the Second World War era. Four-engine monoplanes like the Douglas DC-4 and Lockheed Constellation came into service by the early 1940s. Range and payload had increased significantly by then.

Civil aviation had a landmark period during the mid-1940s. The Chicago Convention (1944) became a milestone in global civil aviation. The system of bilaterally negotiated "traffic rights" between nations, which had applied generally before the war, was reaffirmed by the 1944 Chicago Convention, and the same gave birth to the International Civil Aviation Organization (ICAO) as a UN agency in order to guide and regulate global civil aviation. The International Air Transport Association, with the objective of smooth and efficient commercial air transportation, was formed in April 1945. The Chicago Convention was followed by the Bermuda Agreement in 1946, which set the pattern for most other traffic rights agreements. Development of the radar, with its primary version used in the war, was another major event in the aviation history. The first radar-equipped control tower was installed at Indianapolis in 1945.

Soon, airport runway lengths grew progressively and necessitated more support equipment. By the 1950s airlines had been established as a major mode of transport, particularly for long-haul journeys. By 1957, over the North Atlantic, as many passengers were flying as travelled by sea. Further advancement in aircraft were seen when newer planes came on the scene, such as the DC-7, and runways were extended along with increases in speed – up to 300/330 miles per hour. Along with piston type engines, turboprop aircraft were also in use those days. Very high frequency omni-directional range and finding (VORs and later VORTACs) and the instrument landing system (ILS) were established during 1950s. This decade also saw the commencement of classes of service along with higher operating standards and efficiency of services. Though Europe and the US remained the epicentres of advancement in air transportation, other countries like Japan, Australia and Canada also saw much progress in civil aviation. The Soviet Union also had remarkable achievements in this sector during the same period. By then the jet revolution had begun. In 1955, Pan American Airways placed orders for Boeing and Douglas jets. The Boeing 707, the pioneer jet engine model, went into service in 1958. In 1956 Russia put into service their Tupolev Tu-104 jet airliner. Soon the medium-range Boeing 720 would also enter the scene.

By the first half of the 1960s air transport had slowly advanced to the jet era. But the traffic trend saw a decline in the second half and many airlines were facing losses. Supersonic aircraft was an innovation of the late 1960s. In 1968, BAC/Aerospatiale introduced Concorde, with a speed of up to 2,400 kilometres per hour and a range of 7,000 kilometres. Passenger air transport had grown considerably in this decade. But, by then, airline hijacking or air piracy became a serious issue. In 1970, hijackers throughout the world seized 49 aircraft. Meanwhile, by introducing jet aircraft, tourist class services were launched for crossing the North Atlantic, and fares reduced by 20–25 per cent, which led to an increase of 25 per cent in passenger transportation. This aided the growth of international tourism, with the help of airlines. But, later, in the 1970s, sluggish growth was seen in air transportation. Heavy capital investments, escalating fuel costs after OPEC's formation (1960) and global inflation became the major reasons for the sluggishness in air transportation. In fact, in the 1970s, restrictions in oil production led to a dramatic rise in oil prices. Meanwhile, "Pan Am" became the first airline to offer jumbo jet travel (the Boeing 747), and France and Britain began passenger services with their supersonic transport – the Concorde.

3.4.1 Deregulation

In the following years, the most remarkable transformation in commercial aviation took place; it started in the US. The US air transport system was regulated for a period from 1938 to 1978. The Civil Aeronautics Board (CAB) became the ultimate authority of air transportation, controlling almost all aspects of air transportation during that period, including the commercial aspects and fixing of fares. This created a lack of market dynamism along with delays in processing requests and tasks, and led to talk of deregulation in air transport. In April 1976, the concept of deregulation was agreed in principle, which was promulgated as the Airline Deregulation Act on 24 October 1978. It was enacted with the objective of allowing the marketplace to determine the airlines' business decisions, and to ease controls over airline fares and routes in order to encourage greater competition and better services. Deregulation relied on the principle that the marketplace and free enterprise can better serve the public and the carriers. The primary objective was to have competition to improve efficiency and innovation, lower prices, and encourage price and service options. This could instil managerial efficiency, which could attract more capital and bring other advantages.

After deregulation, competition was a strong factor that determined the structure of the industry. Just after deregulation, most airlines offered similar services and facilities. Also, the major airlines tried their best to keep away new entrants by controlling most of the gates and landing slots at busy airports. Bigger airlines maintained greater market share.

As years went by, LCCs entered the scene which led to stiff challenges for the common carriers. LCCs could easily attract passengers, predominantly due to their low cost. Also, in the US, government agencies like the Department of Transportation pressured airports to provide more space for new entrants. Cargo deregulation was also introduced in 1977. Following the US, ten years later European countries began their own deregulation efforts in a phased manner through three policy "packages" agreed in 1988, 1990 and 1993. Japan's air transport remained regulated until 1996. By 1997, full deregulation came into force. Canada introduced deregulation in 1985 and Australia in 1990. By 1997, full deregulation came into force in the European Union. Due to several reasons, the deregulation efforts in Europe did not result in revolutionary changes. Countries and states continued to fund state-owned airlines, underwrite losses and revive balance sheets. Political interference and heavy unionism prevented many efforts in many countries. Also, airports were required to meet the increase in demand. This was also a slow process. Airport slot allocation was not a smooth and trouble-free process either. Many airlines, especially new ones, had objections due to the monopoly of major airlines in getting the slot.

Other, later effects of deregulation were as follows:

- Privatization in air transportation
- Rise in competition due to entry of new airlines
- Airfare slump
- Surging air travel demand
- Emergence of loyalty schemes
- Improvement of airline productivity
- Increase in air transport employment
- Flourishing of "hub and spoke" system
- Financial issues looming large over airline business
- "Open skies" agreements
- Mergers, takeovers and alliances
- LCCs: a new model of airline business model was established

The deregulated environment resulted in a change in the nature of ownership of aviation businesses, and privatization sprang up as a trend. As a consequence, some of the government-owned or government-controlled companies were fully or partially privatized. This helped the government raise money through the sale and reduce public expenses, enabled companies to become economically viable and encouraged competition. Examples include national carriers such as Air Canada, Air New Zealand, British Airways, Lufthansa and Japan Airlines. Also, deregulation opened up opportunities for investment in airline business for private players. Eventually, it led to the entry of a number of new airlines onto the scene which was controlled by public players alone. The entry of new airlines was like any other sector which experienced a quick transformation from regulated environment to deregulated environment. After the sudden increase in the number of airlines in the market, within a short span of time, many of them disappeared, particularly due to the financial imbalances as a result of extreme competition and fare war. Consequently, in order to beat the competition, most of the airlines entered into "price wars". This caused sudden declines in airfares. Moreover, the industry was able to introduce a wider range of lower, promotional and special fares. The decline in airfare, increase in air routes and services and the similar effects resulted in the rise of demand for air transport. The increase was phenomenal, as services were expanded to newer destinations and other favourable effects of deregulation were experienced.

Escalating competition and travel demand encouraged the industry to retain customers for longer periods; soon the concept of the loyalty scheme was introduced into the airline sector. To enhance the number of travellers and to create loyalty among passengers, airlines started to adopt the frequent flyer programme (FFP) in 1981. American Airlines was the first to do so. Frequent flyer programmes became a key measure of attracting and retaining travelling customers. Further, airline productivity was increased as a result of the dynamism in the air transport sector. Increased use of wide-body aircraft, increasing demand, increased rate of daily usage of aircraft, higher load factors, increases in seating densities, and longer average stage lengths contributed the most to airline productivity improvement. There was a surge in employment opportunities, directly and indirectly, in the air transport sector. For instance, in the decade from 1979 to 1989, airline employment increased from 356,000 people to 556,000 people (The Travel Insider, n.d.). Jobs were created in airlines, airports, aircraft manufacturing companies, travel agents and other related transport sectors. The hub and spoke system, in a limited way, existed even before deregulation, but the post-regulated era saw it flourish. As many airlines were merged and the business environment permitted easy entry and exit, airlines had to depend more on the hub and spoke system to operate international long-haul routes. Airlines could rationalize the efficiency of their services as a result of this in the deregulated environment. Within a short span of time, the haphazard growth of airline businesses began to face financial issues. By 1981, net operating losses spread in the industry, particularly due to rising fuel costs, economic recession and overexpansion in the wake of deregulation. Many airlines struggled to operate services, including Braniff International Airways, Pan American World Airways and Eastern Air Lines.

3.4.2 "Open skies" agreements

Open skies refers either to a bilateral or a multilateral transport agreement between countries, which liberalizes the rules for international aviation markets and minimizes government intervention. Under open skies agreements, airlines of both countries can fly any route they wish between the countries and can continue those flights into third countries (Wensveen, 2007). This was started by the US making agreements with other countries. Removing the barriers to accessing aviation markets abroad and removing barriers to competition were the prime objectives. It provided a free market for aviation services and offered more benefits for passengers, shippers and the economy of the country, on a wide scale.

Though the US made the first formal move toward international open skies in 1979, it became a reality in its true sense only in 1992, when the US signed its first true open skies agreement with the Netherlands, a watershed event in the move to open skies. As of writing, the US had entered into 118 open skies agreements with other nations. Due to these agreements, airlines can have foreign partners, access to international routes to and from their home countries, and freedom from many traditional forms of economic regulation. Air transport demand increased. This gives the airlines of the countries that signed the agreements the right to operate air services from any point in one country to any point in the other, as well as to and from third countries. The granting of rights under these agreements includes rights on routes, destinations, intermediate points, beyond points, etc. Airlines can fly to and from places they want in another nation, stopping where they want, and flying beyond the country, to a third nation. Directly or indirectly, it resulted in increased travel and trade, productivity, economic growth and better employment opportunities.

3.4.3 Mergers, takeovers and alliances

The effect of deregulation was so intense and far-reaching that within a decade so many changes had already taken place. As stated before, a number of airlines faced bankruptcy and losses, and some were merged or taken over by larger surviving firms. The tremendous effect of deregulation took place during mid-1980s when a number of mergers or acquisitions took place in the US; some of them are listed as follows (O'Connor, 2001):

- Delta merged with Western.
- American acquired Air California.
- Northwest acquired Republic.
- TWA acquired Ozark Airlines.
- United acquired the Pacific Division of Pan American.
- USAir acquired Piedmont and Pacific Southwest.

Many airlines have been merged, taken over or gone out of business; the surviving airlines had to look for other strategies to remain competitive. To ensure economic viability, many airlines attempted to be involved in cross-border alliances, partnerships and other cooperative arrangements. Alliances remain a major category among them. Star Alliance, SkyTeam and Oneworld are currently some of the major airline alliances in the world. In an alliance, companies remain separate entities, but the cooperation enables members to improve efficiency, increase customer service, and decrease the cost through sharing of sales offices, maintenance facilities, operational facilities, operational staff, investments and purchases. Alliances enable extended global networks. Customers benefit from lower prices, access to round-the-world tickets at better prices, and mileage rewards on a single account with different carriers. The benefits of cooperative arrangements range from improving efficiency, cost reduction and increasing market share.

3.4.4 LCCs: New model of airline business

Soon after deregulation, the LCC business model emerged in the US. The LCC model is a very cost-effective airline business model with limited services and specific route structure, unlike full-service carriers (FSCs). Such airlines are also referred to as "no-frills". Southwest Airlines was one of the first LCCs, operating from the late 1960s. This had a ripple effect on other airlines. In Europe, Irish company Ryanair, previously a traditional carrier, transformed itself into an LCC. The UK had its first LCC when easyJet began its service. Several other LCCs commenced operation, and by the end of the 1990s LCCs had captured a significant market share.

The air transport sector grew further as a result of the effects of deregulation. In the meantime, the Gulf War started in 1991, which dealt a severe blow to the aviation industry. Consequently, the industry posted a combined loss of $4.8 billion in 1992. Further developments took place technically and comfort-wise. Meanwhile, terrorism became a major threat for the air transport sector. In early 2003, the introduction of Airbus A340–500 and Boeing 777–200 ER aircraft allowed airlines to fly routes of more than 7,000 nautical miles. The September 11th terrorist attacks occurred in the US in 2001, which dealt another major blow to the industry. Prompted by fear, people either cancelled their air travel or preferred other modes of transport, at least for a short time. US airspace was closed for three full days over this period. Many airlines faced significant financial crisis and the industry recorded losses for three consecutive years. To overcome it, the US government granted a multi-billion-dollar relief package. Many airlines cut capacity by 20 per cent and laid off thousands of workers. Also, the Air Transportation Stabilization Board (ATSB) was set up to help the airlines recover and restructure. However, the industry has continued to progress. It saw many other milestones. The largest aircraft, the A380, which can carry more than 800 passengers, was introduced by the middle of the first decade of the new millennium. The Airbus 380 made its first test flight on 27 April 2005. The Airbus 380, the largest commercial aircraft ever built, set a record even when flying empty as the heaviest commercial aircraft to ever fly.

3.5 International regulations

Air transport operation is the only mode of transport that has to follow rules and regulations existing at international as well as national levels, and do so with utmost care. Besides technical rules and regulations, operating services at the international level also have to adhere to certain rules and regulations. Governments engage in a system of bilateral or multilateral agreements, which enables the airlines of those countries to operate services to the other respective countries. At the national level also, necessary approvals from the authorities must be obtained for operating domestic routes. However, the tariffs and fares charged by airlines are less controlled and demand variations heavily influence the fare. The political and regulatory environment of aviation is shaped by different bodies functioning at national, regional and international levels. The regulations existing at the international level, with regard to the freedom of international operations, have evolved over a period of time, through a number of exclusive conferences and conventions.

The dynamism and growth in air transportation after the First World War necessitated commonly acceptable regulations that could provide direction for commercial aviation. Rights and duties of shippers and airlines, airline liability in the wake of accidents and loss of luggage, lack of uniformity of commercial laws of different nations, and issues associated with crossing borders of other countries were the major issues that needed to be resolved through consensus of relevant authorities. Even before the commencement of the First World War, there were attempts to have mutual agreements in air transportation. France took the initiative in 1910 for an International Conference of Air Navigation in Paris. Twenty-one European countries participated and the discussions focused on various aspects associated with flying across boundaries of other countries. The convention focused on agreements among them and it made possible the reconciliation of the divergent views regarding the question of sovereignty of airspace. In 1916, the first Conference of Pan-American Aeronautics was held in Santiago, Chile, where countries argued for unifying their aerial legislation, in order to formulate an international air code of the American Republics. Though it didn't see much progress, it became the background for the 1919 diplomatic conference that framed the Paris Convention.

3.5.1 The Paris Convention

The Paris Convention (Paris Convention for the Regulation of Aerial Navigation – 1919) saw participation by representatives from allied nations and associated nations; ultimately, 38 states became parties to the accord. It became the first international multilateral convention on the regulation of aerial navigation. This convention recognized the principle of airspace sovereignty by stating that the member states have complete and exclusive sovereignty over the airspace above their territory. Apart from the reservation of the sovereignty of airspace by the contracting nations, the convention resulted in the issuance of certificates of airworthiness, each nation's registry of aircraft, the flight of aircraft over the other countries' territories, international air navigation rules, and prohibition of carriage of arms and ammunition. Moreover, the convention also produced the International Commission on Air Navigation (ICAN), a permanent Paris-based organization with a full-time secretariat. This commission was vested with the responsibility of execution, administration and updating of the Paris Convention.

3.5.2 The Havana Convention

The Paris Convention wasn't that effective, as many other states did not ratify, and there were alternatives. The Fifth Pan-American Conference was also held in Santiago, Chile in 1923, and it resolved that an Inter-American Commission on Commercial Aviation be established, consisting of not more than three delegates of each state of the Pan-American Union. It was mooted to formulate a code of laws and regulations. These dealt with commercial aviation, the determination of air routes, the establishment of special customs procedures for aviation, the determination of adequate landing policies, and recommendations with respect to the places at which landing facilities should be established (Wells, 1988). In the meantime, an attempt was made at Madrid, Spain in 1926 to create an Ibero-American Convention on Air Navigation, also known as the Madrid Convention, but the same did not enter into effect. The Inter-American Commission met for the first time in Washington, DC in May of 1927 and prepared a draft code which was revised by the Director General of the Union. The same was submitted to the Sixth Pan-American Conference, held in Havana, Cuba, in 1928 and was ratified by the participating states.

3.5.3 The Warsaw Convention

Later, the government of France made an attempt in 1923 to adopt national laws relating to liability in the carriage by air, but soon realized the need for a unified law at an international level to prevent the unforeseeable conflicts of law and conflicts of jurisdiction. The 1923 event adopted a resolution calling the public's attention to the need for the establishment of a uniform code. The French government took the initiative to have further discussions on the above and representatives of 43 nations met in Paris in 1925. Further amendments and discussions took place on the draft prepared. The conference also established the International Committee of Technical Exports of Air Jurisprudence (Comité International Technique d'Experts Juridiques Aériens– CITEJA) with headquarters in Paris. The draft prepared by the Committee was submitted for consideration at the Second International Conference on Private Air Law held in the Royal Castle at Warsaw, Poland in 1929. Thus the Warsaw Convention, formally entitled Convention for the Unification of Certain Rules Relating to International Carriage by Air came into effect. According to the Warsaw Convention, an airline would be liable for damages in the event of:

- Death or injury to the passengers
- Destruction, loss or damage to baggage or goods
- Loss resulting from delay in transportation of passengers, baggage or merchandise.

It also offered standards for air tickets, airway bills for cargo and other air travel documents. This was amended in a diplomatic conference held in The Hague in 1955. Called

The Hague Protocol, it finalized the compensation limit by doubling the amount. Further revision took place in a diplomatic conference in 1961 at Guadalajara, Mexico.

3.5.4 Chicago Convention

Some other multilateral commissions were also held afterwards: the Buenos Aires Convention of 1935, the Bucharest Convention of 1936 and the Zemun Agreement of 1937. By the time the Second World War commenced focus had moved away from air transport regulations. However, technically, aviation did advance greatly in the war era. Soon after the war, the aviation sector faced a vast array of issues. The majority of issues were either technical or political. The commercial rights of carriers to fly across the territories of other countries were a major issue. Until the end of the Second World War, the negotiation of international routes was left to the individual carriers. It was in 1944 that the US government issued invitations to various nations for an international conference on civil aviation, focused on tackling flying rights over territories of various countries. Representatives of 52 nations assembled in Chicago in November 1944. It was organized with the intention to foster development of international civil aviation in a safe and orderly manner and to promote international air transport services on the basis of equality of opportunity and sound and economical operation.

The Convention has been sometimes referred to as the "Magna Charta for the postwar development of international civil aviation" (Wober, 2003). The Chicago Convention could establish the rules for international aviation operations. The Conference also produced the International Air Services Transit Agreement, the International Air Transport Agreement, drafts of 12 technical annexes to the Chicago Convention and a standard form of bilateral agreement. In addition to the agreements, the Chicago Convention provided recommendations to foster smooth flow of international air transport through inter-governmental agreements. The standard form, the major document of the Convention, has been adopted by many countries as a basis for arrangements. The Chicago Convention affirmed the principle of air space sovereignty and raised for the first time the issues concerning exchange of commercial rights in international civil aviation. The Convention decided to simply create a framework within which the rules regarding international air transportation could be established for regularity of air transport services between pairs of countries. The Bilateral Air Service Agreements (ASAs) thus emerged as the instrument for initiating or modifying international transportation and for regularity of those services. (Odoni, 2009). The Convention made it mandatory to follow the international standards and practices to the highest degree of uniformity by all contracting states in terms of the following (Wensveen, 2007; Wells, 1988):

- Characteristics of airports and landing areas
- Communication systems and air navigation aids, including ground markings
- Aircraft flying rules and air traffic control (ATC) practices
- Airworthiness of aircraft
- Licensing of operational and mechanical personnel
- Registration and identification of aircraft
- Aeronautical maps and charts
- Gathering and exchange of meteorological information
- Customs and immigration procedures
- Aircraft in distress and investigation of accidents of all types
- Matters concerning the safety, regularity and efficiency of air navigation

- Logbooks

The Convention was particular in ensuring the international commonality in airport and ATC facilities, equipment and procedures to ensure the safety and operability of aircraft across other countries. This led to the establishment of a permanent international body charged with coordinating the rules, guiding air traffic operation across the world, developing international standards for air transport facilities and equipment, and overseeing adherence to these rules. The International Civil Aviation Organization (ICAO) came into being on 4 April 1947, and in October of the same year, it became a specialized agency of the United Nations linked to the Economic and Social Council (ECOSOC). ICAO was established with the objective to foster the planning and development of international air transport in accordance with certain enumerated principles. The Chicago Convention superseded the Havana and Paris Conventions and stipulated that all the aeronautical agreements and those subsequently contracted had to be registered with ICAO, and those not consistent would be abrogated.

One of the outcomes of the Chicago Convention, the International Air Services Transit Agreement, was also referred to as the Two Freedoms Agreement. This provided the multilateral exchange of rights flying across the border of another country and non-traffic stops for scheduled air services among its contracting states. This provided two sets of freedoms for those states signing the contract. These freedoms consisted of privileges to fly across the territory of other countries without landing, and to land for non-traffic purposes. Another outcome, the International Air Transport Agreement, came to be known as the Five Freedoms Agreement. This included five freedoms of the air for scheduled international air services. Though this was proclaimed in it, they didn't get much attention then. Moreover, there existed some differences regarding the fixing of airfare, routes and tariffs.

3.5.4 The Bermuda Agreement

In 1946, representatives from the US and Britain met in Bermuda to negotiate a bilateral understanding, which came to be known as the Bermuda Agreement. It helped to incorporate Chicago standard clauses and stipulated that disputes that could not be settled through bilateral consultations had to be put before the ICAO for advisory opinion. The Bermuda Agreement gave a satisfactory reconciliation of the differences that existed in international air policy between the US and the UK after the Chicago conference. After the discussion, a compromise emerged regarding tariffs and routes. Routes were specified and tariffs were agreed to be established by the airlines through the International Air Transport Association (IATA), subject to the approval of both parties. It was decided that capacity would be determined by airlines based on agreed terms and conditions. This, known as the Bermuda Agreement, became the most successful bilateral agreement after the Chicago Convention, and its success became an inspiration for other countries, while the Bermuda Agreement itself became a model. Indeed, many agreements were signed by other countries.

3.5.5 Bilateral agreements and freedoms of the air

A bilateral air transport agreement takes place between two nations, who sign to allow international commercial air transport services between their territories. The commercial access to other markets become possible through the establishment of traffic rights. The

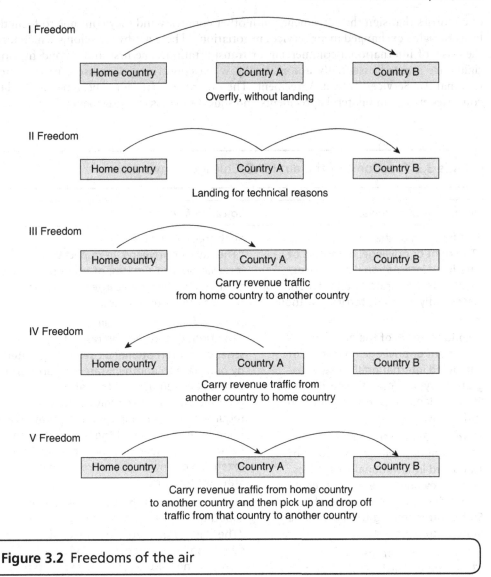

Figure 3.2 Freedoms of the air

Chicago Convention specified the basic traffic rights required for operation in other markets, including foreign countries. A traffic right:

> is a market access right which is expressed as an agreed physical or geographic specification, or combination of specifications, of who or what may be transported over an authorized route or parts thereof in the aircraft (or substitute conveyance) authorized.
>
> (ICAO, 2004)

It denotes the right to transport passengers, cargo and mail, separately or in any combination, and is expressed as a freedom of the air. The first two freedoms of the air were stipulated as per the International Air Services Transit Agreement. Freedoms of the air became the building blocks of air navigation regulations. These are the rights of airlines of countries that sign the agreements with other countries and they continue to form the basis of rights exchanged in air services negotiations. There are five freedoms which form the basis of international commercial air transportation. The first and second freedom rights are granted essentially automatically when countries give consent to the International Air Services Transit Agreement. The other three freedoms become valid when countries engage in bilateral agreements and sign the necessary agreements. The first five

Table 3.3 Freedoms of the air: ICAO/Chicago Convention

Five freedoms of the air	*So-called freedoms*
First freedom of the air "The right or privilege, in respect of scheduled international air services, granted by one State to another State or States to fly across its territory without landing."	Sixth freedom of the air "The right or privilege, in respect of scheduled international air services, of transporting, via the home State of the carrier, traffic moving between two other States."
Second freedom of the air "The right or privilege, in respect of scheduled international air services, granted by one State to another State or States to land in its territory for non-traffic purposes."	Seventh freedom of the air "The right or privilege, in respect of scheduled international air services, granted by one State to another State, of transporting traffic between the territory of the granting State and any third State with no requirement to include on such operation any point in the territory of the recipient State, i.e. the service need not connect to or be an extension of any service to/from the home State of the carrier."
Third freedom of the air "The right or privilege, in respect of scheduled international air services, granted by one State to another State to put down, in the territory of the first State, traffic coming from the home State of the carrier."	
Fourth freedom of the air "The right or privilege, in respect of scheduled international air services, granted by one State to another State to take on, in the territory of the first State, traffic destined for the home State of the carrier."	Eighth freedom of the air ("consecutive cabotage") "The right or privilege, in respect of scheduled international air services, of transporting cabotage traffic between two points in the territory of the granting State on a service which originates or terminates in the home country of the foreign carrier or (in connection with the so-called Seventh Freedom of the Air) outside the territory of the granting State.".
Fifth freedom of the air "The right or privilege, in respect of scheduled international air services, granted by one State to another State to put down and to take on, in the territory of the first State, traffic coming from or destined to a third State."	Ninth freedom of the air ("stand alone" cabotage) "The right or privilege of transporting cabotage traffic of the granting State on a service performed entirely within the territory of the granting State."

Source: ICAO/Chicago Convention (n.d.)

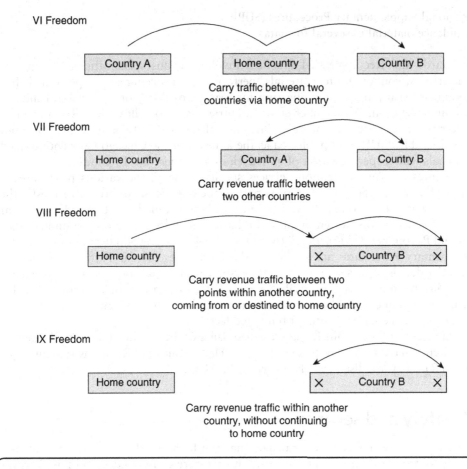

Figure 3.3 So-called freedoms of the air

freedoms are the officially recognized ones by the international treaty. More freedoms were added later. Currently there are nine freedoms. These, as per the ICAO, are provided in Table 3.3.

Open skies agreements are also giving ample rights for airlines of two or more countries to have frequent and less restricted flights in foreign countries.

3.6 Standardization in air transportation

The consistency in standards that must be followed by civil aviation across the world is developed and implemented by the ICAO. These standards are commonly referred to as standards and recommended practices (SARPs). ICAO stipulates the necessary standards and other provisions in the following forms:

- Standards and Recommended Practices (SARPs)
- Procedures for Air Navigation Services (PANS)

- Regional Supplementary Procedures (SUPPs)
- Guidance material in several formats

Standards and Recommended Practices involve various specifications for physical characteristics, configuration, materials, performance, procedures and personnel. It is important to ensure uniform application for reasons of safety or regularity of international air navigation. All member states/countries have to follow this. Recommended practices cover the specifications regarding all of the above, but the uniform application is only desirable. SARPs are published as the annexes of the Chicago Convention. Each annex deals with a specific aspect of air travel; in total there are 18 annexes.

Procedures for Air Navigation Services specify in detail the various procedures to be applied by air traffic service units as part of their services. According to ICAO, this involves various "operating practices and material too detailed for Standards or Recommended Practices – they often amplify the basic principles in the corresponding Standards and Recommended Practices" (ICAO, Making an ICAO Standard, n.d.). Regional Supplementary Procedures are similar to the Procedures for Air Navigation Services, and specify details of all such aspects in the respective regional contexts. Guidance materials, additional to the SARPs and PANs, include the regulations or directions issued as attachments to annexes, policies, manuals and circulars, all of which have the scope of providing guidance with or without binding effects.

Flight rules to follow while flying are called Rules of the Air. In addition to the general rules, aircraft have to adhere to either Visual Flight Rules (VFR) or Instrument Flight Rules (IFR). They are discussed elsewhere in this chapter.

3.7 Safety and security

Among the transport forms, air transport has the highest safety and security threats. As aviation progressed, safety and security threats were compounded and posed critical challenges. The Airport is the hub of air transportation and is the most vulnerable element of air transport in terms of safety and security. Modern airports have multilayered checks and measures which make up a comprehensive system for mitigating threats. Let's look at the safety and security aspects separately. There can be a number of factors that can affect the safety of the airside. Airports take utmost care to avoid safety issues due to such factors. Possible safety issues are discussed below.

Ground and runway safety: this is a very common type of safety issue in air transport. Runway incursion (vehicles, persons or aircraft present in the runway), runway excursion (due to inappropriate exit from the runway) and runway confusion (use of either wrong runway or taxiway unintentionally) are the most common causes of runway-related accidents. Incursion can happen due to human factors, improper instructions from ATC, climatic reasons, like rain and poor visibility, inadequate markings and/or lightings, etc.

Loss of control: loss of control in flight (LOC-I), of late, is a major cause of fatal accidents. It does not take place when a pilot is in a situation in which he/she cannot control anything to avoid an accident. According to IATA (2015), loss of control in flight refers to:

> accidents in which the flight crew was unable to maintain control of the aircraft in flight, resulting in an unrecoverable deviation from the intended flight path. LOC-I can result from engine failures, icing, stalls or other circumstances that interfere with the ability of the flight crew to control the flight path of the aircraft.

IATA further reveals that during 2010–2014, there were 415 accidents, of which 38 were classified as LOC-I. Of the total 415 accidents, 88 were fatal and 43 per cent of those took place due to the reason loss of control (LOC- I), which eventually resulted in 1,242 fatalities (deaths of passengers and crew, in total).

Bird strike: this represents the collision between a flying bird and a flying aircraft, which can be very dangerous. This usually happens near airports, at landing or during take-off. Most airports now undertake land management practices to avoid birds near airports.

Lightning: usually, aircrafts are built to withstand lighting, but in rare cases it can damage aircraft. Aircraft manufacturers usually take adequate measures.

Ice and snow: ice/snow on runway can be dangerous; it can cause a pilot to lose control of the aircraft while landing or taking off. Large quantities of ice on wings can result in the decrease of lift of aircraft.

Sand and dust: the engines have the ability to suck in sand/dust in huge quantities and this is an issue, especially in areas where sand/dust storms occur. Volcanic dust is particularly dangerous for flights. Flights can be disrupted by volcanic dust, with the ash causing significant damage to engines.

Mechanical errors: a range of mechanical errors due to failure of aircraft parts can lead to dangerous situations. Metal fatigue, the effect of cyclical pressure and stress on metal parts, can happen either in the engine or the fuselage. Delamination of composite material is also an air safety concern, especially in the tail sections of aeroplanes. Engine failure has been a safety issue, but nowadays this issue is minimized by the use of multiple engines. Some mechanical errors occur because of a flaw in the plane's design that may result in metal fatigue cracks and wing failure.

Poor weather conditions: this is another common cause of safety issues. Some large-scale air crashes were due to poor weather conditions. For instance, the Flydubai flight crashed (in March 2016) near the runway in a Russian airport due to poor weather conditions and poor visibility, with 62 people dying in the crash. Indonesia AirAsia Flight 8501 was travelling from Surabaya, Indonesia to Singapore on 28 December 2014 when it crashed due to poor weather conditions, killing 162 people.

Controlled flight into terrain (CFIT) and approach and landing (ALA): controlled flight into terrain is a major cause of aviation accidents worldwide. Most of the CFIT accidents occur during the approach and landing phase. Although new developments in aircraft technology increase a pilot's awareness of terrain, it does not guarantee protection from a CFIT or an approach and landing accident. A range of strategies are being undertaken around the world to prevent this kind of accident.

Human factors: a poor decision, lack of care, confusion, negligence, etc. can be fatal. Human error is a major cause of air safety issues. Human errors are of different kinds: decision errors involving procedural errors, poor choices and problem-solving errors; errors associated with skill like the inadvertent activation of controls, and the misordering of steps in procedures; perceptual errors; and violations of rules and guidelines of different kinds (FAA, 2005). Pilot error alone is the most prominent reason in air accidents. One of the most important in this area is situational awareness and control. Use of other electronic equipment while flying can also threaten the flight.

Other causes: there are some other causes of fatal accidents. These include issues associated with the safety management system, midair collision due to lack of separation, issues in air navigation services and air–ground communication, inadequate maintenance and design, and automation-related issues.

It is mandatory for the players involved in air transport, including airport and airlines, to ensure the safety of flight. International rules and guidelines must be followed. Extreme care is taken to avoid any kind of safety issues.

CASE STUDY 3.1

Airport security and aircraft hijacking: a long history

Certainly it's not a new phenomenon: aircraft hijacking began many decades ago. The first reported incident took place on 21 February 1931, in Arequipa, Peru when Byron Rickards (USA) was flying a Ford Tri-motor from Lima to Arequipa. Upon landing, he was surrounded by a group of armed people belonging to a revolutionary group, but later he was freed. Subsequently, hijacking of aircraft has turned into a horrifying reality for the industry, which has killed many people over the intervening years. It's not restricted to any region – it happens in all corners of the world. The September 11 attacks in the US alone caused the death of almost 3,000 people.

In 1948, a flight was on its way from Macau to Hong Kong when it was hijacked, killing all 25 people who were on board when the flight crashed into the Pacific Ocean. Another serious hijacking event took place in 1968. PFLP (Popular Front for the Liberation of Palestine) followers hijacked Flight 426 of El Al Airlines of Israel which was flying from London to Rome. Every hostage was released at different points. Hijacking became a serious issue as the number of aircraft hijacked began increasing. Between 1958 and 1967, almost 50 aircraft were hijacked. In 1977, Lufthansa Flight 181 was hijacked, again by PFLP supporters. All hostages were saved, while two of the hijackers were killed during the rescue operation. A similar incident occurred in 1976 when two PFLP supporters and two members of the German Revolutionary Cells hijacked in midair Air France Flight 139 from Athens. The hijackers' demands were political, including releasing imprisoned supporters. After a commando operation, 105 hostages were freed.

In 1977, a Malaysian aircraft was hijacked. The plane crashed in Kampong Ladang killing seven crew members and 93 passengers. In 1985, Air India Flight 182 was hijacked and the plane went down after a planted bomb exploded, killing 329 passengers. In 1985, an Iraqi Airways flight was hijacked, and 60 people died, and in 1986, an Egypt Air flight was hijacked. Another major incident was the hijacking of Ethiopian Airlines Flight 961, which led to the deaths of 122 people in 1996. And there have been many other deadly incidents in the history of commercial air transport.

After every hijacking, the aviation sector has tried to improve security measures. By the 1970s and 1980s, countries started to have stringent security checks before the commencement of each flight. In 1973, Cuba and the USA entered into an agreement to prosecute hijackers. Better scanning machines had been introduced by then. The number of hijacking incidents dropped as a result of such measures, though they found ways and means of getting around them. September 11th was the result of such efforts. On September 11, 2001, four commercial airline flights were hijacked and used in suicide attacks on major landmarks in New York City and Washington, DC. Boeing 767 aircraft (American Airlines and United Airlines) departed Boston's Logan International Airport and were flown into the 110-storey buildings of World Trade Centre, resulting in the collapse of those buildings and the death of a large number of people. Simultaneously, the other hijacked flight of American Airlines departed Washington, DC's Dulles Airport and was flown into a portion of the Pentagon, the headquarters of the US Department of Defense. Another flight was also hijacked but did not end up in the targeted destination. What set this hijacking apart was that the target of the hijackers was not just the passengers and crew on board, but other people on the ground. The attacks forced the airline industry to renew and strengthen its focus on security. Bulletproof and locked cockpit doors became standard on commercial passenger aircraft. Passengers could not enter the cockpit. Monitoring of cabins is also possible nowadays. Hand luggage and body checks became very stringent, with each and every passenger manually checked. The items one was permitted to carry in hand luggage were strictly limited. Despite having these stringent measures on aviation security in place, a few incidents have occurred in the intervening years.

Read the case study carefully and answer the following questions:

- Discuss the changes in the focus of hijacking attempts since they began.
- Describe how security measures were improved over the last eight decades.

3.7.1 Security

An aircraft is vulnerable to the threat or use of violence. A single person with a weapon inside a flight can control a large number of people while flying. And also, even after landing due to limited exit options, one or a small group of terrorists can control them, and take substantial leverage in blackmailing and negotiating with the authorities concerned for favourable deals. National governments, through their civil aviation authority, have to establish and implement security programmes for their airports and air transportation in the country. Aviation security, according to Annex 17 of the Convention of International Civil Aviation, is "a combination of measures and human and material resources intended to safeguard international civil aviation against acts of unlawful interference" (ICAO Definitions, UVS International, n.d.). Recently it has been more focused on the situations in which passengers are taken as hostages and terrorists take possession of aircraft. There are a variety of security issues, such as: incidents and accidents that occur as part of aircraft operations; bomb blasts; structural fires; natural calamities that affect aviation; national disasters; radiological incidents; sabotage; hijacking; and other unlawful acts.

Aviation security has to be ensured with utmost care. The major components of it, in general, are: intelligence gathering; controlling access to secure air operation areas; screening of passengers and carry-on luggage; screening of checked baggage and cargo; and aircraft protection (including cockpit protection) (Seidenstat, 2004). The airport is the nerve centre of all the safety and security measures. A wide variety of measures are taken in airports to avoid safety and security issues. According to Barnett (2009), security measures are generally classified into three different kinds. They are: the measures to protect the passenger cabin and cockpit; measures to prevent explosions in the baggage compartment; and measures to prevent threats external to the aircraft. Airports, together with airlines, have a significant role in ensuring all of these categories. For baggage compartments, a variety of activities are undertaken to ensure safety and security. Explosion detection equipment and canine teams can be used to ensure that there are no dangerous materials loaded along with the cargo or checked-in bags in the baggage compartment. This exercise is done when the cargo and baggage are still in the airport. Consignments will be verified, and if need be additional security measures will be undertaken, i.e. verified manually, or using sniffer dogs, metal detectors, explosive vapour detectors, etc. The luggage is also screened using x-ray machinery prior to collecting or loading into the aircraft. For carry-on/hand luggage screening, the airline counter will first issue a tag for hand luggage. Hand luggage will be screened using radioscopic (x-ray) equipment. Also, explosive vapour detectors may be used to check carry-on items. For checked baggage screening, all such items have to pass through an automated screening device (usually x-ray machine). It is basically done to check for unauthorized carriage of weapons, explosives or dangerous goods. A manual search is also done. Positive passenger bag matching (PPBM) is a recent measure which refers to a process by which the airline ensures that all checked bags on an aircraft have their respective "owners" onboard as well. Checked luggage is cross-matched with passenger manifests to ensure that no baggage is there unless its owner is on board. Nowadays, known shipper programmes or trusted shipper programmes are also in place in many airports. In order to avoid external security threats, a range of measures are in place in and around an airport.

3.8 Summary

Aviation is an umbrella term covering different aspects of flying. Civil aviation and military aviation are the two prime categories that fall under it. Civil aviation consists of commercial air transportation and general aviation. The air transportation system consists of a wide range of physical as well as intangible elements ranging from human elements to the most advanced technological applications. Airports, airlines, aircraft and air navigation services are the elements of this system. The airport is the hub of air transportation, where passengers can board and disembark flights, airlines can process passengers for travel, aircraft can be controlled for smooth flight, and freight forwarders can process cargo/consignments for shipment. Airlines, which provide various types of air-based transportation services, are the businesses that run regular/occasional services for carrying passengers and goods by air using aircraft. An aircraft, a device used for travelling through the air, helps in connecting people and places, and in transporting things like cargo. Air travel needs a fine-tuned support system for the safe and smooth operation. A range of complexities are involved in air transportation.

The history of air transportation covers a century now. Newer technologies introduced at regular intervals advanced air transportation to become a fast, comfortable and safe mode of transport, accessible to a large section of the population worldwide. Deregulation was a major milestone in the history of modern air transportation and the sector witnessed increased dynamism and competitiveness after that. Expansion of "open skies" agreements and an increase in mergers and takeovers were some of the immediate after-effects of deregulation. The LCC model of air transport was also soon expanded. In fact, smoother and safer air transport became possible due to conventions and summits and to the growth of air transportation generally. The Paris Convention, Havana Convention, Chicago Convention and the Bermuda Agreement were the most significant. The Chicago Convention specified the basic traffic rights (freedoms of the air) required for operation in other markets, including foreign countries. The consistency in standards that must be followed by civil aviation across the world is developed and implemented by the ICAO, which was also formed by the Chicago Convention. Among the transport forms, air transport has the highest safety and security threats. As aviation progressed, safety and security threats were compounded and posed critical challenges. Though aviation safety and security has been prioritized, new challenges continually emerge. The current trends reveal that further evolution and growth of air transport is certain, which will indeed impact tourism greatly.

Review questions

Short/medium answer type questions

- What are the elements of aviation?
- Give a brief account of general aviation.
- Distinguish between civil aviation and general aviation.
- What are the elements of the air transportation system?
- Give a brief account of aircraft structure.
- Describe the impacts of deregulation in air transportation.
- What do we mean by "open skies" policy?
- Give a brief account of mergers that occurred in the airline sector after deregulation.
- What are freedoms of the air?
- What are the Standards and Recommended Practices in air transportation?

Essay type questions

- Discuss the evolution and growth of air transportation.
- Describe the conventions that shaped modern air transport and write down the bilateral agreements in commercial air transportation.
- Write an essay on the safety and security issues in air transport. Be sure to include the common measures undertaken in airports to ensure safety and security of flying.

References

Barnett, A. (2009) Aviation Safety and Security, in P. Belobaba, A. Odoni and C. Barnhart (eds), *The Global Airline Industry*. West Sussex: John Wiley & Sons.

FAA (2005) Human Error and General Aviation Accidents: A Comprehensive, Fine-Grained Analysis Using HFACS, available at https://www.faa.gov/data_research/research/med_humanfacs/oamtechreports/2000s/media/0524.pdf (accessed 15 January 2017).

FAA (2014) The Federal Aviation Administration: The Economic Impact of Civil Aviation on the U.S., available at https://www.faa.gov/air_traffic/publications/media/2014-economic-impact-report.pdf (accessed 16 February 2016).

IATA (2015) IATA Loss of Control In-Flight Accident Analysis Report 2010–2014, Montreal–Geneva: International Air Transport Association.

ICAO Definitions, UVS International, available at http://www.uavdach.org/aktuell_e/3_UVSI_ICAO-Definitions_V01_120813.pdf (accessed 30 August 2016).

ICAO (2004) Manual on the Regulation of International Air Transport, International Civil Aviation Organization, Doc 9626.

ICAO (2009) International Civil Aviation Organization: Review of the Classification and Definitions Used for Civil Aviation Activities, available at http://www.icao.int/Meetings/STA10/Documents/Sta10_Wp007_en (accessed 25 March 2016).

ICAO, Making an ICAO Standard, available at http://www.icao.int/safety/airnavigation/pages/standard.aspx (accessed 16 February 2016).

ICAO/Chicago Convention, Manual on the Regulation of International Air Transport (Doc 9626, Part 4), International Civil Aviation Organization, available at http://www.icao.int/Pages/freedomsAir.aspx (accessed 11 February 2016).

NASA, Airplanes and Parts, available at https://www.grc.nasa.gov/www/k-12/airplane/airplane.html (accessed 25 February 2016).

O'Connor, W. (2001) *An Introduction to Airline Economics*. London: Praeger Publishers.

Odoni, A. (2009) Airports, in P. Belobaba, A. Odoni and C. Barnhart (eds), *The Global Airline Industry*. West Sussex: John Wiley & Sons.

Seidenstat, P. (2004) Terrorism, Airport Security, and the Private Sector. *Review of Policy Research* 21(3): 275–291.

The Travel Insider, A History of US Airline Deregulation, available at http://thetravelinsider.info/airlinemismanagement/airlinederegulation2.htm (accessed 15 April 2016).

Wells, T. A. (1988) *Air Transportation: A Management Perspective*. California: Wadsworth Publishing Company.

Wensveen, G. J. (2007) *Air Transport: A Management Perspective*. 6th edn. Hampshire: Ashgate.

Wober, L. (2003) Postal Communication, International Regulation, in Max Planck Institute for Comparative Public Law and International Law (ed.), *Encyclopedia of Public International Law*. Amsterdam: North Holland.

Chapter 4

Airport

Learning objectives

After reading this chapter, you will be able to:

- Define airport.
- Understand the functions and roles of airports.
- Narrate the evolution of modern airports.
- Identify the customers and revenue sources of airports.
- Describe the structure of an airport.
- Explore the functions of runway, taxiway, apron, air traffic control (ATC) and terminal.
- Learn the certification requirements and regulations of airports.
- Explain the organization and personnel in airports.

4.1 Introduction

Once upon a time, airports were just grass strips where planes could land and take off, with some space for loading and offloading passengers, mail and cargo. Later, by the 1930s, airports had become simple buildings that provided a waiting area along with facilities for landing and take-off. During this period, planes were very light, with low engine power and a tail wheel, and hence a meadow with proper water drainage was sufficient. By the 1940s, airports had improved in terms of scope, operation size, functions and facilities, and later when jet engine flights were introduced in air transportation, further developments took place. Technological advancements, enhancement of socio-economic circumstances of societies, the necessity for improved safety and security measures, policy changes such as deregulation and privatization, etc. provided much impact in the evolution of airports into a modern form. The evolution has been phenomenal; currently an airport is a small city itself, a self-contained metropolis of shops, hotels, banks and facilities complete with their own security and fire departments. It has even been remarked upon as a great "hub of human motion" (Hardaway, 1991). The significance of an airport has been changed from the centre of transportation to a centre of

---

Table 4.1 Leading airports in the world

In terms of passenger transportation		In terms of cargo transportation	
Airport	No. of passengers	Airport	Cargo (metric tons)
Atlanta (ATL)	94,431,224	Hong Kong (HKG)	4,166,304
Beijing (PEK)	83,712,355	Memphis, TN (MEM)	4,137,801
London (LHR)	72,368,061	Shanghai (PVG)	2,928,527
Tokyo (HND)	68,906,509	Incheon (ICN)	2,464,384
Chicago (ORD)	66,777,161	Dubai (DXB)	2,435,567
Los Angeles (LAX)	66,667,619	Anchorage, AK (ANC)	2,421,145
Dubai (DXB)	66,431,533	Louisville, KY (SDF)	2,216,079
Paris (CDG)	62,052,917	Frankfurt (FRA)	2,094,453
Dallas/Fort Worth (DFW)	60,470,507	Paris (CDG)	2,069,200
Jakarta (CGK)	60,137,347	Tokyo (NRT)	2,019,844

Source: CIA (2013)

---

varied economic activities. Furthermore, an airport is a matter of pride and economic advancement of a state.

The number of airports has been growing consistently, and will continue to grow due to the incredible growth in passenger and cargo transportation. There are a large number of airports, but the number of airports in commercial aviation is much less. According to the ICAO, the aviation industry consists of some 1,400 commercial airlines, 4,130 airports and 173 air navigation services providers (ANSPs) (ICAO, 2015). Table 4.1 presents a list of the top ten airports in terms of passenger and cargo movement.

4.2 Concept and definition of airport

Simply, an airport is a created space where flights can land and take off, with facilities for loading and unloading of passengers and cargo. One runway or helipad (for helicopters) is required for an airport. However, an airport exists with a range of other facilities and services as well, in addition to the runways and roads for take-off and landing. It provides all infrastructure needed to enable passengers and freight to transfer from the surface to air modes of transport and to allow aircraft to take off and land (Graham, 2003). Hangars and terminal buildings are common components of an airport. Additionally, an airport may have a variety of facilities and infrastructure, including fixed base operator services, air traffic control (ATC), passenger facilities such as restaurants and lounges, and emergency services. A military airport is known as an airbase or air station. The terms airfield, airstrip and aerodrome may also be used to refer to airports of varying sizes.

In many cases, the term aerodrome is used for referring to an airport. According to ICAO, an aerodrome is "a defined area on land or water (including any buildings, installations and equipments) allocated wholly or in part for the arrival, departure and surface movement of aircraft" (ICAO Definitions, UVS International, n.d.). This is a broader definition that encompasses all sorts of airports and airstrips. Even general aviation landing facilities are included in this. Airports are a subset of aerodromes, as all airports are aerodromes but all aerodromes are not airports. The distinction is based on the criteria for calling an aerodrome an airport. For an airport, all necessary infrastructure and facilities are required as per ICAO specifications. Wells and Young (2004) specify that commercial airports, wherever they are in the world, should satisfy a set of international technical standards intended to ensure aircraft safety and inter-operability across national boundaries. ICAO defines an international airport as:

> any airport designated by the Contracting State in whose territory it is situated as an airport of entry and departure for international air traffic, where the formalities incident to customs, immigration, public health, agricultural quarantine and similar procedures are carried out.
>
> (ICAO Definitions, UVS International, n.d.)

A commercial airport may include runways for take-off and landing, other infrastructure to park aircraft, facilities for maintenance, terminals for passengers and cargo, and other facilities as needed for safety, security, loading and unloading of passengers and cargo, fuelling of aircraft, etc. It is specifically licensed for commercial aviation operation. It is also an entity that offers services mainly for airlines to operate transportation. Moreover, it is a technical and technological centre, which enables aircraft to land and take off as well as help to fly as per the rules and regulations.

An airport has many dimensions and plays a significant role in the socio-economic life of a country. Some of the dimensions of an airport, as suggested by Graham (2003), are as follows:

- It brings together a wide range of facilities and services in order to be able to fulfil its role within the air transport industry.
- It offers a wide variety of commercial facilities ranging from shops and restaurants to conference facilities.
- It provides strategic importance in the region by integrating with the overall transport system and establishing links to key rail and road networks.
- It can bring greater economic development, provide substantial employment opportunities and be a lifeline to isolated communities.

From the above discussion, we can conclude that an airport is a complex set of facilities, services and infrastructure which enables air transport service providers to transport passengers and cargo from one place to another. The essential facilities and infrastructure may include standard runways, taxiways, aprons, safety and security facilities and services, air navigation services, aircraft maintenance facilities, passenger terminals with necessary facilities for passenger handling and travel baggage handling facilities, etc. Commercial services, like duty-free shops and refreshment centres, vary according to the size and nature of the airport. Hence, a commercial airport is a multifaceted air transport infrastructure element encompassing a wide range of facilities and services (technical and commercial) which enables and contributes to smooth, safe and comfortable travel, and to the movement of cargo. Airports are categorized in different ways:

- *Civil aviation airports:* these consist of general aviation airports and commercial service airports.

- *Commercial airports:* these consist of international and domestic airports (depending on the destinations to which services are offered).
- *Hub airports:* these are commercial airports that are considered hubs for air services to many other cities.
- *Regional airports:* these are airports with commercial services in a smaller area.
- *Military airports:* these are built for military/defence purposes.

The following discussion on the functional roles of an airport, particularly a commercial airport, clarifies the concept of airports further.

4.3 Functions and roles of an airport

An airport is an integral part of a nation's overall transport system. There is at least one airport in each sovereign country in the world, which will form part of the overall transport network. A commercial airport won't function in isolation due to the multiple roles it has. The following are the major functional roles of air transport:

- Basic infrastructure needed for air transport
- The location where airlines can undertake flight series
- Interface between land mode and air mode of transport
- A point of national and international connectivity
- A transport hub
- A facilitator for economic development
- A basic infrastructure for international trade
- A facilitator for regional and local development
- An employment provider (direct and indirect)
- A location for cargo handling and its loading and unloading
- Entry and exit point with emigration services for travellers
- Space for safety and security measures in air transportation
- Commercial space refreshments, duty-free shopping, currency conversion, etc.

From a tourism point of view, an airport has much more significance. A tourist enjoys a range of services from an airport. Some of the major services are as follows:

- A port of entry for a tourist visiting a country
- A place for getting a visa wherever visa on arrival (VOA) services are available
- Centre for refreshment options
- Place for booking tourist services such as accommodation, car rental, etc.
- Concierge services and tourism information services
- Shopping location
- Safe transport of luggage
- Place for destination reception, "meet and greet" and tour briefing while arriving
- A platform for tour briefing and seeing off departing tourists
- Currency conversion and limited banking services
- An attraction for tourists and an element in the composite tourist experience
- A place for rejoining friends and making new friends

Table 4.2 National Plan of Integrated Airport Systems (NPIAS) definitions of airport categories

Airport category	Definition
Commercial service airports	Publicly owned airports that have at least 2,500 passenger boardings* each calendar year and receive scheduled passenger service. The definition also includes airports who receive passengers continuing their journey on an international flight for a non-traffic purpose, such as refuelling or aircraft maintenance rather than passenger activity.
Non-primary commercial service airports	These are commercial service airports that have at least 2,500 and no more than 10,000 passenger boardings each year.
Primary airports	These are the commercial service airports that have more than 10,000 passenger boardings each year.
Cargo service airports	These are the airports that, in addition to any other air transportation services that may be available, are served by aircraft providing air transportation of only cargo with a total annual landed weight** of more than 100 million pounds. An airport may be both a commercial service and a cargo service airport.
Reliever airports	These are airports designated by the Federal Aviation Administration (FAA) to relieve congestion at commercial service airports and to provide improved general aviation access to the overall community. These may be publicly or privately owned.
General aviation airports	These are public-use airports that do not have scheduled service or have fewer than 2,500 annual passenger boardings. In this category, national airports are those general aviation airports that support the national and state system by providing communities with access to national and international markets in multiple states and throughout the United States. Regional airports support regional economies by connecting communities to statewide and interstate markets. Local airports supplement communities by providing access to primarily intrastate and some interstate markets. Basic airports link the community with the national airport system and supports general aviation activities (e.g., emergency services). Unclassified airports also provide access to the aviation system.

* Passenger boardings: this refers to revenue passenger boardings on an aircraft in service in air commerce whether or not in scheduled service.
** Landed weight: this refers to the weight of aircraft transporting only cargo in intrastate, interstate and foreign air transportation.
Source: FAA (n.d.)

4.4 Evolution of modern airports

Airports had humble beginnings, used simply as a space for landing and take-off of small planes, requiring only a flat, even surface. Often, they were simply open grass fields.

Dirt-only fields came later, which could eliminate drag from grass. Further improvements came with paved asphalt or concrete surfaces. Aerodrome was the term used for airfields in the beginning. The word comes from the Latin/Greek words *dromus/dromos*, which refer to a race course. Early airports were situated on private property. Built airports began to appear by the beginning of the Second World War in many towns and cities. Before that, airports were steadily increasing in significance as a public utility. The Second World War resulted in many innovations in aviation, including the first jet aircraft and the first liquid-fuelled rockets. One of the earliest aerodromes was Taliedo Aerodrome in Milan, Italy. Opened in 1910, it was transformed into an airport in the mid-1920s and opened to commercial traffic. Later it became too small to cope with the increasing demands of commercial traffic, which led to it being replaced with the Milan Linate Airport (MXP). College Park Airport, Maryland, founded in 1909, is known as "the cradle of aviation". It is the oldest airport in operation and currently serves as one of the gateway airports between Washington, DC and Prince George's County. Shoreham Airport, founded in 1911, was the first commercial aerodrome in the UK. Soon, small airports were built in other major cities.

While airports were expanded along with the increase in demand, the advent of technology and the changes in the social, economic and cultural spheres of human beings brought phenomenal changes in terms of the nature of runways. The length, depth and width of runways increased substantially with the increase in size and speed of aircraft. The first paved runway was made in 1928 at the Ford Terminal in Dearborn, Michigan. Narrow runways were sufficient for earlier aircraft to land and take off. When planes powered by jet engines entered passenger transportation, wide-body aircrafts came into use. This necessitated wider, longer and deeper runways. The first fixed runway lighting appeared in 1930 at Cleveland Municipal Airport, Ohio.

As airports had to respond to growing demands in passenger transportation, both the airside and the landside of airports were expanded, especially after the end of the Second World War. Further airport expansion took place after deregulation, and later, since the 1990s the world has been caught up in the effects of globalization and liberalization. Runway expansion was the prime agenda of airside expansion, particularly during the 1970s, in order to cope with the advances in wide-body aircraft. Terminal expansion also became a matter of concern for airport authorities. The trend of terminal expansion has been widespread since the 1990s when the number of airlines and passengers increased significantly along with changes in socio-economic circumstances. Major airports needed to have runways more than 3,000 metres long. Now airports have runways of up to 5,500 metres. The latest aircraft such as the A380, with much larger capacity, needed larger airports and hence major airports had to upgrade their runways and taxiways, in some cases relocate taxiways and even relocate aircraft stands and buildings to provide sufficient wing tip clearance.

4.5 Socio-economic significance

Apart from the facilities and services offered for transportation of passengers and cargo, airports have many other dimensions of socio-economic significance. Primarily, airports ensure a faster mode of travel for the people travelling into and out of a region. The travel duration is curtailed remarkably by using air transport, which helps to increase accessibility and inter-regional expansion – a boon for community upliftment. Opening up a new airport or increasing existing airport capacities facilitates additional accessibility and this investment can have a positive long-term impact on economic growth. An airport is usually an indication of economic progress of a region as well. In order to have economic progress in a region, airports become necessary. It provides direct, indirect and induced economic benefits. The most obvious parameter of its economic significance is the employment opportunities it provides directly and indirectly. In an airport, there is a wide variety of employment opportunities, including those associated with aircraft operations and maintenance, passenger and freight handling, ATC and safety, transport and logistics, airport management, planning and construction, and various retail and commercial services inside the airport. There are many associated businesses connected to an airport. Associated businesses offer a diverse range of employment in and around the city in which the airport is located. The passengers who are coming into the region also spend on a wide variety of items which will have a multiplier effect in the economy.

Proximity or connectivity of airports is a determinant in investment decisions of many sectors. It directly helps to have more investments in the economy. Movement of cargo by air is an advantage for businesses. Moreover, export industries are benefited directly as well indirectly. Airports enhance business efficiency. As travel duration and logistics time are curtailed, it may result in increased productivity, both directly and indirectly. An airport is also a matter of pride too for the local community. The aviation network identifies the airport and will be shown on the air network map. Airports play a vital role in connecting communities, people and markets, and that enhances the mobility of the population. Moreover, it helps in having a strengthened link between different countries and cultures. Eventually, it also helps to increase international understanding and multicultural cooperation. Increased mobility and access to places is something the community can enjoy through the establishment of an airport.

Apart from these benefits, an airport also plays a key role in/is a catalyst for tourism development and growth. For both inbound and outbound tourism, air connectivity has tremendous significance. For a destination, it helps to increase the flow of tourists into it. Subsequently, tourism benefits the community in a number of ways.

4.6 Airport product and customers

A commercial airport, as a service provider, offers aeronautical services and facilities to airlines. An airport serves a range of customers, directly and indirectly. According to Halpern and Graham (2013), the customers of an airport include airlines, passengers, tour operators, travel agents, freight forwarders, ground handlers, retail concessionaires and to some extent the employees working inside the airports. At the same time, Herrmann and Hazel (2012) attempt to categorize such customers into five categories: airlines; passengers; non-travellers (employees, visitors and retail customers, meeters and greeters, and neighbours); tenants/service providers (retail, car park, ground handling, advertisers); and potential development partners (real estate developers, hospitality, transportation service providers, government). The latter category includes more groups of customers. Airlines are a major customer of airport services. They serve their customers using the services and facilities provided by the airport. Airlines act as a customer and the final consumers of the services are the passengers or those sending cargo. Airlines need services for landing and taking off, space for parking, loading and unloading of flights, baggage handling, check-in, emigration and security check-in services, and other services necessary for operating their flight services. A cargo operator or a freight forwarder also depends on the airport for the movement of their consignments. Here also the final consumers can be the people who send and/or receive the consignments. Moreover, an airport provides services to the commercial agents/firms, like duty-free markets, catering establishments and car parking agents. They are also customers for an airport as they use airport services. Here also passengers constitute the major group of final consumers. The passenger, the final consumer, takes advantage of these services through the airline and expects a smooth and quick check-in and boarding process, along with good waiting area, ambience, etc. At the same time, passengers directly consume a variety of services from an airport.

An airport offers a variety of services to different customers and consumers, yet it is considered a composite product. While the product offered by an airport consists of a supply of services, both tangibles and intangibles, it has different dimensions according to the type of customers, consumers and market segments. The core product of airports with regard to an airline is the ability for aircraft to land and take off smoothly and efficiently, along with the ability for smooth, efficient and quick passenger handling. For the passenger, it is the ability to board and disembark an aircraft for travelling from one place to another using the services of an airline. For freight forwarders, the ability to load and unload freight into and out of an aircraft is the core product. Of late, the service delivery and quality of the services have increased significantly, compared to the earlier era, i.e. prior to deregulation. Currently, as privatization is increasing, airports, too, face competition. Though certain areas like ATC, etc. cannot be altered or modified as they are subject to the state requirements, airports can enhance the quality of many of the services and facilities offered by them. The quality parameters include: the space for queuing and holding lounge space; sufficient check-in space for airlines; comfortable seating in the concourse, departure lounge and gate area; time taken for the security and immigration process; connection/transfer time for connection flights; car parking space and services; equipment for baggage processing; facilities for passengers inside the terminal, including shops and exchange services; complaint response time; baggage delivery time; ground transportation facilities; aircraft turnaround time and delays; number of aerobridges; and others. Total quality management is a norm in the airport sector nowadays.

4.7 Revenue sources

Airports also generate revenue for their competitive survival. Earlier, when airports were treated just as a transport infrastructure and survived in regulated environments, the main source of revenue was the aeronautical activities, which take place on the airfield or in the terminal where airlines operate. As the nature of airports changed, the focus of revenue generation slowly shifted to non-aeronautical activities as well. While aeronautical revenue is dependent directly on aircraft operation and processing of freight and passengers, non-aeronautical revenue is generated from the commercial activities that take place inside the terminal as well as from the rent accrued from space allotted for different entities/activities. Income in the form of landing fees, passenger charges, cargo charges, and from ground services and ground handling activities are all included in the former category. Non-aeronautical revenue sources include: rents; direct sales centres such as shops, catering services by airport concessionaires;

car parking; and other sources such as consultancy services, visitor services, business services, etc. According to Odoni (2009), the following are potential sources of revenue for airports:

- Aeronautical charges:
  - o Aircraft landing fee for the use of runways and taxiways
  - o Terminal area navigation fee for air traffic management services
  - o Aircraft parking and hangar fee
  - o Airport noise charge
  - o Passenger service charge
  - o Cargo service charge
  - o Security charges
  - o Ground handling charge
  - o Concession fees for aviation fuel and oil, etc.
- Non-aeronautical charges
  - o Commercial concession fee by shops and service providers
  - o Rental for airport land, buildings space and equipment
  - o Tolls for automobile parking and rentals
  - o Fee for the provision of engineering services and reimbursable utilities

4.8 Airport ownership and privatization

Most of the commercial airports in the world are still functioning under the government or its agencies. In the very early stages of air transport evolution, airports were privately owned, but with the increasing significance of air transportation governments soon began to take control. After the First and Second World Wars, air transport surged and rapid changes were visible in airport environments. Around the world, ownership remained mainly with the government – directly or indirectly. Some airports were owned and operated directly by government departments, such as civil aviation authorities. Some were managed and operated by semi-autonomous bodies. Others were operated by agencies like companies with public shareholdings, on a concession basis for long periods from national governments.

Deregulation resulted in many changes in airports as well. Commercialization of the airport industry began to take place after the deregulation of public air transport. The increasing cost of building (new) and maintaining (existing) airport infrastructure led some governments to "privatize" or allow the private sector to assume ownership of some airports. In fact, airport privatization began not as a modernization agenda, but evolved due to many pressures and factors emerging in the last quarter of the twentieth century. The need to reduce public sector investment was urgent in many countries. Moreover, it's a widely held view that privatization can enhance the efficiency of operations, encourage greater competition and help in diversification. All of these were essential due to the rapidly changing demand trends during the 1980s and 1990s. The major developments that took place as a consequence of the changes in the air transport sector included airport privatization, commercialization and globalization (Graham, 2008).

While privatization refers to the transfer of management and/or ownership fully or partially to the private sector using different practices, airport commercialization is all about the transformation of an airport from a public utility to a commercial enterprise incorporating modern management principles, practices and philosophies. Privatization is defined as:

> the shifting of governmental functions, responsibilities, and sometimes ownership, in whole or in part, to the private sector. With respect to airports, "privatization" can take many forms up to and including the transfer of an entire airport to private operation and/or ownership.
>
> (Tang, 2017)

Table 4.3 Graham's airport privatization models

Model	Description
Share flotation	Full or partial sale of the airport through the issue and trade of share capital, but can also include long-term leasing (50+ years). BAA PLC, (currently Heathrow Airport Holdings Ltd) is an example of this. Even if the share flotation is 100 per cent, government influence can theoretically be maintained by issuing a golden share to the government so as to protect the national interest.
Trade sale	Full or partial sale to a trade partner or a consortium of investors. In the sale, the expertise of the partner is considered, in terms of management, technical ability and financial capabilities. This includes responsibility for airport development and operations. A number of such sales took place in the UK and in other European countries.
Concession	An airport management company or consortium will purchase a concession or lease to operate the airport for a period of time, say for around 20 or 30 years. The terms and conditions, period of lease/concession, etc. may vary from case to case. Usually an initial investment will be taken from the company that bought the lease, and the economic risk and responsibility of operation, along with future investments, rest with the concessionaire. Governments retain a certain degree of control. Examples of early concession agreements include LaPaz, SantaCruz and Cochabamba airports in Bolivia.
Project finance	This is a common practice nowadays where a private consortium of firms or public–private collaborative agencies build or rebuild an airport and operate it for a certain period of time. When the term ends, the government owners may take ownership. Such arrangements often vary in length (up to approximately 30 years). The cost will be recouped/recovered while operating the airport for the specified period. Usual project finance types include: • Build–operate–transfer (BOT) • Build–transfer (BT) • Design–construct–manage–finance (DCMF)
Management contract	In this case, an agency with technical and management expertise will manage and operate the airport for the contracted period. But the ownership will remain with government and hence the economic risk is shared between government and the managing agency. This practice is used in many airports around the world.

Source: Graham (2014)

Airport privatization has varied dimensions. It may involve the lease of airport property and/or facilities to a private firm to build, operate and/or manage commercial services offered at the airport. Even the airport may not be not privatized fully; privatization can be practised in different airport operations, such as baggage handling, cleaning and ground transportation. Many airports around the world have people working there who are employed originally by other private firms that have been vested with particular airport duties. Some airport management is completely contracted out to private companies. The predominant trend is to contract out a portion of an airport's operations. Airport globalization refers to the evolution of a few global airport companies capable of operating airports in many different countries.

Privatization of airports began in Europe. The transfer of British Airports Authority (BAA) to the private sector transformed the airport sector in the United Kingdom and, eventually, around the world. London Heathrow, London Gatwick, and London Stansted airports were privatized with BAA. In the US, the Airport Privatization Pilot Program (APPP) was established in 1996 with the purpose of initializing private investment in the airport sector. Stewart International Airport in Newburgh, New York, became the first commercial service airport privatized under the APPP. The Canadian government had begun to devolve airport operations by 1992, a process that has since progressed. Most airports in the rest of the world are still owned by governments or governmental agencies.

CASE STUDY 4.1

Experience of airport privatization: British Airports Authority (BAA)

IATA, the global body of airlines, considering airports as the partners of airline business, summed up the privatization experiences of a number of airports around the world. The airport privatization models have been categorized into "sale of airports to private companies and investors" and "trade sales/leasing assets for private operation". The British Airport Authority (BAA), Copenhagen Airport (CPH) (Denmark), Vienna Airport (VIE) (Austria), Zurich Airport (ZRH) (Switzerland), Brussels Airport (BRU) (Belgium) and Auckland International Airport (AIA) (New Zealand) are considered to be in the first category of privatization. In the second category, there are Sydney International Airport (SYD), Perth Airport (PER) (Australia), Ezeiza International Airport (EZE) (Argentina), Juan Santamaria International Airport (SJO) (Costa Rica), Jorge Chavez International Airport (LIM) (Peru) and Athens International Airport (AIA) (Greece).

BAA is an ideal example of airport privatizaion and implementation of effective economic regulation of existing assets. However, it points out that the existing economic regulation of new investment resulted in a sharp rise in airport charges and potentially inefficient investment. It was privatized in

1987 through a public floatation that raised $2.3 billion, and thus became a public limited company. The company, through diversification and by managing airports overseas and taking equity stakes in aviation and non-aviation companies, became very efficient by raising non-aeronautical revenues in particular. The economic regulator had already capped landing and passenger charges at the three largest BAA airports. Effective economic regulation could keep aeronautical charges relatively low with satisfactory service quality. Under BAA, Heathrow and Gatwick airports have been performing successfully with sufficient profit margins.

The key elements in the effectiveness of economic regulation include diverse factors. The independence of the regulator, established in principle through legislation, is one factor. Another factor is the "efficiency improvements generated by incentive-based price regulation", instead of other forms of price regulation such as "rate of return". This could prevent the practice of overestimating various financial aspects, e.g. investment. Measurable quality and service level standards were set in order to ensure the quality of service. However, the costs of other essential customer services (e.g. check-in desk rentals) were not taken under the price cap. The "single till" principle was initiated to make sure that the profits generated through commercial activities by the passengers were considered when setting the level of airport charges. Moreover, strong and informed regulators were used to check the airport's own projections (realistic and reasonable estimates are essential) for asset valuation, operating and capital expenses, traffic forecasts and non-regulated commercial revenues. Over the years of performance, it has been highlighted that the UK economic regulator was successful in extracting value from the existing assets.

IATA highlights some key lessons for airport privatization, such as: engaging customers as key stakeholders in planning and the economic regulation process; efficient management is the key to successful privatization; good governance is more important; independent and robust economic regulation is necessary; it is important to oversee economic regulation by an independent competition commission; economic regulators may not be good at ensuring cost-effectiveness from new investment; mechanisms to incentivize cost efficiency and continual improvements have to be established; establishing service level agreements to ensure that service quality standards are maintained and improved; and preventing unjustified asset revaluations and moves to dual-till accounting.

Source: Pearce and IATA (2005)

Read the above case study carefully and answer the following questions:

- Describe the role of economic regulator in making airport privatization in the UK successful.
- What are the different models of airport privatization? Provide examples.
- Summarize the key point for successful airport privatization.

4.9 Structure of an airport

Ideally an airport can be divided into 3 sections:

- Airside
- Terminal
- Landside

4.9.1 Airside

Airside of an airport is meant for the movement of aircraft around the airport and for landing and take-off. It's the most important area in an airport where all the technical aspects of flying take place. Aircraft can access only this area. The major facilities include runways, taxiways, aircraft parking areas, navigational aids, lighting systems, signage and markings, air rescue and firefighting facilities, snow plowing and de-icing facilities, and fuel service centres. Major components of airside are:

- Runways
- Taxiways
- Aprons/ramp areas
- ATC tower
- Support services and facilities

4.9.2 Runway

The runway is the airport's raison d'être. According to ICAO, a runway is "a defined rectangular area on a land aerodrome prepared for the landing and take-off of aircraft" (ICAO Definitions, UVS International, n.d.). Large airports usually have three or more paved runways of necessary length. A typical runway in an international airport may be about 3,200 metres long, with a width to accommodate the wide-body aircraft. The latest aircraft such as the A380 need longer and wider runways. A runway can be composed of grass, dirt, sand, gravel, asphalt or concrete, depending on factors like location, size and types of aircraft. Nowadays, runways are made up of cement/concrete, with asphalt shoulders – or both are made from asphalt. Runway design and management have to follow strictly the necessary rules and guidelines, especially pertaining to the required length, width, direction configuration, stops, pavement thickness, lightings, markings and signage. Aircraft characteristics are also taken into account when making runways, such as the maximum gross take-off weight, acceleration rate, aircraft type, distance to fly for take-off and wingspan influence. The determinant in the width of the runway is usually the wingspan of the largest operating aircraft. It usually varies from 50 to 200 feet. Pavement thickness varies from 6 inches to over 4 feet. Concrete pavements can remain useful for 20 to 40 years. It is usually better to land *into* the wind. Atmospheric conditions like elevation above sea level are also factors considered in the making of runways. In an airport, there can be a primary runway, which is the runway that is oriented into the prevailing winds. Runways are also sometimes built on a "crosswind" direction. In large airports, there are sometimes parallel, additional runways, but there can also be both parallel and crosswind runways.

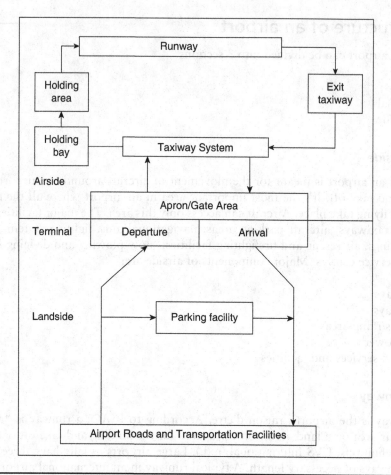

Figure 4.1 Structure of an airport
Source: Mortified from Wells and Young, 2004.

Runway strips appear beyond the shoulder. Runway shoulders are provided immediately beyond the edge of the pavement and the adjacent space mainly to avoid running off the pavement, for drainage, and possibly for blast protection. Edge lights are arranged on the shoulders. A runway strip will surround the runway and ensure the safety of an aircraft or when it deviates from the runway centre line. Runway strips are usually made of grass so that in the event of an aircraft running off the runway, the undercarriage will gradually sink into the runway strip to provide effective deceleration of the plane. Also, on the runway, apart from the "take-off run available" (TORA), a clearway may be provided called "take-off distance available" (TODA), beyond the end of the hard surface. Often a stop way is provided. A "runway end safety area" (RESA) is also provided at the end of a runway strip to avoid any damage to the aircraft when taking off/landing. One of the latest systems is called the engineered material arresting system (EMAS), which is a bed of engineered materials used at the end of the runway to decelerate the aircraft in the event of an emergency. Also, there shouldn't be elevated concrete constructions, sharp embankments for the containment of sewage plants or transport links, etc. in the surrounding area, especially under the approach path. Some countries form a Public Safety Zone (PSZ) near the end of busy commercial runways to control constructions/ other obstacles so as to ensure safer landing/take-off.

Based on runway markings, three types of runways can be seen: visual, non-precision instrument and precision instrument runways. Under the instrument runway category, there are two major types: non-precision approach runway and precision approach runway. Runway lightings are crucial in night-time operations. That may include centre line lights, centre line reflectors, edge lights, edge reflectors, airport beacons and approach lighting. A beacon is meant to indicate the location of an aerodrome from the air. An aeronautical beacon represents an aeronautical ground light visible at all azimuths to indicate a particular point on the surface of the earth. These guide aircraft in properly aligning with the runway while approaching to land. An approach lighting system (ALS) guides an aircraft in properly aligning with the runway while attempting to land.

A pavement, the artificially covered surface on the runways, taxiways and the like, is important as it should have the requisite strength, slope and capacity to match/withstand geological conditions. It means that the airport pavement should comply with requirements. For example, its bearing strength must be appropriate for aeroplanes, it should provide good ride capability of an aircraft and should provide good braking even on a wet surface (Kazda and Caves, 2000). There are different types of pavements. Non-reinforced grass strips are suitable only for the lightest types of general aviation flights. There are also reinforced green strips. Hard surface pavements are in common use in commercial aviation; they have regular year-round operation of heavy aircraft. Cement-concrete rigid pavements and asphalt-flexible pavements are also common.

4.9.3 Taxiways

Taxiways are there to ensure safe, smooth and expeditious movement of aircraft between the runways and the apron or other areas in the airport. They are meant for taxiing of aircraft, intended to provide a link between one part of the airport and another. At very busy airports the taxiway system can be extensive and complex in geometry. Usually in large airports there will be a multi-taxiway system along with high-speed exit taxiways. Taxiways also have shoulders and strips.

Note the following list of facilities in an airport (Urfer and Weinert, 2011):

* Runway
* Runway lighting and markings
* Taxiways
* Aircraft aprons
* Engine testing facilities
* ARFF (Airport rescues and Firefighting) facilities
* Aircraft fuel facilities
* Aircraft maintenance facilities
* Navigational aids
* ATC facilities
* Meteorological facilities
* General aviation facilities
* Helicopter operational areas
* Containment and treatment facilities
* Passenger terminals

- Cargo terminals
- Fixed base operation facilities
- Ground transport interchanges
- Police and security facilities
- Administration building
- Primary and secondary access roads
- Vehicle parking
- Staging areas
- Access roads
- Catering services for flight
- Parking facilities
- Commercial facilities
- Duty-free zones
- Industrial areas

4.9.4 Apron

The term apron is used to refer to the part of the airport, other than the manoeuvring area, meant for parking of aircraft and undertaking turn-around activities before the next flight. A manoeuvring area is that part of an aerodrome to be used by aircraft for take-off, landing, and taxiing, excluding aprons and areas designed for maintenance of an aircraft. The activities include: loading and offloading of passengers; baggage and cargo; refueling; servicing; maintenance; and parking of aircraft. Apron layout is as important as airport design. A properly designed apron is critical to the safety of aircraft, ground support equipment operations, employees, and passengers on and around aircraft parking areas. This area is usually a very active area, and at times congested, particularly in busy airports. The layout, marking, lighting, access for vehicles, fixed or mobile services for aircraft servicing, etc. should follow industry quality standards. Different types of apron layouts include the following:

- Linear
- Open
- Pier
- Satellite

In linear layouts, individual stands are arranged in a row along the terminal building or around it. Stands are seen in rows in front of the terminal building in an open layout, but they are not connected to it. Depending on the distance from the terminal building, vehicles may be used to transport boarding passengers to the flight. Pier layouts refer to the arrangement in which stands are connected to the sides of extensions from the terminal, as rows or more complex forms. In the satellite layout, the stands are arranged like a satellite model, away from the terminal, and connected with the terminal by underground tunnels or by overhead corridors. A terminal area's apron is meant for the enplaning and deplaning of passengers from an aircraft. This can be connected directly to the gate via passenger loading bridges. Otherwise, if they are away from the gates, then air stairs are used for boarding and deplaning passengers. De-icing aprons, cargo aprons, maintenance aprons, remote aprons, general aviation aprons and helipads are other aprons seen in airports. The positions of aircraft parking in stands make different stand types, such as nose-in, angled nose-in, nose-out, angled nose-out, and parallel stands. There may be a holding bay, where an aircraft can be held or bypassed, to enable efficient surface movement of aircraft.

4.9.5 Ramp area

A ramp area denotes the specific space where aircraft park near to a terminal to load passengers and cargo. The term ramp is hardly used, while the term apron is more common. The activities on the ramp include aircraft loading and offloading, baggage sorting, mail and cargo services, aircraft marshalling, security provisions and cabin cleaning.

4.9.6 Hangar

The hangar is an area where aircraft are stored and maintenance work is undertaken. The size, nature and facilities of a hangar can vary, depending on the size and nature of operations of the airport. Moreover, in some airports, there are simple "shade" structures that protect all or parts of the aircraft. Some advanced hangars may have complicated environmentally controlled maintenance facilities.

4.9.7 ATC tower

Air navigation facilities mainly consist of ATC units and associated telecommunication radio beacons, satellite systems and other aids to landing, weather forecasts, airports, computer terminals, etc. Satellites and associated technology have altered the navigation systems, as satellite technology has brought in accuracy and flexibility to navigation along with increasing the range and quality of communication. The functioning of an air navigation system is provided in detail in the next chapter.

4.9.8 Support services and facilities

Aircraft maintenance, pilot services, aircraft rental and hangar rental are most often performed by a fixed base operator (FBO). At major airports, particularly those used as hubs, airlines may operate their own support facilities. Some airports, typically military airbases, have long runways used as emergency landing sites. Many airbases have arresting equipment for fast aircraft, known as rotary hydraulic arrestor gear – a strong cable suspended just above the runway and attached to a hydraulic reduction gear mechanism. Together with the landing aircraft's arresting hook, it is used in situations where the brakes would have little or no effect.

4.9.9 Terminal

The terminal is the most tangible component of the airport. It was once just an interface between landside and airside for passengers and visitors, but has now attained a much more commercial and economic significance. Technically, a terminal is a building that encompasses the provisions for passenger handling and cargo processing prior to the boarding or loading into a flight. The size of the building varies mainly according to the need in respect of the demand or the number of passengers being handled. There are centralized and decentralized terminals depending on the location of passenger processing. Multi-terminal airports are common nowadays. Moreover, in some cities separate terminals are used for domestic and international flights. Shape and the nature of the terminals also vary. E.g. simple, linear, satellite, pier and semi-circular terminals. Large airports may be multi-story and arrival and departure may be arranged on different levels. Passengers on commercial flights access airside areas through terminals, where they can purchase tickets, clear security, check or claim luggage and board aircraft through gates. A passenger passes through a range of activities prior to boarding a flight. The following takes place in a terminal:

- Airlines can process passengers to board flights
- Arriving passengers can enter into a destination
- Baggage handling for departing and arriving passengers
- Services and facilities for entry and exit of foreigners coming into or leaving a country
- Safety and security services
- Cargo handling
- Shopping and refreshments
- Preventing the carriage of banned and restricted items while flying

Example: Basic terminal configuration types in the US
The following configuration types are adapted from NASA and Virtual Skies (n.d.).

Simple terminal
This type is seen in small airports and it consists of one building with a common ticketing and waiting area with multiple exits leading to an apron for boarding.

Linear/curvilinear terminal
Larger than a simple terminal, this type has more gates and more room within the terminal for ticketing and passenger processing. The shape of the terminal can be linear or curvilinear.

Pier finger terminal
"Pier" is an extended path that leads to the space where aircraft are parked in the "finger" slots or gates for boarding. Passenger processing takes place at the simple terminal location; passengers are then routed down a "pier".

Pier satellite terminal/remote satellite terminal
This consists of a single terminal connected to many satellite structures by separate concourses. Aircraft are parked in a cluster at the end of the concourses and passengers have to walk to reach them, or use people-mover systems wherever such are made available.

Mobile lounge or transporter terminal
These have remote aircraft parking and passengers are transported to and from the building to the parked airplane. The mobile lounge can also be used as a holding room for waiting passengers at gate positions. Aircraft are parked in parallel rows.

Terminal structure usually involves departure area, concourses, waiting and gate areas, arrival area and cargo handling area. Access to the aircraft is through the departure area. A passenger has to undergo certain procedures like airline check-in, immigration control and security check-in. The following are the common functional sections, prior to concourses and gates, in an international airport:

- Baggage screening
- Airline check-in and boarding pass collection
- Passport control/immigration
- Security check-in

A concourse, simply an open space where paths meet, represents the long halls with a variety of services and facilities for passengers inside the departure area. This comes after the security check-in section, and contains duty-free shops, restaurants, lounges, seating areas, restrooms and waiting areas. There are gates and waiting areas in all airports where passengers can wait near the gate before boarding. Once a flight has landed, passengers will proceed to the arrival area. An arrival area of an international airport contains the following:

- Arrival gates
- Passport control/immigration
- Baggage claim area
- Customs clearance
- Commercial area

4.9.10 Landside (ground side)

Landside is meant for movement of ground-based vehicles, passengers and cargo from the surrounding area to and out of the airport. Basically, this area is the entry into the

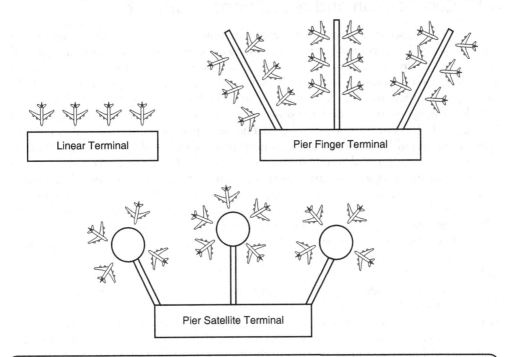

Figure 4.2 Some of the common types of airport terminals

airport that provides access to the airport, without restrictions. Along with the safe and adequate passenger and cargo drop-off facilities, landside provides parking facilities as well. Moreover, some commercial firms such as car rental offices and restaurants can be seen in the landside area. Landside access modes are also important in the modern era of airports. At busy airports, ground access systems can be complex, involving combinations of highway and train stations located under passenger terminals. Major airports usually depend primarily on highways and road networks, and on a combination of private automobiles, rental cars, taxis, buses, trucks and specialized ground vehicles to transport the bulk of passengers, airport-site employees, freight and various supplies to and from the airport. Parking facilities are important as they require a lot of investments and consume valuable, centrally located space.

There has to be a proper system for car transportation in the landside and for access. Taxi services are crucial. Taxis are considered reliable and comfortable, with less luggage handling issues, and they ensure direct transportation between the origin point and the airport departure point. Airports have to make sure that the number of taxi cabs is sufficient to meet demand, and make sure the quality, price levels and security aspects are right. Minibuses are used for transfers, particularly by hotels. They can also provide the door-to-door advantages of a taxi and provide increased security, comfort and speed. Bus services to and from airports are common. There are scheduled services in long and short distances. Local shuttle services are also very common. There is also an increased use of rail transport.

4.10 Certification and regulations of airports

Air transport is a sector bound to strict legal requirements. Each and every component of aviation has to undergo strict verifications and examinations to obtain necessary permits and licences. Airports have to obtain the necessary certification in order to commence operations. Certification requirements have to be considered in the planning stage itself. Development of an airport needs a master plan, which is characterized as a plan for airport development that considers the possibilities of maximum development (Kazda and Caves, 2000). It is considered a set of guidelines for the development of facilities, development and use of land in the airport vicinity, determination of environmental impacts of the development, and determination of requirements for ground access. In order to gain a certificate for operation, an airport must adhere to certain operational and safety standards, depending on the size of the airport and the types of aircraft used, and provide for such things as firefighting and rescue equipment. Airport certification mechanisms will evaluate the compliance with standards and recommended practices with respect to an aerodrome and its local airspace. Compliance with ICAO regulations (obligation of states under the Convention) along with country-specific requirements and the facilities and services will be verified.

In order to get an idea, the steps and practices stipulated by FAA are given in brief. According to the FAA, the inspection begins with a pre-inspection review and it is followed by the finalization of the inspection schedule. Briefing the management of the airport, administrative inspection of airport files, paperwork, etc. constitute the next phase. It is followed by the inspection of the movement area in order to check the runway approach slopes, the condition of the pavement, markings, lighting, signs, abutting shoulders, safety areas, ground vehicle operations, protection measures from possible threats from outside the airport, etc. Further, there is the checking on aircraft rescue and firefighting facilities and services, which involves a timed-response drill, review of personnel training records, checking equipment and protective clothing for operation, condition and availability. Fuelling facilities inspection is the next procedure, which is followed by night inspection which itself involves verification of lighting and signage in airspace, pavement marking, airport beacons, wind cone and obstruction lighting (FAA, n.d.).

4.11 Organization and personnel

Management of an airport is as crucial as the technical operations. Modern airports are typically competitive commercial organizations that need efficient, quality management and an operational team consisting of suitable personnel. Each and every function and operational activity is vital for the efficient, smooth and comfortable running of air transport operations, and the accomplishment of managerial objectives. Jobs vary significantly and serve a broad range of airport customers. Personnel can be classified into the following:

- Airport management personnel
- Ground transportation personnel
- Ground services personnel
- Airport maintenance personnel
- Safety and security personnel

Airport management personnel are involved in the commercial operation and management of airports. They include administrators, finance personnel and public relations employees. Some of the key positions in this category include airport director, finance and administration assistant directors and other personnel, human resources personnel, marketing personnel, etc. The airport director is vested with the responsibility of the overall day-to-day operation of the airport, supervising, directing and reviewing all aircraft operations, building and field maintenance construction plans, community relations, and financial and personnel matters at the airport; and directing, coordinating and reviewing through subordinate supervisors. Ground services personnel, another group who perform various activities airside, ensure the smooth functioning of aircraft landings and take-offs, as well as the essential maintenance of aircraft. Activities include loading of supplies, washing, de-icing, cabin cleaning, aircraft marshalling, toilet servicing, cargo handling, baggage and cargo loading/unloading, aircraft pushback and towing, water service, refuelling, maintenance of the aircrafts at the gate, etc. Usually airports offer ground service providers for airlines, but in some cases, airlines themselves may engage personnel for these activities. Ground transportation personnel are involved in the different transportation activities inside the airport, and to and from the airport. Airport maintenance personnel are also a key personnel category.

An airport has to be maintained with utmost care, and personnel at different levels are involved in this task. The airside has to be kept neat and clean and in top working order. Special care is needed during bad weather conditions. In addition, the terminal is to be kept neat and in working order at all times. The key official in this area develops, directs and coordinates policies, programmes, procedures, standards and schedules for the maintenance of building facilities, coordinates work done by tenants and contractors, inspects maintenance works, foresees future requirements and oversees maintenance

Figure 4.3 Düsseldorf Airport (Germany): airside, with a pier finger terminal structure
Courtesy: Wikimedia Commons

contracts. Safety and security is another crucial area. Security tasks are taken care of by security personnel of different cadres. A government security system will usually be associated with this. Ensuring the safety of airport visitors is another task for a variety of personnel. Emergency services are part of this. Medical services crew are available to handle emergency situations. In addition to these key personnel, there are other groups, such as planning and engineering, certification, rules and regulations, public relations and environmental management.

4.12 Airport codes

Airports are identified through unique three-letter codes, which are used as a location identification/airport identification tool. In some cases, the city has a different code from the airport. It is done to simplify airline operations, to denote airport points of origin and destination, and to avoid confusion due to duplication/similarity of names of airports. In some travel documents, only these codes are mentioned instead of the full names. For instance, a boarding pass for a flight will display only the airport code. These are administered by IATA and the codes once given cannot be changed without strong justification. Some of the codes are abbreviated from the name of the airport (e.g., John F. Kennedy International Airport, New York: JFK) and some are from the city (Harare International Airport: HRE). At times, a common letter is given for all airports in a country (e.g., in Canada, airports are prefixed by 'Y').

> **Table 4.4** Codes and names of some of the busiest airports in the world

Airport code	Airport
ATL	Hartsfield–Jackson Atlanta International Airport – USA
PEK	Beijing Capital International Airport – China
DXB	Dubai International Airport – UAE
ORD	O'Hare International Airport – USA
HND	Tokyo Haneda Airport – Japan
LHR	London Heathrow Airport – England
LAX	Los Angeles International Airport – USA
HKG	Hong Kong International Airport – Hong Kong
CDG	Paris-Charles de Gaulle Airport – France
DFW	Dallas/Fort Worth International Airport – USA
IST	Istanbul Atatürk Airport – Turkey
FRA	Frankfurt Airport – Germany
PVG	Shanghai Pudong International Airport – China
AMS	Amsterdam Airport Schiphol – Netherlands
CGK	Soekarno-Hatta International Airport – Indonesia
JFK	John F. Kennedy International Airport – USA
SIN	Singapore Changi Airport – Singapore
CAN	Guangzhou Baiyun International Airport – China
DEN	Denver International Airport – USA
BKK	Suvarnabhumi Airport – Thailand
SFO	San Francisco International Airport – USA
ICN	Seoul Incheon International Airport – Republic of Korea
KUL	Kuala Lumpur International Airport – Malaysia
MAD	Madrid Barajas Airport – Spain
DEL	Indira Gandhi International Airport – India
LAS	McCarran International Airport – USA

4.13 Challenges

Aviation is a rapidly growing system facilitated by advancements in technology. Moreover, the demand is increasing tremendously along with the socio-economic advancements. The airport is an element in the aviation system and, consequently, just like with the advancements in aviation, the airport sector faces severe challenges. The structure of the airline industry, the major client of airports, is also changing all the time. Demand patterns and consumer behaviour patterns see frequent and significant changes. Airports constitute a very dynamic sector which requires coping with the emerging trends in social, economic, political and technological environments. According to Page (2009), airports face a number of challenges from a visitor experience point of view. Those include: the need to cope with larger aircraft, like the A380s; the need to incorporate the latest technological developments; the need to recognize the changes in consumer behaviours that have begun to reach a mass market; the need to expedite passenger movement inside the airport, along with baggage handling; and the need to address the security and safety issues at airports. In this modern era of air transport, there are a number of factors that act as challenges for airports. The most significant are categorized under the following:

- Technology
- Demand
- Safety and security
- Customer preferences and experience
- Airport expansion
- Eco-friendliness
- Operation and management
- Revenue
- Competition

CASE STUDY 4.2

The challenge of larger aircraft: Changi's preparations for the A380

Airports, in the new millennium, are under stress as a range of factors continue to challenge them, and those airports that fail to cope with the rising challenges are under existential crisis. The new millennium began with a big challenge for airports to have large runways to accommodate larger aircraft. Many airports had to build new runways or expand existing runways to land A380 aircraft. Airports have to restructure their facilities and invest heavily in infrastructure to enable future operations of that aircraft. As of now, the greatest challenge facing the industry is the need to adjust their facilities to accommodate an airplane code F, when most of the major international airports have the required infrastructure for aircraft code E. Despite the Airbus's previous target to operate on runways of code E standard, the later intervention of ICAO stated that A380 belongs to the code F category and urged airports to expand their facilities. Thus, millions of dollars of investment are inevitable. The following is the case study of Changi airport in which the inaugural A380 commercial flight was undertaken.

Singapore Changi Airport, foreseeing the arrival of the A380, began preparations to accommodate it decades ago. The planning started as early as the late 1990s. Along with upgrading of the existing infrastructure at a total cost of S$60 million, new infrastructure was designed to provide high levels of safety, efficiency and service for A380 operation. Runways, taxiways and airfield objects were designed with adequate safety separation to meet A380 requirements. Widening of runway shoulders to provide additional paved area was also completed. Taxiway pavements at turning points were widened to provide additional safety distance between A380 outer wheels and the taxiway edge.

Taxiway bridges were designed from the onset for the next generation of larger aircraft. Shielding was provided along the sides of the bridges. Runways, taxiways and aircraft parking apron pavements were designed for A380 loading. Pre-arrival equipment staging area enlarged by around 30 per cent, fuel hydrant pits adjusted to suit its refuelling inlets and aircraft docking guidance systems were configured. Three aerobridge arms were ensured for more efficient access. Baggage claim belts lengthened to provide longer frontage for presentation of a larger number of bags. Gate holdrooms were expanded by 30 per cent and additional x-ray machines and boarding machines were installed. A new aircraft pushback tractor and upper deck catering hi-lift truck were added. Check-in and passenger facilities were expanded.

The above shows a large airport accommodating a larger aircraft. Smaller airports will obviously have to make huge investments to ensure essential facilities to accommodate larger aircraft like the A380.

Source: Yun (n.d.)

Read the case study carefully and answer the following questions:

- Describe the challenge of larger aircraft for airports.
- Describe the infrastructural modifications made by Changi Airport to welcome the A380.

Every now and then new technologies enter into the realm of aviation and that cannot be sidelined by airports. Air transport is one sector that has to be upgraded to the latest technology for improved safety, security and efficiency of operations. The ever-increasing demand continues to put pressure on airports to increase facilities and services along with the necessary space to accommodate customers. At times, larger airports are constructed when the existing ones have critical constraints in terms of expanding the scope of services and facilities. Ensuring safety and security when there is an increase in threats of various types is a real challenge. Negligence or a new, unconsidered threat can cost the lives of many people. Airports have to therefore incorporate the latest safety measures according to these changes. Consumer preferences change more often than they did in the past; and consumers seek more services and facilities in airports. Airport expansion, both terminal and airside, is a real challenge. "Capacity crunch" is a matter of concern for airports. While terminal expansion is directly proportional to the increase in demand, airside expansion takes place for many reasons, such as an increase in airlines, more aircraft, the advent of larger aircraft, etc. Many airports face congestion and "slot allocation" is of late a major issue. This situation limits entry of new airlines as well. Longer runways are a necessity nowadays. There is also increasing pressure for airlines to be more eco-friendly. Effective and efficient waste management is important. Energy wastage needs to be curtailed. Certainly, their operation and management is of utmost importance for their survival. Notwithstanding these challenges, the dynamism that has emerged in the airport sector is expected to continue for some time yet.

4.14 Summary

Airports have seen a dramatic transformation from simple grass strips where planes could land and take off to large organizations spanning huge areas that offer a wide range of services and facilities to cater to the requirements of travellers. Now, an airport is a complex set of facilities, services and infrastructure that enable air transport service providers to transport passengers and cargo from one place to another. Ideally an airport is divided into three sections: landside, airside and terminal. The essential facilities and infrastructure may include: standard runways; taxiways; aprons; safety and security facilities and services; air navigation services; aircraft maintenance facilities; passenger terminals with necessary facilities for passenger handling for domestic and/or international passengers and baggage; and baggage handling facilities. Commercial services, like duty-free shops and refreshment centres, vary according to the size and nature of airports. A commercial airport won't function in isolation due to the multiple roles it plays.

While airports were expanded along with the increase in demand, the advent of technology and the changes in the social, economic and cultural spheres of human beings brought phenomenal changes in terms of the nature of runways. The length, depth and width of runways increased substantially with the increase in size and speed of aircraft. As airports had to respond to growing demand in passenger transportation, both the airside and the landside were expanded significantly, especially after the end of the Second World War. Apart from the facilities and services offered for transportation of passengers and cargo, airports have many other dimensions of socio-economic significance.

An airport serves a range of customers, directly and indirectly. Airlines, passengers, non-travellers, tenants/service providers and potential development partners are the major customer groups for airports. Income in the form of landing fees, passenger charges, cargo charges, and from ground services and ground handling activities are all considered aeronautical revenue sources. Non-aeronautical revenue sources include: rents; direct sales centres like shops, catering services by airport concessionaires; car parking; and other sources, such as consultancy services, visitors, business services, etc.

Most of the commercial airports in the world are still functioning under the government or its agencies. However, privatization is increasing. Airports have to obtain the necessary certification in order to commence operations. Certification requirements have to be considered in the planning stage itself. The personnel involved in airport operation and management consists of: airport management personnel; ground transportation personnel; ground services personnel; airport maintenance personnel; and safety and security personnel. Airports are identified through unique three-letter codes, which are used as a location identification/airport identification tool. In this modern era of air transport, there are a number of factors that act as challenges for airports. Safety and security, increasing customer preferences and experiences, growing competition, etc. pose severe challenges for airports. Airports are still, nonetheless, on the path of further expansion and growth.

> ## Review questions
>
> ### Short/medium answer type questions
>
> - Define an airport.
> - What are the functions of an airport?
> - What are the services a tourist can avail from an airport?
> - Explain the socio-economic significance of airports.
> - List the customers of an airport.
> - Discuss the revenue sources of airports.
> - Give a brief account of the ownership of airports.
> - Give a brief account of airport runways.
> - What are taxiways in airports?
> - What is an apron? Write down the different types of aprons.
> - Describe the facilities and services in an airport terminal.
> - Write briefly about airport codes, providing examples.
> - What are some of the challenges faced by airports?
>
> ### Essay type questions
>
> - Write an essay on the evolution and growth of airports.
> - Discuss in detail the structure of an airport.
> - Write about the organizational structure in an airport.

References

CIA (2013) The World Fact Book of Central Intelligence Agency of the US, available at https://www.cia.gov/library/publications/the-world-factbook/fields/2053.html (accessed 18 February 2015).

FAA, Airport Categories, available at http://www.faa.gov/airports/planning_capacity/passenger_allcargo_stats/categories/ (accessed 14 December 2016).

Graham, A. (2003) *Managing Airports: An International Perspective*. 2nd edn. Oxford: Butterworth-Heinemann.

Graham, A. (2008) *Managing Airports: An International Perspective*. 3rd edn. Oxford: Butterworth-Heinemann.

Graham, A. (2014) *Managing Airports: An International Perspective*. 4th edn. Oxford: Routledge.

Halpern, N. and Graham, A. (2013) *Airport Marketing*. Oxford: Routledge.

Hardaway, M. R. (1991) *Airport Regulation, Law and Public Policy*. Westport: Quorum Books.

Herrmann, N. and Hazel, B. (2012) The Future of Airports, available at https://www.oliverwyman.com/content/dam/oliver-wyman/global/en/files/archive/2012/20120222_Airport_trends_MAR21.pdf (accessed 22 January 2013).

ICAO (2015) Continuing Traffic Growth and Record Airline Profits – Highlights 2015: Air Transport Results, Press Release of International Civil Aviation Organization, 22 December.

ICAO Definitions, UVS International, available at http://www.uavdach.org/aktuell_e/3_UVSI_ICAO-Definitions_V01_120813.pdf (accessed 30 August 2016).

Kazda, A. and Caves, E. R. (2000) *Airport Design and Operations*. Oxford: Elsevier.

NASA and Virtual Skies, Airport Design, National Aeronautics and Space Administration and Virtual Skies, available at http://virtualskies.arc.nasa.gov/airport_design/7.html (accessed 23 September 2017).

Odoni, A. (2009) Airports, in P. Belobaba, A. Odoni and C. Barnhart (eds), *The Global Airline Industry*. West Sussex: John Wiley & Sons.

Page, J. S. (2009) *Transport and Tourism: Global Perspectives*. Essex: Pearson Education.

Pearce, B. and IATA (2005) Economics Briefing: Airport Privatisation, Geneva: International Air Transport Association.

Tang, Y. R. (2017) Airport Privatization: Issues and Options for Congress, Congressional Research Service, available at https://fas.org/sgp/crs/misc/R43545.pdf (accessed 13 January 2017).

Urfer, B. and Weinert, R. (2011) Managing Airport Infrastructure, in A. Wittmer, T. Bieger and R. Muller (eds), *Aviation Systems: Management of the Integrated Aviation Value Chain*. New York: Springer, pp. 103–134.

Wells, T. A. and Young, S. (2004) *Airport: Planning and Management*. 5th edn. New York: McGraw-Hill.

Yun, A., Singapore Changi Airport: Preparation For & Experience With the A380, available at http://www.aci.aero/Media/aci/file/2008%20Events/ASQ%20Speeches/YUN_presentation.pdf (accessed 15 June 2018).

Chapter 5

Airport operations

Learning outcomes

After reading this chapter, you will be able to:

- Describe the tasks involved in airport ground handling.
- Identify the equipment involved in ground handling operations.
- Learn the passenger handling procedures.
- Better understand the baggage handling by airlines.
- Explain the complex tasks of air navigation services.
- Understand air cargo operation.

5.1 Introduction

Managing airport operations is a challenging task. Airports feature a multitude of tasks and many of them are time-bound, i.e. finished within a stipulated time period. Lately, as a result of privatization, the efficiency of airport operations has become increasingly significant in the airport sector. Moreover, customers seek quality services. Passenger processing, cargo processing and ground handling all have to be managed effectively and efficiently. The turnaround times of aircraft have to be at a minimum. Flight delays should be mitigated. The quality of ground handling services has to meet emerging needs, especially in terms of reliability and resilience, safety and security. Quality and efficiency of services at airports have to be of a certain level, on par with international standards. The following, as described by Graham (2013) reveals the growing significance of quality in airport services and operations:

> Structural changes such as commercialization, privatization, and globalization, together with increased competition between airports, encouraged airports to place more emphasis on quality. Airports which had become regulated in their post-privatization stage, such as the London and Australian airports, also found that their service quality became the subject of increased scrutiny. Moreover, pressure

was coming from the travelling public who were becoming more experienced and demanding consumers of the airport product.

The demand for increased quality levels comes from increasing competition, but also from all the stakeholders of airports. Keeping the business in profit is a daunting task. An airport needs the required revenue for operational expenditure before they can make a profit. Airports face a challenge in generating increased profit, as they are limited mainly by the space available to them and demand patterns. Increasing aeronautical revenue has its own limitations. Competition is a major concern nowadays. Some cities have more than one airport. Furthermore, more airports are being built closer to cities. On one side, there are more and more rules and regulations, and on the other side competition is increasing. Airports have to manage both, without affecting their profit levels. Each and every part of airport operations requires the utmost care. Let's have a look into the major airport operations.

5.2 Ground handling

Ground handling deals with all the activities that are undertaken in order to prepare an aircraft for the next flight (Kazda and Caves, 2000). According to ICAO, ground handling refers to "services necessary for an aircraft's arrival at, and departure from, an airport, other than air traffic services" (ICAO Definitions, UVS International, n.d.). These are the services required by an aircraft for a flight, between landing and take-off. There are a wide range of activities, and all are time-bound. The ground handling activities in the airside includes various services such as aircraft marshalling, toilet and water services, repair of faults, refuelling, wheel and tyre check, ground power supply, de-icing, cooling/heating, routine and non-routine maintenance, cleaning of cockpit windows, wings, nacelles and cabin windows, in-flight entertainment, minor servicing of cabin fittings, unloading and loading of cargo, alteration of seat configuration, safety measures, air conditioning, catering services, deplaning and boarding of passengers, start-up, towing with pushback tractors, etc.

There are two types of ground handling system. One is self-handling, in which the respective airline chooses to provide services for it. This is not feasible in all airports. However, in hubs, airlines may have self-handling ground services. Outsourcing or contracting with a third party is a common practice around the world. In this case, the airline will make an agreement with an agency. The agency that provides the ground handling services to an airline based on a contract can be another airline or it can be a dedicated ground handling company. Swissport Ground Handling is an example of a leading dedicated ground handling company. It provides passenger and ramp handling services at more than 220 stations across the world with a passenger handling record of 224 million per annum (Swissport, n.d.). Care is needed for all the associated activities so as not to damage aircraft or its parts, and to complete them in the allotted time.

Every airline prefers to have less turnaround time so that they can maximize the usage of each aircraft for economic reasons. **Turnaround time** (gate occupancy time) of an aircraft denotes the time taken for preparing for the next departure after the arrival at the gate. In fact, there are different factors that influence the turnaround time. Size of the aircraft, number of passengers, quantity of cargo to load and unload, and itinerary and schedules of the airline are some of them. The less the turnaround time, the greater the benefit for the airlines, as they can utilize the aircraft more.

Table 5.1 Overview of services offered by Swissport ground handling

Service	Overview
Station management and administration	• AFP filing • Flight operations assistance • Irregularity operations support • Liaising with various port authorities • Load control • Station control • Station representation and supervision • Weather briefing
Passenger services	• Airport ticketing sales desk • Arrival and transfer services • Check-in services • Dedicated passenger services • Gate services • Lost and found services • Lounge services • Special passenger and VIP services
Aircraft Servicing and Ramp Handling (Ground Handling)	• Aircraft loading/unloading • Baggage sorting and transportation • Cabin cleaning • Crew transport • De/anti-icing • GPU (ground power unit), push-back • Unit load device control • Toilet and water services

Source: Swissport (n.d.)

Efficient **ramp handling** services, which involve all the activities when an aircraft arrives at the ramp/apron until it departs for further flight, ensure quick turnaround of aircraft and in turn help in maintaining the schedules of airlines. Every second counts in ramp handling services. Ramp handling, part of ground handling overall, involves a series of activities. Supervision, marshalling, start-up, towing aircraft, necessary repair and maintenance activities, safety measures, refuelling, required checks of parts, power supply, de-icing and cooling/heating, toilet servicing, cleaning of cockpit windows, wings, nacelles and cabin windows, and onboard services are some of the major activities performed while the aircraft is on the ramp. Details of major airport operations are discussed below.

5.2.1 Deplaning and boarding

Deplaning is all about disembarking passengers from a flight. Delays in deplaning can cause delays elsewhere, as deplaning and enplaning are also the main factors contributing to the aircraft turnaround time. A series of other activities, such as cleaning, have to be done inside the aircraft after deplaning. Boarding of passengers can be undertaken after these activities have been performed. Stairs or passenger bridges are used for deplaning and enplaning/boarding. In some airports, arriving passengers will be carried by low floor–no step buses from the place the aircraft is parked to the terminal, and vice versa for boarding passengers. If the flight is parked near the gate, there is no need for a vehicle to carry the passengers; instead a passenger bridge can lead to the plane if that provision is available. Air stairs are also an option. They are built into aircraft, particularly wide-body aircraft, and these can be unfolded as needed. Mobile passenger boarding stairs are also very common in airports for boarding and deplaning passengers. Mobile lounges are also in use in some instances.

Passenger bridges or jet bridges are also common for deplaning/enplaning passengers. Gangway, aerobridge/air bridge, air jetty, portal and skybridge are some other terms used for passenger bridges. The official term is Passenger Boarding Bridge (PBB). One end of this is attached to the terminal or gate area, and the other end extends into airside, with the freedom of movement to connect to the aircraft wherever it is parked. The PBB has greater benefits than any other tool used for deplaning/enplaning passengers: it can be used in any climate; it is easy for passengers to move into the aircraft for boarding or into the airport after deplaning; there is no need to climb any stairs (so passengers

Figure 5.1 Boarding via jet bridge: Air India flight
Source: Wikimedia Commons

with disabilities are benefited); and boarding and deplaning will generally be faster. The telescopic tunnel of a passenger bridge is rectangular in shape, made of glass or steel, and can increase or decrease its extension. The rotunda is one end of the passenger bridge. The rotunda assembly is designed as the self-supporting terminal end pivot for the PBB's vertical and horizontal motion. Driven by the lifting and driving mechanism to rotate around the rotunda, the PBB extends smoothly to approach the aircraft until its cab wiggles to conjoin the aircraft's body. There will be a service access, located on the right-hand side of the cab end of the PBB, with a service door and stairs leading to the apron area. This is for the use of authorized personnel only. There is a control station in the cab at the aircraft end which enables a control console and service utilities for PBB operations. A pedestal with undercarriage, crew cab and technological equipment are the other components of a PBB.

As a quick recap, here is a list of ground handling activities:

- Stop aircraft
- Stop engines
- Position passenger bridges
- Supply power
- Air conditioning
- Deplane passengers
- Unload cargo/baggage
- Check airplane
- Service lavatories
- Service galleys
- Service cabin
- Service potable water
- Fuel aircraft
- Load cargo/baggage
- Board passengers
- Start engines
- Power supply removal
- Remove bridges
- Push-back
- Taxi into position

5.2.2 Power supply

While the aircraft is at the ramp, the energy requirements will be fulfilled by supplying the necessary power for the next flight. Aircraft have built-in power generating mechanisms involving mainly generators that are linked to auxiliary engines that will be active while flying to meet the requirements inside. While aircraft are on the ground, during the turnaround time, they still require electrical energy. This can be for flight systems, lights, heating or cooling of the cabin, etc. Such energy can either be provided by the aircraft's built-in auxiliary power unit (APU) or by the ground support equipment (GPU – ground power unit, ACU – air climate unit, and mobile heating unit). The APU, though its efficiency is low (with greater environmental impact), is used most commonly to meet the aircraft's energy requirements due to its advantages, such as independence of the ground source and time-saving (i.e. there is no need to connect/disconnect the ground source). Airports require energy for many other reasons: for lighting systems, radar, communication and meteorological systems, power needs in hangars, buildings and other airport facilities. Co-generation, heating stations that have low-pressure steam turbines and generators are also encouraged in airports in addition to the independent supply of electrical energy. Standby sources like diesel generators or battery power supply are also seen in some airports. Alternative energy sources like solar energy are starting to be used to meet airports' energy requirements.

5.2.3 Cargo and baggage loading

Cargo and baggage loading is also a crucial activity. In wide-body aircraft baggage is transported in containers, which reduces the number of bags going astray because all the baggage going to one destination is stored in one container. After weighing, baggage has to be loaded in the proper way and care has to be taken to secure all the bags inside the compartments so that they don't move while flying. The moving bag conveyer belt brings the checked-in luggage from the point of collection/check-in counter to the bag room, where it is sorted for different flights. Based on the information on the bag tag, the sorted items are placed into the proper bag cart, which can be a unit load device (ULD) or a four-wheeled trailer. They are then carried to the aircraft using a tug. ULD is a general term used to represent both the container and the pallet.

Handling of loose cargo and baggage is very difficult and time-consuming. There are specific rules and regulations for loading of baggage and cargo into a flight. Instructions matching with the aircraft load and trim sheet are provided for proper loading of baggage and cargo. Cargo and baggage can be loaded using containers in wide-body aircraft, which makes the loading and unloading process easier. Some airports have conveyers to transport the baggage from the departure hall directly to the aircraft and vice versa. Care has to be taken for cargo handling. Improper packaging can lead to damage and contamination of other cargo or the compartment. The weighing has to be proper as well. Moreover, all documents and compliance with instructions and applicable laws need to be verified again. The weight needs to be shown on each ULD.

Loading of cargo varies according to the type of aircraft and its relevant parts. Moreover, necessary commodity separation may be required. ULDs and pallets are used in keeping cargo in flight. Loading equipment and aids include tie-down rings, tie-down straps, lashing ropes, supporting planks and platforms, roller platform plastic bags, plastic foil, net bags, pouches for valuable cargo, dry ice boxes, pot kennels, pallets, containers, etc. Palletization is a term used in this context; simply, it is the stacking of shipments or consignments/cargo pallets which can be moved in airports and transported in aircraft easily. Small consignments are stacked on pallets. Containerization is another term used. It is all about the packing of cargo/consignments using containers that can be loaded into aircraft according to convenience and the shape of the aircraft. Containers are shaped to fit the aircraft conveniently and efficiently, and to handle and protect the contents from damage and theft. Some containers are common square-cornered boxes.

CASE STUDY 5.1

Dubai's Al Maktoum International Airport: the largest in the making

The world's largest and busiest airport is being built in Dubai, UAE. According to projections, Dubai's Al Maktoum International Airport, which already began operations after the completion of the first phase, will be able to accommodate more than 200 million passengers per year. As of writing, Hartsfield–Jackson Atlanta International Airport, USA is the busiest airport in the world, handling approximately 100 million passengers per year. A $35.7 billion (£29 billion) investment will be made in Dubai World Central (DWC), which will support the new Al Maktoum International Airport, and other facilities in the south of Dubai.

Once Dubai World Central, a 140 square kilometre multiphase development of six clustered zones, is fully developed, Dubai will be a leading integrated, multimodal transportation platform connecting air, sea and land. The construction works started some years ago and the passenger terminal was built in 2012. In the first phase, a large runway capable of supporting an A380 landing will be built. When it is completed, the airport will have a total of five parallel runways, 4.5 kilometres long, each separated by at least 800 metres. Currently under construction, the ATC tower will be 91 metres tall when complete, which will make it the tallest freestanding ATC tower in the Middle East.

As per the plan, there will be a number of terminals, a large area for cargo and two main entrances. After completion, Dubai World Central will be able to accommodate more than 240 million passengers per annum with an annual cargo capacity of 16 million tonnes. A fully automated baggage handling system capable of handling around 240 million bags yearly is another feature of the airport. Air–sea connectivity would be achievable in four hours. Also, the airport will have 100,000 car parking spaces and an express rail system will connect this airport with Dubai International Airport. This airport will also have hotels, shopping malls, support facilities and high-end maintenance facilities which will make the airport a regional maintenance hub that can handle maintenance requirements of large aircraft, including the A380. The air connectivity, along with the connectivity of other modes of transport, will make Dubai and the UAE at large an important air transport hub in the world.

Source: www.dubaiairports.ae

Read the case study carefully and answer the following questions:

- Write down the prime features of the new airport project in Dubai.
- Describe the significance of this airport when there is already a leading international airport in Dubai.

5.2.4 Gate arrival and push-back operations

Push-back represents the action of moving an aeroplane from a passenger terminal to a runway or taxiway, into a position where it can use its own engines. Extreme care has to be taken during push-back and gate arrival procedures in order to ensure the safety of passengers, crew and personnel involved. Once passengers have boarded, the aircraft can plan to push back. Every employee must be aware of the readiness for push-back. The airline and ground handling staff should follow the procedures properly and priority should always be given for the aircraft movement. A minimum of three push-back crew (two at wing tips and one with direct interaction with flight crew) have to be ready. By this time, all aircraft doors and hatches should be closed, an alert to vehicle traffic near the aircraft should be given (traffic should be stopped if needed), and all ground support equipment (GSE) should be moved away. As per the requirement, a tug and tow bar are attached to the nose wheel of the aircraft. Aircraft tugs of different designs are used to push the aircraft back.

Traditionally, a push-back unit is a combination of a tractor and a tow bar. Varieties of tow bar tractors are used; at some airports tractors are electrically driven. The anti-collision lights should be on and the jetway fully retracted. The pilot has to determine that the aircraft is "ready" for departure, and on receiving confirmation, if things are clear, ATC will allow push-back and start-up of the aircraft. When ready for start-up, ground crew will confirm the hazard-free zone prior to starting aircraft engines, after verifying the safety precautions on hazard zones. The area behind and around the aircraft must be clear of vehicles, equipment and other obstructions. The ground crew should make a visual check for vehicle traffic near the aircraft. With further confirmation in accordance with ATC instructions, and in coordination with the ground crew for the push-back and start-up of the aircraft, the pilot readies for "push-back". Along with the commencement of push-back, the ground vehicle operators have to wait for the aircraft to clear the roadway before proceeding. There should not be cross-bleed start-up until the aircraft completes push-back and it is positioned on the taxiway, parallel to and centred on the taxiway centre line. Tug release points are provided.

During gate arrival, the necessary ground crew has to assemble in the gate area, by which time the amber beacon should be on. The essential ground crew consists of a marshaller and two wing walkers. During this time all vehicles in and around the area should be alerted and moved out of the way. Once the aircraft clears the roadway, the ground service personnel wait until the engines are off, and switch off the anti-collision light (red beacon). Further measures have to be taken to ensure safety, and the deplaning and ground handling activities during turnaround can then begin.

5.2.5 Refuelling

Refuelling of aircraft for the next flight is an activity that should be done with utmost care and safety considerations. Airports usually have adequate measures for refuelling the aircraft. The method/system of refuelling may be different depending on the size, frequency and number of operations, geographical conditions, etc. The two types of fuel most commonly used at airports are (ARCP Synthesis 63, 2015):

- *Aviation turbine fuel (ATF) or jet fuel:* it's kerosene-based and there are a number of different grades.
- *Aviation gasoline ("avgas"):* it's intended for use in reciprocating piston-engine aircraft. As with jet fuel, different grades are available.

Fuel must be treated, and depending on the manner of its transport to the airport, it may be necessary to analyse it. Trained personnel are needed to handle the fuelling activities. Refuelling an aircraft in an airport involves a number of activities but can be summarized into three: receiving the fuel; storing the received fuel; and distributing the fuel to various aircraft as per the need. A brief description of each stage follows.

Receiving the fuel

Fuel is received directly through a pipeline, from tanker trucks, from rail tanks or from marine vessels. Fuel has standardized procedures to ensure safety, which depend on the type of fuel being transferred. The receiving stage involves the filtration, quality testing and checking of volumes delivered. The accounting of fuel quantity and the testing for fuel quality are important aspects of the fuel delivery process.

Storage

The received fuel needs to be stored with utmost care. There are "fuel farms" consisting of storage tanks located at airports. Storage tanks may be underground or overground, the decision being made on the basis of a special study for each case. Double-jacket storage tanks are also used; the cost of the technology is higher, but with lower construction costs. If the storage tanks are single-jacket, then the construction cost can be higher. The quantity has to be accounted for correctly to ensure there is no overfill or spillage, contamination or other potentially hazardous situations arising during storage. Airports should have a reserve, which is the quantity of fuel in storage that may not be used at that time to refuel aircraft.

Distribution

This is the mechanism of fuel delivery to aircraft from storage tanks. The common delivery mechanisms include (ARCP Synthesis 63, 2015):

- Underground hydrant fuelling system
- Stationary platform
- Fueling truck

The hydrant fuelling system is distribution by fixed systems, which can pump fuel directly from the fuel farm to the aircraft through underground pipes. The piping system ends near an aircraft parking space on the ramp and from it aircraft can be fuelled. There is no need for a mobile dispenser unit. Currently, large airports prefer a hydrant fuelling system for a range of reasons including: cost advantages; better safety, particularly from fire safety; operational efficiency; and greener, i.e. more environmentally friendly.

The fuelling truck is a traditional method; the truck or dispenser loaded with fuel from a rack or similar loading area will reach the aircraft to refuel it. The chassis-mounted tank with an integral pump, filter and meter system will help to fill the petrol in the aircraft tanks. Though flexible, this has many limitations. In busy airports, it is not easy to allow for the movement of refuelling trucks. The quantity carried in one tank is obviously limited, whereas large flights require huge quantities. Safety is also comparatively less.

Stationary fuelling platforms are remote stations where aircraft can get their fuel. This mechanism is not often seen in modern commercial airports, as aircraft have to travel some distance for refuelling. However, smaller airports and some general airports do use this system.

5.2.6 Winter operations

Winter seasons can be difficult for air traffic, particularly within or near the airports themselves (Kazda and Caves, 2000). Snow, ice or slush on airfield pavements and drifting snow can lead to aircraft accidents. This kind of contamination can also cause resistance on an aircraft's wheels during the take-off run. Moreover, aircraft braking action can be impacted by the ice deposited, which can also increase the possibility of aircraft sliding off the pavement. Winter storms can also negatively impact air traffic, e.g. reductions in traffic volume, and flight delays and cancellations. In extreme situations, airports can face closure for days. Foggy and cloudy skies can also have consequences on air traffic. Flight delays and cancellations are very common in many airports due to such adverse conditions. It is mandatory for airports to have an effective snow plan. Urgent safety measures are taken for clearing the airside of snow and ice, particularly the runways and taxiways. Ice on the aircraft is another issue. Ice deposited on aircraft parts, particularly on the lifting surfaces, can result in variations in aerodynamic characteristics and flight performance: the weight of the aircraft can go up; and iced sensors can send incorrect indications to the pilots. The removal of ice from an aircraft will also delay the flight.

Ice and snow affecting air transport can be of different types. Dry snow is one type that affects aviation. Dry snow appears when the atmospheric temperature in all layers falls below freezing point. This snow is fluffy and can be blown if loose, or, if compacted by hand, will fall apart again upon release. Also, it can be moved along with wind. Wet snow appears when the atmospheric temperature is just above freezing point and can be compacted by hand so that it sticks together (because of its greater water content). Compacted snow is another type. This snow is in a compressed form, seen as a solid mass. It will hold together or break up into lumps if picked up. Slush snow is in a form that is starting to melt and is thus saturated with water.

De-icing is an activity performed in winter. This is a precautionary procedure carried out in airports to remove ice and snow-related contaminants from aircraft surfaces. Usually a liquid mixture is used, which is a combination of heated glycol and water. De-icing is more effective as a snow/ice removal mechanism. For further prevention of snow/ice build-up on aircraft during flight hours, anti-icing is also required. This is done with a higher concentration of glycol, which ensures a freezing point well below 0 degrees Celsius (32 degrees Fahrenheit). This liquid is added so that it can adhere to aircraft surfaces in order to protect against contamination during active weather events. Polypropylene glycol and ethylene glycol are used to eliminate ice accumulations, depending upon the necessity. A combination of granules of sodium acetate and a solution of potassium acetate is also used for de-icing runway surfaces. Snow removal is another crucial activity in airports. An effective and efficient snow and ice control programme is crucial in reducing the cost and in efficient execution associated with these activities. Prompt removal or control of snow and ice is crucial in aircraft operations, particularly in winter seasons. Appropriate materials are to be used for snow and ice control so as to minimize engine ingestion. Runways, taxiways, aprons, holding bays and other necessary areas are to be cleared off. Snow and ice need to be removed from other areas as well, such as navigation aid locations and equipment. Application of sand after the complete removal of snow, ice and slush can increase surface friction.

In respect of snow and ice control, the following information is included in weather forecasts (Wells and Young, 2004):

- Forecasted commencement of any snowfall
- Duration, intensity and accumulation estimate

- Wind directions and velocities during the snowfall
- Temperature ranges during and after the snowfall
- Types of precipitation expected
- Cloud coverage following the snowfall

There is some mobile equipment in use for snow removal. Mechanical is less expensive and hence preferred more often. Mechanically spread sand on a surface may be heated using a flame-thrower type burner unit so as to melt the ice. Snowploughs, snow blowers/ snow throwers and snow brushes are usually used for removing snow and other similar substances from surfaces airside. Other vehicles and equipment used may include sand/ aggregate trucks, chemical spreaders, tankers and loaders. Chemicals like urea, sodium formate and acetate-based compounds are used for snow removal in areas such as airfield pavements.

5.2.7 Rescue and firefighting

Fire incidents are rare, yet ensuring the necessary firefighting mechanisms are in place is of the utmost importance. It is mandatory for airports to ensure rescue and firefighting services (RFFS) within airports, with a close link to external nearby fire stations and mechanisms. Different materials are used in combating fire-based emergencies. In addition to water, the most commonly used firefighting material, gases, dry chemicals and aqueous film-forming foam (AFFF) are used to fight aircraft-based and other airfield fires. Often a combination of them is used for effective and fast action against fire incidents. Vehicles of different types are used to carry such materials and to approach the location of the fire. Rapid intervention vehicles (RIVs), trucks loaded with firefighting materials and rescue items, are made available and ready in airports nowadays for quick response (within a few minutes). Traditionally a protein agent (e.g. fluoroprotein foam) is used to extinguish fire and cool the aircraft fuselage. Complementary extinguishing agents, like chemical powders, halons and carbon dioxide are used further to suppress fire.

Fire situations are always different and hence the process of fire extinguishing may vary, though certain common steps remain the same. Fire stations inside airports are located usually towards the end of the runways to minimize response time. The number of fire stations can vary according to the size and extensiveness of the runway system. If more than one fire station is there, one will act as primary while the remaining will act as subordinate stations. Necessary firefighting vehicles will also be made available in those stations. Other rescue operations, along with first-aid activities, are also done by the team as and when they are required.

5.3 Ground handling equipment

There is a variety of equipment used for ground handling. According to ICAO, ground equipment refers to "Articles of a specialized nature for use in the maintenance, repair and servicing of an aircraft on the ground, including testing equipment and cargo-and-passenger-handling equipment". A tow bar is used in aircraft manoeuvring from the gate when it is ready to leave. It makes it possible to tow a given aircraft by a tractor that is clipped to the bar. Using a tow bar is more cost-effective as it can be used with universal/ common tractors that can be used with any type of aircraft. Instead of using a tow bar and tractors, push-back tractors can be used. These are more expensive than the other mechanism. Tugs and tractors are very common in airports, used mainly to move heavy equipment and loads. Chocks are used to prevent an aircraft from moving while parked at the gate or in a hangar.

A GPU is used to provide aircraft with electric energy. A forklift is another instrument seen on the airside which is used to carry palettes, especially for freight handling. Dollies are used to carry baggage and cargo from terminal to aircraft. Dollies are used for loose baggage as well as for ULDs and cargo pallets. There are different types, such as container dollies and pallet dollies. Container trailers, pallet trailers, platform trailers and luggage and bulk cargo trailers are also seen in airports. A belt loader is used with conveyor belts for loading and unloading baggage into and out of aircraft. Self-propelled conveyer-belt loaders are used mostly for carrying smaller loads and baggage when these are not packed into containers. A loader is used for bulk loading of heavy loads above 3 tonnes, including baggage containers. Container loaders, with two platforms that can raise and descend separately, are in use commonly for loading and unloading of containers and pallets. Transporters are also used for cargo transportation and for facilitating loading and unloading of cargo.

In addition to the above equipment and vehicles, airside will have many others, including: the air start unit (ASU), which is used for starting aircraft engines when an aircraft's APU is not operational; passenger carrying low floor buses; mobile passenger stairs; waste water disposal vehicles; potable water vehicles; lavatory hoses/vehicles; luggage towing vehicles; luggage delivery wagons; catering vehicles; vehicles for winter operations; fire and rescue vehicles; refuelling vehicles; and all types of ground transport equipment (e.g. mesh, binding band, tray, etc.).

Table 5.2 Major equipment/vehicles used in ground handling

Equipment

Tow bars	Sand/aggregate trucks	Transporters
Push-back tractors	Chemical spreaders	Tractors
Forklifts	Rapid intervention vehicles	Plastic foil
Stairs/Steps	(RIVs)	Net bags/pouches
Ground power units	Tankers	Dry ice boxes
Chocks	Trailers	Pot kennels
Aircraft tripod jacks	Unit load devices (ULDs)	Pallets
Air start units (ASUs)	Tie-down rings and straps	Containers
Waste water disposal	Lashing rope	Luggage towing vehicles
vehicles	Supporting planks and	Luggage delivery wagon
Potable water vehicles	platforms	Buses
Lavatory service vehicles	Loaders	Aircraft service stairs
Catering vehicles	Belt loaders	Other firefighting and
De-icing and snow	Dollies	rescue operations
removing vehicles	Airline service trolleys	

5.4 Passenger handling

Passenger handling is all about the processing activities associated with departing passengers – for boarding the flight for onward journey and enabling the arriving passengers to leave the airport without delay or hassles. Passenger handling primarily takes place in the terminal building, which should provide a convenient facility for transferring from ground to air transport, and vice versa. The terminal is the last point at which passengers from other countries can experience a place (before they get on a plane and fly home). It is also the first point at which incoming foreign passengers experience a country. Hence, the efficiency of passenger handling is determined not just by quick and comfortable movement of passengers from the entrance of the terminal to the boarding place. Many other factors also play a role in the successful management of airports. A departing passenger has to pass through different stages in an airport, particularly in the terminal. A system exists through which passenger movement is sequenced until boarding at the gate area.

5.4.1 Departure procedures

For a departing passenger, he/she enters the departure area, where the check-in concourse is located. Checked-in baggage can be screened through an x-ray scanning machine. In some airports, the baggage screening process takes place later, after the airline collects them. Checked baggage is the luggage that cannot be carried by the passenger in hand and which is stored in the specific place for luggage (the hold) in the aircraft. Free baggage allowance is given to passengers up to a certain weight and size as per the airline's conditions. There are self-check-in kiosks available in many airports and these can be used by passengers who don't have check-in luggage.

   The passenger has to locate the appropriate check-in counter of their particular airline for getting their boarding pass. There will be airport attendants/staff available to help the passenger do this. There are also visual displays available to guide the passenger. There may be different check-in areas for domestic and international passengers. Different airports have different structures of arranging check-in counters. Once the check-in counter is identified, the passenger can approach the counter and the staff will collect the necessary travelling documents, including ticket and passport. Usually airports have check-in counters for individual flights, but some have common check-in counters. If it

Table 5.3 Passenger handling: primary activities and facilities

Activities	Facilities
Arrival of passengers	Information counters
Documents verification and boarding pass issuing	Ticket/boarding counters
Baggage check	Baggage screening facilities
Passport/immigration check	Passenger security stations
Security check	Passport control counters
Departure for boarding	Baggage claim areas and
Baggage claim	conveyor belts
Customs clearance	Customs clearance areas

is individual check-in, then there will be two or more dedicated counters for each flight during the specified check-in time of each flight. The counter staff verifies the details and identification and issues the boarding pass. In the meantime, the luggage will be weighed, and checked baggage will be taken in after proper tagging. Hand luggage is also tagged after weighing. Once the process is complete, the passenger receives their boarding pass and checked baggage counterfoil. It's important to minimize the check-in time in order to be efficient. Long queues for check-in are unwarranted. Displays containing the flight details need to be placed at each counter so that the passenger can easily locate it. In some locations, curb check-in is available, where the luggage is collected upon arrival of the passenger at the airport, before they proceed to the check-in area. This makes it easier for passengers to be relieved of their heavy luggage early on.

With the boarding pass, the passenger has to proceed to the emigration centre, also called the passport control centre. There will be a number of counters with emigration officials. Passengers hand over their documents and the officer in charge verifies them, including the visa. After verification, the exit stamp will be endorsed in the passport to show the departure of the passenger from the country to another country. As soon as emigration clearance and exit stamping is over, the passenger, along with their hand luggage, has to undergo detailed security screening. Hand luggage, electronic devices and other items passengers are carrying are screened and checked separately for anything suspicious. The passenger has to walk through a metal detector, and security personnel may check their body, with the help of the metal detector. After the security check, the passenger enters

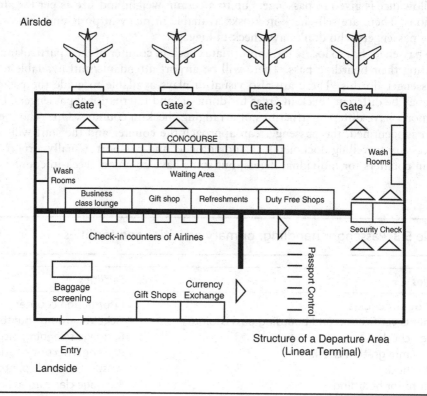

Figure 5.2 Airport departure area

into a concourse with a wide variety of commercial facilities, including duty-free shops, refreshment centres, gift shops, bookshops, etc. From there, after finishing their shopping and/or refreshments, passengers can move to the departure area where the gate is located.

After waiting in the departure area or gate hold room and hearing the boarding announcement, the passenger moves to the gate. Once the verification commences at the gate, the passenger's travel documents will be verified by the airline attendant/gate personnel again and a counterfoil of the boarding pass will be given back to the passenger. The boarding pass and identity verification are extremely important prior to boarding. After pre-boarding verification, the passenger is led to the aircraft by walking, in a transfer vehicle or through a passenger jet bridge. The boarding processing may vary from airline to airline. Some airlines prefer passengers to board based on seat numbers. While entering into the aircraft the flight crew may greet and welcome the passengers and lead them to their particular seats.

Though passengers may move ahead themselves through all the stages as per the information displayed and announced, necessary assistance may also be given when being processed through check-in, security screening, passport control and boarding. A good share of the passengers may be in the airport for the first time, but they should nonetheless feel that it is easy to find the necessary facilities and services. Every passenger will expect to be moved through the respective processes without delay, have space to relax and to refresh in the cleanest environment, with good ambience, beautiful interiors and amenities. Each passenger will also expect warmth during checks and emigration clearances. Efficiency in check-in counters and speed of processing are very important in passenger handling in airports. Long queues are tiring and dissatisfying. Moreover, many airports require a lot of walking. Nowadays, internal transport vehicles, including monorail services, are arranged inside airports to move from one area to another. Elevators, stairs and escalators also need to be in place and functional. Many would also appreciate good shopping options. Other services like banking, information services, etc. are significant, too. A quick check-in process, easy emigration services, shorter distances to walk to reach the gate area, enough space to rest and relax, easy access to gates, good refreshment options, eye-catching interiors and furnishings, efficient staff to deliver the necessary services, good shopping facilities and easy boarding mechanisms are key determinants in the success of airports.

5.4.2 Arrival procedures

There are similar situations during arrival as well. The arriving passenger may want to leave the airport as quickly as possible. Some may want to try out shopping options or arrange accommodation services and car rentals. Others may require banking and currency exchange services. In some busy airports, there are long queues at passport control counters. This really irks arriving passengers who are already tired after their long journey. Let's now take a look at the major arrival procedures in airports.

Once the aircraft lands, passengers are often in a hurry to disembark. First class and business class passengers are permitted to disembark before the rest of the passengers (i.e. economy class) on the aircraft. Everyone will be transported to the arrival gate where they will enter the arrival concourse. From the arrival area, they move to passport verification and visa counters. Once their documents have been verified and stamped with entry permits, passengers move further along. For transit passengers, there is no need to go through the passport control area; there will be separate passage for them. When the boarding announcement is made, transit passengers can move to the departure area (after

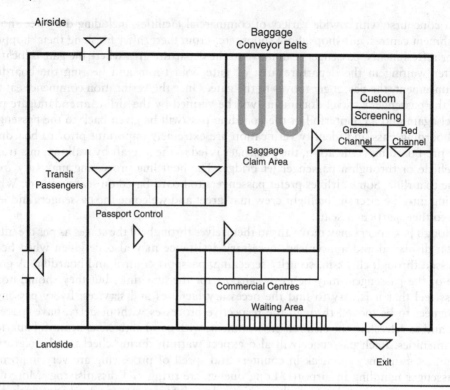

Figure 5.3 Structure of arrival area of an airport

the security check) once again. Arriving passengers have to move to the baggage claim area for collecting their luggage. In large airports there will be a number of conveyor belts and the passenger will have to identify the belt that matches their flight. Necessary assistance can be obtained from the attendants available there or from the office for baggage claim. Passengers can collect their luggage and verify its tags with the counterfoils already issued.

Once baggage is collected, passengers can continue on. There are two ways: the **green channel** and the **red channel**. Usually baggage is screened by scanning machines. If the passenger has nothing to declare, i.e. dutiable goods, he/she can move through the green channel. If there is any item for which duty must be paid, the passenger must move through the red channel and pay the fee accordingly. Some countries maintain restrictions on certain items being brought into the country. In such locations, after baggage screening, officials may physically verify the luggage if they see anything suspicious.

After the customs area, passengers enter into a concourse with a wide variety of commercial service outlets, such as car rental, banking, hotel counters, restaurants, paid taxi services and currency exchange centres. Passengers can make use of any service according to their need, and then can continue on out of the airport for further activities.

5.5 Baggage handling

This is all about the collection, sorting and distribution of checked baggage. The luggage collected from the passenger during check-in has to be moved to the aircraft for loading.

Similarly, the baggage that arrives in a flight needs to be collected and distributed to the baggage claim area via conveyer belts. The whole process should be smooth and mistake-free. Once the airline counters receive the checked baggage, it passes to the central sorting area. Many airports use automated sorting of baggage, which is performed mainly with the help of bar codes. After sorting according to the flight, they will be moved to the respective airlines for loading. Baggage reconciliation is undertaken, which is done to ensure that passengers have boarded the same aircraft into which their baggage has been loaded. In the case of arriving flights, the unloaded luggage will also be moved to the central sorting area and from there it will be moved to the assigned conveyer belts. Those bags for transferring flights will be moved separately. Airports, airlines or outsourced agencies may undertake the baggage handling responsibilities depending upon each airport's policy. Automated systems are there to ensure error-free baggage handling. Baggage claim should be in a convenient location with necessary space and enough conveyor belts.

5.6 Air navigation services

Air travel needs a fine-tuned support system for safe and smooth operation. A range of complexities are involved in air transportation. An aircraft while flying cannot stop and wait for information. It flies very fast and a sudden change in direction or altitude is very difficult. Air navigation services in the system makes air transportation a smooth and safe affair. It involves facilities and services that provide a pilot with information to enable him/her to reach the destination smoothly, safely and on time. The advent of satellites and associated technology has altered the navigation systems. Satellite technology has brought accuracy and flexibility to navigation and significantly increased the range and quality of communication. In the early days, pilots looked out the window and identified routes with the help of maps and landmarks (visual reference). Things have now changed: air traffic has increased, the altitude of flights has increased and the distance covered has also increased. ICAO has an important role in introducing and standardizing the technology aspects in air navigation. Air navigation services have the following components:

- ATC
- Flight information services
- Alerting services

ATC has the function of guiding aircraft into and out of airports, providing pilots with continually updated automatic recordings, detailed information on ground conditions, climate details, runways in use and the state of navigation aids. Pilots get information on what height and direction to take from ATC. The technical services, which are provided from the ground to assist and control aircraft while in the air and during landing or take-off, have a key role in the operation of aviation services. Located in the airport terminal, ATC uses various communication systems, visual signalling and other devices. It is vested with the responsibility to authorize the aircraft to land or take off. The ATC tower may also provide approach control services. Also, visual navigational aids like lighting systems are there to aid the pilot. The pilot can also use a few instruments inside the cockpit while flying. The primary instrument is the flight display or electronic flight information system (EFIS). This provides information on flight situation, position and progress. Another part of the cockpit provides information on aircraft systems conditions and engines performance. There are different sets of rules and regulations for different ways of flying, known as **flight rules**. The two significant flight rules are:

- Visual flight rules (VFR)
- Instrument flight rules (IFR)

Under VFR, a pilot is primarily and exclusively responsible for the observation and visual reference to the ground for the avoidance of obstacles while flying. In the case of IFR, pilots are guided by a set of rules and regulations. Pilots have to take flight along well-determined air routes, called **airways**. Commercial air transportation uses mainly IFR.

There are many flights in the sky and there exists the possibility for collision. Pilots, flying under IFR, have to take airways, also called highways in the air. To avoid collision, pilots must keep a vertical/horizontal distance from other flights in the air. Keeping a minimum distance from other aircraft is referred to as **separation**. Normally, horizontal and vertical separation must be maintained, and under IFR, pilots will get adequate information to maintain the required separation. (Lateral separation may also be considered.) Vertical separation is maintained by flying at different levels (attitudes). One way to maintain horizontal separation is to ensure longitudinal separation, which necessitates keeping a minimum distance between the estimated positions of the aircraft.

Airspace is classified as controlled or uncontrolled. If it is controlled airspace, air traffic controllers maintain separation between aircraft and terrain. Commercial air transport usually takes place in controlled airspace. In uncontrolled airspace, as in the case of VFR, pilots are responsible for separation. In the case of controlled airspace, airspace is divided into three areas: **airway, terminal control area** and **control zone**. When flights are in airway, air traffic controllers will help the aircraft to fly along the predetermined flight path, after it obtains the assigned cruising altitude. The area control centre of ATC will be controlling flights in this area.

> The navigation systems used while 'en route' are often different from those used while on 'approach' to an airport. The en route systems must be capable of longer-range coverage, while the approach systems must have a higher precision to avoid terrain and obstructions at low altitude.
>
> (Hansman and Odoni, 2009)

When the flight reaches the terminal control area, which represents the part of the airspace near airports at least 656 feet (200 metres) above the ground, the approach control unit helps it to land. Traffic density will be high in this area. Terminal area controllers (the approach control unit) provide all aircraft with control, information and alert services. It is usually located within the control tower building. Computers, radio communication and surveillance radar are used for this. In the control zone, aerodrome control takes over from the approach control unit. The control zone is the part of airspace, central in the aerodrome, with a radius of 8 kilometres, with very high density. The tower controller gives instructions to the pilot and gives permission to land. In the aerodrome, visual systems also guide the pilot for safe landing. The instrument landing system (ILS) guides the pilot to the runway using two electronic beams for vertical and lateral guidance. These are supported with lighting systems such as approach lights.

Flight information services include the provision of regular information that a pilot needs and other necessary information such as weather conditions, information on changes in the availability of radio navigation services, changes in airport conditions, any collision hazards, and any other information likely to affect safety. These services are provided when aircraft are within a flight information region (FIR). An **alerting service** is provided when the flight is in trouble, e.g. during a hijacking. Under this service, it will notify appropriate organizations. In such a situation, flight information centres or area control centres serve as the central point for action.

5.7 Air cargo operation

Air cargo operation is another important function of an airport. Cargo is processed in a separate terminal. It can be transported in passenger aircraft, in its belly space, or in cargo aircraft (freighters). There are even super transporters which can carry very larger items, such as helicopters and large machinery. Mail and speed/courier services are also included in air cargo services. Freighter aircraft have access to cargo terminals and loading of cargo will be done there. Palletization, stacking of shipments or consignments/cargo pallets, which can be moved in airports and transported in aircraft easily, is an important task. Usually, small consignments are stacked on pallets. Large ones go into containers and containers can be loaded into aircraft according to the convenience and shape of the aircraft. Containers are shaped to fit the hold of the aircraft and to protect the contents from damage and theft. ULD is the common term for these loading boxes. Various government agencies, like customs, health and agriculture, will be involved in the screening of the freight received or transported. Various activities are involved prior to loading of cargo, like cargo load planning, determining weights, etc. Cargo transportation is an important revenue source for airlines.

5.8 Summary

Airport operations involve a range of activities, of which ground handling is significant. It deals with all the activities undertaken after landing and before take-off and it includes various services such as aircraft marshalling, toilet and water services, repair of faults, fuelling, wheel and tyre check, ground power supply, de-icing, cooling/heating, routine and non-routine maintenance, cleaning of cockpit windows, wings, nacelles and cabin windows, in-flight entertainment, minor servicing of cabin fittings, unloading and loading of cargo, alteration of seat configuration, safety measures, air conditioning, catering services, deplaning and boarding of passengers, start-up, towing with push-back tractors, etc. Airlines prefer to have minimum turnaround times and efficient ramp handling is a prerequisite for this. Deplaning and boarding has to be timely and smooth. While the aircraft is at the ramp, the energy requirements will be fulfilled by supplying the necessary power for the next flight. Cargo and baggage loading is also a crucial activity. In wide-body aircraft, baggage is transported in containers which reduces the number of bags going astray, as the baggage for one destination is stored in one container. Push-back, another activity, is the action of moving an airplane from a passenger terminal to a runway or taxiway, into a position where it can use its own engines. Refuelling of aircraft for the subsequent trip is an activity to be done with utmost care and safety. Airports usually have adequate processes for refuelling the landing aircraft. In some locations, winter operations are very important, particularly in the winter season. Chemicals are used along with mechanical processes for de-icing.

Also, it's mandatory for airports to ensure aerodrome rescue and firefighting services within airports, with close links to external nearby fire stations and mechanisms. In addition to water, the most commonly used firefighting material, gases, dry chemicals and aqueous film-forming foam are used to fight aircraft-based and other airfield fires. A range of equipment is required to manage ground handling activities in airports. This is for maintenance, repair and servicing of an aircraft on the ground and for handling of passengers and cargo.

Passenger handling is all about the processing activities associated with departing passengers for boarding the flight for onward journey and enabling the arriving passengers to leave the airport without delay and hassles. The terminal is the point at which a foreigner has both their first and last impression of a country. Thus, efficiency of passenger handling is important. Passenger handling, baggage handling and cargo operations do matter in the successful operation of airports. Air navigation services involve air traffic control, flight information services and alerting services. A coordinated and efficient functioning of them is vital for smooth and safe air transport operations.

Review questions

Short/medium answer type questions

- What do we mean by turnaround time?
- Write down the activities involved in the ground handling of an airport before the next flight.
- What are ramp handling activities?
- Describe the process of deplaning and boarding of passengers.
- Describe how power is provided to an aircraft while on the ramp.
- Discuss the various aspects of cargo loading in aircraft.
- Explain the push-back operations.
- Discuss the process of refuelling of an aircraft before the next flight.
- Give a brief account of winter operations in airports.
- What are the fire prevention and firefighting operations in an airport?
- What are the major equipment and vehicles used in airport ground handling?
- List the activities involved in passenger handling for an arriving passenger.
- Describe the air navigations services provided for a flight after take-off until landing.

Essay type questions

- Explain the ground handling operations in an airport.
- Describe the passenger handling process in airport terminals.

References

ARCP Synthesis 63 (2015) Overview of Airport Fueling System Operations: Airport Cooperative Research Programme, Transportation Research Board, Transportation research

Board/ Federal Aviation Administration-Washington, available at http://onlinepubs.trb.org/Onlinepubs/acrp/acrp_syn_063.pdf (accessed 22 May 2016).

Graham, A. (2013) *Managing Airports: An International Perspective*. 4th edn. Oxford: Routledge.

Hansman, J. R. and Odoni, A. (2009) Air Traffic Control, in P. Belobaba, A. Odoni and C. Barnhart (eds), *The Global Airline Industry*. West Sussex: John Wiley & Sons.

ICAO Definitions, UVS International, available at http://www.uavdach.org/aktuell_e/3_UVSI_ICAO-Definitions_V01_120813.pdf (accessed 30 August 2016).

Kazda, A. and Caves, E. R. (2000) *Airport Design and Operations*. Oxford: Elsevier.

Swissport, Ground Handling, available at http://www.swissport.com/products-services/products-services/ground-handling/ (accessed 15 April 2017).

Wells, T. A. and Young, S. (2004) *Airport: Planning and Management*. 5th edn. New York: McGraw-Hill.

Website

www.dubaiairports.ae.

Chapter 6

Airline management

Learning outcomes

After studying this chapter, you will be able to:

- Define airline industry and discuss its characteristics.
- Describe the airline product and identify its consumers.
- Understand different types of airlines.
- Comprehend major airline functions such as fleet planning, schedule planning, fleet assignment, aircraft routing and crew scheduling.
- Explain the passenger processing activities.
- Learn the aircraft maintenance activities.
- Understand the organization structure in an airline.
- Identify the major industry practices followed by airlines.
- Explain marketing in the airline sector.

6.1 Introduction

Airlines, the most important element and the most visible player in the aviation sector, are involved in the commercial transport services for the public. It's now one of the largest industries in the world, serving billions of customers annually. Approximately 3.7 billion passengers used the services of commercial airlines in 2016 (IATA, 2017). An airline's basic function is to provide the service (at a price) of transporting passengers, cargo and baggage from one point to another. Though airlines are often linked with passenger transportation, they have categorical significance for cargo and baggage transportation as well. In the case of passenger transportation, the services of airlines are not just on international routes; they also play a key role in domestic transportation, particularly in large countries. Also, the air freight market has been growing. As per recent IATA statistics,

> cargo business generates 9% of airline revenues, representing more than twice the revenues from the first class segment. . . . In 2016, airlines transported 52 million

Figure 6.1 Qantas B744 flight
Courtesy: Wikimedia Commons

metric tons of goods, representing more than 35% of global trade by value. . . . That is equivalent to $6.8 trillion worth of goods annually.

(IATA/Air Cargo, n.d.)

Though airlines can simply be considered organizations that operate and manage the services of transporting passengers and cargo from one place to another, they represent a very challenging business, which involves complex operations requiring a large number of employees at various levels; and hence airlines require efficient management and professionalism for their competitive survival. Airline operations form a network of routes by connecting services between different airports/cities. This network is the domain of airline operations and the customers are transported within the network. Large airlines have vast networks. Also, airlines expand networks through a "hub and spoke system", "code sharing agreements" and alliances. Having broader networks is an advantage for airlines as customers can depend on one airline to travel to more cities.

Airlines do play a major role in the growth of tourism worldwide. Apart from commercial airlines with regular services, tourism is benefited by the services of non-regular airlines also, like those of charter airlines. Large-scale tour operators make extensive use of charter services, particularly for leisure tourism. Some of the regular, scheduled airlines have their own charter services. There are also dedicated charter airlines. Of late, business travel and leisure travel depend on scheduled airline services. The efficiency of airline operations, particularly punctuality of services and quality is quite relevant in tourism.

127

6.2 Airline industry

An industry consists of a number of competing firms having similar products. Airlines also form an industry that provides services for people who intend to travel or send consignments efficiently from one place to another using the air mode of transport. Travel is a fundamental requirement of people and the airline industry ensures smooth, efficient, fast and comfortable journeys along airways. In international tourism, airlines play a crucial role. Though this industry is a major one, it functions as a part of the larger industry of air transportation. The emergence of this industry as a major mode of transport redefined the concept of distance and resulted in the ease and comfort of long-haul travel. Functionally, while transporting people and cargo, the industry connects places across the world. It is "an industry which consists of a vast network of routes that connect cities in different parts of a country/world, and over the network a large number of airlines carry passengers and cargo on scheduled services" (Wensveen, 2012). While an airline forms its own network of operations, the airline industry makes a larger network and the global airline industry integrates all the smaller networks into a global one – with all the cities and towns with airports connected together. This industry network consisting of 1,400 airlines connects 4,130 airports together, with the assistance of 173 air navigation services providers (ANSPs) (ICAO, 2015). This vast network is like the cardiovascular system of a human body, connecting almost every part of the world. Moreover, this is the quickest transportation system for movement of passengers and goods. The passengers and cargo move in all directions within the network.

The role this industry plays in the global economy is amazing. It is a facilitator for many other major industries. For instance, tourism, one of the largest industries in the world, relies heavily on the airline sector. Without the airline industry, tourism would not have enjoyed the same level of growth. Related industries are also dependent on it. The aircraft manufacturing sector depends on the industry, as does the cargo sector. Some cargo products are perishable in nature, which necessitates quick transportation, meaning only airlines can handle it. Travel agents and tour operators are intermediaries of the airline industry. Airlines play an integral role in a globalized business world. Global trade is facilitated by this sector through enhancing access to international markets and allowing globalization and internationalization of business activities. According to an ICAO report, "25% of all companies' sales are dependent on air transport. 70% of businesses report that serving a bigger market is a key benefit of using air services." (ICAO/ATAG, 2011). The industry is treated with a high fixed cost structure with comparatively lower variable costs. Also, it is highly capital-intensive, requiring very specific investment in long-term assets (Wittmer and Bieger, 2011). The airline industry makes use of other industries' products and services for its functioning. In order to operate air services, airlines need the service of airports. Passengers are transported in aircraft, which are the products of aircraft manufacturing companies. Being a price-sensitive sector, the airline industry is affected by variations in its external environments and price is an important determinant in its demand. The industry was completely centralized and regulated in previous years, but developments that took place during the 1970s and later (specifically privatization and deregulation) caused dramatic changes. Privatization became the norm in many countries and some of the large private airlines are now progressing much faster.

The airline industry is a global sector, providing service in almost all countries in the world. Certainly, the industry is an economic force of large magnitude. It plays a significant role in the work and leisure of millions of people. According to the Air Transport Action Group (ATAG, 2016), of the 9.9 million direct jobs created by the aviation sector in 2014, 2.7 million jobs (27 per cent of the total) came from airline industry alone. Moreover, $6.4 trillion worth of goods were transported internationally by air in the same year.

6.3 Characteristics

The following are the major characteristics of the airline industry in general:

- Service industry
- High barriers to entry and exit
- Capital-intensive
- High cash flow
- Dynamic pricing
- Oligopolistic
- Highly regulated
- Non-price competition
- Labour-intensive
- High labour and fuel expenses
- Highly competitive
- Capacity versus demand
- Thin profit margins
- Close government regulations
- Seasonality

Service industry characteristics have been explained elsewhere in this book. Airlines possess all the service industry characteristics, such as intangibility, inseparability and perishability. Akin to many other tourism sectors, airlines are also highly capital-intensive. The start-up cost is extremely high, as purchase of a single aircraft can be very expensive. Even getting licences to commence operations as an airline is not easy. Airline operations require high technology infrastructure as well as technical experts like pilots, technicians, etc. In short, starting out in the airline industry is not easy – barriers of entry are high. Apart from the huge capital required, plenty of governmental regulations have to be adhered to. A range of licences are required. The requirements of technological infrastructure are also very high. High cash flow is another feature of airline business. Everyday operations necessitate large sums of money. Dynamic pricing is also practised by airlines. Indeed, in same flights, different passengers may have purchased tickets for different prices. According to demand fluctuations, prices need to be altered quickly.

Oligopoly denotes that a market is controlled by a small group of firms. The airline industry is characterized by oligopoly. In most of the markets just a few airlines survive in the long run. The main reason for oligopoly is the high level of entry barriers, which limits the entry of new competitors. Also, because the airline industry is highly capital-intensive, with the need to acquire a range of certificates and licences, it is not easy for a new airline to enter the market. Similar to other tourism industries like hotels, airlines are also highly labour-intensive. A wide range of human resources with extremely varied qualifications and skills are required to operate the business. As many of the job positions necessitate high qualifications and skills, the salaries/wages offered are also high. Labour expense is thus significant in the industry. Moreover, fuel expenses are also high. For flying, large quantities of fuel are required.

Being in a highly competitive sector, airlines have to deploy the latest strategies and tactics to remain successful in the market. Due to the issue of "capacity versus demand", it is difficult for airlines to match capacity to demand consistently. Sometimes demand may be less but the operation of the flight still has to take place. At other times, the demand may be high, yet airlines could be helpless to meet this extra demand. Thin profit margins are another concern in the airline sector. Due to extreme competition, airlines usually pursue a competitive pricing strategy and offer products with lesser margins. Usually, the profit level is maintained in high season by hiking the price. Spending on air travel is discretionary. The air travel sector is slow in recovering after a recession. Both pleasure and business travel are curtailed during periods of sharp and sustained downturn. Travel is one of the expenses a business or a person can cut immediately during tough economic times. Close government regulations make it hard for airlines to operate easily. Safety and security is the most important factor in governments' strict regulations.

6.4 Airline consumers and tourists

In the airline sector, the difference between the consumer and the customer is more evident. The actual user of the service and the decision-maker may be different. (It can also be the same.) The airline consumer includes those people who actually travel as well as those who require the service of transporting cargo from one place to another as per his/her need. So the airline customer can be the consumer herself, or the decision-maker. A customer encounters many difficulties in making decisions, especially since this decision is a high-involvement exercise, and is complicated by varied factors, particularly the cost factor. There are other modes of transport which are much cheaper and more convenient. Moreover, the influence of external and internal factors is also relevant, which makes the purchase decision more difficult.

Tourists constitute the major market of airlines. There are also other travellers with a significant share in the airline demand. Among tourists, leisure tourists constitute an important group of consumers. Usually leisure tourists make the travel decisions by themselves. Yet there can be influencers in it. For instance, in a family holiday, children or a spouse can influence the decision of purchasing the travel product. In the case of package tours, the tour operator or wholesaler who makes the travel arrangements may make the purchase of the product as well, which are finally consumed by the tourists. For group inclusive tours (GIT) and fully independent travellers (FIT), tour operators have a significant role to play in the selection of airlines. Frequency of travel by leisure travellers is less compared to the frequency of travel by business travellers.

In the parlance of business travel, though there is a right to choose a product according to the traveller's needs, the decision-making may be done by the decider, not the user. In business travel, the customers are often different from the consumers. Owner-managers of SMEs have the freedom to choose, whereas a personal secretary of a busy businessman or businesswoman takes on the role of buyer and purchases with due consideration for his/her boss's needs and interests. The decision-making with regard to travel can involve different participants in addition to the consumer. For instance, Shah (2007) suggests that there are five types of participants who have roles as decision-making units (DMUs) during the process of air travel decision-making and purchase. They are described in Table 6.1. Some corporate companies have dedicated travel departments that undertake purchasing on behalf of employees. Also, some corporate firms have contracts with travel agents to handle the travel requirements of executives of the respective firms. Airlines,

Table 6.1 Types of participants influencing DMUs in business travel

Type of participant	Description
Deciders	These are the final decision-makers, with apparent need of taking the decision that may be in the best interest of his/her organization.
Gatekeepers	The personnel who control the flow of information to the DMU, such as the secretary of the decider. They can restrict the access of others.
Users	The actual users of the product. They may make efforts to get the suitable product that matches their need.
Buyers	They negotiate the final and best deal, from the perspective of upholding the interests of the organization with suppliers.
Influencers	They may or may not be from the organization; and they neither use the product nor are involved in detailed negotiation with suppliers. But they influence the final outcome of the buying process. An example would be a partner (wife/husband) of a decider.

Source: Shah (2007)

therefore, have to deal not only with the consumer of the product, but other players, including buyers, deciders and influencers. Corporate travel agents, retail travel agents, tour operators, online agents, event managers, etc. are also the customers of airlines, who have their role to play in the decision-making of purchasing of airline seats on behalf of consumers. Another group of customers are freight forwarders. Consumers in this category include those who send the consignments from one place to another using air transport. People can send cargo directly with airlines as well, without using the service of freight forwarders. When using freight forwarders, consumers usually have little choice of airline, as freight forwarders decide which airline to use. Moreover, freight forwarders consolidate small cargo items of different consumers and send them as a single cargo item. Here also freight forwarders act as the customer, with different roles played by personnel working with them.

6.5 Airline product

Airlines certainly provide an intangible product. Moreover, it is "inseparable" in nature and highly "perishable". According to Barnes (2012), an "airline sells air transportation service between two or more cities at a certain price with specified purchase requirements and restrictions". Scheduled flights fly from one place to another and transport passengers and cargo as per a published timetable. Its core product is transportation, either of passengers or cargo, from one place to another. This service aspect begins from the moment of ticket purchase and continues until the completion of the service, when the passenger/cargo reaches the final destination. It means a range of services are expected in between. This expectation can include diverse services (in-flight services), arriving on time, and similar. Services can be augmented/enhanced with, for example, the provision of personalized food and a large variety of in-flight entertainment options. Furthermore, there can be added services to delight customers. Once again, the airline product is a set of services. Indeed, modern air transport consists of increased complementary services and product differentiation. The products of low-cost carriers (LCCs) may have some differences with those of full-service carriers (FSCs). It is mainly the in-flight services that are very different for LCCs.

Quality of in-flight cabin services and ground handling services is an important aspect of airline products. Punctuality in operations, frequency of services, departing and arrival airports and their accessibility, services and features of those airports, etc. also form part of the airline product. Aircraft type and even the carrier's image are components of the airline product. Passenger airline product benefits can include comfortable seats, more legroom, handy baggage compartments, etc. An efficient ticket reservation system, variety of in-flight entertainment options and speedy baggage delivery are also benefits passengers like to have. Apart from the accessibility of airports, other aspects, such as convenient car parking facilities, good waiting lounges, adequate duty-free shops, quick and efficient checking of baggage and baggage delivery, efficient service at reservation counters, efficiency in issuing boarding passes, ease and speed of emigration clearance and security checks, complement an airline's product. Safety is also an important aspect associated with the airline product.

Table 6.2 ICAO definitions of commercial air transportation

Term	Definition
Commercial air transport operation	An aircraft operation involving the transport of passengers, cargo or mail for remuneration or hire. It can be classified into scheduled and non-scheduled operations.
Scheduled air transport (international)	A scheduled international air service is a series of flights that possess both of the following characteristics: • Flights pass through the airspace over the territory of more than one state. • Flights are performed by aircraft for the transport of passengers, mail or cargo for remuneration, in such a manner that each flight is open to use by members of the public. Flights are operated so as to serve traffic between the same two or more points, either according to a published timetable or with flights so regular or frequent that they constitute a recognizably systematic series.
Non-scheduled air transport	This refers to commercial air transport without scheduled air services. A charter flight is a non-scheduled operation using a chartered aircraft. Note the following categories: • Passenger charter flights • Cargo charter flights • Combined passenger–cargo flights Non-scheduled non-charter flights are for the carriage of individually ticketed or individually waybilled traffic (sometimes referred to as on-demand air taxi service).

Source: ICAO (2009)

6.6 Types of airlines

Airlines can be classified based on different factors. Scheduled and non-schedules airlines constitute the fundamental categories. International and domestic airlines form another classification. Major categories of airlines are introduced below.

6.6.1 Scheduled airlines

Scheduled airlines are bound to fly on specific routes at pre-set times on a regular basis: daily, weekly, etc. A published schedule is the basis for operating services regularly between the departing airports and the final ports as per the itinerary. The general public can travel on these, as they are open to direct booking by members of the public. Scheduled airlines may operate within a country or internationally. Some of the scheduled airlines operate both domestic and international services. Cargo transportation is also done by scheduled airlines. The scheduled air transport sector is the most significant among the whole airport industry. In previous years, it was the monopoly of the flag carriers or the national airlines owned and operated by the national or state governments. Later, privatization and deregulation (the US introduced deregulation in air transport in 1978) resulted in competition and dynamism in the industry. Many other countries followed this trend, with "open skies" becoming a buzzword towards the end of the last century.

The airline industry celebrated its centenary in January 2014. By this time, scheduled air transport had carried more than three billion passengers in a single year. The first fixed winged airline service, in 1914, carried only one passenger, as the flight was a single capacity carrier. A hundred years ago, the first service of the first airline launched a new form of commercial transportation – scheduled passenger air transport – from St Petersburg in Florida in the USA. It was organized by the St Petersburg–Tampa Airboat Line, the first scheduled passenger airline service in the world. The first passenger was Abram Pheil, the mayor of St Petersburg. Even before that, there was a passenger air transport service. A passenger airline called DELAG (Deutsche Luftschiffahrts-Aktiengesellschaft, or German Airship Transportation Corporation) began its own operations in 1909. But it was not providing regular scheduled air services then; the purpose in the early period was on holiday transportation. As the years went by, commercial air transport expanded, grew and became a huge industry and arguably the most prominent mode of transport in the world.

Table 6.3 Scheduled air transport: international and domestic

Year	No. of passengers (millions)	Freight tonnes (millions)
2005	2,700	47.0
2010	2,698	47.1
2011	2,865	48.1
2012	2,998	47.4
2013	3,132	48.5
2014	3,303	50.4
2015	3,533	50.7

Source: ICAO (2015)

Over the years, scheduled air transportation has grown and expanded, and different models have emerged in the interim. The following are the most common types of scheduled airlines.

Major airlines
Major airlines are also called trunk airlines, and concentrate on long-haul routes. They operate services between major cities inside and outside the country. Usually these airlines use larger planes with seat capacities of more than 130. Lufthansa, British Airways, Emirates and American Airlines are examples of major airlines.

Regional airlines
These are also certified airlines which provide regular services for scheduled passengers or cargo. They usually provide service between smaller cities and also connect these small communities with major airports. Regional carriers may use small aircraft for operating short-haul routes. They are also called commuter airlines in some regions.

Commuter airlines
These can be considered smaller versions of regional airlines (Purzycki, 2001), which typically fly routes of 400 miles or less. These constitute the smaller airline services, acting as feeders for the major airlines. They operate from smaller airports to major cities (and vice versa), between smaller cities and hubs, and from outlying communities to the associated hub airports to connect with other scheduled airlines.

National airlines
National airlines usually operate services within the boundaries of a country, though they may fly on international routes as well. These include airlines between major and regional carriers. They provide air connectivity between areas of lesser density and also between smaller population centres and major airports.

Flag carrier
These are the airlines owned by the government. They operate services mainly on international routes. They may also operate services within the boundaries of a country.

Full-service carriers (FSCs)
FSCs are also called full-service airlines (FSAs) as well as legacy airlines. They offer a full basket of services to passengers. Services include meals, beverages, lounges, entertainment, etc. They employ more people and cover larger geographical areas due to their 'hub and spoke' agreements with smaller airlines. Different types of aircraft are also used.

Low-cost carriers (LCCs)/low-cost airlines (LCAs)
This type was an addition to the airline sector that evolved significantly towards the end of the twentieth century. They are also called 'no frills' airlines, and have low fares. They operate point-to-point services, and usually on short-haul routes. They don't offer some of the in-flight services, such as food and beverages (at least not as part of the ticket price). Usually they use a single type of aircraft and employ fewer people compared to FSCs. Usually LCCs are single class carriers with standardized treatment for all passengers. No additional features are offered, such as a frequent

flyer programme (FFP), interlining facilities and lounges. Due to quicker turnaround, these planes can make more trips in a day. Leaner crew result in lower labour costs. Also, they cross-utilize their employees. The emergence of LCCs has had significant implications for the growth of tourism (Barrett, 2008). Air Asia (Malaysia), easyJet (UK), Southwest Airlines (US), Air India Express, etc. are examples of LCCs. According to Harvey (2007), LCCs use the following strategies to manage their businesses profitably:

- They fly at off-peak times.
- There is greater focus on less congested airports so as to get lower landing charges and quick turnarounds.
- Point-to-point, short-route services are offered to get higher crew utilization and lower crew costs.
- They provide only basic in-flight service, with no in-flight catering included as part of the ticket price.
- They operate at a higher seat density with less legroom. This means there are more seats available (and a higher load factor).
- They operate with a minimum of staff.
- They operate with only one type of aircraft. This helps to save training costs and leads to gain through the cost saving on spare parts, maintenance, equipment, etc.
- Tickets are sold more online.

Instead of serving in-flight food and beverages, LCCs sell limited items at a relatively higher price. By using small aircraft, less time is needed to get ready for the next flights after landing. As the flight is devoid of food service, time can be saved by not having to load and unload food. Also, less congested and second-tier city airports are mainly targeted. LCCs' fleets include mostly smaller single-type aircraft. This will help to avoid buying different types of spare parts for different aircraft models. LCCs reduce distribution costs by avoiding intermediaries and selling seats primarily though their own websites, own offices and call centres. As many services are not offered, the number of cabin crew needed is also less. Some recruit employees on contract. A variety of items, such as pens, purses, books, etc., are sold inside the aircraft, which brings extra revenue. Mainly to avoid delays and to reduce turnaround time, LCCs usually don't offer connection flights; instead, they offer only point-to-point services. Free baggage allowance is less for such airlines, and by reducing legroom the number of seats can be increased. The price of the tickets is based on the demand and supply of a particular route at a particular time. LCCs usually provide seats for lowest rates for advanced bookings, but the price will increase as time goes on, i.e. closer to the date of departure. In addition, last-minute sales would be possible by altering prices.

6.6.2 Non-scheduled air services

These are also commercial services, but do not follow published schedules for flights. They are permitted to operate services on air routes, but are not on a regular schedule. Demand is the criterion for operation instead of regularity. Charter flight services are good examples of this. Charter flights are usually hired planes that fly from one place to another at a particular time. According to the Director General of Civil Aviation, India, **charter service** constitutes air service operation "for hire and reward in which the departure time, departure location and arrival locations are specially negotiated with the customer or the customer's representative for entire aircraft. No ticket is sold to individual passenger for such operation" (DGCA, 2000). The clients or the consumers consist mainly of tourists, along with other groups, such as members of sports or athletic teams, corporations, government agencies, etc. Charter flights are operated exclusively for certain purposes (e.g. holidays). Tour operators depend on charter services for operating tours to overseas destinations, hiring charter flights exclusively or as a "part-charter". Though the terms non-scheduled and charter (i.e. a contractual arrangement between an air carrier and an entity hiring or leasing its aircraft) have come to be used interchangeably, it should be noted that not all commercial non-scheduled operations are charter flights.

CASE STUDY 6.1

Airline industry: "drivers of change" in the coming decades

The International Air Transport Association (IATA), the global body of airlines, forecast that 7.2 billion passengers would travel in 2035, based on an estimation of 3.7 per cent annual compound average growth rate (CAGR). Between now and 2035, global commercial aviation would face some key risks and opportunities. An IATA study identified 13 drivers that are either likely to have a high impact on the sector by 2035 or a high level of uncertainty as to what that impact would be. The drivers identified are described in brief below.

If they emerge as a competitive alternative for aviation turbine fuel, alternative fuels and energy sources can even disrupt the geopolitical balance of power, and impact how businesses and the public consume energy. There could be far-reaching impacts when the potential of alternative fuels are fully realized and utilized. Along with the growth of the threat itself, cyber security has become an important industry and a major concern in the day-to-day affairs of people and businesses using technology. The boundaries between virtual and physical security are being blurred. Cybercrime is a tool of activists, governments and companies, or simply a disruptive hobby. Environmental activism is spreading and expanding to more communities and groups, and younger people are more likely to participate in online activism than older generations. There is also the possibility that the activists take a more militant stance through provocative marketing strategies. Another driver is the extreme weather events that could occur more frequently and the issues they could cause to air transport. Certain uncertainties prevail in this.

"Geopolitical (in)stability" is a matter of concern, and there is uncertainty as to what type of conflicts may occur and where such conflicts will take place. The degree of conflicts, nature of conflicts, groups involved, range in which conflicts will extend, etc. are also uncertain. Stability can prosper whereas instability can hamper. Infectious disease and pandemics occur more often and the possibilities of these in the future (in addition to their impacts on travel) are also unpredictable. The possible antagonism towards the carbon emissions of air transport and the potential international regulation of emissions and noise pollution are also unpredictable. An integrated supply chain allows manufacturers to look into business processes across multiple suppliers and disparate platforms to follow materials, components and people wherever they are. The uncertainty is all about the nature, ability, etc. of the supply chain in the future.

The changing consumption patterns and the quest for authenticity, greater value, etc. can affect businesses. The oil price has been a major factor that has impacted upon airline business, and the future of the oil price is highly unpredictable. In this unpredictable global economy, as the economic influence of developing nations increases, new markets, competitors and demands will alter patterns of trade, changing what goods are transported, and where they are transported. Tensions between data privacy and surveillance is another driver. For corporations, data breaches and cybercrime could demand novel measures to protect data, and privacy itself could become a valuable commodity. The future threat of terrorism is also uncertain.

All the above factors can be detrimental to the growth of air transport. However, some factors can be supportive and drive the growth instead.

Source: IATA (2017)

Read the case study carefully and answer the following questions:

- Identify the major drivers that are either likely to have high impact or uncertainly with regard to the air transport sector in the coming years.
- Explain how environmental activism, cyber security and geopolitical instability could affect air transport in the future.

6.7 Major airline functions

An airline is a large business organization that has a number of interrelated and complex operations. Most of the functions are time-bound and the success of the business depends to a great extent on the effective and efficient functioning of the operations and various tasks involved. A brief discussion of the major functions follows.

6.7.1 Fleet planning

Fleet planning is a long-term strategic activity. Fleet denotes the total number of aircraft along with their types that an airline has for air transport operations. Aircraft vary, and consequently their capacity, range, size, load factor, etc. also vary. Fleet planning is considered to be one of the most complex and critical planning activities of an airline:

An airline's fleet plan therefore reflects a strategy for multiple periods into the future, including the number of aircraft required by aircraft type, the timing of future

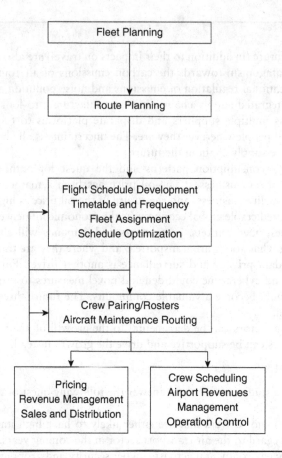

Figure 6.2 Stages in the airline planning process
Source: Adapted from Cook and Billig, 2017

deliveries, and retirement of existing fleet, as well as contingency plans to allow for flexibility in the fleet plan given the tremendous uncertainty about future market conditions.

(Belobaba, 2009)

Fleet planning is a crucial decision-making process for an airline, as the core revenue/profit of an airline is accounted through the efficiency of the operating aircraft's fleet. It's indeed an arduous task to decide on purchasing a new aircraft, especially since it is highly capital-intensive. Based on the future demand factor, an airline plans to select, buy or lease the right type of aircraft at the right time.

Many factors need to be considered in the process of fleet expansion. The factors include an airline's future plans, market expansion potentials, financial position and forecasts, external environmental factors and the abilities of aircraft being considered. Detailed, systematic and in-depth knowledge and understanding of aircraft performance as well as aircraft economics is essential for fleet planning decisions. Analysis and evaluation of market conditions is important for fleet planning. The most important factors

Table 6.4 Elements of consideration in the fleet selection process

Category	Elements considered
Markets and routes	Market size, mix and growth; schedule forecast; airport compatibility, performance and economics, etc.
Operations	Crewing, aircraft mix, extended-range twin-engine operational performance standards (ETOPS), performance of aircraft, etc.
Finance and contractual cost	Purchase versus lease of aircraft, residual value, buy-back possibilities, insurance, price escalation, guarantees, price of spare parts, etc.
Engineering	Inventory of spares, pooling, maintenance facilities, commonality, availability of technical skills, etc.
Regulatory and environmental	Certification rules, standards, environmental aspects, etc.

Source: Adapted from Clerk (2007)

that determine fleet planning are right aircraft type and right time of acquisition. Aircraft economics, performance levels of aircraft from different perspectives and comfort are also factors of influence in the selection of aircraft type. The airline will also take into consideration the demand for travel, the age of the aircraft, the cost of its current fleet and the availability of new aircraft as well as its efficiency which will further determine the right time to expand the fleet.

6.7.2 Schedule planning and development

Route planning, also called **network planning**, is the basic activity in schedule planning, defining an airline's products and network to be sold. "The goal of network planning is to explore potential markets and forecast market demands for certain services, e.g. leisure demand or business demand." (Wu, 2010). This is a long-term process, and "can be viewed as a series of overlapping sequential steps that include scheduling, marketing and distribution" (Jacobs et al., 2012). Schedule planning is the major function that determines the schedules of flying by an airline, and those schedules are central to the planning of entire operations in an airline. According to Wensveen (2016), it is "the art of designing system wide flight patterns that provide optimum public service, in both quantity and quality, consistent with the financial health of the carrier". Schedule is the most fundamental determinant and element of airlines' successful operations and it is planned in order to maximize the long-term profitability of the airline. The common elements of an airline schedule include the following (Grosche, 2009):

- Flights of the airline
- Departure and arrival airports and times of flights
- Days of operation
- Assigned fleet types
- Assignment of specific aircraft
- Maintenance schedule
- Assignment of cockpit and cabin crew

With regard to schedule planning and development, there have been several new methods introduced to improve the schedule efficiency and profitability. Jacobs et al. (2012) describes a few such techniques:

> Integration of crew and scheduling processes to develop more efficient flying schedule; the implementation of demand driven dispatch where fleet assignment changes are made between crew compatible aircraft close to the day of departure to better match passenger demand; and the addition of probabilistic evaluation techniques to better evaluate the likely performance of specific markets.

The process of airline scheduling occurs over time and passes through a number of phases, which need more detailed data requirements at each phase. Abstract and generic forecasts are needed at the planning phase, and later, specific, very detailed real-time inputs are integrated at the execution (operational) phase. According to Mathaisel (1997), though every airline has a different way of handling the process of scheduling, the following common phases can be identified:

- Planning a schedule of services
- Generation of an operationally feasible schedule
- Assignment of specific resources
- Execution of rescheduling (operations control)

The first phase is all about future scheduling, focusing on constructing a basic daily or weekly schedule of services to be flown in air travel markets for a future period. This stage provides a generic service plan, without specific aircraft or crew assignments, and with tentative service times of departure and arrival. The second phase, current scheduling, focuses on creating a feasible monthly schedule of operations for the airline, provided the expected resources are available. The outputs of this stage include: a detailed operational schedule suitable for publishing and the airline's reservations system; optimal rotations for the aircraft and crew; airport gate assignments; station personnel requirements; and others. The next stage, resource assignment, aims to generate optimal work assignments for the airline's specific resources. This stage mainly provides: the aircraft routings with maintenance schedules; crew bid lines and assignments; gate schedules; and station personnel assignments. In the final phase, the focus is on executing the operational schedule at the lowest extra cost, which may happen due to unplanned operational deviations, such as delays, diversions or cancellations. The outputs of this stage include: a modified execution schedule; cancellations, delays, etc.; and reassignment of resources.

Certainly, flight scheduling is the base for all other airline planning and operations. The flight schedule of an airline can reveal its competitive position as well.

6.7.3 Fleet assignment

Fleet assignment is another crucial task in airline operations. It is basically concerned with assigning the right type of aircraft to each flight in the schedule, especially in terms of capacity of aircraft. Different aircraft have different capacity, range and speed. The number of seats in economy class, and other classes may also vary. The forecasted demand needs to match with the type of aircraft. Also, the distance to cover and the time needed are important determinants. Moreover, the required type of aircraft needs to be available for operation without delay. Airlines have to identify the type of aircraft needed for each leg/sector considering both the technical aspects of the aircraft and their availability. The capacity of the available fleet in terms of demand is also crucial in fleet assignment. Moreover, the fleet assignment should not result in reduction in profits; rather, it should help in maximizing revenue while minimizing cost. "An airline's fleeting decision highly impacts its revenues, and thus, constitutes an essential component of its overall scheduling process." (Sherali et al., 2006) The focus of fleet assignment is to "solve the minimum cost assignment problem in order to assign the most suitable type of aircraft for individual flights in the timetable while meeting the maintenance requirements of aircraft" (Wu, 2010). This is done approximately three to four months before the scheduled time. Based on the previous initial schedule, the best possible way to execute the timetable is explored by identifying the available fleets with the lowest operating costs.

6.7.4 Aircraft routing

Aircraft routing is the next process, which is done to allocate a limited number of aircraft of the same fleet type to conduct those flights assigned earlier by fleet assignment. It is "the process of assigning each individual aircraft (referred to as tail number) within each fleet to flight legs. The aircraft routing is also referred to as aircraft rotation, aircraft assignment or tail assignment" (Bazargan, 2010). Aircraft routing involves routing or rotations for each aircraft in a fleet. Routing is all about the sequence of flight covered by a single aircraft and rotation denotes the routing that starts and ends at the same location (Parmentier, 2013). Each aircraft has to visit a maintenance station at regular intervals. Based on fleet assignment, in this stage the objective is to utilize available aircraft in each fleet to operate flights at the right time and between the right airports. In this way, the same aircraft is operated continuously on a particular route, for onward as well as return journeys. This process usually starts one or two months before. Flight continuity is an important factor here, which ensures that the same aircraft can operate those assigned flights in the right order. In continuing, the turnaround time has to match with scheduled arrival and departure times. Flight coverage and maintenance factors in airports also have to be considered in aircraft routings. It mainly includes chronological arrangement of flights on different routes in a profitable manner, along with maintenance schedules.

Table 6.5 Differences between four major airline functions

Airline function	Description
Schedule design	Define which markets to serve and with what frequency, and how to schedule flights to meet these frequencies.
Aircraft routing	Determine how to route aircraft to cover each flight leg with one aircraft and ensure maintenance requirements for aircraft.
Fleet assignment	Specify what type of aircraft to assign to each flight leg.
Crew scheduling	Select which crew will cover each flight leg in order to minimize global crew costs.

Source: Parmentier (2013)

6.7.5 Crew scheduling

Crew scheduling involves crew pairing and crew rostering. Here, crew represents both cockpit and cabin crew. Cockpit crew are also called flight crew, which denotes the technical aspect of conducting flight operation. Usually a flight will have a captain in command as pilot and a first officer as co-pilot. Cabin crew are for providing services on-board, mainly for facilitating safety and emergency procedures. Ultimately it is done to determine the sequences of flight legs and assigning both the cockpit and cabin crew to these sequences. One of the major objectives of this stage is to minimize the total cost of crewing along with allocating suitable crew as per the requirements.

Crew pairing is all about creating a number of crew pairings at the lowest cost. "The objective of crew pairing is to find a set of pairings that covers all flights and minimizes the total crew cost. The final crew pairing includes dates and times for each day." (Bazargan, 2010). Crew pairing is basically the generation of mini schedules, called pairings and crew rostering, which involves pairings that are assembled into longer crew schedules, in the form of "rosters" or "bidlines". The roster is basically a work schedule generated for each crew member according to his/her preferences, capabilities and requirements. "Bidline" is a generic schedule assigned to each crew member. Crew rostering represents the process of building up detailed rosters for individual crew within a particular period. Individual crew members are assigned to crew pairings, usually on a monthly basis. The working hours of flight crew are also regulated as part of safety consideration and fatigue management. In addition, location of crew base is also a factor that is considered. Tour of duty (TOD) is the term used for the working hours of flight crew. According to Wu (2010):

> A TOD may last from 1 to 2 days for a domestic crew, to a number of days for an international crew, depending on flight timetables and airlines networks. If a TOD involves overnights at ports other than the base of a crew, airlines will incur other crewing expenses such as accommodation, grand transport and meal allowance.

In fact, crew constitute the second highest operating cost after fuel for an airline and hence crew scheduling is an important task, and its effectiveness and efficiency translates into savings.

6.8 Passenger processing and flight operation

Passengers usually arrive at airports early enough. By this stage, airlines will have the details of passengers and the required number of check-in counters, etc. Large aircraft necessitate more counters to avoid delays and long queuing. In the beginning, the number of passengers in the queue will be less and hence all counters won't be opened. Later, as passenger arrivals increase, more counters will be opened. Efficiency is needed at this stage as more counters will mean increased cost. There are online check-in options, which many passengers prefer as it allows them to avoid queuing for a long time. For such passengers, airlines offer special arrangements for baggage collection. Airlines should try to reduce dwell time, which is the time between a passenger's arrival at check-in and the scheduled departure time of the flight. If check-in takes place early, passengers will be able to complete the security check and immigration clearance at ease. It is important to ensure passenger boarding at the right time. Delays in check-in can result in delays in boarding and consequently delays in flight operation. The passenger boarding process takes more time in larger aircraft. First-class passengers will be boarded first, followed by business class, and then economy class passengers. Airlines execute a range of activities in an airport. Passengers have to be ready for boarding at the right time. Baggage also needs to be processed simultaneously. Other activities of ground handling may be done directly by airlines, or by an agency on behalf of airlines on the basis of a contract.

All the activities are time-bound. The turnaround time of an aircraft is crucial in ensuring punctuality in operations. Delays in an activity can lead to delays of operation and it can affect the passenger satisfaction as well as further operation of flights. Operations en route consist of aircraft operations on the ground (at airports) and the subsequent operations which are handled by the crew (on the aircraft). Crew have to sign in one hour prior to departure of the first leg. In the case of international operation, crew usually arrive more than one hour before. The flight plan will be prepared, which will have details of various aspects of the flight, such as routing, weather, alternate airport options, fuel requirements, engine numbers, emergency needs, take-off performance and loads. Take-off planning is another task during the preparation of a flight plan, which may be done by a dispatcher or load manager, and if any adjustments to take-off plans are required, those will be done based on the latest conditions.

The crew have to determine the airworthiness of the aircraft. It mainly includes interior and exterior inspection of aircraft. Pre-flight inspection points are usually given in the checklist for the crew. An exterior walk around the flight includes a visual inspection to determine any obvious damage to the fuselage, engines, wings and flight control surfaces. It also includes checking tyre wear and tear, pressure, brake wear indicators, antenna conditions, etc. Interior checks are also done to ensure electric power and air are available on the aircraft. Cabin crew have to check the status of catering and cabin emergency equipment, along with the general cabin condition. Cockpit crew also verify the system conditions and check required documents. The pilot now has to finalize flight parameters by obtaining an update on weather conditions and runway utilization. Flight routing confirmation has to be obtained from ATC.

Once the flight is ready for boarding, passengers are boarded along with the loading of baggage and cargo. Once all doors have been closed, the ground crew does push-back. After the push-back request by the captain, ground staff organize the aircraft from gate to taxiway, and from there the aircraft taxis on the taxiway, waiting in the departure queue, and then taking off. After push-back, communication to ATC/ramp control will be sent for push-back clearance. Once the aircraft has left the gate area, the engines are started. On receipt of permission, the aircraft can taxi into position and hold on the departure runway. Soon, the pilot will receive take-off clearance, and by this time the aircraft will be positioned and necessary measures will be taken. ATC provides all necessary instructions including climb flight profile. The crew will check the necessary flight details as per the given information, such as altitude, etc. Once the aircraft reaches a certain altitude, in-flight services will begin. While the aircraft is at cruising altitude, the crew perform monitoring of aircraft flight path and system maintaining lateral fuel balance within time, cabin temperature and control, etc. As it nears the destination, the aircraft descent must be performed. ATC gives instructions. All information about destination, such as weather, will be provided to the pilot. They take measures to descend. They prepare the cockpit and cabin for landing. They conform to ATC restrictions and plan the approach to landing. In the case of arrival, after landing, the aircraft will undertake taxiing on the taxiway to reach the parking area at the arrival gate.

6.9 Aircraft maintenance

Aircraft maintenance is an important task performed by airlines. Different types of maintenance are mandatory. The most frequent one is the visual check. Routine ramp check, departure check, pre-flight check or post-flight check are the different terms used to refer to this type of check. This routine check happens during the ground time when the aircraft is on the ramp, before/after all flight activities. It is done mainly to get an indication of fuel or oil leaks and obvious discrepancies, like flat tyres, fuselage damage and wing damage. Mechanics walk around and undertake battery checks, landing gear and air pressure checks, cockpit equipment diagnostic checks, detailed checks on engines, exterior or cabin interior, and aircraft logbook checks, which were recorded by the pilot. Service checks are done at major or designated class I stations, usually after every 150 hours of flight time. The check includes checking of oil leaks, obvious discrepancies on external parts, checking of engine oil supply, checking inlet and exhaust areas, checking of landing gear and tyres, checking of exterior lighting, checking of interior water system, etc., and inspection and servicing of cabin compressors, engine accessories, control installations, cockpit equipment, interior lighting, along with other necessary services.

Periodic checks are also mandatory for undertaking air services. Monthly checks are performed at airport gates during the night. They involve detailed checks of body and engines. Once every three months, there is another more detailed check. The C check is done approximately every 12–18 months, usually in a hangar. Until the completion of the check, the aircraft will not be used for service. This maintenance check is usually done at major stations. Major stations, usually in hub cities, will have extensive facilities and a large number of maintenance people will be there to repair the planes. They will also have sufficient spare parts. Complete live maintenance can be undertaken in such stations. This is usually done when the aircraft has completed 500–875 flight hours. (It varies according to aircraft type.) Virtually all operating components are checked and serviced. Overhaul maintenance is the most detailed and important one for aircraft. This is the most detailed check and occurs every 4–5 years. Almost the entire aircraft is taken apart for inspection. It is performed at maintenance base. Maintenance base is the largest maintenance station for aircraft. Here, almost all parts of an aircraft can be repaired. It is considered the "overhaul and modification centre" for an airline's fleet. During the overhaul, the airframe will be opened up fully for thorough inspection and repair. Damaged parts will be replaced. The major overhaul helps to rejuvenate the aircraft into a "like-new" condition. Overhaul of engines and other components are also done. All engine parts are opened, checked and repaired or replaced with new ones if needed.

6.10 Classes of service

Classes of service are based on seating configurations. In international airlines, there may be two or three classes of service. The service, facilities, features, etc. will be different for each class of service. First class is usually the first category of class of service and the most expensive one. Usually, this is located in the front of the aircraft, directly behind the cockpit. Having the widest seats, this class is the most comfortable, with heavier padding in each seat. Seating in this class also features maximum legroom; on some aircraft, the seats in first class can turn into sleeper seats (mainly on long-haul routes). The best in-flight entertainment is offered and a more personalized service is provided, with more attendants available per passenger. The best meal service is provided in first class.

Passengers can enjoy speedier check-in, boarding and special lounge access while in the airports.

Business class is the next category. The target passenger groups include frequent travellers and business travellers. The seats in this category are usually located behind first class. Services and facilities provided are superior to economy class. The seats are wider than economy. There is also a wide range of meals to choose from. Usually, business class passengers are given separate check-in counters and lounge facilities. Speedier check-in, boarding and disembarkation services are offered. Seats are less expensive than first class, but much costlier than economy class. The number of seats will also be limited. Economy class is the largest class of service on a flight. It is also called coach class. Seats are arranged closer together with less seat pitch. All in-flight services are also provided in economy class. However, the variety offered is usually less. Each class is given a separate code in the booking records. For instance, F is the code given for first class, C for business class and Y for economy class. Other codes are also given by some airlines. In-flight services include the following:

- Meal services
- Beverages and liquors
- In-flight entertainment services (movies, music, games, etc.)
- Periodicals and dailies
- In-flight magazines
- Safety and security briefings and assistance
- Duty-free shopping
- Kids and baby care services
- Flight information provision
- Welcoming and assistance for seating
- First-aid services

6.11 Airline personnel and organization

Airlines are large business organizations that have a wide range of employee categories and positions, with a complex organizational structure. The size, complexity of the organization and the number of positions may vary from airline to airline. Before going into the organization and departments, let's have a look at the major types of airline personnel. Employees in an airline can be broadly classified into three areas:

- *Flight operations:* employees responsible for the safe and efficient operation of an airline's fleet. Training staff, flight crew, scheduling and monitoring staff are also part of this.
- *Ground operations:* this group of staff includes people responsible for operation on land for passenger processing, baggage handling, aircraft handling and the support functions necessary for those operations.
- *Commercial operations:* staff in this category mainly include administrative, human resource, and marketing and sales staff.

Flight operations staff can be classified into two categories:

- Flight crew
- Cabin crew

Flight crew, also called the cockpit crew, are responsible for the operation and safety of the aircraft and passengers while flying. A flight usually has a pilot in command (captain) and a flight operation officer (first officer). There may also be a flight engineer. The captain is located in the left cockpit seat and the first officer in the right cockpit seat. Cockpit crew are licensed by their respective national authorities. The captain, usually a senior pilot, is the person ultimately responsible for the flight. He/she makes major command decisions and leads the rest of the crew, including the cabin crew. In case of emergencies, the captain has to lead from the front and also needs to handle any troublesome passengers. The first officer is the second-in-command. He has almost the same responsibilities as the captain, and almost the same experience and level of training as the captain. The presence of the second pilot is for safety purposes, a precaution taken in case of a first pilot's potential fatigue. They have to act if the need emerges, and have the second opinion on piloting decisions. The flight engineer is also a trained pilot, but does not fly the plane. They monitor the aircraft's instruments and calculate figures like ideal take-off and landing speed, power settings, fuel management, etc. Now, in modern aircrafts, there are computerized systems that reduce the need for flight engineers.

Cabin crew are primarily responsible for safety in the cabin while flying. The crew include a flight service director, purser, flight attendants/flight stewards and air hostesses. They are also responsible for providing customer service products like meals, entertainment and assistance while boarding. They are sufficiently trained in the areas of aircraft emergencies, evacuation procedure, medical issues and health hazards, care of special needs passenger, flight regulations and meal service. Air crew training staff are responsible for training flight crew.

Operations control centre personnel are responsible for keeping the actual flight programme as per the schedule published. Responsibilities include movement control, flight planning, load planning, critical decision support, ground management and informing operational departments about the movement of aircraft. Ground operations personnel also include reservation agents who help passengers to make reservations and plan trips. Also, they provide suggestions or information about travel arrangements. Airport check-in staff work at the check-in counter in the airport terminal selling tickets, assigning seats, checking baggage, issuing boarding passes and baggage tags, giving directions and examining travel documents. Gate personnel are responsible for assisting passengers in boarding aircraft, directing passengers to the boarding area, verifying ticket/seat assignments, making boarding announcements and providing special assistance to passengers who need special care, etc. Aircraft maintenance staff include aircraft and power plant technicians and avionics technicians. Ramp personnel guide planes in and out of gates, and load and unload baggage. Responsibilities also include cleaning of aircraft, catering, refuelling, de-icing and maintaining guidelines of aircraft standards. Other personnel take care of crew scheduling.

Commercial operations staff include administrative staff, sales and marketing staff, specialists like lawyers, accountants and PR specialists, and human resources clerical staff. Outsourcing is usually seen in cleaning, fuelling, de-icing, catering and maintenance jobs. There are also other staff categories, such as engineering, safety and security, etc.

Airlines do have a wide variety of departments with specific tasks to perform. Line departments in an airline organization are directly involved in producing and selling air transportation. Flight operations departments develop flight operation policies, procedures and techniques for efficient and progressive operation of aircraft services. This department also develops flight schedule patterns and procedures. Fleet planning is dealt with separately by a department with a strategic approach. The air traffic and safety department develops and recommends ways and means to improve safe, economic and speedy transportation. Programmes for aircraft cabin safety, safe aircraft operations, navigation aids and ground communications are also developed by them. The flight procedures section generates and recommends operating policies, procedures and techniques for the whole fleet. This also directs the flight operations training department and flight standards department. The route planning department deals with an important

Table 6.6 Airline industry: key performance indicators

Key performance indicator	Description
Available seat miles/kilometres (ASM/ASK)	It denotes the annual airline capacity/supply of seats (number of seats available multiplied by the number of miles/kilometres).
Revenue passenger miles/kilometres (RPM/RPK)	Total number of paying passengers flown on all flight sectors multiplied by the number of miles/kilometres which those passengers flew (number of revenue paying passengers multiplied by the number of miles/kilometres flown).
Yield/average unit revenue	This refers to how much an airline earns per passenger mile/kilometre. Also, it is how much an airline makes per mile/kilometre on each seat sold. In other terms, it is the average revenue created while carrying one passenger one kilometre. It's a measure of the average fare paid by all passengers per kilometre or mile flown in a market. This is calculated by dividing passenger revenue by total RPKs for a particular flight (segment, route, etc.).
Revenue per available seat mile/kilometre (RASM/RASK)/unit revenue	It represents how much an airline made across all available seats that were supplied.
Cost per available seat mile/kilometre (CASM/CASK)/unit cost	It is the average cost of flying one seat for a mile/kilometre, calculated by dividing expenses/operating costs by ASK.
Passenger load factor (PLF)	This is a measure of how well an airline is balancing the capacity it makes available with the traffic it could attract. In other words, this measure compares the actual passenger traffic to the capacity available. This is considered the most used performance indicator in the airline sector. For airlines to increase profitability, load factor has to be increased against the decrease of the cost factor. Airlines have to maximize yield, decrease seat costs and enhance load factor.
Freight tonne kilometres (FTK)	In the cargo sector, freight tonne kilometres is an indicator used to show demand. It is calculated by multiplying the number of tons of freight by the number of kilometres flown during a certain period.
Aircraft utilization	This is a measure of aircraft productivity. It is measured as the period during which an aircraft is in use, including the ground taxi type as well as flight times.

function in airline operation. Some airlines may have a separate network operation section. A flying section develops and directs pilot training programmes, analyses the need for pilots within the system to meet schedule requirements, and assigns co-pilots and necessary pilot transfers. The flight crew scheduling section is responsible for developing crew schedules. Customer affairs and services audit is another important department, especially since customer service is a serious affair in the air transport industry. There may also be an international government affairs department which deals with permissions and agreements with governments of other countries. Environmental affairs has also become a separate department. The cargo department handles cargo and freight transportation. The airport services department handles all the required ground handling activities within the terminal as well as airside.

Staff departments basically provide service to the line departments and are primarily located at the headquarters or at major regional offices. A finance department is very important, as the organization's financial survival depends on its efficiency. The staff in this department formulate financial policies, and undertake all accounting and financial activities. The economic planning section plans and controls the factors that affect the economy of the company. The revenue optimization section also contributes significantly to airline profitability and competitive survival. Market research and intelligence gathering are dealt with separately by airlines. Airlines sometimes have an information services section, too. Meanwhile, the marketing and sales department is vital for an airline. The corporate communications department is a powerful section in airlines. Product distribution is separately managed in some airline organizations. Procurement and logistics are also undertaken under an independent department. The HR department is another important section for airline companies. Engineering and maintenance departments play an important role, particularly in ensuring aircraft safety. Security is a crucial area in aviation. There may be a separate section for security at airlines. There may also be a distinct section for facilities design and construction.

6.12 Common industry practices

This highly capital intensive and hyper competitive industry with thin profit margin survives successfully in the market by adopting a range of practices. Some of such common practices are introduced below.

6.12.1 Hub and spoke system

Major airlines prefer to have flight operations from hub cities, instead of point-to-point operations. The hub and spoke system consists of a set of "spoke" routes from the hub city to smaller cities. A hub is a central airport that flights are routed through, and spokes represent the routes from the hub airport to other cities in different directions. Services from these hubs are usually operated to smaller cities, other than the long-haul flight. Several points of departure are fed into a single airport which will act as the hub from which connecting flights operate services to their various destinations along the "spokes". The hub and spoke system consists of at least one hub airport that plays the role of collecting and distributing passenger traffic among flights at an airport (Wu, 2010).

The system is optimized when providing air service to a wide geographic area and many destinations. Passengers departing from any non-hub (spoke) city bound to another spoke in the network are first flown to the hub where they connect to a second flight to the destination. Thus passengers can travel between any two cities in the route system with one connecting stop at the hub.

(Cook and Goodwin, 2008)

In other words, "in hub-and-spoke systems, several points of departure are fed into a single airport (the 'hub'), from which connecting flights transport passengers to their various destinations (along the 'spokes')" (Wensveen, 2007).

Oftentimes, services to smaller airports are undertaken by different smaller airlines. These smaller airlines and the major ones are operated on the basis of agreements between them. This helps major airlines focus on longer routes with better load. Smaller airlines also benefit greatly. Airlines could serve far more markets using the same size fleet. Large airlines may have more than one hub, even up to five, whereas smaller ones may have only one hub. Airlines usually use large capacity aircraft, with non-stop service between hub cities. One major motive of airlines using the hub and spoke system is to increase the average number of passengers on its flights. Due to this system, higher revenue can be earned with better efficiency of operations using fewer aircraft.

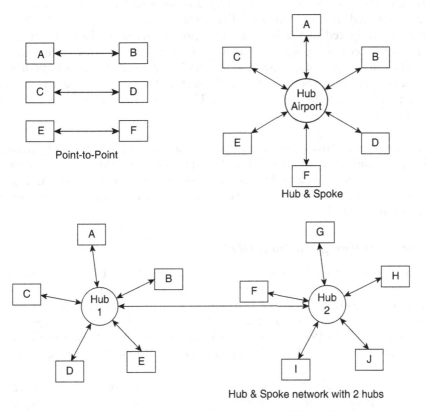

Note: A, B, C, D, E, F, G, H, I and J are airports located at different cities.

Figure 6.3 Hub and spoke system

6.12.2 Code sharing and interlining

Code sharing is an agreement between airlines to enable more choices for passengers. It

> refers to two airlines, usually a major and a regional carrier that share the same identification codes on airline schedules. By code sharing with a regional airline, a major can advertise flights to a much larger market area and expand its market at relatively low cost.

(Wensveen, 2007)

Another definition specifies it's "a marketing arrangement in which an airline places its designator code on a flight operated by another airline, and sells tickets for that flight" (US DOT, 2015). This cooperative agreement between two or more airlines is undertaken to sell seats on each other's flights in order to provide passengers with a wider choice of destinations. The ticket would be booked on the flight code of an airline but the service may be by another carrier. A seat can be purchased from an airline on a flight that is actually operated by another airline with a different code. Still, the passenger is given the code of the airline he/she booked the seat with. Basically code sharing is a kind of agreement and partnership between large airlines and smaller/regional airlines that create an integrated service, linking smaller cities with major cities. Due to this, smaller communities are linked to the large air transport network at the national and international level. Interlining is an agreement between airlines to allow connecting flights between them to be placed on the same ticket. In a journey with multiple flights, the airlines make agreements between them to manage the journey of passengers without making separate tickets for different flights. This is explained by Strauss (2017) in the following way:

> Interlining agreements differ from code-share agreements where a flight is numbered with the airline's code although it is operated by another airline. If you fly for instance from Dubai to New York on Emirates and then carry on to Miami on American, this requires an interline agreement between Emirates and American for you to not have to check in again.

6.12.3 Frequent flyer programme (FFP)

This is an area of customer relationship management (CRM). Large business organizations like airlines have to adopt different strategies to retain customers for repeat purchases. FFPs are a form of CRM practice that has been in use for the last three decades or so. To enhance the number of travellers and to create loyalty among passengers, airlines started to adopt FFPs in 1981. American Airlines was the first to launch a FFP and it was soon followed by United Airlines with its Mileage Plus programme. Simply, it is

> an air carrier program that allows frequent fliers to earn free tickets after accumulating a certain number of miles flown on the carrier. . . . It was a marketing program originally aimed at creating flyer loyalty in response to price competition in the early 1980s.

(Wensveen, 2007)

Frequent flyer programmes became a key measure of attracting and retaining travelling customers. Earlier, it was aimed at attracting business travellers following deregulation and increasing the frequency of same-airline ticket purchases. Through this programme, airlines can encourage loyalty among passengers who choose to fly with the same airline. For each trip, passengers get mileage credit, which will accumulate for earning different kinds of incentives, mainly rewards like free tickets, upgrades and free car rental services (Mak and Go, 1995). FFP passengers can get a range of other benefits as well, such as entry into airport lounges and class upgrades.

6.12.4 Airline alliances

Airlines enter into cooperative agreements to share services, technology and skills, and form alliances for mutual benefits. Larger carriers made an attempt to establish strategic alliances with overseas partners using different measures, including (Debbage, 2005):

- Joint marketing programmes
- Code-sharing arrangements
- Joint CRS operations
- Joint frequent flyer programmes
- Cross holiday arrangements
- Minority ownership

Different alliances have different areas to share and cooperate. Star Alliance, Sky-Team and Oneworld are currently the major airline alliances in the world. In an alliance, companies remain separate entities, but cooperate in order to improve efficiency, increase customer service levels and decrease costs through sharing of sales offices, maintenance facilities, operational facilities, operational staff, investments and purchases. An alliance also enables an extended global network. Customers benefit from the lower price, access to round-the-world tickets at better prices, and mileage rewards on a single account from different carriers. The benefits of cooperation also include an increase in market share.

6.13 Marketing mix in airlines

Airlines face tough competition and marketing and sales have enormous significance for competitive survival. Indeed, all marketing mix strategies have a significant share in the success of airline businesses. Full service carriers may try for differentiation using product strategies as well to compete in the market. Airline product-related decisions usually focus more on seat pitch, legroom, seat width, punctuality of services, meal service, visual entertainment for passengers, quality and variety of beverages, periodicals to be kept, service quality offered on board, etc. Crew communication and interaction, quality of service delivered onboard, etc. also matter in the successful delivery of the service.

Due to the service characteristics and unique features of airline businesses, the process of pricing and inventory control is crucial and complex. Price has to be competitive, but the cost factor, season, demand status, etc. need to be considered when pricing airline products. Airline pricing is defined as "the process of determining the passenger fare levels combined with various service amenities and restrictions, for a set of fare products in an origin-destination market" (Belobaba, 2009). Cost is also major concern in airline pricing strategies. Nonetheless, dynamic pricing is undertaken often.

According to Wittmer and Bieger (2011), due to the extreme perishability of the airline product, "pricing", in addition to other tasks, has an important job to steer demand, making it an important strategic element. The general aim of airline pricing strategy is to target a customer's maximum readiness to pay. Airline cost mainly involves the costs relating to flying operations, direct maintenance, maintenance burden, depreciation and amortization, passenger service, aircraft servicing, traffic servicing, reservations and sales, advertising and other promotional activities, and general and administrative expenses (O'Connor, 2001). Direct operating costs are the cost elements closely related to flying the aircraft, such as fuel. Indirect operating costs involve the ground or terminal costs and overhead expenses. Labour and fuel form the largest share in airline cost. Belobaba (2009) attempts to categorize and compare airline costs on different bases, of which administrative and functional cost categories are noteworthy. Administrative costs include salaries and fringe benefits for personnel, materials purchased (e.g. fuel, passengers' food), services purchased (e.g. advertising, communication, insurance) and additional categories (e.g. landing fees, rental, depreciation). Functional cost categories include flight operation costs (direct operating costs/aircraft operating costs), ground operating costs (e.g. aircraft servicing costs, traffic servicing costs and sales and distribution costs), system operating costs (e.g. passenger servicing costs, publicity costs, general and administrative expenses) and transport-related expenses (e.g. fees paid to regional airline partners.).

Examples of direct aircraft operating costs include the cost for flight operations, flight crew, fuel, and maintenance and overhaul. Indirect operating costs mainly involve administration and marketing expenses, user charges and station expenses, loadings and associated airport charges, passenger security, and administrative and other expenses. Some of them are fixed costs and some are variable costs. Major pricing categories are based on classes of service. First class has the highest level of price offers and it is followed by business class. In each class there may be additional booking classes. Service class distinction is a prime consideration for pricing, and it is done on the basis of product features, such as seat quality and meals. Booking conditions (e.g. early booking and pre-booking, restrictions on cancellation and re-booking) also influence pricing. Previous years' reservation trends are also considered in advance when pricing products. Seasons play a major role. A big chunk of profit is earned during season when higher prices are offered.

Airlines nowadays use advance revenue management systems that can perform forecasting and optimization of booking classes for each flight sector. Airline revenue is usually affected by the price of the product (fare), yield improvement, type of passengers (economy, business class, etc.) and the volume of traffic carried. **Revenue management** is used to maximize profits, or rather to optimize revenues from every operation. Revenue management is an important function within airlines. It focuses on the following two components (Benckendorff et al., 2014):

- *Price differentiation:* different prices with different rules and features for seats in a flight
- *Yield management:* determining the booking limits (the number of seats) for each class at any given time

Differential pricing and revenue management in airlines

Traditionally, the practice of airline pricing is established for travel between origin and destination points (O–D market). After deregulation and through the spread of "open skies" agreements, airlines experienced increased freedom to make their own scheduling and pricing decisions and this freedom led the airlines to embrace the concept of differential pricing. With differential pricing, different prices are offered not only for different classes, etc., but also for identical seats and services within the same cabin. Under this concept, both price discrimination and product differentiation are applied. The willingness to pay (WTP) principle is applied as per the demand and the customer's willingness to pay a higher price. While business travellers may show a willingness to pay higher rates for convenience and fewer restrictions, leisure travellers are usually less willing.

Higher price is targeted at non-price-sensitive travellers by offering attractive service amenities, while low price levels should be low enough to stimulate new demand for low fare travel and fill seats that would otherwise remain empty. The challenge is to prevent the diversion of consumers with higher WTP to the lower fare products. Increased revenue, higher load factors and incremental revenue, which are critical to profitability, are the benefits of this. Low fare products can attract even the passengers who otherwise would not fly at the single fare price.

The implementations of differential pricing faced limitations that even the most effective segmentation schemes were not enough to maximize revenues on their own. Business travellers faced difficulty getting seats as leisure travellers used to book seats in advance for their lower price. The concept of revenue management (RM) thus became relevant. Having the objective to protect seats for later bookings and high fare passengers, it can determine the number of seats to be made available to each fare class on a flight, based on a forecasting of the expected future booking demand for higher fare classes. The limits on each lower fare class are determined. Eventually, it will help in higher yields and increased total revenues. RM systems are set to maximize revenues, by achieving a balance between load factor and yield. A general, ideal system of that kind may include: the capabilities to collect and maintain historical booking data; forecast future demand; make use of mathematical models to optimize total expected flight revenues; provide interactive decision support for revenue management analysts to review, accept or reject the overbooking; and booking limit recommendations. Forecasts and booking levels are revised at regular intervals. In case of unexpected bookings, the system will re-forecast demand and re-optimize booking limits, which will result in the opening or closure of fare classes. This type of fare mix optimization leads to revenue maximization. In addition to the incremental revenue benefits, it helps the airlines to better balance demand and supply at a tactical level. Moreover, the low fare demand can be channelled to empty flights. There are also a range of other benefits due to the use of RM systems.

Source: Belobaba et al. (2017)

Read the above case study carefully and answer the following questions:

- Describe the concept of differential pricing and its components.
- Explain how revenue management helps airlines to maximize revenue.
- Discuss the need and benefits of revenue management systems.

Airline distribution is also an important area to consider. As far as an airline is concerned, the distribution function is critical to the management of its available flights and seat inventory. Its distribution system is also vested with the tasks of tracking sales and revenue generated from passengers, as well as to capture the expected market share by ensuring widespread dissemination of data and information about its services to consumers. Unlike LCCs, FSCs have to depend on multiple channels for distributing the product. Global distribution systems have a significant role in distribution. Both online and traditional channels are utilized by airlines to give final consumers access to their products. The details of travel distribution systems are discussed in detail elsewhere in this book. Airlines utilize various promotion techniques to inform, attract and persuade the target market. Advertisement is the most common tool used by airlines. Public relations and publicity measures are also widely used by airline businesses. Both online and offline media are used for marketing communication and multiple promotion tools are used simultaneously by airlines on target markets.

6.14 Summary

Airlines, the most important element and the most visible player in the aviation sector, play an important role in the global economy. While an airline forms its own network of operations, the airline industry makes a larger network, and the global airline industry integrates all the smaller networks into a larger one, with all the cities and towns with airports connected together. Certainly, the industry is a facilitator for many other major industries, including tourism. In addition to service characteristics, the airline industry has a number of other characteristics including high barriers to entry, capital-intensive, oligopoly, labour-intensive, dynamic pricing, close government regulations, etc. The airline customer can be the consumer himself/herself, or the decision-maker with regard to the travel of a person or transport of cargo. Customers encounter many difficulties when taking decisions, especially since the decision is a high involvement exercise and complicated by various factors, particularly the cost factor. Tourists constitute one of the major markets of airlines.

Airlines primarily offer transportation services between places for passengers and cargo. This service aspect begins from the moment a ticket is purchased until the completion of the service when the passenger/cargo reaches the final destination. Scheduled and non-schedules airlines are the main categories of airlines. International and domestic airlines form another classification. Scheduled airlines operate regular services based on a published timetable. Scheduled airlines include major airlines, commuter airlines, national airlines, flag carriers, FSCs and LCCs.

An airline's organization involves a number of interrelated and complex operations. Most functions are time-bound, with the success of the business depending to a great extent on the effective and efficient functioning of the operations and various tasks involved. Fleet planning, a long-term strategic activity, is done to decide new aircraft purchasing, which is highly capital-intensive. Route planning, also called network planning, defines an airline's products and network to be sold. Schedule planning is the major function that determines the schedules of flying by an aeroplane and those schedules are central to the planning of entire operations in an airline. Fleet assignment is basically concerned with assigning fleet as per demand, especially in terms of capacity of aircraft. Aircraft routing is done to allocate a limited number of aircraft of the same fleet type to conduct those flights assigned earlier by fleet assignment. Crew scheduling involves crew pairing and crew rostering. Passenger processing involves a series of activities within the terminal to make ready the passenger for boarding. Aircraft maintenance is an important task to be performed by airlines.

Classes of services are based on seating configuration and the facilities and services offered to passengers. Flight operations staff can be classified into flight crew and cabin crew. Airlines are large business organizations that have a wide range of employee categories and positions, with a complex organization structure. This highly capital-intensive and hyper-competitive industry with thin profit margins survives successfully in the market by adopting a range of practices. The hub and spoke system, code share agreements and FFPs are the most common practices undertaken by airlines for their competitive survival. Successful airlines effectively utilize marketing mix strategies. Distribution of airlines is now increasingly complicated by the introduction of multi-level distribution systems. Though online distribution is gaining increased significance, traditional intermediaries also have a considerable share in airline product distribution.

Review questions

Short/medium answer type questions

- Define airline and airline industry.
- Discuss the role of the airline industry in tourism.
- Define airline product.
- Describe the characteristics of the airline industry.
- Give a brief account of consumers of airlines.
- Explain the different types of scheduled airlines.
- Distinguish between FSCs and LCCs.
- Briefly explain non-scheduled services.
- Explain fleet planning in airlines.
- Describe the flight scheduling process.
- What do we mean by fleet assignment?
- What is aircraft routing?

- Differentiate between crew pairing and crew rostering.
- Explain passenger processing activities by airlines in airports.
- Give a brief account of aircraft maintenance.
- What is aircraft overhaul maintenance?
- Discuss airline alliances.
- Describe in brief airline marketing and product distribution.
- Describe the hub and spoke system.
- Distinguish between code sharing and interlining by airlines.
- Write down the benefits of airlines' frequent flyer programmes (FFPs).
- What are the different classes of service in airlines?

Essay type questions

- Write an essay on duties and responsibilities of airline personnel.
- Describe the major airline operations.

References

ATAG (2016) Aviation Benefits and Beyond, Air Transport Action Group, available at http://aviationbenefits.org/media/149668/abbb2016_full_a4_web.pdf.

Barnes, A. B. (2012) Airline Pricing, in O. Özer and R. Phillips (eds), *The Oxford Handbook of Pricing Management*. Oxford: Oxford University Press.

Barrett, S. (2008) The Emergence of the Low Cost Carriers Sector, in A. Graham, A. Papatheodorou and P. Forsyth (eds), *Aviation and Tourism: Implications for Leisure Travel*, Aldershot: Ashgate, pp. 103–118.

Bazargan, M. (2010) *Airline Operations and Scheduling*. 2nd edn. Surrey: Ashgate.

Belobaba, P. P. (2009) The Airline Planning Process, in P. Belobaba, A. Odoni and C. Barnhart (eds), *The Global Airline Industry*. Chichester: John Wiley & Sons.

Belobaba, P. P., Brunger, G. W. and Wittman, D. M. (2017) Advances in Airline Pricing, Revenue Management, and Distribution: Implications for the Airline Industry-Discussion Paper, prepared for ATPCO by PODS Research LLC, available at https://www.atpco.net/sites/default/files/2017-10/Full%20version%20-ATPCO%20PODS%20Discussion%20Paper%20FINAL%20Oct02.pdf (accessed 5 June 2018).

Benckendorff, J. P., Sheldon, J. P. and Fesenmaier, R. D. (2014) *Tourism Information Technology*. 2nd edn. Oxfordshire: CABI.

Clerk, P. (2007) *Buying Big Jets: Fleet planning for Airlines*. 2nd edn. Hampshire: Ashgate.

Cook, N. G. and Goodwin, J. (2008) Airline Networks: Comparison of Hub and Spoke and Point to Point Systems, *Journal of Aviation/Aerospace Education and Research* 17(2): 51–60.

Debbage, G. K. (2005) Airlines Airport and International Aviation, in L. Pender and R. Sharply (eds), *The Management of Tourism*. London: Sage.

DGCA (2000) Director General of Civil Aviation, available at http//:dgca.nic.in/cars/d3c-c5.pdf.

Grosche, T. (2009) *Computational Intelligence in Integrated Airline Scheduling (Studies in Computational Intelligence)*. Berlin: Springer, pp. 7–46.

Harvey, G. (2007) *Management in the Airline Industry*. Oxford: Routledge.

IATA (2017) Future of the Airline Industry 2035, available at https://www.iata.org/policy/Documents/iata-future-airline-industry.pdf.

IATA/Air Cargo, available at http://www.iata.org/whatwedo/cargo/Pages/index.aspx.

ICAO (2009) International Civil Aviation Organization: Review of the Classification and Definitions Used for Civil Aviation Activities, accessed at http://www.icao.int/Meetings/STA10/Documents/Sta10_Wp007_en.pdf.

ICAO (2015) Continuing Traffic Growth and Record Airline Profits – Highlights 2015: Air Transport Results, Press Release of International Civil Aviation Organization, 22 December.

ICAO/ATAG (2011) The Economic & Social Benefits of Air Transport, Air Transport Action Group, available at http://www.icao.int/Meetings/wrdss2011/Documents/JointWorkshop 2005/ATAG_SocialBenefitsAirTransport.pdf.

Jacobs, L. T., Garrow, A. L, Lohatepanont, M., Koppelmann, S. F., Coldren, M. G. and Purnamo, H. (2012) Airline Planning and Schedule Development, in C. Barnhart and B. Smith (eds), *Quantitative Problem Solving Techniques in the Airline Industry: A Modelling Methodology Handbook*. Springer: New York, pp. 35–100.

Mak, B. and Go, F. (1995) Matching Global Competition: Cooperation Among Asian Airlines, *Tourism Management* 16(1): 61–65.

Mathaisel, F. X. D. (1997) Decision Support for Airline Schedule Planning, *Journal of Combinatorial Optimization* 1: 251–275, available at https://pdfs.semanticscholar.org/ba56/fe1 9db6a9cb0f60e6ed1bb3a07f3beff8bea.pdf.

O'Connor, W. (2001) *An Introduction to Airline Economics*. London: Praeger Publishers.

Parmentier, A. (2013) Aircraft Routing: Complexity and Algorithms, available at http://cermics.enpc.fr/~parmenta/ROADEF/Rapport_MPRO_Axel_Parmentier.pdf (accessed 25 March 2018).

Purzycki, S. J. (2001) *A Practical Guide to Fares and Ticketing*. 3rd edn. Albany, NY: Delmar Learning.

Shah, S. (2007) *Airline Marketing and Management*. Hampshire: Ashgate.

Sherali, D. H., Bish, K. E. and Zhu, X. (2006) Airline Fleet Assignment Concepts, Models, and Algorithms, *European Journal of Operational Research* 172(1): 1–30.

Strauss, M. (2017) Travel Technology for Dummies: Booking, Waitlist, Ticket, Codeshare & Interlining, available at http://www.travel-industry-blog.com/travel-technology/ticketing/ (accessed 20 April 2018).

US DOT (2015) Code Sharing, available at https://www.transportation.gov/policy/aviation-policy/licensing/code-sharing.

Wensveen, G, J. (2007) Air Transport: A Management Perspective. 6th edn. Hampshire: Ashgate.

Wensveen, G. H. (2012) *Air Transportation: A Management Perspective*. 7th edn. Surrey: Ashgate Publishing.

Wensveen, G. J. (2016) *Air Transport: A Management Perspective*. 8th edn. Oxford: Routledge.

Wittmer, A. and Bieger, T. (2011) Fundamentals and Structure of Aviation Systems, in A. Wittmer, T. Bieger and R. Muller (eds), *Aviation Systems: Management of the Integrated Aviation Value Chain*. New York: Springer.

Wu, C-L (2010) *Operations and Delay Management: Insights from Airline Economics, Networks and Strategic Planning*. Surrey: Ashgate.

Land and water transportation

Part III

Land and water transportation

Land transport and tourism

7.1 Introduction

While the rapid evolution of air transport lessened the importance of water transportation, particularly the ship-based long-haul services, land transport has maintained its prevalence as an essential mode of transport, a trend that continues in the new millennium. Of the two forms of land transport, rail transport could not progress everywhere, but road transport has expanded greatly since the dawn of the automobile in the first quarter of the twentieth century. From a tourism point of view, land transport covers mainly cars/automobiles, coaches/buses, rental cars, taxi services and rail services. While considering the mode of travel to reach destinations, air transport, towards the end of the last century, gained the largest share in international tourism. This occurred due to the declining trend in international water transportation, as well as that in rail transport. However, land transport, combining road as well as rail, remains an important mode of transport in international tourism. According to UNWTO statistics, in 2016, 41 per cent of international tourists used land transport (39 per cent road and 2 per cent rail) to travel to destinations (UNWTO, 2017). Indeed, the share of land transport is much more in domestic tourism, and in developed countries; automobiles, particularly private cars, are used frequently for leisure tourism. Tourist use of rail transport is less, but lately, efforts have been made by some countries to encourage tourists to use more of it.

7.2 Road transportation and tourism

Road transportation is one of the most important forms of tourism transportation. In the last century it has grown tremendously. The road system is still the most important in intermodal transport anywhere, with countries having extensive road transport networks. For instance, according to the US Bureau of Transportation Statistics, public roads in the US, including interstate highways, other major arterials and local routes totalled 4.1 million miles in 2013 (BOTS/US DOT, 2015). Road transport plays a key role in national economies and is the only mode of transport found in almost every corner of every nation. The quality and extensiveness of road infrastructure are considered a determinant in the development of a country. Highways were built once road transport had gained in popularity. The autobahn, a multilane highway built in 1930s in Germany, is one of the earliest highways. Pan American Highway, the longest highway in the world, is 47,958 kilometres (29,800 miles) long. Highway 1, a network of highways that stretches around Australia joining all mainland state capitals, is the second longest highway in the world. The Trans-Siberian Highway has a length of 11,000 kilometres. Road transportation involves a wide variety of modes of transportation. Buses (including coaches), cars, rental cars, taxi services, etc. are the major road transportation modes. Millions of road transport vehicles are on the road for different transportation needs. According to the US Bureau of Transportation Statistics, in the US, government, businesses, private individuals and non-governmental organizations owned and operated about 256 million motor vehicles in 2013 (BOTS/US DOT, 2015). Cities are well connected by road networks. There are adequate links to other regions and places. In most countries, millions of passengers depend on road transport annually. For instance, there were an estimated 5.04 billion bus passenger journeys in Great Britain in the 2015–2016 financial year, and in England alone it was 4.53 billion journeys, of which more than half were in London (Gov.uk, 2017).

Road transport has a significant role to play in tourism. As mobility is the vital aspect in the whole process of tourism, road transport also ensures and enhances the mobility of tourists to move from the origin to the destination and around/within the destination. Though mobility associated with road transport is more significant in intra-destination travel and in domestic tourism, the role of road transport in international tourism in accessing destinations cannot be underestimated. As stated earlier, 39 per cent of international tourists used road transport to access destinations, which is a significant share. The distance to cover is an issue for road transportation. While long-haul travel is dominated by air travel, short-haul international tourism utilizes road transport significantly. Road transport can have a strong presence in intra-regional tourism. For instance, intra-regional tourism in Gulf Cooperation Council (GCC) countries is dominated by automobile travel, as many cities and destinations within the region can be accessed easily through top-class road infrastructure. Private cars are predominantly used for this. For instance, within five hours, a tourist from Muscat (in Oman) can reach Dubai (in the UAE), the most popular destination in the region.

Domestic tourism is dominated by road transportation in most countries. According to the UNWTO, as the destinations are nearer and since the cost of the trips is lower, land transport is predominantly used, up to 88 per cent, in domestic tourism (UNWTO, 2012). In terms of internal transportation in a destination, roads have increased in significance. A destination will have different attractions located in different parts/regions. The success of a destination is also dependent on the nature and efficiency of the transport system in linking all those attractions and locations together. The transport network

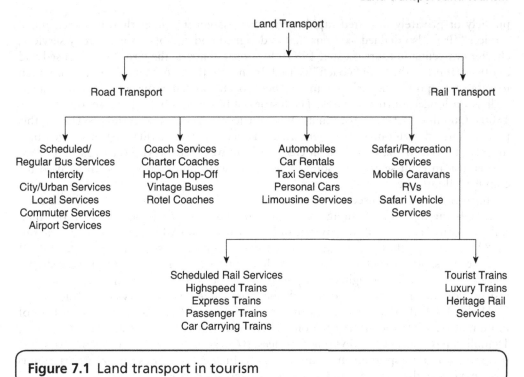

Figure 7.1 Land transport in tourism

has to be scientifically planned and designed so as to ensure smooth access to each one. The road and rail network together forms a large system of transportation within a destination. Other modes can also be part of this. However, the largest share will belong to the land transport network. Road transport has more advantages since it can enable even remote attractions to be accessible for tourists. Frequency of transport and convenience also make road transport more useful for internal transportation in a destination. According to Cooper et al. (2000), in the context of tourism, advantages of road transportation in comparison with railways and other forms of transport include: the control of departure times; ability to carry baggage and equipment easily; ability to use a vehicle for accommodation; control of the route and stops en route; maximum privacy; low perceived out-of-pocket expenses; and the freedom to use the automobile after reaching the destination. Land transport is also more convenient for visiting attractions. Some attractions are spread out geographically and vehicles are needed to travel inside the attractions. For instance, visiting a game reserve requires transport to get there, and once a visitor has arrived different land transport forms are used to get around. Let's now discuss the different vehicles used for tourism road transportation.

7.2.1 Bus services

"Coach" and "bus" are used interchangeably in tourism literature to represent large road vehicles that can carry a number of people, from around 20 to 50 or more. The term "bus" is a shortened version of the Latin word *omnibus* meaning "for everyone". A coach, according to Holloway and Humphreys (2012), represents "any form of publicly or privately operated rapid service for passengers, other than local scheduled services". It is also defined as a bus that is designed and equipped for intercity services, charter or excursion tours (Foster, 1994). In some countries, the term "bus" is used and in other countries the term "coach" is used. In the US, the term "bus" is used more often in public transportation parlance. In Europe, "coach" is used in the context of tourism as well as for longer journey services. The history of buses goes back a few centuries to the 1800s. Omnibus services began in a few countries in Europe and in the US. During this period, horse-drawn omnibuses were used for services. The world's first motorized bus, invented by Carl Benz, was made in Germany and went into service on 18 March 1895. It was just an eight-seater, but soon larger buses were built and started to be used for commercial purposes.

In general, buses are used for urban as well as suburban scheduled travel, with comfort levels varying. The advantage of buses is that they can reach more destinations than railways can. According to the American Bus Association (ABA, n.d.), there were about 32,825 motor coaches providing services for 604 million passenger trips in 2014. Of those services, 40 per cent were for tour/holiday purposes, 24 per cent for airport shuttle services, 20 per cent for sightseeing purposes, 13 per cent for special services and the rest for commuter services. Greyhound, the largest intercity bus service provider in the US, links 3,800 destinations across the US, Mexico and Canada. They have a fleet of more than 1,200 buses in the US alone. Every year in the US and Canada, on average, 18 million passengers use Greyhound services. (Greyhound, n.d.). In many countries, bus transport is more important than rail transport. In some countries bus transportation is more expensive than rail, e.g. in Great Britain, Ireland, Portugal and Greece (Cook et al., 2002).

In Great Britain, bus services have equal importance with other forms of transport. According to Visit England (2014):

> Almost 2.4 million overnight trips were taken by domestic residents as part of an organised coach tour in Great Britain, accounting for 8.6 million overnight stays, contributing £617 million to the domestic tourism economy in 2012. . . . The increasing popularity of day trips in Great Britain saw a further 18 million day trips taken in 2012 as part of an organised coach tour . . . [and] 136 million day trips were taken using a regular bus or coach service for transport.

One popular bus service seen in Britain is the airport shuttle service. Train and bus combined journeys are also operated. A "tourist trail pass", other passes and a variety of tickets with flexible pricing and services are available in Britain. Stagecoach, First, Arriva, Go Ahead and National Express are the major bus service providers in Britain. Euroline is a market leader, operating scheduled European coach services, connecting over 600 destinations across 36 European countries (and Morocco). Euroline offers comfortable services with reclining seats, picture windows and onboard toilet facilities.

Diversity is a feature of bus travel; there is a wide variety of services with different types of buses. For passenger transportation, buses are not just used by low-budget tourists; all sections of society use bus services for various purposes. The type of bus usually varies according to the usage. Motor coaches, tour coaches, commuter buses, double-deckers, school buses, trolley buses, minibuses, midibuses, articulated trams and road trains are the different types of buses used for passenger services. It is important to ask why so many people prefer bus transport to other forms. According to Lundberg and Lundberg (1993), people choose bus transport due to a variety of reasons including:

value for money; ease of access; total experience, including social aspects; better interpersonal relationships; continuous sightseeing throughout the travel; greater learning about the cultural and social vibrancy of destinations; convenience; ease and speed of organization; and comfortable group sizes. Indeed, a random pattern of movement gives greater freedom of travel and choice of destination, which railways and ship services cannot claim. However, many people do not prefer bus tours for a number of reasons including: they are time-consuming (taking longer to reach the destination); there is less space to move around inside and a lack of sleeping facilities; and journeys are tiring. Different types of bus services are offered as part of road transportation. Intercity bus services and general bus services are the most popular scheduled bus services. Commuter services and shuttle services are other public transport services, which are the essential services found almost everywhere. Use of coaches for tourism and special occasions is the predominant segment in coach/bus transportation.

7.2.2 Intercity

Intercity bus services consist of regularly scheduled coach services between cities. These services account for billions of passenger miles worldwide. In addition to linking the cities situated in different regions, intercity bus services provide a vital link between domestic and international transportation systems as well. Bus fares are based on the total mileage between boarding point and destination point. Being long-route services, intercity coaches are better equipped to provide comfort. Greyhound provides the following facilities/services on-board their coaches:

- Free Wi-Fi
- Standard power outlets
- Reclining leather seats
- Extra legroom
- Only aisle and window seats, no middle seats
- Adequate overhead storage for hand luggage
- On-board bathroom

In Europe, international services are offered on coaches. For instance, Euroline offers regular services to cities located in different countries. Its route network consists of more than 700 destinations in 32 countries, with the longest route from Moscow to Lisbon, which covers around 4,500 kilometres.

7.2.3. Regular/general/scheduled bus services

Regular bus services are offered in almost all countries. It includes diverse categories of bus services, including urban/city services, inter-urban services, local services and express services. In the US, the Trailways Transportation System, a federation of independently owned bus companies that market long-route bus services in addition to charter operations under the Trailways name, covers a large portion of the US. Type of bus service may vary from country to country. Some countries have multi-level bus services, varying from local services to international services. In India, for instance, public bus services vary widely. In each state, there are different types of bus services, such as city, intercity, city to suburban areas, suburban to rural areas, within rural areas, and between states.

7.2.4 Commuter bus services

These are common in many countries. They may or may not constitute regular services. In the US, a commuter bus service is defined as a:

> fixed route bus service, characterized by service predominantly in one direction during peak periods, limited stops, use of multi-ride tickets, and routes of extended length, usually between the central business district and outlying suburbs. Commuter bus service may also include other service, characterized by a limited route structure, limited stops, and a coordinated relationship to another mode of transportation.
>
> (US Definitions, n.d.)

7.2.5 Airport transportation

This is different from other public transport services as it mostly involves a single type of service with or without specific schedules. An airport requires a large area, so it is difficult to build one right in the heart of a city. Therefore, many airports are located some distance from their cities. This necessitates frequent transport services from the airports to different parts of the cities and vice versa. Of late, airport bus transportation, one of the most cost-effective forms of transport, has been increasing as more airports have been built and air travel demand continues to grow. It is a very common service in major cities in the world, particularly in Europe and the US.

7.3 Motor coach tourism

As stated before, coaches are comfortable buses and they are used for regional, cross-country journeys and for tours of various kinds. The coaches are graded on the basis of different aspects, e.g. legroom, on-board amenities like kitchens, toilets, air conditioning, cloak rooms, etc. Some coaches have sleeping facilities as well. Coach travel offers a wide range of tourist services, including express coach routes (both domestic and international), private line services, tour and excursion operation, charter services and transfer services.

Motor coach tourism is a term used in tourism literature. Put simply, it represents the hiring of coaches by tour services for a specific period of time. In the US, motor coach tours are becoming more popular and tour operators are offering more package tours that utilize motor coaches (Goeldner and Ritchie, 2011). In package coach tours, motor coach transportation is an important component. Coach tours are of various types; some are full-fledged package tours whereas others are part of general package tours. Coach tours also vary according to the number of holiday days – from day trips to a certain number of tour days. Also, some sightseeing tours can last just a few hours. This complexity of coach tourism is illustrated by O'Regan (2018):

> Even with the development of airborne package tours, coach travel has continued to be an important component of package tourism and has developed strong links to tourism-related companies and destinations. From pairing with airlines to organize transfers and acting with attractions to build access areas to working with destination marketing organizations, accommodation providers, food service organizations, shopping malls, cultural sites, and tour guides, motor coach tourism retains maneuverability and flexibility by taking people where they want to go at a relatively low cost.

Coach tours thus vary widely. Some leading brands also offer various kinds of coach tours. For instance, Eurolines provides city tours, city breaks, Europe4U, wellness and vacation trips (ride and accommodation) along with coach tours to Paris, London, Prague, Vienna, Budapest, Istria, Tuscany, Lake Garda, Costa Brava, etc. In the US, both Trailways and Greyhound operate charter tours as well as package holidays using coaches. There are coach tours available for more than a month as well. The following are the most common types of coach tours:

- Domestic tours
- Short breaks
- Sightseeing/scenic tours
- City tours
- Sports tours
- Attraction visits
- Religious tours
- Inbound tours
- Study/industrial tours
- Overseas tours
- Niche tours
- Affinity group tours
- Shopping tours

In previous years, coach tourism was considered the domain of older tourists. According to the latest theories, coach tourism encompasses all segments of tourists. Families and youngsters (e.g. study tours) are now an integral part of coach tours. Even in the era of widespread air travel, coach tours remain the preferred option for many tourists. Some of the reasons for choosing coach tours include:

- Courier/guide services
- Cheaper and better value for money
- Easy access
- Comfortable group size
- Total experience with a group
- Continuous sightseeing
- Better social environment and interpersonal relationships
- On-board recreation activities
- Door-to-door travel
- Easy and quick to organize
- Convenient stops
- Ease of baggage handling
- No transfer hassles
- Pace of travel as per the need

The term **charter coach tour** is also used in the context of tourism. Charter coach tours are escorted, hosted or even independent tours arranged for groups by hiring motor coaches for a period ranging from hours to multiple days for the purpose of visiting. Bus operators offer more services in response to increasing competition. Wider seats, better outside views, the latest audiovisual equipment, free Wi-Fi services, hot beverage services or even a full galley with a microwave oven are some additional services offered by coach operators to attract tourists. Also, the size of buses has grown from 40 feet to as much as 45 feet in length and passenger capacity has increased from 47 to 55. The sector is poised for further growth along with the growth in transport technology.

Some coaches are attractions themselves, e.g. vintage buses and double-decker buses. Along similar lines, **hop-on, hop-off** city bus tours are common in many major cities. Many branded tour operators operate such bus tours. For instance, Big Bus Tours, a leading city bus tour firm, claims to be the largest operator of open-top sightseeing tours in the world, providing sightseeing tours in 19 cities across three continents. **Vintage buses** are used for tours in many cities. The vintage double-decker bus tours in London, for example, are very popular. **Rotel coach tours** are unique. They are often referred to as "capsule hotels on wheels". The essential facilities and services of a hotel are included in such a coach, along with sleeping facilities. A German tour company, Rotel, has been at the forefront of this sector. There are seats to sit on during the day and sleeping berths at night. The coach also includes a camp kitchen and a single toilet facility.

CASE STUDY 7.1

Coach tourism: the European scenario

Coach tourism is still a prevalent form of tourism in the European Union (EU). It has much socio-economic significance, as it directly employs millions of people in the tourism sector through coach drivers, tour guides, sales advisors, and administrative and engineering employees. Through coach tourism, millions of customers every year contribute billions in revenue. This money is a direct benefit of the coach tourism industry. Indirectly, many other industries, such as hotels, restaurants, and leisure and tourist attractions, depend on coach tourism for their survival. Coach tourism in the EU has a broad customer base: its market segments include senior citizens, corporate travellers, school children, sports teams and inbound tourists. According to European Commission data on passenger transport, 65 coach companies are operating in the EU. Directly it provides 1.55 million jobs and indirectly it supports almost 7.5 million jobs. Tourist attractions, hotels, restaurants, theatres, entertainment attractions and cruise ferries are examples of indirect sectors that depend on coach tourism for employment.

Based on Visit England statistics in 2012 and an RDA review of the German coach tourism market in 2015, on average coach tourists spend more while on a tour (£84 per day per passenger) compared to other tourists (whose holiday expenditure is £63 per day per passenger). This is much more significant for one-day trips in which the average spend per passenger is £42.55 per day, which is 27 per cent higher than the normal expenditure. Coach tourists from the UK alone numbered 1.9 million in 2013 and spent in excess of £752 million in other EU countries. In the same year, there were three million domestic holidays using coaches, which contributed £835 million directly to the UK economy. Some 5.4 million domestic coach holidays generated €3.8 billion for the German economy, with an average expenditure of €716 per person per holiday.

Moreover, coach tours are greener transport forms compared to automobiles, as a single vehicle can carry between 40 and 55 people at a time. A number of cars would have to be used to carry that many passengers. The usage of alternative fuels can make it even more environmentally friendly. Many coaches don't yet provide wheelchair facilities. However, coaches with such facilities are increasing in Sweden, the UK and Germany. For greater progress, this has to be addressed in the policies made in relation to transportation and coach tourism.

Source: EACT (2015)

Read the above case study carefully and answer the following questions:

- Describe the advantages of coach tourism.
- Discuss why coach tourism is important in an economy.
- Write down the benefits of coach tourism.

Different types of **safari vehicles** are also used for tourism. Overland trucks, micro buses, Land Rovers, Land Cruisers, open game viewing vehicles, open four-wheel drive safari vehicles, hatch-top vehicles, etc. are used for safari tourism. **Mobile caravans** are also used for holidays. They are prefabricated structures with facilities for living inside

Figure 7.2 Open loop New York hop-on, hop-off tour bus
Courtesy: Wikimedia Commons

and can be towed/moved with the help of another vehicle. Caravans and trailers are used by holidaymakers. **Recreation vehicles (RVs)** are defined as "motorized (motorhome) or towable (travel trailers, folding camping trailers and truck campers). Off-road vehicles are not included" (RVIA, n.d.). An RV is a vehicle designed as temporary living quarters for recreational, camping, travel or season use. It arrived on the travel scene in the US and Canada. Corollary to the growth of automobile travel, RV camping sites were also developed in Western countries. The RV segment is a strong component of land-based transportation at the beginning of the twenty-first century. Slide-out technology was introduced into RVs during the 1990s, since which time it has advanced further. Slide-outs are available in living rooms, dining rooms, bedrooms and kitchens. At the touch of a button, a portion of the room and other objects in it, such as a couch or a table, slide outward up to about 3.5 feet. Motorhomes, travel trailers, fifth-wheel trailers and even camping trailers are examples of slide-outs. RVs are often referred to as motorhomes or campervans.

7.4 Automobiles and tourism

In the tourism industry, automobiles are an important mode of transportation. The advent of cars provided families in particular with a new freedom of movement, providing a huge increase in opportunities to take day excursions as well as longer trips. Accessibility to interior resorts improved. Car ferry services flourished in Europe. The love affair with the automobile in North America is due to Henry Ford, who ushered in the age of mass automobile travel with the advent of the famous Model T car in 1908. During the period between 1908 and 1923, 15 million Ford cars were sold. Automobiles are the travellers' choice particularly for short distances on relatively uncluttered roads. Privacy, flexibility and variety of routes and destinations are the advantages of automobile travel. Tourists favour the car for holidays for a number of reasons (Sinha, 1997):

- Control of the route and the stops en route
- Control of departure times
- Ability to carry baggage and equipment easily
- Low out-of-pocket expenses of travelling with three or more persons
- Freedom to use the vehicle once the destination has been reached
- Driving itself is a recreational activity, which many are fond of
- Better sightseeing while travelling

Many tourism destinations in the world still depend on private motor vehicles. Tour operators offer self-drive car packages. Automobile owners can leave from their doorstep at any hour of the day or night and travel to a chosen destination. When two or three people travel together, the cost of travel comes down.

Taxi and limousine services are also crucial in tourism. When a tourist arrives at a destination, they may use a taxi service, which could be their first service encounter after landing, causing a first impression of the destination. Quality taxi service is a determinant in the success of a tourist destination. Taxi services are basically intra-city in nature and subject to licensing and rate regulation by authorities. Limousines are very expensive luxury cars driven by chauffeurs. The appeal of such a car is that it has a driver compartment and a separate, rear passenger compartment, with a sliding glass in between so that the conversations of passengers can be private. A limousine service is a unique market niche. Airlines and businesses often contract with limousine services for passengers.

7.5 Car rental

Car rental is the service of supplying automobiles to customers, including leisure tourists and business travellers, for their use for a specific period of time on a daily/weekly rental basis. Car rental, car hire, rental car and rent-a-car are the different terms used interchangeably in the rental sector. Car rental is very popular in the countries wherever tourism is an important industry. In Europe, rental cars from one country can be used in other countries, too. The car rental industry provides a critical link for business and pleasure travellers worldwide. The business of car rental is not new; it has a history stretching over a century. Hertz started its car rental business way back in 1918. Now the car rental industry is a multi-billion-dollar business in many countries. In the US, car rental businesses, with fleets of 2,182,000 cars, generated revenue of $27 billion in 2015 (Auto Rental News, n.d.). Car rental is often required when the passenger has a lot of luggage, small children and/or animals, when the passenger wishes to visit many different places in a given area within a short period of time, or when a passenger wants to visit the countryside, friends, relatives or local people.

The rental car sector is growing significantly, with business travellers constituting the largest segment – some 75 per cent of the customers (Cook et al., 2009). Globally, car rental companies are offering services directly to business tourists, leisure tourists, travel agents, tour operators, airlines, hotels, brokers/middlemen and the public. Generally, consumers of the car rental business include business tourists, leisure tourists, local users (for a replacement vehicle), and city customers for short breaks or visiting friends and relatives (VFR) (Biederman et al., 2008). A car rental service may vary in terms of fleet diversity, service range, geographical region of operation, quality of service and price. Geographically, car rental operations can be seen at different levels, from a global level to a local level. On this basis, car rental businesses can be divided into three categories: multinational, national and local companies. Large car rental companies operate large and varied fleets of cars in thousands of locations across the world. Franchising is a common practice in the car rental business. Some of the large multinational companies provide franchisee licences to operate car rental businesses in those respective regions. Rental cars are available at almost all airports. Indeed, airports are the main source of business for car rental companies. Nowadays, car rental companies offer a range of options for customers. For instance, the types of cars offered by Dollar include economy compact, mid-size, standard, full-size, premium, luxury, standard convertible, minivan, mid-size SUV, mid-size open air all terrain, standard SUV, full-size SUV and premium SUV cars.

Here is another example of a car rental company's (Hertz) offering:

- Green Traveler Collection (more fuel-efficient and less polluting cars)
- Prestige Collection (premium cars)
- Adrenaline Collection (e.g. Dodge Challenger, Ford Mustang)
- Dream Cars (luxury cars)
- Standard Cars (economical car varieties)

- Estate Cars/Wagon Type
- 4WD/SUV/People Carriers
- Convertible Cars (e.g. Chevrolet Camaro)
- Vans (e.g. Nissan NV200, Chevrolet Silverado)
- Special or Customized Cars
- Promotional Cars, Budget Categories
- Other Reservable Models (e.g. Jeep Wrangler)

Efficiency of a car rental business is measured by fleet initialization (number of days a car was rented/number of days a car was available), and daily dollar average (the revenue generated by a car daily). The airport market and leisure market are more seasonal. Other segments are less seasonal. Along with the growth of the car rental industry, car rental companies have expanded services, such as including valet delivery, parking services to avoid shuttle buses, offering on-board computerized navigation systems, drop boxes for return of keys and rental forms, and equipping service personnel with handheld computers to complete rental transactions at the point of return (Cook et al., 2002). Now, a wide variety of services are included, such as wide airport availability, availability at other arrival points (e.g. railway stations), GPS/navigation services, online check-in, corporate offers (exclusive offers for business firms), car share options (using a car only for the required hours), toddler and baby car seats, facilities for people with disabilities, emergency services, multiple pick-up/drop-off points (pick a car up in one country and drop it off in another), chauffer-driven car services, and online or call centre reservation facilities. These may vary from location to location, company to company, purpose to purpose, etc. Insurance is an essential service for car rental businesses, and is offered mainly for collision damage, theft, personal insurance and liabilities. Major car rental brands in the world include the following:

- Hertz
- Vanguard
- Avis
- Enterprise
- National
- Budget
- Alamo
- Dollar
- EuropCar
- Thrifty

Car rental companies distribute products through multiple channels. Major channels of distribution include the following:

- Own desk at arrival points, like airports
- Tourism suppliers like hotels and airlines
- Global distribution systems of intermediaries
- Own office or ally's outlets
- Intermediaries
- Online sources, through own websites and other online platforms

Car rentals are charged on a daily/weekly basis, and if needed, on a distance travelled basis. For longer term usage, leasing is done instead of daily/weekly hiring. Cost for fuel, parking fees, etc. are not included in the price and have to be borne by the passenger. Diverse promotional schemes are used by car rental companies, which may include: discounts, membership schemes, etc. to attract volume business; corporate/business offers; miles system to get benefits from partner services; discounts for online booking; loyalty schemes; weekend offers; partnership schemes; upgrades; and group car offers/bulk discounts.

7.6 Rail transport

Rail transport is the transport of passengers and goods by means of vehicles designed to run along railroads or railways. The train consists of individual bogies/carriages linked together with an engine. Rail transport is considered a mass transportation mode and one of the most energy-efficient. Trains make highly efficient use of space since they travel on two parallel rails and carry hundreds of passengers together with goods. Passenger rail transportation is a component of tourism in many countries. Though the history of modern rail transport goes back a couple of centuries, the earliest forms of railways were actually in use *thousands* of years ago. For instance, in the sixth century BC, Diokos, a 6-kilometre railway, transported boats across the Corinth Isthmus in Greece. Europe is considered the cradle of rail transportation. Over 1,300 years ago, trucks pushed by slaves ran in grooves on a limestone track. The first horse-drawn wagon appeared around 2,000 years ago in Greece and in some parts of the Roman Empire. The first railways in Great Britain were built in the early seventeenth century mainly for transporting coal. In the late eighteenth century iron rails began to appear. In 1802, a railway station was opened in Surrey, arguably the first public railway station in Britain. People were pulled in horse-drawn conveyances on tracks as early as 1807 on the Oystermouth Railway in Britain (Lundberg and Lundberg, 1993). In 1811 the first successful and practical railway locomotive was designed and Blücher, an early railway locomotive, was built in 1814 by George Stephenson. Passenger rail transport commenced soon after in Britain, in 1825. Between 1830 and 1850, in England and other principal European countries, 12,000 miles of railways were built. Rail transport then began to spread, not only in Britain but all over the world. The first rail service for passengers in North America began in 1829. Later, in 1869, transcontinental services began in the US. Railroading spread and changed people's lives forever. Railroads were the first to establish resort destinations to stimulate a travel market. Long-distance rail services were given a boost in US when George Pullman developed the Pullman coach with sleeping facilities for overnight journeys (Cook et al., 2002). The Pullman coach, with sleeping facilities, was a milestone in the history of long-distance travel. Fred Harvey introduced dining cars and legitimate food and lodging facilities in the US in 1875.

Thus, passenger rail service became the most important transport mode and it continued until the 1940s. Soon, major highways were built in the US and automobile travel was able to grow remarkably. Moreover, domestic jet services became popular. In 1967, the postal department in the US stopped using railways for mail services. The rise of car ownership coincided with the decline in the popularity of rail travel. Tourist use of rail travel also began to decline as automobiles emerged as the favoured mode of travel for personal use in Western countries. In the UK, this trend became more prevalent after the nationalization of railways (Holloway and Humphreys, 2012).

While railways couldn't appeal to tourists with innovation, coach travel and private jet travel for holidays progressed side by side with automobiles. But the fuel crisis that took place in the early 1970s revitalized railways. Package tours on railways increased, though by the mid-1980s the trend again reversed. High-speed trains began operating from the 1960s. Recent trends reveal that railway demand is about to increase once more. Moreover, countries are experimenting with high-speed trains and bullet trains which can travel faster and safely. Though many other forms of transport have emerged that offer greater speed, safety and comfort, railways remain an important mode of transport in some countries. The following are the reasons why many people prefer train services to other modes of transport (Cooper et al., 2000; Sinha, 1997):

- Affordable
- High safety standards
- The ability to move around the coach
- Passengers do not lose time "checking in"
- Personal comfort
- The ability to look out of the train and enjoy the scenery en route
- Arriving at the destination rested and relaxed
- Environmentally friendly form of transport
- Centrally located terminals
- Decongested routes
- More interaction with fellow passengers
- Better bathroom and other facilities
- Freedom to engage in simple recreational activities while travelling
- Food and beverage services
- More luxury for higher payment
- Speedier than many other forms of transport

7.7 Rail tourism

Using high-speed trains and luxury train services along with tour packages in collaboration with other suppliers like hotels, rail tourism is being promoted in many countries. Though tourists have been using rail services for many decades, the promotion of rail tourism began only a couple of decades ago. Generally, railways appeal to tourists using two specific strategies: providing classic trains and encouraging travel along classic routes (Holloway and Humphreys, 2012). Rail tourism is a comprehensive concept which consists of rail travel for visiting places and the experience gained through special services in unique trains and routes and by visiting rail-related heritage sites. The concept of **rail tourism** encompasses:

> the experience, and/or symbolic consumption, related to traveling by train (including the experience of railway architecture such as stations, tunnels, and viaducts) and visiting railway museums. Studies on rail tourism acknowledge the heritage value as well as the sociocultural and human geographical dimensions related to train travel, together with cheap or high-end luxury travel.
>
> (Jensen and Bird, 2017)

In addition to general passenger transportation, the trains used in tourism usually fall under one of the following categories.

7.7.1 High-speed trains

High-speed trains could compete with air transport. Some advanced countries are now increasing high-speed rail networks to attract more passengers and tourists to rail transportation. High-speed rail (HSR) is defined as:

> a type of passenger rail transport that operates significantly faster than the normal speed of rail traffic. Specific definitions by the European Union include 200 km/h (120 mph) for upgraded track and 250 km/h (160 mph) or faster for new track.
>
> (Railsystem.net, n.d.)

Certainly high-speed trains are used for tourism in those counties with rail networks. Different terms are used for high speed trains in different countries, like Shinkansen (Bullet trains) in Japan, AVE in Spain, ICE in Germany, TGV in France, Frecciarossa in Italy and X2000 in Sweden.

7.7.2 Luxury trains

These mostly have a specific focus on tourism. Luxury trains are built with elegance and aim to provide a unique experience to tourists. Most luxury trains are nostalgic trains as well, which use old carriages from many decades ago. Vintage carriages, historically significant engines, nostalgic interior designs, etc. are used for making luxury trains more attractive for passengers.

7.7.3 Car carrying trains

These trains carry cars. There will be normal carriages for carrying passengers, but also special carriages for carrying their cars. Tourists or passengers get the car back after the completion of their journey. The advantage is that the traveller can travel a long distance without having to drive it themselves, and then he/she can continue their journey by car. Some European countries offer these services, as do Canada, the US, South Africa and Australia.

Let's go through some of the popular rail travel and tourism options in different countries.

In the US, the importance of rail transport declined after the advent and growth of automobiles. The automobile has overtaken rail transport in every sense and the developments and growth in air transportation have also contributed to the declining importance of rail transport in the US. The declining role of rail service caused authorities to think of strategies and measures to revamp the rail transport system in the US during the second half of the twentieth century. In 1970, when the railway system was suffering through financial issues, US Congress created the national Railroad Passenger Corporation (NRPC) under the Rail Passenger Service Act to subsidize and oversee the operation of intercity passenger trains. The original brand name of NRPC was Railpax, but it was soon changed to Amtrak.

Amtrak, the marketing brand of the National Railroad Passenger Corporation, began service in 1971 serving 43 states with a total of 21 routes. Now, according to Amtrak, it serves more than 500 destinations in 46 states, the District of Columbia and three Canadian provinces on more than 21,300 miles of track. More than 30 million passengers use Amtrak's services annually.

7.7.4 Tourism services of Amtrak

For tourists, Amtrak provides exclusive services and offers. Among them, the all-inclusive train vacation packages are noteworthy. A large number of packages are offered. The following constitute some of the most popular (Amtrak, n.d.):

- Glacier National Park Vacations
- Grand Canyon Rail Trips
- Yellowstone National Park Trips
- Yosemite National Park Trips
- New York City Train Trips
- Washington, DC Train Trips
- New Orleans Train Trips
- Chicago Train Vacations

Regional rail tour packages, with the assistance of listed tour operators, are offered by Amtrak and they encourage passengers to visit more destinations in the US. In order to ensure an easy process of booking and using Amtrak services, two rail passes, USA Rail Passes and California Rail Passes, are offered for passengers. Using the **USA Rail Pass**, all destinations on the Amtrak network are accessible; and 15-day, 30-day and 45-day packages are available. The **California Rail Pass** can be used for exploring California. Using it, the passenger can travel on any seven days during a consecutive 21-day period. Amtrak has a unique **Trails & Rails Program** which gives passengers an opportunity to be educated on the heritage and natural resources of a specific region while travelling by rail. Also in the US, vintage railway tourism experiences are available, such as the steam engine Grand Canyon Railway. Meanwhile, Canada established **Via Rail** in 1977. Currently it operates on a network of 12,500 kilometres and completes 3.97 million passenger trips annually.

As a continent, Europe is leading in rail transport and rail tourism. Railways in Great Britain are the oldest in the world. Railways in the UK were nationalized by the 1940s, but privatization had begun by the 1990s. British Rail, formed after the nationalization of the (then) railway companies London and North Eastern Railway (LNER), London, Midland and Scottish Railway (LMS), Great Western Railway (GWR) and Southern Railway (SR), had begun investing in high-speed trains by the 1970s. There are now 28 different train operators across Great Britain. Britain has an extensive system of railways. According to official reports, the Britain has a network spanning 15,799 kilometres with 2,557 stations. Great Britain has registered substantial growth in rail usage over the last two decades, and rail passenger journeys are now at their highest level since the 1920s. During 2015–2016, there were 1.7 billion rail journeys (an average of 4.7 million journeys per day) in Great Britain. Of all public transport trips, national rail accounted for 20 per cent of passenger journeys and 61 per cent of passenger kilometres (Department of Transport, 2017). The high-speed passenger rail service between London and Paris is a major advancement in rail transportation in Europe. The "Chunnel" (Channel Tunnel) has reduced travel time significantly. The Chunnel operates as a link between England and France through a tunnel under the English Channel, where trains carry passengers, cars, motorbikes, coaches, etc. The Chunnel is 250 feet deep and 23.5 miles long. Eurostar and Eurotunnel operate regular train services through the Chunnel.

Here is a list of high-speed trains in Europe (Eurail, n.d.):

- AVE (Spain) (310 kilometres per hour)
- TGV (France–Belgium–Italy–Germany–Spain–Switzerland–Luxembourg)
- Le Frecce (Italy)
- Railjet (RJ) (Austria–Germany–Switzerland–Hungary)
- Renfe-SNCF (Spain–France)
- SJ (Sweden–Denmark) (200 kilometres per hour)
- Thalys (Belgium–The Netherlands–Germany–France)
- ICE (Germany–Belgium–The Netherlands–Switzerland–Denmark–France) (300 kilometres per hour)
- Eurostar (Belgium–France–Great Britain)
- The Alfa Pendular (Portugal)
- The Altaria (Spain) (200 kilometres per hour)
- Alvia (Spain) (250 kilometres per hour)
- Euromed (Spain) (200 kilometres per hour)
- SuperCity (Czech Republic)
- TGV Lyria (Switzerland–France)

Germany has a large network of railways. Its network consists of regional Express trains (between regional destinations and larger cities); Regional bahn (linking all local towns); Interregional trains; S-Bahn (suburban trains); and InterCity trains. There are also high-speed trains. InterCity Express (ICE) travels at speeds of up to 200 miles per hour (320 kilometres per hour). ICE Sprinter trains are even faster. Additionally, there are two scenic train routes for tourists: the Black Forest route and Rhine Valley route.

France also has an extensive high-speed rail network. France is well connected with its TGV high-speed train network. Trains have an average speed of 200 miles per hour. Spain also has a large network of railways spanning over 16,000 kilometres. Spain now has AVE high-speed trains which run at speeds of up to 220 miles per hour and "hotels on wheels" that serve routes with less traffic. Both are highly convenient, and offer a high-quality experience. In Sweden, rail transport has been privatized to some extent. The national railway company of Sweden is called SJ (Statens Järnvägar – State Railways). There are also a number of private rail companies operating. In Switzerland, the railroad network spans over more than 5,000 kilometres, which mainly consists of standard-gauge as well as narrow-gauge railways. Switzerland is famous for beautiful rail routes across the Swiss Alps and for its trains, including the Golden Pass, the Wilhelm Tell Express and the Glacier Express. Tour packages and rail–hotel packages are also offered for tourists in Switzerland. Italy has high-speed trains such as the Pendolino (250 kilometres per hour). The Trans-Siberian Railway is a network of railways connecting Moscow and European Russia with the Russian Far East provinces, Mongolia, China and the Sea of Japan. Its main route runs from Moscow to Vladivostok via southern Siberia. It was built between 1891 and 1916.

CASE STUDY 7.2

Luxury tourist trains in India at a standstill

After a couple of decades of successful operation of the "Palace on Wheels" – the most popular luxury tourist train in India – authorities introduced a number of new trains to attract more tourists. However, the latest trends point to a subdued luxury tourist train sector. Glancing over a few recent reports reveals the factors that hinder luxury tourist train sector growth in India. According to Deepika (2017), the Southern Splendour, a luxury train run by the Karnataka State Tourism Development Corporation (KSTDC), had to discontinue service due to the inability to break even. There was a lack of consensus between KSTDC and Indian Railways which caused financial issues. The Indian market had just one luxury tourist train some years ago, but this number has grown substantially, which has resulted in supply outstripping demand. Even the best luxury tourist train in India, the Palace on Wheels, had to cancel a trip in March of 2017 due to declining demand. It could still manage to run with only 50 per cent occupancy on average in recent years, but its occupancy rate had been between 95 and 98 per cent between 2005 to 2007.

Another luxury train, the Maharaja Express, launched in 2010 and started with an occupancy rate of 40 per cent. Over the years it has only seen a slow improvement. In spite of the limitations, there are repeat visitors on some luxury tourist trains, such as The Golden Chariot. Some tourists use different tourist trains to experience India at different points in time. As the demand was lowering, some of the tourist train companies tried to offer diverse packages to attract more customers. For instance, The Golden Chariot will soon begin offering short-haul journeys instead of week-long tours and may add corporate and event-based packages along with wedding specials. Low occupancy and high haulage charges are the major burdens on luxury trains in India. Deccan Odyssey, run by the railways in association with Maharashtra Tourism Development Corporation, had only 38 per cent occupancy in 2014–2015, despite the fact that the number of trips had come down from 23 to 13 per year (Dhawan, 2016). Lack of adequate publicity and the negative perception that luxury tourist trains are too expensive for Indians are some other reasons for the decline.

The Standing Committee Report Summary (Tourism Promotion and Pilgrimage Circuit) (PRS, 2018) suggests the same trend. According to it revenue generation has been on the lower side for a few years, and some trains' running costs are higher than the total revenue they're able to generate (like the Deccan Odyssey). Considering the growing problems in the luxury tourist trains sector, it has been reported that authorities are cutting prices of many such trains.

Read the above case study and answer the following questions:

- Discuss how the declining trend in the luxury tourist train market can be improved.
- Explain the issues that mar rail tourism in India.

Rail passes in Europe are very popular, with some aimed at tourists in particular. A brief discussion of the major rail passes follows below.

7.7.5 Eurail Pass

Eurail Pass, offered to non-European Union residents, is a single train ticket to access multiple trains in multiple European countries. Introduced in 1959, it is valid for travel not only on trains, but also on participating ferry and public transport routes in 28 European countries. There are currently three types of Eurail Passes on offer:

1. *Eurail Global Pass:* using this, the passenger can explore five or more countries. There are different options for choosing days, with a minimum seven days of travel within a month to three months of continuous travel.
2. *Eurail Select Pass:* this is customizable with a choice of two, three or four countries according to the need. Passengers can opt for a maximum of ten days within a two-month period. Combinations can be chosen according to the passengers' interests.
3. *Eurail One Country Pass:* this is for visiting only one country. It provides eight flexible days of travel within a period of one month, e.g. Eurail Spain Rail Pass.

7.7.6 BritRail Pass

This enables the passenger to travel extensively across the entire National Rail network of England, with Wales and Scotland. There are different types such as BritRail England Pass, BritRail London Plus Pass, BritRail Spirit of Scotland Pass, BritRail Central Scotland Pass, BritRail Scottish Highlands Pass, BritRail South West Pass and M-Pass ("Mobile Pass", compatible on mobile phone).

7.7.7 Swiss Rail Pass

This provides extensive travel on the Swiss rail network for three, four, eight or 15 days and provides free entrance to over 480 museums and exhibitions.

7.7.8 German Rail Pass

This provides advantages for tourists and other passengers. It offers the passenger unlimited travel on Germany's extensive train network, to over 5,000 locations. Also, some cities in Italy, Belgium, Austria, Czech Republic and Poland may be visited with extended service options.

A few other countries also have separate rail passes for making rail journeys more convenient and to promote tourism. Rail transport is an important mode of transport in Asia, particularly South Korea, Japan, India and China. South Korea has a good rail network and has introduced high-speed trains as well. Japan's rail transportation system is particularly advanced. Early on, it introduced high-speed bullet trains between Tokyo and Osaka. Japan became the first country to create a high-speed rail network when the first Shinkansen (Bullet Train) line was inaugurated in 1964, on the occasion of the Tokyo Olympics. Currently bullet trains run at an average speed of 320 kilometres per hour, with test runs being held for higher speed trains with a speed of 443 kilometres per hour. Maglev (magnetically levitated) trains in Japan set a world record of just over 600 kilometres per hour (373mph) and will soon be introduced on the track. China has the largest high-speed rail network in the world. Among the different types of trains, G

trains move at a speed of 250–400 kilometres per hour, and **C trains** at a maximum speed of 350 kilometres per hour. The Indian railway system is the largest in Asia. Though high-speed trains have yet to be introduced, the existing system is used by millions of passengers daily. Indian Railway is offering one railway pass scheme (Indrail Pass) as part of a promotion for international tourism to India. Some of the rail routes like the Darjeeling Himalayan Railway are nostalgic routes that attract tourists. The longest stretch of rail without a curve is located in Australia, called the Indian Pacific. In some African countries, a few more Asian countries, and New Zealand, there are also advanced rail systems and tourist-focused rail services.

Let's turn now to some of the major luxury tourist trains in the world.

7.8 Venice Simplon-Orient-Express

As the vintage Orient Express ceased operations almost a decade ago, another group of hospitality and transport operators began operating luxury trains. Venice Simplon-Orient-Express is one of the most luxurious trains in the world. This rail service still uses carriages from the 1920s and 1930s and has elegant cabins and suites with single and double/twin bedrooms. The company also offers car or boat transfers between the stations and city centre accommodation (or vice versa) at the start and end of the journey. In addition to the grand, vintage cabins, gastronomic cuisine and lively entertainment are provided on board. This train service offers different routes linking major cities in Europe, including London, Paris, Venice, Berlin, Prague, Vienna, Budapest and Istanbul. It also offers holiday packages, which include accommodation, transport in the vintage train cabins/suites and guided city tours in the destinations. Group tours are also promoted for 12 or more passengers in scheduled luxury train tours. The experience of this luxury tourist train is enhanced by the historic and luxurious carriages, sumptuous cuisine and personal service offered.

7.9 Blue Train

The Blue Train is another luxury tourist train that operates in South Africa. Its flagship route operates between Cape Town and Pretoria, a 27-hour journey of 1,600 kilometres. Along with its luxury travel, the trip offers diverse and spectacular scenery. There is a stopover and an excursion in Kimberley. Another excursion off-train includes a stop at Matjiesfontein. The carriages provide deluxe suites, luxury suites, lounges and boutiques. Fine cuisine, snacks and beverages, and on-board laundry and valet services constitute some of the main services on board.

Other luxury train services include the following:

- Royal Scotsman – a luxury passenger service offering trips from either London or Edinburgh for between one and seven days. It tours England's West Country, Scotland's highlands or specialty destinations. Package holidays are also provided.
- Thalys – a high-speed international train offering quality transport services between Paris and a number of other cities in different countries.
- Al Andalus Express – a luxury train service that uses vintage carriages in Spain.
- Trans-Siberian Express – one of the longest uninterrupted train routes in the world, passing through diverse landscapes and cultures in Russia, from Moscow to Vladivostok.

- Royal Canadian Pacific – one of the finest train trips in North America, offering splendid and varied travel experiences.
- The British Pullman – short trips are offered on a vintage train pulling smart and elegant British Pullman carriages.
- Palace on Wheels (India) – week-long package tours on a vintage train
- Rovos Rail Pride of Africa
- Golden Eagle Danube Express
- Eastern & Oriental Express (Singapore, Malaysia and Bangkok)
- The Belmond Andean Explorer (South America's first luxury sleeper train)
- Deccan Odyssey (India)
- Copper Canyon (Mexico)
- Kyushu Seven Stars (Japan)
- Indian Pacific, The Ghan, and the Great South Pacific Express (Australia)
- Royal Hungarian Express
- Victorian Express and the Reunification Express (Cambodia)
- Trans-Mongolian, Trans-Manchurian and Trans-Siberian Express trains

7.10 Summary

Although air transport is the most prominent mode of transport in international tourism, land transport also plays a significant role, and its relevance has increased in domestic tourism. Coaches, scheduled bus services, automobiles and car rental services are the major types of land transport that support tourism. Motor coach tourism provides tour services in the form of coaches for hire for a specific period of time. Coach tours are of various types; some are full-fledged package tours while others are part of general package tours. Coach tours also vary according to the number of holiday days. Coach tourism now encompasses all segments of tourists. Families and youngsters (e.g. study tours) are now an integral part of coach tours. Charter coach tours are escorted, hosted or even independent tours arranged for groups by hiring motor coaches for a period ranging from hours to multiple days for the purpose of visiting. Some coaches are attractions themselves, e.g. vintage and double-decker buses. Along similar lines, there are also hop-on, hop-off city bus tours in many major cities in the world. Also, rotel coach tours offer a unique experience. Many tourism destinations in the world still depend on private motor vehicles. Tour operators offer self-drive car packages. Car rental services, meanwhile, supply automobiles to different customer segments, such as leisure tourists and business travellers, for their use for a specific period of time on a daily/weekly rental basis. These services are very popular in countries where tourism is an important industry.

Dynamism is prevalent in land transport, as innovative ideas of destinations are being put into practice for attracting tourists. This is the case with rail transport, which has now earned the right to compete with air transport in many countries by enhancing the speed of its trains. France, Japan and China are leading the way with their high-speed trains. Innovative rail tourism products are introduced in many destinations wherever rail transport has strong presence. Using high-speed trains and luxury train services, along with tour packages in collaboration with other suppliers like hotels, rail tourism is being promoted in many countries. Rail tourism is a comprehensive concept which consists of rail travel for visiting places, the experiences offered through special services in unique trains and routes, and of visiting rail-related heritage sites. High-speed trains, luxury trains and car carrying trains make rail travel more attractive for tourists nowadays. Eurail Pass, BritRail Pass, Swiss Rail Pass and German Rail Pass are some of the popular rail passes offered to tourists. The Venice Simplon-Orient-Express, Blue Train and Palace on Wheels are examples of successful luxury tourist trains. Land transport in tourism looks to remain significant for years to come – for reaching the destination and travelling within the destination and attractions.

Review questions

Short/medium answer type questions

- Explain the role of road transport in tourism.
- Write briefly on the different types of road transport.
- Discuss motor coach tourism.
- What are the unique bus tours that attract tourists from far and wide?
- Discuss the role of automobiles in tourism.
- Give a brief account of car rental services.
- Introduce rail transport in relation to tourism.
- What are the advantages of rail services?
- Give a brief account of major rail passes.
- Discuss luxury tourist trains.

Essay type questions

- Explain the significance of road transport in tourism. Be sure to cite suitable examples.
- Describe the role of railways in modern tourism. Provide suitable examples wherever possible.

References

American Bus Association (ABA), available at https://www.buses.org/.

Amtrak, available at www.amtrak.com (accessed 28 December 2017).

Auto Rental News, Market Data (US Car Rental Market), available at http://www.autorental news.com/fileviewer/2452.aspx.

Biederman, S. P, Lai, J., Laitamaki, M. J., Messerli, R. H., Nyheim, P. and Plog, C. S. (2008) *Travel and Tourism: An Industry Primer*. New Jersey: Pearson Education.

BOTS/US DOT (2015) Chapter 1: Extent and Physical Condition of the U.S. Transportation System, data available at https://www.bts.gov/archive/publications/transportation_statistics_annual_report/2015/chapter1 (accessed 9 May 2017).

Cook, A. R., Yale, J. L. and Maryna, J. J. (2002) *Tourism – The Business of Travel*. 1st edn. New Jersey: Prentice Hall.

Cook, A. R, Yale, J. L. and Maryna, J. J. (2009) *Tourism: The Business of Travel*. 4th edn. New Jersey: Prentice Hall.

Cooper, C., Fletcher J., Gilbert, D. and Wanhill, S. (2000) *Tourism Principles and Practices*. London: Prentice Hall.

Deepika, K. C. (2017) On the Slow Track of a Luxury Train, *The Hindu*, 3 March, available at https://www.thehindu.com/life-and-style/travel/on-the-slow-track-of-a-luxury-train/article17401798.ece (accessed 12 November 2018).

Department of Transport (2017) Rail Trends Fact Sheet, January, available at https://www.gov.uk/government/uploads/system/uploads/attachment_data/file/590561/rail-trends-factsheet-2016-revised.pdf (accessed 14 December 2017).

Dhawan, H. (2016) Low Occupancy Slows Down Luxury Trains, *The Economic Times*, 7 August, available at https://economictimes.indiatimes.com/industry/transportation/railways/low-occupancy-slows-down-luxury-trains/articleshow/51725105.cms (accessed 12 November 2018).

Eurail, High-Speed Trains, available at https://www.eurail.com/en/europe-by-train/high-speed-trains (accessed 17 December 2017).

European Alliance for Coach Tourism (EACT) (2015) Position Paper on Coach Tourism & Tourism Economy, available at https://swedishbus.se/upload/pdf/EACT%20Position%20Paper%20on%20Coach%20Tourism%20Nov%2015.pdf (accessed 15 June 2018).

Foster, L. D. (1994) *First Class: An Introduction to Travel and Tourism*. Singapore: McGraw-Hill.

Goeldner, R. C. and Ritchie, J. R. B. (2011) *Tourism: Principles, Practices and Philosophies*. 12th edn. New Jersey: John Wiley & Sons.

Gov.uk (2017) Bus Statistics, available at https://www.gov.uk/government/collections/bus-statistics (accessed 17 June 2017).

Greyhound, About Greyhound, available at https://www.greyhound.com/en/about (accessed 23 November 2017).

Holloway, C. J. and Humphreys, C. (2012) *The Business of Tourism*. 9th edn. Essex: Pearson Education.

Jensen, T. M. and Bird, R. G. (2017) Rail Tourism, in J. Jafar and H. Xiao (eds), *Encyclopedia of Tourism*. New York: Springer.

Lundberg, E. D. and Lundberg, B. C. (1993) *International Travel & Tourism*. New York: John Wiley & Sons.

O'Regan, M. (2018) Motor Coach Tourism, in J. Jafar and H. Xiao (eds), *Encyclopedia of Tourism*. New York: Springer.

Railsystem.net, High-Speed Rail, available at http://www.railsystem.net/high-speed-rail/ (accessed 22 December 2017).

RVIA, Recreation Vehicle Industry Association, available at http://www.rvia.org/?esid=about (accessed 15 December 2017).

Sinha, P. C. (1997) *International Encyclopedia of Tourism Management*. New Delhi: Anmol Publishers.

UNWTO (2012) Some Points on Domestic Tourism, available at http://www2.unwto.org/agora/some-points-domestic-tourism (accessed 15 June 2017).

UNWTO (2017) UNWTO Tourism Highlights 2017, available at https://www.e-unwto.org/doi/pdf/10.18111/9789284419029 (accessed 14 February 2018).

US Definitions, 49 CFR 37.3 – Definitions, available at https://www.law.cornell.edu/cfr/text/49/37.3 (accessed 15 December 2017).

Visit England (2014) Advice Document: Welcoming Coaches and Groups, available at https://www.visitbritain.org/sites/default/files/vb-corporate/Documents-Library/documents/England-documents/guidance_coach_prospectus.pdf (accessed 21 December 2017).

Chapter 8

Cruise tourism

> ## Learning outcomes
>
> After reading this chapter, you will be able to:
>
> - Understand the role of water transportation in tourism.
> - Explain cruise tourism and its trends.
> - Discuss the evolution of cruise tourism.
> - Elaborate on the on-board facilities and services offered by cruises.
> - Identify different types of cruises and cruise tourism destinations.
> - Learn the marketing and distribution of the cruise tourism product.
> - List the environmental impacts of cruise tourism.

8.1 Introduction

Water transportation, one of the earliest forms of transport, still has an important role in the travel and tourism sector. Though air travel has dominated international tourism in recent years, with 55 per cent of overnight travellers utilizing the service in 2016, 4 per cent of international tourists used water transport forms for travelling between origin and destination (UNWTO, 2017). Though the significance of water transportation had been in decline since the end of the Second World War, the emergence of modern cruise tourism provided a respite. Cruise tourism is now one of the fastest growing segments in global tourism. Until the twentieth century when commercial air transportation became widespread, water transportation was the primary mode of transport for international travel. Once people began to use wide-body aircraft for long-haul travel, water transportation, particularly ship-based transportation, started to lose significance. Still, water transportation is the most prominent transport mode for trade-related transport, i.e. for carrying goods and cargo.

8.2 Water transportation

Water transportation, the movement of passengers and goods using various means/vessels through or across water bodies of different kinds, is part of transport networks in most countries around the world. Historically, it was the most prominent mode of transport, playing a significant role in the economic, social and cultural development of societies. Reaching a destination by sailing has been an important method of transport since the first primitive boat was built (Holloway, 1996). Also, long-haul travel and discoveries of new lands and cultures occurred due to the advancements in water transportation. In the ancient era, communities preferred to stay near water, partly due to the fact that water enabled more efficient travel compared to land. During that time, boats of various kinds were used to cross bodies of water. At first people used flat rafts but in time small boats and sailing vessels were built to travel longer distances. Dugout canoes (boats made from hollowed-out tree trunks) were also used. Reed boats and sailing boats were used later when dhows also became a major means for water transport, later succeeded by sailing ships. Still later, steamships became a prominent mode of transport for long-haul travel, followed by cruise travel. Advancements in technology led to the emergence of large, efficient ships that could travel faster and more safely. Traditionally, coastal ports were the primary reason for the emergence of great cities. Ports were the hubs of transport networks of those cities. Indeed, the complex network of connections between coastal ports, inland ports, rail, air and truck routes continues to support material economic wealth worldwide.

As stated before, water transport is still the most important mode of transportation for global trade. According to the International Chamber of Shipping (ICS), approximately 90 per cent of world trade is carried by the international shipping industry, with over 50,000 merchant ships generating an estimated annual income of over half a trillion US dollars. It is the 'life blood' of the global economy and the operation of merchant ships (ICS, n.d.). Even in the new era of air travel, water transportation has both economic and social significance, particularly for those regions near the sea or other connected bodies of water.

Travel by water still offers many unique advantages. In general, it has the advantage of lower price and remains the most cost-effective compared to other modes of transport. Moreover, infrastructure for water transport costs less to build. This is one of the major reasons why water transport is used more for trade, import and export of goods and products. It's an effective means for bulk transportation, e.g. for heavy machinery, cars, etc. As we have already stated, it is indispensable for foreign trade. Moreover, merchant ships can carry goods of any size and weight on the seas and rivers. Certain areas, such as interior regions, some islands, etc., can be accessed more easily by water transport than any other mode of transport. In such regions, water transport has considerable socio-economic significance.

Waterways are still free routes without congestion, which is a major issue for road transportation. Airway congestion is also on the increase. Pollution and environmental impacts are less compared to road and air transport forms. It is also highly fuel-efficient. Water transport is also important in the defence of a country. Furthermore, accident and breakdown rates are low. In certain situations, when other modes of transport are disrupted due to natural calamities, etc., water transport is often the only option to transport people and goods. As with any other form of transport, water transport services are now offering more comfort and luxury. Over the years, safety and speed have increased. Water transportation consists of a wide variety of carrying units/vessels. Different forms of water transport (i.e. other than cruises) have advanced over the last 50 years. Short-sea (ferry) vessels have achieved new standards of comfort on many routes. They attract tourists not just in order to travel from one point to another, but to enjoy a "mini cruise", which provides food and entertainment that was only available on luxury cruise liners just a few short years ago. Technological developments have had the added benefits of reducing high operating costs. In the meantime, new forms of waterborne transport have been developed, such as hovercrafts, jetfoils and the twin-hulled catamaran.

8.3 Water transport and tourism

Though the share of water transport has decreased, it remains an attractive transport mode in the tourism industry. According to the UNWTO, in 1990, 7.7 per cent of international tourists used water transport, while in 2016 this figure was only 4 per cent. Water transport (other than cruises) decreased during the period, but cruise tourism has increased significantly since the 1970s. The significance of water transportation in tourism has slightly shifted from being a means of travel to being an attraction for tourists. Let's elaborate on the point. Transport is not only a means for travelling, as explained elsewhere in this book. It can also be an attraction in itself/in its own right. Cruise tourism is growing not because people want to travel from their origin to their destination by ship. Rather, it is growing because a cruise provides a resort-like experience. It includes facilities for stay, recreation, food and beverage, etc., as per the needs of the tourist. Altogether, the cruise itself *is* a destination and attraction, providing as it does a unique experience. Determinants of cruise selection include the facilities offered on board, comfort and luxury. Hence, in international tourism, the significance of water transport has shifted towards the attraction or experience of water transport in its own right.

Many tourists still use water transport to travel from their place of residence to the destination and back. Ships, ferries, boats, etc. are used to connect the markets in tourism generating regions to destinations. Both domestic and international tourists use various water transport means for onward and return travel. Water transport is significant in intra-destination travel as well. After reaching a destination, tourists can use water transport to visit different attractions within the destination. Inland waterways are relevant to this type of travel. For inter-destination travel also, water transport is used. In multi-destination holidays, a tourist has to travel from one destination to another, and water transport is sometimes used for this. Eventually water transport facilitates all types of travel in tourism. Before discussing other water transport forms, let's look at cruise tourism in more detail.

8.4 Cruise tourism

Cruise tourism, though a buzzword in modern tourism, began several centuries ago. Even before the advent of steamships, many people had undertaken voyages to quench their thirst for new knowledge, to discover new places, and to enhance their understanding of other societies. Five thousand years ago, a trip was conducted in a cruise ship of that era. It is considered the first recorded cruise tour. In 1480 BC, Queen Hatshepsut, the longest reigning female pharaoh in Egypt, made an ocean voyage to the land of Punt (believed to be on the east coast of Africa) for the purposes of peace and tourism (Goeldner and Ritchie, 2003). There were five ships and 210 men, which sailed from Egypt to Punt for the purposes of maintaining good relations. When returning, they brought ivory, ebony, gold, leopard skins and incense, and live animals and trees. The trip demonstrates the grandeur of cruise tourism – even in ancient history.

Since the advent of steamships, ship-based voyages with a recreational focus gained increased significance. By the early twentieth century, recreational cruise tours had become popular among a few sections of Western society. Through the evolution of modern cruise tourism in the last quarter of the twentieth century, the cruise industry has established itself as a key component of global tourism. In 2015, there were 23 million cruise passengers supporting 956,597 jobs and $38 billion in wages and salaries. It created a total economic impact equivalent to $117 billion. The demand for cruising has increased 62 per cent from 2005 to 2015. Now, by 2016, the industry has a total of 448 cruise ships, including 184 river cruises (CLIA, 2016a). As the new millennium began, cruise tourism became one of the fastest growing tourist activities in the world (UNWTO, 2012). Moreover, in the US, between 2008 and 2014, cruise travel outpaced general leisure travel by 22 per cent (CLIA, 2016b), which shows a remarkable change in leisure tourism.

Cruise tourism, of late, has diversified with more market segments. Once cruise tourism was known for wealthy older people who prefered to undertake long-term leisure trips. The cruise market has been expanding and registering significant changes in its nature and characteristics. Lately, the cruise sector attracts markets of all age groups, with varying needs and purchasing abilities. Until two decades ago passenger ships were the forerunners of cruise ships; now exclusive cruise ships are being built with world-class amenities and facilities to satisfy the needs of various market segments. Modern cruises provide unique experiences, diverse services and a large number of facilities and amenities on board. Tourists can engage in a wide range of activities on board. "The enormous scale of today's cruise ships along with the range of on-board activities and amenities expands parameters for what defines a resort experience." (UNWTO, 2012) It is in this context that cruises, lately, are referred to as "floating resorts" and as destination themselves.

Simply, a cruise denotes "a vacation involving a voyage by sea, on a lake, or on a river". (Gibson, 2006). Though the term cruise denotes a holiday by having a voyage on a body of water, destinations are also combined to enrich the cruise tour experience. Certainly, the voyage via cruise touches many shores and excursions onto land are undertaken. During the voyage, cruise ships visit **ports of call** and tourists disembark for a number of hours, even a few days, to visit attractions in the region. These places are usually referred to as cruise destinations. Cruise tours can be defined as an inclusive holiday trip based on preset itinerary for a specific number of days on a luxury ship having necessary hospitality and recreational services and facilities on board, and visiting destinations as part of the voyage. Cruise tourism represents the segment of international tourism in which cruises are used not only for transport to visit destinations, but also for staying and enjoying various recreational and other activities as part of the tour. Considering all these aspects, cruise tourism may be considered leisure tourism. The major cruise destinations are Caribbean countries, the Mediterranean, Alaska, the Panama Canal and Northern Europe. The Caribbean sees the largest share of cruises, attracting half of all cruise passengers worldwide. Caribbean cruises enjoy year-round market demand, although the winter period, when the climate is more temperate than in summer, has the greatest market demand. Recent trends reveal that African destinations and some destinations in Asia are also emerging as popular destinations for cruise tourism. The transit of the Panama Canal remains one of the most famous attractions and the cruises through it either begin or end in San Francisco, Los Angeles or Fort Lauderdale.

Table 8.1 Global ocean cruise passengers: CLIA statistics (in millions)

Year	Cruise passengers (millions)	Year	Cruise passengers (millions)
2010	19.1	2014	22.2
2011	20.5	2015	23.2
2012	20.9	2016	24.7
2013	21.3	2017	25.8 (projected)

Source: CLIA (2016a)

8.5 Trends in cruise tourism

Over the last 50 years, cruise tourism has evolved greatly and seen significant transformation from an unnoticed segment of tourism to a significant one – indeed, one of the fastest growing segments in international tourism. Along with this evolution, a range of innovations and changes have taken place in the industry. Currently, the sector is demonstrating a number of emerging trends. Frey (2011) has identified some interesting recent trends in cruise tourism:

- Global load shifting from the North American market to the European market along with the Asia-Pacific market, in terms of growth rate
- Cruises of branded experiences gaining importance as opposed to a branded ship (e.g. cruises with corporate sponsors like the Elle Fashion Week Cruise and the Amazon Shopping Cruise)
- Growing need for office staterooms to include a functional work environment
- Rapidly evolving shipboard innovations
- Increase in multigenerational travel
- Shorter lead times
- The concepts of floating cities and floating nation-states are on the rise
- Emergence of extreme ship design ideas

Most of them are still relevant today, with the latest trends identified by others also matching with them. The increasing size of the ships, demand for increased privacy and customization, variety seeking, etc. are also pointed out by many authors. For instance, Georgsdottir and Oskarsson (2017) identified a number of trends: increasing size of the cruises; decreasing average age of markets; increasing of features, facilities and services; increasing sense of privacy and diversified experiences; enhancing of quality; and increasing environmental concerns. However, Harpaz (2014) reveals that the industry trend of increasing sizes of ships is actually levelling off now; instead, the industry is gearing up for the need to increase privacy and offer novel experiences and entertainment. CLIA (2017) identifies a range of trends:

- Younger generations – including Millennials and Generation X – will embrace cruise travel more than ever before.
- Travel agents will continue to be the matchmakers between travellers and cruise lines in 2017.

- River cruise demand continues to increase.
- There will be more private islands in itineraries. In 2017, cruise lines were offering ports on a total of seven private islands.
- Cruise demand will continue to increase remarkably.
- Drivable port locations are in favour: cruise passengers like the convenience and cost of driving to a cruise port.
- The number of celebrity chefs will increase.
- Demand for expedition cruises will continue to increase.

In another document, CLIA (2016b) specifies the following trends in cruising:

- Connectivity is on the increase as the cruise industry has made staying connected while travelling a priority.
- The desire for on-board luxury is continuing to increase.
- Big brands are being used by cruises for leveraging cross-promotional opportunities.
- New on-board experiences and amenities (from Broadway productions and designer shops to golf and bumper cars) are in place.
- Overnight stays at ports of call are on the increase.
- There is an increase in popularity due to expansion of amenities and facilities to cater to the needs of every age group of customers.
- Volunteer cruising options are increasing.
- Cruise ships are designed to appeal to passengers' cultures and pay homage to ports of call.

While analysing all of the above, it can be summed up that the major trends in the cruise tourism sector include innovations to delight customers, decrease the average age of customers, expand on-board amenities and facilities, increase demand for river cruises, enhance privacy and luxury on board, and spread their markets and destinations to more regions of the world.

8.6 Why cruise tourism?

Cruise tourism, a segment of international tourism, involves all-inclusive package holidays on cruise ships for a number of days and visiting a number of destinations during the course of the voyage. The industry has recorded a remarkable growth over the last 50 years and its demand is steadily on the increase. Travellers prefer cruises for many reasons. According to Ward (2001):

> cruising is popular today because it takes you away from the pressures and strains of contemporary life by offering an escape from reality. Cruise ships are really self-contained resorts, without the crime, which can take you to several destinations in the space of just a few days.

This definition focuses on the possibility of relaxation, an escape from passengers' busy schedules. Rest and relaxation is a major category of travel motivation. Davidoff and Davidoff (1994) specified the following features of cruise tourism which attract tourists: passengers have the opportunity to visit a number of different places in a short period of time without the issues of other modes of travel; the ships are self-contained;

they include a cruise director and staff whose sole function is to ensure that passengers have an enjoyable time; high-quality food is served in elegant style; and everyone usually begins and ends their vacation on the same day. A tourist can have almost all aspects of a holiday from one service provider and can visit different destinations. A tourist can benefit greatly from cruise tourism. CLIA (2015) has identified a range of relative benefits of cruise tourism among North American cruise travelers:

- Chance to visit several locations
- Relax/get away from it all
- Being pampered
- Explore vacation area/return later
- High-quality entertainment
- Easy to plan and arrange
- Hassle-free
- Variety of activities
- Unique and different
- Fine dining
- Luxurious
- Offers something for everyone
- Good value for money
- Exciting and adventurous
- Fun vacation
- Makes passengers feel special – rich and famous
- Romantic getaway
- Reliable
- Good vacation for the entire family
- Safe
- Cultural learning experience
- Comfortable accommodations
- Good activities for children
- Participate in sports you enjoy

The following reasons explain the increased popularity of cruise tourism among tourists:

- A cruise offers a very relaxing opportunity on board for tourists while sailing.
- A cruise tour is indeed an ideal all-inclusive holiday one can have with various special touches. It simply offers an all-in-one experience.
- Variety is a feature of cruise tourism. A tourist can enjoy a variety of entertainments, sports activities and services on board.
- All travel arrangements are done, and hence there are no hassles and no uncertainty.
- A tourist doesn't have to spend money on each and every item they consume, as the package price is all-inclusive (except for a few offerings).
- Tourists can enjoy the benefit of value and cost-effectiveness by getting the opportunity to enjoy plenty of unmatched inclusive amenities and facilities.
- A tourist can be free of frequent packing and unpacking. They have to pack and unpack only once.
- Most of the services are offered by the cruise operator itself, and hence it is easy to ensure the quality. Quality and professionalism differentiate cruises.

- Tourists can take part in a variety of entertainments and sports activities, and have food and beverages of their choice.
- Modern cruises have aesthetically designed interiors with the highest hygiene standards.
- While on board, cruise tourists can have better safety and security.
- A cruise voyage usually covers different shore trips and a variety of attractions can be experienced in one trip.
- Most of the cruises offer options for families to stay together while enjoying holidays and family-friendly environments are ensured.
- Cruises also have the necessary health facilities.
- Though on board and at sea, tourists can stay connected with their friends, relatives and others.

Destinations promote cruise tourism due to its revenue earning potential. Destinations get a range of economic benefits from cruise tourism. The major revenue sources for destinations due to cruise ship shore excursions include the following:

- Business options for local people for selling goods and services to cruise tourists
- Government earnings through direct and indirect taxes; fees paid by the cruise ship as docking fees and port charges; and revenue from visa, and entry fees at various tourist attractions
- Income generating opportunities through tour guiding services, ground handling services, etc.
- Direct, indirect and induced economic benefits due to tourist spending in the local economy

8.7 Evolution of modern cruises

Though the history of cruise tourism goes back several thousand years, actual cruise-based voyages in an organized manner commenced only a couple of centuries ago, particularly since steam-powered ships began cruising over longer distances. In 1801, the tug *Charlotte Dundas* became the first practical steam-driven vessel. In 1835 Arthur Anderson organized a cruise from Scotland to various destinations including Iceland and the Faeroe Islands. In the same year, there was the first advertised cruise, around the Shetland and Orkney Islands. There was a milestone year in the history of cruise tourism in 1837. That was the year the Peninsular & Oriental Steam Navigation Company, a predecessor of P&O Cruises, was founded. It was subsequently awarded a government contract to run a weekly mail service between Falmouth and the Iberian Peninsular ports as far as Gibraltar. Anderson, along with Brodie Wilcox, founded the famous Peninsular Steam Navigation Company, which later became P&O Cruises, which itself was popular in the early nineteenth century. According to P&O (n.d.), the Peninsular & Oriental Steam Navigation Company first offered voyages known as "excursions" when passengers from England travelled with the Royal Mail to ports on the Iberian Peninsula and the Mediterranean, returning home on other P&O mail voyages. Later, it introduced round trips to destinations such as Alexandria and Constantinople. According to some unverified sources, a cruise ship named *Francesco I*, flying under the flag of the Kingdom of the Two Sicilies (parts of modern-day Italy), was used for pleasure cruising in 1833 (Bryde, 2004).

Later, in 1840, Sam Cunard established the first transatlantic steamship. The first Cunard liner, the *Britannia*, made her maiden voyage in 1840 from Liverpool to Boston.

Figure 8.1 Celebrity Reflection cruise ship in Santorini, Greece
Courtesy: Wikimedia Commons

In 1842, Charles Dickens took the *Britannia* to America, which he described in the second chapter of his book *American Notes*. The popularity of steam-powered vessels increased by the mid-nineteenth century, which led to the development of small cruise ships sometime later. Many developments have occurred in the cruise sector since then. The capacity, facilities and comfort levels of vessels have increased tremendously. A number of players commenced ship-based leisure services. P&O Cruises expanded its services to include voyages to India, Australia and New Zealand.

Prinzessin Victoria Luise of Germany, built in 1900, was considered the first purpose-built cruise ship. By the 1920s, luxurious sea travel had become very popular among wealthy people in the West. A purpose-built vessel class (built exclusively for cruising) was the "Victoria Louise". Cruise services were available mainly from European countries prior to the Second World War. Cruising became popular in the US during the 1930s when alcohol prohibition was in practice. Cruises became a hideout for those who liked to drink, a situation which created the so-called weekend "booze cruises". In 1934, the luxury cruise liner *RMS Queen Mary* was launched. Thereafter, luxurious cruise liners were built in Europe and the US.

The introduction of jet engines in air transportation by the mid-twentieth century changed the travel patterns of people. Air transportation became more popular, which caused a slump in water transport. UK-based cruises recovered by the mid-1960s and later, by the 1970s, cruises became famous for their luxury holiday services. Ship services were not that attractive during the 1960s and 1970s. The large ships that were built during the 1920s and 1930s were stored away or sold for other uses. However, later, new cruise lines were introduced. In 1966, Norwegian Caribbean Line was founded along with the new concept of single-class cruises. The first vessel, *Sunward*, offered cruises into the Caribbean from Miami on a regular basis. Later, in 1987, the company was renamed Norwegian Cruise Line. In the meantime, Carnival Cruise Line was launched (in 1972) by cruise industry pioneer Ted Arison. Carnival Cruise Line took over the *Empress of Canada* and the *Empress of Britain*, which were renamed *Mardi Gras* and *Carnivale*, respectively. Gambling activities were introduced on cruises around this time, which became an important source of revenue. The on-board activities expanded to shopping and shore excursion activities. New cruise companies were established and even fly-cruise was started. New ships entered into cruise services from the 1970s. Also, the size of the ships increased. In the 1970s and early 1980s, ship capacity ranged from 500 to 800 passengers, though there were exceptions like Cunard's *Queen Elizabeth 2* (1,600 passengers). In 1985, Carnival Cruise Line introduced the *Holiday*, with a weight of 46,000 tonnes and capacity of 1,500 passengers. Royal Caribbean International was founded in 1968, and after two years, in 1970, they introduced the industry's first ship built for warm-weather cruising. Later, in 1988, they launched a megaship, *Sovereign of the Seas*, which boasts a five-deck centrum with glass elevators, sweeping staircases and fountains in marble pools, and capacity for 2,850 passengers.

The increasing popularity of cruises after the 1980s resulted in the renovation of many old ships. New ships were also ordered during that period, with Carnival chief among them. Some of the cruise lines like Sitmar could not afford to buy new ships. Holland America Line, another growing company, had taken over the struggling companies. By 1990s, megaships were being introduced for cruise tourism. New ships weighing over 70,000 tonnes with capacity of 2,600 passengers were introduced. Carnival led the trend. In 1997 it introduced the Destiny class, which could carry 3,300 passengers. Voyager class vessels (over 3,800 passengers) were introduced by Royal Caribbean International in 1999. Later, Carnival introduced "Project Pinnacle", which was to have a capacity of 6,500 people including crew. (The ship was never actually built.) Different ship concepts emerged as cruise tourism evolved, including the *Windstar* (1986), *The World* (2002), *Grand Princess* (1998), *Ocean Village* (1989) and *Queen Mary 2* (2003) (Gibson, 2006).

Consolidation in the cruise industry began in the late 1980s. Carnival added a number of agencies like Holland America, Cunard, Princess, etc. In 2002, Carnival Corporation took over P&O Princess. By this time Carnival had 12 cruise lines: Carnival, Holland America, Windstar, Costa, Cunard, Seabourn, Princess, P&O (UK), Swan Hellenic, Aida, P&O (Australia) and Ocean Village (UK). However, all are operated as independent entities. Royal Caribbean Cruises controls three major brands: Royal Caribbean International, Celebrity Cruises and Island Cruises (a joint venture with First Choice Holidays). The Star has joined NCL (Norwegian Cruise Line). The number of cruise passengers has increased dramatically in recent years. The 1970s television show *The Love Boat* featured the Princess Cruise's *Pacific Princess* and did much to raise awareness of cruises as a vacation option for ordinary people in the US. By the 1970s, only 500,000 people took cruise holidays. However, by 2010, this number had increased to 14 million.

Now cruise tourism is accessible to more sections of society and there is an evident shift from cruising as an activity for the rich only to a more popular tourism activity. Services, facilities and amenities have increased along with enhancement of professionalism. The scope of entertainment and sports options improved along with the growth of cruise tourism. Frey (2011) illustrates the changes in this way:

> Throughout its history the industry has responded to the vacation desires of its guests and embraced innovation to develop new destinations, new ship designs, new and diverse onboard amenities, facilities and services, plus wide-ranging shore side

activities. Cruise lines have also offered their guests new cruise themes and voyage lengths to meet the changing vacation patterns of today's travelers.

8.8 On-board facilities and services

Modern cruises have almost all the facilities and services expected of upmarket all-inclusive resorts. The distinguishing facilities on board a modern cruise include a wide variety of services and facilities. They are distributed in different decks of the ship. Accommodation facilities in cruises may include cabins/staterooms, suites, mini-suites, interconnecting rooms suitable for families and friends travelling together, and penthouse suites. A cabin may include: two single beds; twin, double, triple and quad share beds; an extra two upper berths as optional; bedside tables; and writing tables with drawers and a mirror. Staterooms are also arranged on different decks. Facilities for communication, tea/coffee making, etc., along with a TV and radio, are also present inside staterooms. On luxury cruises, there will be more facilities, such as a balcony, lounge and separate dressing area. On some cruises, there is also an atrium on board for exciting views inside.

Food services and facilities in a cruise make it more attractive. Daily food is, usually, part of the package. There is a common dining area. Buffets are common in cruises, arranged on the upper deck. The package doesn't include food that can be taken from specialized restaurants and bars. Large cruises usually have a minimum of two restaurants offering specialized varieties of food. Celebrity chef restaurants are provided on large luxury cruises. There are also bars of various types and pubs on modern cruises.

Entertainment options on board are diverse, and different cruises offer different combinations of entertainment options. Some of the common offerings include theatres and stages for performing music concerts, cinemas, comedy clubs, cabaret and magic shows. Other entertainment options may include different games, bingo, dodgeball facilities, live programmes, game shows, below water viewing chambers, on-board observatories, electronic gaming tournament centres, cook-your-own dinner dining rooms, slash-casters and piano bars. Some cruises prefer to organize wedding events, birthday celebrations and other special occasions. Deck parties and dinner with DJ parties are also arranged as per the need. Casinos are common on cruises for recreation and engaging in gambling activities. Casinos with slots, free drinks, bars, table games, poker, prize games, etc. are common nowadays on luxury cruises. There are also shows and exhibitions (e.g. painting) organized on board. Sports facilities constitute another category of essential features on cruises. There are sports of various types. Minigolf courses, on-board watersports activities, fitness centres and services, jogging tracks, roller skating, basketball courts and bumper cars are available on board many cruises. Other facilities of a similar kind include on-board sky riding, pool decks, whirlpools, solariums, libraries, swimming pools and on-board projected capsules to get a sea view from above.

Health maintenance facilities and services are also offered on cruises. There are equipment and facilities, along with doctors, to handle basic health issues and handle emergency situations. There are also health clubs and gymnasiums on board. Wellness services (e.g. for aerobic exercise, weight-training) are also common on cruises nowadays. Spas are usually found on cruises, and they are a good revenue earner. A variety of other services are offered, such as medi spas, beauty salons, acupuncture, hair and make-up services, facial treatments, massages, thermal suits, etc.

Shops, another major revenue earner for cruises, are also available on board. The diverse range of shops may include jewellery shops, candy/confectionary shops, beauty

Table 8.2 Example of services and facilities on a large cruise

Carnival Vista	
Weight – 133,500 gross tonnage; capacity – 3,934 cruise passengers; crew size – 1,450	
Accommodation	Staterooms – four types, Balcony rooms, Interior rooms, Ocean View rooms and Suites (usually for two guests except otherwise mentioned). Examples of Balcony staterooms include Premium Balcony, Havana Cabana (four guests), Cloud 9 Spa Balcony and Cove Balcony (four guests, with connecting rooms). Grand Suites (four guests, with balcony), Havana Cabana Suite (for four guests with balcony), Family Harbor Suite (for five guests, with connecting rooms) are examples of Suites. Examples of Ocean View staterooms are Cloud 9 Spa Ocean View (walkway view), Family Harbor Deluxe Ocean View (five guests) and Deluxe Ocean View (four guests, connecting rooms). Havana Interior (four guests, connecting rooms), Family Harbor Interior, Interior with Picture Window (walkway view), Interior, and Porthole are examples of Interior staterooms.
F&B services	Services consist of a variety of options and facilities: Seafood Shack, BlueIguana Cantina (Mexican), Guy's Burger Joint, Cucina del Capitano (Italian), Jiji Asian Kitchen, Steakhouse, Guy's Pig & Anchor Bar-B-Que, Green Eggs and Ham Breakfast, Lido Restaurant, Fresh Creations (Salads), 24-hour room service, Shake Spot, JavaBlue Café, Pizzeria del Capitano, etc.
On-board entertainment and facilities	A wide variety of entertainment services and facilities are provided. The major ones include Sky Ride, WaterWorks (on-board waterpark), IMAX Theatre, Havana Bar, The Cloud 9 Spa with Thalassotherapy Pool, Camp Ocean (ocean-themed activities and entertainment for kids and children), Playlist Productions for dance and music, Serenity Adult-Only Retreat, RedFrog Pub with live music, Lip Sync Battle: Carnival, DJ Irie (DJ programme), Seuss at Sea for kids, Hasbro, The Game Show, Club O2 and 'Circle C' for teenagers, and Sports Square with major sports facilities.
Deck plans (major inclusions on different decks of the ship)	Deck 1– staterooms; Deck 2 – staterooms and Family Harbor Lounge; Deck 3 – lobby with restaurants and staterooms; Deck 4 – mezzanine (atrium), casino, restaurants, lounge, sports bar; Deck 5 – Promenade, bar, shops, restaurants; Deck 6 – theatre (multiplex), Circle "C" and staterooms; Deck 7 – staterooms; Deck 8 – staterooms; Deck 9 – staterooms; Deck 10 – pool, bar, restaurants, etc. and staterooms; Deck 11 – restaurants and staterooms; Deck 12 – sports facilities, spas, water park, etc.; Deck 14 – SkyRide, spa and staterooms; Deck 15 – Serenity Adult-Only Retreat.

Source: Carnival Cruises (n.d.)

mini-malls, liquor shops, accessories shops, apparel shops, gift shops, watch shops, art galleries and auctions. Internet services are also available on the majority of cruises. Many cruises offer special facilities and services for those tourists with physical disabilities. Ships may have accessible elevators/lifts, equipped with tactile controls within reach of guests. Audible signals are also provided to guests with limited vision. Photography services and photo books are provided as well. Professional photographers are available to capture memorable moments from the voyage. Some cruises also provide learning and practical sessions. There are now language learning sessions, dance classes, cooking demonstrations, fun game practices and workshops, jewellery making and guest lectures. Competitions are also organized to enliven the trip. Babysitting services are often provided on cruises.

A summary of on-board services a cruise tourist can enjoy, as suggested by Gibson (2006), is provided below:

- Embarkation
- Welcome aboard
- Orientation and induction
- Safety and lifeboat drills
- Accommodation services
- Food and drink services
- Butler services
- Leisure services
- Sport and recreation services
- Entertainments
- Casino
- Nightclub and disco
- Beauty and health treatments
- Shops and boutiques
- Medical services
- Shore excursions
- Port lectures and information services
- Disembarkation services

These services and facilities included in the package are the major revenue sources for cruises. The package price will include the cost of all the elements in the package and it will be received prior to the commencement of the cruise voyage, since the package is sold earlier. However, there are a number of extra payment options for the cruise passenger during the journey. These will enhance the profit margin greatly. Tourists may have to purchase extra items as part of shopping, consumption of beverages, taking part in some entertainment activities, etc. Moreover, different service outlets earn extra revenue for the cruise company by providing extra services and facilities. Most cruises have additional socialized restaurants on board. There are also minibars, specialized recreational centres and facilities, etc. to earn extra revenue. Of late, cruise companies are also promoting the "user-pay" mechanism. Also, most beverages are sold separately. As mentioned earlier, casinos are also a major revenue earner for cruises. Photography services, art auctions, etc. can generate extra revenue as well. Other traditional sources of income include bingo, spas, shops and communication services. Luxury cruises have a wide variety of recreational facilities that generate profits in one way or other. These additional facilities may include golf driving ranges, virtual reality games, pay-per-view movies, in-room video games and yoga facilities. Cruises also earn revenue from shore excursions and port shopping programmes.

8.9 Types of cruises

Cruises are classified in different ways. Some classify cruise vessels on the basis of their features. Others classify them based on the level of services and facilities on board. Purpose and theme of cruise has also become a basis for classification. Let's go through some of the classifications to understand the different types of cruise.

Weight and cruise capacity are used for classifying cruises. Mancini (2000) argues that cruises range from very small or micro cruises (weighing less than 10,000 tonnes and with a capacity of 200 passengers) to megaships (weighing over 70,000 tons with a capacity of more than 2,000 passengers. He places cruises in one of five categories:

- Very small (under 10,000 gross register tonnage – GRT – and capacity of less than 200 passengers)
- Small (10,000–20,000 GRT and between 200 and 500 passengers)
- Medium (20,000–50,000 GRT and between 500 and 1,200 passengers)
- Large (50,000–70,000 GRT and between 1,200 and 2,000 passengers)
- Megaship (70,000 GRT or more and 2,000 passengers or above)

There are also super megaships which weigh more than 100,000 GRT and can carry more than 2,000 and up to 5,000 passengers. Other cruises include Windjammer cruises and barge, river and specialty cruises. CLIA (2011) identifies five types: very large, large, medium-sized ships, small and intermediate/yacht-like ships.

Some classify cruises in terms of different aspects from an industrial perspective. For instance, Gee et al. (1997) classifies cruises as resort cruises, deluxe or luxury cruises, and adventure or exotic cruises. The features of each category of cruise are as follows:
Resort cruises:

- Large vessels, which can accommodate 1,000–2,000 passengers (or more).
- Food and beverage are plentiful.
- Warm climates are usual destinations.
- Markets are highly segmented.
- There are shipboard activities available, such as entertainment, aerobics, bingo, etc.
- Short itineraries – between three and seven days.

Deluxe or luxury cruises:

- Capacities vary from 125 to 950 passengers.
- There is a high level of personal service offered.
- Cabins are usually suites.
- Dining facilities are elegant and stylish.
- Itineraries are 14 days or longer (with some as long as a month).
- Entertainment consists of classical music, shows and educational lectures.

Adventure or exotic cruises:

- These are likely to explore narrow inlets and allow passengers to wade ashore.
- There is on-board interpretation about the place, how to do the adventurous activities, etc.
- Usually older and smaller ships are used.
- Ports of call are unusual.
- There are basic dining services with substantial fare.
- Tourist-type shopping and sightseeing are less important than discovering new places and experiences.
- Passengers are older and well educated; many are professionals.

A similar approach is taken by Ward (2004), who suggests three types of cruise: luxury, premium and standard. The UNWTO (2012) identifies four types of cruise: luxury, premium, contemporary and budget. According to them the fastest growing sector is contemporary, followed by premium. Between 2006 and 2010, 70 per cent of the additional capacity was attributed to these two segments (*ibid.*). Gibson (2006) suggests a similar classification, identifying five types:

- *Luxury:* these cruises are the most expensive, they are the ultimate in comfort and provide high-quality cuisine. They are usually smaller ships.
- *Premium:* these cruises offer good quality food, good amenities and services, and a variety of attractions. The market is a mixed age group.
- *Contemporary:* these cruises use medium-sized to megaships and offer the ultimate on-board entertainment and sports facilities. They are usually equated with floating resorts.
- *Niche or specialty cruises:* the focus of these cruises is special interest attractions and features. Specialties can be of different types, such as adventure seeking, cultural explorations, enrichment activities, etc. The themes can be sports, the arts, hobbies and education. Travellers are usually more experienced and may not opt for any other cruise category.
- *Budget or value cruises:* these are usually mid-sized with lesser facilities compared to premium and contemporary. These cruises offer lower rates and fewer staff. Customers may be relatively less experienced.

Other types of cruises can also be seen in the international cruise tourism sector. Some are introduced here:

- *Theme cruises,* akin to special interest cruises, are operated with an orientation towards a particular topic or interest. The facilities, destinations and services offered will match the theme. Health and fitness cruises, various educational themes and/or recreational activities including wine tasting, cinema, golf, etc. are examples of theme cruises. The spectrum of themes is varied now. Oftentimes theme cruises are used interchangeably with special interest/niche cruises.
- *Innovative cruises* constitute some novel cruises offered to attract tourists who prefer something different. Major cruise companies come up with interesting cruise innovations.

- *Meetings at sea* cruises refer to the conducting of meetings, conferences and workshops at sea on a cruise ship.
- *Casino cruises* usually offer day trips with full-fledged casino facilities on board for a gambling experience. Tables and slots are made available for recreation seekers once the ship enters international waters. They don't travel to any destinations. Many casino cruises promote themselves as offering a "Las Vegas-style casino experience" with a large number of slot machines and a wide choice of casino games.
- *Coastal cruises* focus on marine recreational and adventurous activities, including fishing, diving and sailing.
- *Mini cruises* are short cruises. Amenities and services may be of a similar type to other cruises, but the duration varies from two to five and even up to seven days. These cruises target cruise tourist beginners.
- *Round-the-world (RTW) cruises* travel to a number of countries and last months. Some take more than 100 days for a round-the-world cruise trip.
- *Adventure cruises* aim to sail to destinations where adventurous activities can be undertaken. Smaller ships are used and they are designed and equipped to provide services including visits to remote destinations. According to Smith (2006), types of adventure cruises include nostalgia cruises (e.g. sailing vessels and paddle wheelers, which are a form of heritage tourism), long-haul ferries and yachts, and expedition cruises including icebreakers (mostly industrial ships).
- *Expedition cruises* are operated to infrequently visited, remote destinations to give their customers an exclusive experience. Specially designed ships are used, and at times these trips are undertaken as part of learning/research activities as well.
- In *fly cruises,* air travel is linked with the cruise journey. A certain distance will be covered in flight, after which the holiday will be spent on board a cruise ship. They were introduced in the 1980s and even now they are in high demand in certain locations.
- *Long cruises* are operated for a large number of days. (Short cruises have a cruise duration of only a few days.)
- *Weekend cruises* are operated on weekends (so up to two days).
- *River cruises* involve voyages on vessels of different types in rivers/inland waterways, which are very popular in some locations. They are undertaken in big rivers or waterways, particularly in Europe. Other rivers popular for river cruise tours include the Nile, the Yangtze River and the Amazon.

8.10 Cruise destinations

A cruise destination refers to a location included in the cruise tour itinerary for shore excursions after calling in at the respective port of call. Though on-board facilities and services are key determinants in cruise selection, the destinations included are also important. Season and climate are two major determinants of destination selection by cruise lines. That's the reason why the Caribbean and Mediterranean are getting maximum number of bookings. These regions are sunny during the northern hemisphere's winter and therefore offer a suitable substitute (UNWTO, 2012). The vast majority of destinations in cruise tourism are in the hotspots: the Caribbean, the Mediterranean, western Mexico, the Panama Canal Zone and the South Pacific. Caribbean itineraries are very popular. Europe, North America and Central America together share the vast majority of the global cruise tourism market. Many European cruises sail from the east and west Mediterranean.

The Caribbean, with proximity to North America, is the world's most popular cruise tourism region followed by the Mediterranean, Alaska, the Bahamas, Atlantic islands and northern Europe. The Asia-Pacific region is gaining in popularity. The most visited destinations in order are: Caribbean/Bermuda/Mexico east coast, Alaska/Pacific Northwest, Hawaii, Mediterranean Europe, US west coast/Mexico west coast, Canada/New England, non-Mediterranean Europe, round-the-world cruises, Australia/New Zealand/Pacific Islands, European rivers, Panama Canal, US rivers, Cuba, South America (CLIA, 2017). Traditionally, the major cruise routes have included the Caribbean, Bermuda and the Bahamas, and the coasts of Central and South America; the Mediterranean, divided between the western and eastern sectors; the west coast of North America, including Mexico, the US (including Alaska) and Canada; the Pacific Islands and Far East; the Baltic Sea, northern capitals and the North Cape; West Africa and the Atlantic islands of the Canaries and Madeira; and round-the-world (Holloway, 1996).

For a destination, in addition to the tourist attractions, the port of call is also an important determinant for cruise tourism. The port of call is the intermediate stop for the cruise on its scheduled journey, and is crucial in selecting the destinations to include in the cruise tour itinerary. Ports of call worldwide number more that 2,000 (Frey, 2011). Destinations enrich the cruise tourist's experience. The cruise tour itinerary commences from a port of embarkation and ends at a port of disembarkation (they may or may not be the same). Cruises usually operate for seven, ten or 14 days (corresponding to customer needs). Ports of call are neither embarkation nor disembarkation ports, but rather intermediary ports, where the ships stop and tourists can undertake shore excursions.

Regarding embarkation ports, the US contains some of the most popular. The state of Florida is an important region for cruise tourism. The port of Miami, known as the "capital of the cruise world" and the home to a number of cruise ships, is the largest and busiest cruise port in the world. Fort Lauderdale, Port Canaveral, Tampa, etc. also serve as home ports for some cruise lines. New York City, Boston and Los Angeles are also important embarkation points for cruise tourism. The expansion in the cruise sector has caused the addition of new fleet and new ports of call. A port of call should be able to attract tourists with its facilities and services. In the port of call, the gateway port should have good accessibility to the tourist destination and its attractions. Shopping, recreation and refreshment options of ports of call are important in encouraging cruise lines to include a destination in their itinerary. Ships receive fuel, food, water and other supplies from ports where they stop.

There are port agents in ports of call that render professional local management services in the destination ports. Selecting the ports is crucial; every aspect needs to be verified before finalizing a port. There are hundreds of cruise ports that attract many cruises. Miami, Port Everglades (south Florida), Port Canaveral (Orlando), Nassau (Bahamas), Cozumel (Mexico), Barcelona, Civitavecchia (Rome), US Virgin Islands, St Martin, Venice, the ports of the Balearic Islands, Southampton, Marseille, Naples and Piraeus (Athens) are the some of the major cruise ports (The Telegraph, 2017).

Cruise tourism: impacts, criticism and reputational risk

The report entitled Sustainable Cruise Tourism Development Strategies: Tackling the Challenges in Itinerary Design in South-East Asia by the United Nations World Tourism Organization (UNWTO) and Asia-Pacific Tourism Exchange Center (APTEC) highlights the impacts of tourism in general, criticism against it and the reputational risks faced by cruise tourism, citing some specific examples. Because of visiting cruises, aquatic disruption can occur. Facility construction, ship navigation, discharges and shore excursions are the major reasons. Eutrophication, coral bleaching and mangrove depletion are also possible. Bilge and other waste also have negative impacts. Degradation can disrupt various ecosystem services, including climate regulation. Air pollution can be caused by burning fuel while docked at a destination without adequate purification systems. Noise pollution by cruise ships' engines, propellers, generators and bearings is also possible. Congestion, cultural heritage degradation and community disruption are the common social issues of cruise tourism in destinations. Economic issues can also be possible, as too much of a reliance on cruise tourism (and inevitable short- or long-term reductions in tourist arrivals) have more of an effect.

Destinations can face reputational risk due to the impacts of cruise tourism. Destinations may lose their attractiveness and favour among other segments of tourists due to bad experiences, overcrowding, etc. When the reputational risks and impacts go beyond a certain point, they can cause actions against cruise tourism operators by various groups. A few instances of destination activism, regulations or bans on cruise tourism are introduced here so that we can understand the nature and type of such actions.

Most large cruises were using heavy oil. Svalbard Archipelago (Norway) introduced a heavy fuel oil (HFO) ban, leading to the prohibition on larger cruises entering parts of the Svalbard Archipelago in Norway from January 2015. Crystal, Princess, Regent Seven Seas and Oceania were asked to remove Antarctica from their itineraries for the 2011 and 2012 seasons to abide by the ban on the use of heavy oil by the International Maritime Organization. In 2014, in order to protect a world heritage city in Venice, the Italian government banned large cruise ships from entering the St Mark's Basin and Giudecca Canal. By January 2015, the ban was lifted, with authorities stating that alternative routes needed to have been in place in order to impose such restrictions. The lifting of the ban caused severe concerns among environmentalists and residents. Earlier, in 2003, Monterey Bay (California) banned Crystal Harmony, which was reported for dumping large quantities of wastewater, including grey water, treated black water and processed bilge water, into the National Marine Sanctuary, which is a habitat for 27 species of whale, dolphin and other marine mammals. A citizen's group of Charleston (South Carolina) went into alliance with similar groups in other historic port cities such as Key West (Florida) and Venice, Italy with the objective of protecting their historic port cities from congestion and pollution due to mass cruise tourism. They demanded a ban on cruise ships with capacities in excess of 3,000, reductions in the number of cruise calls and the implementation of a policy for cruise ships to use on-shore power or burn low-sulfur fuel. Due to the protests of the residents in Molokai (Hawaii) against the port calls of cruises on the island to preserve their rural way of life, American Safari Cruises had to cancel multiple Molokai port calls. Meanwhile, citizens of Key West worked towards banning large cruise ships from visiting the city, as it was necessary to dredge the channels, which were delicate ecosystems and the only living coral barrier reef in North America, in order to allow large cruise ships to dock. Considering the increasing protests against mass cruise tourism, UNWTO argued for the scientific and sustainable development of the sector.

Source: UNWTO/APTEC (2016)

Read the above case study carefully and answer the following questions:

- Discuss the reputational risk for destinations due to cruise tourism.
- Identify different types of concerns about cruise tourism by the people and groups.

8.11 Demand and supply

According to the CLIA Annual Report 2016, cruise tourists are estimated to number more than 24 million worldwide in that year. It is stunning to note that "Between 2008 and 2014, cruise travel outpaced general leisure travel in the U.S. by 22%" (CLIA, 2016b). In 1970, the number of cruise tourists worldwide was just 500,000. The growth of cruise tourism has been phenomenal since then, when modern cruise tourism was just in its beginning stages. Cruise tourists, often referred to as cruise passengers in cruise-related statistics/data, are the consumers of the cruise tourism product. Cruise tourists would like to spend their leisure time on a cruise vessel and visit a number of destinations as part of a voyage that may last many days.

Traditionally, cruise tourism had been dominated by older people, mainly retirees. This segment, of late, has begun to change, with passengers characterized by increased health status, energy, time and adventurousness. Dowling (2006) illustrates the shift of cruise tourism demand in this way: "There is currently a globalization of the North America cruise experience. Cruise passengers come from all segments of the population, and there is a high percentage of first-time cruises." The sector witnessed product diversification catering for the various market segments including younger people, families and multigenerational groups (Gulliksen, 2008). Now, retirees are physically more fit and with sufficient income to afford cruise tourism. Also, they have limited household responsibilities, particularly since their children are old enough to support themselves.

Regarding the market segments, baby boomers constitute another major segment in cruise tourism. This segment consists of those who were born, raised, grew up and developed their profession and lifestyle yearnings after the Second World War. According to the UNWTO (2003), the market segments include restless baby boomers, enthusiastic baby boomers, luxury seeker boomers, consummate shoppers, explorers, and ship buffs. Family cruisers with children and theme cruisers are now two major cruise segments. Cultural cruisers constitute another growing segment in the international cruise tourism market (UNWTO, 2012). CLIA, in its 2017 Cruise Travel Report, identified four demographic cruise tourist segments: traditionalists, born between 1917 and 1947; boomers, born between 1948 and 1966; Gen X, born between 1967 and 1981; and Gen Y/Millennials, born between 1982 and 1998. In order to understand the profiles of cruise markets, let's go through some statistics provided by CLIA in its 2014 North American Cruise Market Profile. According to CLIA, 24 per cent of the US and Canadian cruise tourists are in the age group of 50 to 59 years. The share is the same for the age group 60 to 74 years. Some 17 per cent are in the age group 40 to 49 years and 23 per cent are in 30 to 39 years age group. The average age of cruise travellers is 49 years of age. Most cruise travellers are employed (72 per cent), with most of the rest being retired. Some 69 per cent of cruisers have a college (university) education (including postgraduate) and 84 per cent are married. Average household income is $114,000 per annum (CLIA, 2015). A few decades ago, the average age was above 60 years and recently it was 49. Though the older generations still dominate the cruise tourism segment, younger generations have increased their share.

Traditionally, cruise tourism has been dominated by travellers from Western countries. Though cruise tourism has entered other regions, the vast majority of cruise tourists still originate from Europe and the US. The US remains the top cruise tourism market country. The only Asian country that could gain a place among the top ten cruise market countries is China, which is now the number one international tourism market in global tourism. According to CLIA (2016b), the top ten cruise tourism markets in the world in 2014 were the US (11.2 million), Germany (1.7 million), the UK (1.61 million), Australia (1 million), Italy (840,000), Canada (800,000), China (700,000), France (590,000), Spain (450,000) and Norway (180,000). Cruise tourists from the rest of the countries totaled just 2.84 million. Although the rest of the countries have only a marginal share in global cruise tourism, by 2015 Asia could generate 2.2 million, which is more than 9 per cent of the world's cruise tourist numbers.

The cruise product is considered a package of different combined elements. It's a unique leisure product that comprises transport and hospitality activities mainly (Papatheodorou, 2006). As a package, it:

> may include travel to the port of embarkation, an itinerary spanning a defined period of time, an element of inclusive services and facilities (such as meals, entertainment, and leisure areas), accommodation to a specified standard, and various other services that are available at an extra charge.
>
> (Gibson, 2006)

A preset itinerary for a specific number of days is the backbone of the package. Usually the package is all-inclusive and the necessary services are included. Most of the services are provided on board except shore excursions. Being a package of various elements, the cruise product is heterogeneous. Also, each service is produced and consumed simultaneously when the consumer arrives and hence the product is inseparable. Moreover, each cruise package for a particular voyage is perishable as they cannot be stored for future sale. The major elements in the package include accommodation of different types, a variety of food and beverage options, diverse entertainments, options for sports and fitness activities, shore excursions and the required transport services. There are a number of extra services and facilities provided on board which can be provided as per the need and interest of the consumers.

As demand increases, the number of cruises does too. In 2016, 448 cruise ships, including river cruises, were in service (CLIA, 2016a). Moreover, in 2017, 13 ocean cruise ships and 13 river cruises were being delivered. Cruise operators or cruise lines are the firms that operate professional cruise tourism services either by owning or leasing cruise ships. There are three major cruise companies that dominate the global cruise market. Oligopoly is a characteristic of the cruise industry of late, due to the consolidation of major players. Carnival Corporation, Royal Caribbean Cruises and Star Cruises Group together dominate the global market. Lois et al. (2004) explain that the majority of cruise capacity development is from four major cruise lines, and the same cruise lines have been investing heavily on increasing fleet sizes and increasing cruise capacity by building new, larger ships.

Carnival Corporation claims that they handle a good share of cruise passengers in the world. They have a fleet of 102 ships visiting more than 700 ports around the world. A total of 19 new ships are scheduled to be delivered to Carnival Corporation within five years. It employs over 120,000 people worldwide and attracts nearly 11.5 million guests annually, which is about 50 per cent of the global cruise market (Carnival Corporation, n.d.). Their brands include the following:

- Carnival Cruise Line
- Princess Cruises
- Holland America Line
- Seabourn
- Cunard Line
- AIDA Cruises
- Costa Cruises
- P&O Cruises (UK)
- P&O Cruises (Australia)
- Fathom

Royal Caribbean Cruises is another major cruise line. Its six companies employ 60,000 people and have served more than 50 million guests over the past four decades (Royal Caribbean Cruises, n.d.). Their brands are:

- Royal Caribbean International
- Celebrity Cruises
- TUI Cruises
- Pullmantur Cruises
- SkySea
- Azamara Club Cruises

Star Cruises is another popular cruise line. Based in Hong Kong, it has been in operation since 1993, with a fleet of six vessels including SuperStar Virgo, SuperStar Libra, SuperStar Gemini, SuperStar Aquarius, Star Pisces and The Taipan.

Table 8.3 Royal Caribbean International: characteristics of large cruises built recently

Ship	Built	Weight (tonnes)	Passengers	Crew	Cabins	No. of decks
Allure of the Seas	2010	225,282	5,490–6,314	2,150	2,745	17
Anthem of the Seas	2015	168,666	4,168–4,825	1,300	2,098	16
Harmony of the Seas	2016	226,963	5,475–6,314	2,394	2,745	17
Ovation of the Seas	2016	168,866	4,162–4,819	1,300	2,095	16
Quantum of the Seas	2014					
Symphony of the Seas (to commence operations soon)	2018	230,000	5,475–6,314	2,394	2,745	17

Source: Royal Caribbean International (n.d.)

Norwegian Cruise Line is the third largest cruise line operator in the world. It operates the following brands:

- Norwegian Cruise Line
- Oceania Cruises
- Regent Seven Seas

8.12 Cruise organization and personnel

Modern cruises are large organizations with hundreds of staff. Also, cruises have land organizational and on-board organizational structures. The land-based organization may have all the departments in a business organization, like marketing, finance, HR, etc. Regarding on-board organization, different cruises may have different organizational structures. However, the departments generally follow the structure described below.

A Hotel Department handles both accommodation/hospitality services and food and beverage (F&B) services. It has a significant role in the success of a cruise. Hotel managers, cabin stewards, housekeepers, suite attendants, floor supervisors, F&B managers, supervisors, bar stewards, bar waiters, barkeepers, restaurant managers, waiters, sommeliers, public area supervisors for decks and lounges, stewards, butlers, laundry staff, chefs, and crew and officers' mess chefs are the major department personnel who are tasked with delivering the services. If there is no separate guest services division, then the guest services manager, concierge, receptionist and guest relations manager will also be part of this department.

The Deck Department is responsible for navigation, safety and security as well as the integrity of the vessel. All activities fall under the shipmaster (captain). There will also be deck officers. The captain is responsible for navigation. Navigation officers, staff captain, repairman, electrician, plumber, safety staff, security staff, station officer, fireman and desktop publisher constitute the staff categories in this department. The radio controlling division handles all communication in relation to navigation. All are done under the leadership of the chief radio officer and other radio officers.

The Engine Department is responsible for the safe and smooth operation of the ship's propulsion systems, power plant, safety and security systems, mechanical equipment, etc. Engineers connected to each function, staff engineers, electrician, air conditioning staff, ventilation officer, engineering storekeeper, electricians, plumber and oiler are some of the major personnel in this department.

The Administration and Personnel Department is also significant. Staff include managers at different levels, pursers, front office staff including receptionists, shore excursion manager and staff on board, HR manager, etc. There are also personnel in the Information Technology Department. The Entertainment Department, led by a cruise director, deals with entertainment-related activities. There are a variety of staff in this department including stage technicians, musical director, theatre manager, singers, actors, dancers and other artists depending on the type of entertainment activities included on the cruise.

Spas will have a spa supervisor, hairdressers, masseurs, spa front office staff, beauticians and a spa therapist. Casino staff include a casino dealer, host, supervisor and slot attendants. Childcare staff and youth staff are also part of a cruise's organization. There is a medical centre with minimum essential items and staff to handle emergency cases and common diseases. Nurses, doctors and medical secretaries work in this section. Different types of shops are available on board. Each will have sales staff, cashiers and managers. There are also specialized staff (e.g. jewellery specialists) in shops depending upon the type of shop. The Sports Department has a sports trainer, supervisor, sports coordinator and yoga instructors. There are also photographers and videographers. Efficient coordination and quality staff are crucial in the successful management of on-board functions of the cruise. The success of the cruise is mainly a result of the efficiency of on-board cruise management.

8.13 Marketing and distribution

All cruise companies exert considerable effort to establish brand values and design and construct cruise products that meet or, ideally, exceed passenger expectations. Once finalizing the target market, cruises differentiate themselves mostly by enhancing the quality levels and incorporating exciting extra features. While positioning the product, a cruise will be conscious to identify the most suitable aspect to be used for attracting the target market. Finalization of marketing mix strategies is crucial. Product and pricing strategies are important for cruises in positioning the products effectively. Price, destinations included, amenities on board, type of cruise and services offered are the major determinants in cruise selection. As stated before, necessary extra features and benefits will be included when a package is formed to attract customers. As competition is high, product features are crucial in the cruise sector. After ensuring appropriate pricing strategies, cruises offer promotions. Both online and offline platforms need to be utilized effectively. Multiple tools are used for promotion. Print ads are run in the most suitable media and digital advertisements are run on online platforms, including social media. TV ads are also run to promote cruise products. Cruise operators' own websites are visited by potential cruise tourists and can be a major promotion tool for them. According to the CLIA Cruise Travel Report 2017, the influencing sources of cruise tourists in taking decisions in descending order of importance are the cruise's own website, travel information websites, destination websites, word of mouth, people "always wanting to go", spouse or travel companions, travel guides, social networks, travel magazines, travel apps, travel agent recommendations, Internet advertisements, travel blogs, radio/TV ads, magazine ads, direct mail, newspapers and web chat rooms (CLIA, 2017). This clearly reveals that webssite and other online tools are very useful in the promotion of cruise products.

Cruise product distribution is more complex. Cruise companies in the past depended much on travel agents and tour operators to sell their products. Nowadays, multiple channels are used for selling, including online channels. Still, intermediaries, particularly travel agents, have significant role in booking cruise products. The same CLIA report (2017) argues:

> Travel agents play a critical role in the cruise industry, frequently directing vacationers to cruises that are right for them and their families. Up to 82 percent of cruisers have stated that they tend to work with a travel agent when booking a cruise while 18 percent of Cruisers say they never use agents.

The US market shows that up to 70 per cent of customers worked with their agent to secure and book a cruise (CLIA, 2015). This reaffirms the role of travel agents in distributing and selling cruise products. Customer satisfaction rates in the cruise tourism sector are higher than many other tourism forms. Whether a frequent or first-time cruiser, the passenger often has a cruise experience that consistently exceeds expectations. Quality of services offered on board along with exciting extra features, facilities and amenities enhance the satisfaction levels of cruise tourists.

8.14 Environmental concerns of cruise tourism

Cruises produce solid waste, vapours, liquids, particles and energy. The quantity of sewage produced by hundreds of cruise ships operating daily is very large. Fuel consumption produces gases such as sulfur dioxide, nitrogen dioxide, ozone depleting substances (ODS) and volatile organic compounds (VOC) from the ship's smokestacks which pollute the air. Exhaust and sewage can pollute the air and surrounding water. Bilge water, the waste water that collects in the bottom part of the ship with oil leaked from engines and the contaminants, can pollute water very badly. Usually bilge water is treated before discharging; still, there are instances of irresponsible discharge of bilge water. Other waste stuff thrown into the water, such as plastic bottles, can also cause environmental issues. The waste produced by thousands of cruisers, along with grey water, can end up in oceans. Human waste flushed into the sea causes bacterial growths and contaminates fisheries. This waste also contains pathogens, viruses, biocides and toxic substances. One estimate suggests that cruise ships constitute 77 per cent of the marine pollution worldwide (Wind Rose Network, n.d.). For waste handling, Cruises also use incineration, which produces toxic gases.

Noise and light produced from cruises also causes environmental issues. Excessive energy consumption is also a matter of concern. In fact, realizing the impacts of cruise services, operators are striving to ensure measures to ameliorate these issues. According to CLIA (2016c), there are a range of measures taken by cruises to reduce environmental impacts, including: use of LED lighting and solar panels; use of energy-efficient engines that consume less fuel and have reduced emissions; special paint coatings for ship hulls that can reduce fuel consumption by up to 5 per cent; installation of tinted windows,

Figure 8.2 Speed ferry (Muscat to Musandam, Sultanate of Oman)
Courtesy: Author's own photo collection

higher efficiency appliances and heating, ventilation and air conditioning (HVAC) systems and windows that capture and recycle heat; reuse of engine waste heat; the latest wastewater purification mechanisms; efficient cruise itineraries to reduce fuel consumption; and technologies to allow ships to "plug in" at ports to further reduce air emissions when available, as the source of shore-provided power is a cleaner alternative.

8.15 Other water transport services in tourism

Ferries have a long history and are still an important mode of transportation in many parts of the world. Basically, it is a short-distance waterborne transport form, and includes different types: passenger-only ferry services; passenger/vehicle ferry services; passenger train/ferry services (for train wagons and a limited number of foot passengers); cargo/passenger ferry services; and cruise ferries (large luxury ferries). Roll on, roll off (RoRo) ferries are large ones in which vehicles can be carried. Cruise ferries have the combined features of cruises and RORO ferries. Some locations have water buses/water taxis. According to the *Cambridge Dictionary*, a water taxi is "a small boat on a river or other area of water, operated by a person who you pay to take you where you want to go" (http://dictionary.cambridge.org). Roll on, roll off person (RoPax) ferries have large garage intakes and greater passenger capacity. Turntable ferries are also in use. A train ferry is a ship designed to carry railway vehicles. Some other types are also seen in both passenger and cargo transportation. Ferries provide point-to-point transportation and can be used to transport passengers, cargo and vehicles/automobiles across comparatively small bodies of water. Ferry services are usually used by passengers in combination with land transport forms, which carry them from their places of origin to the ferry ports and back to their final destination afterwards.

CASE STUDY 8.2

Urban ferry transport on an upward trajectory

Some of the world's leading megacities rely on inland water transportation to ease congestion on roads. In the US, ferry transport is becoming more important. In 2017, Washington State Ferries published its highest ridership numbers since 2002, carrying nearly 24.5 million people in one year (Workboat Staff, 2018). Washington State Ferries is a division of the Washington State Department of Transportation and it is the largest ferry system in the US. Washington State Ferries planned to update its fleet, soon putting its newest ferry into service on its Seattle/Bremerton line. Cities are now reinventing water transit facilities. In 2017, state ferries completed 161,072 trips and travelled 901,288 miles – nearly four times the distance to the moon.

New York City has experienced significant growth in ferry transportation. Meanwhile, the San Francisco Bay Ferries' ridership has increased 74 per cent over the last five years, to more than 2.7 million passengers annually. As per the current plans, six new vessels, five more routes and another nine terminals are going to be added. Construction work on a replacement multimodal Colman Dock, Seattle's central terminal, began recently. In total, more than nine million riders pass through Seattle's central terminal, along with 600,000 riders on the water taxi. There are plans to add new vessels, five more routes and another nine terminals (Wortman, 2017).

There were more than ten million passenger journeys on the Thames in 2015. Projections suggest there will be 12 million passenger journeys annually on the Thames by 2020. There was a campaign called "Open up London by Boat" to increase awareness of water transport and to encourage people to use it. In Vision 2035, there is a goal to have 20 million commuter and tourist trips annually. Of the 23.4 million visitor trips to attractions beside the Thames, 4.7 million have a direct maritime connection.

The 20-year-old Paris Batobus primarily serves tourists, getting nearly one million riders on the river. In some developing and undeveloped countries, water transportation can be faster and support less congestion on traditional modes of transport. Travelling from one end of Lagos, Nigeria, to the other, a trip by car might take you a day (navigating through clogged streets). However, the recently introduced Metro Ferry takes around 30 minutes only. Currently, it serves 18,000 passengers daily, and ridership is growing (Wortman, 2017). Infrastructure requirements and maintenance to operate a multi-vessel network for ferry services are less. Also, ferries have a quick response rate to changing usage patterns. Along with increases in demand, adding boats and crossings to routes makes for near-infinite scalability.

Source: Workboat Staff (2018); Wortman (2017)

Read the above case study carefully and answer the following questions:

- Discuss the increasing significance of ferry transportation, particularly in cities.
- Describe the benefits of ferries and other water transport services.

Some remote tourist destinations are more easily accessed by ferries. Ferry companies have been developing new routes and tapping regional markets to offer greater choice. There are plenty of famous ferry routes, including English Channel routes, North Sea routes, Irish Sea routes, etc. (Holloway, 1996). Ferry services are still popular in Europe. The English Channel still has regular ferry services from Ramsgate, Dover, Folkestone, Newhaven, Brighton, etc. Australia, particularly Sydney, has a network of ferries to connect different communities. In Hong Kong, there are regular ferries that connect Hong Kong Island, Kowloon and the outlying islands. The Baltic is an important area for ferry operations. The Irish Sea routes, North Sea routes, western Mediterranean routes, eastern Mediterranean routes and ferries to the Canary Islands are also very popular. Ferry boats, or ferry liners, found in many parts of the world, are used for transporting travellers on fresh and salt water. In the US, ferry boats have been used to cross Lake Michigan and for transport between Alaska and the state of Washington, as well as in other locations. River boats are used for holidays. Featuring air-conditioned cabins, restaurants as well as room service and entertainment, river boats are popular in some European countries for vacations. For example, in England, river boats are used for cruising the scenic rivers such as the Avon and Thames and to see the cities, towns and countryside.

A **houseboat** is a boat that has been designed or modified to be used primarily as a human dwelling and for cruising. Houseboats have become increasingly popular in the US. They can be rented, usually on a weekly basis. Indian backwaters are famous for houseboats. Houseboats of Kashmir were world famous, though tourism has been vanishing as a result of terrorism. Kerala (India) is another destination that uses large houseboats. Based on houseboat cruises along networks of rivers and lakes, a new kind of tourism, called **backwater tourism**, has evolved in Kerala. Mini cruises are also on trend. Generally, they are operated along the US Pacific coast from Alaska to California, and the Atlantic coastal areas to the Caribbean. The common characteristics of travellers using mini cruises include: many travel in non-family groups; passengers are predominantly older, married couples with fairly high incomes; many have previous cruise travel experience; they are relatively high spenders on shore (for hotels and food), which benefits other sectors of the travel industry (Gee et al., 1997).

Yachting tourism represents the "use of water vessels or boats for leisure purposes, including cruising, fishing, racing, or the practice of other nautical activities" (Casasnovas, 2016). Yacht tourism includes water sport activities, F&B services, the chance to visit breathtaking islands and recreation activities on shore. There are different types of yachts, including motor yachts, luxury sailing yachts and mega yachts. **Hovercrafts** move over land or water while supported on a cushion of air made by jet engines and are used for different types of recreational activities, including inland racing and cruising on inland lakes, rivers and inshore coastal waters. **Hydrofoils**, boats that move with hydrofoil technology (the hull is lifted out of the water while moving), are faster and more economical.

Figure 8.3 Backwater houseboat in Kerala, India
Courtesy: Manoj Vasudevan, Kerala.

They are also used for travel. **Catamarans** have two parallel hulls. Nowadays, powered catamarans with increased speed are used for cruising and passenger transport. Paddle wheelers are still used in some rivers in North America. Canoes are used for water sports, competitions and touring. Barges are used mainly for carrying cargo. Yachts, both sailing and powered ones, are used for recreation and travel. Line-voyage services/ocean liners offer passenger transport on a port-to-port basis. **Ocean liners** were the primary mode of transport operations, particularly for intercontinental travel, in the early nineteenth century, which continued until 1950, when the air transport sector overtook it. Currently, a number of ocean liners still operate on some routes, particularly transatlantic, Far East and Australia and south and east Africa. **Inland waterways**, a combination of lakes, rivers and canals, have immense potential for passenger transportation and tourism. Different types of boats and other vessels are used for recreation and tourism. The major waterways of the world have long attracted tourists. The Nile, the Rhine, the Mississippi, the Danube, Yangtze and Li rivers, etc., all provide fabulous tourism experiences.

8.16 Summary

Certainly water transport has lost its prominence in tourism. Until the twentieth century, it was a major mode of transport. The advent and advancements in aviation and automobiles have since outdone water transportation. However, lately, water transport, in the form of cruises, has been gaining prominence. Cruise tourism is now a rapidly growing segment in tourism. The cruise market has been expanding along with registering significant changes in its nature and characteristics. Though the term cruise denotes a holiday by having a voyage on a body of water, destinations are combined to enrich the cruise tour experience. Certainly, a cruise voyage touches many shores and excursions onto land are undertaken. Cruise tours can be defined as an inclusive holiday trip based on a preset itinerary for a specific number of days on a luxury ship that has the necessary hospitality and recreational services and facilities on board, and offers the opportunity to visit destinations as part of the voyage. The major cruise destinations are Caribbean countries, the Mediterranean area, Alaska, the Panama Canal and the north European region. The Caribbean has the largest share of cruise tour passengers, attracting half of all cruise passengers worldwide. Along with this evolution, a range of innovations and changes have taken place in the industry. The major trends in the cruise tourism sector include innovations to delight customers, the decreasing average age of customers, the expansion of on-board amenities and facilities, the increase in demand for river cruises, enhancements in privacy and luxury on board, and the spread of market and destinations to more regions of the world.

Destinations promote cruise tourism due to its revenue earning potential. Destinations get a range of economic benefits from cruise tourism. Modern cruises have almost all the facilities and services of upmarket, all-inclusive resorts. Cruises are classified in different ways. Some classify cruises on the basis of the features of vessels. Others classify them based on the services and facilities on board. The purpose and theme of cruises are also a basis for classification. Modern cruises are large organizations with hundreds of staff. Also, cruises have land and on-board organizational structures. Cruise companies in the past depended on travel agents and tour operators to sell their products. Nowadays, multiple channels are being used for selling, including online channels. Intermediaries, particularly travel agents, still have a significant role to play in booking a cruise product. Cruise companies are now competing on the basis of extra amenities and services on board. Some other forms of water transport, such as ferries, also have significance in tourism. Cruise tourism is poised for further growth and expansion into more regions of the world.

Review questions

Short/medium answer type questions

- Define cruise tourism.
- Write about the current trends in cruise tourism.
- Write down the reasons for the rapid growth of cruise tourism.
- Discuss how destinations are benefited by cruise tourism.
- Give a brief account of the evolution of cruise tourism.
- What are the on-board facilities and services for cruise tourists?
- Discuss different classifications of cruises.
- Distinguish between resort cruises and luxury cruises.
- Write briefly about major cruise routes and destinations.
- Explain the demand patterns in cruise tourism.
- Discuss the cruise tourism product.
- Write about the organizational structure of cruises.

- Discuss how cruises are distributed.
- Describe some environmental concerns relating to cruise tourism.
- Discuss the significance of ferries in tourism.

Essay type questions

- Write an essay on cruise tourism.
- Classify cruises and elaborate on cruise tourism services.

References

Bryde, M. (2004) The History of Cruising and Cruise Ships, available at http://www.travel ingwiththejones.com/2014/06/26/the-history-of-cruising-and-cruise-ships/ (accessed 23 November 2017).

Carnival Corporation, Corporate Information, available at http://www.carnivalcorp.com/ phoenix.zhtml?c=200767&p=irol-prlanding.

Carnival Cruises, Carnival Vista, available at https://www.carnival.com/cruise-ships/carnival-vista.aspx.

Casasnovas, A. (2016) Yachting Tourism, in J. Jafari and H. Xiao (eds), *Encyclopedia of Tourism*. New York: Springer.

Cruise Lines International Association (CLIA) (2011) 2011 Cruise Market Profile Study, available at https://cruising.org/docs/default-source/market-research/2011-market-profile-study.pdf.

CLIA (2015) 2014 North American Cruise Market Profile, available at https://www.cruising.org/docs/default-source/research/clia_naconsumerprofile_2014.pdf?sfvrsn=2.

CLIA (2016a) Industry Outlook, data available at https://www.cruising.org/docs/default-source/research/clia-2017-state-of-the-industry.pdf?sfvrsn=0 (accessed 3 November 2017).

CLIA (2016b) Annual Report 2016, accessed at https://www.cruising.org/docs/default-source/research/2016_clia_sotci.pdf?sfvrsn=6.

CLIA (2016c) Environment Sustainability Report 2016, available at https://www.cruising.org/docs/default-source/research/clia_2016_envsust_8-5x11_8-8.pdf?sfvrsn=2.

CLIA (2017) Cruise Travel Report 2017, data available at https://www.cruising.org/docs/default-source/research/clia_cruisetravelreport_2017.pdf?sfvrsn=8 (accessed 23 November 2017).

Davidoff, P. G. and Davidoff, D. S. (1994) *Sales and Marketing for Travel & Tourism*. 2nd edn. UK: Prentice-Hall.

Dowling, K. R. (2006) The Cruising Industry, in R. K. Dowling (ed.), *Cruise Ship Tourism*. Oxfordshire: CABI.

Frey, T. (2011) The Future of the Cruise Industry, available at https://www.futuristspeaker.com/business-trends/the-future-of-the-cruise-industry/ (accessed 24 November 2017).

Gee, Y. C, Makens, C. J. and Choy, J. L. D. (1997) *The Travel Industry*. 3rd edn. New York: Van Nostrand Reinhold.

Georgsdottir, I. and Oskarsson, G. (2017) Segmentation and Targeting in the Cruise Industry: An Insight from Practitioners Serving Passengers at the Point of Destination, *The Business and Management Review* 8(4): 350–364.

Gibson, P. (2006) *Cruise Operations Management*. Burlington, MA: Butterworth-Heinemann.

Goeldner, R. C. and Ritchie, B. J. R. (2003) Tourism Principles, Policies and Practices. New Jersey: John Wiley & Sons.

Gulliksen, V. (2008) The Cruise Industry, *Society* 45(4): 342–344.

Harpaz, B. J. (2014) 6 Cruise Industry Trends to Watch for in 2014, available at https://skift.com/2014/01/25/6-cruise-industry-trends-to-watch-for-in-2014/.

Holloway, J. C. (1996) *The Business of Tourism*. 4th ed. London: Longman.

ICS, Shipping and World Trade, available at http://www.ics-shipping.org/shipping-facts/shipping-and-world-trade.

Lois, P., Wang, J., Wall, A. and Ruxton, T. (2004) Formal Safety Assessment of Cruise Ships, *Tourism Management* 25: 93–109.

Mancini, M. (2000) *Cruising: A Guide to the Cruise Line Industry*. Albany, NY: Delmar, p. 26.

P&O, History of P&O, available at https://www.pocruises.com.au/about/history.

Papatheodorou, A. (2006) The Cruise Industry: An Industrial Organization Perspective, in R. K. Dowling (ed.), *Cruise Ship Tourism*. Oxfordshire: CABI, pp. 31–40.

Royal Caribbean Cruises, About Royal Caribbean Cruises, available at http://www.rclcorporate.com/about/.

Royal Caribbean International, Ship Fleet, available at https://www.cruisedeckplans.com/DP/deckplans/cruiseline.php?line=Royal%20Caribbean.

Smith, L. V. (2006) Adventure Cruising: An Ethnography of Small Ship Travel, in R. K. Dowling (ed.), *Cruise Ship Tourism*. Oxfordshire: CABI, pp. 240–250.

The Telegraph (2017), The 15 Cities with the Most Cruise Tourists – Where Does Venice Rank?, 28 July, available at http://www.telegraph.co.uk/travel/cruises/galleries/the-worlds-busiest-cruise-ports/.

UNWTO (2003) *Worldwide Cruise Ship Activity*. Madrid: UNWTO.

UNWTO (2012) Asia-Pacific Tourism Newsletter, Issue 25, available at http://cf.cdn.unwto.org/sites/all/files/pdf/unwtoapnewsletter25contents.pdf (accessed 29 October 2017).

UNWTO (2017) UNWTO Tourism Highlights 2017, available at https://www.e-unwto.org/doi/pdf/10.18111/9789284419029 (accessed 14 February 2018).

UNWTO/APTEC (2016) Sustainable Cruise Tourism Development Strategies Tackling the Challenges in Itinerary Design in South-East Asia, available at https://www.e-unwto.org/doi/pdf/10.18111/9789284417292.

Ward, D. (2001), *Complete Guide to Cruising and Cruise Ships 2002*. London: Berlitz Publishing.

Ward, D. (2004) *Ocean Cruising & Cruise Ships*. London: Berlitz Publishing.

Wind Rose Network, available at http://www.windrosenetwork.com.

Workboat Staff (2018) Ridership on Washington State Ferries Highest Since 2002, available at https://www.workboat.com/news/passenger-vessels/ridership-wsf-highest-since-2002/ (accessed 15 June 2018).

Wortman, M. (2017) Forget Flying Cars: We Need Floating Ones, 17 May, available at https://www.citylab.com/transportation/2017/05/forget-flying-cars-we-need-floating-ones/526944/ (accessed 16 June 2018).

Website

http://dictionary.cambridge.org.

Part IV

Travel intermediation

Chapter 9

Travel intermediaries

Learning outcomes

After reading this chapter, you will be able to:

- Understand better the nuances of distribution channels.
- Explain the nature of distribution in tourism.
- Recognize the functions of distribution channels in tourism.
- Identify the intermediaries in tourism and their significance in it.
- Elaborate the benefits of having intermediaries in tourism.
- Introduce the different types of tourism intermediaries.
- Assess the challenges faced by intermediaries due to disintermediation and reintermediation.

9.1 Introduction

Business is all about transactions, which denotes that if the transaction or exchange of a "product of value" for money does not take place, the very purpose of undertaking a business may not be accomplished. When a firm produces a product, it has to be transacted and eventually consumed by the final consumer. Some producers can sell directly to the consumer whereas others need to have someone in between them to facilitate that function. The producer's responsibility does not end at producing the product; the product has to be transacted, as the return comes from the sale of the product. Enabling a cost-effective sale of the product is equally important. Making the product available at the convenience of the consumer is a crucial responsibility of the producer or the supplier. In many cases, it is not easy for the producer of the product to ensure smooth and efficient sales due to a range of factors, such as the presence of the consumer in a faraway place, or not owning and operating retail outlets. This gives scope for an intermediary, which accomplishes such tasks with ease and efficiency.

A distribution system may involve intermediaries as well. An intermediary is simply a third party who stands in between two parties and negotiates or facilitates a deal to take place between those parties. In business, it mainly concerns the distribution and transaction and sale of the products that are produced by the principals. Therefore, it denotes an agency or an individual that performs a range of functions, all of which are mainly aimed at ensuring the smooth and efficient distribution, transaction and/or selling of the products and services that are produced by the principals/manufacturers to the final consumers. Intermediary functions are not restricted to distribution and sales, and in certain cases the functions continue even after the sale (after-sales service). For a physical product, an intermediary may be involve in "managing inventory, physical delivery, analysis of services, enabling firms to offer just about everything a buyer wants, from availability, speed of delivery, reliable supply, range of choice in assortment, and so on" (Baines et al., 2008). Usually a distribution channel makes possible the physical flow of products, ownership flow, information flow, payment flow and promotion flow. An efficient channel enables the linking of a producer with buyers, and undertakes marketing communication and sales. Moreover, it can influence the firm's pricing strategy and affect product strategy through branding policies, willingness to stock and customize offerings, install, maintain, offer credit, etc. Distribution is all about the "downstream" section of the supply chain. The players involved in it are called marketing channel partners.

9.2 Distribution channels

Channels of distribution involve a number of intermediaries through which the producer makes available the products to the user or the final consumer. Distribution channel members can help with information and market intelligence gathering, engage in persuasive marketing communication, ensuring customer interaction, matching of consumer needs and modifying the product as per needs, negotiate price and other terms, organize the storing and physical distribution of the products, and finance as part of distribution activities and risk taking with regard to distribution and sales. Intermediaries also help in breaking large deliveries from principals into smaller units and sorting them into diverse items for selling by retailers. They also offer convenient locations for accessing the products. Retailers ensure the selling of products in time. Intermediaries also provide specialist services during and after the sale. Moreover, through intermediaries the ownership of the product is passed on to the final consumers. Traditionally, the distribution mechanism consisting of intermediaries and retailers could add value in the whole process of distribution, transaction and consumption.

In most cases, intermediaries perform more efficiently and more cost-effectively than the producer. In general, a distribution system can be seen in different structures. Direct distribution systems represent the selling of products directly to the customer. It can be electronic as well as physical distribution. As there is minimum involvement of other organizations, principals have maximum control of distribution and increased profit margins along with greater scope of customer relationship management practices. Indirect distribution systems denote the use intermediaries for selling the products. A producer's role is mainly in production. Principals use the skill, infrastructure and efficiency of distribution channels to distribute and sell. Though channels can add value, there is a cost disadvantage. Hybrid distribution systems involve both direct and indirect types of distribution. With this system, more accessibility, more control and more interactivity can be ensured. The following constitute the elements of distribution systems:

- Agents or brokers
- Middlemen
- Merchants

- Distributors or dealer
- Franchisees
- Wholesalers
- Retailers
- Infomediaries
- e-mediaries

Agents or brokers act as principal intermediaries without taking ownership of the product offering. They mainly aim to bring seller and buyer together, and in turn negotiate purchases, sales, or both. A broker does not usually have stock of the product. Middlemen are independent business firms that operate as a link between producers and ultimate consumers or organizational buyers. Merchants act in a similar way to agents, but take ownership as well. Distributors or dealers offer value through services associated with stocking or selling inventory, credit and after-sales service, and their prime duty is to distribute the product. Franchisees hold a contract to supply and market a product as per the requirements of the franchisor.

A wholesaler stocks goods before the next level of distribution and takes both legal title and physical possession of the goods. Usually they deal with other intermediaries like retailers. They are primarily engaged in buying, taking title to, usually storing and physically handling goods in large quantities, and reselling the goods in smaller quantities to retailers or to other buyers. Retailers are the intermediary with the responsibility to sell directly to the consumers. They may purchase directly from the wholesaler or from suppliers/manufacturers. Infomediaries are Internet-based intermediaries with the primary task of providing information. The term e-mediary represents a range of intermediaries present online who engage in one or more tasks of the intermediaries. Some even sell directly to the consumer.

9.3 Tourism distribution

Distribution in the travel and tourism sector is a relatively more important function due to some of its special characteristics. Service characteristics and fragmentation of the industry along with geographic distance of the source markets makes the presence of intermediaries much more significant in tourism. As the tourism world is facing hyper-competitiveness and global-level competition, industries have to face the challenge and find the most efficient distribution of their products to every corner of the world (because the consumers are from varied geographical locations). Though disintermediation is gaining significance, the tourism sector still relies on intermediaries for smooth and value-adding distribution. Distribution channels are primarily meant for making available the product or service to the consumer in a convenient manner. There are, as Kotler et al. (2009) point out, fundamental differences between distribution of goods and services:

> Distribution systems are traditionally used to move goods (tangible products) from the manufacturer to the consumer. In the hospitality and travel industries, distribution systems are used to move the customer to the product: the hotel, restaurant, cruise ship, or airplane.

The inseparability aspect of the tourism industry is relevant here. Consumers have to reach the location where the products are being generated and consumed. Distribution channels enable consumers to access these products in the most convenient manner.

Table 9.1 Needs and wants of distribution channel members in tourism

Distribution channel member	Needs and wants
Outgoing travel agencies/tour operator	Sales volume
	High profit margins/commissions
	Image
	Regular innovation in products
	Standardization in procedures
	Good service
	Prompt commission payments
	Maximum range of products
	Up-to-date information
	Loyal clientele
Tour operators	Sales volume
	High margins
	Producer reliability
	Low risk
	Easily sold products
	New destinations
	Little differentiation
Incoming travel agencies/tour operators/ground handling agents	Sales volume
	High margins
	Active customers
	Reliable partners
	Low risk
	Mixture of large and small operators
	Loyal clientele
	Prompt payments
	Mixture of markets

Source: Buhalis and Laws (2001)

9.4 Functions of distribution channels in tourism

Akin to other industries, distribution channels in tourism also involve a wide range of functions. We discuss the most important in detail below.

9.4.1 Provision of market intelligence

Competitive survival and growth of any industry depends on making use of the most appropriate marketing strategies based on the most accurate and relevant data and information obtained from past customers and from external environments. Gathering the required data and information, called market intelligence, is an arduous task and a costly affair. Large firms may undertake their own exclusive market intelligence gathering exercises, but distribution channels are considered a reliable source of market intelligence. Distribution channels attempt to access relevant, complete, accurate and timely information through both primary and secondary research, using qualitative and quantitative techniques. The data gathered is thus of immense value for all sorts of firms. In the case of tourism, market intelligence gathered by intermediaries is extremely relevant for the suppliers as well. Individual industries conducting market surveys separately is not easy, because after the consumption of tourism products the tourists return to their place of origin, and conducting market surveys in all the source markets is not feasible.

9.4.2 Promotion

Channels also function as a mechanism for promotion of the supplier's products by undertaking persuasive communication. This can be achieved through a variety of means, including the use of brochures, videos, magazine advertisements and websites. Again, since there are a large number of diverse geographical source markets, it is not easy for principals to conduct marketing communication everywhere.

9.4.3 Interactive communication

It is critical that the company establishes contact with its target market in order to be able to communicate effectively the benefits of its product. Apart from the promotional aspect, customers interact for a variety of reasons. For example, they may need to know the details of the products, comparative benefits, etc. This aspect is more important in the case of tourism products especially due to the service characteristics of the products and the location of the products. The potential traveller approaches an intermediary with a wide range of queries. Retailers, particularly, can interact efficiently with costumers on behalf of the principals.

9.4.4 Negotiation with suppliers

Negotiation is a key aspect in the process of intermediation. It's essential to ensure trustworthy agreements and contracts. Moreover, negotiation may be around issues relating to price, operating procedures, etc. Agents, brokers and other intermediaries are involved in negotiations with suppliers. Tour operators, for instance, undertake negotiation for suppliers and customers.

9.4.5 Packaging/consolidation

Tourism intermediaries usually engage in packaging various products of the industry together and making the same available in a more beneficial manner for the potential tourist to consume. This function is similar to the consolidation function of intermediaries. The very survival of the tour operation industry is primarily dependent upon efficient packaging of the products. Lately, customization is more common than before and hence operators have to be more dynamic in order to stay competitive.

9.4.6 Reservation, confirmation, selling

Booking, confirming the booking and issuing the confirmation documents are primary functions of tourism intermediaries. The booking/reservation services are provided on behalf of the principals, e.g. airlines, hotels and cruises. The intermediary, whether it is a travel agency or tour operator, has to perform reservation duties as per the needs of the customers. It is also their duty to see the reservation gets confirmed and the necessary documents mentioning the booking or confirmation are issued to the consumer prior to travel. For instance, when a consumer approaches to buy an airline ticket, it is the duty of the travel agency to reserve a seat on behalf of the customer. Travel agencies usually undertake reservation through global distribution systems (GDSs). Once the seat reservation has been confirmed, the ticket or the electronic record is issued.

9.4.7 Distribution

A distribution system cannot be effective if there are no means of actually delivering the service to the consumer. The channels of distribution are responsible for making the services available and accessible to the consumer easily and conveniently. In tourism, the physical distribution aspect is less relevant due to features of the industry like intangibility and inseparability, yet the distribution is still very relevant, especially since the products exist far away from the consumer. The consumer has to get to the location where the product is available and then consume the product in its place. In order to ensure this can happen, the consumer may have to purchase the product in advance.

9.4.8 Risk taking

The intermediary, especially the consolidator or tour operator, takes immense risk when packaging and selling the product. In fact, the services or the products that are to be included in the package have to be bought well in advance, and in many cases the purchase takes place more than a year in advance. Even advance payments, at least a part of the amount, may be required. This involves a financial risk, since all the products bought have to be utilized or sold in time. Unsold items may become a financial burden for the intermediary.

9.4.9 Payment collection

Retailers or other intermediaries involved in selling the product to the consumer have to collect the payment from the customers as well. The actual transaction of the product takes place here. The collected payment, thus, has to be paid back to the principal. In such cases, the intermediary acts as the representative of payment for the principal.

9.4.10 Customization

Customization is basically about adapting the product as per the specific needs of individual customers. Tour operators and retailers can customize products according to the specific needs of tourists, particularly for free independent travellers (FITs). Heterogeneous products are available, and when the principals offer their products to the masses, tour operators, as part of packaging, can make suitable combinations of products for individual customers. It reveals that, to a certain extent, some of the tourism intermediaries can ensure customization.

9.4.11 Financing

As resources are vital for performing functions, channel members also have to have resources to pursue their activities. If devoid of funds, it may not be possible for intermediaries to establish distribution mechanisms to ensure efficient distribution of the products. Intermediaries, therefore, have to ensure they have the required financial resources for performing their duties as intermediaries in the most effective and efficient manner. For instance, for a travel agent to become an IATA-accredited agency to issue tickets on behalf of airlines, it needs to ensure it has the minimum required financial capability as prescribed by IATA. Tour operators need the necessary financial resources to establish and manage the organization and to design and market tour packages.

9.5 Levels of distribution

As stated before, in tourism, direct, indirect and hybrid systems of distribution are common. From a different perspective, distribution systems in the tourism sector may be understood as different levels: one level; two level; and three level. One-level distribution denotes direct selling by the supplier to the consumer. Walk-ins for a hotel is an example of direct distribution. Through this the supplier enjoys a range of benefits. Since it is direct selling, channels of communication are substantially reduced, which brings in time savings and minimizes chances for making mistakes. Maximum direct interaction is possible and the supplier has a lot of control in the distribution and sale of their product. In addition, the supplier has the maximum liberty to be flexible to change plans. Since there is no commission to pay intermediaries, direct distribution has a cost benefit, which translates into greater profit. However, there are disadvantages as well. The company has to set up a distribution system itself, and this requires capital investment. In addition, existing intermediaries may become hostile, since they have lost the business, and retaliatory actions may be expected. Moreover, suppliers and consumers could be geographically dispersed, which makes distribution more complicated.

Two-level systems involve one intermediary, usually a retailer. The product moves from the supplier to the retailer and the retailer sells it to the final consumer. It also occurs when the wholesaler acts as a go-between for the consumer and supplier. For example, an IATA-recognized travel agent can sell the ticket of an airline, where the airline is the supplier and the travel agent is the retailer. Or, a tour operator, actually a wholesaler, can sell a hotel room to a tourist. There are advantages to involving intermediaries in the distribution system, such as the responsibility of selling being vested with the retailers and the cost required for distributing the products directly by the suppliers can be saved. The customer is benefited greatly since the product can be accessed easily and they get diverse options to choose from. Also, the intermediary acts as a one-stop shop for many of their travel requirements. An intermediary is usually more professional in dealing with customers. This makes the distribution more efficient. In addition, payment and feedback are collected by the intermediary, which gives more freedom to the supplier. At the same time, commission has to be paid to the intermediary for distributing the product. Also, there is less control of the distribution and the supplier may lack direct communication with the customer.

Three-level systems involve two intermediaries, usually a wholesaler and a retailer. For instance, a tour operator buys hotel rooms in bulk, splits them into smaller/single units to include in a package tour and finally distributes the package to a travel agent for sale to the final consumer. Here the travel agent acts as a retailer. The advantages and disadvantages of this are similar to the two-level system, but the customer may have greater benefits due to the presence of a wholesaler. The price to be paid for consuming the product will be less compared to purchasing those products separately. Moreover, the professional service of the intermediaries provides advantages and benefits to the supplier by making the process of distribution more efficient and effective without investing capital for establishing their own system of distribution.

9.6 Intermediaries in tourism

It's not easy to remain an intermediary in tourism, particularly since the emergence of e-commerce, which has led to significant challenges for the sector. The predominance of electronic tools makes it easy for tourists to get the necessary information and suitable products. Once upon a time, getting a flight ticket was rather a difficult task if there was no travel agent nearby. One had to travel to find a general sales agent (GSA) or a travel agent or an airline's own office to purchase a ticket. Now, at any point in time, from anywhere in the world, people can purchase a flight ticket. This hints at the paradigm shift that occurred in product distribution. Yet intermediaries, in the "bricks and mortar" form and in the "click and mortar" form, and e-mediaries are surviving and successful the world over.

Intermediaries in tourism, according to Hudson (2008), are:

> channels of distribution that include travel agents, tour operators, travel specialists and the internet. . . .Through the use of channel intermediaries, a company is able to expand the strength of its distribution network and to reach a much larger portion of its target market.

They are the individuals and businesses involved between the principals and final consumers which are engaged in a range of activities including consolidation, distribution, selling and enhancing the value of the product by adding supplementary services and products. The main task of intermediaries is to make available suppliers' services to the potential travellers or tourists in a cost-effective way. As seen in the industry nowadays, despite the increased presence of electronic distribution channels, hotels and cruises still depend on tour operators and/or travel agencies to handle a significant share of their customer dealings. Such dealings may involve dissemination of information, reservations, accepting payments on behalf of the producers, issuing booking confirmation documents and even promotion of their products. In the process of intermediation, tourism intermediaries add value to the core product by adding a range of supplementary services or by making it easily and more conveniently consumable by tourists. The supplementary services can be the provision of relevant information, product advice, quality interaction, etc. In the whole process of distribution, intermediaries provide benefits not only for the principals, but also for the customers.

The tourism industry enjoys the benefits of intermediaries in many ways. As stated before, direct distribution using the Internet and Internet-based intermediaries pose increasing challenges, but the sector survives by offering value-added services. Even in this era of the Internet, one of the main ways in which the tourism industry communicates, trades and interacts with tourists is through intermediaries, e.g. tour operators and travel agents (Page, 2009). Key functions of tourism intermediaries, according to Buhalis and Ujma (2006) include: enhancing the efficiency of the process of exchange globally; adjusting the quantity and type of products as per the consumer's demand; undertaking routine transactions and establishing a payment mechanism; facilitating the searching process and identifying the most suitable product; and reducing transactional links between suppliers and potential buyers. All these functions contribute in adding value and benefiting customers greatly. Customers get the benefit through reduced prices, increased convenience, enhanced accessibility, increased interactivity and high levels of personalization. Principals also get a number of benefits due to the presence of intermediaries. Tour operators may take on the role of consolidators as well as wholesalers, whereas travel agencies primarily act as retailers. Below are some of the major, specific functions of tourism intermediaries that may contribute in value addition as well (Cook et al., 2009):

- Providing information on types and availability of service offerings
- Contacting current and potential consumers
- Arranging reservations and other travel facilitators
- Assembling services to meet travellers' needs
- Preparing tickets and/or providing confirmation
- Arranging extensive marketing data for tourism suppliers through databases containing targeted consumer behaviour information
- Minimizing costs of acquiring new customers
- Initiating repeat use of supplier channels
- Marketing excess inventories
- Risk taking by buying or booking large quantities of services in advance and then reselling them to the individuals and groups

Table 9.2 Distribution strategies, in terms of intermediary involvement, in tourism

Strategy	Description
Intensive distribution	By using this strategy, the supplier maximizes the exposure of its travel services by distributing through all available intermediaries, in order to ensure high market coverage. Example: Thomson Holidays (now called TUI) in the UK uses this strategy.
Exclusive distribution	There is an intentional effort to limit the number of intermediaries used in distributing the services. The purpose can vary, e.g. enlarging the image of the company, increasing the status of those who consume the products. Example: Canadian Mountain Holidays (helicopter tourism) is one of the pioneers of this strategy.
Selective distribution	Firms use this strategy to make use of more than one but not all of the possible distribution channels. Example: The Rocky Mountaineer employs selective distribution, using sales representation in 18 countries to sell over half a million tours each year.

Source: Adapted from Hudson (2008)

Some of these benefit the suppliers more, whereas others benefit the customers more. The cumulative effect is the added value and cost-effective distribution of the product, and enhancing the tourist experience through the consumption of the suppliers' offerings.

9.7 Why intermediaries are important in tourism

Though the necessity varies from industry to industry, most industries depend on intermediaries of different types. In the case of tourism, due to a range of factors, the need for intermediaries is relatively high. Both direct selling and Internet-based distribution are taking place effectively in travel and tourism sectors. Although many industries in tourism now sell products directly through the Internet, intermediaries have a positive role in the sector. The following are some of the major factors that make the presence of intermediaries more significant in tourism:

- Service characteristics of the products
- Multitude of sectors and interdependence
- Bulk sale
- Cost advantages
- Highly competitive sector
- Geographically diverse marketplace
- Influence in decision-making
- Location of the availability of the products
- Information intensity
- Seasonality
- Strangeness

The majority of tourism products possess service characteristics such as intangibility and perishability. Due to intangibility, the role and significance of the intermediary increase, particularly to convince the customer about the right product for them, and to ensure the purchase. The inability to demonstrate the product in reality and the impossibility of the customer to see, feel or taste tourism products prior to the purchase makes it a challenge for marketers to sell "dreams". The consumer has to develop a sort of belief in the service that he/she is going to consume – with the encouragement of videos, brochures, photos and presentations. The presence of intermediaries can enhance the belief in and more easily convince the customer. This aspect will have more relevance when the potential tourist is relatively inexperienced or a new traveller to a destination. Similarly, due to the characteristic of perishability, suppliers have to sell a maximum number of products as early as possible and in the right time. Due to perishability, unsold product is obsolete after its due time period. As the intermediaries can enhance distribution capability and ensure sales, their presence becomes very important for many industries in tourism. Even the destinations are interested in intermediaries to encourage regular inflows of tourists to their destination.

For tourism, a multi-sector industry with high levels of interdependencies, the existence and survival of one sector is critical for other sectors as well. Some tourism industries offer packages of different industrial products combined, which helps with easier and more convenient distribution of various products. Intermediaries also take measures to ensure quality services are provided by the suppliers, which will have a positive impact eventually. Intermediaries, particularly tour operators, also help to maintain good relationships among the industries through the offering of various services bundled together (as package holidays).

Intermediaries, especially those who act as wholesalers, will buy products in bulk for future dates. This is a relief for some suppliers, especially since they are perishable products, as they don't need to sell these products themselves. The supplier gets diverse cost benefits by engaging intermediaries. Establishing its own system of distribution is a costly affair for a supplier, with significant capital investment required. Apart from that, through bulk sale, a supplier can avoid marketing and selling to customers directly. Intermediaries take care of this. The cost for the same can therefore be saved. Furthermore, the intermediary undertakes interactive communication with the customers and handles payment collection from customers.

Tourism is a highly competitive sector; some of its elements face global competition. In this hyper-competitive business environment, distribution has become an area of competitive advantage for many companies. The competition among airlines is well known. Other sectors face similar issues to airlines. Destinations in the same region or with similar attractions are in competition with one another to attract more tourists. Such an environment necessitates the support of a professional distribution system handled by intermediaries. Tourism markets are geographically dispersed. Direct distribution, except through the Internet, is a difficult task for tourism industries. Every role of an intermediary may not be performed in such a direct distribution mechanism.

Intermediaries do have a certain amount of influence in the decision-making of potential buyers. In tourism, this is more relevant due to the inherent characteristics of tourism products. It has been well established that tourism buying is a high-involvement exercise. Hence, the power of an intermediary cannot be underestimated and is likely to remain strong in the near future. Tourists have to reach the location where the products are available. As stated before, a distribution system in the goods industry makes the products available to the consumer in their place/location, whereas in the tourism industry, the distribution system brings the consumers to the place/location of the products (where they are available) and enables them to consume the products in those locations.

Tourism is a highly information-intensive sector due to the need for diverse, accurate and up-to-date information for potential consumers. At the stage of decision-making to purchase a tourism product, the buyer will search for a variety of information and intermediaries can be a very reliable source. This can, to a certain extent, help tourists to overcome difficulties stemming from the intangibility of the product. As low season affects the tourism sector adversely, intermediaries can play a role in ensuring demand. Package tour operators especially try to sell holidays in low/off season since tourists can enjoy significant cost advantages. At the time of package planning and designing, the demand will be forecast and the special packages will be developed for off seasons with significant price discounts. The suppliers get a lot of advantages, too, especially cost advantages through lower marketing and promotion spending during off season. In this way, steady revenue generated through customer spending is able to meet the operational expenses, and sometimes even reach minimum profit levels. Tourists, being strangers in a destination but with the assistance of intermediaries, gain the confidence to explore destination attractions and enjoy their trip. Escorts, guides or other overseas representatives will also be available in the destination to offer assistance. Furthermore, in the case of emergency, tourists can contact the respective representative. Also, even before taking a decision to visit a place, some will prefer to make bookings, etc. through intermediaries since they have someone who knows details – and someone to complain to if satisfaction levels are not met. Face-to-face interaction may give the potential tourist more confidence to take decisions, especially if they are an inexperienced traveller.

9.8 Reason for decline of intermediaries

As stated before, the intermediary business sector in tourism is facing serious challenges and the sector has declined/contracted over the years. There are a number of reasons for this decline, but some of the most prominent are listed here:

- Declining rate of commission
- Growing rate of disintermediation
- Increasing ease of information access
- Experienced travellers
- Increasing rate of IT and smartphone use by customers

All over the world, suppliers are making efforts to reduce the commission paid to intermediaries, since the alternative options are getting stronger and increasingly reliable. The airline sector provides the best example. Two decades ago, intermediaries were paid large commissions for selling airlines' seats, but now this is almost zero. Even the largest association of airlines, the International Air Transport Association (IATA), initiated a zero commission agenda years ago, and most airlines are following it. Low-cost carriers (LCCs) are emphasizing direct sales and they are reluctant to give commission to travel agents. Such a situation has necessitated travel agents even collecting a service charge. The advent of the Internet made the distribution of the product easier and more cost-effective for the principals or suppliers. Suppliers' own websites and those of other firms provide opportunities for making sales directly over the Internet. Even online intermediaries emerged, which led to the concept of re-intermediation. Yet the traditional intermediaries are now sidelined or bypassed by many suppliers. Selling through their own websites provides increased control over distribution and a significant reduction in distribution/selling cost. This lures the industries to follow Internet-based distribution.

Once upon a time, when a tourist wanted to travel to a distant and strange destination, they depended on intermediaries. Again, the advent of the Internet turned this scenario upside down. Now, information about any places, attractions, tourist facilities, accommodation options, prices of products, etc. is available at the click of a button. At any point in time, from anywhere, any information can be accessed. This has lessened tourists' dependence on intermediaries, and has challenged their very existence. Travel propensity has increased significantly over the last half century due to a wide range of factors. The emergence of multinational companies and global businesses has caused a phenomenal growth in business travel.

Lately, people are gaining experience and more confidence in travelling, even to strange places. The necessity for intermediaries has also declined as a result of tourists having the confidence to travel without pre-arranged itineraries. Furthermore, travellers' computer literacy (particularly in respect of the Internet) has increased markedly. Smartphones have become a window to the world. So much is now available on this personal device. These phenomena have helped to increase the rate of direct booking of hotel rooms and airline seats through the Internet. The information revolution and the significant growth of Internet users have directly or indirectly contributed to the decline of intermediaries in tourism.

The role of intermediaries in community-based tourism (CBT)

Traditionally, intermediaries were integrated in the tourism system. Since the information revolution and the consequent invasion of intermediation by Internet-based tools, traditional intermediaries in tourism have struggled. The number of "bricks and mortar" intermediaries has reduced substantially. However, the phenomenon of intermediation didn't vanish. Online intermediaries emerged strongly through the process of re-intermediation. Some traditional intermediaries met the challenge and still remain competitive. Inherently, tourism is incomplete in the absence of intermediaries. A variety of tourism intermediaries have survived. Here, some intermediaries that are involved in CBT are introduced.

In order to get access to CBT, intermediaries are important, particularly to bridge the gaps in market information, business skills and product design. There are different groups of intermediaries in this area, such as private sector companies operating in a competitive environment, membership associations of CBT groups, public sector agencies and non-governmental organizations (NGOs). The specialty of CBT is developing and promoting indigenous products and packages. Some indigenous communities' exposure to the external world may be limited and they may have limited links to world markets to communicate about and to market their products. Therefore, instead of traditional intermediaries, like travel agents and tour operators, they may need more support from other agencies like NGOs.

Private sector companies with good market information, marketing skills and networks can support CBT activities by offering tourists a new type of tourism and to pursue their social responsibility goals. Membership associations have much more significance, where several such tourism ventures are established together. As the scope for financial earning is limited, they usually rely in part on donor funding, etc. The focus of their efforts is mainly on marketing and capacity building. The public sector has a lot of significance for CBT, as such ventures need its support, and various other kinds of support, too. Apart from financial support, it requires the provision of market intelligence, access to resources, favourable policy interventions, standardization efforts, training and development, etc. from governmental and public sector agencies. Some NGOs view CBT as an additional rural livelihood and support it with capacity building, resources, institution building and facilitating partnerships. Moreover, with limited commercial experience, they are more likely to focus on equity and the participation of the community. Intermediary involvement in CBT ventures may vary, but usually more than one of the above types are associated with it. The private sector may be more involved in ventures with good commercial potential. In such cases, NGOs are more likely to support capacity building. Corporates want high profit margins. Most of the community-based tourism initiatives are small-scale and profit levels are low. The reason is that they usually find it difficult to undertake costly marketing and promotion efforts. In such circumstances, NGOs play a greater role, particularly in gaining access for the community-based private business sector to the tourist markets. Though membership associations have a vital role to play in representing such ventures, they require the support of NGOs, the government and the private sector. Organized support is necessary for the success of CBT initiatives.

Source: Forstner (2005)

Read the above case study carefully and answer the following questions:

- Briefly describe the different types of intermediaries involved in CBT.
- Discuss the role of NGOs in CBT.
- Explain how government can support CBT initiatives.

9.9 Intermediaries and benefits

The primary reason for the existence of the tour operation business is the benefits it can offer to various stakeholders in the tourism industry and the value enhancements it can bring to the entire value chain in the tourism industry. Distinct benefits are enjoyed by different stakeholders. The suppliers in the context of tour operation are a major beneficiary of intermediaries in tourism. Tourists are the other group that benefits from the involvement of intermediaries. Destinations also depend on intermediaries.

9.9.1 Benefits for principals

Intermediaries handle the products and services that are originally produced by the suppliers/principals. Major principals in the tourism sector include airlines and other transport operators, hotels and other accommodation units, restaurants and attractions. All these suppliers, particularly those that are present in the destination, are the primary beneficiaries because of the distance disadvantage of the location of the industries. Those industries are located far away from the destinations, which makes communication with potential customers very difficult. The active involvement of intermediaries in tourism enables them to have a wider coverage of the market. Tourism markets are geographically dispersed and intermediaries make it easy for them to get in touch with consumers prior to their arrival. Intermediaries bear the risk of selling the stock, as they buy a significant share of the products in advance. Wholesalers, mainly the tour operators, assume the responsibility for products/services bought in advance in bulk, which are then made into smaller units for individual consumption. This is an immense relief for the principals, which are freed from the risk of selling the products/services in time. Furthermore, the intermediaries ensure convenience for selling the products/services. It eventually ensures consumers can access the products easily. Usually intermediaries, and particularly retailers, will be present in the same location as the consumers, which would be very difficult for the principals to arrange.

Intermediaries can help in reducing the cost of marketing and promotion. As tourism markets are geographically dispersed and located in different corners of the world, it is hugely expensive for the supplier to ensure efficient marketing communication directly. Intermediaries take up the responsibility of promotion on behalf of the principals in many cases. This helps to lower the marketing cost of the principals. Furthermore, marketing costs will be substantially reduced when the intermediaries ensure the sale of a good share of products and services. In addition, the principals enjoy a reduction in operational costs as well. For instance, intermediaries will collect the payment for the products sold from the consumer and the required amount will be transferred to the principal. In this process, the principal gets the sum of the amounts instead of individual amounts, which reduces the labour needed for direct payment collection. Moreover, intermediaries in tourism act as genuine sources of market intelligence. In the case of packaged holidays, though the services are delivered by the principals, tour operators receive customer feedback as well as complaints. The regular and intense interaction with the market provides them with very relevant information principals require for marketing efforts. Here, the intermediary acts as a source of increasing knowledge of markets, as a mediator and as a catalyst in ensuring quality services.

9.9.2 Benefits for other stakeholders

For any intermediary to survive there have to be benefits for the consumers. Here, the ultimate consumers of tourism products, the tourists, also get a range of benefits from the presence of intermediaries in tourism. Price advantages, reliability and quality, minimized uncertainty, easy access and convenience are the major benefits that tourists can enjoy when buying products from intermediaries. Most of the time, it is actually economical to buy packaged tourism products from intermediaries. Because the products are bundled into one package, the price will be lower compared to the sum of individual products included – the intermediaries get them more cheaply because they purchase them in bulk and in advance. Consumers also get the benefit of convenience in purchasing the tourism products from intermediaries. Either a tour operator or a travel agency which distributes the package tour may be available at a location near to the consumer, making it easier for the tourist to access the products.

One of the primary objectives of an intermediary is to provide ample and the most relevant information to the tourist, along with the necessary suggestions. A potential tourist is usually in search of a lot of information and the access of such is made easy and more cost-effective by intermediaries. Even the uncertainties associated with the consumption of various tourism products can be minimized to a great extent by the presence of intermediaries, as tourists can interact with intermediaries as and when it's needed. Moreover, intermediaries can convince potential tourists of the right product and receive complaints to take further action. A tour is a complex process and it involves diverse activities. Buying a package holiday always provides the tourist with the convenience of getting various elements of the tour together. In addition, tour operators always try to include quality/branded items in the package offered in order to make the product more attractive and worthwhile. This ensures the quality of the service. Such attempts are the usual strategies undertaken for the competitive survival of the business.

Destinations also gain a lot of advantages from tourism. Emerging destinations' dependency on tour operators is always high. Tour operators can ensure regular flows of tourists to a destination, which becomes particularly relevant in the off season. Destinations also gain much advantage in terms of marketing and promotions, as it is very costly for them to do it themselves – particularly in light of the fact that tourism markets are geographically dispersed. Here, the network of tour operators assists destinations in reducing the costs of marketing and promotion.

9.10 Types of tourism intermediaries

Tourism is supported by a range of intermediaries. For the airlines sector, for instance, selling happens through different channels. Airlines will have their own offices/branches in major cities. In other areas, general sales agents will act as representatives of airlines; they may issue tickets themselves, or they may do it through IATA-recognized travel agencies. In rural areas, sub-agents that are not IATA-recognized will help customers to obtain tickets. Electronic ticketing provision is very popular and has changed the travel product distribution system significantly. In the tourism sector, the range of intermediaries includes wholesalers, consolidators, infomediaries, e-mediaries, retailers and the like. Travel agents and tour operators are the most visible businesses that perform the functions of intermediaries in tourism.

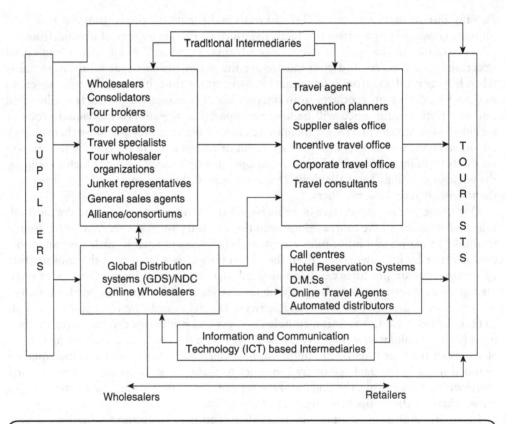

Figure 9.1 Intermediaries in tourism

9.10.1 Consolidators

Consolidators are basically the intermediaries that sell the products of the suppliers at sizeable discounts. They usually specialize in specific areas and will have contracts with one or more principals to distribute products at discounted rates. While some consolidators act strictly as wholesalers by selling the products only through retail agents, some others sell directly to the public, usually at a higher rate than the wholesale price. Therefore, they function as both a wholesaler and a retailer (Goeldner and Ritchie, 2003).

9.10.2 Wholesalers

Wholesalers deal directly with principals, buy in bulk and negotiate prices. In this hyper-competitive market, tour wholesalers are becoming key players in the distribution system (Kotler et al., 2009). They are primarily involved in assembling packages with transport and accommodation. They can provide package holidays to the public at prices lower than an individual can arrange since they buy services such as transportation, hotel rooms, sightseeing services, airport transfers and meals in large quantities at discounted prices.

9.10.3 Tour operators

As stated before, a tour operator is a prime intermediary in tourism. Traditionally, tour operators purchase tourism elements separately – transport, accommodation and other services that are essential for a tour, and then combine them into a package, which can be sold directly or through travel agents to potential tourists. Also, they manage tours en route, depending on the type and terms and conditions of the package sold. They take up the role of wholesaler, consolidator and distributor of tourism products. Details of tour operation are discussed later in this book.

9.10.4 Travel agents

Travel agents, in general, are considered the retail agents from whom the consumer can buy the tourism product. However, travel agents also assume many other roles. The concept of the travel agent evolved a few centuries ago, when such agencies sold tickets for railroads and steamships on a commission basis. The concept evolved further, and became a major intermediary in travel and tourism by diversifying its activities and tasks. Until the 1990s, travel agents enjoyed decent commission from suppliers, primarily airlines. As the Internet era dawned, the sector shrank due to dynamic and dramatic changes taking place in the industry. Airline commissions were the main source of revenue for travel agents, but the emergence of online ticketing and disintermediation had a huge impact on the sector, threatening its very existence. However, travel agents remain a strong influencer in the system, through the further diversification of their activities and functions. This is also discussed in detail later.

9.10.5 Convention/meeting planners

Convention and meeting planners plan and coordinate meetings, seminars, conferences, summits and similar events on behalf of companies, trade associations, professional bodies, governmental agencies, etc. MICE (meetings, incentives, conferences and exhibitions) tourism, more commonly called business tourism, depends a lot on convention and event organizers. Of late, business tourism has been a major component of international tourism. Event planners have a significant role to play in the distribution and sale of associated products.

9.10.6 Tour brokers

Tour brokers are associated with short-term tours. They are seen more in organizing coach tours, both scheduled coach tours and those organized in seasons. In addition to arranging transport and accommodation, tour brokers have an important role in selling the services of hotels and restaurants.

9.10.7 Travel specialists

Travel specialists are the "intermediaries that specialize in performing one or more functions of a company's distribution system" (Hudson, 2008). They are specifically equipped for handling those functions and their focus of activities is basically on their areas of specialization, such as hotel booking, entertainment arrangement in destinations visited and transport arrangements.

9.10.8 Hotel representatives

Hotel representatives, like travel specialists, function exclusively for booking rooms in specific regions. They specialize in representing hotels, motels, resorts and destination areas. Tourism markets are located far away, international hotel representatives have traditionally been reliable and economical options for the accommodation sector to distribute their products.

9.10.9 Tour wholesaler organizations

Some industry associations also act as intermediaries through their network. The **National Tour Association (NTA)**, **United States Tour Operators Association (USTOA)** and **European Tour Operators Association** are examples of industry organizations that promote the intermediation and support the intermediary sector for its competitive survival.

9.10.10 Supplier sales offices

Airlines usually set up their own sales offices in major cities and locations. These are supplier sales offices. Their primary duty is to sell the products directly, coordinate sales activities in those regions and promote their products.

9.10.11 Incentive travel firms

Incentive travel firms organize incentive holiday activities by designing, promoting and executing incentive travel programmes on behalf of corporates, companies and agencies. These are the agencies or departments that provide incentive travel, offered to employees or distributors as a reward for the performance they have shown. Incentive tours can be of various types, such as providing all-inclusive packages or offering accommodation in an upmarket hotel or resort.

9.10.12 Corporate travel departments/offices

Large corporations have their own travel sections as well. They typically provide the same services as those of travel agencies. The scope of business travel is on the increase day by day, which creates the need for corporations, transnational firms and multinational companies to have their own departments to arrange the travel needs of their employees.

9.10.13 Automated distribution

Automated kiosks are seen in many strategic locations offering potential consumers access to products. This is more convenient for consumers as they can purchase the products when they are free or at a convenient location. Automated ticketing machines (ATMs) are owned by airlines and located in major airports for passenger convenience. This is a good example for this kind of facility. Train tickets, Bus tickets, etc. can also be purchased this way.

9.10.14 Travel consultants

A travel consultant acts as a mediator or an agent helping the customer to arrange their travel needs, such as booking hotel rooms, booking flights, arranging tours, etc. without hassle. Travel consultants are mainly used for ensuring that all aspects of a client's travel are seamlessly arranged. They help to provide quotes and find the options available at the best value and make bookings for transport, accommodation, sightseeing activities and other travel-related activities that a client may need.

9.10.15 Junket representatives

These representatives mainly offer services to the casino industry as intermediaries for premium players. They maintain lists of gamblers who like to visit certain gaming areas and work for one or two casinos rather than the whole industry on a commission basis (Hudson, 2008).

9.10.16 Global distribution systems (GDSs)

Global distribution systems are the most important distributors of airline products. A customer who purchases a flight ticket does not usually know about the role of a GDS, but even if they purchase the ticket through a "bricks and mortar" agent or directly from an airline's website, GDSs play a crucial role in accessing the product. GDSs are the new incarnation of the traditional computer reservation systems of airlines, which were predominant after the 1970s. There are a number of GDSs in the market, but the main ones are Galileo, Amadeus, Sabre and Worldspan. Abacus dominates the East Asian market.

9.10.17 DMSs and public sector agencies

Destinations, in order to remain competitive and to attract tourists from far and wide, establish destination management systems (DMS) with the main objective of information dissemination. Markets require timely and accurate information that reflects the individual needs of travellers. Demand patterns also change as contemporary, sophisticated and wired travellers seek new experiences, often based on information. It is therefore technology and demand that have driven the realization of DMSs. The role of DMSs has widened, as nowadays they provide product distribution on behalf of the suppliers in the destinations. The ability of destinations to efficiently satisfy the information and reservation requirements of buyers, by providing appropriate and accurate information online, will be critical for their future attractiveness. Initially, different DMSs supported different functions, depending on the requirements of the destination concerned. Increasingly, DMSs have supported multiple functions, drawing on central product and customer databases. Today we are starting to see more vertically integrated DMSs, systems consisting of a set of browser-enabled software modules, accessed across the Web from the remote servers of application service providers or internally through intranets. DMSs are collections of computerized, interactive information accessible about a destination. DMSs typically include information on attractions and facilities and often incorporate the ability to undertake some reservations. They are usually managed by destination management organizations, which may be private or public.

9.10.18 Travel and tourism call centre

A potential tourist can make a toll-free telephone call to gather information and book hotel rooms and similar tourism products. The advancements in technology and telecommunication make the purchase of products easy. Call centres are becoming more and more popular nowadays, as a customer can easily access the product by making a phone call. A travel call centre is a virtual location where travel and tourism firms can sell their products over the phone.

9.10.19 Alliances/consortiums

Alliances are in vogue nowadays. Some alliances perform distribution functions as well. Due to the wider geographical representation, consumers from different areas can undertake bookings and purchase products through alliance members. This means that members of the alliance can enjoy access to diverse markets through other members located in different parts of the world.

9.10.20 General sales agents

General sales agents (GSAs) have traditionally been a major intermediary in tourism, especially for airlines. For an airline GSAs are responsible for selling all products in the designated region, which includes flight tickets and cargo space, on the basis of commission. In appearance, they may look the same as the original company. They also pursue marketing and promotion activities, depending on the agreements between the airline and themselves. For the supplier, they provide local infrastructure, market intelligence and a sales system along with marketing and promotion services.

9.10.21 Reservation systems of hotels

The Internet is now one the most prominent distribution channels, functioning at a relatively low cost but open to markets across the world. We now have the reservation referral system, fundamentally an international organization that processes requests for room reservations on behalf of referral member hotels. Integrated property referral is a system in which one member property recommends another's rooms to a guest. There are also affiliate reservation systems which represent hotel chain reservation systems. Some chains run a central reservation system on behalf of the members. Every member hotel can get the benefit of the global booking facilities using this.

9.10.22 Online agents

There are different types of e-mediaries online, which act as both wholesalers and retailers. Online travel agencies have a significant share of travel and tourism suppliers' sales. Hotel booking has become easy; it can be done through websites and mobile apps. Holiday packages are also transacted via online agents of different kinds.

9.11 The challenge of disintermediation and re-intermediation

As the term denotes, disintermediation is all about eliminating the intermediaries from the distribution system. It has gained much significance due to the cost-saving advantages for the suppliers through cutting the payments made to intermediaries. By the advent of the Internet and the consequent emergence of e-commerce, the stage was set for disintermediation on a large scale, i.e. worldwide. In addition to higher profit margins due to cutting of commission, suppliers began to sell directly to customers. Suppliers could attempt increased customization through direct selling. Because of its tempting benefits, disintermediation on a large scale is happening in travel, tourism and hospitality sectors as well.

All the major principals in tourism, particularly airlines, hotels, resorts and tourist attractions now support selling of their products through their own websites. Every airline now sells tickets via their own websites. LCCs in particular depend on online distribution to a great extent. Hotels and resorts have their own networks and central reservation systems that can be accessed from anywhere. For instance, chain hotels with units in a large number of cities across the world, like Marriot Hotels (www.marriott.com), intercontinental hotels (www.intercontinental.com) and Hilton Hotels and resorts (www.hilton.com) have their own sites to distribute their products. Tourist attractions also now distribute products directly. UAE's top attraction, the Burj Khalifa, the tallest building in the world which attracts millions of visitors, now uses discriminatory pricing even for online bookings. Those who purchase tickets via their site (www.burjkhalifa.ae) pay less. Disintermediation is widespread in the tourism sector and traditional intermediaries are facing challenging times. Customization, product diversification, value addition, quality service assurance, discounted price offers, etc. are different strategies taken by traditional intermediaries to meet the challenge of disintermediation.

While disintermediation takes place at a higher rate, new intermediaries utilizing the potential of the Internet are also gaining an increased presence in the global distribution and retailing of products, particularly with the support of mobile-based distribution. The term re-intermediation basically denotes the emergence of additional or new intermediaries into the distribution channel. The Internet is used to reassemble buyers, sellers and other partners in a traditional supply chain in new ways. The phenomenon can be considered the re-emergence of, or reintroduction of, middlemen or intermediaries to the process of distribution. The Web has now become a space for online retailers in which B2B (business to business), B2C (business to customer) and C2C (customer to customer) types of transactions take place. The platforms nowadays bring buyers, sellers, traders and intermediaries together for the purpose of transacting the goods or service offerings. They have become hubs for undertaking various marketing mix strategies as well.

Online intermediaries of various kinds are now dominating the global distribution of products. Some retail service sites sell almost all types of products. The trend, though it commenced more than a decade ago, has evolved greatly in recent times and now has significant influence in the distribution of products across the world. Online intermediaries perform a variety of functions. Supplier search, product evaluation, price comparison, etc. are some of the prominent services offered online. Online intermediaries are now enabling the suppliers and principals to reach a much wider audience with their products and offer customers a "value-added" experience. A variety of e-marketing strategies can be easily undertaken with the help of online intermediaries. Affiliate marketing is one example. It is an e-marketing strategy in which suppliers can utilize affiliate sites to sell their products. Online intermediaries can establish "affiliate marketing" programmes online which enable products to be promoted and sold by almost anyone for a commission.

Re-intermediation is also happening as a byproduct of e-business or e-commerce. In the usual e-commerce model, shipping small quantity orders is time and resource consuming. Moreover, maintaining your own e-commerce mechanism is not easy. Distributing the product using online intermediaries opens up the global market as well as providing easy distribution and delivery of the products. Moreover, the cost for maintaining your own mechanism of both Web-based and traditional distribution systems has become expensive. Also, more customers are now visiting online intermediary platforms. Now, hotel rooms, airline tickets and package tours are also available on online intermediary sites (e.g. www.booking.com). Online travel agencies, such as Expedia, now have a significant role in travel product distribution. As in the case of disintermediation, in order to compete with online agencies, traditional intermediaries have to take up diverse strategies to remain competitive in the market.

9.12 Summary

Distribution channel members can help in information and market intelligence gathering, engage in persuasive marketing communication, ensuring customer interaction, matching of consumer needs and modifying the product as per needs, negotiate price and other terms, organize the storing and physical distribution of the products, and finance as part of distribution activities and risk taking with regard to distribution and sales. Traditionally, the tourism sector has featured a dominant role for intermediaries. Even in the Internet era, intermediaries in tourism play a significant role. Service characteristics and fragmentation of the industry along with distance/location of the source markets make the presence of intermediaries much more significant in tourism. Like other industries, distribution channels in tourism also involve a wide range of functions such as provision of market intelligence, promotion, interactive communication, negotiation with suppliers, payment collection, customization and financing. Distribution systems in the tourism sector can be classified on the basis of different levels, one level, two level and three level, depending upon the number of intermediaries involved in tourism.

The intermediary business sector in tourism is facing serious challenges with the sector having declined over the years. There are a number of reasons for this decline, and the declining rate of commission, including: the emphasis on disintermediation; the increasing ease of information access; the increasing experience of travellers; and the increasing rate of IT and smartphone use by customers. The primary reason for tour operators is the benefits they can offer to various stakeholders in the tourism industry and the value enhancements they can bring to the entire value chain of the tourism industry. Distinct benefits are enjoyed by different stakeholders. The principals/suppliers in the context of tour operation are major beneficiaries of intermediaries in tourism. Tourists constitute the other group that gets a range of benefits due to the involvement of intermediaries. Destinations also depend on intermediaries for their success.

Different types of intermediaries in tourism include consolidators, wholesalers, tour operators, travel agents, convention/meeting planners, tour brokers, travel specialists, hotel representatives, tour wholesaler organizations, supplier sales offices, incentive travel firms, corporate travel departments/offices, automated distribution mechanisms, travel consultants, junket representatives, global distribution systems (GDSs), DMSs and public sector agencies, travel and tourism call centres, alliances/consortiums, GSAs, reservation systems of hotels and online agents. Disintermediation and re-intermediation both challenge the existence of intermediaries in tourism. Notwithstanding these challenges, the sector, through value addition and diversified services, continues to have success.

Review questions

Short/medium answer type questions

- Define distribution system.
- What are intermediaries?
- What are the different levels of distribution in tourism?
- Describe the significance of intermediaries in tourism.
- Cite the reasons why tourism intermediaries continue to face a decline.
- What are the elements in the distribution system?
- Write down how suppliers are benefited by the involvement of intermediaries.
- Define disintermediation and re-intermediation.

Essay type questions

- Explain the functions of intermediaries in tourism.
- Describe the role and types of intermediaries in tourism.

References

Baines, P., Fill, C. and Page, K. (2008) *Marketing*. Oxford: Oxford University Press.

Buhalis, D. and Ujma, D. (2006) Intermediaries: Travel Agencies and Tour Operators, in D. Buhalis and C. Costa (eds) *Tourism Business Frontiers: Consumers, Products and Industry*. Burlington, MA: Elsevier Butterworth-Heinemann.

Buhalis, D. and Laws, E. (2001) *Tourism Distribution Channels: Practices, Issues and Transformations*. New York: Continuum.

Cook, A. R., Yale, J. L. and Marqua, J. J. (2009) *Tourism: The Business of Travel*. 4th edn. New Jersey: Prentice Hall.

Forstner, K. (2005) Choosing a Middleman – the Role of Intermediaries in Community Tourism, available at http://www.eldis.org/document/A45764 (accessed 25 June 2018).

Goeldner, R. C. and Ritchie, B. J. R. (2003) *Tourism Principles, Policies and Practices*. New Jersey: John Wiley & Sons.

Hudson, S. (2008) *Tourism and Hospitality Marketing: A Global Perspective*. London: Sage Publications.

Kotler, P., Bowen, J. and Makens, J. (2009) *Marketing for Hospitality and Tourism*. London: Prentice Hall.

Page, J. S. (2009) *Transport and Tourism: Global Perspectives*. Essex: Pearson Education.

Chapter 10

Travel agency management

Learning outcomes

After reading this chapter, you will be able to:

- Describe travel agency from different perspectives.
- Recognize different types of travel agencies.
- Specify the functions and activities of travel agents.
- Explain the organization and management or travel agencies.
- Explain the Billing and Settlement Plan (BSP).

10.1 Introduction

Traditionally, travel agencies have had an important role, as they are the primary retailers that could make the distribution and transaction of travel and tourism products easier, more convenient and smoother. Before the widespread use of the Internet, the travel and tourism industry depended a lot on travel agencies to sell its products. The same was true of customers. Most customers booked travel and tourism services through travel agencies. Earlier travel agencies were known as passenger sales agents. Even before the emergence of air transport, there were travel agencies which could provide the travelling population with access to the required services. The first known travel intermediary, Cox & Kings, was started in the UK way back in 1758 (Swain and Mishra, 2012). Later, the legendary Thomas Cook expanded the business of travel intermediation greatly. In the twentieth century, along with the evolution of air transport, the travel agency business was also expanded. The beginning of the new millennium has posed new challenges for the sector due to potential tourists' reliance on the Internet and the tremendous developments in online transactions.

10.2 Travel agency: different perspectives

The travel agency has been defined from different perspectives: as an intermediary, as a location for easy access to travel products and information, as a sales outlet and so on.

Many authors have taken different perspectives when defining travel agencies. One definition says that a travel agency serves as an "unbiased representative or agent to various suppliers of travel products" (Purzycki, 2001), from which they earn commission. The suppliers mainly include airlines, cruises, hotels, resorts, car rentals, other transport services and tourist attractions. Being a primary intermediary between the travelling public and suppliers, it is viewed as a retail service, selling the travel-associated products directly to the public. In order to understand the concept and functional aspects of a travel agent, a discussion on various perspectives of the travel agency business is given below.

10.2.1 Intermediary that acts as a retailer

Travel agents act as sales outlets for selling the travel and tourism products to the customer. The product selling can be single products or a combination of varied products. Goeldner and Ritchie (2006) view it from the perspective of an intermediary selling the product or a combination of products, such as a package tour; in other words, it is "an intermediary selling the wholesome travel products or parts of products or a combination of the parts to the consumer".

10.2.2 Location for easy access to products and information

Another prominent view of travel agencies is that they primarily provide a convenient location for sale of the travel products. Page (2009) suggests that a travel agency is "a physical location that offers a convenient place to purchase travel products". The location aspect has particular significance, as tourism products are situated away from tourism markets. Suppliers like airlines and hotels are located far away from the locations of the consumers. Traditionally, accessing their products was not easy for a consumer as they would have to travel a long distance to reach the office or a sales outlet of the relevant supplier.

10.2.3 Marketing agent for a supplier

A travel agent can be viewed from a marketing perspective as well. A travel agent takes on the role of marketing and promotion of suppliers' products. This role is highly significant in the case of travel and tourism products, especially since most of the products are intangible in nature and located far away from the point of sale. Moreover, tourism markets are geographically dispersed, and undertaking marketing communication in every market is difficult for suppliers. Travel agents interact with consumers effectively and make the interaction easier and more convenient, especially since they are the agencies in the distribution system that contact customers directly, prior to the consumption of the products. A travel agent, to a certain extent, can encourage a potential consumer to choose a specific product, or indeed discourage them. Brochure display itself is considered a significant promotion effort undertaken by a travel agent. Travel agents display brochures in order to garner the interest of the walk-in customers.

10.2.4 Catalyst of transaction between the principal and the final consumer

A travel agent is able to facilitate the transaction process for principals more easily than the principals can themselves. They can bring suppliers and consumers together. Whatever the marketing or promotion activities undertaken, if they do not result in transactions, then the efforts are futile. The benefit eventually comes from the purchase of the product by the final consumer. Being an agent of the principal, a travel agent facilitates the sales process responsibly. Hudson's (2008) definition is the one that focuses on this aspect, saying that travel agents are "marketing intermediaries that offer the tourism customer a variety of services, including everything from transportation plans and tour packages to insurance services and accommodation".

10.2.5 "Real-time" intermediary

Travel agents also act as "real-time intermediaries" since the transaction takes place as and when the consumer approaches, though possession of the product is still with the principal. On the other hand, in legal terms, they are agents of the principals, e.g. airlines, cruise companies, etc. A travel agent is an agent middleman, acting on behalf of the clients and receiving commissions from them. Biederman et al. (2008) define a travel agent from this perspective, i.e. as a "real-time intermediary between customers and suppliers, the latter being airlines, hotels, rental car companies, cruise lines, and trains". A travel agent acts on the basis of demand and ensures access to travel products from the suppliers. Holloway and Taylor (2006) emphasize this point:

> [A] travel agent's role is dissimilar to that of most other retailers. Only when a customer has decided on a travel purchase do agents approach their principal on their customer's behalf to make a purchase. The travel agents do not, therefore, carry "stock" of travel products.

The above suggests that travel agents are real-time intermediaries.

10.2.6 Reliable source of assistance

For a traveller, a travel agency is a dependable source for various kinds of assistance. A travel agent has to be an expert, knowledgeable about schedules, routing, lodging, currency, prices, regulations, destinations, and the similar aspects of travel and tourism options. Traditionally, travel agencies were the source of information. But in the Internet era, information access is freely available. Still, a travel agency retains the responsibility of providing accurate and reliable information. Furthermore, a travel agency facilitates many travel services, such as arranging visas, insurance, the currency required for travelling and so on. Travellers, particularly international travellers, have many reasons to contact a travel agent, and it becomes the responsibility of the agency to arrange those services. It means, in addition to their roles at point of sale, travel agents arrange various travel facilitators as well. When consumers complain, travel agents are the ones at the receiving end, meaning they are tasked with assisting and trying to solve the issues.

10.3 Types of travel agencies

Though travel agencies are the retailers, there are different types based on the nature of operations. Cook et al. (2009) identified eight types of travel agencies: independent agencies, agency chains, agency channel franchisees, consortium-affiliated agencies, specialty agencies, corporate travel agencies, corporate travel departments and home-based agencies. A brief discussion of the major types of travel agencies follows.

10.3.1 Retail travel agent

Travel agents are fundamentally classed as retailers in the distribution system of the travel and tourism industry. The main concern of a retail travel agent is the choice of location to ensure ready availability of the principals' offerings. Hence the primary duty is to sell the products of the various principals. There are also retail agents for selling the products offered by tour operators. In general, retail travel agents handle the products of both the principals (e.g. airlines and hotels) and the wholesalers (e.g. tour operators). They depend more on commission. They sell directly to the public, arrange all travel documents and act on behalf of the suppliers. They also display the products of the suppliers in order to grab the attention of customers visiting their offices.

10.3.2 Wholesale travel agent

Though travel agents are classed as retailers, some of them act as wholesalers as well. They purchase services of suppliers in large quantities in advance. The same are sold in smaller/individual units as per customer needs. These agents depend more on the volume sales margins instead of commission. Akin to tour operators, they may also sell packages combining the purchased stock. However, the primary focus is on selling the products directly to the customers.

10.3.3 Corporate travel agency

Business travel has progressed at a tremendous pace, meaning corporates now require exclusive agencies to handle the travel requirements of their employees. Corporate travel agencies offer services mainly to business clients. They may have branch offices on site at major clients' locations. In addition to arranging basic travel requirements like airline and hotel bookings, these agencies may have to arrange car rentals, transfers, post-meeting excursions and similar. At times, they may have to organize professional meetings and similar events as well. Business travel decisions are not taken too far in advance and hence last-minute bookings and arrangements are more frequent in the area of business travel.

10.3.4 Specialty travel agency

These agencies offer services for "niche" markets. The activities and operations are focused on specific aspects of travel, a particular tourism sector or a specialist tourism product. Handling a single product, a specialist travel agent can offer the best service due to their exclusive expertise and knowledge in that area. Moreover, the quality of product and unique experience can ensure high levels of repeat business. Examples include specialist travel agencies for the cruise sector and meetings, incentives, conferencing and exhibitions (MICE) travel.

10.3.5 Online travel agent (OTA)

Lately, online travel agencies have had a significant share of the distribution of air travel products. As "re-intermediation" has progressed, more and more online agencies are appearing in tourism distribution. Some of the traditional agents have online media as well in order to meet the challenges of disintermediation and re-intermediation. Online travel agents focus more on the provision of reservations and booking of travel, tourism and hospitality services. Expedia, Priceline.com, Orbitz Worldwide, and Travelocity are perhaps the main online travel agents.

10.3.6 Other types

According to Cook et al. (2009), **independent agencies** are small agencies that are unaffiliated to large organizations and privately owned, traditionally serving customers from walk-in locations or over telephone. They are normally found at single locations, but sometimes outlets of independent agencies can also be seen in other locations. **Agency chains**, meanwhile, are wholly owned mega agencies that have a large number of branch offices in many countries. **Agency channel franchisees** are semi-independent agencies affiliated with each other through franchise organizations. **Consortium-affiliated agencies** are independent agencies that link together through a consortium to increase their buying power. **Corporate travel departments** are found within corporate companies and function as a travel agent for the organization (for its employees' travel requirements). **Home-based agencies** conduct services from their place of residence, mainly using electronic technology. This may be independent or affiliated with some organizations.

10.4 Functions and activities of travel agents

Travel agents perform a wide range of services and activities for travellers as per their needs. They engage primarily in arranging for the needs of travellers. Booking of air seats, transport services, accommodation, recreation and entertainment services, etc. constitute some of the functions of a travel agent. Moreover, a travel agent may have to arrange travellers' travel documents, e.g. passports and visas. An inexperienced traveller will seek a lot of information from an agent. There are a number of complementary services that are undertaken by a travel agent. A detailed discussion of each of the functions of a travel agent in general follows.

10.4.1 Reservation functions

One of the primary duties of travel agents is to make bookings and reservations with principals on behalf of clients. A travel agent is the ideal person/organization to contact for booking a hotel room as they know the quality of the service provided by each hotel. In the past, airline seat reservations were also made primarily by travel agents. Additional services are sometimes booked by travel agents, such as cruise bookings, car rental services, train seats, etc. Since the booking or reservation is done through a travel agent, it is the agent that bears the responsibility to ensure quality services by the suppliers.

Airline seat reservation is an important function of travel agencies across the world. In a travel booking with an airline, the term "journey" is used for representing the entire routing in a ticket/travel record. Traditionally, it was the main function and the most important source of revenue for travel agents. Nowadays, a global distribution system (GDS) helps travel agencies to handle almost all types of bookings. Though GDS is primarily meant for airline reservation, it has additional options to book hotels, cruises, car rentals, railways and the like. **Overbooking** is a common practice of airlines, used

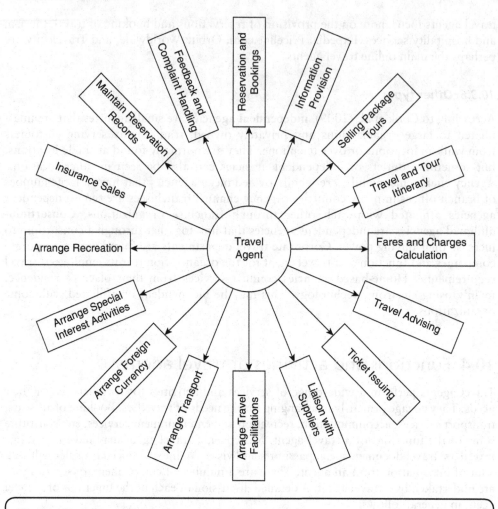

Figure 10.1 Functions of a travel agent

to sell more tickets than are actually available on a route, expecting last-minute cancellations and "no-shows" (passengers who don't check in despite having confirmed their reservation). If the no-shows are fewer than expected and more passengers show up than can be accommodated, the service is referred to as "oversold". The passengers who are left behind are then "bumped" and may be given priority on the very next flight. If the next flight is not there within a certain time frame, then the passengers are entitled to "denied-boarding compensation", where the conditions may vary from airline to airline. In the past, hotel reservations were done over the telephone. However, as technology has advanced, this kind of manual reservation has been sidelined.

10.4.2 Information provision

A tourist or a traveller is an intensive information seeker. This is more relevant for leisure tourists as well as inexperienced travellers. Such tourists may be travelling to strange places where many things will be unknown to them. Moreover, making the right choice about where to go, what to see, where to stay and the like also requires a range of information. For many, a travel agent is a source of reliable information about travel options, travel facilitators (travel documents) needed, places to visit, suitable hotels, amount of money required while travelling and so on. The Internet is now available for getting this information, though the most specific and reliable information can easily be had from a travel agency, making it worthwhile even in the Internet era. A traveller may be curious to know about many things. Also, they may be unaware of some important aspects of travelling. For instance, an airline passenger has to know the items that cannot be carried in hand luggage, and of course the quantity of luggage (and its weight) that may be carried on a particular airline free of charge. The number and size of bags/luggage and their total weight that a passenger is permitted to carry free of charge while travelling is called **free baggage allowance**. Ticket charge is inclusive of baggage allowance for the permissible quantity. For international flights, it is usually around 30 kilograms of checked baggage and 7 kilograms of hand baggage. If the piece method is applicable, the size and number of baggage items will be specified, e.g. two pieces of checked baggage and one or two small pieces of luggage as hand luggage which can be stored in the overhead compartment or under the seat during the flight. A travel agent should ensure that the passenger who purchased a ticket from them is aware of such information. Hence, a travel agent has to know a varied and broad range of the most accurate, specific and timely information about any transport associated with travel and tourism.

10.4.3 Travel plan/itinerary planning

When one travels to different locations, it is always recommended to have the expertise of a professional to prepare the itinerary in order to ensure smooth travel, avoid double routing, reduce the travel expenditure and avoid any hiccups while travelling. Having the specific geographical knowledge is an advantage for a travel agent so that they can prepare the travel itinerary that suits the requirements of the traveller. While preparing air travel itineraries, a range of areas needs to be considered, such as minimum connecting time (MCT), time needed to transfer from terminal to terminal in the case of large airports, time needed for transfer from airport to hotel and back, etc.

CASE STUDY 10.1

Travellers are returning to travel agents

When the Internet took over travel intermediation, travellers' preference was for online booking. After some years of making bookings over the Internet and the simultaneous information boom, some Internet-savvy people began to return to travel agents to make their travel arrangements. Certainly, some people have grown weary of online searches and the excessive consumption of their time for this searching, and indeed purchasing. Some are confused about what is available and find it difficult to decide and make a purchase, as there is such a large volume of information and options available to them online.

Certainly, the number of travel agencies has reduced drastically: Internet travel and booking sites began to take their business nearly 20 years ago. In the US, according to an estimate of the Bureau of Labor Statistics, there are currently about 70,000 full-time travel agents operating there. In 2000, that number was 124,000. Different survival strategies were adopted by the surviving travel agencies. Many trained to become specialists in various travel products, like adventure, multigenerational/group, cruise and luxury. By adopting different operational practices, they reduced the cost of operation and began charging for rendering services. They are active as and when they are needed, disregarding the time, and have become saviours during all sorts of travellers' crises. Moreover, they can suggest the right choice without travellers having to mine the large volume of information online.

Travellers are returning to travel agents because they can be recommended the right choice according to their preferences.

> [T]hey are returning to travel agents, relying on their expertise to do the research, the comparing, the vetting, the suggesting of the right place, the right time, the right price, and all those other details the DIY planner may have either sweated for days or forgotten altogether.
>
> (Schensul, 2016)

Clarity and curation requirements lead people to approach travel agents. According to MMGY, a travel and hospitality marketing firm, in 2015, 18 per cent of travellers worked with an adviser, a 50 per cent jump from the previous year. Millennials are now a major customer segment. In MMGY's 2015 Portrait of the American Traveler report, 34 per cent of the millennials consulted a traditional travel agent in the year preceding the survey and 39 per cent were planning to do so in the next two years. Some potential travellers search on the Internet to find a suitable travel agent as well. According to the report, 22 per cent of Americans making $50,000 or more made bookings through an agent in 2015. Many people go to travel agents to plan more complex trips, international trips or trips to places they have not yet been. Innovative ideas are introduced by travel agents to attract customers as well. Another important fact is that the majority of the face-to-face travel consultations result in bookings.

Source: Schensul (2016)

Read the above case carefully and answer the following questions:

- Identify the reasons why travellers are returning to travel agents for bookings.
- Briefly discuss the changing scenario in travel intermediation.

10.4.4 Airfares and charges

Airfare calculation was once a laborious task. There was a very complex formula used to prepare the most economical fare for multi-destination travels. Airfare calculation became easy through the use of GDSs and less significant when e-ticketing services became common, though many of the traditional rules are still followed. Travel involves many other charges as well. For example, the traveller may need to use the services of tour guides and rental cars. There are some additional charges to pay while travelling, such as entry fees needed for entering museum or other attractions. Hence, prior to travel, the traveller has to know how much money they are required to carry and to pay for these services. Once again, travel agency services will be of use to an inexperienced traveller especially.

When manual ticketing was in practice, the personnel who calculated the fares had to have adequate knowledge, expertise and skill. They had to be able to identify, locate and name countries and cities, prepare itineraries, identify local currencies, code and decode the city, airline and country codes, and interpret the terms, definitions and codes used in air transportation. Passenger Air Tariff (PAT) was the source of information for calculation of fares. It has come as a set of four books: Maximum Permitted Mileages, General Rules, Worldwide Fares and Worldwide Fare Rules. These were published periodically. Fare construction formula is used to calculate the fares of multiple destination travel itineraries, and such an approach is called journey concept. Pricing unit concept is the other type, in which fare was calculated as a single pricing unit. Apart from origin and destination, an air travel journey can consist of intermediate points (transfer points) which are classified as either **intermediate stop over point** (break for more than 24 hours) or **intermediate no stop over point** (arrives and departs within 24 hours). A stop over refers to the break in the journey, at an intermediate point, which lasts for more than 24 hours. It is basically a transfer point. Types of journeys identified for airfare construction are discussed below.

One-way trip (OW)

This is a usual, simple, one-way journey from one place to another. The journey commences from origin, ends in a destination, and does not either return to the origin or proceed to another destination.

Round trip (RT)

This journey consists of travel from one point to another point and return to the original point, and which has only two flight legs. The passenger has to return to the origin place itself. Ultimately this consists of an outbound trip and an inbound trip back to the point of origin. Onward routing and the return routing are the same.

Circle trip (CT)

This journey consists of travel from a place and return to the same place, after a continuous, circuitous air route. Origin and return points are the same and two or more cities other than the origin are included in the journey, which is circuitous in shape. There can be two or more stop overs, as the routing in each direction involves different intermediate cities and/or airlines, e.g. Rome (ROM)–Paris (PAR)–Zurich (ZRH)–Madrid (MAD)–Rome (ROM).

Open jaw (OJ)

In this type of journey, there will be a surface transport in between. A passenger may take one or more surface transport legs in between and the journey may still be a round trip or circle trip, which is interrupted by a surface or non-air in the routing. Open jaw occurs when a return flight may be from a different airport than the one the passenger arrived to. It can also occur when a passenger returns to a different airport than the airport of departure for the onward journey. Furthermore, it can occur when both of the above happen together. Two types of open jaws, single open jaw and double open jaw, are described below:

- *Single open jaw (SOJ):* this consists of one surface transport sector in between. The following types can be seen in it:
  - o Turnaround single open Jaw (TSOJ): the outward point of arrival and the inward point of departure are different, e.g. London–Dubai/Muscat–London.
  - o Origin single open Jaw (OSOJ): the inward point of arrival and the outward point of departure are different, e.g. London–Bangkok/Bangkok–Paris.

- *Double open jaw (DOJ):* this consists of two surface transport sectors, one at the origin and the other at the turnaround point, e.g. London–Kuala Lumpur/Singapore–Paris.

Airfares are divided into two categories: normal fares and special fares. Normal fares are usually without restrictions, and in certain cases, there are a few restrictions in terms of number of stop overs and transfers, seasonal/day of week application and flight application. There are full refunds for cancelled tickets on unrestricted normal fares. Special fares are promotion fares, with a number of restrictions applied, including the period of stay, advance purchase requirements, reservations and payment limits, day/time of travel, eligibility restrictions, refundability and changeability. Public special fares and inclusive tour fares are some examples of special fares. Public special fares are usually meant for late booking. Advance purchase excursion (APEX) fares need advance reservation with advance payment and confirmed reservation for all sectors. Excursion fares are offered during certain seasons and with specified minimum and maximum stay durations. Inclusive tour fares and reduced fares for specific reasons are also offered. Discounted fares are usually restricted fares. Negotiated fares are the special discounted prices on the basis of negotiations, usually between an intermediary and airline. This can happen between corporations and airlines for their executives' frequent travel. Fares will be much discounted. Consolidator fares are offered to consolidators, who buy tickets from airlines in bulk at wholesale rates and sell tickets at discounted rates. Discounted fares are given to certain categories of passenger, e.g. senior citizens, military personnel, children, students, etc. Fares are usually published or shown in the local currency of the country of commencement. However, there are countries where fares are published in dollars or euros. But for fare construction, this would be difficult to calculate in different currencies, and hence a neutral unit of construction (NUC) was used, when fare was calculated manually. The conversion will be done only at the end of the fare construction process. The IATA Rates of Exchange (IROE), which is published regularly, is used for conversion of airfares into local currencies. Fare construction is a process consisting of a series of sequential steps. The published fares, mileage, mileage surcharge, etc. have to be obtained from the documents. A sample fare construction formula for a round trip/circle trip is shown in Table 10.1.

Table 10.1 A sample fare construction formula on IATA for a round trip/
circle trip

Sl. no.	Steps	Activity
1	FCP	Identify fare construction point (FCP) of the fare component after selecting a fare break point.
2	NUC	Quote the NUC (neutral unit of construction) from the origin to the final point based on GI (global indicator), fare type and carrier code.
3	RULE	Follow conditions of the rule. Check for specified routings.
4	MPM	Note the maximum distance between the FCPs (MPM – maximum permitted mileage).
5	TPM	Add up the TPMs and compare with MPM (TPM – ticketed point mileage).
6	EMA	If TPM is greater than MPM, look for a TPM deduction (EMA – excess mileage allowance).
7	EMS	If the EMA is nil or insufficient, find out the excess mileage surcharge (EMS) by dividing TPM by MPM.
8	HIP	Look for a higher intermediate point (HIP) fare in the direction of the fare component.
9	RULE	Follow the rule of HIP fare, particularly the number of stop overs, transfer, seasonality or day of the week, flight application conditions, including blackout dates.
10	AF	Identify the resulting applicable fare (AF) in the NUC for the entire journey.
11	SUB TTL	Find out the sum of outbound and inbound AF NUCs.
12	CHECK CTM	Look for the highest RT NUC from the origin to the highest rated stop over point in the whole journey. If the CTM > SUB TTL NUC, find "Plus Up" by deducting SUB TTL from Highest RT NUC.
13	TOTAL	Sum up all the NUCs including Plus Ups.
14	IROE	Multiply NUC by the IROE (IATA Rate of Exchange) of the local currency. Drop trailing zeros, if any.
15	LCF	Round off the resulting local currency fare, with exact decimals.

Source: Adapted from IATA (2008)

10.4.5 Arranging tickets/booking documents

Once a seat is booked by a travel agent on behalf of an airline, then it is that agency's responsibility to issue the confirmed ticket to the traveller. In the same way, when a hotel room is booked, then the document containing the confirmation of the room has to be arranged for the traveller. For all bookings and reservations made, the travel agent has to provide the proof or a document to the traveller so that they may receive those services.

Air tickets are issued by both airlines and authorized intermediaries. Manual tickets were replaced by electronic tickets (e-tickets) some years ago. E-tickets are used to document the sale and track the usage of passenger transportation electronically. When travel agents issue manual tickets, they are validated, which is done with identification plates provided by the authorities, e.g. IATA. For a travel agency, a unique code is given for validation. The ticket validation is done using a "ticket imprinter".

Traditionally, airline tickets were small rectangular-shaped booklets containing coupons meant for specific purposes. They were issued by travel agents accredited by airlines. The ticket booklets consisted passenger coupons, flight coupons, audit coupons and agent coupons. Passenger coupons were meant for the passenger as the record of payment. Flight coupons were used for travel in each sector of the travel itinerary. A travel agent could retain the agent coupon and the audit coupon was for accounting purposes. An agent coupon was detached as and when the ticket was issued and filed by the agent, while the audit coupon was attached with a sale report to be given to airlines for their use. Traditionally, before the widespread use of the Internet and GDS use, the ABC World Airways Guide and Official Airlines Guide (OAG) were used as part of air travel itinerary design, fare calculation and ticketing.

Currently, an e-ticket or electronic record is provided which is a summary of the travel itinerary with essential details including fares, class of travel, date of issue, origin and destination points with terminal names, expected time of arrival and departure (ETA and ETD), tax, passenger name record (PNR), ticket number, ticket status, free baggage allowance, airline codes, airport codes and essential applicable conditions of travel. Also, travel agents traditionally issued a miscellaneous charges order (MCO) as a prepaid voucher, valuable like a bank cheque, for making payments for excess baggage, car rentals, surface transportation, etc. Prepaid ticket advice (PTA) is issued by travel agents asking airlines to issue a ticket for a passenger who begins a journey from a location other than from where the payment was made. Someone else can also make payment on behalf of the passenger from another location and PTA may be used. An open ticket is issued at times. This is a ticket that does not specify the date on which the service is to be performed, leaving the passenger to secure a reservation at a later date.

10.4.6 Advising on travel services

Similar to information provision, a travel agent is considered to be a reliable source of advice on travel options and other services. Travellers, especially first-time travellers, need a wide range of advice. When one travels to a strange place, the relevance of advice is elevated. Travellers may be worried about how much extra money they will need, and what currency they should carry when travelling to an unfamiliar country. Immigration formalities and requirements, customs formalities, currency conversion rates, etc. are all essential information to be communicated to the traveller prior to the trip. A travel agent can certainly provide the necessary advice, which may not be easily obtainable otherwise.

10.4.7 Communication and negotiation

The travel agent negotiates the rates for the services provided by the suppliers. Also, it is important to ensure the quality of the services to be provided. The travel agent has the power to negotiate with clients, as it is a major source of bookings, reservations and customers. Furthermore, the travel agent communicates effectively with suppliers and other clients to make the distribution and sale of the products easy and to ensure quality services are delivered to the customers. Travel agents' communication is critical in the entire value chain, as it is the agency that deals with a potential traveller. Also, it can provide valuable feedback to suppliers, which will be very important from a marketing point of view.

International travel and time calculation

Identifying local times and total transportation times while travelling from east to west and west to east is a difficult task, since such travel often crosses different regions and different time zones. Greenwich Mean Time (GMT) is the base used for calculating local times. On either side of the meridian line are 12 time zones, each with a one-hour difference between them. GMT+ and GMT− are used to represent time zones on the east and west of the meridian line, respectively. In order to calculate the local time, it is essential to know the time zone in which the country or destination is situated. The following example will make it clear.

If the local time in Buenos Aires (BUE), Argentina is 15:25 (3:25 pm), what will the local time is New Delhi (DEL), India be then?

> BUE is GMT − 3 and DEL is GMT + 5.5
> The time difference between these countries is 8.5 hours (3 + 5.5).
> Therefore, the time in New Delhi will be 8 hours and 30 minutes ahead of the time in BUE.
> In other words, the local time in New Delhi is 23:55 (11:55 pm) on the same day.
> (If both countries are on the same side of the meridian line, then the time difference is taken by subtracting the GMT figures).

Another responsibility for the travel planner is the calculation of total transportation time. The flight ticket issued will show the local times of departure and arrival. To get the total travel time, the local times have to be converted into GMT and the difference has to be identified. The following example will make it clear.

A flight leaves at 19:27 (7:27 pm) on a Tuesday from Montreal (YMQ), Canada and arrives in Dubai (DXB), UAE at 22:30 (10:30 pm) the next day, with two stops in between. Find out the total transportation time.

> First Step: Convert local time into GMT.
> YMQ = GMT − 5
> Departure time = 19:27 + 5 = 24:27 (i.e. 00:27 the following day)
> DXB = GMT + 4
> Arrival time = 22:30−4 = 18:30.
> Next step: Find out the difference between the times
> 18:30−00:27 = 18:03
> > (During summer, some countries advance their standard time by 1 hour, which is called daylight saving time.)

Interestingly, when the International Date Line (IDL – the imaginary north–south line through the Pacific Ocean) is crossed, a difference of one day takes place. When the movement is from the west, and crosses the IDL, even if the journey is for a short duration, the traveller will reach their destination on the following day. The opposite will take place (they will gain a day) when the traveller travels from east to west over the IDL.

Consider the following activity to learn about international travel and time calculation:

- Search for airline schedules and attempt to calculate total transportation times from scheduled times of departure and arrivals of various flights.

10.4.8 Arranging travel documents

In addition to flight tickets and hotel room bookings, an international traveller needs some other travel documents as well. A visa is an essential document for a traveler, as it is a prerequisite for entering a foreign country. Similarly, it is important/recommended to have travel insurance when travelling to a foreign country. For some countries, health/vaccination certificates are also required. A travel agent is vested with the responsibility to arrange such travel documents for the traveller. A traveller arranging all such documents by himself/herself will be time-consuming and a waste of energy. In most cases, the offices that issue such documents are in different cities.

A passport is a document issued by country authorities that proves that the bearer is a citizen of that country. It establishes the identity of the traveller and their nationality and authorizes them to travel outside the country, as well as indicating protection rights for them while travelling aboard. The validity of the passport is specified in a passport. Visas are endorsed in a passport. Different types of passports are issued. Information included in a passport essentially includes full name, parent(s) name(s), nationality, passport number, validity, date of birth, date of issue, place of issue, authority of issuance, address, spouse and children, signature and photograph. A travel agent should verify the passport validity, emigration status, minimum validity required for getting visas for visiting foreign countries, etc. For visiting some countries, specific ID cards are also issued.

A visa is another requirement for visiting a foreign country. It's an endorsement by authorities of the country the traveller wishes to travel to and is issued for a specific period of time and purpose. In certain cases, it is initially issued as a separate document obtained in advance of the trip and the stamping is done at the time of entry into the country. A valid passport is the most important prerequisite for obtaining a visa. A visa specifies the period of validity and the number of entries allowed into the country, along with the type of visa or purpose of the visit. Even if a visa is issued, the final decision regarding the entry is vested with the emigration officials at the passport control office at airports, etc. Travel agents have to advise the traveller on how a visa can be obtained, documents to submit with the visa application, passport validity, etc. Details about passports and visas are provided in another chapter in this book.

A travel agent should also be familiar with the health conditions, vaccinations required, etc. for the country in question. Health is a major concern while travelling through foreign lands. For those countries where immunizations are required, the traveller must record vaccinations or other health measures in a document called "international certificate of vaccination". The necessary health certificates need to be arranged for making the travel possible and smooth. Arranging the required insurance is also important. Travel insurance is available for death, permanent disablement, medical expenses, luggage, personal effects and travel documents, personal liability, cancellations, hijacking, travel trade indemnity and legal expenses.

10.4.9 Mediator when customer complains

Variability is a feature of tourism products. Performance variation and service delivery quality fluctuation may be experienced in service products. Also, it's a people industry in which customer satisfaction depends greatly on the "moments of truth" and the people who deliver the service. Hence, the possibility of receiving complaints on service delivery may be greater. A travel agent, in such cases, acts as a mediator who can handle such complaints efficiently. Both travellers and suppliers of services can utilize travel agents in order to have an amicable settlement to the complaints raised.

10.5 Organization and management

Efficient management and quality service are necessary for the competitive survival of travel agencies. Setting up a travel agency necessitates care in terms of the location, as it is a retailer. The accessibility of it is crucial since the public has to reach the office to make a purchase. Adequate space is required within the office not only for its functioning, but even for the display of suppliers' products. Financial soundness and financial standing of the agency are important, particularly for getting accreditation for issuing international air tickets. Accreditation parameters differ from country to country. Basic requirements of starting a business are applicable for this as well. In addition, ticket issuance accreditation of IATA or the respective authority needs to be obtained. Having proficient staff with IATA/UFTAA qualifications is a basic requirement for getting accreditation. In some countries, recognition of national authorities is also required. Necessary physical facilities for starting an agency are prerequisites as well. In addition to the location and accessibility of the office, security, visibility and appearance are also important in the establishment of a travel agency.

There are proprietorship, partnership and corporate types of organization in the travel agency business. Franchisees are also common. The organizational structure varies; however, in general, an agency may have a managing director, supported by vice presidents for operations and marketing. Other staff may include general manager for operations, sales managers, branch managers, advertising director, agent supervisor and customer service manager. There may be specific staff for operations ranging from air ticket bookings to travel documents arrangement. The staff should be well versed in various travel-related information and knowledge. Providing inaccurate information can cause an agency to be seen as unreliable by customers and can cause those customers to switch to other firms. The staff in the agency should have the knowledge about the "best buys", and the ability to read timetables and other various data sources. Furthermore, good communication skills are a fundamental requirement for travel agency staff. The knowledge required for being a front office staff or sales staff is very high compared to the same personnel selling physical products. Travel agent staff should have adequate knowledge and the ability to gather and read travel data sources, GDS proficiency, knowledge about products and customers, communication skills, packaging skills, presentation skills, customer relationship management abilities and organizational skills. Well-trained staff are an asset for a travel agency. Traits like passion for working, punctuality, positive personality, creativity, etc. can enhance the quality of service delivery.

All accounting procedures must also be carried out. Basic journals such as the cash receipts journal, accounts receivable journal and a cash disbursement journal are maintained in travel agencies. Ledgers also need to be ensured. ARC/IATA/BSP Ledger, tax records and employee records are also maintained in travel agencies. Nowadays, all are computerized though hard copies are also used. The cash disbursement file, asset and liability files, etc. also need to be kept. Financial reports including financial statements, operating statements and cash flow analysis are maintained. Travel agencies have the following types of accounting-related books and records.

Travel agencies mainly survived through the commission of principals. In the past, air ticketing was the main source of commission, as airlines offered decent amounts of commission for the sale of each ticket. Travel agency commission from airlines was significant in the early era of air transport growth. Until the end of the twentieth century, the practice continued to prevail. When the e-ticketing facility emerged along with the growth of Internet use and the entry of low-cost carriers (LCCs), things turned upside down. LCCs do not usually promote the sale of their seats through travel agents; instead, websites and other online intermediaries are their primary distribution channels. The International Air Transport Association (IATA), the most prominent international association of airlines, has even been discouraging airlines from giving commissions. They set up a zero commission agenda some years back to avoid the commission burden on airlines as the airline business is characterized by thin profit margins. Hence travel agencies are diversifying their offerings and finding new services through which to earn income. There is commission for arranging other tourism services, such as booking hotel rooms and cruises. Also, travel agencies earn service fees for arranging travel facilities. Nowadays, retail agents charge a nominal fee for issuing airline tickets in some locations. To summarize, commissions from different suppliers such as airlines, cruises, tour operators, car rental agencies, hotels and resorts, and bulk booking discounts and service charges constitute major income sources for travel agents. Incentives, override commissions (given when an agency surpasses a certain quota set by the supplier) and mark-ups on tours also contribute to revenue. The financial transactions with airlines are carried out separately through a unique mechanism called the Billing and Settlement Plan (BSP)

10.6 Billing and Settlement Plan

The (BSP) is a unique mechanism used by airlines and IATA-approved travel agencies to settle sales accounts. By using the services of electronic data processing centres (DPCs), a BSP makes the process of reporting and remittances easier for the IATA agents. IATA-initiated BSP is a system designated to facilitate and simplify the selling, reporting and remitting procedures of accredited travel agents and similar intermediaries that directly purchase airline products and consequently improve the financial control and cash of participating airlines. Intermediaries need to settle the accounts once a week or every fortnight only. In this way, a standardized mechanism is in place for the settlement of tickets of airlines. Ticket sales agents like travel agents can make use of this for settling the amounts of tickets sold, through a designated clearing bank. IATA agents can issue standard traffic documents (STDs) on behalf of all the participating airlines. With the help of DPCs, BSP can calculate the billings and amounts that the IATA agents remit to the designated banks and divide the total amount into each airline's account.

Settlement services have been provided since 1971, when IATA introduced its IATA Settlement Systems (ISS). in the past, in the US, ARC network undertook airline-related matters on behalf of IATAN (International Air Transport Association Network). There, ticket revenue was obtained by airlines through the Airline Reporting Corporation (ARC), through a system of networked banks. Travel agent sales report is an important one. Weekly/fortnightly sales reports are prepared. In the US, traditionally they were prepared as ARC sales reports. ISS is a service network consisting of BSPs for passenger transport services and Cargo Accounts Settlement Systems (CASS) for cargo transport.

BSP is now relevant in more than 140 countries. This makes it a cost-effective system for selling the tickets of participating airlines, by reducing product distribution costs of airlines and by reducing administrative overhead costs of both parties. Settlement of the amounts due to airlines became more efficient through this system. Without BSP, travel agents have to report and settle the amounts of each airline separately. With BSP, travel agents can issue STDs and prepare a single consolidated report and send one remittance to the clearing bank. The non-IATA airlines can also be part of BSP, provided they adhere to the rules of the BSP. The agent can prepare a single AST (agency sales tracking) for all sales for the specific period, say one week or 15 days, and the same AST with supporting documents is forwarded to the DPC. Electronic sending is in practice now. From the DPC, after analysing and preparing agents, billing analysis for each agent for each airline is forwarded to them. Using the STD, this common document can be used for all airlines, instead of an individual airline's own stocks. BSPlink is available, which enables the settlement of financial transactions between travel agents and airlines.

Recently, IATA has introduced a new financial settlement system which is more efficient and has increased capabilities and benefits for both airlines and travel agents. Called NewGen ISS, it aims to modify the current ISS business model so as to deliver faster, safer and more cost-effective and relevant financial settlement services and solutions to both the supplier and the intermediary. While airlines are benefited through faster settlement, safer funds and lower costs of distribution, travel agents can have more personalized products and services, enhanced customer support and more cost-effective solutions. According to IATA (n.d.), this new business model consists of the following features:

- Three levels of travel agent accreditation, enabling agents to choose the most suitable option
- A Remittance Holding Capacity (RHC), which can ensure a safer selling process
- Global Default Insurance (GDI), which will offer travel agents a flexible financial security option and help to reduce default losses for airlines
- IATA EasyPay, a new secure and cost-effective "pay as you go" e-wallet solution for agents to issue tickets via the BSP

10.7 Summary

Traditionally, travel agencies play an important role in travel and tourism business. A travel agent has been defined from different perspectives: as an intermediary, as a location for easy access to travel products and information, as a sales outlet and so on. There are different types of travel agencies, including independent agencies, agency chains, agency channel franchisees, consortium-affiliated agencies, specialty agencies, corporate travel agencies, corporate travel departments and home-based agencies. Travel agencies undertake a range of tasks. Booking and reservation of tourism services is the most important among them. Also, they provide vital information for travellers, advise them to take decisions, suggest and prepare travel itineraries, etc. In addition to flight tickets and hotel room bookings, an international traveller needs some other travel documents as well. A visa is an essential document for a traveller, as it is a prerequisite for entering a foreign country. Similarly, it is recommended and important to have travel insurance when travelling. In some countries, health/vaccination certificates are also required for entry. Moreover, travel agents also function on behalf of the suppliers in distributing the products and in ensuring transactions. The Billing and Settlement Plan (BSP) is a unique mechanism used by airlines and IATA-approved travel agencies to settle the sales accounts. By using the services of electronic data processing centres (DPCs), BSPs make the process of reporting and remittances easier for IATA agents. As disintermediation and re-intermediation have progressed, traditional travel agencies have begun to face severe challenges. Their competitive survival depends on the diversification of their functions and ensuring quality services.

Review questions

Short/medium answer type questions

- Conceptualize travel agencies from different perspectives.
- Write short notes on different types of travel agencies.
- List the functions of a travel agency.
- What are the different types of journeys in air travel and airfares?
- Give a brief account of visas and passports.
- Discuss the operation and management of travel agency business.
- Describe the Billing and Settlement Plan (BSP).

Essay type questions

- Describe the functions of a travel agency.

References

Biederman, S. P., Lai, J., Laitamaki, M. J., Messerli, R. H., Nyheim, P. and Plog, C. S. (2008) *Travel and Tourism: An Industry Primer*. New Jersey: Pearson Education.

Cook, A. R., Yale, J. L. and Marqua, J. J. (2009) *Tourism: The Business of Travel*. 4th edn. New Jersey: Prentice Hall.

Goeldner, R. C. and Ritchie, J. R. B. (2006) *Tourism: Principles, Practices and Philosophies*. New Jersey: John Wiley & Sons.

Holloway, J. C. and Taylor, N. (2006) *The Business of Tourism*. 7th edn. Essex: Prentice Hall.

Hudson, S. (2008) *Tourism and Hospitality Marketing: A Global Perspective*. London: Sage Publications.

IATA (2008) International Air Transport Association-IATA-UFTAA Foundation Course Study Material. Montreal: IATA.

IATA, NewGen ISS, available at http://www.iata.org/whatwedo/airline-distribution/pages/newgen-iss.aspx?tab=5.

Page, J. S. (2009) *Transport and Tourism: Global Perspectives*. Essex: Pearson Education.

Purzycki, S. J. (2001) *A Practical Guide to Fares and Ticketing*. Albany, NY: Delmar Learning.

Schensul, J. (2016) Why Travellers are Returning to Travel Agents, available at https://www.usatoday.com/story/travel/advice/2016/11/18/travel-agents/94028838/ (accessed 15 June 2018).

Swain, K. S. and Mishra, J. (2012) *Tourism: Principles and Practices*. New Delhi: Oxford University Press.

Travel distribution systems

11.1 Introduction

The travel industry is a major user of data and information of all kinds. As Poon (1993) states, IT has been immersed deeply into the tourism system. Certainly, the growing application of information and communication technology (ICT) in tourism has transformed the industry. The phenomenal expansion of air transportation owes much to the development of the jet engine which substantially improved aircraft productivity by increasing the number of passengers carried over much greater distances, which itself augmented tourism development. Experts are also of the opinion that the computer reservation system (CRS) has had an equally significant impact on productivity in the travel industry, specifically in respect of marketing. CRSs became an essential component of travel distribution systems (Buhalis and Licarta, 2002). IT advancements have transformed the CRS into a much more comprehensive GDS. By the 1980s, it had re-engineered the entire marketing and distribution system of airlines.

CRSs/GDSs constitute the hub of IT applications for commercial purposes in airlines and GDSs now provide the backbone for communication between principals and intermediaries. GDSs offer flight schedules, availabilities, passenger information (e.g. PNR, name of the passenger, address of the passenger, phone numbers), fare quotes and rules; and they offer facilities for printing tickets as well. Nowadays, ICT and internal CRSs are used extensively to support the Internet distribution of airline seats. CRSs are accorded with transaction processing systems (TPSs). The influence of IT has continued and led to the expansion of scope and functioning of CRSs. They have been transformed into GDSs. Sabre, Amadeus, Galileo and Worldspan are the leading GDSs in the world, which are also referred to as travel supermarkets (Go, 1992). In the meantime, other technology solutions like videotext systems have entered the scene. The advent of mobile devices has revolutionized the communication process, and soon they will also became part and parcel of travel distribution.

Some of the leading online travel intermediaries are listed below:

- Expedia
- Booking.com
- ebookers.com
- eDreams
- FlightSite
- Flyin.com
- Opodo
- Orbitz
- lastminute.com
- Webjet
- MakeMyTrip
- Travelocity
- Priceline.com
- Travelstart
- FlightHub
- JustFly
- KAYAK
- Orbitz
- Wotif.com
- Travelgenio

11.2 Electronic distribution

The Internet, being a universal and interactive means of communication, has influenced the electronic travel distribution system dramatically, especially considering consumers can undertake their entire tourism product search and booking over the Internet. This has created a lot of opportunities for businesses. The increasing scope of product transaction and distribution led to the formation of Web-based travel agencies. An online travel agency specializes in online sourcing and online bookings. Some of the online travel agencies are owned and managed by leading GDSs. A few major travel agencies have developed their own online travel distributions (e.g. www.thomascook.com). Internet portals have also developed online travel distribution, often by sourcing their travel context from external online agents and suppliers (Buhalis, 2003). Of late, along with disintermediation, re-intermediation is also gathering pace. There are now a range of online intermediaries acting in different ways via the Internet. Benckendorff et al. (2014) have identified a range of online intermediaries:

- Online travel agents (OTAs)
- Meta search engines

- Aggregators
- Trip planning sites
- Affiliates
- Group buying sites
- Opaque sites
- Product review sites

Apart from these, GDSs, destination management systems, social media platforms and mobile apps of various travel intermediaries are also playing key roles in travel distribution. In fact, there are GDSs behind most of the online and traditional travel intermediaries, though they rarely involve direct sale to travellers. The most interesting development in air travel distribution is the emergence of the New Distribution Capability (NDC) of International Air Transport Association (IATA). Let's now learn more about the important electronic intermediaries in tourism, particularly in the travel sector.

11.3 New Distribution Capability

IATA has taken a revolutionary step towards transforming the supplier–intermediary transmission and enhancing electronic air travel distribution to the most advanced levels through the introduction of the NDC. According to IATA, the NDC is a travel industry-supported programme ("NDC Program") launched by them for the development and market adoption of a new XML-based data transmission standard ("NDC Standard"). This can enhance the communication channels between airlines and intermediaries, particularly retailers. This IATA-led collaborative industry initiative to build an open, Internet-based data exchange standard primarily supports current and enhanced airline distribution capability. This new technology solution can eliminate the current distribution limitations, such as lack of scope for product differentiation and time to market, limited access to full and rich air content, lack of transparent shopping experience, and high distribution costs (IATA, n.d.).

Currently, airlines push the contents to intermediaries, like GDSs, who finally create the product offerings for the travel agents and travellers. In this long process, many of the product attributes like fare, inventory, etc., which are extremely dynamic in nature, do not reach the end customer in the right time. The existing travel distribution technologies, to a large extent, are based on decades-old legacy technologies. Due to this, a range of products and services that airlines sell directly are not reaching the final customer. GDSs are limited in terms of innovation in offering enhanced shopping capabilities. Furthermore, airlines have limited control only in their own products while being distributed via GDSs. In addition, GDSs use age-old teletype messaging protocols for transmission. In most of the other sectors, distribution systems have advanced features. Moreover, the existing system of air product distribution via GDSs is costly as airlines have to offer transaction fees and a fixed fee per message exchanged to the network providers (SITA/ARINC) due to the legacy nature of the messages.

Belobaba et al. (2017) describe the key changes due to the arrival of NDC in the following way:

> The most important change contemplated by NDC is that requests for seat availability and fare quotes can be sent to the airline for real-time evaluation. In essence, NDC will provide for the equivalent of "direct connect" between the airline's own

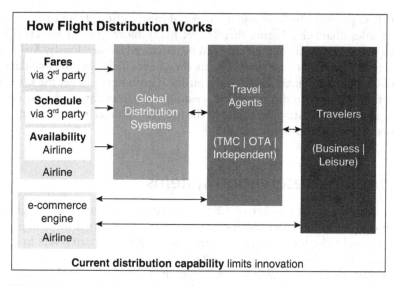

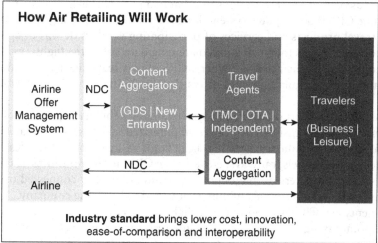

Figure 11.1 Overall shopping landscape of airline shopping before and after NDC
Source: IATA – NDC, June 2018 (Printed with permission)

inventory in its PSS and all distribution channels, both direct and indirect. "Indirect" channels that involve travel agencies (whether traditional or on-line) as well as GDS providers will receive real-time availability and fare quote information from a new "airline pricing and merchandising engine" that will reside with the airline. The airline's direct distribution channels, including its own web site and reservations call center, will similarly receive information in real-time.

Airlines can increase personalization in product offerings and simultaneously travellers can get access to personalized offers, real-time fares, a full suite of ancillary products and services such as priority check-in and a variety of meal options from the airline through the indirect sales channels. Agents thereby get many more options to serve passengers and the quality of service from their side can be enhanced tremendously. Airlines are also able to open up the sales of all the products they have, including the ancillary services, through all the distribution channels of the airline. Customers can get the same shopping experience that is provided directly to the customer. Airlines can get better control over the content and differentiate their brand in the indirect channel as well. Moreover, distribution costs can be substantially reduced.

11.4 Computer reservation systems

The airline industry is the pioneer of CRSs. Reservation systems were originally developed by air carriers to deal with the increasing volume of information and processing of their own internal ticketing processes. In general, a CRS as a term refers to a computerized system set up for booking of services/facilities offered by businesses. These systems emerged as transaction processing facilities/systems (TPF/S) that could handle large volumes of data as part of the transactions that happen in the business. According to Foster (1994), airline CRS is a computer system designed for use by booking agents to facilitate the sale of travel products and services of participating vendors. It was designed to provide an automated means for storing and managing data about the flights, available seats and fares controlled by their airline owners. CRS allows real-time access to airline fares, schedules and seating availability and offers the capability of booking reservations and generating tickets.

Many sectors are incorporating such systems mainly for making the booking/selling of the services/facilities easier. These are computerized systems, which can process the reservations through a database that handles details of inventory, schedules and prices, among other details. Hotels, railways, etc. also use CRSs in their businesses. CRSs run on mainframes, minicomputers or microcomputers and are usually connected through data communication links to terminals within various branches of the company.

Travel agents use CRSs to find relevant flight information and to make a reservation directly without having to telephone an airline reservation office (Klein and Langenohl, 1994). Airlines enable CRS to allow direct access through terminals for intermediaries to check availability, make reservations and print tickets (Buhalis, 2003). This usage of CRS basically facilitates the product distribution and it is made possible through computerized or videotext system terminals. CRS enables travel agencies to update information constantly, to obtain specific and accurate information, to make bookings and issue tickets, and to obtain a wide range of related products.

Archdale (1993) argues that two categories of intermediaries can be identified when we look at them from a perspective based on CRSs. They are:

- Those who were in business already providing some kind of service and have automated their systems to provide a better service to their existing clients.
- Those who enter or are seeking to enter the market by offering a "new" service usually based on a technology application.

An example of the first type is Utell, one of the world's first and largest hotel representation companies. It is a company that has consistently been at the forefront of technical and related commercial development in the business of making hotel reservations and acts as the intermediary between a travel agent in one country and a hotel in another. Avis is an example of the second type of intermediary. It is a company that developed its own central database and established communications links with the major CRS companies. Having done this successfully it has seen a business opportunity to recoup some of the investment it had made and to profit from the expertise it has gained.

The Hotel Industry Switch Company (THISCO), a joint venture set up by a number of the largest US hotel chains, is another innovative initiative of this kind. THISCO was set up in order to provide a simple connection between the various central reservations offices (CROs) of all these hotel companies and the different CRS systems. Its objective was to reduce the cost and complexity of developing and maintaining such links.

11.5 Evolution and growth of CRS and GDS

In the early years of aviation, with a limited number of carriers and available flights, airlines simply presented their scheduling and pricing information to customers by distributing timetables and advertising in newspapers. As the industry expanded, the practice of interlining became commonplace, which necessitated the industry to create a comprehensive, multi-carrier guide that would provide passengers with the detailed information necessary for them to make an informed purchase decision. Consolidated reference guides were formed involving multi-carrier schedulers or tariff guides (e.g. Official Airline Guide – OAG). Travel agents then became the main intermediary and played an important role in travel product distribution. The travel agent's primary sources of information on airline schedules were publications such as the OAG.

Air transport was growing at a tremendous pace, as was the case for information technology as well. Handling large volumes of data (e.g. on flight schedules, fares, seat availabilities, passenger reservation, etc.) became a cumbersome activity. During this time, airline reservations were made over telephone or at airports and airline offices. Airlines disseminated information through timetables and advertisements. Soon, more airlines entered the market. Existing airlines expanded operations. Airlines started to use innovative measures to handle increasing volumes of information. American Airlines used a "request and reply" system before the 1950s, which enabled reservation agents to phone a central location for availability information. Teletype was sent as responses. Some airline reservation offices depended on wall-sized availability boards to monitor and process reservations (Sheldon, 2003). Manual processors were used for updating. "Lady Susan" was another manual method followed by airlines for making reservations (Inkpen, 1998).

American Airlines was the pioneer in automating reservations. C. R. Smith, the president of American Airlines, and R. Blair Smith, a senior sales representative for IBM, met on an American Airlines flight from Los Angeles to New York in 1953. The idea of developing a data processing system that could create and manage airline seat reservations and instantly make that data available electronically to any agent at any location generated from the conversations they had with each other during that journey (www.sabre.com). A partnership was developed between American Airlines and IBM in the same year to develop the first computer system to handle airline reservations, ticketing, schedules, seat inventories and PNRs. Many studies and much research were conducted over some years. After six years, the idea that had generated from a flight journey became a reality when American Airlines and IBM jointly announced their plans to develop a Semi-Automatic Business Research Environment (SABRE). It was the first and most important milestone

Airlines and other suppliers

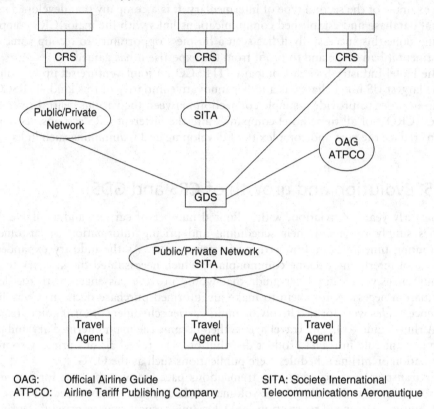

OAG: Official Airline Guide   SITA: Societe International
ATPCO: Airline Tariff Publishing Company   Telecommunications Aeronautique

Figure 11.2 GDS architecture
Source: Werthner and Klein, 1999

in the history of global travel product distribution. This revolutionary system was the first real-time business application, and it allowed American Airlines to replace the hand-written passenger reservation system of the time with this automated reservation system of the future.

By the 1960s, many airlines had installed computer systems to store flight schedules and fares and to handle reservations. Still, the system was not sufficient to handle the complicated reservation requests and product distribution. Continual experiments were held to design and implement a better system to handle the information requirements and data processing. An initial computer centre was installed in Briar Cliff Manor, New York in 1960. Computerized reservations and ticketing procedures offered airlines significant improvements in productivity over the cumbersome and time-consuming manual process involving telephones and telexes.

CRSs were originally developed by the major airlines for enhancing the efficiency of their own internal reservations systems. More CRSs were introduced by the beginning of the 1970s. Galileo had its beginning in 1971 when United Airlines of America introduced the Apollo, a CRS for their own use. In 1972 the SABRE system (now styled "Sabre") moved to a new consolidated computer centre in Tulsa, Oklahoma, which was designed to house all of American Airlines' data processing facilities. Another milestone in the history of CRS was reached in 1976 when the Sabre system was installed in a travel agency for the first time, which triggered a wave of travel automation. In the same year, 130 locations could access the Sabre system. At this time, a travel agent's set, which is the data terminal of a CRS in a travel agency, was hooked up to a CRS with a teletype machine via a telephone line.

Following deregulation in the US in 1978, travel agents started using CRSs widely, and that changed the CRS usage scenario in the country. CRS vendors began to attract more travel agents and healthy competition emerged, which expanded the scope of the systems. As deregulation was implemented, scores of new airlines entered the market offering a wide range of fares, as had been predicted, and consequently the number of travel agency locations also increased tremendously. At the time of deregulation in 1978 there were 14,804 travel agency locations, accounting for about 40 per cent of airline ticket sales. But by 1982, almost 82 per cent of the nation's travel agencies, which had increased to 20,000, were linked to one of the major CRSs in existence (Truitt et al., 1991). By 1985, CRSs started to offer a wide range of travel services and the development enabled travel agents to offer a range of travel and tourism services, including issuing of tickets and boarding passes, booking of hotel rooms and rental cars, selling of travel insurance, transmitting of itineraries, etc. Also, travel agents could utilize the CRSs more effectively to manage their offices by adding more features, like computerized accounting and payroll. The increased usage of CRS resulted in better productivity. Corresponding to the developments that occurred in technology, the scope, nature, dimensions and ability of CRSs reached greater heights.

The advances in CRS technologies have resulted in more efficiency and economy in the operation of travel agencies. It eventually led to increased bookings and reduced fare levels resulting from deregulation. Global distribution systems (GDSs) emerged, which are basically super switches connecting several CRSs. A GDS will be powered by a large mainframe computer that performs many of the end-user functions that are delivered to travel agents using PC-based terminals (Inkpen, 1998). Amadeus, a major GDS, was formed in 1987 by Air France, Lufthansa, Iberia and SAS. In April 1995, the Amadeus Global Travel Distribution acquired the technical system of System One, another GDS that came into existence in 1982. Galileo International turned out to be the global distribution company to provide two core systems: Apollo in the USA and Galileo throughout the rest of the world. Within each country, Galileo had a national distribution company with the responsibility to market and sell the Galileo service within that country. Worldspan was formed from two of the world's most important CRSs, namely Delta Airline's Data II and TWA/Northwest's PARS (Passenger Airline Reservation System). DATAS was formed in 1984 by Delta Airlines. Before that System One was created by Eastern Airlines. Now Worldspan is owned by Delta Airlines, TWA and Abacus Distribution Systems. Abacus is owned by Singapore Airlines, Cathay Pacific and Dragon Air.

11.6 CRS and information-based strategies

The increasing competition and sophistication in the airline reservation and product distribution sector encouraged CRS vendors or owner airlines to adopt information-based strategies for effective marketing. The strategies used were: display bias, the halo effect, code sharing and commission overrides (Truitt et al., 1991; Bennett, 1993).

11.6.1 Display bias

"Bias" in relation to CRS competition is referred to as the practice of programming a CRS to give the flight services of host airlines a superior display position. Many studies have revealed that during the 1980s and 1990s a good majority of all flight bookings were made from the first line of listings displayed while the lion's share of bookings came from the first screen. Travel agents also have the tendency to select the first option displayed which meets the customer's stated criteria. Virtually all CRSs listed their host flights first. This also generated protests from the "have-not" airlines.

11.6.2 The halo effect

Travel agents had more confidence in the accuracy and timeliness of the information provided by the CRSs' parent airlines than the competing carriers. It is referred to as the "halo effect". Studies have revealed that CRS dramatically increased the incremental bookings for their parent airline and it made CRS very valuable to their parent companies, especially since a small increase in passenger load can dramatically increase profitability. This too raised debates across the world.

11.6.3 Code sharing

As far as CRS is concerned, it's difficult for smaller players to compete with larger players. The "code sharing" agreement helped small airlines to use the code letters of bigger partners and link up their flight schedule. The small airlines benefited from this, as they received an advantageous display position, which enabled them to attract a much wider market. Both partners can enjoy an enhanced schedule by coordinating their services. The bigger airlines gain significant economies of scale, the added power that accrues from serving numerous markets and broad market segments. The benefit of code sharing was great, particularly from the point of view of additional sales as well as the increased market penetration at "hubs".

11.6.4 Commission overrides

"Override" in this context represents extra commission paid to encourage travel agents to sell a particular airline's seats rather than those of another carrier. They are usually awarded to travel agents by the airlines in return for increases in volume or market share. CRS helps airlines track agent bookings on other carriers as well as their own sales so that airlines can observe whether travel agencies are favouring any particular airlines by receiving override commissions (Truitt et al., 1991; Bennett, 1993).

11.7 Global distribution systems

The term global distribution system refers to a network of one or more CRSs for distributing product offerings and functionalities of the participating organizations in different countries across the world (Werthner and Klein, 1999). CRS and GDS form one of the major players in value chains. They provide the main electronic link between big supplier groups and the travel agent/tour operator community. According to Amadeus, GDS refers to

> the reservation tool travel agents use when making an air, hotel, car or other travel service booking. And not only do GDSs power the content of "traditional" travel

agency platforms, but they also provide pricing, availability and reservation functionality to many online travel agencies (www.amadeus.com).

According to Vialle (1995), the major functions of a GDS are the following:

- Maintenance and search facilities for flight schedules and availability
- Information on other travel and tourism products and their availability, like package holidays, car rentals, ferries, etc.
- Seat reservation and selling
- Ticketing
- Maintenance of user information based on PNR
- Maintenance of and search facilities for fare quotes and rules
- Management functions both for intermediaries such as travel agents and for airlines.

A GDS will have a very large number of interconnected companies from the supply side as well as from the demand side. According to Werthner and Klein (1999), there are three different ways of processing reservations submitted by a travel agent. They are: sell on status, direct access and seamless connectivity. Each of the modes is discussed in brief below.

11.7.1 Sell on status

Airlines transmit their availability and flight status to the GDS, using SITA. When a travel agent sends a request, the GDS contacts the airline inventory system. As and when the airline replies, GDS will send confirmation to the travel agent.

11.7.2 Direct access

Here, when a travel agent makes a request, it will be handled at the GDS itself. After the same is processed, the reservation will be transmitted to the airline's system. The most important thing is that the airline's inventory be consistent with that of the GDS.

11.7.3 Seamless connectivity

In seamless connectivity mode, all the transactions done at the GDS are duplicated immediately on the carrier's system.

GDSs have become an indispensable tool for any type of travel intermediary. Over the years, it has been proven that the investment in GDS will certainly bring returns. The most important of these returns are (Buhalis, 2003):

- Gross income from commission generated by the system and subscription
- Assistance in the promotion of the parent company through preferential display
- Participation and rental fees
- Organizational and information management benefits from the improvement in the efficiency

11.8 Major global distribution systems

A brief discussion of the major GDSs, involving history, products and services, features and advantages of using the systems follows below.

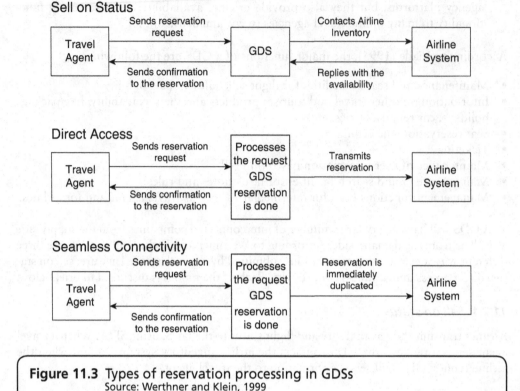

Figure 11.3 Types of reservation processing in GDSs
Source: Werthner and Klein, 1999

11.8.1 Travelport/Galileo and Worldspan

Galileo and Worldspan, formerly separate GDSs, now function under the Travelport. Galileo, formerly a subsidiary of Cendant Corporation, is a high-end technology solution that basically connects travel buyers and sellers through CRSs. The history of Galileo dates back to 1971 when United Airlines of America introduced the Apollo, a CRS, for their own use. The Apollo Travel Service (ATS) division was created later and Apollo CRS was marketed to travel agencies in North America and Japan. Apollo launched Inside Link, which provided instant confirmation and last seat availability to travellers. In 1986, ATS was renamed Covia, an independent affiliate of United Airlines. The need for CRS automation was on the increase during the latter half of 1980s in Europe and the Galileo Company Ltd was incorporated in England and Wales by shareholders including British Airways, Swiss Air, KLM Royal Dutch Airlines, Alitalia and Covia. In America, the Covia partnership was created by selling 50 per cent of Covia to US Air, British Airways, Swiss Air, KLM and Alitalia. In Canada also, Air Canada joined Covia. Again in Europe, more airlines such an Austria Airlines, Aer Lingus, TAP Air Portugal, Sabena and Olympic Airways joined the Galileo distributions system. By 1990, Covia was involved in car aid hotel bookings. Simultaneously, the Galileo Company launched "Release 3" onto the system, making it the first fully operational European-based CRS. Galileo soon expanded to Arab countries. "Global Fares", a new fare system designed for Apollo, Galileo and Gemini users worldwide, was introduced over this time.

In 1992, the world's first GDS – GALILEO – was formed, when the European and North American owners of the Galileo Company Ltd and the Covia partnership signed a letter of intent. Apollo Travel Services formed as Galileo International's national distribution company for the US and Mexico. The facility for live availability pricing and instant information on tour packages was incorporated, and then another facility to provide real-time availability directly from an airline's own system was incorporated. The data centre, which mainly consists of mainframe computers, was moved to Denver, Colorado from Swindon, UK in 1993. Asian operations began in 1994 when an office in Hong Kong was registered. Leisure Shopper Cruises launched on Apollo, providing agents with real-time, global access to cruise company products. Galileo Canada formed to replace the Gemini partnership by linking Air Canada with Galileo International. Galileo extended its operations to India in the same year.

As technology advanced, more and more features were added to the Galileo products. Apollo travel service was acquired by Galileo after the formation of Galileo International. Galileo further expanded tremendously and more services have been incorporated since then. The Cendant Travel Distribution Services division has been transformed into Travelport, which now owns both Galileo and Worldspan. Together, it has become one of the world's largest GDS providers. Galileo is currently one of the leading GDSs.

Worldspan, founded in early 1990 by Delta Air Lines, Northwest Airlines and TWA, intended to serve customers through sophisticated global communication systems and networks. With its headquarters in Atlanta, Georgia, Worldspan primarily offers technology solutions to deal with travel-related products globally. In mid-2003, Worldspan was sold by its owner airlines to Citigroup Venture Capital and Ontario Teachers' Pension Fund. It is now a part of the Travelport GDS business. In December 2006, Travelport agreed to acquire Worldspan, but decided not to merge it with Galileo. The acquisition was completed on 21 August 2007. On 28 September 2008, the Galileo and Apollo GDS systems were moved from the Travelport data centre in Denver, Colorado to the Worldspan data centre in Atlanta, Georgia (although they continue to be run as separate systems). Worldspan is another technology leader in Web-based travel e-commerce, offering solutions for conducting all facets of travel business online. It enables travel distribution, technologies and services for thousands of travel companies worldwide, including travel agencies, corporations, travel suppliers and travel websites. Travelport is now a major technology solution provider for the travel industry as a whole. Its product range is provided in Table 11.1.

11.8.2 Amadeus

Amadeus is a leading provider of technology solutions to the travel and tourism industry with corporate headquarters in Madrid (Spain). Airlines such as Air France, Lufthansa, Iberia and SAS founded Amadeus as a GDS company in 1987. Recently, in 2015, it acquired Abacus, a leading GDS in the Asia-Pacific region. Since its inception as a CRS, it has advanced to become one of the leading providers of technology solutions to almost all players in the travel trade. It primarily aims to connect travel stakeholders such as airlines, airports, car rental agencies, corporations, ground handlers, hotels, travel insurance providers, online travel agencies, railways, tour operators, travel agencies and travel management companies to the travel marketplace and to assist in working with their travel partners. The suppliers can ensure their content is available through all channels and the sellers can access the richest, most relevant travel content. Currently, Amadeus serves more than 190 countries and claims to be the largest distributor of leisure packages worldwide. Its data centre is one of the largest data centres in the world. More than 3.8 billion transactions are undertaken on the platform every day during peak season.

Table 11.1 Various technology solutions offered by Travelport

Technology solution	Description
Travelport 360 Fares	This is a global fares and pricing system that powers all fares and pricing transactions for Travelport's GDSs.
Best Buy Plus	It enables the monitoring of bookings and searching for the best available fare.
Travelport Smartpoint	It can redefine the selling experience.
Travelport Rapid Reprice	This enables automated ticket reissues.
Global Exchange Manager (GEM)	It automates the ticket exchange/reissue process.
Travelport e-Tracker	It's an efficient e-Ticket management tool.
Travelport e-Pricing	It helps to instantly shop, compare pricing and book from one of the broadest spectrums of available itineraries and low fares, with one powerful availability request.
Search Control Console	A new search tool that can empower travel agents.
Travelport Mobile Agent	Travelport's GDS can be accessed via smartphone or tablet using this solution.
Galileo e-line	Galileo is an iframe solution that offers business to business (B2B) and business to customer (B2C) systems and online reservations to IATA member travel agencies.
Travelport Universal API	This is probably the first truly universal API, giving access to a world of content and functionality through a single API connection.
Travelport ViewTrip Mobile	It provides a personal travel concierge service for travellers.
Travelport ViewTrip	It's a flexible online itinerary resource.

Source: www.travelport.com

For airlines, Amadeus offers a range of advanced technology solutions. Amadeus Global Merchandising System and the Global Retailing and Distribution Systems together strengthen the Amadeus Global Travel Ecosystem. Airline Core Systems form the basic information system that is at the heart of airlines' commercial operations. There are three modules, Altéa PSS Suite, revenue management and financial solutions. Altéa Suite involves reservation, inventory, a departure control system, ticketing and ticket changer disruption. Revenue management involves dynamic pricing, income management, network planning and scheduling, and revenue integrity. The financial solution module integrates revenue accounting, payment, revenue integrity and ticketing. Both the Global Merchandising and Retailing and Distribution Systems are fully integrated across the above Core Systems. Its Digital and Direct Retailing Systems link airlines with call centres, city/airport ticket offices and digital solutions for all their direct channels.

Global Distribution and Indirect Retailing enables smoother access to new markets, partners and technology, to personalize and differentiate an airline's offering and deliver a consistent shopping experience. Its components include Digital Traffic Acquisition, LCC Distribution, Content Processing, Booking and Fulfilment and Channel Revenue

Optimization. Its Global Merchandising System enables clients to pursue advanced merchandizing techniques, including personalization, dynamic pricing and packaging, anytime merchandizing, new distribution capability of IATA, search and shopping, dynamic content and indirect merchandizing. The Travel Intelligence and Personalization System is also offered by Amadeus, providing each airline with actionable and unique business insights that can be fed into it in order to deliver a customized and contextualized passenger experience across the entire journey.

11.8.3 Sabre

Sabre serves airlines, airports, car rental companies, corporations, cruise lines, developers, hotels, meta search engines, online travel intermediaries, rail carriers, tour companies, travel consolidators, government agencies and travel management companies. For airlines, a wide range of software and data solutions are offered to enable them to market themselves, sell their products in both the direct and indirect channels, serve their passengers and operate efficiently. More than 425,000 travel agencies use Sabre GDS for accessing products of all the major tourism suppliers and they can use the products and services of Sabre to manage every aspect of their business, including personalizing their customers' needs (www.sabre.com). Car rental companies, cruises and rail carriers can make use of the potential of Sabre technology solutions mainly for distributing their products. Corporates can simplify travel sourcing while also ensuring extraordinary savings. Technology developers can power their applications with Sabre technology. Government agencies can make use of this technology for their travel bookings and the like. Using Sabre solutions, hotels can ensure seamless distribution, operations and marketing solutions to save costs, increase revenues and personalize their service to guests. Meta search engines can make use of the shopping services of Sabre to enhance their marketing and user experience. As of writing, Sabre provides online travel agents (OTAs) with access to 400 airlines, 175,000 hotel properties, 17 cruise lines, 40 car rental brands, 200 tour operators and 50 rail carriers for distributing and selling their products. For tour operators, Sabre ensures easy access to all the suppliers for accessing their products for packaging. Travel consolidators and travel management companies can also make use of Sabre technology solutions for optimizing their business potentials.

Trends in online intermediation: Excerpts from Euromonitor study findings

- There has been consistent performance of online intermediaries and a remarkable move of traditional tour operators to the online channel.
- Leading organizations, such as Google, Facebook, TripAdvisor and the meta search engines, are playing an increasingly important role in the travel industry, driving online traffic and causing competition among industry players.
- Increasing consolidation is seen in the OTA sector, with Expedia and Priceline.com emerging as its dominant players.
- OTAs from emerging markets, such as Ctrip and MakeMyTrip, are gaining ground.

- Leading tour operators (e.g. TUI Travel and Thomas Cook) are changing their business models to make their websites their main distribution
  platforms.
- The environment is changing rapidly, with new trends visible, such as
  peer-to-peer services expanding to more travel sectors, online travel
  marketing becoming increasingly personalized and wearable electronics
  going mainstream.
- There is strong growth in mobile-based transactions.
- There has been a move from OTAs to mobile travel agencies (MTAs); due
  to the surge of mobile channels and of in-destination tourist services,
  online travel agencies are expected gradually to adopt an MTA model.
- The Asia-Pacific region leads in estimated growth of online travel distribution over 2008–2018 period.

Source: Euromonitor (2014)

11.9 GDS new entrants

GDS new entrants, also known as global new entrants, provided more cost-effective distribution services for airlines. These GNE companies "target low cost distribution with
their systems, which recognise the need to aggregate content for all kinds of different
sources" (Merten, 2008). Farelogix, G2 SwitchWorks and ITA Software are the leading
GNEs, which are sometimes also called alternative content access platforms (ACAPs).
GNEs have been envisaged as more powerful to make distribution more competitive.
They aim to provide sophisticated technology solutions for airlines for distribution at
cheaper rates. They also have direct links with airline inventory and access to all fares,
both public and Web fares. A brief discussion on Farelogix follows which can provide
insight into the nuances of a GNE.

Farelogix operates an airline distribution mechanism with advanced technology solutions that have multiple facets. Its SaaS Airline Commerce Gateway (the "Gateway")
extends the potential of airlines to distribute products with the options for creating,
controlling, optimizing and delivering personalized and differentiated offers via multiple
channels. These channels include airline websites, check-in kiosks, mobile apps, travel
agencies, meta search engines (e.g. KAYAK) and consumer online travel sites. Its clients
include Air Canada, American Airlines, Austrian Airlines, Brussels Airlines, Delta Air
Lines, Emirates, Eurowings, flydubai, Hawaiian Airlines, Lufthansa, Olympic Airlines,
Qatar Airways, Swiss International Air Lines, United Airlines, Virgin Atlantic, Virgin
America and WestJet. The following components are part of its Gateway (www.fare
logix.com):

- *FLX Open Connect:* it permits making and managing bookings and reservations out
  of the airline reservation system for users.
- *FLX NDC API:* this is an integrated delivery API for accessing the airline's full suite
  of content for all users.
- *FLX Merchandise:* this is airline-controlled merchandising and enables airlines to create tailored product and service offerings for distributing through various channels.

- *FLX Shop & Price:* this offers airlines a state-of-the-art airline shopping, offer and pricing engine.
- *FLX Availability Calculator:* this permits an airline to fully calculate its own availability, without taxing the passenger service system (PSS), while retaining full airline IP over its proprietary rules algorithm.
- *FLX Schedule Builder:* this ensures control over schedule building for the airline by opening the door to new revenue opportunities for dynamic, personalized schedule building and optimization of the most profitable connections and routes.

11.10 Airline reservation systems

Airline reservation systems (ARSs) used by airlines are Web-based booking engines connected with GDSs. Through this integration, ARSs can provide better inventory and rates to the end-customers and travel agencies with 24/7 online availability, along with real-time bookings. In order to understand the difference between ARSs and GDSs, the following extract is useful:

> An ARS shows the schedules for a single airline, whereas a GDS shows many carriers' schedules. Furthermore, ARSs are used by airline staff while GDSs are used by airline travel intermediaries to source and book seats. It is important for an ARS to connect to other systems such as GDSs and Internet booking engines (IBEs).
>
> (Benckendorff et al., 2014)

Such systems consist of the exchange of data through GDSs. Major GDS companies and similar firms do also offer standard ARSs. An airline system fundamentally has the following components:

- *Flight schedules:* days and times for flights operated by the airline.
- *Availability:* seat availability on a flight by service class.
- *Fares:* fares and the corresponding rules for journeys are stored and provided as per the need.
- *Passenger information:* passenger information for each booking is stored and retrieved for various purposes, like reservation, ticketing and check-in. PNR format is used for storing the required information for each booking.
- *E-tickets:* the system provides e-Tickets as well for each reservation for further use by the passenger during the entire process of travel.

11.11 Online travel agents

Towards the end of the last century, realizing the increasing potential of online distribution, some of the leading technology solution providers in the world established Internet-based travel agencies to sell the travel, tourism and hospitality products directly to consumers. It soon became a trend and many such Internet-based travel agents, called online travel agents (OTAs), emerged. OTAs primarily market and sell travel-related products and services directly to customers through its own and other online channels. Customers can directly access the products of airlines, hotels, car rentals companies and cruises through OTAs. They can also provide pricing information about airlines, hotels, car rental companies, cruise lines, vacations/holidays and last-minute travel packages, and other travel-related services. Compared to traditional travel agencies, online agents have the capacity to offer a vast range of products from all over the world. Expedia, one of the pioneer OTAs in the world, was established by Microsoft as Microsoft Expedia Travel Services in 1996. Sabre owned Travelocity, another leading OTA, and it is currently owned by Expedia itself.

OTAs follow different business models, like the merchant model and agency model. In the merchant business model, which is the most common, the suppliers sell their products to OTAs in bulk at discounted or wholesale prices. While selling the products, OTAs benefit by getting a marked-up price. This has increased risk for OTAs as they have to make sure they sell all of the products they bought in advance. The agency model is a commission-based model. Suppliers provide commission to OTAs for the business generated. Some of the intermediaries use an advertising model wherein the income source is primarily the revenue from advertising fees. Some of the OTAs adopt both the merchant model and the agency model, depending on market conditions. Mobile-based apps are also developed by many OTAs for easier and more convenient booking by travellers.

CASE STUDY 11.1

Why online travel agencies?

While disintermediation loomed large over traditional intermediaries, spearheading a new trend of re-intermediation, OTAs began successful operations. Both suppliers and customers prefer OTAs due to a range of reasons. One of the major advantages of an OTA is its capacity for global reach and influence. Traditional travel agents have a limited coverage area of operation. For instance, Expedia has 150 travel booking sites in over 70 countries with websites localized in more than 30 languages. The number of people using smartphones and computers for online booking is steadily increasing. Moreover, inexperienced travellers, particularly the new generation of travellers, prefer online purchases, even if they are first-time overseas travellers. The rate of growth of OTAs is also faster, as they are expected to expand gross bookings twice as fast as the overall market, particularly in emerging regions in Latin America, Asia-Pacific and Eastern Europe. The expansion is augmented with investments in multilingual, culturally relevant displays as well as alternative payment systems. Organic growth and international acquisitions enable them to gain local knowledge. For example, Expedia and Priceline.com have over the last ten years made a series of significant international (non-US-based) acquisitions and partnerships, particularly in Europe and China. Mobile websites are a priority for OTAs now as more and more people prefer to transact over smartphones. Travellers, even when they are travelling, can check and change itineraries, read reviews, share experiences, undertake last-minute transactions and choose restaurant options, hotel accommodations, tours and activities. Mobile bookings may grow at a double-digit rate over the next two years.

OTAs have increased customization and therefore consumers, especially younger travellers, typically prefer the depth and breadth of OTAs, compared to supplier direct channels. They can choose the most suitable options that fit their preferences and budgets and prefer to cross-shop. Online reviews, mapping services and overall comparative capabilities of OTAs help consumers in the process of decision-making and purchasing. OTAs are like one-stop shops because of their breadth of content across multiple travel segments, such as carriers (air, rail and bus), lodging (hotels, B&Bs and rental properties), cruises, rental cars, ground transportation and attractions/activities.

OTAs also help to connect travellers who are not always brand-loyal, are searching for value as well as amenities, and who prefer deals. Although multinational hotel chains have their own websites, only a segment of the travelling population is actually faithful to a particular hotel brand. Also, some OTAs have their own loyalty programmes that reward bookings made with any supplier. OTAs have advantages beyond just distribution. They have some marketing influence, similar to search engines and meta search sites. They have even extended their influence through mobiles. OTAs in the US spent nearly $700 million on advertising in 2013, and that figure is expected to jump 8 per cent over the next two years. According to PhoCusWright research, consumers use OTAs to shop nearly as much as they use search engines. Leisure tourists are more likely to use OTAs. Business travellers may book through a travel management company (TMC) and/or GDS. The advantages of using OTAs is not just for consumers, but for suppliers as well.

Source: Carroll and Sileo (2014)

Read the above case study carefully and answer the following questions:

- Describe the strategies that are used by OTAs for expansion of the business and market.
- Explain the reasons why OTAs are preferred by some customers.
- Discuss the advantages of using OTAs for travellers.

11.12 Mobile travel agents

In this new era of m-commerce, mobile-only travel agents, or mobile travel agents (MTAs), are gaining increasing significance. In the near future, MTAs may increase their role in travel distribution as smartphone-based e-commerce is steadily rising. People depend on their smartphones and other mobile devices for searching and booking. According to Rossini (2014), MTAs are:

currently niche players focusing on tonight-only bookings made by travellers on the go. However, in an increasingly competitive mobile travel arena, the most successful mobile-only players are expected to reach the mainstream market in the next few years, gaining share at the expense of traditional OTAs.

CTrip, Hotel Tonight, Blink, JustBook and Hot Hotels/ReallyLateBooking are examples of MTAs. Experts are of the view that all travel players also have to have mobile-based services to cope with with the challenging technology environment in the coming years. According to Euromonitor (2014), mobile channel-based bookings see the fastest growth, and the prime reason for this is the growing trend among consumers to use smartphones and tablets for searching as well as booking. Travel companies are increasingly allowing bookings and payments through smartphones (Euromonitor, 2014).

11.13 Destination information systems

A destination information system (DIS) is considered a very comprehensive and integrated option to process and disseminate information in the most efficient and economical manner for the maximum number of stakeholders in the tourism industry. It has been defined as a comprehensive electronic database of a destination's facilities which can be accessed by travel counsellors and/or travellers themselves, either in the destination or in the region (Sheldon, 2003). Of late, such systems are integrated with booking and reservation services as well, on behalf of various suppliers, and thus take part in the distribution of travel and tourism products. They can offer facilities to tourists for local and ancillary services. Tourism information system is another term used to refer to an information system for a destination. A well-established tourist information system will benefit local business, the community and local residents as well as tourists. Destination management system (DMS), destination marketing system, etc. are other terms used in this context, though the functions may vary slightly. These systems also offer new tools for destination marketing and promotion. Nowadays, more advanced systems are developed at the destination level by the respective national tourist offices (NTOs) or destination management organizations (DMOs). A DMO establishing a business system to utilize the potential of the Internet would be necessary for the destination to remain popular. Consider some of the services offered by a standard DIS/DMS below:

- Information search – by category, geography (using geographical information system – GIS), keyword, etc.
- Itinerary planning
- Reservations
- Customer/contact database management
- Customer relationship management (CRM) functions
- "Push" marketing
- Market research and analysis
- Image library
- Publishing on electronic and traditional channels
- Event planning and management
- Marketing optimization and yield management
- Data editing and management
- Financial management
- Management information systems and performance evaluation
- Economic impact analysis
- Access to third-party sources, such as weather, transport timetables and travel planning, theatre and event ticket reservations

DMSs have become a major promotion, distribution and operational tool for both destinations and local industries. Buhalis (2003) defines DMSs as the collection of computerized, interactively accessible information about a destination. The following extract defines a DMS as a:

> dynamic web-based platform that integrates a wide range of information about a destination's tourism products. It also provides an infrastructure to support different types of e-commerce (e.g., B2B, C2B, and G2B) in the destination. Additionally, it allows interaction with different stakeholders (e.g., suppliers, visitors), data collection and information visualization.
>
> (Estevao et al., 2011)

Such systems generally provide tools and measures required to compete in the tourism marketplace and will enable the tourism sector in the destination to make use of the opportunities of IT. DMSs facilitate the interface between the tourism enterprises in and around the tourist destination and the external world. Essentially a DMS consists of a product database and customer database, and a mechanism to connect them. Transaction applications through DMSs are on the increase. Currently, they include online reservations, sale of tickets/entry passes of attractions, etc.

11.14 Other online intermediaries

There are a number of other online intermediaries in tourism. **Meta search engines** also have a role in the distribution of travel and tourism products. These, which provide results based on a combination of results from other search engine databases, assist travel customers to find a suitable option as per their needs. A customer's query is sent to multiple existing search engines and OTAs and once the results are received from them, they are merged into a single ranked list. The merged list is presented to the customer. In fact, meta search engines do not offer provision for booking; rather, they will enable the customer to search, compare and choose the best option, and finally lead the customer to the sites where booking can be done. KAYAK, Trivago, Webjet and Flight Centre are examples of meta search engines in the travel and tourism sector.

Travel aggregators primarily aim to aggregate travel, tourism and hospitality inventories from different sources like GDSs, and give users access as per their need. They can show all the best deals on a single platform and ensure quick results along with easy and convenient access. GNEs are considered aggregators. Personalized itinerary makers online, called trip planning sites (e.g. MyGola) are also gaining ground. **Affiliates** market online travel intermediaries' content and offers and drive bookings to them. OTAs' offers are usually advertised on affiliate sites. Affiliate sites usually charge for driving bookings to clients. Customer reviewing is gaining increasing significance in tourism nowadays. Potential tourists often visit review sites to get past reviews and comments of past customers. Review sites like TripAdvisor are very popular among travellers. **Opaque sites** are other booking channels which offer the unsold/distressed travel products. As the inventory is in the "distressed" category, a higher discount is offered. The supplier will be hidden until the completion of the transaction. Hotels and airlines offer last-minute sales through opaque sites. Group buying sites also have a role in selling travel and hospitality products.

11.15 Hospitality distribution

Electronic distribution is gaining increased significance in the hospitality sector as well. OTAs, online aggregators, other online agents and mobile apps have a significant role in contemporary hospitality distribution. Direct distribution is equally significant among hotels and resorts. There are powerful reservation systems and websites for chain hotels to ensure speedy and efficient online reservation from anywhere in the world. GDS-based distribution is also important for the hotel and resort sector. Usually hotels will have a central reservation office (CRO), where reservations are processed. Following CROs, hotels started to develop centralized reservation systems mainly to handle reservations and a lot more information, other than GDSs. Hotels can use other forms of technology to facilitate reservation systems. For example, an application service provider (ASP) environment is used to deliver a complete booking system tied to the hotel's inventory in real time via the Web (Walker, 2004). According to Buhalis (2003), there are four types of hotel reservation systems: in-house CRSs and property management systems (PMSs) (e.g. MICROS, Fidelio), hotel chain CRSs, independent reservation systems and representation systems of strategic alliances and consortiums.

11.16 Summary

Tremendous developments in technology has impacted travel product distribution greatly, and due to the same, the process has become faster and easier. The increasing role and relevance of the Internet caused the emergence of e-mediaries in travel and tourism. There are now a range of online intermediaries acting in different ways on the Internet, such as online travel agents, meta search engines, aggregators, trip planning sites, affiliates, group buying sites, opaque sites and product review sites. All the industry's components depend on Internet to distribute their products easily, more conveniently and efficiently. Even traditional intermediaries are now coming up with their own online travel agencies. IATA has taken the revolutionary step to transform the supplier–intermediary transmission and to enhance electronic air travel distribution to the most advanced levels by introducing the New Distribution Capability (NDC).

The advent of computer reservation systems was one of the most significant developments in the history of the travel industry. Airlines or groups of airlines had taken initiatives to develop a computer reservation system to deal with the increasing volume of information and its processing and dissemination, along with the internal ticketing process. The consistent developments in technology have offered greater opportunities for CRSs and hence CRSs have advanced further to include more products and services and to ease operations. CRSs have traditionally been undertaking different information-based strategies, such as display bias, the halo effect, code sharing and commission overrides. Eventually, through the expansion of their scope and range, CRSs have been transformed into GDSs. There are four major GDSs in the international travel sector: Galileo, Amadeus, Sabre and Worldspan. Galileo and Worldspan are promoted by Travelport now. In addition, in the Asia-Pacific region, Abacus has also emerged as a major GDS. All these GDSs offer a wide variety of products and information services as well as technology solutions, which make the travel products distribution an easy process.

GDS new entrants, also known as global new entrants, provided more cost-effective distribution services for airlines. Farelogix, G2 SwitchWorks and ITA Software are the leading GNEs, which are sometimes also called alternative content access platforms

(ACAPs). Airline reservation systems, which are web-based booking engines connected with global GDS systems, are used by airlines. Online travel agents primarily use them to market and sell travel-related products and services directly to customers, though they use other online channels as well. Customers can directly access the products of airlines, hotels, car rental companies and cruises through online travel agents. Furthermore, mobile-only travel agents, also called mobile travel agents (MTAs), are gaining increasing significance. Apart from all of these, there are a number of other online intermediaries actively involved in travel and tourism distribution. Online intermediation is poised for further advancements in the years to come.

Review questions

Short/medium answer type questions

- Identify major electronic distribution channels in travel and tourism.
- Give a brief account of the New Distribution Capability (NDC).
- Explain the basic concept of a computer reservation system (CRS) in airlines.
- Write a short note on the early stages of evolution of a computer reservation system.
- What are the information-based strategies of CRSs?
- Define global distribution system (GDS).
- Write down the functions of a GDS.
- What are the different ways of processing reservations submitted by a travel agent in CRS/GDS?
- Give a brief account of any two of the major GDSs.
- What is a GDS new entrant (GNE)?
- Differentiate between a GDS and an ARS.
- Write a short note on online travel agents (OTAs).
- What do we mean by mobile travel agent (MTA)?
- Write down the role of destination information systems in tourism distribution.

Essay type questions

- Describe in detail electronic distribution in travel and tourism.
- Explain the roles and functions of global distribution systems.

References

Archdale, G. (1993) CRS and Public Tourist Office, *Tourism Management* 14(1): 3–14.
Belobaba, P. P., Brunger, G. W. and Wittman, D. M. (2017) Advances in Airline Pricing, Revenue Management, and Distribution: Implications for the Airline Industry-Discussion Paper, Prepared for ATPCO by PODS Research LLC, available at https://www.atpco.net/sites/default/files/2017-10/Full%20version%20-ATPCO%20PODS%20Discussion%20Paper%20FINAL%20Oct02.pdf (accessed 5 June 2018).

Benckendorff, J. P., Sheldon, J. P. and Fesenmaier, R. D. (2014) *Tourism Information Technology*. 2nd edn. Oxfordshire: CABI.

Bennett, M. M. (1993) Information Technology and Travel Agency: A Customer Service Perspective, *Tourism Management*, August: 259–266.

Buhalis, D. and Licarta, M. (2002) The Future of e-Tourism Intermediaries, *Tourism Management* 23: 207–220.

Buhalis, D. (2003) *e-Tourism: Information Technology for Strategic Tourism Management*. Essex: Prentice Hall.

Carroll, B. and Sileo, L. (2014) *Online Travel Agencies: More Than a Distribution Channel*. New York: PhocusWright.

Estevao, J. V., Carneiro, M. J. and Teixeira, L. (2011) The Role of DMS in Reshaping Tourism Destinations: An Analysis of the Portuguese Case, *Information Technology and Tourism* 13(3): 161–176.

Euromonitor (2014) Online Travel Intermediaries: A Fast Changing Competitive Landscape, available at https://news.wtm.com/online-travel-intermediaries-fast-changing-competitive-landscape/.

Foster, L. D. (1994) *First Class: An Introduction to Travel and Tourism*. Singapore: McGraw-Hill.

Go, F. (1992) The Role of CRS in the Hospitality Industry, *Tourism Management* 13(1): 22–26.

IATA, New Distribution Capability, available at http://www.iata.org/whatwedo/airline-distribution/ndc/Pages/default.aspx (accessed 12 January 2018).

Inkpen, G. (1998) *Information Technology for Travel and Tourism*. 2nd edn. Essex: Longman.

Klein, S. and Langenohl, T. J. (1994), Coordination Mechanism and Systems Architectures in Electronic Market Systems, in W. Schertler, B. Schmid, A. M. Tjoa and H. Werthner (eds), Information and Communication Technologies in Tourism, Proceedings of the 1st International Conference, Innsbruck, Austria: Springer-Velag.

Merten, P. S. (2008) Transformation of the Distribution Process in Airline Industry Empowered by Information and Communication Technology, in C. Van Slyke (ed.), *Information Communication Technologies: Concepts, Methodologies, Tools and Applications*. London: IGI Global.

Poon, A. (1993) *Tourism, Technology and Competitive Strategies*. Oxford: CAB International.

Rossini, A. (2014) The Rise of Mobile Travel Agencies, Euromonitor, available at https://blog.euromonitor.com/2014/01/the-rise-of-mobile-travel-agencies.html.

Sheldon, J. P. (2003) *Tourism Information Technology*. Oxfordshire: CABI.

Truitt, J. L, Teye, B. V. and Farris, T. M. (1991) The Role of CRS: Internal Implication for the Travel Industry, *Tourism Management*, March.

Vialle, O (1995) Global Distribution Systems in the Tourism Industry. Madrid: WTO.

Walker, R. J. (2004) *Introduction to Hospitality Management*. Essex: Pearson Education.

Werthner, H. and Klein, S. (1999) *Information Technology and Tourism – A Challenging Relationship*. Vienna: Springer Verlag.

Websites

www.amadeus.com.
www.farelogix.com.
www.sabre.com.
www.travelport.com.

Tour operation business

Part V

Tour operation business

Chapter 12

The business of tour operation

After reading this chapter, you will be able to:

- Conceptualize tour operations.
- Understand the evolution of the tour operation business.
- Identify the product, suppliers and consumers in the tour operation business.
- List different types of tour operators.
- Appreciate the benefits of tour operation for tourists, destinations and suppliers.
- Discuss the risks involved in the tour operation business.
- Understand the organizational structure of tour operators.
- Explain the influence of environments on tour operation.
- Explain the buying behaviour in tour operation.

12.1 Introduction

Almost 200 years ago, a novel entrepreneurial attempt was made to arrange an organized tour, also called a "holiday". To be precise, it was actually a group "excursion" that was organized, on 5 July 1841, for a price of one shilling per person, by one of the greatest visionaries in tourism, Thomas Cook. It paved the way for organized tour ventures, which are considered the first organized tour operation. Later, his business expanded by adding a number of innovations. More entrepreneurs ventured into this arena with novel ideas and gradually a new business sector, called tour operation, emerged as an exclusive sector with ample scope for global expansion.

Tour operation basically involves a wide range of activities associated with arranging facilities and services for travellers while on a journey; and designing, marketing, selling and executing package tours in keeping with the number and characteristics of potential tourists. While acting as an intermediary in the whole system of tourism, tour operators focus on facilitating the travel of a tourist and on enhancing the touristic experience. There is an element of value addition in the whole system of tourism because of the involvement of a tour operator. Indeed, tour operation has more dimensions than just coordinating a journey on behalf of a tourist.

12.2 Tour operation: the concept

People travel for many reasons, but when it is for visiting it can be called a tour. Basically, it is defined as a journey with a purpose of visiting. Touring has been a recreation and leisure activity since the earliest times. In fact, leisure and recreation are used interchangeably and are considered an essential aspect of a healthy life. While leisure indicates free time, the term recreation often denotes the activities that one can engage in during free/leisure time. Indeed, one can spend leisure time in a number of ways, of which tours are prominent nowadays; hence, touring is also referred to as a recreation activity. Touring as a recreation activity was less important in the past than it is now. Moreover, it was largely limited to the wealthy and aristocratic class. Nowadays, it has become commonplace. There were many reasons for the non-prominence of touring as a recreation activity, such as the limited amount of leisure time, less discretionary income, limited transport options, unfavourable social and family circumstances, lack of awareness about places to visit and so on. Things changed in the post-Second World War era and now tourism is accessible for a significant share of populations across the world, with some engaging in tourism more than once a year.

The United States Tour Operators Association (USTOA) defines a tour as

> a trip taken by a group of people who travel together and follow a pre-planned itinerary. Most tours include accommodations, a number of meals, sightseeing, land transfers, and other forms of transportation to get you quickly and efficiently from place to place.
>
> (USTOA, How to Select a Tour/Vacation, n.d.)

This definition includes the aspect of a pre-planned itinerary which is necessary in a common tour programme. Yet it distinguishes tours from independent trips, which, according to them, are vacation packages. Whereas a tour is the activity undertaken for visiting, tour operation is about organizing a tour for a potential traveller. This means the complexities of travelling for the purpose of visiting for many days can be minimized through the process of tour operation. Tour operation is primarily about organizing a traveller's or a group of travellers' journey for the purpose of visiting, and arranging the services and facilities needed to enjoy the tour, in a professional way. While a tour is a pre-arranged trip to a destination for a short term, the major activities in tour operation include developing, marketing and managing tours as per the demands of various markets. Organized tours or holidays are carefully designed and developed by professionals. Often they are sold as packages. The very existence and survival of tour operation businesses depends on the efficiency of packaging. An efficiently designed package can attract customers, ensure high enough profit levels and can eventually add value to the tourism value chain.

A tour operator is basically an individual or an agency that organizes package tours and/or facilitates travel by arranging the necessary facilities and services. To the tourist, the tour operator takes on diverse roles, such as organizer, advisor/consultant, facilitator and one upon whom the tourist can depend during a journey. When viewed from other perspectives, tour operation can be defined in different ways. For instance, the following, rather technical definition specifies the basic function of a tour operator and points out how the product is sold to customers, the tourists. A tour operator basically puts together a tour and all its components, and sells the tour through his or her own company, through retail outlets and/or through approved retail travel agents (Goeldner and Ritchie, 2006). Page (2007) describes it in similar terms, suggesting a tour operator fulfils a number of roles, but basically organizes travel, packages and different elements of the tourism experience, and then offers the products for sale to the public through brochures, leaflets, advertisements or the use of electronic media. According to Laws (1997), a tour operator is "a company specializing in packaging the elements of inclusive holidays for sale to clients". Here, the focus is on how the product offered by a tour operator is created, and specifies that the tour operator's product is something that is created by packaging: an efficient combination of various essential components that are required for a tourist to enjoy the tour.

The Federation of Tour Operators (FTO) defines tour operators as the "organizers and providers of package holidays" (FTO, n.d.). They make contracts with principals such as hoteliers, airlines and ground transport companies, and then print brochures advertising the holidays that they have created. Here also, the focus is on the packaging aspect of tour operation. Furthermore, some other intermediary roles of a tour operator, such as making links and agreements with principals and promoting the transformed form of the offerings, are also hinted at in the description. Hudson (2008) describes tour operators simply as "organizations that offer packaged vacation tours to the general public".

Another detailed definition is suggested by Yale (2001), who says that a tour operator is

a person or a company who purchases the different items that make up an inclusive holiday in bulk, combines them together to produce package holidays and then sells the final products to the public either directly or through travel agencies.

(Yale, 2001)

Table 12.1 Different conceptual viewpoints on tour operators

Viewpoint	Description
Wholesalers	They buy in large quantities from principals/suppliers so as to sell in smaller quantities.
Principals	They gather necessary elements from suppliers, package a series of them into single whole new product, termed an "inclusive tour", and sell to the consumer. Here, the product is actually new, by changing the nature of those individual products.
"Light assembly" business	The tour operator assembles various travel and tour products and presents a competitively priced and convenient package to the customer for purchase.
Intermediary	The tour operator acts as an intermediary in enabling the consumer to purchase the products of the principals easily and conveniently.

Source: Adapted from Holloway and Taylor (2006)

In this definition, the emphasis is more on the role of a tour operator as an intermediary in the whole process of tourism. It makes it clear that the tour operator procures the required items from the suppliers in large quantities and then breaks them into smaller quantities suitable for consumption by an individual tourist or a group of tourists.

Moreover, the product is not just sold in the same way it is procured from the suppliers; instead, the small quantities of different items are combined to form a new product, called a package tour or a package holiday. In addition, it describes how it is transacted with the final consumer. The product is either sold directly by the tour operator to the potential tourist or through retail agents. However, for a retail travel agent, the tour operator can also be considered a supplier, but in the wider context it is equated with a wholesaler.

According to Kotler et al. (2009), tour wholesalers "assemble travel packages usually targeted at the leisure market. . . . in developing a package, a tour wholesaler contracts with airlines and hotels for a specific number of seats and rooms, receiving a quantity discount." Tour operators usually purchase services and products offered by various components of the tourism industry in advance, at substantial discounts. As wholesalers, they obtain the necessary components in large quantities from the principals, often from the transportation and accommodation industries, and convert these into individual packages as per the needs of the targeted potential travellers. The packages formed are marketed and made accessible to the final consumers through retailers like travel agents, online media or even directly. In this process, the tour operator simultaneously takes care of the interests of the suppliers as well as the consumers with almost equal responsibility. As the package tour is organized, the benefits are shared among all those involved in the industry. Principals can assure the sale of a good portion of their products far in advance and the tour operator can obtain such products and services at significantly discounted rates. To a certain extent, the principals, particularly small and medium establishments, get a financial advantage in terms of marketing and promotion costs, since a good share of their products and services are sold in advance. The tour operators provide a guarantee of sale of a portion of their products. This will enable the tour operators to achieve economies of scale by gaining discounted rates through bulk purchases. The price of the package tour is usually very economical from a customer's point of view. The wholesaler role of tour operation is the prime reason for its relevance in the context of tourism. Tour operators have to be efficient in acquiring the product components at a competitive price and reselling them at a price lower than what customers have to pay when they purchase each component separately.

Also, a tour operator is one who acts on behalf of principals in order to make the efficient sale and transaction of the products with the final consumer. Being the most relevant intermediary in tourism, this business provides advantages not only to principals like airlines and hotels, but also to the retailers and the final consumer – the tourists. Therefore, all the players in the tourism value chain appreciate the presence of tour operators. Another aspect is that a tour operator is a facilitator who arranges products and services in a very convenient and appropriate form for consumption. The consumer enjoys easy access and smooth consumption along with some financial benefits. An easier supply of the products is thus ensured by the tour operator.

12.3 Reasons for starting a tour operation business

Besides the role and relevance of the tour operation business as an intermediary, there are a number of reasons for starting a tour operation business as an entrepreneurial venture, whether the focus is on inbound or outbound operations, or both. In fact, the entry barriers are less in tour operation compared to other sectors, such as the airline industry which has a wide range of legal and operational entry barriers. A tour operation business, unlike other major tourism industries, is a less capital-intensive sector. Though it depends on the level of the business – whether small, medium or large – the capital investment required is much less compared to many other sectors in tourism. Even an individual can have a start-up tour operation business at a micro level quite easily provided they have adequate knowledge, experience and expertise to carry out the business. In the beginning, they require only very limited facilities, like a computer, Internet connection, telephone and stationery. Although the capital requirements are less, the potential profits are good for many reasons. From the sale of each package, from each tour participant, a certain amount of profit is accrued. On top of that, as an intermediary, the tour agency receives a commission from all the suppliers whose services are used. The commission thus accrued supplements the profits from package sales.

Besides the advantage of limited capital requirements, the operational cost or working capital is also relatively less. The number of employees required is relatively low for tour operation. In fact, tour operators achieve economies of scale by obtaining highly discounted prices on their bulk purchases. This makes it possible to break even much earlier, and provides higher profit potential. The profit margin will increase when the sale exceeds the minimum target number of sales for a group package. For instance, when a package is designed for 40 people with a reasonable profit margin, and after the marketing and promotion efforts, they can sell it to 60 people, the profit margin (from the extra sales) will be higher than the pre-set level. In addition, medium and large players offer a range of products and frequent trips. Such operators depend on volume sales for increasing profit, whereas specialized operators focus on niche market strategy with higher margin levels from each sale to maximize profit. Mass tour operators usually keep the profit margins low for each package sale. At the same time, they attempt to sell as many packages as possible, and profit maximization is achieved through volume. Large tour operators sometimes make an attempt to convert domestic holidays into international ones by conveying images of low-cost holidays. Moreover, consistent efforts are always made by large operators to increase market dominance. Competitive positioning is also undertaken to beat the competition (Page, 2007). The niche market players are also referred to as special interest tour (SIT) operators. Both large and niche players operate long-haul and short-haul tours. While some tour operators believe several short breaks each year benefit them more (Syratt and Archer, 2003), others emphasize long-haul holidays.

In addition, being an intermediary in tourism, the tour operator also gets the opportunity to travel to many destinations. This is of interest to those who are curious to travel. Usually destination promotion agencies and national tourist offices (NTO) offer familiarization ("fam") tours to intermediaries in order to acquaint them with the attractions and places. Such trips are also offered by other players, such as hotels and resorts. In addition, principals or suppliers like airlines and accommodation centres usually provide incentive tours to the most successful tour operators. Some key personnel can go as tour directors/managers/escorts, depending on the nature of the tour. All such opportunities give ample scope for travelling to many places. It is a challenging sector and the quality of services will often bring in high levels of customer satisfaction and eventually it will pave the way for expansion and growth. Even vertical and horizontal integration strategies are used by tour operators for growth and expansion, enabling them to become major players in the market, even at the international level.

12.4 Evolution of tour operation

Travel is one of the oldest activities in human history. Though early travel was for reasons such as trade, recreational travel soon emerged. Some forms of recreational and educational travel existed in ancient times, e.g. in Egypt under the pharaohs. Innovations and inventions of that era indeed changed the nature of travel. Sailing vessels are one example. The invention of the wheel and currency benefited travel immensely. The Romans established a well-maintained road system. Even inns, stables for animals, and crude maps or itineraries were established as part of ancient travel. Thus the phenomenon of travel gradually evolved into a major activity. Along with this evolution, people began to arrange their required travel and stay facilities well in advance. Organized travel thus emerged and the traces of tour operation in a limited manner can be seen in history. Some ancient travel proceeded in an organized way. For instance, the ancient Persians and the Egyptians travelled in this manner. People travelled long distances even during the Roman era, with prior arrangements having been made. According to Feifer (1985), imperial Rome was "the first culture genuinely to produce mass tourism, in both the letter and spirit of the term". That progressed further, with Pond (1993) suggesting that the organized travel activities existed in the early years. "The first 'package tours' were likely those available during the medieval period, from Venice to the 'Holy Land', when a trip's cost would include passage, meals and wine, accommodations, donkey rides, and bribe money for protection." (Pond, 1993)

The spread of religions, especially Christianity, also contributed to the development of travel. Even a form of package tour was organized for religious purposes. Later, the Industrial Revolution was a catalyst for travel. Simultaneously, the grand tour – for cultural exploration in an organized manner – flourished in Europe. During their grand tour, a traveller was accompanied by a tutor, a kind of scholarly escort.

12.4.1 Thomas Cook pioneered tour operation

Still, organized tour operation began in a professional manner only when Thomas Cook conducted the first well-organized tour in 1841. Thomas Cook is regarded as the father of modern tour operation (Reilly, 1991). He organized that tour for 570 people travelling from Leicester to Loughborough using a hired train. That successful trip gave the impetus to move ahead with the novel venture of professional tour operation. Many of his ideas became success stories and his business developed into a large one with regular innovations. Initially, in order to make the tours a success, he personally escorted the tourists himself. He was primarily depending on the railways, and bought tickets that he then resold to the travellers. He prepared itineraries and other tour documents. Until the 1860s, Cook focused on domestic destinations. He was also the person who introduced travel vouchers. It was a revolutionary act, as using a travel voucher in the travel and hospitality industry became common practice for many years. He introduced the "circular ticket" using rail transport, "hotel coupon" for accommodation payment and the "circular note" for exchanging of foreign currency. Later, overseas offices were started in Cairo and Alexandria, Egypt. Thomas Cook started the first travel newspaper as well, called *The Excursionist,* with English, French, German, Indian and Australian editions. Diversification of product offerings was a success factor in his business. He expanded his tour business by adding a variety of options, including tours through Europe, luxury rail journeys to India, and cruises along the Nile river. The company grew rapidly, providing escorted tours to Europe and to other continents, and it continued for many years. In

Figure 12.1 Statue of Thomas Cook near Leicester railway station
Courtesy: Wikimedia Commons

fact, it remains a major international brand, though there were some changes to its ownership and management in the later stages of its growth. Some of the major milestones in the Thomas Cook era of tour operation are provided here:

- 1845 – Thomas Cook started commercially operated tours to Liverpool.
- 1855 – Thomas Cook commenced excursions to Europe.
- 1856 – Thomas Cook organized his first tour of Europe.

- 1867/1868 – Thomas Cook introduced hotel coupons.
- 1871 – the company name becomes Thomas Cook and Sons.
- 1872 – at a price of 210 guineas, he offered round the world trips.
- 1874 – Cook's circular note, an early form of the traveller's cheque, launched.
- 1878 – banking and money exchange services began.
- 1886 – his son, John Mason Cook, took the first American tour.
- 1890 – John Cook began to popularize Egyptian tours.
- 1891 – *The Business of Travel: A Fifty Years' Record of Progress* was published.
- 1892 – Thomas Cook dies at the age of 83.

12.4.2 Other legendary entrepreneurs in tour operation

Once Thomas Cook's venture became successful, some other entrepreneurs also entered the realm of tour operation. There were innovations in these attempts as well, and all such contributed to the evolution of the tour operation industry. Among them, Ward G. Foster and Henry Lunn deserve special mention, as their ventures paved way for new forms of tour operation. Even before that, in 1850 Thomas Bennett started a travel agency business in Europe. He established the business as a "trip organizer" and his offerings included itineraries, transport arrangements and a travel kit along with accommodation arrangements. Ward Foster started travel services under the brand name Ask Mr Foster in St Augustine, Florida in 1888. Sir Henry Lunn started the first winter sports tourism in 1898. Henry Lunn was the founder of Lunn Poly, once a large travel firm in Europe. He also founded Co-operative Educational Tours in 1893. Many recreational associations and clubs were started in that era. These mainly focused on sports activities. For instance, in 1878, a cycling club was formed which organized the first continental tours in the following year, and in 1888, the Polytechnic Touring Organization organized the first cruises to Norway. It was in 1891 that American Express introduced the traveller's cheque. It later became an invaluable instrument in overseas tours, a trend that continued for many decades.

By the beginning of the twentieth century, a new form of transport, aviation, entered the travel scene. Commercial air travel began by the second decade of the twentieth century. Many experiments were undertaken in aviation during the First and Second World Wars which strengthened air transport. Newer flights, which were initially used for transportation of arms and ammunition, were later used for passenger transport. Once passenger air transport began, people's propensity to travel increased greatly. Charter flights for tours were soon introduced. Airline companies, such as United, Western and Pan Am, were established in the 1920s and a number of airports were constructed soon after the end of the First World War. Arthur Tauck, another legendary figure in the tour operation business, commenced operations in 1925. He started guided tours, river cruises, safaris and similar tours from the US. He is often referred to as the pioneer of adventure tours. By the 1920s, the Thomas Cook Company had begun offering the first flights to Paris, and in 1939 it offered a "round the world tour" by flying boat. The Second World War caused sluggishness in the tour operation sector. Once the war was over, things started to change rapidly. Air transport developed into a major mode of transport at that time. Package tour business using air transport became more economical once larger flights started to be used for passenger travel. Vladimir Raitz, who started Horizon Holidays in 1949, has been credited with establishing the mass charter air transport to "sun" destinations for the first time. All-inclusive skiing holidays emerged towards the end of the 1940s. In 1948, Erna Low came up with exclusive ski tour packages to Murren, Switzerland, and that too widened the product range in tour operation.

Soon after the end of the Second World War, air charter package tours began and the 1950s saw a gradual increase in the popularity of such package tours. Package holidays to warm sunny destinations in the Mediterranean began sometime towards the end of the 1940s. It was during this time that the paid holiday concept became common practice. By 1945 almost 14 million British workers were receiving paid holiday entitlements. Growth in paid holidays, particularly in Europe, contributed to the rapid development of tour operations after the Second World War. Entrepreneurs like Vladimir Raitz started to use old turboprop planes for charter services. In 1952, Horizon Holidays offered charter services. This helped tour operators to offer long-haul tours. In the same year, airlines introduced "tourist fares" and the first "economy fare" appeared in 1958. Air transport recorded another milestone around this time when jet engines were introduced to the aviation sector. Jet engines brought increased speed, range, load carrying capacity, reliability and comfort. The first jet engine aircraft, the Boeing 707, was put into use in 1958. Charter airlines also began using jet aircraft later. Package tours, especially mass tours, increased in popularity as a result of the use of large airplanes. In 1963, Caledonian and Donaldson Lin introduced the first inclusive tours to the US, and Hapimag popularized the "timeshare" concept in holidaying. A number of tour companies had emerged by the end of the 1950s, especially in Europe. Outbound tourism expanded well, especially after the advent of long-haul tours and with the advancements in the air transport sector. Outbound tour operation had grown continually, though it faced some setbacks at certain points along the way.

12.4.3 Growth and the challenges after the Second World War

As more and more tour companies started tour operation businesses, players in the sector faced stiff competition. Airlines and tour operators were engaged in high level competition and the price of packaged holidays was lowered. Though the industry was progressing, there was a collapse for a short period after the 1960s, especially in the UK. The reasons for the decline, according to Holloway and Taylor (2006), include the following:

- Rapid growth, over-borrowing for expansion and even, in some cases, lack of management expertise
- "Price war" and consequently underpricing in order to survive
- Impact of external forces: fuel price hike, political unrest in some destination countries, and economic downfall

The increasing price war alarmed the travel industry and consequently some regulations were formulated in order to mitigate the effects in Europe. The regulations, as spelt out by Yale (2001), are as follows:

- Clients stay for a specific or minimum duration at their destination.
- A minimum or maximum advance booking period is imposed.
- Minimum prices for selling "inclusive tours" are ensured.
- Charter flight services are restricted only to certain types of passengers.

The post-war era saw the emergence of cruise tourism as well. Shipping liners were one of the major transport modes until the 1950s. Cruising emerged as the most promising opportunity for declining shipping services, and some began offering cruise tourism. By then, fly-cruise packages to the Mediterranean were being offered by Cunard.

Cruising was quite expensive and its major market segment was senior citizens. Cruise tourism remains one of the fastest growing segments.

Meanwhile, during the 1970s, the industry faced a stiff challenge. The formation of OPEC and the corresponding rise in oil prices severely affected the transportation sector and this impacted holidaying as well. In 1974, the price of oil doubled and travel costs increased by more than twofold, which had a knock-on effect for the entire travel sector. The ensuing price war and increasing travel costs triggered financial crises for many tour operators. Some of them were closed down. Those that could survive had to think of strategies to overcome the crises. Innovative concepts soon emerged and diversification became a norm in the sector. Special interest tourism turned out to be the focus of many firms, especially small and medium organizations. Specialized tours, also called "niche holidays" emerged during this period. Slowly, the industry prevailed over the challenges. At the same time, due to severe financial difficulties, the industry had witnessed several mergers and acquisitions, and the emergence of some multinational firms.

While tourism has been progressing well since then, there have been some incidents that halted that growth. The Gulf War that took place in 1991 also posed difficulties for the sector, followed by the 9/11 attacks in the US, which severely affected the travel sector for some time. The spread of diseases like Ebola, severe acute respiratory syndrome (SARS), etc. have also affected travel in many regions. Natural calamities like tsunamis have also had an impact on the growth of tourism. At the same time, the pervasiveness of the Internet had became a threat to the tour operation industry. The tendency of travellers to make online purchases of travel and hospitality products is growing steadily. Online itinerary planning and similar activities are also very common nowadays. However, the tour operation sector remains competitive.

12.4.4 Growth factors

There are many factors that have contributed to the growth of outbound tours/overseas holidays. The post-Second World War period has seen significant changes in social, political and technological spheres of life. Many countries started to enjoy increased political freedom, especially after the end of colonial rule. Democracy became more prevalent. The improved relations among countries also contributed to the exponential growth in tourism. Countries also started developing tourism substantially. East Asian countries began aggressive tourism developments in the 1960s. More destinations started developing infrastructure for tourism. Such developments enabled long-haul tourism to grow. Deregulation in key business sectors occurred and liberalization efforts gained momentum. Transnational businesses became widespread as part of the globalization movement. The emergence of information technology (IT) had a very significant influence on the growth of travel. New destinations emerged on the world tourism map as more and more countries started developing and promoting tourism. Economic standards of people in many regions improved as a result. The increase in leisure time and greater discretionary income in developing countries also contributed to the growth of holidaying.

One of the primary reasons for tourism's growth is the advancement that has taken place in transport technology. Speed, comfort and safety have increased steadily. Long-distance travel has become more enjoyable. Revolutionary development of information technology and the integration of it with communication technology has become another significant cause of the remarkable growth of overseas touring. Information technology became part and parcel of the tourism industry. Though it varies, every operation in all the elements of the tourism sector is now benefiting from information technology applications. Tourists now have increased access to quality information from every corner of the world. Product information, which was initially only available from intermediaries primarily, became very easily accessible. The travel propensity is influenced greatly by tourists' IT use as well. The socio-economic changes which happened after the Second World War directly influenced the growth of tourism. As employment and income opportunities increased, so too did travel. Overall health indicators became more favourable for travel. Better health standards have a direct relationship with travel propensity. Early retirement from services also helped the growth of travel. Early retirement provides more free time and better health conditions, both of which are favourable to long journeys. Education levels have also risen around the world. The increase in education has a direct bearing on the propensity to travel too. Better education levels always increase people's propensity to travel, and influence the nature of holidaying. The paid holiday concept soon became a norm in the industry, with the objective of enhancing productivity of employees. In addition, the amount of free time people had also rose gradually.

As income levels of the population across the world increased, the lifestyle of people also improved, and that directly or indirectly became favourable to travel. Across the world, the rate of urbanization increased gradually. As urbanization increased, so too did travel, particularly outbound travel. The ever-advancing transport technology enables safer, more luxurious and speedier travel. This also contributes to the growth of tourism. Transport infrastructure has improved tremendously over the last 50 years or so. Transport facilities like airports have also changed substantially. As competition increased, the price of travel and tourism products came down, making the products accessible to a larger section of the population. Increasing competition also resulted in enhancing standards in product offerings and in maintaining quality levels. Furthermore, the diversity in product offerings was expanded, attracting more people to visit. Creativity and innovation became a strategy in the tourism sector, and dynamism turned out to be a determinant in the success of tourist destinations. Every now and then, new attractions and destinations enter the tourism realm. Experienced travellers may prefer variety and uniqueness, which helps the newer destinations get established in the international tourism scenario.

The evolution of tourism was also helped by the regular addition of new market segments. While some are geographical segments, the others are demographic. For instance, retired people in good health constituted a major market segment which increased the quantity of tourism. Travel propensity started to penetrate almost all societies in the world. The phenomenal evolution of business travel is one major reason for the quick growth of tourism, particularly since the 1990s. By this time modern globalization had begun its march across the world, meaning countries the world over were forced to adopt liberalization policies. This spurred the growth of business travel tremendously. A section of the business travel sector also depended, partially or fully, on the assistance of the tour operation industry, and that too caused the growth of the tour operation business. Altogether, the tour operation sector evolved into a major element of the tourism industry, with a significant contribution to the growth and development of tourism around the world.

12.5 Tour operation: the product, suppliers and the consumer

For any business, there will be a product of value that can be transacted with consumers. While discussing the nature of tour operators' products, the "overall tourism product view", suggested by Medlik and Middleton (1973), is particularly relevant. It says, "as far as the tourist is concerned, the product covers the complete experience from the time he leaves home to the time he returns to it". They further state that tourism products are an amalgam of three components: attraction, facilities at the destination and accessibility. Here, a tour also encompasses the complete experience one can have from the time of commencement of the journey until the time the traveller is back home. It also encompasses an amalgam of product components. It was in that context that Middleton et al. (2009) pointed out the "components view" of travel and tourism products. In their view, such a product is "a group of components or elements brought together in a 'bundle' selected to satisfy needs" of the tourists. They further state that "the bundle may be designed, altered and fitted together in many different ways calculated to match identified customer needs" (Middleton et al., 2009). The tour operator also focuses on the ideal "bundle" to be offered to the tourist. Moreover, the appropriate bundle is developed that matches the target group's needs and interests.

The tour operator adds value to the process in different ways, which results in the form of benefits for tour operation and advantages for consumers. In the tourism business, a tour operator acts as an intermediary. At the same time, when we consider the tour operator separately, we can see that they produce a product with certain characteristics and distribute it to the final consumer. Here, the operator plays the role of a producer of a product by taking inputs from the suppliers and regrouping and arranging them into a new form that can be sold in a more convenient mode, with easier access, to the consumers. For example, when a tour operator makes a package, they purchase rooms, airline seats and some other services from suppliers, and create packages to be consumed by tourists in a more affordable and convenient form. This will be distributed to the potential tourists either through an intermediary like a retail travel agent or sold directly. As a result, the role of a tour operator becomes more significant, much more so than that of a simple wholesaler. The product ultimately is a combination of the products of different suppliers.

The idea of the package being the chief product of a tour operator is clarified in the following extract:

> In every case the packages that tour operator assemble are drawn from the five basic elements of the overall tourism product, plus whatever added value of their own operations is built in, such as price guarantees, convenience, accessibility to the customer, image and branding, high standards and sense of security in dealing with a reputable company.
>
> (Middleton et al., 2009)

Hence, the primary product of a tour operator is a bundle of components called a package. It is a combination of two or more of the elements of the tourism system. Those elements included are chosen according to the requirements of the individuals or groups who wish to visit a destination for a period not less than 24 hours. Transportation and accommodation are the most commonly included elements. Some other elements may include sightseeing, activities, optional tours, shopping, food services, entertainment and interpretation/guiding depending upon the nature of the tour and the requirements of the consumers.

Conceptually and from a marketing perspective, the product is considered to have different layers based on product offering. While some authors identified three layers of offering, some others came forward with more levels. In the three-layer concept, as suggested by Kotler et al. (2009), the levels are seen as a continuum, with the product's most basic benefit at one end and a range of add-on benefits at the other end, not directly related to the product's essential purpose. The core product, tangible product and augmented product constitute those layers. **The core product** represents the most basic "need function" served by the generic product and what a customer is really buying. This is the most fundamental level and it may be a sort of intangible aspect of the product. The core product is directly connected to core competencies of the companies. For instance, in the hospitality industry, it can be the experience offered for "rest and relaxation". **The tangible product** is used when describing the specific features and benefits involved in the product itself, like the quality level, service features, styling, brand name, design, packaging, etc. There are some other features or add-ons that are extrinsic to the product itself, but may influence the decision to purchase, and are referred to as the **augmented product**.

Levitt (1981) proposed a similar theory, called the customer value hierarchy concept which involves five product levels, each adding to customer value. In his analysis, the first level, the core product, represents the same as above. The second level is called the **basic** or **generic product**. In this level, the marketer turns the core benefit into a basic product, as in the case of a hotel, where the core benefit, "rest and relaxation", is converted into a product with facilities including bed, bathrooms, toilets, towels, etc. According to Levitt, the third level is the **expected product,** which involves a set of attributes and conditions that a customer expects to purchase. In the same example, the customer expects to buy a clean bed, fresh towels, a degree of quietness and the like. The **augmented product** is one which the marketer may prepare to exceed the customer expectations. Product positioning can happen at this level. In a hotel, arranging a smart TV in the room, placing fresh flowers and ensuring prompt room service can make the augmented product. The **potential product** is the highest level, which includes all possible augmentation and transformation a product might undergo in the future. In this, the marketer searches for new ways to satisfy the customer and distinguish that offer. Aiming for customer delight is an expectation in this level.

Similar levels need to be identified in tour operation as well. While marketing the package tour and other products, it is essential to identify such levels. In both of the above concepts, by engaging in tourism, the vital benefits a tourist seeks may include the travel, stay and sightseeing which form the core product. The generic product may include the needed mechanism to provide the services to the tourist. Expected product could be when the customer expects comfortable travel and stay, pleasant sightseeing, etc. The augmented product level can be identified when the tour operator prepares to exceed the tourist satisfaction by offering something special, such as free travel bags, good entertainment programmes, grand dinners, high-quality accommodation services. Higher levels of service and facilities can also be offered to delight customers. According to the concept suggested by Kotler et al. (2009), the quality of services, brand name of various service providers and that of the operator, services actually offered in the package, etc. become part of the tangible component of the package tour. The augmented product can be the add-ons and those may influence the buying behaviour, such as credit terms, insurance offered, briefing documents, luggage offers and similar. Marketers can make use of the identified product levels in each of their products so as to beat the competition and achieve their marketing objectives, with a perspective that looks towards the future.

As we have already learnt, the consumer and customer of a tourism product may not always be the same. A customer is one who pays for and purchases a product. Yet, a customer need not necessarily be a consumer. In some cases, the product purchased by one may be consumed by another, in which case the customer and the consumer are two different people. A consumer is the one who purchases a commodity or a service and uses it personally. It doesn't mean the consumer always pays for the product. For example, a flight ticket for an executive in a corporate company to attend a business meeting in another city may be purchased by another executive who looks after such activities in the company, in the administration department. The decision that led to the purchase may have been taken by another manager. But the executive who attends the meeting is the consumer, as they are the real traveller. The tour operator, too, purchases the product components in advance, breaks them down, regroups them into a new form, and sells them to the final consumer directly or through an intermediary. The tourist is always the ultimate consumer in the system, and they experience the phenomenon of tourism during the course of their journey until they arrive back to their place of origin. Tour operators primarily focus on packaging the elements in a way that can be conveniently consumed by a tourist who is the final consumer.

Suppliers provide their product offerings as demanded by the tour operator, who likes to include various elements in a package according to the customer's needs and interests. While some tour operators offer all-inclusive packages, others offer travel and accommodation alone in their packages. Choosing the right supplier is a difficult task for tour operators. Hotels, resorts, airlines and restaurants are some examples of suppliers in the context of tour operation. Tour operators also have the responsibility of ensuring the quality of the suppliers' products included in their packages. Moreover, the products are consumed at locations far away from the location of the tour operator and that, too, poses a challenge in ensuring standards and quality. The tour operator usually makes an attempt to take maximum advantage of discounts. The terms and conditions also have to be favourable to the tour operator before signing the agreement with the suppliers.

A wrong product included can harm the entire package irrespective of the quality of other products. The satisfaction level of the consumer is critical for the long-term survival of a tour operator. Therefore, the tour operator has to design and develop the product with the utmost care and diligence. Professional and efficient design and execution of a package is a determinant in the success of tour operation. It is not just purchasing the product elements from suppliers in bulk and selling them in small quantities. It is about careful planning, design and development of a product using expertise and efficiency. The tour operator ensures the smooth execution of the tour with the assistance of professional escorts/managers, through overseas representatives or with the help of inbound handling agencies. Professionalism and expertise are key in making the most suitable product as per the needs and interests of consumers. Tour operators' products have certain characteristics in common:

- Intangibility
- Perishability
- Inseparability
- Variability
- Discretionary products
- Heterogeneous

12.6 Types of tour operators

There are different types of tour operators. Some of the major ones are introduced below.

12.6.1 Inbound tour operator

An inbound tourist is one who arrives from a foreign country for the purpose of visiting. Inbound tour operators are those who deal with and handle directly inbound tourists and provide them with the required services in the destination, such as local transportation, transfers and sightseeing trips. The clients may include travellers coming from overseas markets with an interest in a specific destination or activity. The main product consists of packaged tours/holidays for groups or independent travellers belonging to markets in foreign countries. Mostly, the packages are designed in-house, with some services from ground operators and local service providers. As an inbound tour operator's responsibility of handling a tourist begins at the arrival point in a country, the tour operation activities commence with the transfer of arriving tourists from the arriving airport to the hotel. The duty of an inbound tour operator ends with dropping the tourist at the exit port. The activities of inbound handling include "meet and great", transfer, accommodation arrangements, excursions, optional trips, shopping assistance and specialist services.

Usually an itinerary will be followed during the whole trip, though in certain cases the duties are limited to arranging some facilities only. Some inbound tour operators act just as ground handling agents, arranging accommodation and transport facilities along with "meet and greet" activities. Usually, they are small-scale operators. The main focus of marketing will be on foreign countries and developing products and services to cater to the requirements of those populations. In some cases, inbound operators handle tours on behalf of other tour operators situated in the market country. Marketing of inbound tour operation is more complicated, as the market is far away from the location of the operator. In order to avoid complications, an inbound operator attempts to have links with outbound operators functioning in the source markets. Usually, the product is sold through outbound tour operators. Sometimes, they may pursue direct sales as well. Resellers, retailers, web portals, online agents, e-commerce sites, etc. are also considered for sales. Online marketing activities are carried out by inbound operators more often than outbound operators. The following are the usual services rendered by inbound tour operators:

- "Meet and greet" at the airport
- Onward and return transfers
- Hotel check-in and orientation
- Sightseeing tours
- Accommodation arrangements
- Guide services
- Courier services
- Concierge
- Secretarial services
- Theatre services and arranging conferences
- Special interest holidays
- Food and beverage holidays
- Reconfirmation of flight reservations
- Travel documentation assistance
- Assistance during emergencies

12.6.2 Outbound tour operator

Whilst an outbound tourist represents someone who departs their country in order to visit other countries, an outbound tour operator denotes a tour operating agency that organizes tours for residents of a country to visit another country. They sell package tours to groups of people or individuals who are local residents, which facilitate travel to another country or multiple countries. They arrange the required services and facilities in a foreign country that customers would like to visit. The domestic or regional market is the source market and therefore the focus of marketing activities is inside their home country. The target market may be people with specific interests to visit certain places or attractions, usually a defined audience, in the domestic market. The primary product is packaged tours to a variety of destinations for groups or independent travellers. They operate both group packages as well as individual customized tours. Furthermore, they may offer variety, with different packages consisting of diverse destinations/attractions. Planning, designing and developing the product according to the needs and interests of the targeted market segments takes place in the home country itself. Sometimes products are sourced from inbound operators, or may be designed in-house with assistance from inbound operators, ground operators and local service providers in the destination country. Others work with partners in the destination.

Being an agency from the same region, outbound operators can have in-depth knowledge of customer preferences, trends and interests. With the availability of potential customers in and around the location, marketing the tour may be easier for an outbound operator than for an inbound operator who would have to overcome the challenges of marketing in foreign countries. Activities like market research and marketing communication can be done with less difficulty. Outbound operators may undertake direct sales to consumers, sell through resellers or portals, or through specialized agencies. Targeted marketing is also carried out using different channels. Social organizations and associations are other sources for target marketing as affinity group travel can originate from such organizations. Targeted marketing through direct mail (of catalogues, brochures), via websites and customer loyalty programmes, and at travel fairs is also considered by outbound operators. Outbound operation is more laborious, as the matters related to international travel also have to be dealt with by them. The major functions of outbound operators include:

- Designing tour itinerary
- Travel advice and consultations
- Arranging accommodation
- Travel facilitation services
- Travel arrangements
- Developing package tours
- Marketing and sales activities
- Organizing package tours
- Ensuring overseas operations
- Assistance during emergency situations

12.6.3 International and domestic tour operators

A tourist's country of origin and the intended destination is the basis for the classification of tourists, into domestic and international. Likewise, tour operators are classified into domestic and international on the basis of the country in which the tour is executed. An international tour operator plans, designs and executes tours to overseas destinations.

Both inbound tours and outbound tours are basically international tours as they involve crossing of country borders. Domestic tour operators organize tours for residents of a country to visit destinations situated within the boundaries of that country. The country of origin and destination are one and the same. Domestic tour handling is easier, as it doesn't involve many of the hassles associated with travelling abroad. While international tour operation is associated with air transport, domestic is often associated with coach tours, though railways and flights are seen widely nowadays.

Domestic tour operation is also an important segment in the tour operation industry. In large countries with ample tourist locations spread over different areas, domestic tour operators play a key role in facilitating tourism within the country. The origin and destination of the tourist in this category remains the same. Tour operation and marketing are relatively easier since the travel takes place within the country and the source market is also the same country. Some domestic tour operators carry out the same duties as outbound operators, whereas others act as ground handling agents. Bigger firms usually undertake both functions. Coach tours are predominant in domestic tours. However, railways and flights are also widely used.

12.6.4 Ground operator

In the parlance of tourism, the term "ground operator" is used to refer to the small-scale agents who arrange the required services and facilities for incoming tourists through tour operators or independent travellers in a destination or a region. In general, ground operators provide services required by tour operators in the destination where they do not have a local branch/office or are not dealing directly with the suppliers over there. These operators, unlike tour operators, rarely conduct direct sales or sell packages. Instead, they operate primarily for outbound tour operators as they are their main clients. However, package tour services or necessary tour arrangements are done in the destination for those who have already arrived in the destination independently, not through any other kind of tourism intermediary. Services of local suppliers are resold or used as part of their operation. Usually these companies do not actively market their services directly to customers in foreign markets. Though target marketing at international level is not done, these operators undertake some local advertisements or similar marketing communication techniques along with some online efforts.

12.6.5 Local service providers

These are also similar to ground operators, but the operation is at the local level specifically. Their business, to a large extent, depends on the inbound tour operators, and sometimes the outbound tour operators as well. They carry out services in a locality, not on a large scale or at the country level. Most commonly, they undertake local services such as rental services, accommodation arrangements, organizing cultural performances and the like. The service is rendered to the independent tourists who have already arrived in the destination as well. The tour operators are contacted for getting the business, yet in order to attract independent tourists already in the country, some kind of marketing communication tactics will be used at the local level.

12.6.6 Mass market tour operator

Mass market operators prefer to have group tours to established and well-known destinations. While offering highly packaged products, they ensure standardized packages for sale. Most of the activities constituting the holiday in the destination are prearranged. The profit is earned from volume sales as the margin from each sale is less. The commission they receive from the suppliers may vary, but the rate can be higher depending on the quantity of operation and the reputation of the operator. "Economies of scale" is very relevant in the case of mass operators as they purchase in bulk and the discount they receive is much higher. Usually they sell package tours at cheaper rates as they can buy the product elements at discounted rates due to advance bulk purchases. In general, mass operators are medium and large firms, comparatively, though small firms also exist in the market.

12.6.7 Specialist operators

Special interest tourism is a trend in this modern era. Experiential tourism is also gaining increased significance. Unlike mass tourism, specialist tours are not to established destinations or attractions; rather, they are initiated for people with specific motivations to experience something different in their life, or as part of a passion. Distinguished tourism products are consumed in this category. Unique locations and niche attractions are preferred. Usually medium- or small-scale operators are interested in SITs. Customers are placed in the special interest category and the price range is usually higher than that of mass tours. Moreover, the tour operator has to be well versed in the attractions and destinations as the tourists are more inquisitive during purchase decision-making and even during the trip. In certain cases, they also have to acquire the necessary skills for operating such tours. For example, it would be better for an adventurous tour operator to know how to do the activities involved in the tour.

12.6.8 Other types

Tour operators are also classified on the basis of the mode of transport used. There are a number of transport-based tour operators in the holiday sector globally. **Coach tour operators** use buses/coaches for conducting a tour, usually within a country. This can be to various locations where a group tour is arranged. A coach has many advantages as a medium for transport which were discussed earlier in this book. A tour leader, an escort or a courier can easily be accommodated to travel with the group. Specialist guides will be involved as and when required. Multiple locations can be visited as part of coach tours. Coach tours are still a major sector in the whole tourism industry. For example, according to the Coach Tourism Council (CTC, n.d.), it is

> one of the UK's biggest travel sectors. Around nine million people take a coach tour each year while in the UK; coaches contribute £2.35 billion to the UK economy. CTC members play a major role in meeting the increasing demand for day excursions, short breaks and holidays by coach which offer unbeatable value for money.

Rail tour operators constitute another type. Some operators conduct tours using rail transport. Domestic tours are more suitable for this type, though there are many international rail-based tours operated by various agents. Rail tours are comparatively cheaper (except luxury tourist train trips), and trains have many advantages as a mode of transport. These are also usually escorted tours, with necessary guiding services wherever they are required. Some of the rail companies themselves organize luxury tourist trains exclusively for tourism purposes. **Ferry tour operators** are also available. They use ferries for transporting tourists from the point of origin to the destination. They are usually short-haul tours. Some tour operators use charter services for conducting package tours. **A charter tour operator** is one that sells or operates tours using charter flights. Either they hire a charter aircraft and organize tours using that, or they use part-charter arrangements. Long-haul tours are used more often in the charter tourism scene. **Cycle tour operators** are also prevalent, particularly of late. Tours using bicycles are also a common trend nowadays. Cycle tourism is spreading to almost every part of the world. Usually these tours are organized to the countryside. Youngsters are the main market segment of this type of tour, which is also comparatively cheaper. Good health and interest in experiencing the nuances of village life and the natural environment are prerequisites for cycle tours. A **safari operator** offers safaris to different geographical areas, such as into forests and deserts. Automobiles are used in certain cases. Animals are also used in some cases, like a safari into a forest or a game reserve.

12.7 Contributions and benefits of tour operation

Based on the fundamental functions involved in tour operations, the major contributions of tour operators in the whole tourism value chain, as suggested by Laws (1997), include the following:

- Enhance accessibility of tourism industry
- Make tour components more affordable
- Select and package tour components
- Organize sightseeing and entertainment
- Establish and monitor quality standards in supplier services and offerings
- Promote and distribute tour products/components
- Disseminate destination information
- Manage relationships with principals/suppliers and distributors

The benefits gained by the stakeholders of a tour operation sector are diverse. Even in the era of globalization where online buying is so prevalent, the tour operation sector survives and is competitive, due particularly to its capability to enhance value in the entire value chain and to provide benefits to all the key players in the process of tourism. The very existence of this business owes much to the advantages it provides to tourists, suppliers as well as destinations. Each of the stakeholders gets different benefits from the tour operation process. For example, tour operators play a crucial role in the competitive survival of a tourist destination. This is particularly true for new and emerging destinations that have to ensure regular inflows of tourists in order to become a noted international destination. Such destinations usually find difficulty in attracting enough tourists, especially since the tourism markets are dispersed and located far away from them. Moreover, marketing the destinations in different market countries is not an easy task. Mass tour operators prefer to operate tours to established destinations. Seasonality minimization is indeed essential for a destination and the presence of tour operators help in this regard. Tour operators can also ensure tourist arrivals in the off season, which helps the sustainability of the associated industries. Tourists, the final consumers of the tourism product, certainly enjoy a range of benefits by purchasing package tours. The same is the case with suppliers. Let's go through the benefits of each of them in detail.

12.7.1 Benefits to tourists

Tourists are the main beneficiaries of this business process. The major benefits a tourist gains from consuming a package tour are discussed below.

Expertise and knowledge

Tourists benefit immensely from the expertise and knowledge of a professional tour operator while travelling to a strange place. In this era of the Internet, one can find almost limitless options to choose from while making a purchase decision. Choosing the most appropriate product is indeed a time-consuming and difficult task. The "intangibility" of the product complicates the decision-making process further. Whilst a tourist runs down the list of possible options – the places to visit, hotel to stay, guide to interpret for him, etc. – the expertise of a tour operator will be very valuable. Professional operators have intimate knowledge of destinations and can suggest activities to take part in. A tour operator gains the knowledge through many years of regular operation to the respective destinations and through market researche.

Time efficiency

Package tours are designed by professionals to provide time efficiency, thus minimizing the wastage of time throughout the trip. The utmost care is taken while designing a tour itinerary and that helps to significantly minimize time wastage. The tour is held as per the planned schedule, which will ensure the optimum utilization of time in terms of the clients' requirements.

Ease and convenience

An overseas holiday is not an easy affair. It involves crossing borders, booking and arranging the services and facilities required, engaging in activities in a strange place, etc. The tour operator acts on behalf of the tourist. Arranging travel documents and tour components is the responsibility of the tour operator. The tourist is free from any currency exchange issues, booking of services and facilities, finding out about suitable restaurants, accessing the right shopping locations, getting the right tour guides and the like. Internal transportation in a destination is also a hassle that, usually, is taken care of by the agent. As all the essential needs are taken care of, the travel takes place far more easily and conveniently.

Economical

Tour operators are wholesalers as well. They buy products in bulk at discounted prices and form packages from these. Tour components such as transportation and accommodation are usually bought at wholesale rates, far in advance, and hence the package tours can be provided at very economical rates to the clients. Certainly, this arrangement is more economical than individual arrangements. If one books everything oneself, from air travel to tour guides, the total amount would be much higher. While buying package tours, tourists benefit by divided costs as well, in addition to the benefit of wholesaling.

Less planning time

Tourists do not have to bother about making bookings and arrangements. They do not expend travel planning time other than their necessary personal arrangements. Tours are bought when arrangements are already made by the operator. Tourists spend less time planning their trip compared to a free independent traveller (FIT). It takes a lot of time for a tourist to ensure all their own travel arrangements. It's a lot of work to identify the most suitable option, find out about availability with service providers, compare the costs and services, choose the right option, book services, make advance payments and arrange other services.

More safety and security

There is a chance that safety and security issues could occur while travelling to unknown destinations. Individual travellers, in general, are more at risk of safety issues than travellers in organized group tours. While in a group tour with a professional tour operator, the chance of being confronted by safety and security issues is much less. Usually, all possible measures would have been taken by the tour operator before venturing into travel. Yet, there is an element of uncertainty in any kind of travel, and many of the safety and security issues are unpredictable. In the events of an emergency, tour operators will have representatives to take care of it. This minimizes the risk for the tourist while travelling.

Social

In a group tour, a unique social environment may be automatically formed. Group tours offer opportunities for strengthening friendships and/or making new friends. Group tours are more enjoyable for those who like to be in such a social environment. Affinity groups and SITs usually form a pleasant social environment. The shared interest among members in the affinity group makes the journey more pleasurable.

More sightseeing/activities

Most of the package tour elements are well suited, with diverse attractions and activities, and organized in an efficient manner. Due to "time efficiency", participants can cover more attractions and engage in more activities than they could travelling alone, without the assistance of a professional agency. Improperly planned travel can result in wastage of time and some of the attractions could be left out. Also, a package tour follows a more or less fixed schedule which enables the tourists to cover more attractions and activities.

Assistance or guidance throughout

In most package tours, there will be an escort, tour manager, tour director or guide who will accompany the tour participants during the entire course of their journey. In some cases, overseas representatives will be there to assist tourists when required. Tourists get adequate assistance and guidance throughout the journey due to the presence of any one of them.

More relaxing

The package tour reduces the burden of travel arrangements and results in more pleasure due to less stress. The coordination and organization of the tour is vested with the tour operator. The tourists can relax more and enjoy the travel much more easily. The uncertainty associated with travelling can be minimized, to a large extent, by the efficiency of the tour operator.

12.7.2 Benefits for destinations

Destinations, especially the mass tourist and special interest destinations, benefit greatly from tour operation. In addition, tour operators' service is essential for an emerging tourist destination. The following benefits are enjoyed by destinations.

Regular arrival

Regular tourist arrivals in destinations are critical for destinations to survive in the long run. This is crucial for newer, burgeoning destinations as they may face difficulty in getting tourists due to less awareness in tourist markets. Due to regular tourist arrivals, seasonality can also be minimized. The role of tour operators in ensuring tourist arrivals is significant for any tourist destination.

Entrepreneurial activity

The more the tourists come, the greater the expansion in the supply environment. Moreover, the supplementary/ancillary sectors will also flourish. Altogether, local entrepreneurship will be enhanced due to the inflow of tourists.

Base for infrastructure development

As tourists are brought in regularly by tour operators, destination managers will be able to estimate the future requirements of infrastructure and other facilities. Tour operators act as a source for an approximate forecasting of future tourist arrivals. This becomes the basis for infrastructure development.

Savings in marketing expenditure

Since tour operators bring tourists in large numbers, destination management organizations and other tourism marketing agencies save a share of marketing expenditure. In fact, undertaking marketing communication in all the market countries is not an easy task. The role of tour operator in bringing tourists, even without the support of marketing efforts of the destination marketing organization (DMO)/NTO, is very high. Tour operators, to a great extent, can persuade potential tourists to visit the destinations. Emerging destinations benefit more from this service.

Employment and income

Employment opportunities in tourist destinations will certainly increase along with the increase in tourist activities and the growth of the tourism industry, as tourism is a labour-intensive sector. Moreover, the cascading effect of tourist arrivals and their expenditure in the destination results in greater income-earning opportunities.

12.7.3 Benefits to suppliers

Suppliers and the other principals in the tourism sector get a range of benefits due to inbound tour operation. We discuss some of the more important below.

Reducing uncertainty

Lead time in tour operation is very large. Therefore, as part of developing a package tour, the tour operator has to contact, negotiate and finalize the deal with the suppliers far in advance. This happens many months before the date of departure for the tour, which helps the suppliers to ensure sales of their products much earlier and to minimize their uncertainty about future sales. Suppliers then need to market and sell only the remaining products.

Forecasting

Suppliers may depend on the current trends in tourist arrivals while forecasting future requirements and expansion. For them, forecasting becomes easier when they get tourists regularly through tour operators. Moreover, they will have a clear idea about how many products can be sold through tour operators, who are the ones carrying out advance bookings.

Savings in marketing expenditure

When a tour operator contracts a certain number of products months in advance, the suppliers only have to do marketing and promotion activities for the remaining stock of products. This enables suppliers to reduce marketing costs significantly. Small-scale operators receive immense benefits from the support of tour operators, as marketing on a larger scale in different source markets is very difficult. The tourism industry has this difficulty in general, yet the multinational chains have the freedom in marketing at international levels.

Easy payments

Making payment to the suppliers is the task of the tour operator. This is much easier for the suppliers as the amount is received collectively. For instance, the tour operator will make payment to a hotel for all the tour participants' rooms for the duration of the tour. Collecting payments individually is more difficult in terms of the labour and time required. Moreover, there is surety for the payment owing to the agreement made between the tour operator and the service provider.

Minimizing seasonality

Seasonality is a feature of tourism which causes tourist arrivals in a destination to fluctuate. During peak season, suppliers can meet the sales targets easily. A fall in demand is very common during off season in tourist sectors. Suppliers will face difficulty in managing the businesses during the off season, and managing the cash flow. Tour operators may prefer to operate tours during the off season due to the availability of low tariffs and this helps the suppliers to get essential revenue to manage the business. Tour operators are also benefited from this since they get more discounts during the off season.

12.8 Disadvantages

Although a tour operation generates a number of benefits, there are a few disadvantages for stakeholders. Some of them are discussed here. While being part of a package tour, tourists usually get a fixed schedule, called a tour itinerary. The itinerary is decided far in advance and the tour has to proceed according to it. Tourists rarely have the freedom to modify it according to their interests, except in customized packages for affinity groups. Everything is fixed, from the flight dates and the time of pick-up. Moreover, in the case of group package tours, interests may vary from person to person. Hence it won't be feasible to make a flexible itinerary that suits the preferences of everyone. At times, some tourists may wish to spend a bit more time in a place than others do. Also, in every destination there may be some other interesting attractions, in addition to those included in the itinerary. The tour manager may have limitations in that regard as they are bound by the contract to proceed further and to finish the tour as per the pre-set itinerary. This gives fewer chances for optional tours as well.

Custom-designed packages for a group have less room for independent choices. In fact, a mass tour itinerary may try to include the maximum number of attractions to enhance the "pull" of a package. This makes the itinerary packed. Packed itineraries necessitate frequent intra-destination travel, along with tedious walking from one attraction to another in a short span of time. Furthermore, tourists may have to change accommodation often and frequent packing and unpacking creates difficulty and exhaustion. A very professional method of itinerary preparation can be used to minimize this, though it cannot be avoided as mass package tours more often than not cover a great many destinations. Moreover, as individual preferences have less significance in a group tour, everyone has to compromise a lot to make the tour a success.

Usually, room allocation is done based on the concept of twin sharing. For this reason, in a group tour one tour participant may have to share a room with a stranger. Time for shopping is always included in a package tour. Yet, the time allotted for shopping will be limited and may not always be sufficient. Some prefer long shopping hours whereas others need less time. Moreover, tourists are allocated time for shopping, in many cases, according to the decision of the tour manager or escort. A tour manager or escort can take the tourists to a shopping centre where they earn commission for sales occurring on account of his charges' visit. The success of the tour also depends on the cooperation and compromises of everyone. If any participant causes trouble, the mood of the whole tour will be affected. Moreover, choosing the right package is not easy. A wrong itinerary or inefficient arrangements by a tour operator can cause immense dissatisfaction among tourists. The industry also faces some disadvantages. The suppliers have to compromise on room rates for tour operators since they supply tourists regularly. Tour operators negotiate very hard to get the services at the cheapest rates. The discount to be offered can affect the profitability of the accommodation provider. Also, if demand increases, the suppliers cannot meet the increased requirement since a part of the accommodation premises is already booked by the tour operator. The destination certainly has disadvantages as mass tourism causes a plethora of problems. Regular flows of tourists necessitate infrastructure development and increased transportation along with many other activities, and all of them can cause social, cultural and environmental concerns, unless and until the destination authorities and the industry take extreme caution in minimizing the impact.

12.9 Tour operation and risks

There is always risk associated with any business. This is true for the tour operation sector as well. Tourism organizations take increased risks due to some of their unique products and industry characteristics. Moreover, the sector is facing challenges posed by the Internet, along with hyper-competition. Tourism businesses are quite sensitive to external/environmental factors. Experience and expertise also matter when chasing success in the tour operation business. The successful running of the business is challenging. There are many risks associated with tour operation. Some of the major risks are discussed here.

12.9.1 Financial risks

As stated before, any business has a financial risk. Financial risk is related to the use of financial leverage and debt, and that will have significant impact on the viability of the business. Large amounts of money have to be invested, though the tour operation business may require a relatively smaller amount. However, the success of the business depends on many factors, and tour operators being small or medium businesses mostly, the chances of failure are high. Also, after start-up, most of the profits are usually reinvested. In many cases, the investment amount required may have been borrowed from banks, venture capital firms, etc. The changes in interest rates, non-payment of mandatory amounts, etc. can elevate the financial risks. The tour operation industry is highly impacted by external factors and any changes severely affect the business. Even a natural calamity in the destination can cause the postponement or cancellation of tours, which has huge financial implications. Tourists will demand reimbursement of the amounts paid and tour operators may have booked hotel rooms and flights. On cancellation, a good amount of money may be lost. An economic recession or a financial issue in the market can cause cancellation of bookings by tourists.

12.9.2 Career risks

An entrepreneur in the tour operation business may take a career risk as well. Establishing a tour operation business requires time, energy and focus. During the process, the opportunity of pursuing other careers may be lost. Questions about re-employment after an eventual failure must be considered for a tour operator. This risk is particularly acute for well-paid specialists and people close to retirement.

12.9.3 Performance risk

Though tour operators design and sell package tours, the actual services are delivered by the principals like airlines and hotels. The quality of service delivery/performance cannot be assessed in advance. Here, the tour operator doesn't have any control over the quality of the service delivery. If a hotel provides below-par standards in service quality, the tourist may not be satisfied with the experience and it will eventually affect the overall customer satisfaction. Here, the tour operator's reputation will also be at stake.

12.9.4 Social risks

The tour operator faces social risks as well. Starting a business venture expends much of the entrepreneur's energy and time, which creates potential conflict in the entrepreneur's family. It can be worse when the family is not involved in the process. Another risk is linked to the negative image of failed entrepreneurs. If a business fails once, the image of a failed entrepreneur will remain with the entrepreneur for a long time.

12.9.5 Physical risk

There are many factors that cause physical risk, such as health, political instability, terrorism, strange food, crime, etc. Some of them have very serious implications for a tour operation business. While weather variability and extremes have always existed, recent history shows that extreme weather events are becoming more frequent and intense. Even a natural calamity in a destination can pose severe challenges for the business. Terrorism is a common physical risk factor nowadays.

12.9.6 Health risks

Entrepreneurs may experience more job stress and psychosomatic health problems than other professionals. Would-be tourism entrepreneurs should make sure that they can cope (physically, emotionally and mentally) with the demands and challenges of starting and running a business.

12.10 Organizational structure

Tour operation firms can have different organizational structures depending on their size, scope and nature of functions. In tour operation businesses, Sarbey de Suoto (1985) has identified three different organization structures: vertical structure, horizontal structure and mixed structure. The vertical structure is one that represents group division, in which the entire process involved in tour operation is handled by a single professional from the stage of planning until the execution of the tour. One person is responsible for all activities, but this kind of structuring is usually seen in smaller organizations. This particular professional will have thorough knowledge about the tour which enables them to run the tour smoothly. In the horizontal structure, the functions are organized laterally and there are separate divisions for separate functions, such as planning, costing, marketing, etc. The tour packaging process passes through each and every division and ends up with the division that handles post-tour wrap-up activities. This kind of structure is characterized by specialization in each function, yet thorough supervision is mandatory for making the tour programme a success. The mixed structure is a combination of both vertical and horizontal structures. In this, some functions are performed together by one division or a person while others will be carried out by another division. For instance, one person/division may be an expert in designing and costing a tour and all activities involved, including planning. Another person/division may be responsible for marketing, brochure printing, distributing, negotiation with clients, etc. Hence all such will be undertaken by that particular person or division.

Functional departmentalization is also common in tour operation companies. In such cases, the following departments may be seen:

- Accounting department
- Administration department
- Reservation department
- Sales and marketing department
- Overseas department

Regardless of whether the firm is a micro, small, medium or large firm, expertise in group tour packaging is essential for the smooth functioning of a firm. The number of personnel required in a tour operation company depends on the size and volume of the business. In a medium-sized firm, there will be different positions at different levels. The following areas of expertise are crucial for a tour company, and hence personnel with one or more of the skills are necessary (Sarbey de Suoto, 1985):

- Itinerary preparation
- Negotiation with suppliers and bookings
- Tour costing and pricing

- Handling client queries and reservations
- Preparation of tour materials
- Selecting tour manager and briefing/debriefing
- Preparation of promotional literature
- Controlling a tour project

Personnel are also needed for administration, marketing-related activities, sales, accounting and related functions in an organization.

12.11 Business environments and influence

A tour operation business is influenced by diverse factors that occur around it. Factors may influence either positively or negatively, with varying effects. As in other businesses, internal factors in an organization or industry have a certain degree of influence on the organization, be it positive or negative. External environment factors do exist outside the organization or the industry and they, too, have a significant influence on the organization. The tour operation industry has no control over these factors and sometimes their effect can be damaging. Some of the factors with a significant impact on tour operation business are mentioned below.

12.11.1 Economic factors

Economic factors such as the economic policies of the government, overall economic circumstances, economic growth (or recession) of the country and currency fluctuations have both adverse and facilitating effects on tourism. Positive economic circumstances are always positive for tourism. We discuss some of the economic factors that have a substantial impact on tour operation below.

Currency issues
The "lead time" in the tour operation sector is rather long. Currency exchange rates can vary substantially within that period between tour planning and tour execution. The tourism industry is a sensitive industry and the impact of currency fluctuations, at times, can trouble a tour operator significantly. If the currency value of the origin country decreases, the tour operator has to spend more money for the tour than forecasted, and vice versa. This will affect the profit level as well. Usually tour operators take precautionary measures, like not finalizing prices until the last possible moment or including a clause on change in the published price in the wake of huge currency fluctuations.

Inflation
Inflation relates to the sustained increase in price of products, in general. Inflation, whether in the origin market country or in the destination, can affect the tour operator severely. Inflation makes people poorer which will force them to be more economical. Tourism is a discretionary product and the level of disposable income is a matter of concern for tour operators. Meanwhile, inflation in the destination can also impact tour operation. If the destination's inflation is high, more money needs to be spent on purchasing services and goods in the destination, thereby affecting the tour operation business.

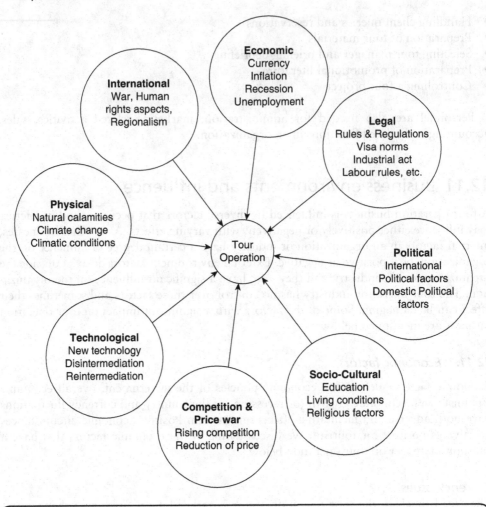

Figure 12.2 External factors affecting tour operation business

Economic recession

An economic recession, at any level, can dampen the scope of the tour operation sector. Increasing unemployment levels, decreasing business prospects, lowering profit margins, etc. are some of the features of economic recession. All these factors can affect the tour operation sector negatively. For instance, the United Nations World Tourism Organization (UNWTO) and International Labour Organization's (ILO) Report on Economic Crisis says:

> The 2008–2009 global economic crisis severely affected international tourism, causing in 2009 a decline of 4% in international tourist arrivals and a decrease of 6% in international tourism receipts. The crisis actually caused the first serious downturn faced by international tourism in decades, a sector accustomed to a long-term average growth rate of about 4% a year.
>
> (UNWTO and ILO, 2013)

Unemployment level in tourist market

When unemployment levels increase, the economic status of many in tourist markets can also be affected. Moreover, the increasing rate of unemployment can cause a decrease in the number of potential buyers. Tour operators' products are discretionary products and the amount of disposable income is a determinant in buying behaviour. A good economic environment will have more employment opportunities and hence more potential buyers for the tour operators' products.

12.11.2 Legal factors

Rules and regulations existing in a country, both directly and indirectly related to tourism, have some bearing on inbound and outbound tour operations. The regulatory environment in the destination country has some impact on tour operators' business. For example, changes in visa regulations and currency restrictions have a direct impact on tourism. When visa regulations became more onerous, tour operators faced more difficulties in obtaining visas for travellers. Of late and all over the world, visa regulations are being eased, in order to promote tourism. Moreover, online visa or e-visa options are now becoming a trend among countries. In the origin country, there can be many laws, labour rules and regulations, etc. that affect tour operation business in one way or another.

12.11.3 Political factors

There are a number of political factors that directly affect the tour operation business. Political turmoil in a country can severely dampen their tourism sector. International political issues can also badly affect tourism. For example, when the Gulf War broke out in the early 1990s, tourism and travel were severely affected. Even a destination country's political relations with an origin country can influence the tour business. Terrorism is another factor that severely impacts tourism. Most terrorism activities are directly or indirectly politically motivated. Political stability in a country, the attitude of the political parties to the industry, the nature of the political system and system of governance, political risks, national security, authority centre, corporate influence in politics and influence of foreign political elements are some of the political factors that influence tour operations.

12.11.4 Socio-cultural factors

Socio-cultural circumstances in the tourism generating regions have significant influence on travel propensity. Better education, lifestyle, living conditions, health parameters, etc. facilitate the growth of tourism in a country. This will create a favourable environment for the outbound tour operation sector to flourish. Cultural factors and religious aspects affect tourism in a varying manner. Moreover, some of the demographic factors also greatly influence travel propensity.

12.11.5 Competition and price war

At different points in history, the tour operation sector has faced much competition and the consequent price wars. The entire industry was affected negatively and saw structural changes when the price wars were at its peak. The emergence of multinational companies and oligopoly were some of the after-effects of the price wars, while many existing players closed down over this period.

12.11.6 Technological factors

Due to the advancements in information technology and mobile technology, the industry is facing severe challenges, even in respect of its survival. Technology brings both opportunities and challenges. Online transaction opportunities were a blow to intermediaries, particularly tour operators and travel agents. Online agents are flourishing and travellers' direct purchases through websites are on the increase. At the same time, the industry has to make maximum use of the opportunities in order to enhance the effectiveness, efficiency and optimization of operations. Moreover, information and communication technologies (ICT) can be effectively used to gain competitive advantage in the market.

12.11.7 Physical forces

These include the geographical and environmental factors in the destination region that can affect tour operation business. In some destinations where climatic factors are the main attractions, the dramatic/unexpected changes in weather conditions can adversely affect tour operations. For example, the decline in snowfall can cause issues for tourism in a winter destination, while torrential rain can cause planned tour cancellations. A volcano eruption can affect travel for many days. A pleasant climate, on the other hand, can enhance the tourist experience. Climatic conditions can therefore affect the performance of the business as well.

12.11.8 International factors

These are the factors that exist at the global level or at least in two or more countries. Global recession, regional wars, international rules, laws, human rights issues, regionalism, etc. can pose challenges for tourism as well.

There are also other factors that influence tour operation business, like an epidemic that spreads in a destination, which can dampen the scope of tourism there. Other external factors include the following (Yale, 2001):

- Foreign exchange rates
- Inflation at home and abroad
- Unemployment rate in the tourist market
- Outbreaks of diseases
- War and civil war
- Airport delays and aircraft accidents
- Weather and climatic conditions at home and abroad
- Interest rates at home and abroad
- The cost of aviation fuel
- Political changes at home and abroad
- Natural disasters
- Terrorist activities
- Fashion
- General bad publicity

12.12 Growth and emergence of large-scale tour operators

Over the last one and a half centuries the tour operation sector has grown from humble beginnings in 1841 to a major business sector taking a key role in the whole tourism system. Tour operators played a significant role as intermediaries while adding value in the process of tourism around the world. The sector suffered serious setbacks at different points in history. The widespread use of the Internet became a threat for the sector as people began booking rooms and flight tickets directly. There are some statistics available at regional levels that indicate the growth of organized holidays around the world. For instance, according to an estimate by the European Travel Agents' and Tour Operators' Associations (ECTAA), there are 77,549 tour operators and travel agents in Europe (www.ectaa.org). The Mintel study (in Travel Weekly, 2009) reports that, of the total holiday sales, 41 per cent are package holiday sales, with around 20 million package sales per year. This gives an indication of the share of package tour operation compared to independent arrangements. According to ABTA, one of the leading travel associations in the UK, in 2012 nearly half (48 per cent) of the British population travelled abroad as part of outbound package tour operation. This is compared to 42 per cent in 2011 and 37 per cent in 2010 (ABTA, 2013). The latest report shows the same trend:

> The preferred method for booking a holiday abroad remains a travel company or agent, with 45% of people booking a holiday overseas in this way. For domestic holidays, people prefer to book on a general holiday booking website (52%) or directly with the service providers, with almost half (48%) of people doing so.
>
> (ABTA, 2018)

All these point to the relevance of tour operation business in this modern era.

Whenever this sector has experienced setbacks for a while, it has recovered from these by introducing innovation, diversification and various business expansion strategies. These practices began from the 1970s onwards, and from 1990 onwards such practices gained momentum. As a result, a number of large-scale players emerged that have operations in many countries on different continents. Vertical integration and horizontal integration strategies were used widely for expansion of tour operation businesses to become large organizations.

Note below the UK experience of focusing on integration and consolidation in the tour operation sector (adapted from Page, 2009):

- Expansion via acquisitions
- Integration of air and hotel businesses
- Widening of distribution channels
- Expanding geographical coverage of markets and tour operating firms entering into strategic alliances or mergers
- The impact of the euro that enabled operators to purchase capacity cheaper from weaker currencies, providing lower-priced holidays
- Gradual levelling of package holiday prices across the European Union
- Increased cost controls and yield management practices
- Introducing new strategies like diversification, a greater alignment of business activities matching changing buying behaviours

Historically, vertical integration has always been a major expansion strategy in the tour operation sector. Using vertical integration, some of the players expand their operations by taking control of either the supply of products and services or distribution. Vertical integration takes place at different levels. When the integration or control of businesses occurs upwards or expands upstream, it is called backward integration. On the other hand, when the expansion takes place downstream, it is called forward integration. For instance, when a tour operator likes to take control of the distribution of products by taking over a retail travel agent, it can be referred to as forward integration. By doing this, the tour operator gains advantages: the price of the product can be reduced by eliminating commission; the profit level can be increased by avoiding intermediaries; better interaction with customers can be possible as the tour operator sells its products directly to the customer; better customer relationship management strategies can be possible; and unfair practices of distributors or favouritism can be eliminated. On the other hand, with backward integration, a tour operator aims at having their own control over the supply of products and services. For instance, when a tour operator owns or operates hotels, resorts, charter flight services, etc., it is referred to as backward integration. By doing this, the tour operator gains a range of benefits: the control over the supply becomes effective; the cost can be reduced substantially; the profit levels can increase; the product features can be increased (creating uniqueness); and product differentiation becomes easier.

Horizontal integration has also been in vogue. It happens when the expansion takes place in the same area. It means a firm expands by taking over or acquiring firms that offer similar products. When a tour operator acquires, or merges with, another tour operation firm, there is horizontal integration. Most of such are mergers of competitors. In the history of tourism, at different stages of tour operation business development worldwide, many firms have been taken over by, or merged with, other firms. Some of the current leading tour operators became such large firms after passing through expansion stages that utilized both vertical and horizontal integration strategies.

CASE STUDY 12.1

New challenges of tour operators

Faced by the severe threat of online intermediaries, traditional tour operators are forced to choose from specialized and personalized services that provide unique customer experiences, i.e. not always offered. Consequently, offering an enhanced travel experience has become a niche market for tour operators. Though personalized service is an advantage for traditional tour operators, they have to keep up with technological advancements to efficiently manage client expectations. In addition to the low utilization of IT, lack of brand awareness is another challenge for tour operators. Online agents such as Booking.com, Expedia, TripAdvisor, KAYAK and Skyscanner have been able to build huge brand presence and continue to invest in brand awareness and reinforcement. Brand preference and loyalty is an advantage for luring potential travellers. In order to compete, tour operators have to make some investments in digital technology, such as customer relationship management solutions, to enhance their online presence and manage their reputation while providing personalized services.

Digitization can lead to enhanced user experience and the major online travel intermediaries are great at personalizing their promotions and services to the customer on their websites. Such online agents can configure a trip (based on choice of activity, interest or destination) and automate follow-up emails. By digitizing, customizing an itinerary, selling a pre-packaged tour, or creating and promoting their own holiday packages, etc., tour operators can ensure smooth and enhanced productivity, efficiency and customer retention. An active presence on social media can also help to create brand awareness cost-effectively while engaging with the target audience. This is also important for getting new customers. An efficient social media strategy, along with digital customer relationship management (CRM) platforms, is very useful. Building credibility and trust is very important in this sector, and it is a challenging task. Also, to minimize human errors, tour operators can make use of IT tools. Poor credibility can quickly lead to negative reviews and testimonies.

Working with multiple systems is another challenge, particularly when multiple systems aren't necessarily fully integrated. Switching between platforms means increased work, which can lead to delays in providing quick and accurate information to the customer. Using new generation booking and CRM platforms can reduce this burden substantially. Modern technology solutions providers can enable tour operators to work efficiently by automating repetitive tasks, maintaining accuracy and working smarter, while enabling the management of products, prices, suppliers and business accounts all in one system. By doing this, tour operators can check on the health of their business and be able to identify areas that need improvement for quick response.

Source: Óladóttir (2017)

Read the above case study carefully and answer the following questions:

- Discuss how IT solutions can help tour operators to face challenges.
- Explain the new challenges for tour operators to remain competitive.

There are currently a number of large-scale operators. TUI is a leading leisure tourism business agency, based in Germany. It turned into a major agency once it started adopting business expansion strategies and practices. Currently, it includes some strong tour operation brands such as TUI Deutschland, 1–2-FLY.com, Airtours, Wolters Reisen, Thomson and First Choice. It expanded vertically to have six proprietary airlines: TUI fly, Thomson, TUI fly Nordic, Jetairfly (now part of TUI fly Belgium), Corsair and Arke (now TUI fly Netherlands), with a fleet of 136 medium- and long-haul aircraft. In addition, they own 300 hotels with 210,000 beds in 24 countries. Retail travel agencies include 1,800 agencies and leading online portals. Moreover, it has 13 cruise liners and countless incoming agencies in all major holiday destinations around the globe (www.tuigroup. com/en/about-us/glance). Another firm, Thomas Cook, following its development from a simple tour operator in the nineteenth century, became a major operator in the 1950s and its growth continued. It has become a large tour operator using all sorts of expansion strategies. In 1982, it took over Rankin Kuhn Travel, while retail travel agent chains such as Frames, Blue Sky and Four Corners were acquired between 1985 and 1990. Thomas Cook became a wholly-owned subsidiary of WestLB in 1995. Later, it acquired Sun-world, Time Off and Flying Colours and soon was merged with Carlson Leisure Group's UK travel interests to become JMC (including JMC Airlines) in 1999. In 2001, it was acquired by C&N Touristic AG. Later, in 2007, Thomas Cook AG and MyTravel Group plc merged to form Thomas Cook Group plc. Another merger followed in 2011, when its UK high street travel and foreign exchange businesses merged with those of the Co-operative Group and the Midlands Co-operative Society, thus becoming the UK's largest retail travel network with more than 1,200 shops. As of now, Thomas Cook Group plc is a leading holiday group with 27,000 employees and operating in 17 countries, handling more than 20 million customers (Thomas Cook, n.d.). The tour operation sector continues to expand, and remains a major tourism industry component all around the world.

12.13 Summary

The tour operation sector is still an important tourism-related business. It offers the opportunity for ample innovation along with good profit potential. Tour operation is primarily about organizing an independent or group journey for the purposes of visiting and arranging the services and facilities needed to enjoy the tour, and doing so in a professional way. A tour operator is basically an individual or an agency that organizes package tours and/or facilitates travel by arranging the necessary facilities and services. Tour operators usually purchase services and products offered by various components of the tourism industry in advance, at substantial discounts. Tour operation has a long history. Professional tour operation began only when Thomas Cook conducted the first well-organized tour in 1841. Soon other entrepreneurs entered the realm of tour operation. There were innovations in these attempts, and all such innovations contributed to the development of the tour operation industry. Plenty of factors contributed to the remarkable evolution of the tour operation industry.

The tour operator adds value to the process in different ways, which benefits the consumers. Tour operators' products are often viewed as a bundle of services, called a package. It is a combination of two or more of the elements of the tourism system. Transportation and accommodation are the most commonly included elements. Some other elements may include sightseeing, activities, optional tours, shopping, food services, entertainment, and interpretation/guiding depending upon the nature of the tour and the requirements of the consumers.

Inbound tour operators deal with and handle directly inbound tourists, and provide them with the required services in the destination, such as local transportation, transfers and sightseeing trips. An outbound tour operator refers to a tour operating agency that organizes tours for residents of a country to visit another country. They sell package tours to a group of people or individuals who are local residents to travel to another country or a number of countries. The term "ground operator" is used to refer to small-scale agents who arrange the required services and facilities for incoming tourists through tour operators or independent travellers in a destination or region. Mass-market operators prefer to have group tours to established and well-known destinations. Unlike mass tourism, specialist tours do not involve travel to established destinations or attractions; rather, they are initiated for people with specific motivations to experience something different, or as part of a passion. There are also other types of tour operators.

Being a challenging sector, the operator has to ensure strategic growth and efficiency in its overall functions. The luring benefits of tour operation are not only playing a key role in and adding value to tourism, but they are also indicators of sustained future growth of tour operations across the world. The benefits of having tour operators for travel arrangements and group visits are not just for tourists; the suppliers and destinations also enjoy a range of benefits from organized tour operation. Tourists gain the benefits of a tour operator's expertise and knowledge, time efficiency, ease and convenience, lower price and planning time, more safety and security, better social environment, more sightseeing/activities, assistance or guidance throughout and more relaxation. Regular arrival, entrepreneurial activity, base for infrastructure development and savings in marketing expenditure are major benefits enjoyed by destinations. Destinations still depend on tour operators to ensure regular inflows of tourists. This is more relevant for emerging destinations. Suppliers benefit through reduced uncertainty of sales, savings in marketing expenditure, easy payments and minimizing seasonality. On the other hand, tour operators take risks (e.g. financial risks, career risks, physical risks and health risks) while carrying out the tour operation business. Tour operators may have different organizational structures, such as vertical structure, horizontal structure and mixed structure. Tour operation is a sensitive sector, vulnerable to external environments and forces. Package tours are sold via online media as well. Still, traditional tour operators add value in the tourism process.

Review questions

Short/medium answer type questions

- What is tour operation?
- Discuss the role of Thomas Cook in the evolution of tour operation business.
- Identify important entrepreneurs/figures in the history of tour operation.
- Give a brief account of the growth of tour operation business after the Second World War.
- Identify the factors that stimulate the growth of tour operation.
- Conceptualize the product of a tour operator.
- Discuss the nature and characteristics of a tour operator's product.
- What are the functions of inbound tour operators?
- Write briefly about outbound tour operators.
- What do we mean by ground operator?
- Distinguish between mass tour operator and niche tour operator.
- What are the benefits of tour operation for tourists?
- "Emerging destinations depend on tour operators for regular inflows of tourists." Comment on this statement.
- What are the benefits for suppliers of using tour operators?
- Discuss the disadvantages of purchasing a package tour.

- What are the risks of the tour operation business?
- Discuss the influence of economic environment on the tour operation business.
- Write about how large-scale tour operators emerged.

Essay type questions

- Conceptualize tour operations and describe the benefits to various stakeholders of having tour operators.
- Discuss how business environments impact tour operation business.

References

ABTA (2013) Travel Trends Report 2013, available at https://www.abta.com/sites/default/files/media/document/uploads/Travel_trends_report_2013.pdf.

ABTA (2018) Holiday Habits Report 2017, available at https://www.abta.com/sites/default/files/media/document/uploads/Holiday_Habits_Report_2017_0.pdf.

CTC, Coach Tourism Council, available at http://coachtourismcouncil.com/component/content/article/271 (accessed 15 September 2015).

Feifer, M. (1985) *Going Places: The Ways of the Tourist from Imperial Rome to the Present Day*. London: Macmillan.

FTO, Federation of Tour Operators, available at http://www.fto.co.uk//operators-factfile/tour-operators/ (accessed 15 June 2015).

Goeldner, R. C. and Ritchie, J. R. B. (2006) *Tourism Principles, Practices, Philosophies*. New Delhi: John Wiley & Sons.

Holloway, J. C. and Taylor, N. (2006) *The Business of Tourism*. 7th edn. Essex: Prentice Hall.

Hudson, S. (2008) *Tourism and Hospitality Marketing: A Global Perspective*. London: Sage Publications.

Kotler, P., Bowen, J. and Makens, J. (2009) *Marketing for Hospitality and Tourism*. London: Prentice Hall.

Laws, E. (1997) *Managing Packaged Tourism: Relationships, Responsibilities and Service Quality in the Inclusive Holiday Industry*. London: International Thomson Business Press.

Levitt, T. (1981) Marketing Intangible Products and Product Intangibles, *Harvard Business Review*, May/June: 37–44.

Medlik, S. and Middleton, V. T. C. (1973) Product Formulation in Tourism. *Tourism and Marketing* 13.

Middleton, V. T. C., Fyall, A., Morgan, M. and Ranchhod, A. (2009) *Marketing in Travel and Tourism*. 4th edn. Oxford: Butterworth-Heinemann.

Óladóttir, M. H. (2017) Five Challenges Facing Tour Operators in 2017, available at https://kaptio.com/blog/five-challenges-tour-operators-2017/ (accessed 13 July 2018).

Page, S. (2009) *Tourism Management: An Introduction*. Burlington: Butterworth-Heinemann/Elsevier Science.

Pond, L. K. (1993) *The Professional Guide: Dynamics of Tour Guiding*. New York: Van Nostrand Reinhold.

Reilly (1991) *Handbook of Professional Tour Management*. 2nd edn. New York: Delmar Publishers.

Sarbey de Suoto, M. (1985) *Group Travel Operations Manual*. Albany: Delmar Publishers.

Syratt, G. and Archer, G. (2003) *Manual of Travel Agency Practice*. Oxford: Butterworth-Heinemann.

Thomas Cook, Thomas Cook History, available at https://www.thomascook.com/thomas-cook-history/.

Travel Weekly (2009) Package holiday market still "huge", says Mintel, available at http://www.travelweekly.co.uk/articles/30468/package-holiday-market-still-huge-says-mintel.

UNWTO and ILO (2013) Economic Crisis, International Tourism Decline and its Impact on the Poor, available at http://www.ilo.org/wcmsp5/groups/public/@ed_dialogue/@sector/documents/publication/wcms_214576.pdf (accessed 14 May 2017).

USTOA, How to Select a Tour/Vacation, available at https://www.ustoa.com/resources/how-to-select-a-tour-vacation (accessed 2 September 2015).

Yale, P. (2001) *The Business of Tour Operations*. Essex: Longman-Pearson Education.

Websites

www.ectaa.org.
www.tuigroup.com/en/about-us/glance.

Package tours

After reading this chapter, you will be able to:

- Define package tour.
- Understand different types of tours.
- Identify the elements of a package tour.
- Comprehend the planning and designing of a package tour.
- Explain types of supplier contracts/agreements.
- Elaborate on the costing and pricing of a package tour.

13.1 Introduction

Some 5,000 years ago, in 1480 BC, a cruise ship of that era set off on a trip for the purposes of peace and tourism. Considered the first recorded cruise tour, Queen Hatshepsut, the longest reigning female pharaoh in Egypt, made the ocean voyage to the land of Punt (believed to be on the east coast of Africa) (Goeldner and Ritchie, 2003). There were five ships with 210 men that sailed from Egypt to Punt in order to maintain good relations with the people in the destination, and upon returning they brought ivory, ebony, gold, leopard skins and incense, and live animals and trees. There were other organized trips of that kind over land and water at that time, but they were not reported as tours. Over the following millennia, travel for the purposes of tourism developed and evolved. During the grand tour era, there were remarkable changes in the nature of touring. While the Industrial Revolution was taking place, holidays also became the vogue, but the primary purpose of travelling was for learning, and for spiritual and cultural reasons. The grand tour era began sometime in the seventeenth century with tours by the wealthy, aristocratic and privileged classes seeking education, culture and pleasure in major cultural centres of Europe. That marked the beginning of a popular movement of tour travelling. Though recreational travel was limited, the concept of the tour had gained significance by then. As discussed in the previous chapter, Thomas Cook made history when he organized a tour with a professional approach. The success of that venture paved the way for others to innovate, which contributed to the evolution of the tour business.

Tours thus gained significance for individuals, but would only see social and commercial significance later, after the end of the Second World War. Along with its continued development, the nature and scope of tours and holidays were transformed. There were also expansions in product lines. During the last quarter of the twentieth century, diversification became crucial to the survival of holiday businesses and in the strategic growth of the tour operation sector. While there was significant competition between organized tours and online platforms in tourism (as potential customers' buying behaviours evolved), diversification, customization and specialization became the pillars of the tour operation sector's competitive survival. Before going into detail about the nuances of a tour and its organizing, let's have a look at various types of tours or holidays seen in contemporary tourism.

13.2 Tour classification

The tour operation sector sees myriad types of tours and giving a common base for those classifications is not an easy task. Nonetheless, some types of tours can be brought under some common bases. For instance, business tours and leisure tours are a classification based on the purpose of travelling internationally. **Overseas tour** and **domestic tour** are other classifications based on the country of origin and destination. Citizens of a country visiting a foreign country are on an overseas tour, while tourists visiting places within their own country are on a domestic tour. Depending on the number of people travelling, tours can be categorized as foreign independent tour or group inclusive tour. **Inbound tour** and **outbound tour** are the most commonly used terms in the tour operation sector. Classification depends on the direction of travel, from country of origin to the destination. When a tour takes place from a foreign country to the destination country, it is referred to as an inbound tour. When a tour takes place from the home country to a foreign country, it is an outbound tour in relation to the host country. The same trip is an inbound tour for the people living in the destination country. For overseas tours, according to Sarbey de Suoto (1985), there are three kinds of tour groups: group travel for pleasure, for business and for a specific purpose (like special interest tours – SIT). The first category is for people seeking pleasure and they can be from any society. The second category covers a range of clientele, including those who travel for conventions, meetings, trade fairs, incentive holidays and training programmes. The third category is for people who travel with a very specific interest in mind, to seek something that is not very common in tourism. Like inbound tours and outbound tours, leisure tours and business tours are also common categories. The following discussions provide an introduction to some of the major tour types seen in different world tourism contexts.

13.2.1 Foreign independent tour

Travelling independently is challenging and thrilling. It is a popular category. Independent travellers like to experience the flexibility that comes from being on one's own. They prefer not to be in a group and make arrangements according to their needs. They depart on any day and return when they like; there is no set schedule. Independent travellers can make the necessary travel and accommodation arrangements themselves, and engage in activities they're interested in. Alternatively, the required arrangements can be carried out by intermediaries. Independent tours are a category of tours that give maximum autonomy to the participants. These tours are usually popular among leisure tourists, particularly experienced ones seeking something special.

Poynter (1989) specifies that a foreign/free independent tour (FIT) represents a "travel programme designed to tailor-fit the specific needs and interests of the traveler". If it is arranged by an intermediary, it looks similar to a package tour, with ground arrangements like transfer, stay, meal services, sightseeing, local/ground transportation, special facilitation services, etc. given due preference in terms of the traveller's needs and interests. Though many independent tourists' travel is based on an itinerary planned with necessary flexibility, many independent tourists may not choose a fixed itinerary; instead they may move as and when they need/want to. The pace of travel is set by the tourist. Some prefer to visit multiple destinations while others prefer to roam within a single destination and explore it in detail. Types of accommodation also vary; a traveller may not necessarily stay in one category of accommodation within a destination. While discussing the market segments in FIT, Poynter (1989) identifies two major groups of clients: "empty nesters" and "the adventuresome". According to him, the FIT market is dominated by elderly people and youngsters who prefer adventure, primarily. However, he mentions other segments as well, which are briefly described in Table 13.1.

13.2.2 Custom designed/tailor-made tours

FITs are basically custom-designed tours as they are designed exclusively to meet the specific requirements of the traveller. Simply, these "are those designed to fit the specific needs of a particular market or affinity group" (Pond, 1993). Since the tour elements are arranged as per the needs of the tourist, they have a good amount of control over the elements and the overall activities of the tour.

13.2.3 Group inclusive tour

As the name specifies, a group inclusive tour (GIT) is an organized tour programme targeted at a group of tourists. A group tour, simply, is organized for a number of participants using scheduled or non-scheduled forms of transport. The size of the group varies. There are specific pre-set itineraries, usually provided by travel intermediaries like tour operators and travel agents. The members of a tour group will travel together. This constitutes the major market, usually referred to as the group travel market, of tour operators across the world. Since it is an inclusive tour, travel and accommodation arrangements are usually done by the operators. The tour proceeds based on a pre-set itinerary with fixed departure and return dates. These are organized for and aimed at groups of participants, which constitute the so-called "group travel market".

There are many reasons why travellers take part in GITs. Cost is a major factor. Usually, GITs offer lower rates than independently organized tours. Tour operators and other intermediaries who organize GITs gain cost advantages due to the advance bulk purchase of tour elements. This results in a lowering of package prices. A GIT also provides a sort of belongingness and a social environment. Group tours, especially for affinity groups, provide a social environment in which tour participants can enjoy companionship and form new friendships. Sharing experiences, having fun among the members, etc. can be a positive experience for participants. Moreover, GITs have the advantage of a fixed itinerary. When there is a fixed itinerary, the chance of omissions (of attractions, etc.) is

Table 13.1 Poynter's list of FIT tourist segments

Segment	Description
Empty nesters	Aged above 50 with little family responsibilities, but with adequate financial resources to take up travel. Their children are old enough to lead independent lives. Having ample time, they seek more touristic experiences, often with special interests.
The adventuresome	Usually belong to the young age group, but not always. They prefer adventurous activities, and physical involvement in touristic activities will be high. This group is more educated and mostly employed. They have a good amount of disposable income. Many of them seek a tour operator/travel agent's expertise in order to make the trip smoother.
The family reunion	Family members who live far away from each other may on occasion get together and enjoy a reunion in an attractive destination or while engaging in a touristic activity. It is concerned with parents and grandparents wishing to be with younger family members. They find readymade FITs tempting for adding spice to their lives and giving their children memories that will last a lifetime.
The specially interested	The tourists with very specific interests belong to this category. SIT is gaining increased significance with tour operators now offering many packages for this segment. The packages are for exclusive special interest tours suitable to various kinds of tourists. They seek or explore their own specific interests.
Sports enthusiasts	These tourists travel to experience sports activities that are not present in their usual environments. For instance, people travel for game fishing, playing golf, skiing, surfing, etc.
Business professionals	A small portion of business travellers seek an FIT operator's expertise to get tailor-made travel experiences.

Source: Adapted from Poynter (1989)

minimized. Also, tour operators are better aware of what attractions are worth seeing, and hence all the major attractions can be covered within the tour's limited period of time. Safety is another major reason travellers choose GITs. As tourists go with a group and there are experts to help them throughout the journey, the safety and security factor is much higher. Moreover, international travel lasting many days requires myriad arrangements prior to and during the journey. When it is an inclusive tour, it is the responsibility of the tour operator to make these arrangements, so the traveller can avoid the hassle. Additionally, the whole tour programme is able to run more smoothly.

13.3.4 Mass-market tours

Movement of people on a large scale for the purpose of visiting is often referred to as mass tourism. The lion's share of tourism in the world belongs to this category. According to Kelly and Nankervis (2001), it is "sometimes referred to as 'mainstream' tourism, refers to the large scale movement of people to and from leisure travel destinations, often

Table 13.2 Tour packaging: differences between GIT and FIT

GIT	FIT
Fixed dates for departure and return	The choice of dates is according to the convenience of the tourist
Tour price is less	Tour price is relatively higher
Less profit margin per sale	Single sale profit margin is higher
Pre-set tour itinerary, usually rigid	May or may not be with a fixed itinerary, usually flexible
Attractions to visit are pre-set, as per the itinerary	Tourists have the freedom to demand them
Less personalized, everything is set for a group	Individual's preferences constitute the norm
No hassle of travel and stay arrangements	If not a packaged one, then the arrangements have to be done independently
Social environment exists within the group	Travel independently and hence chance of social environment is less
Long lead time as planning is done far in advance	Less lead time
The pace of the tour is as per the itinerary	Tourist can more or less decide the pace
Limited possibility for optional tours	Optional tours or the number of options and time required are according to the tourist
Tour leader needs to follow the itinerary and hence less pressure in managing the tour	Flexibility in the tour puts more pressure on the operator
Documents related to travel and stay are handled by the tour leader	Tourist may have to handle those documents as well
More safety and security	Safety and security may be less, comparatively
No choice for accommodation	The hotel choice is based on the tourist's preference
Larger vehicle for ground transportation	Ground transportation may be in a car or on a shared basis in a larger vehicle.

making use of tour packages incorporating travel, accommodation and sightseeing". In the area of tourism, mass-market holidays or tours involve mainly traditional GITs, which are organized on a regular basis. Poon (1993) defines mass tourism as a large-scale phenomenon, packaging and selling standardized leisure services at fixed prices to a large clientele. Success of such tours depends on the volume of sales as the profit margin is less. Hence, tour operators aim to organize as many tours as possible with group sizes at the maximum extent. Preferred destinations are popular ones and lower prices are a feature. Professionalism is a prerequisite in designing and managing these tours in order to get a wider appeal, include the maximum number of attractions without affecting the itinerary and ensure cost-effectiveness.

13.3.5 Special interest tours/niche tours

Special interest tours (SITs), as the name implies, are organized based on specific themes, interests and motivations. They do not have mass appeal as in the case of mass tours. The traveller choice is based on specific motivations, and correspondingly the major determinant in tourist satisfaction is the level of the experience the tourist can have from the place visited based on the specific need or interest they had prior to the visit. Travel can be to specific locations with unique attractions, sites with certain activities, etc. A tourist's prime motivation is to enjoy an experience related to a particular interest/hobby, activity, theme or destination. "Niche tour" is another term used to refer to this kind of tourism. Niche tours are "travel and tourism products without a mass appeal, appealing to special interests and tastes" (Biederman et al., 2008). The target market size for niche tours is smaller compared to other types. The target market is, however, more easily identifiable and measurable. The operators, usually, are also smaller in terms of size, turnover and market share. Archaeology, cycling, bird watching, fishing, golfing, hiking/trekking, hot-air ballooning, wildlife safaris, rafting, whale watching, wine tours, etc. are examples of special interests that tours may be organized around. The popularity of SITs is on the increase and innovation is a feature of the category. Another feature of SIT is that it is more experiential in nature and tour operators require deep knowledge about the focus area to ensure the best tourist experience.

Some of the examples of SITs/niche tours already mentioned are described below:

- *Bird watching tours:* watching birds in their natural habitat is a passion for many, particularly for seeing rare species in remote locations
- *Bicycle or cycle tours:* tours with long bicycle rides in the countryside or in remote locations with limited tourism infrastructure
- *Golf tours:* travel to destinations where there are good golf courses to play
- *Skiing tours:* winter tours with a specific focus on skiing and associated activities
- *Adventure tours:* adventure tourism can be a niche tourism category when it is being offered exclusively for those keenly interested people with the necessary skills and knowledge to enjoy the adventure activities
- *Historical tours:* visiting places with historical importance, with the initial choice to travel motivated by learning and education
- *Literary tours:* travel to places associated with literary works or figures for people passionate about literature
- *Music tours:* travel to see music concerts, festivals, places where musicians lived, sites of music history, etc.
- *Culinary tours:* travel with a motivation to understand, consume or even prepare food and drinks that reflect the local heritage and culture of a place
- *Wine tours:* visiting palces with a passion to experience vineyards, wineries, breweries and wine festivals.

13.3.6. Long-haul and short-haul tours

This is a classification based mainly on the duration of travel between origin and destination countries. Long-haul tours are packaged tours to places far away from the origin locations. Exact flight durations for long-haul tours are not specified, but the general understanding is that the flight duration can be ten hours or more. For a destination, tourists are from far-away markets. For example, for countries in Europe, typical long-haul destinations would include Asian countries, such as India, China, Singapore, Malaysia and Thailand, and South American countries. Long-haul tours became more popular after the arrival of jet aircraft, which can cover long distances and carry a large number of passengers. By the 1980s, the popularity of long-haul holidays had gained much momentum. However, because the destinations are located far away from the markets, in order to lure tourists the attractiveness of the destination needs to be high, or it needs to represent a unique opportunity. Alternatively, attractions have to be highly rated in order to influence the tourist's buying decision. Scheduled flights are common for long-haul travel, but of late, charter flights have also become popular for this category.

On the other hand, short-haul tourists are from relatively nearby markets. These tours refer to holidays in places in proximity to tourists' origin locations, where the travel duration is just a few hours. Five hours is usually considered the maximum length of time for short-haul travel. Some of the short-haul tours are for a weekend or short break. The number of nights spent in the destination may vary from two to a few more. In contemporary international tourism, this is a crucial segment, as the number of short-haul tourists is much greater than that of long-haul tourists. Intra-regional tourism in Europe is short-haul in nature, though the number of days spent in the destination varies considerably.

13.2.7 Single-centre/multi-centre holidays

Here, the tours are differentiated by the number of destination countries covered in a single tour. A single-centre holiday refers to a tour to a single destination/resort. Summer tours and winter tours are the main types within this category. The tour duration is usually a week or two weeks; rarely do single-centre holidays last more than two weeks. Multi-centre holidays involve tours to two or more destinations in one trip. Obviously, the destinations are nearby ones and the distance between them is a determinant in the decision-making of the tourist. Though destinations here represent multiple countries, it can mean multiple destinations within a single country. It means that multi-centre tours can be trips to two or three destinations within a country of larger size. Moreover, the destinations may be different types in terms of its primary attractions. Some examples of multi-centre holidays include Miami and Orlando in USA, Singapore, Kuala Lumpur and Hong Kong in the Far East, Florence, Venice and Rome in Italy, New Delhi, Goa and Kerala in India, and Cairo and Dubai in the Middle East. These are also common in the package tour industry, as many of the packages cover more than one destination. A **touring holiday** is similar to a multi-centre holiday, but the stay duration in each destination may be comparatively less, say three or four nights per destination or country. The focus is on sightseeing at major attractions in different locations/countries/destinations. For example, a package tour may cover India, the Maldives and Sri Lanka over 15 days.

13.2.8 All-inclusive tours

An all-inclusive holiday is a packaged holiday/tour in which almost all the tour elements are included in the single price paid by tourists. All elements are combined together into one package. Some of the all-inclusive tours are fully inclusive packages, i.e. they include alcohol and entertainment costs. According to Yale (2001), "all-inclusive holidays make it possible for tourists to spend their entire stay in their hotel complex without venturing outside, perfect for those who are wary of getting to grips with a different culture". According to the Club Med (n.d.), a leading all-inclusive holiday resort chain:

> All-inclusive holidays are exactly that – they include everything! One booking takes care of every detail including your flight and transfer to the resort, beautiful

accommodation, meals, drinks, entertainment, sports and recreational activities. It even includes free Wi-Fi, taxes and tips.

By paying a single price, the traveller knows exactly what the tour cost will be, and doesn't have to worry about keeping an amount in reserve for unexpected expenditure. Usually the price is less than the sum of all the expenditures when paid separately. Many international tour companies and resorts offer all-inclusive packages. In addition to travel, transfer and stay, all-inclusive packages usually include buffet meals, soft and alcoholic drinks (with restrictions), day-time activities, including sports, aerobics, dance classes, etc., and entertainment activities in the evening.

13.2.9 Guided, hosted and escorted tours

Group tours usually have someone accompanying the tour participants throughout the programme. It can be a tour leader, professional tour guide or an escort. A guided tour programme includes a professional guide orienting the participants within the sites and attractions using explanations, interpretations, guidance and assistance. The primary purpose of the guide is to inform participants about the attractions and sites and to interpret, though the tour guide may also take up different roles, including tour leading, PR and day-to day managing. The tour guiding style may also vary.

In an escorted tour, a professional tour manager or leader will escort the tour throughout the programme. These are typical group tours with most of the tour elements prearranged and with a pre-set itinerary. A tour escort is sometimes called a tour manager, tour director or tour leader. The escort has the responsibility of directing the tour, and acting when emergencies arise on behalf of the tour operator. The pace of the tour is as per the itinerary and all other activities are under their control. Though the escort is capable of providing some primary information about the places and attractions being visited, whenever there is a need, a local tour guide may be hired and utilized for interpreting the nuances of the attractions.

Unlike an escorted tour, a hosted tour does not necessarily have an escort all the time, only when one is needed. It is "relatively unscheduled, features a host stationed in a designated location and available for assistance" (Pond, 1993). The host provides the necessary assistance and guidance in the places visited, but does not usually accompany the tour. In many cases, the host will be available at the hospitality desk in the accommodation centre to provide the necessary guidance. A hosted tour is more or less similar to an independent tour. The host will be a representative of the tour operator or a ground handling agent. Single destination or multiple destination options are available. In each location, a host will need to be arranged.

13.2.10 Affinity tour

This tour references the relationship among the members of a tour. When a group tour has participants from the same institution or social organization, the members have a kind of affinity, which creates a warm social environment for them to enjoy. It means the participants have a common identity. Reilly (1991) defines an affinity tour as a "tour whose membership is composed of individuals sharing some common affiliations, like membership in a club or organization, or associationship with an educational institution or church". When the members of a social organization or a recreational club go on a group tour, it can be called an affinity tour.

13.2.11 Safari holidays

A safari holiday refers to travel to a remote location. The tour is usually equipped and guided, with arrangements made for food and drink. A safari is basically a thrilling journey into an exotic location. Safaris often target young populations. There are limited amenities on tour, but it does include comfortable accommodation and transport, along with an opportunity to experience the wilderness. The travellers' purposes can vary from photography to adventure, etc. Safari experiences also vary; examples include: guided, mobile, self-drive, walking, hiking, fly-in, elephant back, camel back, four-wheel drive, drive into deserts, river-boating, horseback, balloon, night game viewing, photographic and mobile tented journeys. African destinations are famous for this category of tour. Game safaris are about observing and photographing wild mammals and birds in their natural habitat. Chalets with basic facilities are provided as accommodation in the area and transport is arranged in specially designed four-wheel drive vehicles with pop-up roof hatches (Horner, 1996). Safari vehicles will be painted to match the environment, and have adequate seating that allows tourists to view the wildlife without obstruction. African countries are the most popular safari destinations. Kenya, Tanzania, South Africa, Zambia, Zimbabwe and Botswana are known for their wildlife and safari tours. Some game parks arrange accommodation on-site, with comfortable facilities that also allow visitors to watch the wildlife from their rooms. Desert safaris are very common in Arab countries. These require four-wheel drive vehicles for travelling over sand dunes deep into the deserts.

13.2.12 Combination tours

Some of the tours have a combination of transport forms for convenience and recreation. One major mode of transport is used for international travel, and it will be combined with another mode of transport for the rest of the travel. This makes it more interesting. Some examples follow below.

Fly cruises

Air travel is linked with cruise journeys. A certain distance will be covered on an aircraft, and then the holiday will proceed on board a cruise ship. Fly cruises were introduced in the 1980s and even now, they are in high demand in some locations.

Fly/drive holidays

This consists of a flight along with hiring a car or camper. In other words, it's round trip air travel combined with a rental car or self-drive car arrangement in the destination. The tourists enjoy the freedom of having a rented vehicle in the destination when they arrive.

13.2.13 Summer tours and winter tours

Summer and winter both appeal to tourists. Summer tours/holidays are the most traditional forms of holidays. Summer holidays are primarily recreational tours. Enjoying the summer on beaches is common across the world. Beach-related tourism is often marked by the letter "s", specifically sun, sand, sea and surf. Both long-haul and short-haul tourism involve summer tours. This is a major market segment in international tourism and people of all ages take part in this. Nowadays, summer tours are combined with more activities including surfing, yachting, snorkelling and scuba diving.

Winter holidays are primarily meant for travelling to locations where the winter season is enchanting, and where winter sports and activities are offered. Visiting snow-clad locations is interesting for many people, particularly those who are from warmer regions. Skiing is the most important winter sport, and ski tours are very popular around the world. Many European countries are known for skiing tourism. Traditional ski resorts and purpose-built ski resorts are two types of common skiing locations (Horner, 1996). The former is usually situated in picturesque places in rural settings with the necessary skiing facilities. The latter involves a ski lift that is designed professionally in order to accommodate more skiers and operate as quickly and as efficiently as possible. Glacier skiing, heli-skiing (reaching the tops of mountains/ski slopes by helicopter, and then skiing down from there), cross-country skiing (skiing across flat surfaces), backcountry skiing (skiing in remote areas where it may or may not be part of a resort and outside ski area boundaries), etc. are some different skiing activities seen in winter tourism. Après-ski is a term used in skiing tourism which refers to the social activities after a day's skiing or evening entertainment in the resorts for skiers and their companions. The term "winter holidays" is also used for going on winter breaks, including visits to warmer places when a tourist's place of origin is experiencing winter. When a tourist from a winter location visits a summer location, it is called winter sun holidays.

13.3 Tours based on mode of transport

13.3.1 Cruise tours

In the beginning of this chapter, we briefly discussed the first recorded cruise trip. Cruise tours have been around for millennia. However, modern cruise tourism only became a trend in the second half of the twentieth century when cruise operators began offering modern, inclusive holidays on ships for long durations. Currently it is one of the fastest growing tourism types. Usually, the price of a cruise holiday includes almost everything a tourist would need for the whole course of their journey. At times, the cost of shore excursions and drinks are charged separately. Shore excursions are short trips onto land when the ship reaches the ports of call. Cruise tours are known for luxury, relaxing times, good cuisine and lots of fun and recreation. Mediterranean cruises, Baltic cruises and Caribbean cruises have been some of the most popular. There are also round-the-world cruises, which last much longer. A detailed discussion on cruise tourism is provided elsewhere in this book. River cruises are also very popular in some locations. They are undertaken along big rivers or waterways, particularly in Europe. Other rivers popular for cruise tours include the Nile, Yangtze and the Amazon.

13.3.2 Charter tour

Charter flights have been used for tour operation since the 1920s. They are still used by large-scale operators, mainly for all-inclusive package holidays and other package tours. Simply, a charter tour is a tour organized by an agent, wholesaler, carrier or tour operator that hires an aircraft, or part of one. The primary advantages of this include freedom and convenience for transport, and economy. Some of the vertically integrated tour operators have their own charter flights, which make it much more economical and easier for operations.

13.3.3 Rail tours

Rail tours are package tours offered by railway companies. There are some luxury rail tours that are particularly unique and attract people from all over the world. The tours commence from a single point and pass through a number of destinations, where there will be excursions. Food and accommodation are found inside the train itself. The Bernina Express, Venice Simplon-Orient-Express, Danube Express and Palace on Wheels are some examples of this. Many train journeys, like the Trans-Siberian rail journey, are unique and attractive for tourists.

13.3.4 Coach tours

These are tours that use coaches/buses, ranging from minibuses to large coaches with toilet and bar facilities. Tour durations on coaches are usually long, from five to 14 nights. Customers are commonly in age groups above 40 years. There will be courier/driver guides throughout.

13.3.5 Self-drive packages

Self-drive packages are provided when the tourist would like to travel in their own cars, but the rest of the arrangements are made by tour operators. The tourist can enjoy the freedom of travel and the scenic views throughout the trip with ample opportunities for sightseeing. In addition to the freedom of pace and movement, the tourist can carry as much luggage as they can fit in their vehicle.

13.4 Business tours

Business tours, MICE (meetings, incentives, conferencing and exhibitions) tours, convention tours and incentive tours are some terms used in the context of business tourism, which is now a major category in international tourism. On a broader spectrum, business tourism covers off-site face-to-face meetings with business partners, while incentive trips are about rewarding and motivating employees or as part of sales promotion, with travel involved so as to participate in large-scale conferences, conventions, exhibitions and trade shows (UNWTO, 2013). MICE is a common term used in this regard. Planned travel with the intention to attend or participate in meetings, conferences and/or events is called a MICE tour. An incentive tour is another type which is offered to corporate employees, intermediaries, retailers, customers, etc. with the objective of motivation or as a reward for achieving particular targets. A convention tour, as defined by Pond (1993), is the "excursion provided for persons attending meetings and conventions". Another definition suggests that a convention tour is an exclusive tour planned for attending conventions or similar events and for taking part in excursions during free time.

Note below some tour classifications by purpose/nature of attractions:

- Cultural tours
- Educational tours
- Religious tours, spiritual tours
- Health tours
- Business tours
- Agricultural tours
- Farm tours/plantation tours
- Ethnic tours
- Photographic tours
- Creative tours
- Recreational tours
- City tours
- Rural tours/urban tours
- Anthropological tours
- Bicycle tours
- Culinary tours

Here are some further tour classifications, with some examples provided:

- *Wedding tours:* tour packages which enable couples to get married in a foreign country (unlike other package tours, this includes extra visits as well as arranging facilities and other required items)
- *Honeymoon tours:* exclusive package tours for newly married couples to stay in romantic environments
- *Sports tours:* exclusive arrangements for taking part in sports activities like golf
- *Adventure tours:* tours for partaking in adventurous activities
- *Space tours:* a recreational expedition into space

13.5 Package tours

A package tour is a planned and prearranged form of travel from one place to another for the purpose of visiting, with a variety of features/services packaged and offered as a single product to an individual or a group of people. A tourist needs to pay a single price for all the services included in the package. It is defined as "a vacation plan arranged by [a] tour operator or wholesalers which provides, for a set fee, all or most of the required services: transportation, accommodation, sightseeing, attractions, and entertainment" (Pond, 1993). In many cases, packages are called "all-inclusive" when they encompass most of the travel elements. It doesn't mean that a package tour covers all the tour elements. If a planned tour is offered at a single price and includes transport and accommodation, then it can be called a package tour. It means that in order to consider a planned tour a package tour, a minimum of two of the important services have to be covered and the package has to be offered to the customer at a single price. Usually a tour operator gets the services at lower, negotiated rates from the suppliers due to bulk purchases. Negotiation with suppliers is a major activity in the process of packaging. This cost saving will be reflected in a lower price for tourists. Tour operators work with all segments of the tourism industry to negotiate rates and coordinate myriad details relating to tour packages at an inclusive price.

CASE STUDY 13.1

Reasons to book a package tour

According to the United States Tour Operators Association (USTOA), there are ten principal reasons to book a tour. By buying in bulk and negotiating special rates for various services like accommodation and transportation, tour operators achieve substantial savings, which are passed on to the consumer. Thus, the holidays become affordable for different strata of society. Tourists can have additional savings when the packages include select meals, hotel tips and sightseeing. A properly planned package and a tour operated by a professional team will minimize tourist uncertainty. Trust in a proficient operator, the presence of an escort or other assistants in case of emergencies, advance payments made for the package, etc. all add to the comfort of the tourist. Tourists don't have to wait for services as such would have been arranged in advance, and thus tour operators can provide unparalleled access to services and facilities.

Nowadays, tourists prefer to go beyond the tourist hotspots and experience the colourful history, unique culture and distinct tastes of a destination. Professional tour operators provide some exotic experiences in addition to the usual stuff. This can enhance the tourist experience. Tourists have a lot of variety, as tour operators offer a large number of itineraries to choose from, and there are even customized packages to suit their requirements. Diversity of offerings makes the tour operation business more attractive. By providing a package tour, the tour operator can guarantee accommodation. Quality of accommodation and services provided as part of it is a prerequisite for the success of a tour. Tour operators have the responsibility to ensure this. Moreover, all elements of a tour are conveniently available to the tourist since the tour operator is vested with the responsibility of arranging them. The provision of knowledge is also a responsibility of a tour operator. The details of attractions and the places visited are arranged with the support of local experts, which will enhance the quality of the tourist experience.

Nowadays, itineraries are created with increased flexibility which provide enough time to explore particular points of interest on one's own. Local tour guides can assist in this context. This flexibility can help to enhance the tourist experience. USTOA ensures protection from financial issues, in case a member tour operator goes bankrupt or becomes insolvent, so booking a tour will not end up with the potential tourist losing their money. "In addition to protecting consumers' vacation dollars, these operators must meet strict requirements of ethics and integrity in their tour offerings and advertising."

Source: USTOA (n.d.)

Read the case study carefully and answer the following questions:

- Identify USTOA's ten reasons for booking a package tour
- What are the services that can enhance the tourist experience?

13.6 Elements of a package tour

13.6.1 Return travel

Travel is the most fundamental aspect of tourism and a package tour usually includes travel from the tourist's place of origin to the destination and back. Air transport is the most commonly used form of transport in package tours. However, other modes of travel are also used, depending on the destination being visited and availability and convenience of transport forms. Some tours are designed to attract more tourists by offering interesting combinations of transport forms, such as fly cruises in which travellers fly to an embarkation point and then board a cruise ship for the rest of the tour. Some tours are even named after the main transport modes used. If the trip is a multi-centre holiday, then the inter-destination travel will also be arranged.

13.6.2 Transfer

Transfer denotes the transport of arriving passengers from the airport/seaport to the accommodation centre, and vice versa. In package tours, this is an important item since the incoming tourists are strangers in the destination, which makes it difficult to locate the hotel. Prearranged transfers are very convenient for them. If the tour operator does not have offices in the destination, then the transfer arrangements will be made by overseas representatives, inbound tour handlers or ground handling agencies. A separate bus will come for a group tour of reasonable size. At times, the inbound handlers may use buses on a sharing basis. Smaller vehicles are also used depending on the need.

13.6.3 Accommodation

Most package tours include accommodation arrangement as well. Type of accommodation included, category of the accommodation units, etc. depend on the price, nature of the tour and the needs of the tourists. Ensuring quality accommodation is a determinant in the success of tours. Usually hotel rooms are booked several months in advance and hence tour operators get significant discounts on the cost of the rooms. In group tours, sharing accommodation is encouraged. Separate rooms may be provided if the traveller is ready to pay extra for it.

13.6.4 Sightseeing/excursions

Almost every tour package consists of sightseeing trips. Some tours (e.g. escorted) will have more sightseeing options. For group tours, separate vehicles, usually buses, will be arranged for short trips to attractions, events, trade fairs, etc. as per the itinerary. In the tour, along the routes, attractions may be added according to the interests of tour participants, when the itinerary is designed. When the tour takes place, the tour leader will try to adhere to the pre-set itinerary. Wherever needed, local guides will be used for explaining further about specific attractions.

13.6.5 Food/meals

Meals are an important aspect of packaged tours. Included meals in a tour package will increase the tour cost, and hence, in some cases, tour operators may reduce or eliminate meals provided in the tour as part of the package. At times, buffet meals are offered in order to save costs. Breakfast is usually provided as part of accommodation. In many packages, either lunch or dinner is included. In others, neither is provided. Meal plans are sometimes in accordance with the accommodation centre's practice, or they may follow any one of the established plans: American Plan, Modified American Plan, Continental Plan or European Plan. When they follow any one of these, the room tariff includes the cost of meals as per the plan. Specification of meal arrangements will be included in the tour brochure and tourists will be aware of what meals are included and what meals are not.

13.6.6 Other elements

Other elements include the following:

- Insurance
- Activities
- Entertainment
- Guide services
- Car rental for business and leisure passengers

In addition to the above elements, there can be extra elements according to the policy of the company. Here are the most significant:

- Optional tours
- Gratuities
- Baggage handling

Table 13.3 Meal plans/terminologies

Terminology	Explanation
American Plan (AP)	Includes all three meals: breakfast, lunch and dinner. Also called full board.
Modified American Plan (MAP)	Includes breakfast and either lunch or dinner.
Continental Plan (CP)	Only continental breakfast (bread with butter/jam/honey, cheese, meat, croissants, pastries, rolls, fruit juice and various hot beverages) is included.
European Plan (EP)	No meals included.
English breakfast	Full breakfast of cereal, bacon, sausages, eggs, toast, juice, tea and coffee.
Family Plan (FP)	This plan offers discounted meals for children.
Bed and breakfast	Only breakfast is provided.
Half Board (or Half Pension)	Breakfast and dinner are included.
À la carte	Food served as per the guest's order from the menu. It is not a set meal. Each item is priced.
Buffet	A meal with several dishes, laid out on tables, from which guests serve themselves.
Table d'hôte	A fixed-price meal, with few (if any) choices.

- Service charges, fees and taxes
- Welcome events
- Complimentary dinners, etc.

Note some common inclusions in a travel insurance policy:

- Health/medical insurance
- Personal baggage and lost money
- Personal accident
- Personal liability
- Medical emergency, repatriation
- Missed departure/departure delay
- Hijacking or missing person
- Cover for natural calamity
- Home care
- Legal advice and expenses cover
- Scheduled airline failure

Inclusion of the elements in the package depends on the policy of the tour operator, needs of the tourists, nature of the group, price of the package, type of destination, intensity of the competition and obviously the package type. The success of the tour package to a great extent depends on the right combination of these elements. Furthermore, the elements included are useful for marketing the package as well. The tour brochure, the key tour marketing tool, will usually highlight the accommodation included, major attractions covered, insurance options, entertainment and activities. Services offered and the experiences from each of the included elements contribute to the ultimate tourist experience, which is the determinant of tourist satisfaction. An underperforming element can add to dissatisfaction. Besides, adding elements without considering the cost and the scope of the package can reduce the profit or can lead to loss.

13.7 Package tour: planning and designing

The package tour, the product of a tour operator, has to be designed, promoted and sold in the market. Meticulous planning is a prerequisite for preparing a package tour and a series of steps have to be followed prior to making the final package. A number of factors need to be considered in the whole process of planning. Professionalism is of utmost significance. The wrong combination of elements, wrong choice of destination, inappropriate attractions included, inclusion of elements without considering the cost, inclusion of activities and entertainment without considering the age group/nature of the target market, etc. can lead to failure. Selection of hotels in wrong locations, buses without air conditioners, inappropriate/unprofessional guide/tour manager, pace of tour (too fast or too slow), poor quality food, unsafe destinations, etc. are some other factors that can negatively impact a tour. Besides financial implications, a failed tour results in serious consequences, because an unhappy tourist will often be critical of the tour operator with other people, i.e. talk about their bad experience. Planning and designing a package demands knowledge, skills and expertise. Usually experienced staff in the organization are entrusted with the task of packaging the tour. Different sources can be used for information in the planning stage of packaging:

- Tour operator's own repository
- Websites, travel blogs, virtual communities and online intermediaries
- Familiarization ("fam") trips, previous experiences
- Destination promotion materials and marketing communication
- Visitor bureaus, overseas tourist offices, national tourism offices (NTOs)
- Encyclopaedia, published books, travel guides, travelogues
- Trade associations, professional organizations
- Libraries and learning resource centres
- Destination management systems
- Educational/interpretation programmes
- Maps and atlases

While designing a package, it is important to include destinations and local resources that appeal to tourists. Destination selection criteria may be different for different types of tours. For instance, for an SIT, the choice of destination will depend on the availability of the specific interest-related attractions. Webster (1993) identifies six important determinants in selecting a destination for a GIT:

- *Popularity:* for a GIT, popular destinations are preferred as they are considered easier to sell. For FITs, it may be different.
- *Adequate facilities:* availability of convenient and comfortable transportation, variety of accommodation, quality and necessary basic infrastructure are critical for selecting a destination for a common group tour.
- *Wide appeal:* including a variety of attractions and activities can generate appeal in most market segments.
- *Far away:* people may be more familiar with nearby destinations and hence they can take trips by themselves. The distant destinations may be more attractive.
- *Climate:* year-round destinations, where climate is favourable most of the year, are chosen more often. If destinations have an adverse climate, tour operation may not be possible.
- *Agent recommendations:* the agents' own experiences will give an indication.

In large firms, the packaging process passes through different professionals who have expertise in specific areas. Some are involved in identifying the attractions and activities to be included. Once the destination selection has been done, the travel plan needs to be prepared. Others may have expertise in costing and pricing. Negotiation with suppliers is also an important task handled by professionals. Moreover, packaging commences after market research, which is also undertaken with professionalism. Identifying the mistakes that happened in previous tours is important so that those mistakes can be avoided for future ones. Therefore, packaging a tour or a holiday is a process that requires meticulous planning and the involvement of experts.

Tour planning is carried out far in advance. It is essential to have an adequate time frame to undertake all the activities involved, from the planning stage until the execution of the tour, in a sequential manner. Some agencies commence tour planning several months in advance, even up to 18 months in advance. This period, the advance time between initiating a tour and its departure date, is called the **lead time** in package tour operations. Usual lead time in the tour operation sector is one year minimum. Different stages of the tour packaging process happen at different points in the lead time. Prior to commencing packaging activities, it is necessary to review the feedback, past activities,

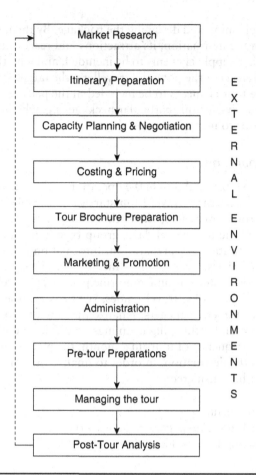

Figure 13.1 The tour packaging process

experts' opinions, experience of other tour operators or tour managers, and industry news releases. The stages of tour packaging are provided in Figure 13.1.

13.7.1 Market research

A successful package is also the result of careful and appropriate research. A wide variety of aspects come into consideration when carrying out research. There are two major focuses for the research. One is the destination and its elements, which constitute the major component of the product. This is more intense when a new package is formed with a new destination. Choosing the right destination is crucial. Destination research should try to determine why tourists would visit that destination and what the attractions and benefits would be over other destinations. The destination selected has to match the needs and interests of the target market as well. The second focus is usually on the demand and supply. All the trends, changing interests of customers, buying behaviour, etc. can be studied along with searching various aspects associated with the supply side. This stage is done almost a year in advance of the tour execution. The outcome of this provides the base for planning and designing the package. By then, the tour operator will have gained clarity on the destination, its attractions and reasons for choosing it, different attractions and other supply elements to be included, and who the potential travellers are. The needs and interests of the potential travellers (the target group) are assessed and then matched with the tour elements to be included in the package. In addition, this will help to finalize the objectives of this particular package, e.g. whether to earn profit, to be a leader in the market or to increase market share.

13.7.2 Itinerary preparation

The tour itinerary is the most vital tool in the operation and marketing of a package tour. Simply, it's a "planned pattern of travel from start to its completion" (Ryan, 1991). Its elements include the route, distances, travel times, activities and sightseeing. Once we identify the destination, the number of days, group type, type of attractions to include, etc., we can proceed with itinerary preparation. Information from different sources can be used for making itineraries. These sources include old itineraries, wholesaler itineraries, competitor itineraries, information from principals, NTOs, websites, feedback from past customers, fam trips, books, travel guides, overseas representatives, ground handling agencies and tour leaders/managers. Finalize the date of departure, date of return, time for both departure and return, flight timings, check-in and check-out times in the accommodation units, frequency of tours in a month, the place of departure, and accommodation locations in the destination. In order to finalize the date of departure, the following factors have to be considered:

- The convenience for clients
- Availability of tour leaders/managers/guides/escorts
- External environmental factors, like political changes
- Weather patterns
- Seasons
- Availability of special events
- Public holidays and vacations

In addition to the major inclusions, a package can include local cultural features which are unique, such as local rituals and local events. Finalize the main locations and highlights that visitors will experience. Specify the flora, fauna, history, culture and other items to consider. Be sure of the activities and attractions included, and their working times, entrance fees, additional costs required for the visit, etc. While making the list of attractions and activities to be included in the package, specify the reasons why each has been chosen and why others were not chosen. Then, establish a route on a map along with a timeline and a logical order for the movement of the tour. Try and map the locations in sequence in order to use the travel time efficiently. The time frame should be day-based, and then hour-based in a day. The travel time, nature of the group, distance to travel, etc. then need to be considered. There should be enough time provided for travelling to, visiting and explaining about the places, and for buying some local souvenirs, etc. There should be enough of a time gap for rest and meals. On some tour days, the tour group will stay in the same hotel to avoid too much packing and unpacking and travelling with luggage. If the next day's attraction is not too far, then it is better to stay in the same hotel. If it is far, moving to the new location for stay should also be feasible. (Basically, there should be enough time to travel to attractions and to return to the hotel that same day.) It will of course be tiring. Think of the time required for meeting and greeting, and for transfers. Keep in mind the potential for small flight delays, too. There needs to be enough rest/sleeping time provided before the commencement of the tour.

Note below some of the points of concern when planning a package tour (Mitchell, 2005):

- Ensure that it includes all aspects.
- Present the benefit of using your services.
- Price the tour to compete with other destinations' offerings, similar services or experiences.
- Pace the tour with your clients' safety and comfort in mind.
- Pay attention to details and offer a quality package.
- Allow flexibility in the tour programme.
- Ensure that the customers are fully informed of what they will experience on the tour.
- Try to make the tour package as unique as possible.
- Develop fair refund and payment conditions and schedules.
- Ensure that the package is profitable.

Try to visualize the movement of the tour and make sure the movement is smooth and not too tiring. Also, fix the inter-destination modes of transport. At times, rail journeys can be included wherever possible. Different modes of transport can be included to maintain the interest of the tour party. Once the route, timings, and attractions and activities have been determined, prepare a rough itinerary. It has to be developed in a day-by-day format. While setting the itinerary, the distances between places, attractions and accommodation centres should be known. The average time to reach each important location should be known. Climate, local time, usual shopping hours, etc. should also be known. Time is usually worked out on a 24-hour clock. While planning the itinerary, the distance, location, air routes, land routes, etc. have to be taken care of. Also, airfares need to be considered before planning the itinerary. The number of possible stops, transit, economical flights and flight schedules are also considered. Include shopping facilities, variety of attractions, etc. The inclusions may sometimes become excessive, as there are so many items that could be included. Now the itinerary has to be reviewed based on real-time availability, cost factor, variety and the general character of the group. Wherever needed, eliminate, add or limit the needed items and try to fit them into the given budget and time frame. Fine-tune the itinerary again with further discussions with other experts. The itinerary can be made in different forms, as described below.

Inclusive itinerary
This type of itinerary involves each and every activity included in the tour along with all relevant data, including hotel contacts, transfer details, details of meals, etc. This is the one that is used for the costing and tour planning and even for the execution of the tour. These are vital tools for escorted tours. Some other types of itineraries are prepared based on the inclusive itinerary.

Semi-inclusive itinerary
This, with fewer details, is prepared based on the inclusive itinerary. Every tour participant is provided with a copy of the semi-inclusive itinerary for their information and preparations before and on tour.

Abstract itinerary

This is a shorter itinerary with only essential items included – the highlights. An abstract itinerary is a concise form that is intended to appeal to the clientele. This may also form part of the tour brochure.

Preliminary itinerary

The preliminary itinerary is prepared as an initial version of the itinerary, before details are finalized. It is important for the early stages in the package designing process.

13.7.3 Guidelines for preparing the itinerary

An itinerary is the essence of a tour and the backbone of all tour-related activities. Moreover, it has a significant role in the tourist experience and their satisfaction. Therefore, itinerary preparation has to be carried out with extreme care and diligence. We discuss some of the important aspects to consider during the process of itinerary preparation below.

Needs and interests of the target market

The ultimate objective of an itinerary is to ensure tourist satisfaction, and hence extreme care needs to be taken to understand the needs and interest of the target market. In group travel, it is not easy: most general needs and interests may be prioritized, but individual ones also need to be considered (without affecting others), as far as this is possible.

Pace

This is all about the speed of tourist movement while they are in the destination. The movement of tourists on tour has to be comfortable, but faster movement can be tiring, and slower movement can be boring. Time may be provided for shopping, the occasional nap, washing clothes, meal times, and time for selfies and photographs. The distance to walk, distance to travel, nature of attractions and nature of activities also have to be considered. Certain attractions need to be well interpreted and hence the necessary time must be provided for learning about them. Climate is also a factor. If it is very hot, activities in the middle of the day (when it is often hottest) must be considered carefully. Similarly, if it is very cold, morning activities should be included only if necessary.

Too overloaded

The volume of activities every day should also be carefully considered. A tour itinerary that is loaded with activities can be tiring and tedious. There have to be activity inclusions and the time in the destination needs to be well utilized. However, this doesn't mean that from morning until night there have to be activities running continuously. There needs to be enough time for resting and relaxing and for getting to the next activity, and group characteristics must be considered as well.

No frequent packing and unpacking

Try to minimize the need for constant packing and unpacking in hotels. Intermittent travel and changing hotels is tedious, at times. Hotel stays should last more than one night, so that travellers are able to arrange luggage properly, to sleep late at least one morning, etc. If they have to pack everything and move to another hotel in the next location every day, it will be tiring and frustrating/annoying. While making the itinerary, it is therefore necessary to consider accommodation in locations where travellers can stay for longer than a day, until it is necessary to relocate to another hotel in another location.

Details

Pay attention to each and every detail of the tour, like check-in and check-out times, transport times, ground handling organizations, holidays, etc. For instance, if the arrival time is during the night in the destination but check-in time at the hotel is 12 noon, it's a wastage of one night's room rate. If the tour party arrives in the morning, then they can occupy the room around 12 noon and that day can be used for other activities as well. The same can happen with check-out times. Whenever excursions/visits to attractions are planned, ensure that they are open for the visit. If the guide chosen for interpretation does not possess the required professionalism, it can negatively affect the tourist experience. There are many such aspects that may not look very important but that have to be considered, as they all contribute to tourist satisfaction and ultimately the success of the tour.

Energy levels

The energy levels of tourists has to correspond with the tour activities, such as walking and climbing. It is important to note how much walking certain trips within the destination require, whether or not there is climbing involved, if tourists are travelling alone or with family members, etc. As mentioned above, the age group of the tour must also be considered, as should health levels of participants when deciding what activities to include. In group travel, some participants may move quickly, while others may not be able to. If it is an adventure tour, the energy levels of participants will be higher, and hence the itinerary can include activities that correspond to them.

Routing

In a package tour, interesting and efficient routing is a major component. Routing deals primarily with the direction of travel. When finalizing the routing of the tour after arrival in the destination, there should not be backtracking, doubling back, routing in a circle, etc. A practical approach is needed. It is better to finish trips in one direction before leaving in another direction. Once the group has left a hotel and gone to another hotel in another location, returning to the previous location after the visit to the new one is a waste of time and energy.

Balance

An itinerary should have balance in terms of attractions and activities, especially for a group package tour. In a group, there are different types of participants. If it is an affinity group, make the itinerary according to their needs. If it's a common kind of group, then there will be heterogeneity among participants. In this way, a variety of interests may be accommodated. It has to be understood and diversity can be ensured. A mix of different activities, including recreational, educational, and frivolous activities will make the tour interesting. Some of the attractions can be serious, some entertaining, some can generate wonder, etc. Some are pleasing for the eye, relaxing and light-hearted, while others may be educational. A balanced itinerary can be more interesting for the tour group compared to having the same type of accommodation, etc., which can lead to monotony.

Optional tours

Though for an all-inclusive tour, the itinerary is preset and fixed, it is better to have some opportunities for optional tours. Optional tours are the short trips the tourists can go on after arriving in a destination, as per their tastes. Usually, once tourists have reached the destination, they find attractions they're interested in which are not included in the itinerary. Going on optional tours is up to the tour participants themselves, but time slots for such have to be included in the itinerary.

Evening activities

There have to be interesting activities on some evenings during the tour. They can be occasional and varied, including parties, concerts, shows and fun activities. Some unexpected activities can also be arranged. For instance, if any of the tour members' birthdays fall on a tour day, a birthday celebration can be arranged without their knowledge, which can create enthusiasm and excitement for everyone in the tour party.

Social activities for boring hours

Including social activities can be useful for improving the social mood on tour. In order to start the tour on a positive note and to break the ice, an early social get-together can be arranged. During long coach journeys within the destination, travellers will invariably get bored. The tour escort or guide can initiate some games and social activities to minimize this boredom. Also, parties can be arranged for alleviating the fatigue.

Shopping

Regardless of the type of tourist, shopping is an important activity when they visit a place. The type of products they purchase and volume can vary. Some may go for small-scale purchases, mainly souvenirs, while others may be interested in buying more. Some search for indigenous items, and some look for products that cost less compared to their home shopping locations.

First impression

The first days are crucial for ensuring the tour is pleasurable. According to Sarbey de Suoto (1985), "the first forty-eight hours are so important because this is when first impressions are made; friendships are initiated among passengers; and a relationship of trust and respect is cemented between the tour manager and the passengers". Hence, arranging ice-breaking sessions, welcome parties, orientations, etc. are crucial. The enthusiasm and warmth of the rest of the tour depends on the first impression created.

Final night and lasting impressions

The final night is crucial for leaving lasting impressions. It needs due consideration and it's important to organize social events in order to create happy memories. Usually a very large dinner and entertainment are organized on the last night. Lasting impressions are a major element in tourists' memories and crucial for ensuring positive "word of mouth" publicity.

Day 01 – Los Angeles

On arrival, transfer to hotel. Check in and free day for leisure.

Day 02 – Los Angeles: City Tour (Duration: 6–7 hours)

City tour of Los Angeles, a drive through the "entertainment capital of the world", Hollywood, Hollywood Walk of Fame, Beverly Hills, Grauman's Chinese Theater, Sunset strip, Rodeo Drive for the world's most expensive shopping, and Chinatown. (Meals: B)

Day 03 – Los Angeles: Universal Studios Hollywood (Duration: 8 hours)

Join us today for a tour of Universal Studios which has always been known for its innovative rides and attractions, and is designed to let visitors experience the movies like never before. A trip to Universal is like a trip into the heart of Hollywood. (Meals: B)

Day 04 – Los Angeles: Disneyland Park (Duration: 8 hours)

Today you will visit Disneyland Park, where storybook fantasy is everyday reality, and Disney classics are brought to life. From the moment you step onto Main Street USA, you are transported to a place where the cares of the outside world seem to magically melt away.

Day 05 – Los Angeles–SeaWorld San Diego (Duration: 8 hours)

Today we proceed to San Diego to visit SeaWorld. This theme park is one of the most fascinating marine life parks in the world. Here you will discover SeaWorld's many attractions. We dare you to take a one-of-a-kind water coaster thrill ride through the mysterious lost city of Atlantis. Soar through danger on a jet copter ride to the Wild Arctic. Touch, feed or get face to face with awesome and amazing wild animals.

Day 06 – Los Angeles–Buffalo

Free day for leisure and shopping. Evening transfer to airport to board the flight to Buffalo. Overnight on board.

Day 07 – Niagara Falls USA: Maid of the Mist

Transfer to the hotel. Today you will board the famous boat ride "Maid of the Mist", which takes us close to the thundering falls and around the American and Horseshoe Falls (varies based on season). Return to the hotel to freshen up after your damp ride. In the evening enjoy the illuminating falls dazzled by thousands of lights that will leave spectators in awe.

Day 08 – Buffalo–Washington, DC: City Tour (Duration: 8 hours)

Fly to Washington, DC. Explore the capital city of the USA. Enjoy the sights of the White House, Lincoln Memorial, Supreme Court Building, the Capitol Building, Smithsonian Museum, the Air and Space Museum, Union Station, World War II Memorial Building, the Pentagon and the Washington Monument.

Day 09 – Washington, DC–New York

Today you are proceeding to New York. Known as "The Big Apple" or "The City that Never Sleeps", New York is America's largest city, with millions of visitors each year. Upon arrival at the airport, you will be transferred to the hotel. Enjoy an illumination tour of Times Square in the evening.

Day 10 – New York: City Tour (Duration: 8 hours)

Today you will proceed for a city tour of New York. The sightseeing will include USA's famous landmark Statue of Liberty via ferry ride with a spectacular view of the New York City skyline. Later enjoy/appreciate visits to the Rockefeller Center, Wall Street, Ground Zero and Central Park, Times Square, United Nations and Trump Tower. In the afternoon, experience the view of a lifetime from the 86th floor of the Empire State Building.

Day 11 – Departure

After breakfast, we will depart for the airport so that you can board your flight to your next destination or return home.

Figure 13.2 A sample tour itinerary to the USA (10 nights/11 days)
Source: Courtesy of Intersight Holidays (P) Ltd, Cochin, India

13.8 Capacity planning and negotiation

Tour capacity planning and identifying the requirements for services of suppliers in the future – for anticipated packages – is another crucial task in the packaging process. It is necessary to specify tour capacity for all further activities. Forecasting capacity requirements and determining how many beds and flight seats are required is a somewhat cumbersome project. Some tour operators book large numbers of rooms in destinations far in advance, based on rough estimates. They allocate the required number of rooms as per the need for each package tour. As they book rooms so far in advance, they can enjoy substantial discounts. Once forecasting is complete, and while the tour is being planned, tour operators will have a clear idea of the requirements of service from suppliers in the destination. Once the service needs have been identified, negotiation with suppliers must be carried out before entering into contracts with them. Major suppliers in the destination include hotels, ground handling agents and transport services. Airlines or other transport operators used for onward and return journeys also need to be contacted for further discussions and for entering into contracts. The selection of suppliers requires utmost care, as the quality of services they provide ultimately determines customer satisfaction. Also, tour costs include the payments made to the suppliers.

Selecting the most appropriate hotel is a daunting task. The hotel is one of the most important service providers for a package holiday. The quality of the service provided by the hotel is an important determinant in tourist satisfaction. The factors to consider in the hotel selection process include the following:

- Client preferences
- Group/client type
- Location of the hotel
- Accessibility
- Image and brand
- Rates and discounts
- The method of booking and reservation
- Check-in and check-out times
- Hotel ratings
- Food and beverage (F&B) services
- Meal plans
- Housekeeping
- Ease of baggage handling
- Room size and facilities
- Motor coach parking and loading facilities
- Suitable space for representative's desk, notice board, etc.
- Extra facilities, such as gym and spa
- Commission level
- Safety and security
- Services offered
- Entertainment options
- Wi-Fi connectivity and Internet options
- Quality of services
- Cooperation and assistance
- Availability of different restaurants
- Ambience and cleanliness
- In-room entertainment
- Concierge and information services
- Tax, tips (gratuity), service charges, etc.
- Availability of special facilities, if required
- Possibility of free or subsidized accommodation for accompanying representatives, escorts/guides, etc.
- Booking and cancellation terms
- Modes of payment

For hotel contracts there are three common practices: commitment, allocation and ad-hoc basis (Horner, 1996; Yale, 2001). Prior to entering into contracts, it is important for operators to estimate seat and room requirements. Negotiating for the best product at the cheapest rate is the ultimate objective. But the financial risk also needs to be considered. Large agencies may have their own offices or overseas representatives for negotiation and for putting contracts together. Smaller ones may depend on ground handlers. We will briefly describe each type of hotel contract below.

13.8.1 Commitment

This is a common type of agreement between hotels and tour operators, particularly large ones. It denotes the commitment from the side of the tour operator to buy a certain number of beds during a particular time of the year. The agency is committed to pay for an agreed number of beds/rooms. By making this agreement, the tour operator takes up the risk to make the payment for all the beds they have agreed to use. Even if the actual requirement is less, the agency will have to bear the cost of it. The advantage of this agreement is that they will receive the lowest possible rates.

13.8.2 Allocation

In this category, the tour operator agrees to an allocation of rooms/beds up to a specific date and if they are not needed by that date, the non-required rooms/beds will be released back to the hotel so that they can resell them accordingly. The release date is a specific date agreed between the agency and client, after which the supplier has the freedom to resell them. Until the release date, the rooms are blocked for that tour operator. For instance, one tour operator may agree to book 1,000 rooms in a hotel in a destination for the holiday season, which may commence from 1 April. They will negotiate a cut-off date, say 15 February, when they will have to release the rooms. After estimating the exact room requirements, the tour operator realizes that only 600 rooms are required, so by 15 February the non-required rooms (400) can be released back to the hotel and 600 can be confirmed. For this type of agreement, hotels may offer higher rates than the commitment category. Allocation is also very common with large players.

13.8.3 Ad-hoc basis

In this case, rooms/beds are booked as per the requirement and as and when they are needed. Due to the fact that this booking is made much later than both commitment and allocation types of contracting, the rates of rooms for this category are often the highest among them. However, for the operator this is the least risky contracting option. Though not so common among mass tour operators, "upmarket", "niche" or specialist tour operators may opt for this kind of arrangement quite often.

Hotel bookings can be done directly, through a central reservation system (CRS)/global distribution system (GDS), through a chain's sales offices, through hotel representatives or through overseas representatives. Moreover, some hotels have central reservation offices.

Selecting the transport provider is also an important concern. Tour operators may use scheduled airline services or charter airline services. Scheduled carriers are preferred more for complex travel itineraries that have multiple destinations, such as "open jaw", "circle trips", etc. Major airlines usually have holiday divisions as well. They gain many advantages from this. Also, scheduled services are used more for long-haul tours. Selecting the most appropriate airline for contracting is the primary task. Airline contracting for tour operation is a crucial activity in which a number of factors have to be taken care of:

- Schedule frequency
- Departure and arrival time
- Direct flight/stop over/transit with connecting time

Table 13.4 Comparison of hotel contract types

Type	Advantages	Disadvantages
Commitment	Rooms/beds will be made available at the best prices. The tour operator has more negotiating power. There is no release date for the operator. It offers the lowest price for rooms. It is highly profitable in good seasons/years.	The tour operator has to make payment for all the rooms contracted. If there are unsold beds/rooms, the cost of them have to be borne by the tour operator, which can reduce the profit margin. The tour operator has the risk of selling all the contracted rooms. It represents the highest financial risk.
Allocation	There is more negotiating power compared to ad-hoc basis. There are reasonably good prices for rooms. The tour operator doesn't have to make payment for released rooms. It is less risky for the operator.	Bargaining power is less than commitment contracts. Prices are higher than commitment contracts. It is less profitable compared to commitment contracts. There must be proper communication about the number of rooms/beds at the right time. A lack thereof will result in cost increases.
Ad-hoc basis	The tour operator bears no risk about unsold rooms/beds. There is no need of bothering about release dates. The case of reverting rooms does not arise. Lowest financial risk.	This represents the lowest bargaining power. Prices are higher than allocation and commitment types. It is less profitable, unless the package is priced high.

Source: Horner and Swarbrooke (1996); Yale (2001)

- Reputation and image of the airline
- Location of airport (if there are multiple airports)
- Airport services, ease of use
- Cost (fare) and fare basis
- Terms and conditions of booking and cancellations
- Group booking facility
- Commission and override commissions/discount level
- Group booking offers
- In-flight services and entertainment options
- Flight capacity
- Punctuality of services
- Attitude and cooperation of key staff
- Seat comfort

While selecting the airline, it is also important to identify the most suitable airfare. Though GDS-based seat booking is the normal mode of airline seat distribution, large operators may negotiate with airlines to gain a price advantage. Airline policies and airline industry competition do matter in this process. Traditionally, "group fares", "excursion fares", etc. are used for overseas tour operation. "Special fares" are useful in this category. Most airlines use IT (inclusive tour) fare and GT (group tour) fare for contracting with tour operators. But such options are given to large-scale tour operators who can handle booking in large numbers in advance. Also, there will be conditions, such as days of journey, seasons, etc. The agreement for booking seats is made between the airline and the tour operator, and the booking may not be done through a GDS. Also, there are some fare types suitable for tour operators that can be booked through a GDS. However, not all intermediaries can obtain those fares through GDSs. Traditionally, the term "ITX" has been used to refer to special fares of scheduled airlines. ITX stands for inclusive tour excursion fare. Tailor-made packages also make use of ITX fares or other fares of scheduled services. In this era of modern airline pricing philosophy, airfares vary quite often depending on the demand. For ad-hoc booking, tour operators prefer to conduct off-season tours – when demand is less and price levels are low. While booking with airlines, it is imperative to see the terms and conditions for date changes, cancellations, free tickets, luggage, and booking periods. Low-cost carriers (LCCs) do not encourage this type of booking.

Mass tour operators, especially large-scale leisure operators, opt for charter services for overseas tours. The term "ITC" (inclusive tour charter) is used for undertaking tours using charter services. ITC is usually used by large operators and specialist operators (SITs). Some of the vertically integrated large operators in developed countries own charter flights as well. Using charter flights has many advantages. Charter services are cheaper, more convenient and they offer the needed flexibility to adjust with the changing circumstances. The usual charter contracting methods, according to Yale (2001), are: time series chartering, part chartering and ad-hoc chartering. The following sections look at all three types.

Table 13.5 Difference between scheduled flights and charter flights: a tour operator perspective

Scheduled flights	Charter flights
The cost of the flight is high.	They are cheaper than scheduled flights.
Flexibility is much less as the tour operator has to follow the schedules of the airline.	They are very flexible; even destinations can be altered as per the need.
They are suitable for multi-destination tours.	They are suitable more for single destination tours.
In-flight services make the trip more enjoyable.	Relatively speaking, in-flight services are less, so flights are more boring.
They are more suitable for long-haul tours.	Usually used for short-haul tours, but can be used for long-haul tours as well.
Different classes of services are available.	Such distinctions are rarely seen.
They are used by all types of tour operators.	They are mainly used by mass operators as well as specialist operators.

13.8.4 Time series chartering

In this type, also called time share contracting, a charter aircraft is fully contracted for a specific period, usually a season. Back-to-back operations are undertaken using this chartered flight by the tour operator. Though there is the risk of unsold seats, maximum utilization of the aircraft will add to profits. In order to avoid the "empty-leg" issue during the first and the last trips to a destination, a tour operator may opt for long-term contracts. For the back-to-back operations, the return journey after the first trip to a destination will be empty. "Back to back" is a phrase used when an aircraft has a group of passengers to carry to a destination and has another group of passengers to carry back on the return journey. "Empty leg" means that there will be passengers for the initial journey but will return empty. For the next trip, both legs will have passengers. On the last trip to the destination, the onward journey will go empty and bring back the remaining tourists to the origin place. So, in a series of trips to a destination in a season, there may be two empty legs. It provides the operators with the lowest possible prices, but carries the highest element of risk. In addition, unused time can be used for subcontracting the flight to another agency if the opportunity exists.

13.8.5 Part chartering

Instead of contracting the whole plane, some tour operators prefer to charter only a portion of the capacity. This is also called "allocation", which denotes that a certain number of seats are allotted to a particular tour operator. This is up to the tour operator, according to their requirements (usually the volume of the business), whether to use the allocation or time series category. It is the tour operator's responsibility to fill the seats.

13.8.6 Ad-hoc chartering

Ad-hoc chartering allows a tour operator to contract a specific number of seats for specific dates, not for a period. This is undertaken as and when it is needed. It is costlier than the other types of contracting. Usually, smaller companies prefer to buy seats on specific routes on specific dates, for fixed prices, and on an ad-hoc basis. However, generally speaking, ad-hoc chartering has become more popular over the last few years.

Selecting a suitable ground operator or ground handling agent is also an important task. There can be many operators available in a destination. They can handle inbound tour activities on behalf of a tour operator from another country. The outbound operator has to consider a range of factors for choosing the ground operators. The major factors are included here:

* Services offered
* Cost of services
* Quality of services
* Reputation and image
* Proven track record
* Cooperation and assistance
* Quality of the personnel
* Language and communication skills
* Public relations abilities

Table 13.6 Comparison of air charter contracting types

Time series	Part chartering	Ad-hoc chartering
Contracting the whole flight	Contracting a part of the flight	Only the needed seats are booked
The contract is for days, weeks or even a year	The contract is for days, weeks or longer periods	It is for specific dates
The tour operator carries the risk of selling all the seats	The risk is selling the allocated seats only	The risk of selling seats does not arise
Highly risky for the tour operator	Less risky for the tour operator	There is no financial risk
Most economical for the tour operator	Equally or less economical, compared to time series	It is the least economical
Highly flexible for the tour operator	Less flexible for the tour operator	Least flexible for the tour operator
Destinations can be altered easily	It is more difficult to change the destination	This issue is less relevant
The lead time for contracting is rather very long	The contracting lead time is long, but less compared to time series	Booking can be done as per the availability of the seats

Source: Based on Yale (2001)

- Availability of vehicles
- Interpretation skills

A similar type of care has to be undertaken when contracting with other service providers, such as guides, cruise companies, local transport providers and even overseas resort representatives.

13.9 Costing and pricing

Once contracting and booking are done, the next stage in tour packaging is costing. Determining exchange rates, identification of cost elements, estimating the total cost and finalizing the package price after including the margin/markup are the major activities involved in this stage. Cost/price is a major determinant in tourist buying behaviour and hence costing and pricing must always consider the economic levels of potential customers. Moreover, price, along with being a main element of profit, is also a marketing tool. Inappropriate pricing can result in loss. Pricing follows costing, which is a laborious activity. Each item included in the package that has to be paid by the tour operator should be identified during costing. Costing is the first activity; pricing comes later. While costing deals with finding out the total cost, including that of administrative and commercial activities, for conducting of the tour, pricing is about the finalization of the price the customer will pay for purchasing a package tour. Pricing is carried out to set the selling price. It's a method of determining the value that a consumer has to spend to obtain the goods and services. Price, which includes profit share as well, is the amount that comes into the business when a sale takes place. Cost is the amount spent for various items.

Meticulous costing is a prerequisite for successful pricing. Costing, which involves elaborate work, concerns a series of critical tasks. The primary task is to identify all the cost elements. Cost elements in the case of a tour package are all the items that require payment or necessitate expenditure directly or indirectly. Multi-centre holiday costing is more complex. Also, the complexity increases with the length of stay. As in the case of other business activities, costing of package tour operations also involves fixed and variable costs. Fixed costs involve those cost elements that remain constant regardless of the quantity of goods or services produced. The amount does not vary according to the demand or supply variations. Meanwhile, variable costs change according to changes in the level of production or supply of goods or services. For example, rent of a building where production takes place does not change, but the labour cost or material cost may change according to the variation in production. Variable costs in package tours include all the costs associated with each participant. Here are some examples:

- Cost for accommodation
- Travel expenses/air tickets
- Meals/food and beverage
- Visa fee
- Taxes and entry fees, etc.

Fixed costs associated with tour operations are more or less related to the entire tour project, not determined by participant. Here are some examples of fixed costs:

- Cost for brochure production
- Salaries and wages
- Administrative expenses
- Marketing and promotion costs
- Rent for the buildings, etc.
- Maintenance expenses, etc.

Costing is very important, as an omission or incorrect identification of a cost element could cause significant financial losses for the operator. Identification of cost elements is a cumbersome task. Usual cost elements include the following:

- *Administrative expenditure:* It includes all the expenses for managing the business of tour operation with regard to that particular package. It can include the cost associated with the salary of employees, rent for the building, electricity expenses, stationery, IT facilities, communication, other equipment related expenses, etc.
- *Marketing and sales:* expenses includes cost for:
  o Brochure production
  o Brochure launch event
  o Promotional activities including advertisements
  o Promotional evenings
  o Sales activities

- Expenses for retailers – this includes costs for agency training/fam trips, commissions for retailers, etc.
- Banking and currency conversion
- Accommodation expenses – this is usually costed on a night-by-night basis. In group package tour accommodation, it is often provided on the basis of twin bed/double bed rooms, or shared rooms. Tourists can opt for a single room, and for that the "single room supplement" can be arranged for an additional charge. All required taxes, service charges, etc. have to be considered along with the cost of accommodation. If any refreshments/snacks are provided, that also needs to be accounted for.
- Transportation – international travel cost is a major element in package cost. The mode of transport can be land, air or water
- Meals – the inclusion of the cost of meals varies according to the meal plans of hotels. Some of the package tours do not include meals. If included, then the cost for each meal other than that available as part of meal plans for participants has to be accounted for. Tips and other extra charges, if required, have to be included as well
- Transfers – costs for transfer from the airport to the hotel and return to the airport after the tour, along with any other transfers
- Other transport costs – coaches may be hired or ground handling agents may be contracted for such services. Make sure the cost is on a per person basis or per trip basis. Other transport costs, such as those for boats, cruises, ferries, etc., need to be included
- Sightseeing/excursion costs – expenses other than transport costs and entry fees (these are shown separately) for day trips to attractions, if any
- Fees to enter palaces, zoos, museums, etc.
- Taxes – include duty amounts wherever applicable
- Tour manager's salary and expenses
- Expenses for tour guides
- Overseas representative/ground handling agency cost
- Entertainment/social activities and special evening costs
- Visas, permits and feed
- Complimentary trip costs
- Markup or profit margins (usually added after totalling the cost elements)
- Miscellaneous

Costing is usually done on minimum enrolment figures, which is the minimum expected group size. It means the minimum number of tour participants required for conducting a particular project. There will also be a maximum enrolment amount, which is the threshold limit; anyone above the limit cannot be accommodated. If costing is done on the basis of the maximum number, then there can be financial implications for the agency. While the minimum is the required number for carrying out the project, the agency can accommodate more people up to the maximum capacity. However, even if the maximum number of bookings is not reached, a tour can still be run with adequate profit. Whenever more than the minimum level is sold, then the profit will be much higher. However, if costing is done on the maximum, then selling anything less than that could result in less-than-expected profit or even a loss. This is illustrated with sample data and assumed rates and figures in Case study 13.2. The profit factor must also be considered when costing is done. Hence, during costing, net figures are taken and profit is estimated on the basis of those figures. A net figure represents the non-commission rates. Earning has to be anticipated from the markup, as commission may vary. Hence every tour costing and pricing should consider adequate markup to earn profit. Commissions can be extra earnings. Also, while costing, it is important to think of earning or profit for the entire group tour project, not just per participant. It is necessary, while costing, to think of the income level of the target group. Cost elements have to be identified in net terms, i.e. with no commission. Wherever extra expenses are required, include them, e.g. luggage handling in a railway station.

CASE STUDY 13.2

Tour costing and pricing: an example

Costing with minimum and maximum enrolments: Comparison

Assume that ABC tour company has designed a tour package with a minimum expected enrolment of 40 people. However, the tour can accommodate up to 60 people. Assume that they have worked out the total cost for 40 participants to be $20,000. Let's see how much profit there can be from the sale of the package for 40 people.

> Cost for 40 participants = $20,000
> Markup (20%) = $4,000
> Total = $24,000
> Price per participant (24,000/40) = $600
> Total revenue from sales (600 × 40) = $24,000
> Profit (24,000–20,000) = $4,000

Assume that the company could sell the package to 60 participants. The variable cost will increase, but the fixed costs will remain the same. Assume that with the increased variable costs, the total cost has risen to $25,000.

> Then, the revenue will be = $36,000 (600 × 60)
> Profit = 36,000–25,000
> = $11,000

Now consider that the package was costed and priced for a maximum number of participants (60):

> Total cost = $25,000
> Markup (20%) = $5,000
> Total = $30,000
> Price per participant = $500 (30,000 ÷ 60)
> Total revenue = $30,000 (500 × 60)
> Profit = 30,000–25,000
> = $5,000

Here the profit is reduced by $6,000 even if the number of tourist enrolments is 60.

One more situation can emerge if the operator cannot sell to 60 people. Assume that they could achieve only 50 sales; then the revenue would be $25,000 (50 × 500).

In this case, the net result will be a situation with no profit, as the cost itself is $25,000.

Read the case study carefully and answer the following questions:

- Discuss the benefits of conducting package tour costing with minimum enrolments.
- Explain the issues of package tour costing based on maximum enrolments.

One of the ultimate objectives of pricing is to target the profit. In fact, a tour operator has multiple sources of revenue. The most important are listed here:

- *Markup:* Markup certainly constitutes the largest share of a tour operator's profit. Also, during costing and pricing, only markup is considered for targeting the profit.
- *Commissions:* commissions add to the profit. Possible sources of commission include suppliers, shopping centres, sale of travel insurance options, etc.
- *Savings:* this includes savings from the direct distribution of products, foreign currency transactions for tourists, and the interest for deposits. (A deposit is the amount paid by the potential traveller to book a tour package; they are usually refundable).
- *Cancellation charges:* cancellation of bookings carries charges, as per the terms and conditions specified in the brochure. This is considered extra revenue since the same product can then be sold to another person.
- *Sale of ancillary products and optional tours.*

Table 13.7 Differences between costing and pricing

Costing	Pricing
Operational task	Managerial task
Done under operational manager	Done under the higher level/marketing
Costs deal more with expenses to bear	manager
Costs deal with what goes out	Price focuses on profit aspect
Costing focuses on what the operator has to pay to clients for various services offered	Price involves the profit margin the company gains after the cost
Costing yields no profit	Pricing focuses on determining what the tourist has to pay
	Pricing is what yields profit, mainly

Source: Adapted from Sarbey de Suoto (1985)

The hyper-competitiveness existing in the tour operation industry forces companies to offer competitive prices to attract the maximum number of tourists. Therefore, along with other strategies, agencies will usually try to reduce price in order to be competitive. For tourism, being a discretionary product and price elastic to a large extent, reducing price is very important, though the quality of services cannot be compromised on. The following are some strategies that tour operators can use to reduce price:

- Minimize the meals included.
- Compromise on accommodation level.
- Costing may exclude fees for visa, entry into attractions, etc., which can be communicated to tourists clearly.
- Try to sell directly to tourists, i.e. avoid retailers to save on commission.
- Utilize online platforms for marketing and sales.
- Bargain and negotiate with suppliers.
- Utilize early bookings.
- Expand business using vertical and horizontal integration, particularly the former.
- Manage charter flights efficiently by minimizing empty legs, selling surplus seats, etc.
- Try to retain past customers for future sales, at least for different packages.
- Reduce brochure costs and use digital brochures more.
- If essential, pursue costing on the basis of higher minimum expectation.
- If possible, include optional tours at additional cost.

Common pricing strategies are also used by tour operators. Cost-oriented pricing is quite common. For cost-plus pricing, one kind of cost-oriented pricing, the seller's costs are calculated and the price is set by adding a margin. Demand-oriented pricing is based on demand trends. Skimming pricing, which is usually much higher, is often used when products are unique in a newer market, so they are offered to customers initially at a high price, but then the price comes down over time. Penetration pricing, with a lower level price, is applied when a seller wants to get established in a new market. Discriminatory pricing is also applied in specific circumstances – when different prices can be set for different customers. Competition-oriented pricing is common in the hyper-competitive tour operation sector. With this strategy, pricing is based on what the price of competitors' products are. Other pricing strategies, such as premium pricing, are also used by tour operators depending on the market and demand conditions. Price is set months in advance, which can cause other issues. Currency exchange rates may change in the interim period, which can increase or decrease profit. Any variations in certain external factors (e.g. economic downturns, political turmoil) can impact an operator's sales and profitability. Surcharges may be levied on the customer, in necessary situations, such as a serious devaluation in a particular currency. This happens because costing is done so far in advance. However, these surcharges could seriously disappoint tourists, so it should be specifically mentioned in the brochure. Moreover, the minimum number of sales has to take place in order to run a tour. Inflation in the destination is another major issue that tour operators face. All these factors affect costing. Adequate forecasting has to be carried out in order to overcome any such issues.

13.10 Summary

The package tour is the prime product in a tour operation business and it represents a planned and prearranged form of travel from one place to another for the purpose of visiting, with a variety of features/services packaged and offered as a single product to one or a group of people. In many cases, packages are called "all-inclusive" when they encompass most of the travel elements. Tours are classified in different ways. Some of the most common include: foreign independent tour (FIT); group inclusive tour (GIT); mass-marketed tours; special interest tours (SITs)/niche tours; long-haul and short haul tours; single-centre/multi-centre holidays; guided, hosted and escorted tours; affinity tours; safari holidays; and summer tours and winter tours. A package tour includes two or more of the tour elements, such as return travel, transfers, accommodation, sightseeing, and food and beverages. Inclusion of the elements in the package depends on the policy of the tour operator, needs of the tourists, nature of the group, price of the package, type of destination, intensity of the competition and obviously the package type.

Meticulous planning is a prerequisite for preparing a package tour. A series of steps are followed prior to making a final package: market research; itinerary preparation; capacity planning and negotiation; costing and pricing; tour brochure preparation; marketing and promotion; and administration. An itinerary is the essence of a tour and the backbone of all tour-related activities. Therefore, itinerary preparation must be carried out with extreme care and diligence. For hotel contracts, there are three common practices – commitment, allocation and ad-hoc basis. While selecting the airline, it is also important to identify the most suitable airfare. Mass tour operators, especially large-scale leisure operators, opt for charter services for overseas tours. The term "ITC" is used for undertaking tours using charter services. ITC services are often used by large operators and specialist operators. There are three types of ITC contracting – time series chartering, part chartering, and ad-hoc chartering.

Cost/price is a major determinant in tourist buying behavior. It is therefore important to consider the economic levels of potential customers. Meticulous costing is a prerequisite for successful pricing. Usually costing is done on minimum enrolment figures, which is the minimum expected group size. The hyper-competitiveness within the tour operation industry forces companies to offer lower prices to attract as many tourists as possible. Well-designed packages combined with efficient staff who can market and manage a tour effectively can ensure the success of a tour operation business.

Review questions

Short/medium answer type questions

- What is a free independent tour?
- What do we mean by group inclusive tour?
- What are niche tours?
- Differentiate between long-haul and short-haul tours.
- What is the difference between single-centre and multi-centre holidays?
- What do we mean by escorted tour?
- Briefly describe an affinity tour.
- What are summer tours and winter tours?
- Define package tour.
- Describe the elements of a package tour.
- What are the different types of tour itineraries?

- List the factors to consider in the hotel selection process.
- Write briefly about the three hotel contract methods.
- What are the factors to consider when choosing a scheduled airline for a package tour?
- Differentiate between time series chartering and part chartering.
- Explain the process of costing and pricing package tours.

Essay type questions

- Describe in detail the planning and designing of a package tour.
- Describe itinerary preparation and the guidelines one needs to follow.

References

Biederman, S. P., Lai, J., Laitamaki, M. J., Messerli, R. H., Nyheim, P. and Plog, C. S. (2008) *Travel and Tourism: An Industry Primer*. New Jersey: Pearson Education.

Club Med, All-Inclusive Holidays, available at https://www.clubmed.co.uk/l/all-inclusive-holidays.

Goeldner, R. C. and Ritchie, B. J. R. (2003) *Tourism Principles, Policies and Practices*. New Jersey: John Wiley & Sons.

Horner, P. (1996) *Travel Agency Practice*. London: Longman.

Horner, S. and Swarbrooke, J. (1996) *Marketing Tourism, Hospitality and Leisure in Europe*. London: International Thomson Business Press.

Kelly, I. and Nankervis, T. (2001) *Visitor Destination*. Milton: John Wiley & Sons.

Mitchell, G. E. (2005) *Travel FREE as an International Tour Director*. Charleston, SC: The GEM Group.

Pond, L. K. (1993) *The Professional Guide: Dynamics of Tour Guiding*. New York: Van Nostrand Reinhold.

Poon, A. (1993) *Tourism, Technology and Competitive Strategies*. Wallingford: CAB.

Poynter, J. (1989) *Foreign Independent Tours: Planning, Pricing and Processing*. Albany, NY: Delmar Publishers.

Reilly, T. R. (1991) *Handbook of Professional Tour Management*. 2nd edn. Albany, NY: Delmar Publishers.

Ryan, C. (1991) *Recreational Tourism: A Social Science Perspective*. London: Routledge.

Sarbey de Suoto, M. (1985) *Group Travel Operations Manual*. Albany, NY: Delmar Publishers.

USTOA, USTOA's Top 10 Reasons to Book a Tour in 2013, The United States Tour Operators Association, data accessed from https://www.ustoa.com/r/ustoa-filemanager/source/press-kit/Top-10-Reasons-to-Book-a-Tour.pdf (accessed 24 March 2014).

Webster, S. (1993) *Group Travel Operating Procedures*. New York: Van Nostrand Reinhold.

Yale, P. (2001) *The Business of Tour Operations*. Essex: Longman Pearson Education.

Chapter 14

Tour marketing

Learning outcomes

After studying this chapter, you will be able to:

- Describe the importance of brochures in the tour operation business.
- Comprehend how to design and produce a tour brochure.
- Explain market segmentation in tour operation.
- Elaborate on buying behaviour in tour purchases.
- Better understand marketing and distribution in the tour operation sector.

14.1 Introduction

Marketing is certainly a crucial function for a tour operator. Being in the service sector, tour operators face challenges in marketing the product. The features of tour products such as intangibility, inseparability and perishability make the job of marketing difficult. Moreover, "word of mouth" has extreme significance in the tour operation sector. The success of tour operation depends to a large extent on the quality of the services provided to the tourists while they are on tour. Here, a tour operator has a limited role in providing quality services as those are provided by the suppliers. Usually, tour operators try to include services of reliable suppliers only while planning the package tour. Still, there can be issues of poor service delivery. Tourist satisfaction is critical for the long-term survival of tour operation businesses. Indeed, tourist satisfaction can be affected by poor performance of any element included in the package. A tour operator takes the utmost care in ensuring quality of services by all the suppliers. Hence, along with marketing, it is crucial to ensure quality as well. Even in this modern era filled with information and communication technology applications, tour brochures have an important role. Intangibility necessitates customers purchasing the tour package without having the opportunity to verify it, and often from a base of very inadequate knowledge (Holloway and Taylor, 2006). In this circumstance, brochures act as the cardinal means to inform customers about the product and to persuade them to buy it. Let's begin the marketing discussion with tour brochures, which have been the most important tool for a tour operator in the marketing and promotion of their products.

14.2 Tour brochures

A brochure is a folder, booklet or small book with information and pictures. It is common in all businesses and primarily acts as a tool for providing information to the clients and to create interest. However, for a tour operator, it is a necessary tool with diverse objectives to accomplish. According to Horner and Swarbrooke (2005), "tour operators still rely very heavily on their brochure, which is often a thick, glossy, full-colour catalogue, designed to persuade people to purchase the product". Due to the product characteristics, particularly "intangibility", a tour operator depends significantly on tour brochures to inform potential customers about the product, to convince them about the product features and benefits, to create interest in the target market, to enter into contracts with clients, to communicate the terms and conditions related to the package tour, to generate sales, to garner the attention of the clients through intermediaries, etc. A tour brochure, simply, is a publication with the relevant and necessary content for potential clients about a tour. A tour operator needs a brochure before it begins its product promotion. Its importance has not been diminished even in this modern, digital era. Traditionally, it is a widely used and attractive information source for tourists (Holloway and Plant, 1988; Wicks and Schuett, 1991; Yamamoto and Gill, 1999). Even though its digital version can be transmitted cheaply, the print version remains significant as it is the primary tangible evidence that can be used to convince a potential buyer, who it has been argued is influenced by promotional brochures in their travel-related decisions (Moeran, 1983). In short, it is vital because it is the chief means of knowing the tours that are being offered to potential tourists. Certainly it is the most important sales tool for a tourism operator and should contain the necessary information to persuade the client to purchase a holiday. It also creates and reinforces the company's image with its clients.

Tour brochures had a humble beginning; in the past they were simple sheets that described the product. As the industry progressed, the need and scope of tour brochures also expanded, and the post-Second World War era witnessed tremendous developments in the making of tour brochures. By the 1960s, there were dramatic changes, with glossy cover pages and colourful and artistic designs. Contents in brochures also changed, as modern brochures included a variety of information, which we will describe later. With the evolution of modern tour brochures came different types of tour brochures. Some are large, some are small, and some are of medium size with varying quality levels. They can be in a variety of formats, e.g. leaflet, centrefold, booklet, saddle-stitched, side-stitched, etc. Brochures, predominantly, are colourful and created with the utmost professionalism and diligence. They can vary according to purpose, scope, cost and target group. Although tour brochures are prepared in order to target potential travellers, their target market also includes retailers (e.g. travel agents), suppliers (e.g. hotels) and other stakeholders.

Usually, a tour operator makes different types of tour brochures. The general tour brochure, also called the comprehensive tour brochure, includes all the packages or some of the packages of similar nature that are offered by the tour operator. While covering all the products, only limited information can be provided for each product in the brochure. However, the catchy, interesting and necessary details will be included to attract the attention and to create interest. Usually, these are thick brochures and artistically

PACIFIC TOURS - Seeing Seattle

FACTS WORTH KNOWING

Seattle was first settled in 1851.

Business district wiped out by fire June 6, 1889.

First shipment of gold from Alaska and Klondike arrived 1897.

PARKS: Seattle has 44 parks, 31 miles of scenic boulevard, 24 playground sites. Combined recreation facilities, 1820 acres. Golf is played every day in Seattle, over five wonderful courses.

Graded streets, 749 miles; paved streets, 294 miles. Sidewalks, 1140 miles; sewers, 505 miles.

CITY WATER PLANT: Reservoirs, capacity 271,137,000 gallons. Average daily consumption, 32,593,932 gallons. Supply mains, 63 miles. Distributing mains, 655 miles. Analysis demonstrated water is pure as ever obtained in natural state.

ELECTRIC LIGHT: Seattle has 15,633 street lights, and 32 miles of cluster lights. Electric power rates on a parity with Niagara Falls. Total miles of illuminated streets—1126.

AREA OF SEATTLE: (Sq. Mi.) Water—35.91; land—53.66.

Figure 14.1 Examples of brochures used in the 1920s and 1930s
Courtesy: Wikimedia Commons

Figure 14.1 Continued
Courtesy: Wikimedia Commons

designed with a greater number of (multi-colour) pages. Along with comprehensive brochures, tour operators prepare separate/exclusive brochures, also called "dedicated brochures" for each package tour. Comparatively, these have fewer pages, but are more attractive, with multi-colour prints on high-quality paper for persuading potential buyers. Such brochures may attempt product differentiation as well. Since this is prepared focusing on the target market, the details included are based on the needs and interests of that group of customers.

Note the following roles of printed materials, including tour brochures (Middleton and Clarke, 2009):

- Creating awareness
- Promotional (messages/symbols)
- Promotional (display/merchandizing)
- Promotional (incentives/special offers)
- Product substitute role
- Access/purchasing mechanism
- "Proof" of purchase/reassurance
- Facilitation of product use and information
- Providing education

14.2.1 Importance of tour brochures

As stated before, a tour brochure is not just a booklet containing information about the Product. It has diverse roles to play and different functions to perform. Page (2007) summarizes its importance as follows: it is prepared to obtain sales; to provide information to assist in decision-making; to provide cost-effective distribution through intermediaries like travel agents; and to offer an effective means to enable agents to sell tour packages with product details and booking codes. It also acts as a kind of contract between the tour operator and its customers. While it plays a role in stimulation of travel need, it also assists in reducing the intangibility effect of a tour operator's product. It educates the potential traveller about the tour and its features, and can be used as a tool for negotiation as well as for distributing and selling. A few other factors can also be identified, but the major factors of a tour brochure are as follows:

- It introduces the tour operator and its products.
- It's an important document that communicates the image and professionalism of the company.
- It's the main tangible means for convincing a customer about the product.
- It provides the necessary information for a potential tourist, which can eventually help in tour decision-making.
- It specifies the details of booking, like terms and conditions, and cancellations.
- It's a form of marketing communication.
- It's a tool for creating interest and in persuading a customer to buy their product.
- It can be used to differentiate the product from that of competitors.
- It's used as a means for distribution of the product through the intermediaries.
- For an intermediary, particularly for a retailer, it is the prime selling tool.
- It's a means for negotiation with suppliers.
- It helps to maintain uniformity of details while undertaking sales presentations.
- It acts as a simple document of agreement between the tourist and the tour operator.

14.2.2 Contents of a tour brochure

A tour brochure should contain the minimum details to be conveyed to the tourist to stimulate the need, to generate interest and to persuade them to buy. Contents may vary according to the type of the brochure. A comprehensive brochure usually includes an introduction of products on offer, but it may not contain booking terms and conditions, and other similar details. A dedicated brochure is supposed to include all the necessary information. For any brochure, a cover page is crucial. It should contain the name of the package, the name of the company and its logo, signature items and tour date, along with attractive photos. Common contents of a tour brochure include the following:

- A brief about the company
- Trademark, logo, legal identity, affiliations
- Duration of tour, date, place and time of departure
- Tour highlights and features
- Destination general information
- Glimpses of attractions and a few illustrations of attractions. (Photos have more "immediate impact". The pictures should appeal to the target customers, their needs and interests, etc.)
- Travel arrangements – international, intra-destination and inter-destination travel arrangements
- Accommodation details (type of hotel, rooming, etc.)
- Meals included and not included
- Excursion, picnics, sightseeing, optional tours
- Price and items included in the price, and those not included. (While including price, if any extra amounts are required, it should be mentioned. Also, if there is price variation according to currency fluctuations, it must also be clearly mentioned.)
- Simple itinerary
- A simple tour map
- Specification on overseas representatives
- Details of special arrangements
- Health aspects, vaccination required, etc.
- Terms and conditions – brochures have some legal aspects as well, as they are a kind of agreement between the customer and the company (All care must be taken, especially in respect of the wording. Terms and conditions should also be specified clearly.)
- Amount of deposit and payment dates.
- Details about how to make bookings
- Cancellation and refund terms and conditions. (The terms and conditions, as well as other legal aspects, should be mentioned, e.g. clause on cancellations, price changes)
- Special offers
- Tour essentials, clothing, baggage, *dos* and *don'ts*
- Limits of the agency's responsibilities
- Information of complementarities
- Reservation forms – usually a reservation form for registering the tour will also be included, separately or as part of the brochure. (The essential information required for booking a tour must be there in this form.)

Note the following points to consider in brochure preparation (USAID, 2007):

- The front cover should be interesting and eye-catching.
- The front cover should be able to convey the crucial messages.
- The front cover should show the company name and logo.
- The choice of picture on the front cover can make it clear the type of products on offer.
- The main part of the brochure should be clearly structured so that clients can easily identify the details they require.
- A contents page may be appropriate for brochures with a lot of pages.
- General information may be given at the rear of the brochure.
- The text in the brochure should be carefully constructed.
- Photographs should portray the destination and products in a positive light.

14.2.3 Qualities of a good brochure

Being a vital tool in marketing and selling a tour programme, the brochure should have certain qualities. An effective brochure is the one that can bring in a good response, create an appeal for the customer, attract the customer to the product, convince them of the qualities and features of the product, and create a positive image and cost-effective tool in promotional efforts. Major qualities of a tour brochure follow below:

- *Right contents:* selecting the content of a tour brochure is a serious activity. A brochure filled with too much, or with irrelevant content, can make it ineffective and boring. Necessary, valuable and interesting content should be included. By reading the brochure, the potential customer should be convinced to take the decision to buy the product. Moreover, selection of content needs to be based on the objective of the brochure and the needs and interests of the target group.
- *Attractiveness:* the brochure has the necessary attractiveness so that it can be picked from a travel agent's rack and read. Attractiveness is a combination of different factors like quality of design, photographs, layout, content, paper, colour, etc.
- *Clarity and legibility:* ensure the matter is clear, specific and crisp. Use bullet points instead of long paragraphs. This will keep customers' focus on what you are trying to communicate. Avoid jargon and complicated sentences. Easy-flowing language is better. Also, the text/font size needs be legible enough and the backgrounds should not be too dark, as this makes the text difficult to read.
- *Layout and design:* the design of the brochure needs to be appealing so as to compel customers to stop and look at what you have to offer. The design includes a wide range of factors, such as the texture of the paper, colour, font styles, illustrations and layout. Creativity is of utmost significance. When designing the brochure, the theme of the tour, nature of the audience, image of the tour operator, etc. need to be considered.
- *Photographs:* photographs are certainly part of tour brochures. These can convey a lot of information and focus attention and appeal on the attractions included in the tour. Pictures are economical, as they can convey something at a glance that would take a great many words to accomplish on their own. The right images complement the matter in the brochure, and are able to attract customers.
- *Uniqueness:* the more unique a tour brochure, the greater the attractiveness of it. Valuable messages may not be conveyed in the intended way if the brochure is not

presented in a unique way. Uniqueness of a brochure cannot be defined easily, yet the creativity, right content, design, layout, colour, photographs, etc. contribute to the uniqueness of a tour brochure. Uniqueness of the brochure can ensure its distinctiveness among competitors.

- *Credible:* the contents included in the brochure have to be reliable and should not exaggerate. Misleading facts should be avoided. Inaccurate or biased information can lead to consequences, including litigation.
- *Persuasive:* a tour brochure is a selling tool and it should have the ability to persuade a potential buyer to take a decision in the business's favour. All the above points are complementary in making a brochure persuasive.

14.2.4 Brochure design process

Being a crucial promotional material, a brochure needs to be designed with diligence and prudence. Furthermore, it's a creative piece of work and high-quality professionalism is warranted. Usually, a professional individual or group can be engaged to design and print it. Engaging an advertising agency for this is very common practice. Some of the large operators may design and prepare brochures in their own creative departments. Also, digital brochures of different formats are essential. Tour brochures are prepared well in advance, before the commencement of marketing and promotional efforts. All the administrative activities are started only after the brochure has been launched and distributed. Meticulous planning is a prerequisite for making a tour brochure. Different activities are involved and they follow a sequence, as described here:

- *Understanding the target market and the product:* prior to starting the design work, it is necessary to understand the target market. Their motivation, the benefits sought from the product and what the needs are that can be satisfied by the product being offered should be understood clearly. Likewise, it is crucial to learn about the product. The knowledge thus acquired forms the base for the brochure since it is going to address the target market with the details of the product. By this time, it is also important to finalize objectives, target group and the scope of the brochure specifically.
- *Idea generation:* based on the knowledge of the customers and the product on offer, create a general idea about the brochure. Further activities will be based on this creative idea being formed. This can also be shared with the respective personnel of the tour operator so that they have a notion of the brochure's creative concept. Some agencies prepare a "creative brief" for further proceedings.
- *Plan layout:* on the basis of the creative concept or idea, an initial layout is planned and prepared. While preparing this initial layout, it is important to keep in mind that the brochure needs to grab the attention and interest of potential customers, and ultimately persuade them. The layout has to be creative and unique and represent the professionalism of the company.
- *Gather the data and photographs:* all the necessary matter to be included in the brochure has to be obtained from the company. Available photos must also be collected. If needed, more photos may need to be arranged from external sources. Consent to reproduce the photographs and copy must be obtained. Booking details, terms and conditions, and other necessary information are also gathered as per the need.
- *Finalize the front over:* the front cover is the most important part of the brochure. It should reflect the quintessence of the tour. It should be able to grab the attention and interest of potential clients so that they pick it up from the racks and read further.

The cover page can include only very limited information, yet it should provide the essential information in a captivating way. It should be very attractive as it is the first thing a potential tourist sees. Its layout must therefore be eye-catching, with crucial messages and attractive photographs.

- *Finalize brochure details:* before proceeding further, it is important to finalize the technical details of the brochure including the size, length (number of pages), typeface (font), paper quality and colour types. Usually glossy paper is used. The thickness/weight of the paper for both the cover page and inside pages need to be finalized.
- *Prepare the initial draft version with layout for approval:* the layout design with necessary photographs and text needs to be prepared into an initial draft version. Finalize the matter, headings and subheadings. Use these "inside headlines" to hold their attention and move them through the copy. The matter has to be well written, i.e. readable, interesting and crisp. The most attractive and representative photographs need to be included. The initial draft version needs approval from the agency side as well as from the respective department of the tour operator, with any suggestions for modifications made at this stage.
- *Corrections and modifications and approval:* once the initial consent is obtained for the draft, necessary corrections have to be carried out. Also, modifications can be done with the layout. Further proofreading is then undertaken. Once this has been completed, a copy of the brochure should be taken for approval of both matter and layout.
- *Prepare final layout and design and get approval:* after making all corrections and design modifications, the finalized copy of the whole brochure can be sent to the tour operator and all its relevant departments for final consent. The price panels are integrated and the final proof and design are agreed by this stage.
- *Prepare digital version and print necessary copies:* once the designed brochure has been finalized after further checking and proofreading, the same will go for printing. A digital version will be supplied to the tour operator in the required formats, e.g. PDF.

14.2.5 Brochure launch

A tour operator may organize a brochure launch as the first step towards the marketing of tour operation. Some firms will release the brochures early, whereas others will wait to see the nature and content of their competitors' brochures. At times, an introductory brochure will be released first and the detailed one will follow it. Brochure launches are sometimes organized on a larger scale to garner publicity. Distribution of brochures will follow the launch. Printed brochures will be immediately distributed to travel agents or other retailers. If possible, posters and other display materials can be supplied to intermediaries. It is crucial to effectively and efficiently use the brochures to sell the products, especially due to the cost involved in producing and distributing them. Simultaneously, digital brochures are distributed to all potential customers and clients on their database.

14.3 Market segmentation and target market

Market segmentation is basically the division of markets into various homogenous groups of customers so as to target them for designing and marketing the product. Each segment identified may react differently to promotion, communication, pricing and other variables of the marketing mix. Theoretically, the buyers included in an identified market should have similar needs and interests. The segment identified should be measurable, accessible, relevant to the product, congruous and distinguishable from other segments. Such an effort can help the tour operator make the product-related decisions easily; develop the most appropriate marketing mix strategies and actions; understand the customer needs and interests easily; develop the product to satisfy specific needs; make suitable pricing strategies; undertake targeted marketing, positioning and differentiation; identify where and how to sell the product; enhance the effectiveness of facing competition; and ensure good customer relations. While choosing a market segment, the factors a tour operator should consider, according to USAID (2007), include:

- Growth rate of the market segment
- Size of the market segment
- Existing competitors in the market and their market share
- Profitability of competitors in the same market segment
- Costs involved in market entry
- Ease of communicating with the sector
- Necessary resource availability for the segment
- External influences

Different approaches are used by tour operators to segment the market. Geographic segmentation is very common in tourism. Outbound package tours definitely have a geographic perspective since tour operators do focus on tourists from the same geographic area when developing overseas packages. Geographic segmentations help in effective implementation of marketing strategies. Geographic bases can include countries, states, regions, districts, cities, localities, urban/rural spaces, and sales or distribution territories. Demographic segmentation is also widely used by tour operators (Horner and Swarbrooke, 2005). Many of the products are made considering the age group of the customers. For instance, adventurous package tours are designed for young tourists and cruise tourism primarily targets older customers. The bases of demographic segmentation include age and life cycle stage, gender and sexual orientation, marital or co-habitational status, family size, occupation, etc. Examples for demographic segmentation-based marketing include family holidays, singles holidays and youth holidays. "Empty nest" is a common market segment term used in tourism which represents the older, often retired population whose children have grown up and left home (leaving them with less financial burden). They are a major market segment in tourism and prefer long-term holidays including cruise tours. Yale (2001) identified three distinguished market segments, based on the demographic variables, in the tour operation sector:

- *Youth market:* this consists of tourists aged between 16 and 30 who are unmarried. They have the lowest level of family commitments and the highest level of discretionary income. Among them, the student group enjoys more leisure time, but their spending power is less. The other group in the youth market are those in their late 20s who are employed and have higher income levels. They go on long-haul tours and travel more often.
- *Family market:* the family market includes those who are in the age group between 25 and 50. Summer sun and winter sun are preferred by this category. Though they have higher income levels, their discretionary income varies. They are highly price-conscious and often travel seasonally.

- *The "third age" market:* this includes tourists older than 50 years of age. Their discretionary income is higher. There are two divisions: those who are relatively young and healthy, and those who are much older. Winter holidays to warmer regions, lakes and mountain holidays, cruise tours, etc. are more popular in this group.

Psychographic segmentation is based on dividing markets in terms of lifestyle, personality, values, beliefs, attitudes, etc. It is noted that many people buy holidays matching their everyday lifestyles. Socio-economic segmentation is also done in the tour operation sector. In this segment buyers are divided into groups based on their social class and income. The income level of buyers and the price of the packages often correlate. A tour operator's product is a discretionary product and hence the income level and disposable income of customers are very relevant to their buying decision-making. This is one major reason for fare war in the tour operation sector, especially where large numbers of tour operators are operating. Also, online agents pose serious competition by using lower prices than "bricks and mortar" tour operators. At times behavioural segmentation is also carried out in the tour operation sector. Travel purpose-based segmentation is very common as well. It can include holidays for pilgrimage, health, education, business and learning new experiences.

The market segments identified finally turn into target markets in which the marketing efforts can be concentrated. For a package tour, especially for a group inclusive tour (GIT), the potential travellers involved in the target market may have similar needs and interests and the product being offered to them has to match those needs and desires. A tour operator cannot make a product that can be sold to every potential customer in a market. Not all packages are meat for all types of tourists. Moreover, marketing communication, rather, the promotion of the product, is a costly affair; no one can afford to target all markets through their marketing and promotion activities. The target market, the market a company wants to sell its products and services to, provides the ultimate focus of all marketing activities, and by determining the target market, the marketing mix efforts can be much more cost-effective than marketing to an entire population, i.e. without a focus. For a niche tour operator, it is easier to identify the target market due to the product characteristics. Mass operators may have to undertake reviews, evaluation, analysis and surveys to identify and finalize their target market.

14.4 Tourist buying behaviour and the role of tour operators

Learning the buying behaviour of tourists is of utmost importance, particularly because of the characteristics of tourism products. The same is true for tour operators' products. Tourist purchase decision-making is a process with a series of sequential stages. The most significant activities related to marketing are how a consumer makes a judgement call while choosing a product and the influences. Schiffman and Kanuk (2009) consider buying behaviour as "the process of making purchase decisions based on cognitive and emotional influences such as impulse, family, friends, advertisers, role models, moods, and situations that influence purchase". Engel et al. (1995) argue that it is a process by which a consumer chooses to purchase or use a product or service. Other perspectives can also be seen in the literature of tourist buying behaviour. Details and number of stages differ between authors. Lovelock and Wirtz (2007) have divided the buying behaviour process into three stages: pre-purchase stage, service-encounter stage and post-encounter stage.

The first stage is all about decision-making, which involves awareness of need, information search, evaluation of alternatives and making choices. It is followed by "moments of truth" and most importantly the service delivery. The post-encounter stage includes the evaluation of service performed during service delivery and further intention formation. Another viewpoint is that buying behaviour is a process of sequential stages such as need recognition, search for information on various products according to these needs, formation of alternative choices, evaluation of alternatives, the act of purchase and consumption, and post-purchase behaviour (Foxall and Goldsmith, 1994; Kotler et al., 2009; Horner and Swarbrooke, 2007). Ideally, the stages involved in tourist buying behaviour with regard to the purchase of a tour operator's package can be summed up as follows:

- Need recognition
- Information search
- Formation of alternatives
- Evaluation of alternative choices
- Buying decision
- The act of purchase
- Product consumption
- Evaluation of tour experience
- Recollection and sharing of experiences, memories, etc.

Before making a decision to go for a tour, a potential tourist has to feel or recognize a need for the same. Tourism is always based on a need which leads to a tourist motivation to visit places and experience various aspects of it. Tourist motivations can be of different types, as discussed elsewhere in this book. Usually, through various marketing strategies, an attempt can be made to initiate or realize a need for taking part in a tourism activity available in the industry. The move of buying a tourism product theoretically commences with the recognition of a need existing or initiated.

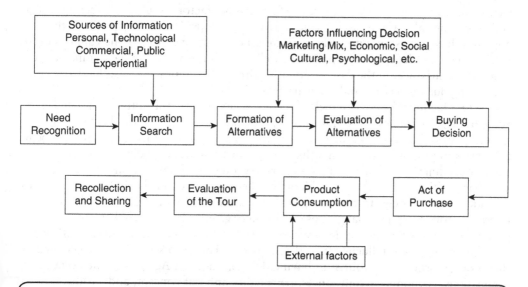

Figure 14.2 Tourist buying behaviour

Once the need is identified, the search begins to find a solution that can satisfy the need. The sources of information also vary. Currently, the Internet is one of the most popular sources of information. Intermediaries are traditionally reliable sources of information for potential tourists. Books, television, guidebooks, friends, colleagues and relatives are other dependable sources of information. Marketing communication measures have also become important sources of information for tourists. The potential tourist, particularly a less experienced one, will search for information intensively. As part of the search for information, based on the need and motivation, the potential tourist may identify a variety of options for selection. These are the various alternatives formed of which the most suitable one may be chosen. Based on the need, motivation, internal and external determinants, availability of time and money, etc., the potential tourist will try to evaluate each of the alternatives formed. While evaluating the alternatives, the objective characteristics (e.g. the features and functionality of the product) as well as the subjective characteristics (e.g. perception and perceived value of the brand by the consumer or its reputation) are taken into consideration.

Usually, the number of alternatives will be more when the potential consumer is more involved in the decision-making, which is more relevant to tourism products. The most appropriate option will be chosen, leading to purchase of the holiday or some elements of it, based on the need. Once the planned travel process begins, the consumption of the product will take place. The experience of tourism thus commences and once the tour is over, the tourist returns to their place of origin. The post-purchase process begins with the memories and the good feelings generated from the tour. Of course, there can also be complaints. It depends on the level of satisfaction. It may be that the experience was below expectations. If there is a high satisfaction level, the tourist will have a positive opinion that may lead to fewer stages in their buying behaviour for future purchases. On the other hand, if the satisfaction level is low, the negative opinion of the product may be passed on to others and the next purchase process may be more stringent in order to ensure the most appropriate holiday option is chosen.

Every purchase decision can be affected by a number of factors that are intrinsic as well as extrinsic. Theoretically, there are four distinct factors – cultural, social, personal and psychological – which can influence buying behaviour. The service quality in the tour operation business is an extremely intricate affair. Tour operators alone cannot ensure service quality. It depends on suppliers as well. Tourism services also have some tangible aspects. For instance, in the case of hotels, bedrooms, facilities, etc. also have relevance in ensuring quality service, and these are tangible.

The first factor, cultural, can include a consumer's culture, subculture and social class. Some of these factors can also influence a potential tourist. The cultural environment of a tourist can be influential in their decision while choosing a destination. While a subculture refers to groups with similar values or similar lifestyles, including religions, nationalities and ethnic groups, a social class refers to groups with similar characteristics and in a similar position within the social hierarchy. These two factors also influence a tourist's decision-making. Social factors are primarily external factors, which include groups – reference groups, aspirational groups and member groups. Family members, friends, peer groups, etc. have significant influence on tourist buying behaviour. An individual's social roles and status often influence their decisions too. The third set of factors, personal, is the most important for a tourist in buying decision-making. Age group, life cycle stage, occupations, economic circumstances, personality and self-concept, and various aspects associated with lifestyle, can be some determinants in tourist buying behaviour. The economic status of a person is one of the most significant determinants in tourist buying behaviour. Above all, the psychological factors may also influence the decision-maker. A potential tourist's perception, motivation, attitudes, beliefs and learning are some of the common determinants of tourist buying behaviour. For a package tour purchase, there can be some specific determinants, in addition to many of the common factors.

Tourism buying decision-making is a high involvement and complex process (Horner and Swarbrooke, 2007; Laws, 1997) due to the inherent characteristics of tourism and its products. Tourists may face a great deal of buying dissonance (anxiety) if they are uncertain about their purchases and when they had a difficult time deciding between alternatives. The following reasons make the decision-making and buying of tour operators' products a high involvement process:

- *Expensive:* many of the components of tour products, mainly air travel and accommodation, are relatively expensive. Making a decision for buying an expensive item is definitely a serious activity.
- *Time-consuming:* consumption of tourism products needs specific time durations. Spending that much time should be worthwhile.
- *Less frequent purchase:* buying holidays is not a frequent purchase item and taking a decision for a rare purchase item has its own complexities.
- *Intangibility:* the product cannot be tested prior to consumption and uncertainty prevails until consumption.
- *Lead time:* long lead times can cause unexpected things to occur in the meantime.
- *Commitment:* there is a higher level of consumer commitment in decision-making and the following stages make it more difficult to take a decision.
- *Risky:* travel and stay and the overall tourism also involve risk factors, such as financial, health, social (e.g. image of the destination and tourist's personality perception), economical and emotional risks.
- *Uncertainty about customer satisfaction:* tourist satisfaction is a combination of a wide range of factors and the "moments of truths" are difficult to predict.
- *Involvement of others in decision-making:* the act of decision-making and purchase of a tour product may involve others as well. For instance, leisure tourism decision-making may be influenced by family members or friends. Business tourism buying is usually influenced by a number of people, and consumers and customers are often different people in business tourism.

A tour operator has an important role to play in this high involvement process of tourist buying behaviour. There are many determinants of the buying behaviour of tourists, which include social, cultural, economic and environmental factors. Moreover, the health status, political factors, psychographic factors and demographic factors can also influence the buying behaviour of a tourist. The uncertainty prevailing in the decision-making can be minimized by providing the necessary information and advice. The intangibility effect can be minimized by showing detailed brochures and past tour participants' shared experiences. Also, highlighting the quality of services and the brand image of suppliers included in the tour can reduce the anxiety of the buyer greatly with regard to the performance of the product. Tour operators can offer products more cost-effectively and can include the most suitable options in them. During the tour, a maximum number of attractions can be visited due to the professional design of tour itineraries. Tours are led by professionals or resort representatives, who are available for support at any point during the tour process. This can eliminate confusions and risks associated with the buying of a tour operator's product. Certainly, along with persuading, a tour operator has to interpret the tour details and instill confidence in the minds of the potential tourists to take the most appropriate decision for buying a holiday.

14.5 Image, branding and positioning

Image is significant in tourism, as potential travellers regard it as very important in the destination selection process. Many of the tourism products compete on the basis of image. According to Pike (2004), destination image is part of a repertoire of brand associations held in the mind of the traveller. Destination image is highly developed in destination selection and positive images about the destination are crucial in tourist buying behaviour. Destinations undertake deliberate efforts in developing a positive image among populations in different tourism markets. In addition to the destination image, the image of the tour operator is also vital in the selection of a holiday package or the use of services. Tour operators attempt to use image in their favour. Gunn (1988) suggested two levels of image: organic and induced. The former is developed through an individual's daily assimilation of information, which may include a wide range of mediums, from school geography readings to mass media to actual visitation. The induced image level is developed through the influence of promotions undertaken by marketers. Usually, the induced image is formed when the individual starts an information search during the early stages of buying decision-making. A tour operator can have a role in this: deliberate efforts can be made to create an induced image among the potential buyers.

Usually in the tour operation industry, branding focuses on the firm, instead of their different packages. Branding helps customers to decide which products to buy. Brand attempts to convey attributes, benefits, quality of service, values, personality, culture and the standard of users. Almost all the sectors in tourism attempt to develop own brands. Airlines and hospitality sectors have world-renowned brands. Tour operators also attempt to incorporate suppliers with good brand names into their packages. This can add value to the package offered. In the tour operation sector, there are some international brands which have already created a brand image among consumers internationally. Such brands stand out from others and give a clear idea about the nature and quality of the product being offered by them. Also, brands allow easy identification by customers. When a tour operator is renowned as a brand, it is easy for customers to select their services. A travel agency may have rack space for a number of brochures of different products. The name, trademark, logo or design would help potential customers to pick particular brochures. Images placed in the brochure can also be useful in identification of the brochures. In addition, taglines and slogans are used, some of which are memorable and some of which are stunningly attractive.

Positioning tour products is not an easy task. Brand positioning illustrates how a brand can effectively compete against a particular set of competitors in a specific market (Keller, 2003). Indeed, every firm makes an attempt to create a distinctive place in the target market's mind. The target market and every customer in it form and keep an image about the tour operator and its products. Successful companies are able to create an image that is very different from that of competitors and very favourable for them. Positioning of the products requires the consideration of a number of factors. The differences, compared to the products of competitors, that are to be promoted constitute a major decision in respect of positioning. The position of a product is a combination of various attributes customers are looking for from an offering. It can include the quality, benefits, value, strengths, features and the like. Different positioning strategies can be used, such as attribute positioning, benefit positioning, quality positioning, price positioning and product type positioning.

"Niche" operators' positioning strategy will be decidedly different from that of mass-market operators. The focus of niche operators is on special interest products and the images being created are more experiential in nature, ensuring experiences with authentic products. Mass-market operators may try to position with different strategies, including price, benefits and the like. When positioning once the target market has been identified, operators have to be sure of what the target consumers expect and believe to be the most important considerations in the buying decision-making. As soon as the most appropriate product, here the package, is formed, tour operators evaluate the positioning and images, as perceived by the target customers, of competing products in the selected market segments. This will give a clear picture of competitors' ways of positioning their products and what differences can be made to position their own products. Selecting the most appropriate image that can clearly distinguish their product from that of the competitors is a crucial task. It is of utmost importance to ensure that the chosen image matches the expectations of the target customers. Once these aspects are set, intensive marketing communication can be undertaken to position the product.

14.6 Marketing mix

One of the most popular definitions of the marketing mix is that of Kotler, who writes that it is "the mixture of controllable marketing variables that the firm uses to pursue the sought level of sales in the target market" (Kotler, 1984). The "controllable variables" mentioned in the definition are product, price, promotion and place, which are collectively known as the four Ps. Each P represents a mix of crucial strategies that can be planned and adopted to generate the highest level of consumer satisfaction along with meeting the organizational objectives. Recently more Ps have been added to it: people, physical evidence and process. The right combination of marketing mix strategies is fundamental in the competitive survival of a tour operator. Product, the first element, is all about creating a product that matches with the consumer needs, wants and benefits sought. There are different elements in the product and in tourism. Middleton and Clarke (2009) include the following components of the tourism product:

- Fundamental design of all the components that are put together as an offer to tourists
- Style and ambience of the offer (it's mainly a function of design decisions creating the physical environment, and ambience/'physical evidence' suitable for the product's image and price)
- The service element (e.g. training, attitudes and appearance of staff engaged in service delivery)
- Branding activities associated with a particular product which help to identify particular a set of values, a unique name, image and expectation of the experience to be delivered

Elsewhere in this book, we have already discussed designing a tour operator's product and the care required. Here, though the package is the product designed by the tour operator, the service elements included in it are offered by different suppliers and therefore the tour operator has to be efficient enough to include the most suitable elements so as to create a high level of customer satisfaction. Selecting the right elements in the package is crucial for the success of a tour operator.

Price, the amount charged for the product offering, is a key determinant in the sale of a package tour. The process of pricing and common strategies used for pricing by tour operators are described elsewhere in this book. A tour operator's product is a discretionary product and that intensifies the need for the most appropriate pricing decisions. It's very important to decide whether to adopt a cost-oriented pricing strategy or a demand-oriented pricing strategy. Moreover, competitors' price is another challenge for the tour operator. While considering the competitors' price, the cost factors cannot be neglected in order to reduce the price to compete in the fare war. All cost elements should be included while costing. Missing even a single cost element can result in loss. In addition, including lower quality services in the package with the objective of reducing cost can backfire in the long run. The long lead time is another challenge, as changes in the economic environments in the interim can cause issues in profitability.

14.6.1 Promotion

Promotion is the most visible form of all marketing activities. The sale of a product depends very much on the effectiveness of promotion activities. It's all about the marketing communication activities undertaken to create awareness of the products, to generate interest towards the product, and persuade potential buyers to purchase the product. Primarily promotion is carried out to "convince potential customers of the benefits of purchasing or using the products and services of a particular organization" (Horner and Swarbrooke, 2005). It is basically the marketing communication undertaken by firms to influence the consumer attitude and behaviour that create interest, desire and attention to purchase the product at a particular price. Through promotion, a tour operator communicates in an effective way with its target customers. Tour operators use a variety of marketing communication activities to achieve its marketing objectives. Essentially, the right mix of those communication activities is vital in the success of the firm. Major promotion tools used by tour operators are introduced below.

Fam tour

A familiarization tour ("fam tour", also called "fam trip") is a direct or indirect marketing communication tool. Though the tours are organized with different purposes, they are undertaken primarily to familiarize participants with the features of the concerned products/attractions, with an ultimate objective to promote it. At times, fam tours are held as part of incentive programmes of suppliers as well as tourism intermediaries. They are also organized for other groups of tourism stakeholders, such as journalists, travel writers, media representatives, bloggers, etc. They may be able to write travel stories, experiences or travelogues based on the knowledge and experience gained through such tours. Furthermore, they will help to get supportive media coverage. This can eventually help in building destination image and in promoting the tourism products. The other target groups of fam tours include travel consultants, tour operators and travel agents, and working professionals of tourism industries. Tourism suppliers frequently organize such trips to a variety of stakeholders. The following are the major tourism suppliers who usually organize fam tours:

- Destination management organizations (DMOs) and national tourist offices (NTOs)
- Tour operators and travel agencies
- Airlines, cruises and other tourism transport carriers
- Accommodation establishments

- Attraction agencies, tourism bureaus
- Convention promotion bureaus

A tour operator organizes fam tours to some of the stakeholders mentioned above with the objective of product familiarization and promotion. Most frequently, tour operators provide fam trips to retain travel agents because they are the people who have direct contact with consumers during the process of selling. Those who gained expertise with the tour elements through fam tours may be able to convince and persuade the potential buyers in a better manner. Also, tour operators organize fam tours as incentive programmes for the employees and professionals of the intermediaries to motivate them further to achieve better targets in marketing and selling their products. Other stakeholders, like media representatives, are also given fam tours by tour operators.

Advertising

Advertising is the most commonly used form of promotion by tour operators. Though it's a costly affair, advertising is considered indispensable by the industry. Simply, it is a sponsored form of non-personal communication of the offerings. It is defined as "a paid, mediated form of communication from an identifiable source, designed to persuade the receiver to take some action, now or in the future" (Richards and Curran, 2002). An advertisement is created with the purpose of promotion and placed in the media to be conveyed to the targeted group of people. The space in the media is purchased for this purpose. This is one-way communication; the parties, those who advertise and the target audience, do not get together and do not interact in this form of communication. According to Horner and Swarbrooke (2005), there are advantages and disadvantages of advertising:

- Advantages:
  o Very flexible form of communication
  o Can target the mass market as well as precise market niches, as per the need
  o Can be cost-efficient since it can reach a large number of people at a low cost per person
  o It is possible to repeat the message as and when it's needed through different media
- Disadvantages:
  o Expensive
  o Relatively difficult to monitor its effectiveness mainly due to its long-term objectives

Traditionally, mass-media forms have been used for advertising. Print media as well as broadcast media were used primarily. Since the advent of the Internet as a global medium, online advertisements have become essential for the competitive survival of organizations. Moreover, there has been a shift from the mass media to the new media of mass communication. This has helped in reducing the cost advertisements. Obtaining space in mass media like television and newspapers is expensive. Online advertisements offer significant cost advantages. Yet traditional forms of advertisements are still used by all forms of tourism agencies. The following media are used for advertisements by tour operators nowadays:

- Television
- Radio
- Newspapers

- Periodicals
- Social media
- Mobile apps
- Online agent sites
- Others' websites
- Yearbooks and other publications
- Billboards, signboards, walls, etc.

Usually advertising agencies are engaged by tour operators to carry out creative planning and execution, media planning, media space contracting, advertisement production and releasing, and implementation of agreed campaign elements and materials. Large operators may also have creative departments to undertake many of the above activities. Small- and medium-sized tour operators have limitations in undertaking advertisements often and in different media due to the cost factor. Advertisements usually require good budget allocation. Decisions regarding the use of advertisements and adequate allocation are made well in advance. Moreover, media selection is done with the utmost care so as to reach the right customers. The wrong media selected for advertising with an improper message can be a total waste of money and effort. It is also important to measure the effectiveness of advertisements to make suitable decisions with regard to promotion and advisements in the future.

Public relations (PR) and publicity

Public relations is another promotion strategy used by tour operators to get a favourable public opinion. According to Deuschl (2006), PR is the "management staff function that uses truthful two-way communications and operates in the public interest to influence public opinion in order to earn good will and understanding for the organization". In the past, good PR was considered more publicity. Since then there has been a shift from that focus. In this modern era of marketing, publicity is more about attracting the attention of the public and the tools used, including generating news stories, articles and event information. Moreover, publicity is part of public relations. As per the Public Relations Society of America, "public relations is a strategic communication process that builds mutually beneficial relationships between organizations and their publics" (PRSA, n.d.). Here, focus is given to building symbiotic relationships between the firm and its stakeholders. A tour operator would certainly like to have mutually beneficial relationships with its stakeholders. A tour operator functions within a system consisting of a variety of stakeholders. It should have good opinion among the publics. There has to be a good rapport with suppliers. Deliberate efforts are taken nowadays to generate public relations with the publics. Different tools can be used for PR. Some of the most common are listed in Table 14.1.

Direct marketing

Tour operators interact with target customers directly through cost-effective measures. Direct marketing has its own significance in the tour operation sector. According to Middleton and Clarke (2009),

> direct marketing links producers with their customers in a two-way communication, using individually addressable media (such as mail, telephone and e-commerce). Interaction is organized through a database recording unique details of actual and

Table 14.1 Standard PR tools and the most common travel/tourism PR tools

List of PR tools

Press releases	Editorial board meetings
Websites	B-roll
Publications	Frequently asked questions (FAQs)
Feature articles	CD-ROMs
Special events	Fact sheets
Open houses	Exhibits
Press conferences	Audiovisuals
Video news releases	Radio actualities
Op-eds	Photography
Letters to editors	Speakers' bureaus
Tours	Speeches
Public service announcements	Statement stuffers

Source: Deuschl (2006)

prospective customers, including their geo-demographic profile, product purchasing behaviour and their responses to different communications media.

It can have a variety of tools such as mailing brochures, advertisements, publicity, etc. Brochure emailing is a very common practice among tour operators. Other published materials in digital form are also sent by email. Mail is sent to potential customers, previous customers, heads of social organizations and other relevant groups. Complimentary trips will be offered to the heads of the organizations for arranging a minimum number of participants for an affinity group tour. Postal mailing, telemarketing and point of sale interactions are also carried out by tour operators.

Promotional evenings/events

Organizing promotional evenings/events is common among tour operators, with the intention to create interest among a select audience. This is possible only for the local market and outbound tour operators can do this effectively. It aims at converting attendance into sales. Road shows are another practice seen in the tourism industry. Proper planning is critical in the success of a promotional evening. It should be lively, interesting, and short and sweet, and should involve presentation, distribution of adequate materials, refreshments and, if possible, some entertainment. Videos/photographs of the tours may add to its liveliness. Sometimes, gifts, souvenirs, etc. will be given.

Sales presentations

Sales presentations are also common among tour operators. A sales presentation is a deliberate and organized presentation before an invited audience. It is the intention to expose them to a product offering, and ultimately to persuade them to purchase that offering. Tour operators carry out such presentations in social organizations, professional bodies, industry associations, clubs, etc. where they can target an affinity group. It can also be done with dinner party/refreshments. Making presentations lively and interesting can be more useful.

Word of mouth

It's common for a satisfied customer to tell others about their experience with the consumption of the product. Customer satisfaction is key in the success of tourism industries. Personal recommendations by friends and relatives are still a crucial determinant in the decision-making of a tourist for buying tourism products. Only satisfied customers can provide positive opinions and suggestions. In the tourism sector, word-of-mouth publicity is crucial. The opinions, suggestions and ideas of tourists' friends and relatives are highly valued. It is important to ensure good word of mouth and important to take advantage of this, so tour operators ensure they follow up and maintain interaction.

Other methods

Trade fair and exhibition participation is common. Tour operators participate and exhibit products in dedicated stalls in trade fairs, particularly travel trade fairs. A stall in a trade fair has to be in a good location, with necessary promotional materials, and well arranged. Moreover, it should be manned by experienced and knowledgeable personnel from the company with good communication skills and personality traits. Exhibits and displays have to be eye-catching and provide necessary space for interaction with potential clients. Endorsement by famous people or specific customers in their promotional materials is also used. Different types of promotional materials are provided by tour operators to be displayed at the point of sale locations. Use of mobile platforms for interaction and persuading customers is common nowadays. Social media-based promotional efforts are also undertaken by tour operators. Even a boosting of a post by a social media agent can help to gain attention and customers.

14.7 Distribution system

Traditionally, package tours have been sold through travel agents, who remain a key intermediary in the distribution chain. Along with the distribution of tour products, a tour operator's distribution system involves the flow of payments, information and promotion materials to ensure the availability and accessibility of products to the consumers at the proper time. The "forward flow" involves the promotion materials, booking materials, payment details, etc. from the tour operator to the consumer through an intermediary. Meanwhile, the "backward flow" is all about the details of bookings, payments received, customer suggestions and opinions, etc. flowing to the tour operation by the intermediary, mainly the retail travel agent. In both directions, the flow of the information, negotiations and finance is common. In fact no physical products are distributed to the customer. Rather, they deal with an intangible product and are convinced about the product through the provided brochure and other materials and documents. The information required to be communicated to the customer is also provided to the intermediary. The intermediary agency will be well versed in the product so that they can explain it to the tourist. At times, the personnel interacting with the customer may have experienced a fam tour as well, and hence they will be much more familiar with the tour. The experiences along with the information about the tour can be shared with the tourist. The channel of distribution is the term used to represent the distribution/delivery arrangement by the tour operator. Here are the functions of channels in the tour operation sector (USAID, 2007):

- Provide advice and assistance for the potential tourist to take a decision to purchase.
- Distribute information about the product and its features.
- Distribute promotional materials to the potential customers.
- Act on behalf of the tour operator for marketing and selling the product.
- Act as a point of sale and ensure easy access to the product.
- Display the promotional materials such as brochures to attract the potential buyers and to choose easily.
- Arrange booking of products of tour operators.
- Collect payments and transfer to the tour operator.
- Gather feedback from the tourists.
- Collect travel, stay and other documents and transfer them to the tourist.
- Arrange ancillary services, such as insurance.

Akin to the tourism distribution system, a tour operator's distribution system also involves different levels of distribution. In one-level distribution, tour operators sell the product directly to the tourist. It is also called direct selling. Tourists can visit a tour operator's office and purchase the product. In this way, a tour operator can have maximum interaction with the customer and the control of sale is in the hands of the tour operator. Channels of communication can be reduced which helps to save time and minimize the chances of making mistakes. Commission saving is the primary advantage of direct selling. At the point of sale, expert knowledge can be made use of and more control of product distribution can be ensured. There is also less wastage of brochures, market segmentation is easier and direct contact with the customer is possible by having a customer database for future marketing and customer relations. Furthermore, tour operators can distribute products through their own websites.

Two-level systems involve one intermediary, the retailer. In the case or tour operators, travel agents are the common retailers. Online travel agents (OTAs) also do the retailing for the tour operator. They will list the tour products and allow the users to search and book directly with the tour operator. Some of the leading online travel agents and travel retailers include:

- Expedia
- Viator
- Adventure Finder
- Travelocity
- Priceline.com
- Lastminute.com
- Cendant Corporation
- Opodo

A retail travel agent primarily undertakes two main roles: providing detailed knowledge of the tour product and persuading the customer to buy the product (Davidson et al., 1988). Once there is a travel agent, then the responsibility of selling will be taken care of by it. A tour operator can be freed from distribution and the cost involved in having sales outlets for selling the products. The following are the common functions carried out by retail travel agents on behalf of tour operators while acting as intermediaries for the tour operators:

- Providing information
- Providing advice
- Understanding visitors' needs
- Displaying tour brochures
- Encouraging visitors to choose brochures
- Persuading customers
- Face-to-face marketing
- Undertaking promotional activities
- Tour booking and payment collection
- Feedback gathering and complaints handling

A tourist gets the benefit of easy access and the professional services of the travel agent. The most important disadvantage is the lack of control over sale of the product, cost disadvantage due to commission, and the lack of direct interaction with the tourist. The following are the advantages and disadvantages of having retailers in the distribution system of a tour operator:

- Advantages:
  o Wider marketplace representation
  o More convenient to sell
  o Increased promotion
  o Reduction in marketing expenses
  o Fewer staff needed
  o Less administrative work
  o More convenience for buyers
  o More focus on packaging
- Disadvantages:
  o Less profit due to commission
  o Lack of interaction with customers
  o Fam trips for retailers' employees
  o Staff have to be trained and motivated
  o Too much dependency on retailers
  o Smaller database of customers
  o Limited control over sales
  o Limited control over brochure distribution
  o Issue of bias of retailers

More levels can be seen in the distribution of tour operators' products. The following, according to Lenoir (2016), are some of the common distributors in this modern era filled with information and communication technology:

- Traditional travel agents
- Inbound tour operators
- Concierge services of accommodation units
- Tourist information centres and visitor information centres

- Hostels and restaurants
- DMOs, NTOs and their websites
- OTAs
- Agencies' own websites
- Social media sites
- Mobile communication platforms
- Destination management system and its online links
- Online review sites and advising/recommender sites, such as TripAdvisor

14.8 Summary

Tour operators attempt to address the challenge of disintermediation by ensuring quality services and customer satisfaction along with a range of value-adding services benefiting both customers and suppliers. As "word of mouth" has extreme significance in the tour operation business, tour operators have to be on guard throughout the process of tour operation, from the planning stage until the post-tour stage. Even in this digital era, tour operators have particular significance in the tourism sector. Due to the product characteristics, particularly "intangibility", tour operators depend a lot on tour brochures for informing potential customers about the product, to convince them about the product features and benefits, to create interest in the target market, to enter into contracts with clients, to communicate the terms and conditions related to the package tour, to generate sales, to garner attention of the clients through intermediaries, etc. A comprehensive brochure usually includes an introduction of the products on offer, but it may not contain booking terms and conditions and other details. An effective brochure is one that can bring in a good response, appeal to the customer, attract the customer to the product, convince them of the qualities and features of the product and create a positive image. In short, it is a cost-effective tool in promotional efforts. There are a series of steps in the design and production of tour brochures.

Market segmentation is another important task in tour operation. It can help the tour operator make product-related decisions easily; develop the most appropriate marketing mix strategies and actions; understand customer needs and interests easily; develop the product to satisfy specific needs; make suitable pricing strategies; undertake targeted marketing, positioning and differentiation; identify where and how to sell the product; enhance effectiveness in facing competition; and ensure good customer relations. A tour operator has an important role to play in the high involvement process of tourist buying behaviour. Buying behaviour is a process of sequential stages: need recognition; search for information on various products according to these needs; formation of alternative choices; evaluation of alternatives; the act of purchase and consumption; and post-purchase behaviour. In many of the stages, a tour operator can influence the potential tourist to select the right product and to purchase. Marketing is also a challenge due to the service characteristics of a tour operator's products. Well-designed marketing mix strategies provide an edge for them. Online and traditional platforms are used for marketing communication with the target market. Along with the distribution of tour products through travel agencies, a tour operator's distribution system involves the flow of payments, information and promotional materials to ensure the availability and accessibility of the products to the consumers at the proper time. In the whole system of tourism, the tour operation sector has an important role, which is expected to continue for many years to come.

Review questions

Short/medium answer type questions

- What is a tour brochure?
- Describe the importance of a tour brochure.
- Write some brief notes on the different types of tour brochures.
- Identify the contents of a tour brochure.
- List the qualities of a good tour brochure.
- Explain the tour brochure design process.
- Describe the significance of brochure launches in the tour business.
- Give a brief account of market segmentation in the tour operation business.
- Describe tourist buying behaviour and the role of the tour operator in it.
- What do we mean by fam tour?
- Discuss the distribution of a tour operator's product.

Essay type questions

- Write an essay on marketing package tours.

References

Davidson, R., William, S., Sweeney, D., Jones, T. and Stampfl, R. (1988) *Retailing Management*. 6th edn. New York: John Wiley & Sons.

Deuschl, E. D. (2006) *Travel and Tourism Public Relations: An Introductory Guide for Hospitality Managers*. Oxford: Elsevier Butterworth-Heinemann.

Engel, F. J., Blackwell, D. R. and Miniard, W. P. (1995) *Consumer Behavior*. Chicago, New York: Dryden Press.

Foxall, G. R. and Goldsmith, R. E. (1994) *Consumer Psychology for Marketing*. London: Routledge.

Gunn, C. (1988) *Vacationscape: Designing Tourist Regions*. 2nd edn. Austin, TX: Bureau of Business.

Holloway, J. C. and Taylor, N. (2006) *The Business of Tourism*. 7th edn. Essex: Prentice Hall.

Holloway, J. and Plant, R. (1988) *Marketing for Tourism*. London: Pitman.

Horner, S. and Swarbrooke, J. (2005) *Leisure Marketing: A Global Perspective*. Oxford: Elsevier Butterworth-Heinemann.

Horner, S. and Swarbrooke, J. (2007) *Consumer Behaviour in Tourism*. 2nd edn. Oxford: Butterworth-Heinemann.

Keller, K. L. (2003) *Strategic Brand Management*. Upper Saddle River, NJ: Prentice Hall.

Kotler, P. (1984) *Marketing Management: Analysis, Planning, Implementation and Control*. Upper Saddle River, NJ: Prentice Hall, p. 68.

Kotler, P., Bowen, J. T. and Makens, J. (2009) *Marketing for Tourism and Hospitality*. London: Prentice Hall.

Laws, E. (1997) *Managing Packaged Tourism: Relationships, Responsibilities and Service Quality in the Inclusive Holiday Industry*. London: International Thomson Business Press.

Lenoir, S. (2016) Distribution Channels for Tour Operators, available at https://wavehuggers.com/wp-content/uploads/2016/01/REZDY_distribution_channels_for_tour_operators.pdf (accessed 22 July 2017).

Lovelock, C. and Wirtz, J. (2007) *Services Marketing: People, Technology, Strategy*. New Jersey: Pearson Prentice Hall.

Middleton, V. T. C. and Clarke, J. (2009) *Marketing in Travel and Tourism*. Oxford: Butterworth-Heinemann.

Moeran, B. (1983) The Language of Japanese Tourism, *Annals of Tourism Research* 10(1): 93–108.

Page, S. (2007) *Tourism Management: An Introduction*. Oxford: Butterworth-Heinemann.

Pike, S. (2004) *Destination Marketing Organisations*. Oxford: Elsevier.

PRSA, About Public Relations, available at http://apps.prsa.org/AboutPRSA/publicrelations defined/.

Richards, J. I. and Curran, M. C. (2002) Oracles on "Advertising": Searching for a Definition", *Journal of Advertising* 31(2): 63–77.

Schiffman, L. G. and Kanuk, L. L. (2009) *Consumer Behaviour*. New Jersey: Pearson Prentice Hall.

USAID (2007) The Business of Inbound Tour Operators, United States Agency-International Development, available at https://www.pdffiller.com/jsfiller-desk6/?projectId=187858495&expId=3425&expBranch=2#951cdcf6d2374840b341d917a79964b3 (accessed 21 March 2017).

Wicks, B. and Schuett, M. (1991) Examining the Role of Tourism Promotion Through the Use of Brochures, *Tourism Management* 12(4): 301–312.

Yamamoto, D. and Gill, A. (1999) Emerging Trends in Japanese Package Tourism, *Journal of Travel Research* 38(2): 134–143.

Chapter 15

Pre-tour preparations

15.1 Introduction

Once marketing and promotion activities are started, the tour operator has to be ready for tour bookings and further proceedings. Before the tour departs, a number of sequential steps have to be undertaken by the administration department of the tour operator. Administration activities prior to the tour departure involve handling of tour enquiries, tour booking, handling payments, booking of supplier services, arranging documents for travel, dispatching tour documents to tourists, interacting with tourists and getting them ready for travel, and arranging pre-tour meetings. Each stage is important in the success of the tour. It is necessary for the tour operator to have adequate staff for carrying out the administrative activities, including pre-tour preparation activities. For each task, necessary skills are required. Seasonality is a factor in the tour operation sector. Hence, the tour operator may need extra personnel during peak season, when demand is highest. In administration there may also be requirements for additional staff depending upon the number of packages being marketed and the demand. The staff who handle the administration process, which includes reservation, accounting, arranging and dispatching tour documents and the like, require adequate knowledge about the whole process. Moreover, in addition to the administrative skills, they have to possess specific skills necessary for each task. For tour execution, additional staff may again be required as per the demand. For tour execution in season, additional staff may be required for tour managing, to act as tour guides, to manage overseas tour activities, etc. Many tour operators recruit reservation staff, guides, resort staff, sales representatives, international agents and so forth on a temporary basis or for a season (at most). Specific skills required for each staff will be discussed as we progress through the chapter. The following are activities involved prior to the tour departure stage and tour execution.

- Work scheduling
- Handling enquiries
- Tour booking
- Payment handling and sending invoices
- Reserving supplier services
- Arranging tour documents
- Handling cancellations (if there are any)
- Verifying the tour details and documents again
- Dispatching of tour documents to agents, and from there to the tourists
- Booking forms filed for audit, and then stored
- Engaging the tour operating department to prepare for the departure
- Preparing for the new season

15.2 Tour booking and administration

Before entering into the administrative activities, a proper work schedule should be finalized. It can be kept in electronic or hard copy format. The activity schedule, which includes dates of all activities to be processed before tour, should be ready by then. Deadlines and due dates of each and every activity should be included in it. Since the lead time is long, its necessity is very high. All activities and tasks accomplished should be rewarded periodically. One traditional approach is 90-day, 60-day and 30-day reviews, prior to departure. A work schedule is all about the identification of various activities to be carried out to complete the task assigned. Each activity, its starting time, total duration needed, the activity in relation with the previous activity, and the target completion dates are given specifically in a work schedule. Also, the appropriate number of workers required for the jobs during each day of work is earmarked as part of it. This helps the staff to know what their activities are and when they are working. Ultimately it will help in focusing on their job and essential tasks can be covered at the right time.

Handling enquiries is the task that immediately follows marketing. Once marketing has started, inquiries will come. It is important to take down contact details and other details relating to the enquiry, and to ask whether potential customers need hard copies or soft copies of brochures, etc. Respond quickly to the queries and provide proper information. Those who are handling queries should be thorough in respect of the tour and its details. People contacting you to find out about the tour will be very curious to know as many details as possible, and may be confused about what to choose. It is very important to learn their needs and interests. Knowing this can help the tour operator offer them a suitable product. Many will make contact over the telephone. Some may come online to chat if there is a provision available on the particular operator's website. Others will send emails. Walk-ins are also a possibility. All potential customers have to be treated well to persuade them to buy the product. This query handling is carried out mainly when the tour operator is interested in direct selling. If the product is sold through a retailer, query handling will be conducted mainly by the intermediary. If the customer comes to the office, provide them with the brochure along with reservation forms and ensure they understand the mode of payments, deposits, etc. Those who make contact over the Internet can also be provided with all such documents in digital format.

Among the many potential customers who make contact in order to know the tour details, some will turn up for booking. Once the booking process has started, staff need to be vigilant and properly record everything that happens. It is also important to make sure that the customer is aware of the tour they have chosen – its details, price, terms and conditions, etc. Otherwise, it can result in confusions and issues at a later stage. Once the customer is convinced about the package they are going to book, they will be supplied with the booking forms and other documents to fill in. Soon after, the customer may fill in these forms and return them to the tour operator. Though reservation is done using automated systems, there will be a written agreement/form that will be signed by the tour operator and client. The terms and conditions will be included in it, as issues can arise, e.g. cancellation. It is important for written registration and collecting deposits. At this stage, the staff have to verify the details entered in the booking form whether they are written correctly or not. Before this, price details, what items are included/not included should be communicated to clients.

Sometimes tour operators collect deposits from the customer during the booking, especially when the booking is done early. Some operators collect advance amounts along with the booking. Sometimes, although rare, the whole payment is made by the customer. This depends on how early the booking is done. If the booking happens closer to the departure date, then the whole payment may be collected in order to ensure participation. Acknowledge all bookings as soon as possible and provide receipts. Once the booking form is verified and documented, a tentative booking confirmation document or message is given. Confirm the booking only when things are ready for sale. Also, invoices have to be prepared, the balance has to be collected and tentative confirmations sent. Billing formats vary from company to company, but all essential items of entry should be there. The invoice or bill can be sent electronically along with other necessary information. Hard copies can also be sent. As per common practice, the second information bulletin will go along with this. The agency has the right to set the mode of payment, provided it is clearly communicated in advance. Whether it is a cheque, cash, bank transfer, online transfer or credit card transaction, send the invoice at the right time, i.e. by the stipulated dates. The invoice should be complete and clear. Along with the invoice, send the covering letter, including deadlines for final payments and cancellation, etc. Also, remind clients about the required travel documents.

If the booking happens through the agent, the agent may send the deposit to the tour operator quickly, assuming the tour operator issues an interim invoice. If advance payment or part payment is done, then the invoice has to mention the balance to be paid and it has to be initiated to make final payment by the customer. The final invoice will be issued once full payment is made. If the booking is done through the travel agency, be sure to verify the booking details, collect payments timeously and send invoices and the processed documents to the travel agency in time. When sending the invoice or bills, make sure that they contain the invoice number, date, date of payments, name and address, tour package code/name/details, departure dates and times, transport details, accommodation details, price of package, details of supplements/compliments, terms and conditions, rules of cancellations and due dates. Provide all necessary information on all stages to the client without delay. Traditionally such information provision was done using information bulletins, which were sent at three different times (Sarbey de Suoto, 1985). Along with acknowledgement soon after booking, the first one should go, and it should contain the details of necessary arrangements to be done. It should be designed in a manner to provide necessary answers to customers' possible queries. The second one usually goes with the invoice and should contain a brief of further details of the tour. The third one should be the most detailed and go along with the final documents. It should cover almost all the details tour participants would want to know, including travel advice. Such efforts drastically reduce frequent queries through different media from the participants.

Once the number of participants has been confirmed, it is necessary to confirm all the supplier services as early as possible. Hotel rooms have to be confirmed – how many are needed along with the type of services and facilities. Flight seats have to be confirmed by this stage. Once the list of participants is ready, the tickets can be issued for each participant. Nowadays, reservation and booking are done using computerized systems or modules of global distribution systems (GDSs). Small agencies may sometimes use manual bookings as well. The rooming list should be finalized 30 days in advance. Computerized lists will serve the purpose more efficiently. If printed early, additional revision can be made accordingly. Though reservation is done using automated systems, there will be a written agreement/form which will be signed by the tour operator and the client. The terms and conditions will be included in it, as issues can arise in the wake of cancellations or similar. The brochure is an important document as it also consists of vital terms and conditions. Customer complaints have to be dealt with properly. The brochure and other agreements signed should be followed properly.

There will be late bookings. These happen a few weeks before the departure date. Late bookings have to considered very seriously as can cause issues associated with hotel rooms and flight tickets. A staff member has to dedicate time to make the necessary arrangements for including these late bookings into the proposed tour.

If any clients need to cancel, it should be done as early as possible, since last-minute cancellations bring more damage. In many cases advance payments may have been made to the supplier, and if so, the cancellation is more complicated. Cancellation terms and conditions should have been communicated to customers well in advance. As we mentioned, these can be included in the tour brochure as well. Regardless, there can be issues

Table 15.1 First information bulletins: essential coverage of items

Passport	Visa
Rooming arrangements	Security check-in at airports
Camera restrictions	Travel insurance
Vaccination	Health insurance
Flight seating	Land transport
Airfare restrictions	Smoking restrictions
Cancellation and refunding policy	Payment modes
Use of credit/debit cards	Currency exchange
Shopping possibilities	Hints on extra spending
Clothing and winter clothes	Luggage and packing
Duty-free shopping	Customs and immigration rules
Hand luggage restrictions	Care for valuables
Hotel/other accommodation	

Source: Sarbey de Suoto (1985)

during cancellation, as some customers will demand to be reimbursed the whole advance or amount paid for the tour. Specify cancellation and refund policies. It is important to have written request for cancellation. The financial liability of the tour operator may not be considered if they have not communicated the terms and conditions to clients. In the meantime, a proper filing system has to be followed in a tour operator's office. The copies of major documents, in hard copy, should be retained. It is true that there is software to undertake almost all the functions of tour operation. All data and information can be stored in it as well. Yet hard copies should be filed for records, too. At each stage of the tour operation process, copies of the necessary documents are stored. Once the tour is over, the file will be comprehensive, with almost all details of the tour accounted for. It can then be used for future reference and for planning and forecasting. Major items to include in the file of a particular tour programme include:

- Market research details and summary of findings
- Tour details and comprehensive itinerary
- Notes and minutes of meetings
- Brochure and details of its printing and dispatching
- Essentials of marketing and promotion activities
- Supplier negotiation details and contracts
- Correspondence with all suppliers before and after contracts
- Cost sheets and price details
- Sales documents
- Retailer-related details and commissions
- Booking details of each tourist
- Payment details
- Tour escort and overseas staff details, and remuneration/payment details
- Supplier payment details
- After-tour reports, etc.

Computer systems will keep soft copies of each tour as well. Separate files may also be maintained for each tour participant – to keep records of bookings, payments, details of travel documents, etc. For each tourist, a folder can also be maintained in the system for easy retrieval and reference.

15.3 Travel documents

Arranging the travel documents and dispatching to the tourist is the next important stage in the tour operation administration process. A tour operator has to collect all the necessary documents about confirmation of supplier services. Moreover, travel documents of the tour participants also have to be ready. Flight ticketing processing will be undertaken and tickets will be ready by then. The utmost care is needed in arranging travel documents. Even a small error can negatively affect the travel plan and lead to dissatisfaction. The travel documents needing to be arranged are discussed below.

15.3.1 Passport

The passport is basically the proof of citizenship of a country. It is issued by the competent authority at the national level to the nationals or residents of the issuing country.

It establishes the identity of the traveller and their nationality and authorizes them to travel outside the country, along with indicating a request for protection for them while travelling abroad. The validity of the passport is specified in the passport itself. A visa is endorsed in a passport. This is a passenger's prime document while travelling abroad. That means it provides evidence of legal entry into another country. The information in passports includes full name, nationality, date of issue, date of expiry, date of birth, issuing authority, address, holder's signature and photo, place of birth, sex, ECNR (emigration check not required)/ECR (emigration check required) intimation, etc. Though it is a basic requirement for international travel, citizens of some countries can travel to neighbouring/other countries without a passport, provided both countries have a mutual agreement in place for inter-country travel without a passport and visa. In such cases, other proof of national identity may be required for crossing the border. It is primarily the responsibility of the traveller to obtain a passport, but a tour operator can assist in getting it for them. The passport is the most important travel document, so a tour operator has to ensure early on whether the traveller has a valid passport or not. Also, the validity of the passport, availability of blank pages for stamping visas, ECR status, etc. need to be verified prior to proceeding with the booking of the tour. Some of the common aspects of normal passports are listed here:

- It's a proof of identity of a citizen of a country.
- It is issued by the competent authority at the national level in each country.
- It remains the property of the authority who issued it.
- A passport issued to a citizen can be withdrawn at any point for certain reasons.
- Every passport has a validity period (usually 5–10 years), beyond which it is not accepted as a proof of identity.
- An adequate validity period (usually a minimum of six months) is required for getting a visa to travel to another country.
- A visa, the mandatory evidence for visiting another country, is stamped in a passport.
- Along with visas, entry and exit stamps are placed on available blank pages inside a passport during border crossings.

There are different types of passports issued by authorities. The common types of passports that are issued by respective national authorities are as follows:

- *Normal/regular passport:* this is issued to common citizens/nationals of a country.
- *Official passport:* this is issued to an official or employee of the government travelling abroad to carry out official duties.
- *Diplomatic or consular passport:* this is issued to diplomatic and consular staff, and people with diplomatic status or comparable status travelling to carry out diplomatic duties on behalf of the government.
- *Alien's passport:* this is issued to residents of a country who are not citizens or nationals of that country.
- *Special travel documents:* these are issued by international organizations like the United Nations (UN) and International Committee of the Red Cross for specific reasons. They are usually valid only when the passengers carry their national passports as well. For instance, the UN laissez-passer (UNLP) is issued to UN staff, but for international travel the holder also has to carry their national passport. There are additionally other documents issued instead of passports. For example, children's identity cards are issued by some countries for minors/children.

15.3.2 Visas

For entering another country, permission is certainly required. A visa is issued for this purpose. It allows citizens of one country to enter another country. This is a conditional permission granted by a country to a foreigner. There are exemptions to this. But in general, visas are issued by countries for citizens of other countries to enter, visit and work (or for another reason). Usually as part of visa issuance, the visa is stamped in the passport of the passenger concerned by the official authorized for it. In it, information including authorized length of stay, period of validity, number of entries allowed during the period, and purpose of visit category of the visa is included. This, usually a stamp or a sticker in the passport, gives the passport holder the permission to enter or leave a country. Yet the permission is, in many cases, at the discretion of the officer in charge of emigrations. Usually a fee has to be paid when applying for a visa. Tour operators often arrange visas for tourists in the case of group inclusive tours (GITs) as well as for free independent travellers (FITs). In such cases, the tour operator should verify all the necessary pages in the passport and the documents needed for applying for a visa. The documents required for obtaining a visa and the guidelines, etc. vary from country to country as well as from one type of visa to another.

The different types of visas are based mainly on the purpose of entry. Instead of formal visas, some countries issue other types of entry permits or travel documents that allow the citizens of specified countries, on the basis of mutual bilateral relationships and agreements, to enter their territory. Common types of visas are tourist visa, employment visa, transit visa, diplomatic visa and business visa. When issuing a visa, the country concerned may verify the passport details of the applicant, their purpose of entry and their ability to pursue the purpose after visiting the country. For example, an employment visa seeker may need the necessary qualifications and experience to get the job applied for. Different countries have different visa types. Though there are some common types, there are a variety of visas. A few visa types relevant to tourism are introduced below.

Visitor/tourist visa

This is issued for the purpose of a short-term visit and provides the right of entry into a country. Visitor/tourist visas are issued by the embassies or consulates of countries. Some countries offer "on-arrival visitor visas" for citizens of specific countries. In such cases, the visitor can arrive at the entry point of that country and get the visa from the emigration authorities situated within the entry point, e.g. airport. Officials may require visitors to prove they have enough money to support themselves for the duration of their stay, proof of prepaid return travel, and sufficient validity in their passport. Some countries require a visa to be granted before arrival. For instance, the UK requires the issuing of a standard visitor visa for citizens of many countries prior to entering the country. This visa, according to UK emigration authorities (Gov.uk, n.d.), is issued for three specific reasons:

- For leisure, e.g. people on holiday or seeing family and friends
- For business, or to take part in sports or creative events
- For another reason, e.g. to receive private medical treatment

Of late, some countries have been trying to ease visitor visa restrictions and liberalize visa regulations so as to attract as many tourists as they can. Very strict visa rules for visitors are considered a bottleneck for tourism development. Even some conservative countries are now easing visa restrictions.

Transit visa

This is a very short-term visa, which gives right of entry into a foreign country; but it is given so that travellers can make connections onward to a third country. The visa period may be up to a few days in some countries, so travellers with a transit visa are often able to visit the nearby attractions. It is usually issued if the connection time is more than four hours, though it varies from country to country.

Example: Tourism-related visas (visitor visas) issued by the US

The US has a number of visas issued to non-immigrant and immigrant categories of visitors. They are usually represented by letters, and in each of the categories different types are issued. For instance, all tourism-related visas are classified under the category B, termed as "visitor visas". It includes B-1 and B-2. While the former is issued for the purpose of business tourism, the other, B-2, is issued for the leisure category of tourism.

The B-1 visa is issued to tourists who have one of the following purposes for travel:

- Consult with business associates
- Attend a scientific, educational, professional or business convention or conference
- Settle an estate
- Negotiate a contract

The B-2 visa is issued to tourists who have one of the following purposes:

- Tourism
- Vacation/holiday
- VFR (visit friends or relatives)
- Medical treatment
- Participation in social events hosted by fraternal, social or service organizations
- Participation by amateurs in musical, sports, or similar events or contests – if they are not being paid for participating
- Enrolment in a short recreational course of study, not for credit towards a degree.

Source: Travel.State.Gov (n.d.)

Schengen visa

This is issued by 26 European countries in the Schengen area, which envisages "borderless" travel for its citizens. This area covers the majority of European countries, except for the UK, Romania, Bulgaria, Croatia, Cyprus and Ireland. Non-EU countries such as

Norway, Iceland, Switzerland and Lichtenstein are also part of it. This visa allows free movement for its holder within and between these countries.

15.3.3 Health vaccination

While travelling to foreign countries, travellers have to take precautions against contagious diseases. Some destinations have compulsory vaccination requirements and require tourists to have vaccination certificates in order to enter the country. Examples of contagious diseases that require vaccinations include malaria, yellow fever, hepatitis, typhoid fever and cholera. International certification of vaccination formats can be used in this regard.

15.3.4 Travel insurance

Travel insurance is a recommended option for people travelling abroad as it can cover the costs relating to accidents, theft and other events which may take place while on tour. Provided over the short term, it may offer medical coverage, health and accident coverage, loss or delay of travel documents, damage or injury to people or property, cancellation or missed departure, baggage loss or damage, legal expenses, or even the expenses required in the event of death.

15.3.5 Hotel vouchers

For certain tours, hotel vouchers are issued which enable tourists to stay in a hotel. As the tour operator has already made payment for the tourist's stay in the hotel, they don't have to make payment to the hotel, except for certain extra services or facilities used. A hotel voucher, being a form of "receipt", means tourists can then claim the service that has been paid for. Though it represents a proof of an amount already paid for the stay, at times the voucher may also indicate that the tourist has to make the necessary payment amount.

15.3.6 Baggage tags

Tour operators usually provide common baggage tags for all the participants on a tour. The primary purpose of these is easy identification of the checked luggage. In busy airports, there are many conveyor belts and a large number of luggage items move along them. Having a common baggage tag attached to every luggage item of all the tour participants can make it easier to locate the luggage as it arrives via the conveyor belt. Usually such tags will be colourful and easily identifiable. Apart from the purpose of identification, common baggage tags are an important tool for promotion. The label prominently displays the company name and logo in public. Attractive baggage tags can make a good impression for the tour operator.

15.3.7 Passenger manifest

A good passenger manifest is an essential tool for the smooth operation of a package tour. It is a listing of the essential details of all passengers booked on a tour programme. It is usually in a simple format, easy to read and understand so that the transport operator can easily understand when and where the service has to be provided. For an airline, while handling tourists as part of a package tour organized by a tour operator, it will make the checking procedure easy and smooth. Using the latest IT solutions, such things are easy for tour operators and the airline. Ready-made software packages are available for preparing passenger manifests according to the need.

15.3.8 Rooming list

Rooming list is an important document required for the accommodation unit and also for the tour leader. It's a list that includes details such as the names of tourists, room allocation and type of rooms. Copies of this will be kept by the tour manager, the tour operator's overseas representative, ground handling agents and the hotel. The accommodation centre needs it to assign the right tourists to the same room and to use it as a blueprint for where the rooms should be located relative to each other. The tour manager/leader should have a copy to ensure the provision of the rooms to the right people and the smooth process of room allocation when they reach the accommodation centre for stay in the destination.

15.3.9 Documents with other relevant information

A simple document with important information regarding the tour also has to be provided to the tourist. Information about how much cash to carry should be communicated. Though there are many electronic payment methods nowadays, certain amounts of liquid cash may need to be carried while travelling. Currency exchange information, value of the currency, approximate amounts needed for certain unavoidable products/services, etc. can be communicated to the tourist prior to departure. Give proper information on currency issues. Also, not all currencies can be converted into all other countries' currencies. It is therefore better to carry currency that is transacted more widely, such as the US dollar or euro. Also, before landing in the destination, some amount of local currency should be in hand. Details of customs regulations also have to be provided to travellers. Documents specifying customs regulations deal with the transport of articles and species from one country to another. There are restrictions, guidelines and prohibitions on certain articles or species when transported from other countries. One aspect of regulation may protect the population of a country from the spread of dangerous infectious diseases from the articles or species being transported from other countries. Also, duty may be paid on carrying/importing some articles when exceeding certain limits. Some possible extra taxes levied on travellers, in addition to those included in the package price, need to be communicated to tourists. Other relevant information, like cultural uniqueness and differences, customs and traditions, usual shopping items and centres, climate and clothing to carry, extra care to take, etc. should also be communicated. Promotion leaflets, including duty-free shopping discount vouchers, can also be sent to the tourist.

Once all payments have been made, the travel documents have to be ready. All bookings made, sales received, preparations undertaken, etc. should be reviewed. Also, within this period it is important to match the sales with the space booked and tour capacity. If they don't match, take necessary action. After that, all documents are dispatched and the flight manifest is prepared and sent to the airline. If travel agents are involved, format agreements, specifying terms and commission, should be signed. The flight manifest with passenger details should be prepared in advance and confirmations should be ensured. The same can be provided to the airline, with details of the tour manager as well. Also, the hotel should be given proper information and room bookings have to be confirmed. The rooming list should also be prepared. Some may prefer to have a proper tour roster.

A typical tour roster may contain the names, addresses and passport details of travellers; details of room sharing; flight ticket details; preferences for optional tours; and remarks on each passenger. Review the bookings made by the reservations department again and confirm that all are done.

During the whole process of tour operation, reviews have to take place periodically. Usually 90-day, 60-day, 45-day and 30-day reviews are undertaken. Traditionally, review forms were used for periodical reviews. Nowadays, the software used provides electronic review forms as well. During the whole process, tourists will have a number of doubts and it is mandatory to handle each enquiry and clarify these doubts. Now the travel documents will be ready and they can be dispatched to agents, and from there to the tourists, or directly to the tourists in the case of direct selling. Once the administrative work is over and the documents are filed, the package is ready for pre-tour preparations and tour execution. In the meantime, hotels should be properly informed about arrival time, travel plans, meal preferences, rooms to be used, special arrangements required, payment details, etc. Moreover, provide all details to the ground handling agents. The documents handed over to the ground handling agents can include the tour roster, optional tours, sightseeing preferences, arrival and departure times, their expected services, guide needs, payment details, shopping preferences, tour schedule and itinerary.

15.4 Tour manager briefing

The professional who accompanies a tour is referred to by different names, such as tour manager, tour leader, tour escort and tour director. Regardless of the title used, the duties and responsibilities are relatively consistent. Here, let's use the term tour manager. They lead from point to point and coordinate and control the tour. Sometimes, tour companies recruit tour managers. In some other cases, they may hire an experienced freelancer for the purpose. They are responsible for the smooth conduct of a group tour. Service of a tour manager helps in better coordination and smooth conduct of the programme. The package tour has to follow the pre-set itinerary and hence the tour manager is necessary. Once the tour reaches the destination, tourists become strangers, and hence the tour manager has to play a role to minimize this strangeness. They act as local support and link with suppliers and destination services. Also, tourists gain confidence in the presence of tour managers to visit new places and try new activities, which helps them to enjoy the tour more. A tour operator arranges various services and contracts with their providers. A tour manager can ensure the services are offered as per the contract and the quality of the service is on par with the expectations.

During the course of the tour, tourists may have different complaints. A tour manager can patiently listen to them and find solutions. Emergencies may occur at any point in time during a tour. Having a tour manager can minimize the consequences of such situations and tourists can depend on them. The job of the tour manager is varied, as different tasks have to be fulfilled and different roles have to be played. Their ability is critical in the success of the tour programme. Though tour operators engage their own professionals as tour managers, at times they may have to engage tour escorts from outside their organization, e.g. freelancers or travel agency staff.

Tour manager briefing is an important activity. All the arrangements and tour details must be communicated to the tour manager. The staff in charge can discuss with the tour manager and let the tour manager read the itinerary and relevant materials. The tour manager should also be made familiar with payment details. Other aspects to be introduced to the tour manager include: tips for handling emergencies; how to act in case of emergencies and loss of valuables, luggage, etc.; the amounts earmarked for celebrations and social events; and the tour group's nature, needs and interests. The following should be handed over to the tour manager to ensure an efficient tour:

- Flight manifest
- Tour roster or rooming list
- Group flight itinerary
- Flight details, such as flight number(s), airports, estimated time of departure (ETD), estimated time of arrival (ETA) and meal service
- Copies of tour questionnaires filled in by participants
- Baggage tags
- Sample set of passenger material, already provided to them
- Payment modes for suppliers, vouchers, payment proofs
- Booking confirmation details
- Required stationery
- Other documents required for a tour manager

The tour manager has responsibilities not only towards the tour operator. Indeed, for a tour operator, the tour manager has to conduct the tour as per the itinerary and ensure that the tour is executed with maximum efficiency and quality. They have to maintain good relationships with service providers as well. Also, the quality assessment has to be done on behalf of the tour operator. Customer satisfaction is also an objective of a tour operator, and here, the tour manager, on behalf of the tour operator, has to ensure that the tourists are satisfied. Ultimately, profit making is the objective of any business, and here the tour manager can contribute a share towards it. However, the tour manager has an equal responsibility to the tourists. For a tourist, the tour manager plays a range of roles, including that of facilitator, supporter, information source and interpreter. All these roles need to be handled well by the tour manager. Moreover, the tour manager has to ensure smooth services from suppliers, make sure the participants get what they paid for and enhance their experience. The responsibilities of tour managers do not end with the above. They are also responsible to the supplier. A tour manager acts as the link between consumer and supplier, ensures smooth consumption by participants and provides good opinions about services to the tour operator. Apart from all the above, a tour manager is also responsible to the society and the environment, by ensuring sustainable practices throughout the tour process.

15.4.1 Duties of a tour manager

Duties of a tour manager include the following:

- Accompany the group.
- Establish relationships early. Get acquainted at the beginning.
- Find out check-in procedures at airports in advance.
- Introduce the participants to everyone.
- Liaisons between tour participants and the company.
- Verify their name with the master list.
- Count the individuals and their checked bags.
- Describe check-in procedures to the tourists.

- Brief the passengers about the details of facilities inside airports and point them in the direction of gates for boarding.
- Confirm the meeting point after landing.
- Upon arrival, get in touch with the ground handlers.
- After baggage collection and customs procedures, proceed to the coach.
- Load luggage, board and perform a head count.
- In the coach, provide essential instructions.
- Upon reaching the hotel, rush to registration.
- Get introduced, provide the booking details and verify the rooming list.
- Let the participants enter the hotel, register independently or provide keys as per rooming list.
- Inform tourists to reassemble at a particular place after rest.
- In case any issues associated with the rooms arise, settle them quickly.
- Ensure all registered have occupied rooms and luggage is completely taken with them from the coach.
- Verify all the facilities inside the hotel.
- Freshen up and plan for further activities.
- If needed, a service desk may be operated near the front office for helping the participants.
- After rest, reassemble, have the meal as per the plan and provide necessary instructions.
- Remind tourists of valuables (not to keep them in room).
- Remind tourists to be punctual.
- Ensure that the coach comes at least 15 minutes prior to the trip commencement.
- If someone comes late regularly, handle this amicably and in private.
- Inform tourists about extra services in the hotel.
- Keep track of the luggage.
- If someone appears with more luggage, warn them of luggage restrictions, especially when flying.
- Inform tourists about dutiable items.
- Proceed with the tour as per the master itinerary.
- Accompany tourists for sightseeing and shopping.
- Make balance payments to the suppliers.
- Keep records of every occurrence.
- Ensure the quality of supplier services.
- Make the tour interesting for the tourists.
- After the tour, collect all the tour records and feedback.
- Assist tourists on various issues encountered.
- Act as a host at times.

15.4.2 Roles of the tour manager

The job of the tour manager is varied, as different tasks have to be fulfilled and different roles have to be played. Their ability is critical to the success of the tour programme. The following are the roles played by a tour manager during a tour:

- *Leader:* directs and leads the tour as per the pre-set itinerary.
- *Administrator:* manages the tour as envisaged and set out by the tour operator.
- *Interpreter:* interprets various attractions and other sites during sightseeing trips particularly; and makes cultural comparisons, encourages respect for the local culture, explaining customs and traditions.

- *Coordinator:* organizes all the activities and ensures services are received in time – all participants look to the tour manager to "get things done".
- *Motivator:* inspires tourists to visit and learn about new places, encourages them to buy souvenirs and to go for optional tours so as to enhance their tourist experience.
- *Entertainer:* helps in energizing the tour and reducing "the boring time"; and ensures entertainment activities are organized for tourists.
- *Complaint handler:* listens to the issues of participants and provides possible assistance.

15.4.3 Qualities needed for a tour manager

For undertaking the tour and handling various roles, a tour manager should possess certain qualities and qualifications. A tour manager should also have a good understanding of situations and of dealing with people of different statuses. The following are the essential qualities needed in a tour manager:

- Leadership skills
- Knowledge
- Communication skills
- Language proficiency
- Commonsense
- Logical and reasoning ability
- Experience
- Punctuality
- Social abilities
- Organizational skills
- Sensitivity
- Hardworking and diligent
- Decisive
- Positive outlook
- Tactful
- Honest and loyal
- Patient and calm
- Warm and pleasant
- Clean and neat appearance
- Forecasting skills
- Empathetic
- Healthy and hygienic
- Flexible, yet assertive
- Commitment
- Wit and virtuosity
- Control and firmness
- Knowledge
- Ability to handle emergencies

The job of a tour manager is challenging and different problems will be encountered during the process of tour operation. In addition to professional challenges, a tour manager has to face a range of personal problems as well, such as tedious work schedules, the need to exercise extreme patience, the monotony of visiting the same places again and again, the possibility of health issues due to tiring travel and frequent breaks in routine, and leaving one's family for regular and extended periods. A tour manager hence needs good mental and physical capacity to handle such stresses.

15.4.4 Dos and Don'ts

Being the most important person responsible for the success of a tour, a tour manager, in addition to their duties, has to follow certain *dos* and *don't*s, as listed below:

- Smile and be cheerful.
- Lead without compulsion.
- Dress neatly and consider one's appearance.
- Be patient and empathetic.
- Be respectful, but not servile.
- Be prepared.
- Learn the group characteristics.
- Always remember that you are in a professional role, not on vacation.
- Try to learn the names of the participants.
- Be flexible yet firm.
- Always remember that you are on the job.
- Treat all equally – give equal time and attention to all.
- Keep a sharp eye on elderly members.
- Don't become emotionally attached to anyone.
- Never discuss personal problems with members.
- Don't assume all participants are experienced travellers.
- Go in groups, not with individuals.
- Do not become *too* close to members and form personal relationships.
- Don't party too much with tour participants.
- Avoid quarrels with tourists; rather tackle issues with wit and humour.
- Do not alter an itinerary without good reason.
- Correct difficulties before they get out of hand.
- Don't show too much authority; rather be diplomatic.
- Don't bluff.
- If you don't know something, admit it.
- Always be ready early.
- Don't consume alcohol or other substances that have a similar effect.
- Expect that unexpected things will occur at any point in time.
- Have a few surprises, such as gifts, games, etc.
- Don't take participants shopping so as to earn personal commission.
- Don't lie and cover up the truth in difficult situations.
- If you are physically unfit, don't take the tour.
- Do not encourage tips or gifts from passengers, but do not be rude in the event that they do give you something.

15.4.5 Tour manager preparations

An assigned tour manager has to make the necessary preparations for the tour. They have to go through the itinerary and identify possible hitches. This will help to identify all the requirements during travel and allow them to lead and better manage it. Each and every tiny detail has to be considered, all necessary documents put together and preparations carried out. The following details for a tour escort/leader/manager for a GIT operation must be brought/considered:

- Contact details of all people involved in the tour, including overseas representatives, ground handling agents, tour operator and supplier representatives
- Itinerary in detail to proceed with the tour, and the map
- Details of payments to be made to suppliers and service providers
- Names and addresses of hotels, restaurants and shopping centres, with contact persons
- List of tour options/choices and possible entertainment
- Rooming list with names of each tour participant accommodated in each room of the hotels
- Passenger list with essential details, such as name, address, mobile numbers, email addresses, IDs, passport details, details of accompanying spouse, health aspects, food habits and the people to be informed in case of emergencies
- Tipping suggestions
- Some details of attractions, and cultural, social and geographical features
- Baggage list containing the number of luggage items for each passenger
- Details of people to contact at destination for transfer, shopping, food and beverage, entertainment, tour guiding, transport and accommodation. (The list may also include the details and contacts of travel bureaus, embassies/consulates, and police and hospitals for handling emergencies.)
- Confirmation documents from all the suppliers including accommodation, food, entertainment, etc.
- Report forms to record the daily happenings, expenses, attractions covered, etc.
- Miscellaneous information, such as friends list, extra copies, etc.

15.5 Pre-departure meeting

The pre-tour meeting is crucial for the smooth operation of the tour. The departure bulletin can be sent to the tourists prior to the pre-tour meeting. Essentially, it should contain: the time and place of the pre-tour meeting and orientation; flight details; details for completing baggage tags; instructions for check-in and security check and immigration; details of wearing identification marks; contact details; and reminders. The tourists have to be well prepared for the tour and be equipped physically and mentally for it. Also, they have to know what preparations are necessary and what items to carry during travel. The meeting will be led by an expert from the tour operator's office in the presence of the tour escort/manager. This will be done a few days prior to the tour so that the tourist will have sufficient time to prepare. The following are the major objectives of a pre-tour meeting:

- To orient tourists to the whole tour
- To familiarize tourists with the tour escort/manager and the proceedings of the tour
- To establish the authority of the tour manager to handle the tour and ensure its success
- To introduce all tour participants to one another – to have an idea of who is travelling with them
- To hand over the travel documents

- To collect due payments, if any balance amount is pending; or if any extra amounts need to be collected due to sharp currency variation
- To provide *dos* and *don'ts* throughout the tour
- To provide travel tips and tour checklist
- To provide complimentary items, such as tour bag, tour caps and other promotional materials

In the pre-tour meeting, provide all the details of the tour. Let the tourists be prepared and be confident to travel. Also, they have to be motivated to enjoy the tour with a group of people and to get along with the other tour members. Being a group tour, there will be people from different backgrounds with different attitudes and behaviour patterns. The success of a tour is also dependent upon the social environment developed inside the group and the understanding among members while on tour. Tourists have to be clear on the details of the accommodation centre, and the rooms, facilities, services, meals provided, etc. The rooms are usually twin-based. Communicate the type of hotel, location and contact details to the tourists. Also communicate the details of single room supplements. The tour plan/itinerary, functions and activities, arrival and departure patterns are dealt with in the pre-tour meeting. At this point all travel documents have to be verified again and handed over to them after verification. Make the tourists aware of insurance documents and the relevant coverage items. Remind them to carry their passport. Check the visa and ECR stamps inside passports again. Also, if children and a spouse are travelling, check whether their names are endorsed in the respective passports, if needed. Verify visa stamps, and the periods given. Provide travellers with luggage tags with the name and address of the agency, with bright or unique colour patterns for easy identification.

It is always recommended to provide an idea about tour guides being used for interpretation during sightseeing. Airport security is another important item to be communicated to tourists in the pre-tour meeting. Educate them about the "don't carry items". Also inform them about items not permitted in handbags and carry-on luggage. Getting the seats everyone wants may not always be possible on flights. Therefore, do not assure them of that! Also, for motor coach seating, care has to be taken for seat rotation on different days. In some places cameras may not be permitted. Photography/videography equipment may be restricted in some attractions. Also, there may be cultural differences in some countries in taking photos or videos of locals. Some tips will be included in the tour price, which should be mentioned. In some places tips may be very significant whereas in others it may not be. Provide adequate information on tips and service charges. Also, it is necessary to make travellers understand how much cash is required and should be carried for the duration of the tour. It should also be clear to everyone how much additional cash (approximately) may be required. Additionally, possible items for shopping and approximate costs can be communicated. It is also important to inform travellers about how much hard currency they should carry and options to get cash, e.g. credit cards, traveller's cheques, etc. It may also be useful to provide some advice about how to control spending so that they still have money left in the latter parts of the tour. Details about baggage are also very important. Give an idea about what kind of baggage may be carried, how much to take, weight limits, and the size and weight limit of hand luggage. Packing suggestions are sometimes gratefully received, too. Sometimes complimentary bags are given. Uniformity in luggage is recommended. Tourists should remember to carry mobile chargers, plug adapters, clothing needs for different occasions, etc. A suggested wardrobe checklist is also recommended.

Inform tourists of health-related aspects and the care that should be taken. Try to ascertain if anyone has health conditions, e.g. heart disease, high blood pressure, etc. In such cases, insist on the tourist getting written permission to travel from a physician. Remind them to carry the necessary pills and medicines and to acquire them in advance if needed. Also, in order to minimize jetlag-related issues, advise them to take it easy the day before they are due to depart, eat light foods on board and minimize alcoholic drink consumption. If possible, preparations should be made days in advance. Make suggestions for carrying valuables, and mention places notorious for pickpocketing, etc. Talk about what good buys there are in the country they're visiting. Educate the participants on customs and immigration rules and procedures. Moreover, encourage them to do some background reading about the places they will be visiting. Provide them with some good links/websites where they can learn more about the places. Some good books can also be suggested. Give the tourists a checklist before departing from their residence so they don't forget to carry some essential documents and have a smooth and memorable tour. This will also help to overcome the tendency to forget something due to the busy schedule prior to the trip. A departure information bulletin consisting of the essentials of all the above details can also be given to the tourist along with the checklist.

15.6 Departure procedure at the airport

The tourists should be informed about the exact times of departure and the times to arrive at the airport. The tour manager has to arrive at the airport well in advance. Before going inside the airport, go through the entire programme and make sure that all documents as per the list are there and overseas operators are being informed about the arrivals and schedules. Also confirm that the person who will meet at the airport upon arrival will be there, and ensure transfer arrangements. Review each function inclusive of sightseeing activities, and confirm arrangements at the hotel(s), including VIP rooms, facilities, social schedules and room courtesies.

Arrive well in advance, introduce yourself to participants, provide the full details again to passengers, tell them which queue to stand in, what documents they need to provide, etc. Before that, ask all tourists to ensure that they have all tour-related documents and remind them to keep them safe while travelling. First impressions are lasting impressions. During the first meeting, try to exhibit professionalism and create a positive impression. After a head count, assemble the tourists in an appropriate place, greet them, introduce them to each other and have a briefing about airport procedures. Provide information to tour members for airline check-in, help them do it and educate them on various check-in and security check procedures. Also inform them about jetlag, climate-related issues, delay possibilities, and brief them on the destination airport and procedures. Ensure they all have boarding passes and baggage tags. Let the participants have same bag label or complimentary T-shirts. Ensure everyone has a boarding pass, luggage tags, handbag tag, etc. and show them the way to the security check, immigration counter, duty-free shops, coffee shops, gates, etc. If there are "no-shows", there is no need to wait an longer; try to contact the agency and the tourist without delay. Make sure that no one faces any issues checking in, during the immigration process or security check. Once all the tour members have completed the airport procedures, they can proceed to the gate area. If anyone needs refreshments, they can get these here. Also, if needed, some duty-free shopping can be done. The tour is now ready for departure.

15.7 Summary

Pre-tour preparations involve critical tasks, each and every one of which must be performed with due diligence. Administration activities prior to the tour departure involve handling of tour enquiries, tour booking, handling payments, booking of supplier services, arranging documents for travel, dispatching tour documents to the tourists, interacting with the tourists for getting ready for travel and arranging the pre-tour meeting. It is necessary for the tour operator to have adequate staff with necessary knowledge and skill for doing the administrative activities along with pre-tour preparation activities.

The travel documents have to be arranged as early as possible. Passport, visa and vaccination certificates (if needed) are the most important documents to be arranged. Ensuring travel insurance is advisable for any tour. Tour operators' essential documents to carry along with the tour include hotel vouchers, baggage tags, passenger manifest and rooming list, which are prepared once the booking process is over and payments have been collected.

Also, at this stage, the tour manager has to be identified and finalized. The professional who is accompanying a tour goes by different names, e.g. tour manager, tour leader, tour escort and tour director. Regardless of the title that is used, the duties and responsibilities are somewhat consistent. They are critical to the success of the tour and should be capable enough to handle the group throughout the journey. A tour manager should be properly informed about all aspects of the tour in order to avoid any confusion during its execution. Prior to the commencement of the tour, a tour manager has to interact successfully with the group members and discuss various aspects of the tour. This will provide a positive prelude for the tour and create rapport between the tour manager and the tour participants which can instil confidence among them for the tour ahead.

Review questions

Short/medium answer type questions

- Elaborate on the process and procedures of tour booking.
- Write about various travel documents needed for foreign travel.
- Write briefly about different types of passports.
- Describe the different types of visas.
- What are the documents that need to be handed over to tourists while travelling on a package tour?
- What do we mean by tour manager briefing?
- What are the documents needed by tour managers for the efficient conducting of the tour?
- List the duties of a tour manager.
- What is a rooming list?
- What do we mean by passenger manifest?
- Explain the roles a tour manager is required to play.
- Write down all the qualities needed for a good tour manager.
- Describe the pre-departure meeting.
- Write briefly about departure procedures in airports.

Essay type questions

- Describe the tour preparation process after the commencement of a package tour booking.
- Discuss the duties and roles of the tour manager in the efficient management of a package tour.

References

Gov.uk, Standard Visitor Visa, available at https://www.gov.uk/standard-visitor-visa.

Sarbey de Suoto, M. (1985) *Group Travel Operations Manual*. Albany: Delmar Publishers.

Travel.State.Gov, Visitor Visa, available at https://travel.state.gov/content/visas/en/visit/visitor.html.

Chapter 16

Managing the tour

Learning outcomes

After reading this chapter, you will be able to:

- Comprehend the tourist arrival procedures in the destination airport.
- Understand the emergency handling procedures in general.
- Explain how to manage the tour.
- Identify the post-tour activities.
- Recognize different types of overseas tour representatives.
- Describe the duties, roles and qualities of tour guides.
- Appreciate the significance of customer satisfaction in the tour operation sector.

16.1 Introduction

"Well begun is half done" – Aristotle

As the preparations for the tour are now complete, the time has come to execute the plan. It is easy to implement a plan which is properly set, though the right people are required to carry it out. The real tour operation commences from the arrival of the tourists at the airport for proceeding to the destination. The tour group proceeds through the airport after the formalities have been completed for boarding the flight. If all documents are proper and the necessary planning has been done, then the check-in formalities inside the terminal will be hassle-free and the tourists can enjoy the flight. There are further formalities at the arriving airport. It is important that all of the tourists are properly aware of what needs to be done in the airport for emigration clearance and customs formalities.

In long-haul travel, jet lag can cause some uneasiness for travellers. When passengers travel a long distance, and from east to west or west to east, they face a kind of physical discomfort which is called jetlag. In such situations, the passengers have to pass through many time zones, and when they reach the destination, the time (or perhaps even the day) will be different. But the body may not respond well to the rapid change in time; the "body clock" may get confused. This will result in fatigue and related symptoms. A tour manager may have provided all necessary information to passengers to enjoy the flight and to minimize the fatigue of travelling. The details of the remaining procedures and tour operations are described in the following sections.

16.2 Arrival procedures

Once the flight lands, ensure that every tour member easily clears immigration. Let them have their passports, disembarkation cards and visa ready for verification and stamping. Tourists can verify the details of the visa stamped and entry and exit dates given in the stamp. As the immigration process is now over, and the visa has been stamped, tourists can move to the baggage claim area. There may be a number of conveyor belts. The tour manager may help them to locate the exact conveyor belt to collect their checked baggage. The common baggage tags provided will enable the tourists to identify their luggage easily. If promotional bags were provided, then the baggage collection process will be that much easier. Those who collected the baggage can move ahead through the customs area and, if asked to do so, open the luggage for further checking by the customs authorities. There are duty-free shops there, where items can be bought quickly without delaying the tour. At this point, the tour manager can ask everyone to assemble in an area (not crowded) to wait for the transfer. The tour manager can perform a head count and confirm that everyone has arrived. In the meantime, the tour manager should have contacted the ground handling agent/overseas representative to inform them of their arrival. The driver of the transfer vehicle should also have been contacted without delay. The activities of a single centre tour after arrival at the destination are listed here:

- Transfer to hotel
- Hotel check-in
- Day activities
- Optional tours
- Shopping
- Last night dinner and entertainment
- Check-out and transfer to airport
- Tour wrap-up
- Post-tour activities

Let's now discuss the details of the activities.

Transfer to the hotel is usually by coach. If the tourist is a free independent traveller (FIT), the vehicle can be a car or shared coach. Once the vehicle arrives, the tourists' luggage has to be loaded safely. Let them board the vehicle. Once everyone has boarded, the tour manager does another head count. Now is an ideal time to brief the tourists about hotel accommodation and the day activities. All the necessary instructions can be given during the briefing. The coach reaches the hotel and the tourists are offloaded and led to the hotel registration counter.

Once the hotel has been reached, proceed quickly to the reception, make introductions and ensure smooth registration. A tour manager collects the room numbers and allocates them to the rooming list. Let the tourists get registered as per the need and distribute the room keys to them. If needed, establish a hospitality desk to be staffed for the duration of the tour at pre-arranged times. Prior to that, a tour manager can clarify each and every aspect during the stay, such as meals schedule, rules and guidelines, and facilities. Before tourists occupy their respective rooms, all details regarding stay, food, starting time, hotel rules, etc. must be communicated to them. Also, provide further instructions about the next procedures, and tell them their room number. Once they have their key, they can proceed to their respective rooms. The tour manager can ensure that all rooms are well equipped and all facilities are working properly. The tour manager can then occupy their room, relax and see the proceedings of the day. It is important to match the itinerary with timings provided. In between, the tour manager can visit the facilities at the hotel, such as restaurants, bars and shops. Confirm food arrangements as per the bookings. Take care of the safety of rooms and valuables and remind members about things to be done.

To continue orientation about the day's activities, arrange for everyone to meet in a separate restaurant or hall. After relaxing, let the tourists come for the refreshments/meal as per the itinerary. The orientation meeting can be held in the same restaurant if there is space; otherwise it can be held at another convenient location. Ensure further activities like sightseeing. Advise participants on time, dress codes, valuables, luggage, cameras, tip policies, etc. Tourists will have a wide range of queries. Reply to them patiently, without causing delays to the tour. By this point the tour manager should already have contacted the tour guide so that the tour can commence on time. It is important to make sure that the local guide and the coach come at the right time. A local guide is made available usually as part of the package arranged by the tour operator. The cost of the guide is built into the overall cost of the tour. Local guides are preferred in many destinations where local customs, traditions, and other cultural and natural aspects have to be described in detail. They also help in giving directions, parking vehicles, etc. At times, the driver of the coach acts as the guide as well. They also help to handle baggage. It is recommended that the tour operator choose a guide who is cooperative.

Tourists must be well aware of the tour's starting time. After the refreshments, and without delay, the tour manager leads the tourists to the coach. If tourists are in their rooms, it is better to call them a few minutes before the time of departure to remind them when day trips leave. The tour manager should be ready well in advance. Once the tour members arrive, greet them with a smile and enquire about their stay, required refreshments, etc., and then lead them to the coach, which is ready with the driver and guide. It is necessary at this point to do a head count to ensure that everyone is present. Usually there won't be any luggage to carry except for some snacks, extra clothing and other essentials for the travel. If some tourists are carrying luggage, let them load it into the relevant space for keeping luggage. As everyone has now occupied their seats, the tour manager can provide a brief – where they are heading to and what they are going to see. If needed, the guide can also provide a brief about the nuances of the attractions they are going to visit. As they travel, the guide and tour manager can provide commentary about the geography, unique aspects of the place, things they can see en route, etc.

Once they have reached the location, let the tourists move to the attraction. In cases of there being an entry fee, make the necessary arrangements for it. Make sure that the vehicle is locked properly, and in case tourists have brought valuables along, let them carry these items with them. The guide can take up the roles of leader and interpreter. It is also important to provide authentic information and interesting titbits to the tourists. Ensure the minimum time needed to visit the attraction is given to tourists; don't rush them through the attraction. Respect local customs and traditions. For instance, if footwear must be removed prior to entering a holy place, ensure tourists adhere to this. The dress code must also be followed. After the visit, if it is mealtime, take them to the right places. Care must be taken when choosing suitable restaurants or food centres. Cleanliness, quality, variety, speed of service, ambience, cost, etc. have to be considered. Allow tourists to enjoy the meals in their own time, but remind them what time the tour needs to move on.

After the meal, the tour can travel to the next place. If needed, allow the guide to do their commentary, but restrict it according to the mood of the group. To avoid the inevitable monotony of the coach journey, invite tourists to take part in entertainment activities and games, especially if it is a long way to the next stop. Provide scope for rest of the tour and for toilet facilities, etc. If possible, allow for stops at good locations to take advantage of photo opportunities. In the meantime, when they stop for sightseeing, small-scale shopping for indigenous souvenir items can also be done. However, this should not take too much time from the tour. Don't have daylong sightseeing trips and avoid back-to-back days of travel. In the evening, possible entertainment options may be provided depending on the available time. For entertainment, there must be variety. The times of the entertainment elements are important. Entertainment should be organized at night, so that it does not interfere with daytime activities, e.g. sightseeing, shopping etc.

Providing a shopping slot is very important in an overseas tour. An adequate time period has to be provided for it. Shopping options can be included for a few hours en route, a few minutes after lunch, one or two evenings or even half a day. The timing should be controlled. Local guides, the tour manager and hotel staff can also provide the necessary tips for shopping. A shopping centre is the most appropriate venue for this; the local guide's/tour manager's personal interest should not be the reasons for choosing a place for shopping. Moreover, it is unacceptable for a tour manager or guide to attempt to get commission from shops for bringing tourists there – it can inspire a lack of trust in the tourists.

In respect of tips, provide tourists with proper instructions. As mentioned elsewhere, some tips and service charges are included in the cost of the tour package; hence it will be dealt with by the tour operator directly. In other cases, the tour manager can provide advice about where a tip may be given, where it should not be given, the usual amount given, etc. The norms vary from place to place, and it is not mandatory. Package tours usually provide a slot for optional tours as well. The tourists are free to decide what optional tour they would like to participate in. The cost for this may need to be carried by the tourist. The manager has to provide proper guidance. If needed, arrangements can be made for tourists based on their request. Some may want to visit their friends or relatives staying somewhere near the destination, and if time permits, this can be arranged.

If the tour lasts for many days, it is important that it follows the itinerary. On evenings, provide the necessary entertainment and variety of items. Though hotel bookings can be shifted if the tour moves to a distant place, changing of hotels too often will cause problems for tourists, who have to pack and unpack often. Also, on some days let them wake up a bit later than usual. If they have to get up early every day and go sightseeing, the tour can become a bit mechanical.

The night before the final day of the tour is very important. It is something that can create a lasting impression in tourists' minds. Usually, on this night, a grand dinner and entertainment options are arranged. This is usually part of the package. Make sure that there is a variety of food served, and that the food is what the tourists like. Buffet is usually preferred. Drinks may also be provided, but it may be at an extra cost for the tourists. Along with this, an entertainment programme is also arranged. By this stage, tour members would have developed a very good rapport and understanding among them, so a warm, friendly social environment may be created on that night. The partying may go on late into the night. However, a very late night can cause problems for the next day's activities. The tour manager therefore has to make sure that the tourists don't return to their rooms too late. Besides, it is important to give instructions for the next day's departure and related activities.

Obviously, the tourists are often late the next day morning, but the itinerary prepared would have anticipated that. The manager has to plan the check-out procedures and should have communicated these to the tourists in advance. There may be a visit to a final place before transfer to the airport. The starting time should have been communicated. Remind the tourists again and again about the departure time; a reminder call at least one hour before departure time may be given. Usually, tourists will check out from the hotel and go for a short sightseeing, and then proceed to the airport directly from the location. This depends on the check-out time of the hotel. If there is time, they can return and check out. A head count must be performed whenever they leave and return. If checking out, make sure all luggage has arrived and that nothing has been left in the rooms. The coach has to be ready by this point. Also, the tour manager has an important duty to settle the bills of the hotel. If any tourists have consumed extra services from the hotel, the amount to be paid by them has to be communicated early; it is also important that they make the payments themselves. All other payment settlement as per the contract should have been done by this point. Provide a pre-check-out briefing time for communicating transfer details, airline seating, check-in details and duty-free shopping details, and ensure that all documents are ready with the tourists. Once they reach the airport, give instructions again on how to proceed through airport check-in, passport control and security check. Also, duty-free shopping can be done inside the airport.

One thing which is very important is that the tour manager records all activities that happen during the tour, at the right time. Delays in recording can cause omissions for some activities, and later it can cause difficulties for the tour manager when reporting back to the tour operator. Also, each and every payment made by the tour manager should be recorded and all bills/receipts should be collected and kept. Again, if any payment is made without a receipt, then the tour manager may have to cover the expense him/herself.

16.3 Handling emergencies

During the tour, the tour team can encounter different kinds of problems. A variety of emergency situations may emerge, all of which have to be handled with the utmost professionalism and diligence. In fact, a tour manager may come across a wide variety of issues on tours that they will have to manage. Their tact, experience and knowledge will come into play in handling the situations with minimal harm to the tour and the company. First of all, let's look at some of the common difficulties a tour manager may face:

- Poorly planned itinerary
- Flight delays
- Overbooked flights
- Lost luggage, damaged luggage
- Difficult members to handle
- Unpleasant attitudes of the local people/host
- Strikes/roadblocks/unrest

- Currency fluctuation
- Extra surcharge or fee hike, or additional tax
- Negative reviews of chosen destination
- Vehicle breakdown
- Missing tour members
- Participant complaints
- Getting ill
- Culture shock
- Misplacing/loss of travel documents
- Loss of cash and personal items (e.g. gadgets)

An unprofessional itinerary can lead to various issues. It can cause unnecessary repeated visits on certain routes, too much packing and unpacking because of changing hotels, wastage of time at some attractions and lack of time at others, monotony of seeing the same type of attractions and the like. As a tour manager, you are permitted to alter the tour itinerary, and discuss possible solutions with the tour members and with the tour operator. Care has to be taken that the changes do not lead to extra expenses. Flight delays is a common issue; if it is more than a couple of hours, then the necessary information has to be provided to the tour operator, who can communicate the same to the suppliers on an urgent basis. Necessary steps can be taken to change the schedule. However, it is better not to alter the return arrangements since such a situation will be costly for the tour operator.

Last-minute booking of flights can be very expensive. Within the time, necessary modifications can be made so that the tourists can visit all the places and enjoy the tour to the maximum extent. Overbooked flights can cause problems, as some passengers may only be able to fly on the next available flight. In order to avoid such situations, tour operators should confirm the reservations well in advance. Also, check-in has to be done as early as possible. If it does happen, a tour manager may take action to support that passenger who misses the flight as a result of overbooking. Luggage issues can also occur. Luggage can disappear, be misplaced (in a bus, train station or on a flight). Loss of baggage during flights has been reduced substantially in recent years, since modern, IT-based solutions for baggage handling have been utilized. However, tourists' baggage still gets lost on occasion. For a tourist, it can be a frustrating or even embarrassing situation. They may not have enough clothing to wear, and in the meantime, while they are waiting for their bags to turn up, the tourist may find it difficult to enjoy their tour in the absence of many of their essential items. A tour manager can assist the tourist in retrieving the luggage as soon as possible. It is important to have a regular count, and ensure the bags are properly tagged and numbered, etc. If luggage is lost, take immediate steps with the carrier to try and retrieve it. Moreover, tourists should be instructed not to keep valuables in their checked luggage.

The presence of a difficult member in the group tour can spoil the mood of the tour. A difficult member is someone who does not follow the common protocols, manner and customs of the tour. There are different types of difficult members. Some tour members may consume too much alcohol too often. Others may be tardy all the time. Some may take extra time in visiting places and don't follow the instructions of the tour manager. Some can display an indifferent attitude to the tour. A tour manager has to be diplomatic and tactful when handling such people, so as not to hurt these people's feelings; but at the same time manage them so that others' freedom and enjoyment are not negatively affected. Tours sometimes encounter strikes/roadblocks/unrest. Vehicle breakdown is another common issue. The tour manager should try to take stock of the situation with the help of the ground handling agent or overseas resort representative. If the situation is going to be worse, it is better to alter the route, etc. Decisions can be taken in consultation with tour members as well.

Financial situations in a destination can vary. Inflation is one factor which can affect the profitability of the tour. Also, tourists may find it difficult to purchase items not included in the package. Prior to the commencement of the tour, a tour operator can review the economic aspects in the destination. They can do the same for currency fluctuations. If there are any surcharges, fee hikes or additional tax, a tour manager has to be careful to manage these without affecting the tour's profitability. Tourists may also be levied after making them understand the situation, particularly in light of possible negative news reports about the destination. A tour manager has a role to play in making the tourists understand the situation and go ahead with the plan.

Sometimes a tour member goes missing. In such a situation, the action taken depends on where the member went missing. Always try to have members' phone numbers, email addresses, copies of identification, etc. Also, check with family members, the agency and friends. All tourists can carry the phone numbers of some fellow tourists as well as the tour manager. The tour manager can search for the missing tourist, and if it becomes necessary police authorities can also be informed. There is the possibility of some tour participants getting ill as a result of pollution levels, food poisoning, allergies, etc. The tour manager should always have a stock of common medicines. The tour manager/overseas representative ensures that the tour participant who is sick consults a doctor and is hospitalized if necessary. They also ensure the participant gets the proper treatment, informs the authorities, and updates the participant's relatives and dependents on their condition. If necessary and possible, they can claim from the insurance provider for covering the treatment expenses. If necessary, the tour manager may stay back to assist the sick tourist.

Misplacing/loss of travel documents and loss of cash and personal items (e.g. gadgets) are common issues during travel. Necessary instructions should have been provided to participants during the commencement of the tour itself about the possibilities of such incidents. If items are lost, check everywhere again. If they don't turn up, contact the nearest police station and the relevant embassy (in the case of lost travel documents). It is always useful for the tour manager to have a copy of the relevant travel document pages of the tour members. Regarding cash, it is always better to carry other forms of money, e.g. credit cards, cash cards, etc. Culture shock is caused by experiencing unexpected cultural aspects of a destination. The tour manager has to prepare the tourist before the commencement of the tour for such cultural aspects so that the tourist is able to adapt to/absorb the strangeness. Participants complaining is also common. Some complaints can be resolved easily, whereas others may take more time and effort. Complaints about suppliers are more difficult to handle. Such complaints should still be taken seriously and attempts made to resolve them as satisfactorily as possible. In future, such suppliers may be avoided.

Most of the issues described above will be familiar to all tour operators. But there are other more severe issues that a tour manager must handle more seriously. Such emergencies are, to a large extent, beyond the control of the tour manager or tour operator. There can be a variety of emergency situations, though they are less common than those already described. The following are some of the emergencies that are possible on a tour:

- Death of a tourist
- War and political turmoil

- Terrorist activities
- Natural disasters
- Accidents and emergencies, etc.

The death of a tourist is obviously a serious issue. A lot of formalities and procedures have to be followed, and other tourists may not be able to wait for such procedures to be completed. The tour manager also has to look after the other tourists. The ground handling agent can help a lot in this situation. When a death occurs, it is of utmost importance to inform the local authorities, with the help of ground handling agencies. Essentially, a tour manager has to contact the relevant embassy and police, and inform the tour operator to make the necessary arrangements and inform the deceased's family, as well as carry out any other related activities. Also, all necessary formalities need to be completed with the assistance of local representatives. The hospital, local municipal authorities, police, etc. need to be consulted for undertaking all activities. An important task is also booking the flight for carrying the body home. The tour manager will often have to lead from the front. The remaining part of the tour can be handled by another professional from the ground handling agency or another suitable person. The tour manager is not in a position to handle crises like natural disasters, war, political turmoil, etc. Instead, they can make all efforts to understand the situation, consult with the tour operator as well as the tourists and take necessary steps with due consensus of the tourists. Consult with local handlers, police, etc. Also, keep updated with the latest news. Act according to the intensity of the issue. Also, if possible, a tour may be diverted to another location. If that is not possible, it better to leave the place when it is safe to do so. The same is the case for terrorism activities. Contacting the respective embassy for assistance is necessary in all such situations. Local authorities can also be contacted.

Whatever the situation, the tour manager has to show character and leadership qualities. It's imperative to use commonsense and experience, with the support of tourists. The tour manager and overseas representative have to act quickly and efficiently in the event of a crisis. They must ensure they understand everyone's distress. Try to get the cooperation and support of local agencies as well, including ground handling agents. Someone responsible, with proper linkages and knowledge, should take charge to coordinate the crisis management activities. When the problems are beyond the tour manager's control, it is important to maintain a calm demeanour so that the tourists don't panic.

16.4 Post-tour activities

The tour manager reports back on everything that happened during the tour. The tour record will be handed over to the tour operator, along with the payment receipts. The tour operator, without delay, pays all outstanding bills to suppliers. The feedback forms are collected and analysed for evaluating the effectiveness and efficiency of tour preparations and to take necessary precautions in the future. In the meantime, the department concerned has to calculate the profit accrued as part of the tour operation, and see if profit is not generated or is less than expected. In this case, they will have to find out what went wrong. **Debriefing** the tour manager will be done to understand the tour's level of success. The tour manager has to be given enough time to briefly describe all the activities in the tour. Their feedback and opinion are collected, along with descriptions of what worked and didn't work during the whole tour process. A written report is also usually collected. This process is very important for future preparations. Also, the tour manager needs to be appreciated for their time, efforts and hard work, and for (hopefully) making the tour a success. In the meantime, all tour members have to be contacted again with the help of the mailing list created (the existing database of past customers will have been expanded by then), so that the tour operator can convey their gratitude for joining the tour and for their cooperation for making it a success. If possible, organize a reunion of all the tour members. This will help in getting more of their opinions and to form long-lasting relationships with them. The tour file is now ready to close. Before that, however, all the documents have to be gone through again, along with forwarding of all client referrals to the sales department. Before this process, the tour planning department might have started planning and designing activities for future tour projects. The essential findings of the post-tour evaluation will be passed on to them to make the necessary adjustments for future tours.

16.5 Overseas tour representatives

Overseas tour representatives are those who look after tourists who come on a package tour and arrange the required services and facilities on behalf of the outbound tour operator. With the exception of large tour operators, many cannot afford to have their own branches to handle the visiting tourists. Also, it is not possible for a tour operator to have their own office in each of the destinations they operate in. Overseas tour representatives are utilized in these circumstances. Their job is to ensure that the tour runs smoothly and efficiently, and that tourists enjoy their stay. There are different types of overseas tour representatives. The following are some of the most common:

- *Tourist/customer service representative:* they act like a host to assist tourists who are on a holiday in the destination and arrange the required services and facilities for them.
- *Resort representative:* they perform almost all duties of an overseas tour representative, but do so from a resort.
- *Children's representatives:* they offer dedicated childcare services for tourists during the day in particular.
- *Entertainment representatives:* they provide different entertainment programmes for the tourists to enjoy during the trip.
- *Transfer representatives:* they accompany tourists during transfers.
- *Young people's representatives:* they arrange services for young tourists, including entertainment and recreation activities.
- *Club representatives:* they are a type of resort representative, e.g. "Gentils Organisateurs" (GOs) of Club Med (Club Méditerranée).
- *"Mobile resort representative"/courier:* they are like guides, accompanying tourists during sightseeing trips and providing commentary during travel times, especially on coach trips.

A wide variety of activities are undertaken by overseas tour representatives. When tourists arrive, they meet and greet them at the airport and arrange transfers to the hotel. Also, necessary assistance is given for check-in at the hotel. They also ensure the services are at the customer's expected level of quality. They have relationships with suppliers and ground handling agents and act as liaisons for such, and they sell or arrange sightseeing tours and transport services on demand – as per the needs of the tourists. If needed, they also escort tourists on sightseeing trips. Moreover, an overseas representative handles client issues and manages the crises that occur as part of the tour. Having good relationships with other tourism stakeholders in the destination, overseas representatives can be instrumental in ensuring a hassle-free tour. Also, it is mandatory to act as a concierge and maintain in-depth knowledge of the facilities and services in and around the destination in order to answer tourist queries. Other types of assistance are also provided for tourists, such as childcare during the day, organizing entertainments, etc. Horner (1996) provides a number of reasons for engaging overseas representatives for an outbound tour in a destination:

- Meet and greet the group on arrival at airport/resort.
- Provide the accommodation centres with rooming lists.
- Facilitate the participants to occupy rooms in hotels.
- Help participants to enjoy the holiday.
- Act as concierge, provide information on local facilities.
- Sort out any potential problems.
- Take care of children, on demand, where children's clubs are provided.
- Help to organize entertainment programmes.
- Assist the tourist with medical requirements, if and when it is necessary.
- Make arrangements for those who need repatriation.
- Escort clients to the departure point at the end of the tour.
- Help clients to prepare a company report.

16.6 Tour guiding

Among the different types of travellers, tourists are the most curious. Curiosity to know, feel and learn something different is a prime motive for tourists. While visiting, tourists will certainly look for information about what they see and experience. A tour guide is the term used for a professional who can assist a tourist to learn about the nuances of a tourist attraction. Though it only emerged as a profession in recent times, tour guides of different types have been around for centuries. Interpretation is the basis of tour guiding, but guiding has wider functions. There are interpreters in some attractions that require detailed explanations for tourists.

16.6.1 Interpretation

Before elucidating the concept of tour guiding, let's examine interpretation and its significance in tourism. Interpretation requires deeper knowledge and has more of an educational function. Basically, interpretation in tourism is about explaining and attempting to educate tourists about the natural, cultural or historic values attached to attractions, and to enable tourists to gain an understanding of various aspects associated with those attractions and their conservation. The Society for Interpreting Britain's Heritage (1998) defines it as "the process of explaining to people the significance of the place or object they have come to see, so that they enjoy their visit more, understand their heritage and environment better, and develop a more caring attitude towards conservation". According to Rennie, in tourism interpretation aims to increase tourist understanding, awareness and appreciation of various resources. Communicating a message with regard to nature and culture is another objective. Involve people in nature and history through first-hand experience with the natural and cultural environment; provide an enjoyable and meaningful experience; increase the public's understanding and support for the agency's role, its management objectives and policies; and encourage the behaviours and attitudes of people on the correct use of natural resources, the preservation of natural and cultural heritage, and the respect and concern towards the environment – both natural and cultural (Rennie, in Knudson et al., 1995). Randall and Rollins (2009) argue that interpretation is a form of education that concentrates on meanings and relationships by employing original objects, first-hand experience and illustrative media rather than by communicating factual information. Interpretation has its own significance in tourism. Along with the educational aspect, interpretation in tourism absorbs other aspects. Moscardo and Woods (1998) identify the following important aspects of interpretation in tourism:

- It can educate visitors about the nature of the attractions and places they are visiting and inform them of the consequences of their behaviour, with the aim to inspire them to act in more appropriate ways.
- It can enhance cooperation and support of visitors for environmental conservation and management activities.
- It can reduce crowding in sensitive areas and relieve pressure on sites by encouraging visitors to move to less sensitive or crowded places and by providing them with alternative experiences.
- In its entirety, it can help to enhance the quality of visitor experiences, adding value to tourism products.

Interpretation thus has much significance in tourism. There are various kinds of interpreters in tourist attractions. A tour guide is different from an interpreter, but the role does encompass that of an interpreter on a limited basis, i.e. whenever it is needed. A tour guide, compared to an interpreter, has diverse roles. In most cases, a tour guide travels with tourists and talks about the features of attractions. Interpreters, meanwhile, are based at a particular site and provide specific information with authority. A tour guide may have wider knowledge and disseminate information about different attractions during a sightseeing trip. A comparison of tour guides, interpreters and tour managers is provided in Table 16.1.

16.6.2 Tour guide

Some authors have equated tour guides with other tourism professionals, such as tour leaders, tour managers, tour escorts, local guides, docents and interpreters (Hu, 2007). Certainly, there are different types of tour guides, but the role is different from that of a tour manager, tour leader and tour escort. The World Federation of Tourist Guide Associations (WFTGA) makes clear distinctions between a tour guide and other professions, saying that a tour guide is "a person who guides visitors in the language of their choice and interprets the cultural and natural heritage of an area which person normally possesses an area-specific qualification usually issued and/or recognized by the appropriate authority" (WFTGA, 2003). On the other hand, based on the definition of the European Committee for Standardization (CEN), a tour manager, tour director or an escort is specified as "a person who manages an itinerary on behalf of the tour operator ensuring the programme is carried out as described in the tour operator's literature and sold to the traveller/consumer and who gives local practical information" (quoted in WFTGA,

2003). Here, it is also pointed out that a tour guide is a person with the necessary qualifications and with a licence issued by an authority to act as a guide.

A tour guide is usually a licensed professional who interprets and explains the features of attractions to tourists when they are on a visit. Guiding may be considered both a formal and informal sector activity, with variation in the degree of formality (Cukier, 1998). Tour guides have been called "orphans of the travel industry" (Pond, 1993) due to the nature of the job. A tour guide usually works independently, as a freelancer. Some work regularly with reputable tour operators; and some are included in the national tourism office (NTO)/destination marketing organization's (DMO) list of professional guides. Some are part-timers who do it as extra work to earn more money. Some are full-time professionals. Seasonality is an important factor. Getting full-time employment as a guide is difficult in some destinations. As a professional who enhances the tourist experience, a tour guide demands remuneration at a similar level to higher level tourism professionals. Laws (1997) defines a guide as "a destination based person who accompanies holiday makers during local excursions and who interprets aspects of local culture and other points of interest". A tour guide is usually a person who comes from the destination the tourist is visiting and interprets various features of the attractions while travelling along with the tourists on their excursions. A tour manager, on the other hand, is the one vested with the responsibility to lead and manage the tour based on a pre-set itinerary. Mancini (2001) defines a tour guide as someone who takes people on sightseeing excursions of limited duration. This makes the point that tour guiding is for a limited period of time, i.e. not for the entire tour. Therefore, the tour guide performs their duty for a shorter length of time compared to the tour manager. The time allocated for guiding is pre-scheduled, so the tour guide will join the tour group as per the schedule. Some of the authors have pointed out that a tour guide is responsible for directing and leading tourists in the process of a tour. For instance, Chilembwe and Mweiwa (2014) write that a "tour guide is responsible for directing and leading tourists on a tour or sightseeing".

In certain cases, a tour guide may also lead the group. In an escorted tour, this function is limited. Though a professional tour guide is able to carry out a variety of responsibilities, the roles played depend on the setting, the visitor, the purpose of the visit and indeed the tour guide. It reiterates the fact that tour guides are also expected to share certain managerial responsibilities as and when the need arises, depending upon the setting and circumstances. At times, they are expected to take care of the entire tour, starting from receiving the guest and ending at seeing them off. A guide acts as a link between the tourist and local people. Necessary public relations activities are undertaken by the guide. They have to ensure that the tour will be enjoyable and as safe as possible. Furthermore, a tour guide is vested with the responsibility for creating a positive image of the destination and the country. The tourists are strangers in the destination and local cultural features may seem very odd to them. A tour guide can help them to understand the local culture and enable them to adjust to it. As a tour guide has to take up different roles, they have to be multiskilled, too. Various roles, skills required and qualities of a professional guide are explained later.

Based on the above discussion, a tour guide can be defined as a destination-based professional who accompanies a group of tourists or an individual tourist on sightseeing trips with the intention of explaining and interpreting various aspects of the region and its attractions, and creating interest and a favourable image of the destination in their minds.

Tour guiding is a very important activity in the tour operation process. Its significance is not restricted to tourists. A tour guide is also an important professional for a tour

Table 16.1 Tour guide, interpreter and tour manager: the differences

Tour guide	Interpreter	Tour manager
Travels with the group of tourists	Does not travel with the group	Travels with the group of tourists
Joins the group when needed	Performs interpretation when tourists reach a site	Accompanies the tourists throughout the journey
Primarily a communicator	Primarily an educator	Primarily has an administrator's role
Plays diverse roles and has diverse responsibilities	Limited roles and responsibilities, comparatively	Plays a number of roles, with the prime focus of running the tour smoothly
Needs wider knowledge along with detailed knowledge on different attractions	Needs authentic and specific knowledge about a particular site	Does not necessarily possess detailed local knowledge
Guide can be an interpreter as well, as per the need	Interpreter need not be a tour guide	Takes up the roles of interpreter and guide on rare occasions in a limited way
Limited responsibility in the successful conduct of the tour	Interpreter seldom involved in the conduct of the tour	Tour manager is the ultimate personnel in the successful conduct of the tour

operator, as they interact directly with tourists at perhaps the most important stage of the tour. The quality and efficiency of the tour guide's service certainly matter for the overall success of the tour. For tourists, they are very important people to know in the destination, for seeking help, for receiving guidance, for understanding the local culture, for knowing about the features of the places visited, for getting advice and so on. The tour guide is also very significant for a destination. They act as a kind of cultural ambassador and image booster for the region. Guides interact a lot with tourists during their travel around a destination. During the interaction, a guide has to attempt to interpret the cultural features of the destination and the society at large in a positive way, and try to foster respect for the local culture among the tourists. Ultimately, the tour guide should attempt to boost the image of the destination through guiding. An efficient tour guiding process contributes to the tourist experience and eventually helps to generate favourable "word of mouth" after the tour. Thus, the tour guide acts as marketer for the destination. Moreover, by stimulating interest among tourists to see more places, a guide can help in extending a tourist's stay in the destination. Also, by encouraging tourist behaviour to be eco-friendly, a tour guide helps to ensure the tourism process in the destination is sustainable. A guide can also stimulate interest in buying different products and souvenirs from the destination. Ultimately, a tour guide adds value to the whole tourism process.

16.6.3 Evolution of tour guiding

Different sorts of tour guides existed at different stages in tourism history. The profession evolved over centuries, and when modern tourism began, the modern tour guiding profession started to take shape. An analysis of the history reveals that tour guides were more than simply leaders of expeditions to strange places and interpreters. They were seen in other forms as well, like the "mentor" tour guides during the grand tour era. The guides during the grand tour in Europe were more professional compared to previous guides. They were called "Cicerones". Cohen's (1985) theory of the evolution of modern guides is the most discussed piece of literature about the evolution of tour guides. Cohen illustrates that the professional guide is an evolved form of the "original guide", and the modern guide descends from "pathfinder" and "mentor" lineage. The pathfinder is equated with the geographic guide, who leads the way. Examples include mountain guides, safari guides, etc. Pathfinders were basically guides who "showed the way" and led visitors to places for which the visitors lacked orientation, or through socially defined territories with little access for visitors. Fundamentally, the pathfinder is the guide who leads others through social and natural areas unknown to their followers. They mainly pointed out the routes and were mostly the natives of the destination region. They seldom elaborated on tourism features of a destination and were seen in relatively undeveloped regions with more natural attractions and resources. Meanwhile, the "mentor" category of guide has more diverse and complex roles. The mentor is embedded within the concepts of personal tutor and spiritual advisor. A tour guide is like a specialist or guru to the seeker, aiming at creating insight and enlightenment.

Cohen identifies the spiritual advisor in a pilgrimage tour, and the personal travelling tutor, who was seen in the grand tour era, is a typical mentor guide. For mentor guides, organization, practicality and entertainment are of minor importance; they were seen more in established tourist locations. He clarifies that an "original guide" is like the simple pathfinder, with instrumental responsibilities, and a "professional guide" is more sophisticated, with increased relevance for communication (Cohen, 1985). As the years passed and modern tourism continued to evolve, tourists' expectations of tour guides grew. Tour guides had to make tourist trips interesting, comfortable and convenient, and provide interpretation services. Modern tourism therefore evolved, with increased roles, responsibilities and skills.

16.6.4 Roles of the guide

A tour guide takes up different roles in the process of tour guiding. For playing each role, a guide needs separate skills. Different authors have identified different mixes of roles for tour guides. For instance, Pond (1993) identifies five important roles of a tour guide: the leader, the educator, the public relations representative, the host and the conduit. Cohen (1985) had already identified four distinct roles:

- *The instrumental role:* the focus is on providing directions, navigation, access to the territory and safety.
- *The interactional role:* the focus is on representation of the area in a non-threatening manner and organization.
- *The social role:* the focus is on social roles, which include tension management, social integration and cohesion, humour and entertainment, used to maintain and build group morale.
- *The communicative role:* the focus is on the dissemination of correct information, translating the unfamiliar and selecting points of interest for the group.

A modern tour guide synthesizes and applies a range of roles to ensure utmost satisfaction for the tourist and to remain competitive. Some of the roles of a tour manager are also undertaken by the tour guide. Some of the identified roles are:

- *Leader:* joins the tour and leads the tourists through the destination and coordinates the visit in an enjoyable manner
- *Communicator:* ensures interactive communication, presents the facts and stories about the attractions and highlights
- *Educator:* interprets cultural and natural features and educates the tourists about various aspects of the destination
- *The host:* being the local person, and a professional service provider, they have to receive the guests and act as the link between tourists and locals
- *Motivator:* inspires, motivates and gives confidence to the tourists to visit and enjoy the tour
- *PR representative:* acts as a cultural ambassador and creates a positive image for the destination and the country
- *Entertainer:* creates interest and enlivens the tour activities
- *Sustainability confirmer:* is required to promote eco-friendly practices, create social, cultural and environmental protection awareness and ensure that tourists follow sustainability practices
- *Complaint handler:* offers assistance to the tourists to resolve their issues and to get quality products and services
- *Concierge:* provides a variety of information about local services and facilities
- *Advisor:* provides advice for many different activities, like shopping, optional tours, etc.

16.6.5 Tour guiding: Various aspects

Guiding is undoubtedly an art form. A tour guide has to perform before tourists using their inherent characteristics and enhanced skills, while remaining professional, so as to stimulate interest among tourists to learn about the destination and its features. The performance of a tour guide is also a determinant in the success of a tour programme, and for a tourist it is imperative to have a memorable tourist experience. A wide range of aspects can be identified in tour guiding, which highlights the complexity of the profession. Guiding is not an easy job as it needs a wide range of skills, a good knowledge base about different aspects of a destination, several personal qualities and commonsense. Tourists are in an unfamiliar context with limited knowledge of local community life for only a short time. They have different cultural backgrounds and it is the tour guide's job to acquaint them with the local culture. The job of a guide is not just to educate visitors about a monument or destination; it also includes helping visitors understand and appreciate the destination. For a tourist, a guide is an expert on everything in a destination. Besides being responsible to tourists for providing high-quality experiences through interpretation and education, a tour guide has to act as the ambassador of the community as well as a representative of the tour company. These three stakeholders (tourist, destination and tour operator) expect maximum contribution from a tour guide.

Being a responsible citizen and a tourism professional, a tour guide has to act responsibly as a representative of the country and the people. Tourists are strangers in a destination. While guiding, a tour guide must explain the local customs and traditions properly and sensitively. A tour guide must be motivated to stimulate the tourist's interest to delve deeper into the culture. Also, the cultural features of the region have to be interpreted in a positive way so as to foster a sense of respect among the tourists towards the cultural features of a country. The need for religious sensitivity must be communicated to tourists and necessary information should be provided before entering religious sites/buildings. For instance, the dress code for visitors in religious sites must be followed by everyone.

Similar to an interpreter, a tour guide is entrusted with the responsibility to create awareness about cultural and environmental protection. Moreover, they have to make sure every activity/assignment is fun while at the same time respecting the environment, wildlife, sights and monuments, and local customs and traditions. Necessary instructions and dos and don'ts in terms of social, cultural and environmental sustainability need to be communicated to tourists before they enter a site. A tour guide can attempt to modify and correct visitor behaviour to ensure that it is environmentally responsible and reflects environmentally sensitive attitudes. Also, a tour guide has to act as a watchdog to ensure that tourists and the tour process do not harm nature or society in any way.

While explaining, it is important to distinguish the truth from stories, legends and traditions. There will be different stories associated with a site. Some may be based on historical facts. Others may just be stories or myths. It is the tour guide's job to distinguish them. However, interesting stories can add to the appeal of an attraction/destination for tourists. Having said that, never take advantage of tourists' ignorance. A tour guide should enlighten the tourists by providing the appropriate and correct information. It makes the visit more meaningful and worthwhile for tourists. Also, a tour guide has to be honest when proving the information. Being a stranger in the destination and being curious, a tourist may ask questions for clarity and to know more. A tour guide has to be equipped with the knowledge and be patient enough to answer them. Educate your guests about objects of interest, artefacts, natural or cultural assets of the destination, events, people, etc. Showing a disregard for queries and becoming irritated will put tourists off from the process and discourage guide–tourist interaction. There may be some situations in which you are unable to answer a tourist's question. Use common sense and be honest by saying, "I don't know, but I can find out for you". Don't pretend you know the correct answer and then give false information.

A tour guide has to stay updated to avoid embarrassing situations in front of tourists. In this era of information technology, getting information is very easy and is usually at one's finger tips. If tour guides provide outdated information and tourists realize it, the guide's respect may be damaged. Moreover, knowledge enhances a guide's confidence. One important point to always remember is that tour operators and tourists always seek tour guides who can provide specific, interesting, factual and authentic information. It is good to have reasonable knowledge on current affairs and local and global news and environmental issues. A tour guide is also responsible for the safety of tourists while they are in a destination. Some of the sites pose risks, and negligence can turn dangerous. While guiding, a tour guide must provide the necessary safety information to avoid risks and take precautions. It is important to provide the relevant information so as to encourage safety and comfort. This way, tourists know how to cope with and better manage encountered difficulties and correctly interpret the warning signs.

CASE STUDY 16.1

Detour: a mobile tour guide

A tour operator needs a range of information and communication technologies (ICT) for its successful operation and effective marketing, and to remain competitive in the market. According to Buhalis (2003), a wide range of applications of ICT is possible for tour operators. They need ICT for strategic and operational tools to coordinate their departments and improve internal efficiency. Electronic management of inventory with the principals is also a requirement in tour operation. Technology solutions are used to keep watch on the external environments. In order to manage the tourists' journey while they are on it, tour operators may have to rely on ICT. Moreover, ICT can be used for enhancing customer satisfaction as well. Customer relationship management (CRM) in this modern era is not possible without electronic relationship and retention practices. Tour operators also have to make use of CRM. ICT is of great use for core managerial functions, like accounting, HR, etc. Furthermore, ICT has an important role to play in marketing, distribution and sales. Extranets can be developed with separate clients, like hotels, travel agencies, etc. IT use in market intelligence gathering and market research is also significant, as it is for destination research, product design, customization and in providing value-added services.

IT applications in tourism are expanding and mobile tour guides are an innovative way of enhancing the tourist experience. Basically, mobile guides are location-based systems (LBSs) developed in the area of tourism. They combine geographic information systems (GIS) and tourism information and deliver relevant information to tourists on the spot. Geographic data in the form of maps include a special form of data that can be delivered to tourists. These maps provide a snapshot of the tourists' environment at a particular location and time, and are able to enhance the tourists' activities and enjoyment. The latest examples of these applications have increased services.

Detour is one example of a mobile tour guide application that can virtually replace traditional tour guides..It's an audio guide that reacts to the user's actual location. Using the mobile phone's GPS to pinpoint the user's location, the app can offer an insider perspective of destinations, often with interviews of people a tourist can meet in person on their journey. Headquartered in San Francisco, Detour was launched in February 2015 with 150 immersive audio walks in 17 cities. Tours can be bought individually or tourists can buy a yearly pass for $20. Currently, Detour provides audio guides to many cities across the world, matching the narrations to the specific locations using a phone's GPS. Moreover, audio cues prompt the tourists to pause and listen to the narration. The addition of interviews and interactions with local people or experts can certainly enhance the tourist experience greatly. For example, the tour of San Francisco's Fisherman's Wharf explores the working side of the wharf. The user can see where fishermen unload their daily catch, and learn about hidden gems in the area, including a vintage arcade with working games from the 1800s. When the tourist arrives at a stop, the narrator explains its significance, etc. and then leads them to the additional land-marks, vistas, museums and restaurants. The biggest advantage for a tourist is that the tour can proceed (move from place to place) at their own pace instead of that of a traditional guide. Also, unlike traditional guiding, consistent performance can be expected from mobile tour guides. Detour also plans to release creation tools to the public so that anyone can "make a Detour".

Source: Buhalis (2003); www.detour.com

Read the case study carefully and answer the following questions:

- What do we mean by mobile tour guide?
- Explain the features of Detour.
- Give a brief account of ICT applications in tour operation.

Before commencing, tour guide introduces him/herself and other professionals to the tourists. First impressions are significant in efficient tour guiding; are formed rapidly; and are often highly accurate. Appearance, dressing style, demeanour, a proper introduction, way of greeting, confidence, command of language, etc. contribute to a good first impression. Receive tourists as you would guests in your home. A guide has to make the necessary preparations for the presentation. Try to learn what the guests would like to know and be informed about. It will provide enough hints to make the presentation. Necessary research can also be carried out. Be organized and be clear about what has to be done. Attempting a presentation without due preparation can lead to ineffectiveness and reduce tourist satisfaction. As stated before, tour guiding is an art form. Presentation is the most important element of guiding. Before a presentation, the guide has to be well aware the nature of the audience, and make decisions about where to stand, what tools to use, the time to take for the presentation, and the amount of information to be presented to the audience. Perfect presentation depends a lot on the techniques used. Several factors need to be pointed out in relation to this. It's always better to be on a raised platform while delivering the explanation about a site. Every tourist can see the guide when they are on a raised platform, and it helps in effective communication. The guide should not commence the presentation until the whole group has assembled. The guide has to bring everyone to the place where the talk is going to be held before the presentation begins. Otherwise, some tourists may miss a lot of information and some will ask the guide to repeat it, which can cause delays.

The guide needs to follow the essential communication principles and qualities. Both verbal and non-verbal communication techniques should be used while guiding. Ensure the speech is slow enough for the people to follow. Guides should have good communication skills and clarity of speech. Language proficiency is also a significant factor. Moreover, pronunciation should follow international standards. Tourists need to know in advance which language is going to be used by the guide. The presentation should also be stylish. Eye contact is an important element of effective communication. Care needs to be taken with regard to posture and distracting mannerisms. During the presentation, be aware of necessary voice modulation and pitch control. The presentation has to be audible enough for everyone to hear clearly. Clarity of speech, pace, proper pronunciation, language proficiency and crispness of the speech are the essential features of a good presentation. During the presentation, it is better to use simple vocabulary and grammar. Mixing of humour, as stated earlier, is vital and the presentation should not be too long. The right body movements are needed for good presentations and appropriate technology tools may also be utilized to make it interesting and easier to understand. Along with the facts, some interesting highlights can be included, along with myths, stories, etc. As we have already mentioned, authenticity of information is crucial, and necessary preparations should have been carried out for ensuring this. While presenting, a guide should also listen to the audience, for their questions and opinions and to make the presentation more interactive. Tourists may be encouraged to respond to the details given and to ask questions. The guide has to remain calm and confident throughout the presentation and in all other situations. Avoid jargon and use simple, well-enunciated words. Ensure everyone can hear what is presented. Presentations must seem spontaneous but be well prepared. They should also be well paced and delivered audibly in order to hold the audience's attention. Multilingual skills are also useful.

Note below the gold standard behaviours for a tour guide, according to Mitchell (2005):

- Courteous words instead of sharp replies
- Smiles instead of bored looks
- Enthusiasm instead of dullness
- Response instead of difference
- Warmth instead of coldness
- Understanding instead of closed minds
- Attention instead of neglect
- Patience instead of irritation
- Sincerity instead of being mechanical
- Remembering details instead of forgetting them
- Creative ideas instead of humdrum
- Giving instead of getting
- Action instead of delay
- Appreciation instead of apathy

A guide has to make adjustments based on the needs and desires of the tourists. They need not be rigid in their approach. Necessary changes have to be carried out by the guide according to the mood of the tourists, the circumstances, general tourist behaviour, climatic conditions, available time, number of tourists in the group, knowledge level of tourists, etc. Understanding tourists is essential for a successful guide.

An efficient tour guide can make the guiding process livelier. In some cases, actual experiences can be created so that tourists can participate in activities, e.g. heritage walks, adventures, art gallery visits and educational activities. Instead of one-way talks, these activities will enhance the tourist experience. Good tour guides mix humour during the communication process. A good sense of humour is a useful tool to have. However, the guide cannot be humorous all the time; they need to read every situation and then consider the most appropriate action. Being responsible to the tour operator, it is important for the guide to gather and provide feedback to the company. Keep the tour operator informed of the tour and its progress as often as you can. The feedback from the tour guide is an important resource for the future, specifically when designing new tour packages and selecting attractions and suppliers.

There can be crises at any point in time. The guide has to be aware of how to handle such situations. In the event of a crisis, a tour guide cannot be idle and avoid responsibility, even if the tour manager is available. Instead, the guide and tour manager have to work together to support the emergency efforts and undertake all such activities efficiently. Tourists will have their own issues during the tour. At times, they may complain or they may seek help. Whatever the situation, the tour guide has to empathize with the guest and try to resolve the problem without delay. Showing due concern is important and making efforts to resolve their issues will be appreciated.

Punctuality is mandatory for a tour guide. Before tourists arrive, the guide has to be ready. Professionalism is key in tour guiding. In addition to the qualities and qualifications, a guide should have acquired the necessary skills to exhibit professionalism. Guiding is a multiskilled activity and training at regular intervals is required to remain competitive. Because they deal with tourists from various cultures, tour guides have to demonstrate standard etiquette and manners. The style of communication needs to be reviewed often, and, if needed, modified. Good body language is a sign of a professional tour guide. A guide needs to be well groomed all the time and wear appropriate clothing. A tour guide should, obviously, be inclined to meeting people and interacting with them. Being social and extroverted is crucial for a guide. Good health is also a prerequisite for becoming a guide. A guide needs good energy levels and they have to exhibit liveliness and energy throughout the tour guiding process.

Always act with tact and diplomacy when dealing with guests. An impartial approach is always recommended. Though a tour guide has to demonstrate professionalism, it is important to be oneself as far as this is possible. When making decisions, consider everyone and act for the benefit of the majority. However, try not to hurt any individual's feelings. A general awareness of basic human behaviour and attitudes can help in dealing with tourists in a group. Knowing the group composition as early as possible can be useful in this context. It is recommended to know the names of guests, etc. and address them by their names. Handling difficult people on tour is very important. There can be people in a group who are regularly late, make trouble for others, complain often, are short-tempered, consume alcohol and drugs, etc. Experience, using a psychological approach, etc. can be helpful in containing such tourists.

Prior to the commencement of the tour, review the tour itinerary and check areas of concern. Review transport arrangements, timings, driver, etc. All arrangements can be reconfirmed. The next day's itinerary can be reiterated to the tourists every evening. Also, tourists can be thanked for their patient listening and cooperation. They can also be informed about the stops possible for refreshments, etc. while travelling to different sites in the destination. It is better not to do excess work and become disorganized. Also, care has to be taken not to be too rigid or too flexible, not to party too much with tour participants or spend too much time with someone, overextend them, or cover up the truth while explaining. Also, if you're not physically fit, it's better to avoid the trip and engage someone else for it. While guiding, proper care has to be given to the tour members. Respect their age, particularly senior citizens. A professional guide should be proficient in first-aid activities, and they should carry the details of hospitals and doctors in case they are required.

16.6.6 Traits/qualities of a tour guide

There are many essential traits of a successful guide. The major traits are listed here:

- Enthusiasm
- Willingness and passion

- Genuine interest
- Honesty and sincerity
- Dedication
- Approachable
- Outgoing and social
- Confident
- Integrity and self-esteem
- Active and energetic
- Responsible
- Empathetic
- Sensitive
- Flexible, yet assertive
- Self-control
- Punctuality
- Organizing skills
- Cooperative
- Pleasant
- Sense of humour
- Authentic
- Good communication skills (verbal, non-verbal as well as listening ability)
- Good presentation skills
- Analytical and decisive
- Healthy
- Leadership qualities
- Charismatic
- Patience
- Commonsense
- Dresses well
- Appreciative
- Ability to handle emergencies
- Positive personality
- Love of country
- Good sense of humour
- Sensible and dedicated
- Resourcefulness
- Good knowledge
- Rapport with clients
- Environmentally responsible

16.6.7 Types of tour guide

Different types of tour guides can be found in international tourism. Some of the most common are listed below:

- *On-site guide:* a professional, competent enough to guide in a certain locality or area, they conduct tours for a specific duration at a specific setting such as a building, limited area or attraction
- *Urban guide/city guide:* a guide who specializes in interpreting various features and highlights of cities (large cities may need very specialized guides)

- *Docent:* undertakes interpretation, mostly on a voluntary basis, in a confined location of historical and heritage environments
- *Step-on guide:* a guide joins a coach tour as per the demand and performs interpretation for a small segment of the tour, based on the directions of the tour manager
- *Freelance guide:* functions as a freelancer, is not permanently connected to a tour operator or any other intermediary who organizes a package tour
- *Government guide:* a guide, either full-time and part-time, employed by governments, NTOs and DMOs
- *Specialist tour guide:* a guide who specializes in interpreting certain specific fields such as botany, architecture, environment, marine life, etc.
- *Business or industry guide:* a specialized guide for interpreting various aspects associated with some interesting manufacturing processes in an industry or business
- *Staff guide:* a guide who is permanently associated with a tour operator or any other intermediary who operates package tours; they receive a monthly salary
- *Driver guides:* drivers who act as guides as well
- *Adventure guide:* specialized guides for leading adventure tour groups and helping tourists engage in adventurous activities
- *Local guide:* a person competent enough to guide in a certain locality
- *Personal or private guide:* a guide who operates based on the client's needs and takes tourists in their vehicles or arranged vehicles for sightseeing
- *Shore excursions guide/ship tour guide:* a guide who works for cruise ships and undertakes guiding during shore excursions

16.6.8 Challenges of tour guiding

The tour guiding profession has been facing issues and challenges of various kinds. Some of the most common, current issues and challenges of tour guiding are introduced below:

- *Seasonality:* due to seasonality, the tour guiding profession often cannot sustain full-time employment. Ensuring the quality and professionalism in part-time guides is also a challenge.
- *Updated information:* tourists are able to access the latest information, which is available at their fingertips. Hence, guides should have the latest and most *authoritative* information and knowledge.
- *Technological challenges:* nowadays, there are mobile apps capable of replacing tour guides. Many destinations develop such apps. There are also technological developments such as the global positioning system (GPS), geographic information system (GIS) and destination management system (DMS) which can assist tourists visiting sites without tour guides. All these remain a challenge and actual guides have to be increasingly efficient in delivering their guiding services.
- *Training and development:* tour guides need to regularly refresh and enhance their skills and frequently develop their managerial abilities. The latest presentation techniques have to be acquired and getting effective training is crucial.
- *Lack of qualified guides:* many a time, getting guides with the necessary qualifications is a difficult task. Usually a licence is mandatory in guiding and many destinations face a shortage of licensed guides.
- *Gender issues:* gender issues prevail in some destinations. Female tour guides in some locations are not common.

- *Social stigma:* in many societies, tour guiding still can't acquire the due social status, though recent trends suggest it is gaining in prestige.
- *Travellers are more experienced than before:* hence guides have to be better equipped to face them. Many travellers do not actually need guides.
- *Authenticity:* tourists prefer authentic information and experiential tourism is a trend nowadays. It is a challenge to provide the most authentic information and experiences.
- *Lack of uniformity and national frameworks:* different countries and destinations within countries have different levels of standards for tour guides. Ensuring standardization is still a challenge.
- *Salary and pay:* as stated before, tour guides are often referred to as "orphans" in tourism and many work as freelancers. There is sometimes little regularity in salary/pay, except for staff guides or government guides.
- *Health and dynamism:* a tour guide always has to maintain a high level of health and be dynamic. Being a human being, it is a challenging task to always remain so.

Note below some of the *don'ts* of tour guiding:

- Treating customers indifferently
- Standing or sitting too close to tourists
- Flirting with tour members
- Avoiding tourists when they approach for assistance
- Being cold to customers
- Viewing a topic as uninteresting
- Criticizing those who ask questions, etc.
- Being very rigid with pre-set itinerary and norms
- Treating tourists as ignorant people
- Neglecting tourists' mood, age, health, etc.
- Walking and leading tourists too quickly during sightseeing
- Listening only for facts and faking attention
- Prejudicial or racist remarks
- Arriving later than tourists
- Drug and alcohol consumption
- Undertaking guiding without due preparation

16.7 Need of quality and customer satisfaction

Customer satisfaction is dependent on quality. The service quality in tour operation is an extremely intricate affair. The tour operator alone cannot ensure service quality; it depends on suppliers as well. A tour operator's product involves different services, which are offered by different suppliers. Providing excellent service quality is widely recognized as a critical business requirement (Voss et al., 2004). The same is true of tour operation. The most important task of a tour operator is to identify the right suppliers who can deliver quality services to the tourists. For most of the products with an intangibility aspect, this is a tough task for the operator. Previous experiences, customer feedback, market surveys, etc. can help in identifying the right elements and service providers in the package. Moreover, it is also the duty of operators to interact with suppliers and ensure that the services are provided with utmost efficiency. Even minor negligence from one supplier can negatively affect the mood of an entire group of tourists. Customer satisfaction is directly related to service quality. Indeed, customer satisfaction is based on a range of factors, including customer expectations. Identifying customer expectations before selecting suppliers is crucial. Customer dissatisfaction can be due to a range of factors. When the products and services do not match the customer expectations, there can be dissatisfaction. Service delivery and quality of products and services offered are serious determinants in customer satisfaction. At times, tour operators exaggerate aspects of a tour that in reality are very different. This can happen as a result of poor marketing communication. Inclusion of the correct elements in a package is vital for the success of a tour and in keeping customers happy. There can be customer dissatisfaction due to the inefficiency of a tour manager, tour guide or other overseas representative. The level of quality and experience on the previous tour can also be a measure for judging the current tour. If the tourists feel that the current tour is not up to the mark of the previous one, they will be dissatisfied.

Even if all suppliers are good and service delivery was of expected quality, still there can be some factors that can lead to dissatisfaction in tourism. For instance, if the climate in the destination is bad and if unexpected rain in large scale takes place, then tourists may not be able to enjoy the tour. Assume that some unexpected incidents occurred during the tour or there erupted a political crisis soon. Any of such external factors can dampen the tourist satisfaction. Hence, customer satisfaction in tourism is not only depending on the supply factors, even the uncontrollable external environmental factors can cause dissatisfaction.

A competent tour operator can usually predict such eventualities, and take the necessary precautions to prevent them. Effective market research is necessary prior to the designing of each package tour. Post-tour evaluation has its own significance. The tour manager's report, debriefing of the tour manager, feedback received from tourists, etc. can help the tour operator to minimize future tourist dissatisfaction. Tour planning and designing require the utmost professionalism and expertise. Extra care is needed when selecting the suppliers and service providers from the destination. Quality and professionalism should be the essential criteria for choosing them. While making a tour brochure and designing marketing communication, care has to be taken to provide clear, non-exaggerated and correct content. The staff, including the tour manager, need to be provided with the necessary training to acquire skills to perform their tasks. Their motivation is also a matter of concern. Customer complaint handling is also crucial. All necessary effort is required to resolve their issues and complaints in the best possible manner. The package has to offer a good balance of price and quality, and possible extra features may be added to excite the potential customers. Moreover, the necessary information relating to possible destination turmoil and threats should be provided to tourists in advance. This can minimize customer dissatisfaction if any threats occur. Also, tour participants should be involved in the decision-making process in the aftermath of an emergency. All such can help in reducing the possibility of customer dissatisfaction. A dissatisfied tourist will share their bad experience with many more people than a satisfied tourist will share their positive one. Also "word of mouth" is still a major determinant of success and a useful marketing tool in the tour operation sector.

16.8 Summary

Managing a tour requires quality leadership, and each task in a properly prepared tour requires diligent implementation. Following the pre-set itinerary is important for the success of a tour programme. It needs strictness but also flexibility at times. Sometimes situations will require changes to the plan. The efficiency of a tour leader is important in ensuring tourist satisfaction. Forming part of international travel, tour operation includes a number of procedures to be completed during the journey. Upon arrival at the airport, a tour manager has to ensure the speedy completion of passport and visa verification procedures for all tour members. Baggage collection is another important task. If the tour operator provides a uniform tag, identification of tour members' baggage will be much easier. Once the luggage has been collected, the tour manager should ensure hassle-free customs clearance. Every tour participant should have been told the necessary precautions to take prior to the commencement of the tour. If this has not happened, a delay at any counter (e.g. customs) is possible, which could delay the whole tour. Necessary briefings should be carried out by the tour manager whenever possible. Smooth hotel check-ins should also be ensured. Moreover, emergencies of various types can occur at any moment. Emergency handling demands the utmost professionalism and diligence.

Post-tour activities are also important from a future perspective. The tour manager has to be debriefed and feedback of participants collected. These are valid for forthcoming tour programmes. Outbound tour operators have to ensure reliable overseas tour representatives. Tourist/customer service representatives, resort representatives, children's representatives, entertainment representatives, transfer representatives, young people's representatives, club representatives, mobile resort representatives/couriers are the common types of overseas representatives. A tour operator can choose representatives as per their need.

Tour guiding is an important task. A tour guide is usually a licensed professional who interprets and explains the features of attractions to tourists when they are visiting. They can be a destination-based professional who accompanies a group of tourists or individual tourist during sightseeing. Their role includes explaining and interpreting various aspects of a particular region and its attractions and creating interest and a favourable image of the destination in tourists' minds. A tour guide has to be an efficient person with the requisite skills, knowledge and qualifications. A tour guide is an important person in tour operations, who has a significant role in determining tourist satisfaction. All the suppliers' services in a package tour help to ensure tourist satisfaction. Hence, the most important task of a tour operator is to identify the right suppliers who can deliver quality services to the tourists and to include them in the package.

Review questions

Short/medium answer type questions

- What are the arrival procedures on a tour?
- Discuss the tasks to be carried out by the tour manager upon arrival at the destination airport.
- List the possible difficulties/emergencies on a foreign tour.
- Discuss how to handle emergencies on an outbound tour.
- What are the post-tour activities?
- What do we mean by debriefing of a tour manager?
- Briefly describe overseas tour representatives.

- List the reasons for engaging an overseas representative.
- Define tour guide.
- Distinguish between interpretation and guiding.
- What are the differences between a tour guide and a tour manager?
- Give a brief account of the evolution of tour guiding.
- What are the roles of a tour guide?
- Discuss the points to consider while guiding a group tour.
- What are the qualities of a tour guide?
- Identify the different types of tour guide.
- What are the challenges faced by the tour guiding profession?
- Discuss the need for quality and customer satisfaction in the tour operation business.

Essay type questions

- Describe the tour managing procedures after arrival at the destination airport.
- Write an essay on tour guiding and the important aspects to be taken care of in the process of guiding.

References

Buhalis, D. (2003) *eTourism: Information Technology for Strategic Tourism Management*. London: Pearson.

Chilembwe, M. J. and Mweiwa, V. (2014) Tour Guides: Are They Tourism Promoters and Developers: A Case Study of Malawi, *IMPACT: International Journal of Research in Business Management* 2(9): 29–46.

Cohen, E. (1985) The Tourist Guide: The Origins, Structure and Dynamics of a Role, *Annals of Tourism Research* 12: 5–29.

Cukier, J. (1998) Tourism Employment and Shifts in the Determination of Social Status in Bali, in G. Ringer (ed.) *Destinations: Cultural Landscape of Tourism*. London: Routledge.

Horner, P. (1996) *Travel Agency Practice*. London: Longman.

Hu, W. (2007) Our Guides and Sustainable Development: The Case of Hainan, China, available at http://hdl.handle.net/10012/2732.

Knudson, D. M., Cable, T. T. and Beck, L. (1995) *Interpretation of Cultural and Natural Resources*. State College, PA: Venture Publishing.

Laws, E. (1997) *Managing Packaged Tourism: Relationships, Responsibilities and Service Quality in the Inclusive Holiday Industry*. London: International Thomson Business Press.

Mancini, M. (2001) *Conducting Tours*. 3rd edn. New York: Thomson Learning.

Mitchell, G. E. (2005) *Travel FREE as an International Tour Director*. Charleston, SC: The GEM Group.

Moscardo, G. and Woods, B. (1998) Managing Tourism and the Experience of Visitors on Skyrail, in E. Laws, B. Faulkner and G. Moscardo (eds), *Embracing and Managing Change in Tourism*. London: Routledge, pp. 307–323.

Pond, K. (1993) *The Professional Guide: Dynamics of Tour Guiding*. New York: Van Nostrand Reinhold.

Randall, C. and Rollins, R. B. (2009) Visitor Perceptions of the Role of Tour Guides in Natural Areas, *Journal of Sustainable Tourism* 17(3): 357–374.

Society for Interpreting Britain's Heritage (1998) Interpret Britain, *Interpretation* 3(2): 27.

Voss, C., Roth, A. V., Rosenzweig, E. D., Blackmon, K. and Chase, R. B. (2004) A Tale of Two Countries' Conservatism, Service Quality, and Feedback on Customer Satisfaction, *Journal of Service Research* 6(3): 212–223.

WFTGA (2003) What is a Tourist Guide?, available at http://www.wftga.org/tourist-guiding/what-tourist-guide.

Website

www.detour.com.

Part VI

Impacts and prospects

Chapter 17

Impacts of travel and tourism

Learning outcomes

After studying this chapter, you will be able to:

* Understand the environmental impacts of aviation.
* Explain the impacts of tourism on economy, society, culture and environment.

17.1 Introduction

Travel is certainly a wonderful recreational activity with varied dimensions. Its significance is on a steady ascent, and the social phenomenon that has evolved out of travel,
i.e. tourism, is also progressing at a remarkable pace; so much so that tourism is being
promoted by countries as a solution for many of their economic difficulties. Tourism
undoubtedly has the potential to produce myriad social and economic benefits for destinations. However, the haphazard development of tourism could have a range of consequences spanning across social, cultural and environmental arenas. Indeed, the negative
impacts of tourism have been a matter of discussion and debate for several years. The
impacts took on a new dimension when climate change began to be taken seriously.
Travel contributes to negative environmental impacts and the tourism industry in general
continues to be criticized for this.

Among the tourism industries, the transport sector contributes a significant share of environmental impacts, particularly global warming and climate change. The burning of fossil
fuels in automobiles and other transport forms cause carbon emissions, which have environmental consequences. Common impacts of tourism are introduced here. We begin with a discussion of the environmental impacts of aviation, one of the largest tourism transport forms.

17.2 Environmental impacts of aviation

Air transportation affects the environment at the local, regional and global levels (Marais
and Waitz, 2009). The effects on people who live close to airports and under flight paths

are always a concern of airport development. Pollution, increasing noise levels, soil erosion, landscape destruction, additional congestion due to airport travellers and increasing quantity of waste are the major impacts of airport development. According to Graham (2014), the environmental impacts/consequences of airports can be divided into five categories: noise; emissions; water pollution and use; waste and energy management; and wildlife, heritage and landscape. A discussion of the major consequences of airport development follows.

17.2.1 Noise

Air transport and airport operations cause disturbing noise levels for the inhabitants around airports. Noise in the vicinity of the airport includes tests of aircraft engines, supersonic booms, and the noise of aircraft during landing and take-off (as well as the noise generated en route). Modern aircraft technology has significantly reduced the noise from aircraft. For example, the area on the ground affected by a particular level of noise from modern jets is approximately five times smaller than that affected by similar aircraft in the 1960s (Kazda and Caves, 2000). A comprehensive global level has been attempted to reduce the noise levels, which includes the reduction of aircraft noise at source, introducing better operational procedures that can reduce noise levels, land use planning and management measures, and imposing possible local-level restrictions on noise-related operations.

17.2.2 Emissions

Air pollution occurs mainly due to the emissions of engines, by operation of vehicles in the airport, from transportation to and from the airport to other sources in the airport such as heating. Aircraft emit a number of different pollutants that alter the chemical composition of the atmosphere, changing its radiative balance and hence influencing the climate. Emissions include carbon dioxide (CO_2), nitrogen oxide (NO_2) particles (mainly soot) of sulfur oxides, carbon monoxide and various hydrocarbons (Graham, 2007). Emissions from aircraft, airport transport and stationary airport sources adversely affect air quality. According to the FAA Office of Environment and Energy (2015), aircraft emissions include:

> carbon dioxide (CO_2), which comprises about 70% of the exhaust, and water vapor (H_2O), which comprises about 30%. Less than 1% of the exhaust is composed of pollutants like nitrogen oxides (NOx), oxides of sulfur (SOx), carbon monoxide (CO), partially combusted or unburned hydrocarbons (HC), particulate matter (PM), and other trace compounds.

Aviation emissions cause long-distance transfer of air pollution, greenhouse effect and depletion of the ozone layer. Also, these emissions contribute to climate change by increasing the level of greenhouse gases. The main "greenhouse gas" emission from aviation is CO_2, though water vapour also contributes. The exact effect of emissions is yet to be studied fully. Of late, emissions are being reduced through the use of advanced engines that release smaller quantities of pollutants, utilization of improved airframes that need less thrust to fly and improved operational procedures that enable more efficient use of aircraft (NRC, 2002, reported in Marais and Waitz, 2009).

17.2.3 Water pollution

There is excessive use of water at airports. Moreover, water quality is affected by the discharge of a variety of chemicals and waste disposals. Run-off from aircraft, airfield de-icing operations, fuel leaks, spills, and solid and liquid waste contribute to water pollution in and around the airport. Imperfect treatment of waste waters is also a major cause of water pollution. According to the British Airports Authority (BAA, 2003), the major water pollution sources of airport operations are as follows:

- Chemicals used for aircraft de-icing
- Aviation fuel spills
- Inadequate storage, handling or disposal of oils and other chemicals
- Use of pesticides and herbicides for controlling plants and pests airside
- Water used for firefighting operations
- Surface run-off from ground transportation areas
- Leaks and spills from the fuel arm and fuel supply facilities
- Construction and contractors' compounds
- Waste water containing chemicals after washing an aircraft

17.2.4 Waste and energy management

Waste management is a major concern. Improper waste treatment results in different kinds of impacts. It can affect air quality, soil composition, water contamination and some social issues. Airports are a major source of waste – of solid, gaseous and liquid types. Some waste is biodegradable like food waste. Non-biodegradable waste is substantial in quantity. Energy requirements for airports are extensive, mainly for heating, air conditioning, lighting and ventilating. The possibility of energy wastage due to inefficient use of energy exists, and that leads to far-reaching consequences. Utmost care needs to be taken in terms of energy consumption.

17.2.5 Wildlife and heritage

Inhabitants in the vicinity of an airport are affected by noise, the expansion of the airport, air pollution, water pollution and soil pollution. Reduction in the type and extent of habitats, bird strikes and roadkill, disturbance from noise and vehicle movement, the degrading air quality impact on biodiversity, habitat loss and degradation, etc. are the major effects. There are also social effects due to airport operations. Monuments especially can be damaged by the air pollutants in the long run.

17.2.6 Airport construction

Airport construction necessitates huge land takeovers. This may lead to evacuation of people from their lands. Proper rehabilitation of evacuated people for airport development is a daunting task, and in many a cases it ends up as a social issue. Moreover, construction results in excavating of soil and soil erosion. Landscape structure and beauty can be severely – and negatively – affected. Visual pollution is also a consequence of airport construction. Interference with ground water channels and rivers is another possible effect of airport construction.

17.3 Economic impacts of tourism

Despite the fact that tourism contributes a range of benefits, there are some economic consequences as well. Some of the commonly discussed economic impacts of tourism are:

- Inflation
- Migration of labour
- Overdependence on tourism
- Opportunity cost
- Seasonal character of jobs
- Job-level friction
- Economic inequality
- Leakage of economic benefits

Tourism is a major determinant of inflation in geographical regions where mass tourism is established. Inflation in tourist destinations is primarily related to the increases in prices of land, houses and even food which can occur as a result of tourism. Prices for these commodities can increase when tourists place extra demand on local services in a tourism destination. Tourists are a group of consumers from outside the economy and their stay in destination is for a limited period of time. Tourists bring additional financial resources into the economy, and if the supply of goods and services cannot adapt according to the increased demand, the general price levels will increase. Their knowledge of the prices and bargaining capacity has a limit. Moreover, in peak seasons the demand for various tourism products and services will be at its maximum. These circumstances lead to inflation which the local community also has to bear. It is also common that the same product has different price levels in a tourism destination and in a non-tourist area. When there is tourism development in rural areas, the possibilities will arise for migration of labour towards the tourism sector. In such areas, primary sectors of production such as agriculture, fishing, etc. would have been the major source of employment before the arrival of tourism. The primary sectors may suffer due to the drain of skilled labour and there can be further economic consequences, like rises in labour costs.

Tourism becomes the main economic sector in some tourist destinations and the dependence on it reaches its maximum level when the destinations are established for mass tourism. Overdependence on tourism can occur in, for example, small states where tourism is seen by the government as the best method of development. Over a period of time, the emphasis on tourism becomes such that there is virtually no other approach to development. As a result, the country becomes dependent on tourism revenue to the extent that any change in demand is likely to lead to a major economic crisis. Opportunity cost is another economic aspect which refers to the cost of engaging in tourism compared to another economic activity. Investment in the tourism sector can take away investment in other sectors. There is a cost associated with engaging in tourism rather than another form of economic activity. Public resources spent on subsidized infrastructure or tax breaks can also reduce government investment in other critical areas such as education and health. The use of capital resources in the development of tourism-related establishments precludes their use for other forms of economic development.

Many of the tourism development activities consume resources in large quantities. Human resource requirements in peak season are often at their maximum, while they are at their minimum in off season. For this reason, some industries provide jobs more on a contract basis. Moreover, low-paid jobs are also a common feature in some tourism-related industries. In developing or undeveloped regions, local communities may be able to acquire jobs in the lower strata of the job hierarchy. In such cases, many of the jobs occupied by local people in the tourist industry are at a lower level, such as housemaids, waiters and gardeners, while the higher-paying employment opportunities go to sophisticated outsiders of the economy. Economic differences between the locals and the visiting population can lead to friction as well. Though the tourism sector utilizes local resources, the possibility of economic "leakage" from the local economy is very high when the destination supply is dominated by large-scale operators and "enclave tourism". In order to get maximum benefit, destinations have to ensure maximum local entrepreneurship and participation from small and medium-sized enterprises (SMEs) from the locality.

17.4 Social consequences

Tourism as an economic activity brings many opportunities for employment and income generation. More people in the locality will get employment and the opportunities for starting enterprises will also increase. This will lead to the generation of increased income for the society which ultimately leads to better living conditions and better lifestyles. The development of infrastructure for tourism will also provide enough facilities for the local people. Regional development is sometimes a result of tourism. Through it, a population's primary facilities (education facilities, health facilities, etc.) necessary for living can emerge. Altogether, the social benefits of tourism cannot be neglected. Especially in undeveloped countries, tourism has been promoted as a means for poverty alleviation and regional development. At the same time, tourism's social consequences are well debated around the world. A range of issues have been identified. The major social impacts of tourism are:

- Demonstration effect
- Changing attitudes of the host population
- Increasing social menaces
- Displacement of local communities
- Irritation within the local community as a result of tourist behaviour
- Overcrowding
- Tourist intrusiveness and intensive interaction

The likelihood of the host community in a tourist destination being exposed to the nuances of diverse cultures from different parts of the world is high when tourism is established. This has both positive and negative aspects. On one hand it helps in learning about other cultures and in cultural exchange. On the other hand, the vulnerability of local communities of being lured by the "extravaganza" exhibited by tourists and the possibility of being influenced by it is high. The phenomenon which causes the occurrence of indigenous and rural communities and cultures adopting foreign styles and behaviours that they are exposed to due to regular tourist visits is referred to as the demonstration effect. Local people become attracted to the material possessions of tourists and aspire to associated lifestyles. Local people may emulate a leisured and wealthier lifestyle which is unrealistic and unaffordable. In the longer run, it can lead to behavioural changes in the resident population (Williams, 1998). According to Burns (1999), the demonstration effect refers to the process by which traditional societies, especially those which are particularly susceptible to outside influences, such as youths, will voluntarily seek to adopt certain behaviours (and accumulate material goods) on the basis that possession of them will lead to the achievement of the leisured, hedonistic lifestyle demonstrated by the tourists. This is particularly relevant in undeveloped and developing (especially traditional) societies.

Mass tourism can bring different changes in the attitudes of a self-contained, small community with a simple, basic lifestyle who live in remote locations. Usually attitudes and others will change very slowly. This can be positive also, but generally it has resulted in some negative impacts. Some areas of attitudinal and behavioural changes due to tourism are discussed below.

Even a peace-loving, nature-friendly host population can react with hostility towards tourists who constantly clash with the traditions and customs of the country they are visiting. In religious aspects, this dominates and in some places continuous tourist–host conflicts and clashes are reported. Another possible response of the host population to tourists is that of imitation. In the context of commercialization and in retail businesses, the host community involved will only concentrate on selling and making profit. Pleasing tourists and forcing them to buy as many products as possible will be their main concern. This circumstance may lead to locals having pseudo behaviours throughout their approach towards tourism activities. The relationship between the host population and tourists can become a commercial one, with tourism becoming a business.

In many areas, tourism encourages anti-social activities. From a sustainable point of view, such situations are important issues and should be controlled. Prostitution is one such area on which wide discussion has been going on worldwide. The presence of large numbers of tourists carrying relatively large sums of money and valuables with them provides a source of illegal activities, including drug trafficking, robbery and violence. There have been complaints that tourism opens the gates for male and female prostitution. Child abuse is another area that relates to social impacts of tourism. Apart from these, increasing drug abuses, mafia activities, gambling activities, etc. have been creating many problems for sustainable tourism development. International tourists are sometimes easy victims of crime where they are clearly identifiable by language or ethnicity and may be assumed to be carrying significant sums of money with them. Tourism development can directly or indirectly displace local communities from their habitats. At times it happens forcibly and in quick succession. Gradual displacement as tourism industries expand is very common.

CASE STUDY 17.1

The growing menace of child sex tourism

Among the various social menaces of tourism, the worst is the child sex tourism (CST), for which millions of children are being trafficked for the pleasure of tourists. CST, which is growing steadily, is a subtype of child prostitution. Child prostitution is vast, with a large number of victims across the world. It is not only paedophiles who take part in child abuse. Child sex tourists also involve other categories of people who do not have a clinical disorder, but who find pleasure in engaging in such activities when they get an opportunity to do so. Being a commercial activity, the product offered is in fact the service provided by the suppliers, i.e. supplying children younger than 12 years of age, mainly, for sexual satisfaction. There is supply in selected hotels, resorts, brothels, massage parlours, casinos and other similar establishments in many tourism locations across the world. The Code, an agency that works against such practices, defines child sex tourism as "acts perpetrated by those who are traveling or using their status as tourists in order to sexually exploit children. It is considered to be a sub-type of child prostitution with clear links to the tourism industry" (www.thecode.org).

According to ECPAT, another agency that acts against CST (www.ecpat.net), it:

> involves the exchange of cash, clothes, food or some other form of consideration to a child or to a third party for sexual contact. CST occurs in multiple venues, from brothels in red-light districts to beaches or five-star hotels and in urban, rural or coastal settings.

Commercial sexual exploitation of children (CSEC) is a growing crime the world over and tourism becomes a catalyst and facilitator for its expansion.

Comprehensive statistics on CST are not available. A rough estimate of more that a decade ago suggests that more than two million boys and girls are exploited in the CST industry. Some statistics quoted by ECPAT based on studies follow. In Mexico, 20,000 minors were involved in prostitution by 2005. Colombia has up to 35,000 child victims. Up to 30,000 girls between the ages of 12 and 14 years are exploited in tourism industries in Kenya. Asia, particularly South East Asia and certain countries in South Asia, has long been the target of child sex tourists. In the Philippines, an estimated 100,000 child victims are involved. In Moscow, estimates of children victimized in prostitution have reached between 20,000 to 30,000 (ECPAT, 2016). If you include common prostitution and sex work using children in the figures, the number would be much larger. For example, in India the United Nations International Children's Emergency Fund (UNICEF) has estimated that around 1.2 million children are exploited through prostitution, in general. According to government information there are at least 100,000 children exploited through prostitution every year in the United States (*ibid.*). The pressing need is to curtail its expansion and minimize child trafficking.

Source: Dileep (2015)

Read the above case study carefully and answer the following questions:

- Give a brief account of child abuse in tourism.
- Discuss how to minimize CST and child prostitution.
- Write down the role to be played by the tourism industry to minimize child trafficking for sexual pleasure.

Tourists, out of ignorance or carelessness, often fail to respect local customs and values. When they do so, they can bring about irritation and stereotyping. Recurring cultural and social clashes and tourism behaviour can cause irritation among local people. **Doxey's Irridex** of tourist irritation is a model that describes the changes in local people's attitudes towards tourists at different phases of tourism evolution in a destination. It says there are four distinct stages and in each stage local people behave differently (Doxey, 1976):

- *Euphoria:* soon after the initial development of tourism, visitors and investors are welcome, locals are excited over tourists' visits and there is little planning or control mechanism. Local people feel happy to welcome tourists.
- *Apathy:* along with tourism development, visitors are taken for granted and contact between residents and outsiders becomes more formal (commercial). Locals become more indifferent to tourists, and planning mostly concerns marketing.
- *Annoyance:* as tourism becomes established and the saturation point approaches, "hosts" have misgivings about tourism and get irritated at the tourists' presence. Policymakers attempt solutions through increasing infrastructure (rather than limiting growth).
- *Antagonism:* where residents become tourist-averse and tensions, conflicts and anti-tourism feelings become widespread. Irritations are openly expressed since visitors are seen as the cause of all the problems. In this stage planning becomes remedial and promotion is increased to offset the deteriorating reputation of the destination.

In mass tourism destinations, crowding is a major issue. This affects the quality of the tourist experience. Moreover, local people are overcrowded and disturbed. Roads face congestion. Parking spaces will be occupied by tourist vehicles. Traffic congestion is an inevitable consequence of some tourism activities, such as special events. A new project can increase traffic congestion in its vicinity. Increasing tourism in a rural location can cause intrusions by foreigners into their lives. Local people's social life can also be affected by regular tourism beyond a certain limit. Moreover, tourism of this kind can cause intensive interaction between tourists and the local community, which can lead to some social and cultural consequences for the latter.

17.5 Cultural impacts

For many, tourism is, in fact, a bridge between peoples, fostering communication, mutual understanding and a desirable redistribution of wealth. To others, tourism is a negative factor destroying traditions, customs, manners and the environment. They view tourism as cultural imperialism. It has been proven that improperly planned tourism generates different socio-cultural negative impacts in addition to the environmental hazards. Although it is difficult to generalize, socio-cultural impacts will typically depend upon the degree of cultural similarity or dissimilarity between the tourists and hosts (UNWTO, 2011). The major cultural impacts are:

- Commercialization
- Commoditization
- Staged authenticity and "pseudo-events"
- "Human zoos"

- Cultural changes and "acculturation"
- Reduction in cultural diversity and homogenization of culture
- Cultural clashes

Tourism contributes to preserving art and art forms. However, at the same time and in some cases, it leads to mass commercialization of art and art forms. In one sense it is good that people earn a livelihood, but in another, art production loses its sanctity and perfection, which may spread a distorted image of the art form. Trivialization of culture is another term used in this regard. It also means that the traditional ceremonies and rituals are reduced or modified to tourist products. Commoditization has a similar effect. When a destination is promoted as a tourism product, the increasing demand for souvenirs, art, entertainment and other commodities begins to exert influence, and basic changes in human values may occur. It has been reported that, in many of the fragile and ancient cultures, indigenous people's art and culture have been over-commoditized. Culture becomes a commodity for financial transactions. It causes

> the presentation of an entity as a market product available for sale. Problems occur when the entity was not intended to be for sale, where there are non-market values attached to it, and where ownership does not lie with any individual or organizations
>
> (Kelly and Nankervis, 2009)

Mason (2009) defines commoditization as when "demand for cultural aspects and performances have become packaged for convenient consumption by visitors". The traditional objects that are marketed as new products may not have the true value and meaning. There can be "reconstructed ethnicity" as part of this. It happens when tourism turns local cultures into commodities when religious rituals, traditional ethnic rites and festivals are reduced and sanitized to conform to tourist expectations. Religious sites, objects, cultural features and rituals may not be respected when they are perceived as goods for trade.

Staged authenticity and "pseudo-events" are widely discussed effects of tourism. Similar to commercialization, in order to attract tourists, "cultural shows" are performed that are devoid of intrinsic meaning. These are referred to as "staged authenticity". It denotes adapting of cultural expressions and manifestations to the tastes of tourists or even performing shows as if they were "real life". MacCannell introduced this concept in tourism with ample illustrations in his book *The Tourist: A New Theory of the Leisure Class* (1999). It has been a trend nowadays to organize such cultural shows for tourists, particularly when mass tourists arrived as part of package tours. Regular inauthentic performances can lead to forgetting of the true meaning and significance of the practice or event. The commoditization has led to pseudo-events that share the following characteristics: they are planned rather than spontaneous; they are designed to be performed to order, at times that are convenient for tourists; and they hold at best an ambiguous relationship to real elements on which they are based (Mason, 1995; Williams, 1998). Also, of particular concern, as Williams notes, is that these pseudo-events eventually become the authentic events and replace the original events or practices. They hold at best an ambiguous relationship to real elements on which they are based (Mason, 1995).

"Human zoo" is another term used in a similar context. Indigenous people on display, their customs on exhibition and their attire for showing: this was a practice, with a racial component, too, that occurred in some parts of the world and are recorded in the annals of history. People were kept in cages or inside fenced areas, and exhibited in the same way as animals. Others watched them with much enthusiasm due to the strangeness of colour, customs, costumes, traditions and so on. The term "human zoo" is used to refer to this barbaric form of entertainment. In some locations, exhibitions of varying levels, similar to those primitive performances, are arranged for tourists, who get the pleasure of seeing the "strangeness" of some communities.

The overall cultural features of a society can be influenced by continuous mass tourism over a long period. The reasons for this can differ. The society interested in tourism activities may adapt to new cultures so that they can entertain tourism activities effectively. Such a change is often remarked upon as "acculturation". Williams (1998) defines acculturation in this way: "When two cultures come into contact for any length of time, an exchange of ideas and products will take place that, through time, produce varying levels of convergence between the cultures; that is they become similar". Tourism services are now promoted in the same manner in most locations in the world. Many aspects of tourism are becoming homogenized. Hospitality is one example. The style of food served, services offered, facilities, etc. are becoming similar everywhere in the world. The food sector is another example. Almost all destinations have some products in common. Homogenization is all about the spread of Western ideas and values to indigenous and rural communities across the world. Dressing styles are now becoming homogenized. Modern art forms are also becoming similar. This results in a reduction in the cultural diversity in the world. In some cases, cultural clashes can occur. Cultural clashes can take place as a result of differences in culture, ethnicities and religions, values and lifestyles, languages and levels of prosperity. Tourism is a social process that leads to the mingling of different cultures. Moreover, when tourists do not respect the value and spirit of local cultures, the possibility of cultural clashes is high.

17.6 Environmental impacts of tourism

The environment, whether it is natural or man-made, is the most fundamental ingredient of the tourism product. However, as soon as tourism activity takes place, the environment is inevitably changed or modified either to facilitate tourism or during the tourism process (Cooper et al., 2000). Different kinds of tourism activities affect the natural and built environment. There is a complex interaction between tourism and the environment. Many studies have shown that tourism has immense impact on the physical environment and that little has been done to remedy or control the assault on the ecology. The environment in which tourism takes place is important to the quality of the tourist experience. Both the natural environment in the form of land, water, plants and animals and the man-made environment, which includes buildings and streets, form the foundation of the tourism industry. In the absence of an attractive environment tourism rarely succeeds, because it is one of the vital elements which tourists look for in a destination.

Environmental impacts of tourism are usually site-specific. Yet, some are seen widely. There are some factors that act as determinants of environmental impacts of tourism. Here are some of the most significant:

- *Where it takes place:* location of tourism, such as urban or rural, etc.
- *Type of tourism activities in the destination:* some cause more damage
- *Nature of tourist infrastructure:* the type and nature of tourist facilities in a destination
- *Extent of tourism development:* vulnerability increases along with increase in tourism development
- *When the activity occurs:* such as seasonal variations

- *The density of population*
- *Duration of visitation:* visitation for longer periods may experience more damage
- *Duration of season:* if the seasons are short, damage may be less
- *Fragility of location:* the more fragile, the more vulnerable
- *Resilience of ecosystem:* to withstand and recover

Much of the damage done to the environment as a result of tourism is caused simply by the volume of tourists arriving at the destinations, which are not used to supporting people in great numbers, and the improper planning and infrastructure development. A variety of negative environmental effects are reported from tourism areas all over the world and the types of impact vary according to many factors. In general, the more ecologically fragile a destination is, the greater the chances for damages. Fragility and environmental (ecological) damage have a direct relationship. Like economic and socio-cultural impacts, environmental impacts of tourism development can generate indirect effects in addition to direct ones. The following constitute some of the major environmental impacts of tourism:

- Pollution
- Physical damage
- Waste disposal and sewage
- Erosion
- Depletion of natural resources
- Loss of biodiversity
- Deforestation and disturbance to animals
- Emissions and climate change
- Aesthetic pollution/visual pollution/architectural pollution

Mass tourism leads to different kinds of pollution. It affects the quality of water, air and noise levels. Hotels' sewage disposal, disposal from boats and other motorized water transporting vehicles, etc. pollute the water. Vehicle (and other) emissions pollute the air. Night camps, discos, transportation, etc. create noise pollution and when the destinations are in forest areas, it will disturb the fauna in the forest. The following types of pollution can be attributed to tourism:

- *Air pollution*, e.g. from transport
- *Water pollution*, e.g. disposal from boats, waste, chemicals from gardens, airports, etc.
- *Noise pollution*, e.g. from airplanes, cars and buses, as well as recreational vehicles such as snowmobiles and jet skis, etc.
- *Soil Pollution*, e.g. waste disposal, littering, chemicals from different sources, etc.

Landscape destruction and loss of natural beauty is a common impact around the world. The development of tourism can involve sand mining, beach and sand dune erosion, soil erosion and extensive paving. Deterioration of ecosystems is a common issue and tourism's contribution to it in destinations is significant. Crowding and congestion is another issue that leads to environmental damage. Over-usage of the infrastructure will pose problems. Hunting and fishing have obvious impacts on the wildlife environment. Sand dunes can be damaged through overuse. Littering by tourists can raise many environmental problems. Waste disposal is a serious problem; improper disposal can cause further environmental issues. Sewage is another problem.

CASE STUDY 17.2

Too much tourism: Antarctica in trouble

The focus of the annual Antarctic Treaty meeting in 2014 in Brasilia was the concern for tourism there. Antarctica's environmental hazards are not just due to tourism; there are other activities that harm the most pristine, iciest land on earth. But, of late, people have raised a hue and cry due to increasing tourism activities. According to Cool Antarctica (n.d.), the threats to Antarctica are varied but mainly include: global warming, resulting in a loss of sea ice and land-based ice; oceanic acidification, which results in the loss of some marine organisms; increased tourism, which the accompanying pollutants ships and aircraft bring; the possibility of oil spills and the effects of lots of people and infrastructure on wildlife and the wider environment; overfishing; pollution due to (among other things) chemicals produced thousands of miles away; invasive species and organisms that are not native to Antarctica being brought there on ships (*ibid.*).

The impacts are far-reaching and can be at a global level. Even the melting of ice at a nominal level can result in floods and raise sea levels substantially. According to the Inter-Governmental Panel on Climate Change (IPCC) (Church et al., 2013), it is not easy to estimate the future sea level due to the effects in the Antarctic. However, its total sea level contribution is projected to rise 16 cm this century. The contamination can harm the ecosystem severely and also lead to the extinction of many species. WWF Global (n.d.) reports that the massive Arctic and Antarctic ice shelves have been disintegrating and breaking away, such as the now-famous break away of the Larsen B ice shelf in Antarctica in 2002.

A study of the British Antarctic Survey and the UK Antarctic Heritage Trust who operate Port Lockroy on Goudier Island in Antarctica reveals that there is an impact on animal species due to tourism and warns that if tourism increases in this manner, it will end in huge impacts on the wildlife in the near future (www.discoringantarctica.org.uk). Tourist activities in the destination are expanding and that is the focus of concern. In the 1980s and 1990s, the tourist segments mainly consisted of older travellers who would arrive in small groups. Lately, the scenario has changed, with various age groups now visiting and keen to participate in diverse activities like paragliding, waterskiing, diving, fishing and so on. The visitors' time spent there (i.e. duration of stay) has also increased. The tourism community across the world, led by the UNWTO and other responsible agencies including professional bodies, have to intervene and help to implement stringent measures so as to minimize the environmental impacts in the polar regions due to tourism.

Source: Adapted from Dileep (2014)

Read the above case study carefully and answer the following questions:

- What are the environmental impacts of tourism in the polar regions?
- Identify the tourist activities that lead to environmental issues in Antarctica.
- Discuss the measures that can be taken to minimize the impacts of tourism in polar regions.

Erosion takes place in different contexts. For instance, in coastal areas it is more as the vegetation clearance exposes the beach to sea storms. Construction activities of various kinds on different locations cause erosion when it rains. Overdevelopment may cause landslides/slips, damage to river banks and sea coasts. Large-scale tourism activities create issues in relation to natural resources especially when resources are scarce. It has been reported that tourists' water consumption is much higher than that of local people. Loss of biodiversity is more serious in nature-related tourism and tourism in forest areas. Rich natural resources naturally attract more tourism and consequently it can severely affect the biodiversity there. Though at times large animals are protected, smaller living beings and floral diversity may be neglected in many cases. Regular tourist arrivals, construction, facilities and services, souvenir collection, etc. can hurt biodiversity.

Forests are vulnerable to the impact of tourism. Mass movement of tourists is always a problem for wildlife. Regular disturbance by tourists will force animals to migrate to other places. The free movement of animals will be disrupted by tourist activities. Tourists are always fond of souvenirs, and when they are exotic, the attractiveness will increase. In destinations near to forest areas, souvenir makers may need to kill small or even large animals for their skin or other parts in order to make their products. Some purely profit-minded tour operators near to forest areas use unethical methods to attract animals to be shown off to tourists or even to provide hunting opportunities. Land clearance for roads and construction, trampling of delicate ecosystems by walkers, vehicle movements and plant souveniring are other impacts. Consider the following consequences:

- Species diversity is affected – less resistant plants may be displaced by the introduction of new plants
- Disruption of habitat equilibrium
- Animal's foraging routes and feeding habits are disrupted
- Breeding areas are abandoned because they are unsafe

Aesthetic pollution is another impact of tourism. Basically, it refers to the loss of natural beauty or traditional architecture, etc. due to construction. High rises often dominate hotel construction and resorts of disparate designs can look out of place in any natural environment. They may also clash with indigenous structural designs. These are so common in coastal tourism as well as in hill stations. "Visual pollution generally refers to those elements of the landscape that the community finds unattractive, including badly maintained buildings, advertisements (hoardings), business signs, telephone and utility poles, weeds, garbage dumps and litter." (Albuquerque Environmental Society/CPR Envtl. Edn. Service, 2001) Tourism can cause all such aspects that lead to visual pollution. The effect of inappropriate development of buildings is also referred to as architectural pollution, such as the constructing of high-rise hotels on beachfronts. Tourism is a significant contributor of carbon emissions. It also contributes to ozone layer depletion, which leads to climate change. The aviation sector in particular contributes a large share.

17.7 Summary

Though travel is an amazing recreational activity, the associated activities generate impacts of various kinds. Travel necessitates transportation, which is a sector that causes severe and irreversible consequences, particularly on nature. All transport forms cause impacts. The aviation sector is the leader among them, with wider and deeper impacts. Air transport causes issues associated with noise, emissions, water pollution and use, and waste and energy management. People and other inhabitants in proximity to airways and airports are badly affected by aviation activities. Tourism, though once perceived as a "smokeless industry", is, of late, being criticized for generating a wide range of impacts in a number of areas: economy, society, culture and environment. In the economy it causes inflation, migration of labour, overdependence on tourism, opportunity costs, seasonal character of jobs, economic inequality and leakage of economic benefits. The impacts on society include demonstration effect, changing attitudes of host population, increasing social menaces, displacement of local community and the irritation directed towards tourists. Cultural impacts are also diverse and include commercialization, commoditization, staged authenticity, human zooification, acculturation, reduction in cultural diversity and homogenization of culture, and cultural clashes. The environment is affected badly by tourism in many ways. Pollution is a common issue in tourism. Other issues include physical damage, waste disposal and sewage, erosion, depletion of natural resources, loss of biodiversity, deforestation and disturbance to animals and emissions contributing to climate change. However, a number of measures have been suggested to mitigate the impacts of tourism and, around the world, developers are increasingly considering these measures while developing tourism. As tourism and its elements are highly prone to crises of varied kinds, it is extremely important to have crisis management plans and crisis management teams in place to take action immediately when the need arises. Being a sensitive sector, it is crucial to restore normalcy and to regain confidence among the stakeholders for the sustainability of tourism's growth.

Review questions

Short/medium answer type questions

- Describe the environmental impacts of air transportation.
- Write down how air transport contributes to global climate change.
- Describe the economic concerns of tourism development.
- How does tourism cause the "migration of labour"?
- What do we mean by "opportunity cost" in tourism?
- Discuss the social consequences of tourism.
- What do we mean by "demonstration effect"?
- Discuss how tourism results in the displacement of local communities.
- Define "commercialization" due to tourism.
- What do we mean by "staged authenticity" in tourism?
- Discuss "human zooification" as a consequence of tourism.
- What is "acculturation"?
- What are the factors that determine the environmental impacts of tourism?

Essay type questions

- Explain the impacts due to tourism development.
- Discuss in detail the environmental impacts of tourism.

References

Albuquerque Environmental Society/CPR Envtl. Edn. Service (2001) Environmental Studies, Chennai, India: Environmental Society/CPR Envtl. Edn. Service.

BAA (2003) British Airports Authority Heathrow, Airport Water Quality Strategy 2003–2008. Lickfield, East Sussex: Beacon Press.

Burns, P. M. (1999) *An Introduction to Tourism and Anthropology*. London: Routledge.

Church, J. A., Clark, P. U., Cazenave, A., Gregory, J. M., Jevrejeva, S., Levermann, A., Merrifield, M. A., Milne, G. A., Nerem, R. S., Nunn, P. D., Payne, A. J., Pfeffer, W. T., Stammer, D. and Unnikrishnan, A. S. (2013) Sea Level Change, in T. F. Stocker, D. Qin, G.-K. Plattner, M. Tignor, S. K. Allen, J. Boschung, A. Nauels, Y. Xia, V. Bex and P. M. Midgley (eds), *Climate Change 2013: The Physical Science Basis. Contribution of Working Group I to the Fifth Assessment Report of the Intergovernmental Panel on Climate Change*. Cambridge: Cambridge University Press.

Cool Antarctica, Human Impacts on Antarctica and Threats to the Environment – Overview, available at https://www.coolantarctica.com/Antarctica%20fact%20file/science/human_impact_on_antarctica.php.

Cooper, C., Fletcher, J., Gilbert, D. and Wanhill, S. (2000) *Tourism: Principles and Practices*. London: Prentice Hall.

Dileep, M. R. (2014) Too Much of Tourism: Antarctica in Trouble!, available at https://www.linkedin.com/pulse/20140617163529-75171222-too-much-of-tourism-antarctica-in-trouble/ (accessed 16 July 2018).

Dileep, M. R. (2015) How Many Tourists Do Seek Children for Sexual Pleasure? *Destination Kerala* 18(4): 8.

Doxey, G. V. (1976) When Enough's Enough: The Natives are Restless in Old Niagara. *Heritage Canada* 2: 26–28.

ECPAT (2016) Global Study on Sexual Exploitation in Travel and Tourism, available at http://www.ecpat.org/wp-content/uploads/2016/10/SECTT_Region-EUROPE.pdf.

FAA (2015) Federal Aviation Administration – Aviation Emissions, Impacts & Mitigation A Primer, available at https://www.faa.gov/regulations_policies/policy_guidance/envir_policy/media/Primer_Jan2015.pdf (accessed 5 January 2018).

Graham, A. (2007) *Managing Airports: An International Perspective*. 3rd edn. Oxford: Butterworth-Heinemann.

Graham, A. (2014) *Managing Airports: An International Perspective*. 4th edn. Oxford: Routledge.

Kazda, A. and Caves, E. R. (2000) *Airport Design and Operations*. Oxford: Elsevier.

Kelly, I. and Nankervis, T. (2009) *Visitor Destinations*. Milton: John Wiley & Sons.

MacCannell, D. (1999) *The Tourist: A New Theory of the Leisure Class*. London: Macmillan.

Marais, M. K. and Waitz, A. I. (2009) Air Transport and the Environment, in P. Belobaba, A. Odoni and C. Barnhart (eds), *The Global Airline Industry*. London: John Wiley & Sons.

Mason, P. (1995) *Tourism: Environment and Development Perspectives*. Godalming: World Wide Fund For Nature.

Mason, P. (2009) *Tourism Impacts, Planning and Management*. Oxford: Butterworth-Heinemann.

National Research Council (NRC) (2002) reported in Marais, M. K. and Waitz, A. I. (2009) Air Transport and the Environment, in P. Belobaba, A. Odoni and C. Barnhart (eds), *The Global Airline Industry*. London: John Wiley & Sons.

UNWTO (2011) *Policy and Practice for Global Tourism*. Madrid: United Nations World Tourism Organization.

Williams, S. (1998) *Tourism Geography*. London: Routledge.

WWF Global, The Antarctic, available at https://www.wwf.org.uk/where-we-work/places/Antarctic.

Websites

www.thecode.org.
www.ecpat.net.
www.discoringantarctica.org.uk.

Chapter 18

The prospects

Learning outcomes

After reading this chapter, you will be able to:

- Describe the carbon emissions reduction strategies in the aviation sector.
- Understand the sustainable tourism development aspects of tourism development.
- Describe the various commonly practised strategies and measures for mitigating the environmental impacts of tourism.

18.1 Introduction

Tourism is certain to grow consistently for many years to come. Tourism Towards 2030, a long-term forecast of UNWTO (2011), reveals that there is still a lot of potential for further expansion in the coming decades. Every year, international tourist arrivals increase by some 43 million on average, and by 2030 international tourist arrivals are expected to reach 1.8 billion. In 2017, the number of international arrivals reached 1,322 million (UNWTO, 2018). Global tourism is facing a paradigm shift in its geographical focus, as the East and other emerging economies are forecast to lead world tourism soon. China has become the number one tourism market and top destination. The phenomenal rise of the East in tourism is due to a range of factors. Many Asian destinations have seen incredible economic progress and consequent changes in lifestyle, education and health conditions in the last a couple of decades. China and India have advanced greatly and these countries are becoming important source markets. Tourism development has become a priority for many countries. Countries like China, Malaysia, Thailand, Singapore, Turkey, UAE, India and Indonesia have become major international destinations within a small span of time. Air travel will also grow consistently. A recent estimate of the International Air Transport Association (IATA) predicts that by 2036 more than 7.8 billion passengers will use air transport services for travel, based on a 3.6 per cent average compound annual growth rate (CAGR) (IATA, 2017). China, the US, India, Indonesia and Turkey are expected to be the fastest growing air transport markets. The forecast also suggests that the biggest driver of demand will be the Asia-Pacific region, and hence the region will be the source of more than half of new passengers over the next two decades.

As tourism, along with air transport, is poised for further growth and expansion, it is important to have measures to ameliorate its consequences. Indeed, the quantum of impacts are also growing at a rapid rate and this leads to social, cultural and environmental issues of various kinds, as discussed in the previous chapter. Climate change is a serious concern, and transport and tourism sectors are exploring ways of eliminating the impacts. The tourism sector has been searching for suitable alternatives to develop the industry sustainably and some of the measures that are in wide practice are introduced here. The aviation sector is still in the research and experimentation stage to determine the most effective solution for minimizing emissions. Other transport sectors are also trying to adopt suitable measure to reduce emissions. The automobile sector, for example, may move more rapidly towards electric sources of power.

18.2 Carbon emissions reduction strategies in the aviation sector

The aviation sector has taken the issue of air transport impact seriously, and measures are being developed and implemented to mitigate the negative effects as much as possible. The reduction of our carbon footprint is the most important target of such efforts across the world. Global bodies involved in aviation have been taking serious initiatives in reducing the environmental impacts of the sector. ICAO, the most important organization in the civil aviation sector, started efforts to minimize impacts several years ago. In 2004, it established three major goals: to limit or reduce the number of people affected by significant aircraft noise; to limit or reduce the impact of aviation emissions on local air quality; and to limit or reduce the impact of aviation greenhouse gas emissions on the global climate (ICAO, Environmental Protection, n.d.). Recently, at the 39th Session of its Assembly in 2016, a new agenda called the Carbon Offsetting and Reduction Scheme for International Aviation (CORSIA) was adopted. Its primary objective is to address any annual increase in total CO_2 emissions from international civil aviation above 2020 levels and contribute to the industry's commitment to carbon neutral growth from 2020 ("CNG2020"). Airlines have to buy carbon offsets to compensate for their growth in CO_2 emissions and they have to monitor their fuel consumption emissions with subsequent reporting to authorities concerned. ICAO has developed the Carbon Emissions Calculator, a methodology to calculate the CO_2 emissions from air travel for use in offset programmes. The ICAO Green Meetings Calculator (IGMC) is another innovative measure which is a tool designed to support decision-making in reducing the carbon emissions from air travel to attend meetings. The ICAO Fuel Savings Estimation Tool (IFSET) was also introduced to assist countries in estimating fuel savings in a manner consistent with the models approved by the Committee on Aviation Environmental Protection (CAEP) and aligned with the Global Air Navigation Plan. The ICAO Global Framework for Aviation Alternative Fuels aims to develop and use sustainable aviation fuels. In 2013, ICAO, at its 38th Assembly, adopted a policy to address the impacts of international aviation on the global climate, with a global aspirational goal of improving annual fuel efficiency by 2 per cent, and stabilizing the sectors' global CO_2 emissions at 2020 levels (carbon neutral growth from 2020). It recommended a "basket of mitigation measures" to reduce CO_2 emissions. The following are the measures included in it:

- Advancements in aircraft technology
- Operational improvements
- Sustainable alternative fuels
- Market-based measures

Note below the minimum sustainability requirements for aviation sustainable fuels, according to the ICAO Sustainable Aviation Fuel User Group (SAFUG) (n.d.):

- Jet fuel plant sources have to be developed in a manner which is non-competitive with food and where biodiversity impacts are minimized.
- The cultivation of those plant sources should not jeopardize drinking water supplies.
- Total life cycle greenhouse gas emissions from plant growth, harvesting, processing and end use should be significantly reduced compared to those associated with fuels from fossil sources.
- In developing economies, development projects should include provisions for outcomes that improve socio-economic conditions for small-scale farmers who rely on agriculture to feed them and their families, and that do not require the involuntary displacement of local populations.
- High conservation value areas and native ecosystems should not be cleared and converted for jet fuel plant source development.

According to ICAO (2016), aircraft built currently are about 80 per cent more fuel-efficient than those produced during the 1960s. Technology upgrades are evidently continuing. The new standards aiming at drastic reductions of CO_2 emissions will apply to new aircraft type designs from 2020 and to aircraft type designs that are already in production in 2023. Operational measures are also important; they have to be ensured by authorities at national levels. The ICAO Global Air Navigation Plan (GANP) involves improved operational measures to reduce CO_2 emissions. Development of sustainable aviation fuels has made good progress. Biofuels are being developed and are currently mixed with jet fuels. A number of airlines began using biofuels. Most biofuels are developed mainly from feedstock, but now it has been decided to use biofuel sources that are sustainable, do not affect food requirements, biodiversity and social sustenance of farmers, etc. Alternative fuel sources are also being explored and used for aircraft movement and airport operations. Global Market-Based Measures (MBM) have been envisaged to play a complementary role to fill the emissions gap.

The International Air Transport Association (IATA) has also initiated airline reduction targets for carbon emissions. Its current targets include (IATA, n.d.):

- An average improvement in fuel efficiency of 1.5 per cent per year from 2009 to 2020
- A cap on net aviation CO_2 emissions from 2020 (carbon-neutral growth)
- A reduction in net aviation CO_2 emissions of 50 per cent by 2050, relative to 2005 levels

In order to achieve its target, IATA has devised several strategies including an Alternative Fuels initiative, the Carbon Offset Program, Environmental Assessment (IEnvA), the Fuel and Emissions Database (FRED), and Cargo Sustainability.

Aircraft manufacturers are continually engaging in research and experiments to develop alternative fuels. Boeing reports that in 2008 the first commercial aviation flight using a sustainable biofuel mixed with traditional kerosene-based fuel was undertaken by Virgin Atlantic and GE Aviation. Sustainable biofuels are being experimentally used for reducing carbon emissions with the help of other aircraft engine manufacturers, like Pratt & Whitney and Rolls-Royce. Solar cells are being developed and used. Also, fuel cells that can directly convert hydrogen into heat and electricity without combustion are being developed for commercial use. They can reduce the need for conventional fuels, eliminate emissions and lower noise (Koehler, 2008).

18.2.1 Example: FAA strategy for reducing aviation emissions

The US Federal Aviation Administration (FAA) relies on a five-pillar comprehensive and integrated approach to set the specific initiatives needed to achieve aviation environmental goals. The following is adapted from FAA (2015), Aviation Emissions, Impacts & Mitigation: A Primer.

I: Improved scientific knowledge and integrated modelling
Its various elements include: collaboration with centres of excellence (COE) to leverage the combined resources available for aviation research and maximize technological competence; initiating the Alternative Fuel Effects on Contrails and Cruise Emissions (ACCESS) programme of NASA; applying the Aviation Emissions Characterization (AEC) Roadmap for understanding and quantifying aircraft emissions; the industry-driven Airport Cooperative Research Program (ACRP) to develop near-term, practical solutions to problems faced by airport operators; and the Aviation Climate Change Research Initiative (ACCRI) to evaluate the impacts of aviation emissions on climate change.

II: Air traffic management modernization
It aims to develop and integrate advanced operational procedures and infrastructure improvements for more operational efficiency, improving energy efficiency and thus mitigating environmental impacts. Other elements include Performance Based Navigation and required navigation performance (RNP) routes to reduce fuel burn, emissions and flight times; Optimized Profile Descents (OPD) to reduce noise, emissions and fuel consumption; and transforming the air transportation system. (NextGen capabilities are being developed which will mainly guide and track aircraft more precisely and efficiently in the air and on the ground to save fuel, decrease emissions and manage the impact of noise on communities.)

III: New aircraft and airport technologies
This pillar attempts to generate advances in engine technology and airframe configurations to lay the foundation for the next generation of aircraft with quieter, cleaner engines that can operate more efficiently and with less energy. The Continuous Lower Energy, Emissions, and Noise (CLEEN) programme is aimed at accelerating technology development, and the Voluntary Airport Low Emission (VALE) programme and Zero Emission Airport Vehicle and Infrastructure Pilot (ZEV) programme are its major components.

IV: Sustainable alternative aviation fuels
Developing and deploying sustainable alternative aviation fuels that have the potential for environmental improvements, energy security and economic stability for aviation is the main objective of this pillar. The Commercial Aviation Alternative Fuels Initiative

(CAAFI) is a major element of this. Currently the following three alternative jet fuels have been approved for blending with jet fuel:

* Fuels from biomass, coal or natural gas (Fischer–Tropsch – FT – jet fuel)
* Fuel from fats, plant oils and greases (Hydroprocessed esters and fatty acids – HEFA – jet fuel)
* Fuel from fermented sugars (synthesized iso-paraffins – SIP – jet fuel).

The Farm to Fly programme was initiated to ensure the availability of a commercially viable and sustainable aviation biofuel industry in the US, increase domestic energy security, establish regional supply chains and support rural development. The Unleaded Avgas Transition (UAT) Plan is also part of it.

V: Policies, environmental standards and market-based measures
This pillar aims to develop and implement suitable policies, standards, programmes and mechanisms for quick integration of advantageous technology and operational innovations into the commercial fleet, the airport environment and the entire national aviation system. The Aviation Sustainability Center (ASCENT) was initiated to explore ways to meet the environmental and energy goals for NextGen. The Partnership for Air Transportation Noise and Emissions Reduction (PARTNER) was formed to encourage collaboration in order to advance environmental performance, efficiency, safety and security.

18.3 Sustainable tourism development

As the concept of sustainability became a norm for development, tourism also had to embrace it without delay. The most common definition of sustainability is "meeting the needs of the present without compromising the ability of the future generations to meet their own needs" (WCED, 1987). Indeed, the tourism sector, during this time, was being criticized severely for its social, cultural and environmental consequences. Searching for alternative forms of tourism was in practice during the 1980s and 1990s. Towards the mid-1990s, sustainable tourism emerged as a new form of tourism development. Even the UN agencies concerned wanted the tourism sector to adopt sustainability principles. Giving an exact definition for sustainable tourism is difficult. When we consider the social, cultural and environmental elements of the tourism system, sustainable tourism can be defined as "the mass tourism which is economically viable, but does not destroy the resources on which the future of tourism will depend, notably the physical environment and the social fabric of the host community" (Swarbrooke, 2003). The definition speaks of mass tourism, but sustainable tourism has to be ensured in all forms. Small-scale "niche tourism" is also considered important in the realm of sustainable tourism.

The United Nations World Tourism Organization (UNWTO), a promoter of sustainable tourism around the world, specifies it in this way: "Sustainability principles refer to the environmental, economic, and socio-cultural aspects of tourism development, and a suitable balance must be established between these three dimensions to guarantee its long-term sustainability" (UNWTO, n.d.). Sustainable tourism is, thus, considered a model form of economic development that is designed to improve the quality of life of the host community, provide high-quality experiences for visitors, and maintain the quality of the environment on which the host community and the visitor depend. This type of tourism has to be one that considers the future, namely in respect of the social, cultural, economic and environmental aspects. The needs and expectations of the tourist community and the host community should be taken into consideration. The UNWTO/United Nations Environment Programme (UNEP) (2005) specifies the following principles to be followed while promoting sustainable development in tourism:

- Make optimal use of environmental resources that constitute a key element in tourism development, along with maintaining essential ecological processes and helping to conserve natural resources and biodiversity.
- Respect the socio-cultural authenticity of host communities, conserve their built and living cultural heritage and traditional values, and contribute to inter-cultural understanding and tolerance.
- Ensure viable, long-term economic operations, providing socio-economic benefits to all stakeholders that are fairly distributed, including stable employment and income-earning opportunities and social services to host communities, and contributing to poverty alleviation.
- Sustainable tourism development requires the informed participation of all relevant stakeholders, as well as strong political leadership to ensure wide participation and consensus building. Achieving sustainable tourism is a continuous process and it requires constant monitoring of impacts, introducing the necessary preventive and/or corrective measures whenever necessary.
- Sustainable tourism should also maintain a high level of tourist satisfaction and ensure a meaningful experience for the tourists, raising their awareness about sustainability issues and promoting sustainable tourism practices amongst them.

Sustainable development of tourism needs to ensure different types of sustainability. Mowforth and Munt (1998) identified four different types of sustainability: ecological, social, cultural and economic. Environmental sustainability refers to the sustainability of the ecological and other environmental parameters. There are different dimensions in this such as sustainable use of resources, elimination of impacts, creation of environmental awareness, and maintenance and management of natural features, etc. in a sustainable manner. Effective and efficient use of resources is the most crucial aspect in this. Natural resources need to be used sparingly, with effective and efficient utilization. Possible impacts should be assessed at the planning stage and effective measures have to be ensured to avoid such. Moreover, regular monitoring is necessary once the project comes into effect. Social sustainability is the next one. Tourism causes diverse social impacts. Sustainable tourism should not lead to such impacts; rather it should ensure equitable distribution of economic benefits among everyone in a society. Harmony between tourism and the societal objectives, and between tourists and the local people, should be initiated. A mutually beneficial tourism with zero impacts on society can endure for a long time. Social disharmony may cause barriers for tourism as well. Effective local community participation is essential in ensuring social sustainability.

Cultural sustainability is also an element of sustainable tourism development. Tourism has an incredible capacity to rejuvenate old art and art forms, preserve heritage sites and safeguard history. Moreover, tourism helps in cultural exchange. However, tourism can lead to excessive commercialization, commoditization, human zooification, trivialization of culture, etc. Properly planned tourism can enhance the positive impacts and minimize the negative impacts. Cultural sustainability refers to cultural aspects related to tourism being maintained at a certain level. Economic sustainability is the fourth type of sustainability to be assessed during tourism development. Sustaining economic viability is the basic concept here. Tourism in destinations has to be economically viable and survive over the long term. Moreover, it should ensure equitable distribution of economic benefits among everyone in the society. Leakage of the income generated needs to be restricted, and small- and medium-scale businesses have to be promoted to ensure maximum local entrepreneurship and income generating opportunities for the local people. The benefits of tourism can be enjoyed more by the local community than large-scale investors from abroad.

18.4 Carrying capacity

Sustainable tourism development is possible not just through the implementation of scientific planning and strategic development. A range of measures have to be undertaken to minimize the impacts and aim for sustainability. Carrying capacity is one such measure commonly used during the planning and development stages of tourism in a destination. The nature of impacts may vary from one destination to another. Impacts happen more quickly and deeply in highly fragile areas. The concept of carrying capacity has an important role in this context. Carrying capacity assessment/analysis (CCA) is a specific technique that was born in the 1960s as a method of numerical/computerized calculation for prescribing land-use limits and development control (Clark, 1996). The term "carrying capacity" was originally used in range management, in which context it referred to the number of stock that could be supported by a unit of land. Given this definition, it can therefore be inferred that every destination is subject to a carrying capacity.

Carrying capacity analysis is a basic technique used in tourism to determine the upper limits of development and visitor use, and optimum exploitation of tourism resources. Within a country, carrying capacities need to be established generally for the planning area and calculated more precisely for each development site at the community planning level (Inskeep, 1991). The concept of carrying capacity has its base in resources and their management, and the carrying capacity of a site, resort or even a region refers to its ability to be used for tourism without deteriorating. Cooper et al. (1993) say that "there may be a threshold level of tourist presence beyond which the impacts become unacceptable or intolerable". It shows the level of tourism activity or other similar parameters that can be sustained in the long term without creating serious or irreversible problems in a destination. When carrying capacity is exceeded, it is reported that the negative impacts will increase and positive impacts will diminish. Carrying capacity can basically be defined as "the amount of tourism a destination can handle" (Goeldner and Ritchie, 2006).

UNWTO (1981) defines it this way:

> the carrying capacity of a tourist resort may be defined as: the maximum number of people that may visit a tourist destination at the same time, without causing destruction of the physical, economic and socio-cultural environment and an unacceptable decrease in the quality of the visitors' satisfaction.

Wall and Mathieson (2005) have a similar opinion. According to them, carrying capacity is "the maximum number of people who can use a site without an unacceptable alteration in the physical environment and without an unacceptable decline in the quality of experience gained by visitors". Basically, carrying capacity is about developing or promoting tourism without causing a deterioration in nature, culture or the social fabric of destination communities, focusing on the threshold limit of the site. Resources and resource management are primary aspects in this. The site should be developed adhering to its capacity, and resources should not be overutilized. Swarbrooke (2003) states that there are several types of carrying capacities in respect of a destination, including: physical carrying capacity, environmental carrying capacity, infrastructure capacity, perceptual capacity and economic carrying capacity.

18.5 Environmental impact assessment

Destination planning nowadays also involves impact assessment. Environmental impact assessment (EIA) was introduced as a tool in the planning process, as a part of environmental management initiatives. EIA procedures are being increasingly applied throughout the world to all types of development, including tourism projects, to ensure that any negative environmental impacts are identified in advance, analysed and minimized. With increasing concerns about the environmental impacts of development, the EIA procedure has been set out to assess the impacts of the proposed development projects. EIA is considered to be one of the primary tools (to date) for the environmental manager and a useful guide for decision-making (Khoshoo, 1991). It has been used by national decision-makers in their efforts to prevent further environmental degradation.

The EIA process is seen as a means of identifying potential impacts but also of enabling the integration of the environment and development (Green and Hunter, 1992). EIA is primarily carried out to identify risks, minimize adverse impacts, determine environmental acceptability and obtain environmentally sound proposals through research, management and monitoring, and also to manage conflict and public participation (Peiyi, 2000). According to Middleton and Hawkins (1998), EIA is designed to prevent the degradation of environments by giving decision-makers better information about the likely consequences that the development actions could have on the environment. It thus informs planning decisions and will ensure that decision-makers take environmental issues into account when making development control decisions. The most significant benefit of EIA is the ability to compare the developmental options and the screening of alternate sites for locating development projects. For getting maximum benefits, EIA must identify measures to minimize effects and evaluate both the beneficial and adverse environmental impacts of the development project (Khoshoo, 1991).

Generally, the identification and measurement of potential impacts assessed to varying degrees of precision depends on the nature of the project and the data available. At the planning stage of a proposed project, the significant environmental impacts can be identified and examined, and measures suggested for their prevention or mitigation. There is no set structure for the EIA process, but it is generally assumed that EIAs have to assess future levels of noise pollution, visual impact, air pollution, hydrological impact, land use and landscape change associated with the development. Holden (2000) states that most of the EIAs involve five stages, such as identification of the impact, measurement of the impact, interpretation of the significance of the impact, displaying the results of the assessment and the identification of appropriate monitoring schemes. Checklists are widely used as a technology for conducting EIAs. They are somewhat useful for undertaking a preliminary assessment, but have limitations as a complete tool for the EIA. Matrices will be a useful technique for evaluation which summarize and synthesize the impacts so that comprehensive evaluation can be carried out for all factors. Also used are systems and network diagrams, which attempt to describe more comprehensively the cause and effect relationship, listing impacts and how these are generated through the effects on resources. In this context, modelling and computer simulation are sometimes utilized with mixed results. Map overlays are also used in this context; they are intended to identify areas of lesser conflicts among resources, the use of alternatives and environmental values. By superimposing on top of maps, they can depict various uses for values such as vegetation, water resources, unique wildlife habitats, etc. It is often possible to screen areas which have to be exempted in locating the projects. But this doesn't reveal relationships and is not good enough to differentiate among impacts. The Delphi study is one of the techniques which can be used for EIA. Adaptive environmental assessment and management (AEAM) is one of the recently developed tools used in the context of EIA.

18.6 Environmental auditing

Environmental auditing can be defined as a process comprising of a systematic, documented, regular and objective evaluation of the environmental performance of any aspect of an organization. The term auditing is generally referred to as a methodological examination involving analysis, tests and confirmation of a facility's procedures and practices with the goal of verifying whether they comply with legal requirements, internal policies and accepted practices. In the context of tourism, it is important for organizations to ensure environmental performance, recognize the specific problems of an organization and have a ready means for self-regulation of its environmental performance. The essential purpose of environmental management systems in particular is to ensure that commitments made are implemented, that environmental standards are met, and that relevant procedures are in place and are being followed. The concept of environmental auditing is a relatively recent development and an evolving technique.

18.7 Visitor management

Number of visitors is a cause of impact generation. When a destination has more tourists than its carrying capacity, it leads to increased impacts. In such cases, visitor management measures can be applied to minimize the impact of excess visitor concentration. These measures primarily focus on restricting and managing the visitor flow and their activities in a destination. Visitor management measures are broadly classified into two: "hard measures and soft measures" (Page, 2007). The former places extensive and permanent restrictions on visitor activity. The latter involves improving marketing, interpretation, and planning and visitor coordination. Visitor management models involve the recreation opportunity spectrum (ROS), carrying capacity model, visitor activity management programme (VAMP), visitor impact management model (VIMM), the limits of acceptable change (LAC) and tourism optimization management model (TOMM) (Hall and McArthur, 1998).

18.7.1 Recreation opportunity spectrum (ROS)

This is a land zoning system identifying the environmental setting and offering guidelines for appropriate activities and visitor experience. It provides a framework that is widely used to guide outdoor recreation planning and management. Developed back in the 1970s, it helps to classify and monitor existing and desired recreation settings, and in identifying and determining the diversity of recreation opportunities for a natural geographical location, based on the idea that for visitor services, quality is best assured by offering the group of opportunities suited to the full range of expected tourists. From a visitor's perspective, the output is providing opportunities to participate in preferred activities in the appropriate physical, social and managerial setting. Veal (2002) illustrates ROS in this way:

> Classification of areas in which people might seek outdoor recreation along a continuum from the totally undeveloped, such as pristine wilderness ("primitive"), to the highly developed, such as a fully serviced camping site and recreation area ("modern"). Against this are set the sorts of activity which the management and users of these areas might engage in to maintain the appropriate ambience of the site and compatibility with visitor expectations.

It provides a means for classifying the range of recreational opportunities and managing that range. It is a flexible and adaptable approach and valuable for integrated planning, particularly for analysis and planning in a region with a range of natural attractions. Ultimately, using an ROS will provide a mechanism to inventory existing opportunities, analyse the effects of other resource activities, assess the consequences of management decisions on planned opportunities, and develop standards and guidelines for planned settings and monitoring activities.

18.7.2 The limit to acceptable change (LAC)

This focuses on the management of visitor impacts by identifying, first, desirable conditions for visitor activity to occur, and second, how much change is acceptable. Basically it's a framework for establishing acceptable and appropriate resources and social conditions in recreation settings (Stankey, 1984). This process identifies appropriate and acceptable resource and social conditions and the actions needed to protect or achieve those conditions. Monitoring programmes determine whether desirable conditions are within acceptable standards, and determine the management actions required to achieve the desired conditions. It is ideal in deciding the most appropriate and acceptable resources and social conditions in natural areas. Moreover, it incorporates opportunity classes based on the concepts of ROS. Ultimately this provides a strategic and tactical plan for the area based on defined limits of acceptable change for each opportunity class, with indicators of change that can be used to monitor ecological and social conditions (Nilsen and Tayler, 1998).

18.7.3 Visitor activity management programme (VAMP)

VAMP is a planning system which integrates visitor need with resources to reduce specific visitor opportunities, and is designed to resolve conflicts and tensions between visitor, heritage and heritage managers. It requires the heritage manager to identify the provider for and market to designated visitor groups.

18.7.4 Visitor impact management model (VIMM)

VIMM focuses on reducing or controlling the impacts that threaten the quality of heritage and visitor experience. It is an eight-step sequential process for assessing and managing visitor impacts aimed at: identification of problem conditions (unacceptable visitor impacts); determination of potential causal factors affecting the occurrence and severity of the unacceptable impacts; and selection of potential management strategies (Graefe et al., 1990). It uses explicit statements of management objectives and research. Also, it monitors to determine heritage and social conditions and then generates a range of management strategies to deal with the impacts.

18.7.5 Tourism optimization management model (TOMM)

This focuses on achieving optimum performance by addressing the sustainability of the heritage, viability of the tourism industry and empowerment of stakeholders. It covers environmental and experimental elements, the characteristics of the tourist market, economics conditions of the tourism industry and socio-cultural conditions of the local community. It contains three main parts: context analysis, a monitoring programme and management response system (Hall and McArthur, 1998).

18.8 Growth of travel and tourism and the challenges

Tourism is growing at a remarkable pace. Although it is often faced with challenges, it shows extreme resilience to bounce back. We discuss some of the modern challenges tourism faces here.

18.8.1 Terrorism

Terrorism is a very serious issue for tourism. Tourism is a highly sensitive sector. A terrorist attack or just the fear of a possible attack can keep tourists from visiting destinations. Many tourist destinations are already dealing with consequences of terrorism, e.g. France, Turkey, Egypt and many others. Terrorism has the potential to curb tourism's remarkable growth significantly. Indeed, recurring terrorist attacks can ruin a tourist destination. A single bomb blast can hamper tourism in a place temporarily or even permanently. In 2002, Bali, an island tourist destination in Indonesia, was struck by massive bomb blasts killing more than 200 people. It led to a fall in tourism there for a few years, and many people lost jobs as the economy suffered. France has seen a number of terrorist attacks in recent years, as have countries in the Middle East.

18.8.2 Communicable diseases

The spread of communicable diseases is a major issue for tourism. The threat of such diseases, which occur at regular intervals, has impeded the progress of tourism in many parts of the world. Severe acute respiratory syndrome (SARS) curbed the flow of tourists to Asian countries for a short period, while the spread of the Ebola virus in West Africa kept many tourists from visiting countries in the region. More recently, tourism in Latin American countries was threatened by the Zika virus outbreak. Similar incidents are likely to occur in the future as well.

18.8.3 Political instabilities

Political instabilities are always serious issues in tourism. The intervention of political issues has stalled tourism progress on many occasions in history. After the First and

Second World Wars, political instabilities occurred at different junctures at different locations in the world. The nature and degree of political issues can vary. Notwithstanding the varying nature and depth, any issue can pose a threat to tourism. There are plenty of examples in the contemporary history of tourism as well. Currently, tourism in Iran, Turkey, Tunisia and Egypt is negatively (and considerably) affected by political turmoil. In its recent history of tourism, Thailand has also experienced political unrest in recent years, though it was short-lived.

18.8.4 Economic downturns

In the years following 2008, the world suffered through an economic depression, which impacted tourism directly. The number of tourist arrivals decreased considerably over this period. Similar events in history have caused tourism levels to fall. This is because tourism's progress is directly linked to economic progress. So as economic downturns occur, the tourism sector experiences similar setbacks.

18.8.5 Climate change

Climate change can be a major challenge for tourism in the future. Increasing temperatures, rising sea levels and unpredictable climatic conditions can harm tourism at any point. Changes in seasonality, threats to winter tourism and beach tourism, further increases in temperatures in warmer destinations, etc. are the major challenges tourism is expected to face in the future. Indeed, destinations and countries have to keep an eye on this and prepare long-term plans well in advance. Tourism itself is even a contributor to climate change. According to NASA (in Page, 2007), climate change is the change in the average or typical climate of a region or city, or even that of the earth's surface. Due to climate change, extreme variations in climate can occur. Increases in the average temperature of the earth's surface has been an ongoing phenomenon for the last few centuries and is called global warming. The effects of climate change can be summed up as follows:

- Rising of average global temperature
- Rising sea levels
- Increasing frequency of extreme climatic events

The depletion of the ozone layer is a prime reason for those phenomena. Excessive emissions of greenhouse gases lead to the depletion of the ozone layer and climate change in general. The burning of fossil fuels emits greenhouse gases in large quantities. Many tourism activities also lead to harmful gas emissions. The transportation sector contributes the largest share, with aviation the main culprit.

Apart from its contribution towards climate change, tourism may face a number of consequences as a result of climate change. Increasing temperature is going to create many issues for tourism. Due to this phenomenon, the seasons can be extended in some destinations; while they may be shortened in others. Due to temperature variations, some communicable diseases can be more easily spread. Polar regions may face the melting of ice. As a consequence, more water will flow into the sea and sea levels will rise. It can also lead to floods. Increasing sea levels may lead to the submerging of some islands under the sea. Beach tourism may be affected more by climate change. Rising sea levels can affect beaches severely. Erosion can also be a problem. Reduced water supplies and more sandstorms are some other effects. Coral reefs may face increasing levels of bleaching and even extinction due to global warming. Beach space may be shrunk. Decreasing snow cover and shrinking glaciers can cause many other issues. Winter tourism may be badly affected due to lack of snow in winter sport destinations and increased snow-making costs, shorter winter sports seasons and reduced aesthetics of landscapes. Due to loss of snow and ice in lower regions, greater numbers of visitors could flock to destinations at higher altitudes.

Seasonality in destinations can be affected. Seasonality variations in destinations can cause social and economic impacts for destinations. Short seasons may cause economic problems. Increasing frequency and intensity of storms can pose risks for tourism facilities, increased insurance costs/loss of insurability, and business interruption costs. Torrential rains, cyclones, floods, tsunamis, etc. often severely affect tourist arrivals. They can also affect the natural and cultural heritage. Monuments and other heritage aspects/ sites may be damaged. More frequent and larger forest fires, loss of natural attractions, greater flooding risk, damage to tourism infrastructure, soil changes (e.g. moisture levels, erosion and acidity), loss of archaeological assets and other natural resources, with impacts on destination attractions, etc. are just some of the tourism consequences of climate change (UNWTO–UNEP–WMO, 2007)

18.9 Crisis management

Recurring crises trouble tourism often. Natural calamities are more frequent nowadays. Man-made issues also occur quite often. The tourism sector at all levels, from the national level to the local level and industry levels, has to be ready to tackle the issues as and when they occur. Anticipatory mechanism and crisis management plans are necessary. Preparing efficient crisis management mechanism is a challenge for the agencies involved in tourism management.

Crisis management is all about the prevention of a crisis or the efficient management after the events of a crisis, with the objective of minimizing the impacts and recovering from the situation without delay in order to restore the normal conditions. It is defined as "a systematic attempt by an organization and its stakeholders to manage or prevent crises from occurring, such that key stakeholders believe the success outcomes outweigh the failure outcomes" (Pearson and Clair, 1998). Crisis management should put in place a preparatory action plan as and when a crisis occurs. The range of actions after a crisis should be appropriate to the circumstances. The unpredictability of crisis is what makes the task of crisis management so difficult. Along with the preset preparations, quick decisions are fundamental in responding to a crisis. A crisis management plan is a prerequisite in any type of organization. Effective communication and coordination are key in the success of crisis management.

The travel and tourism industry is prone to crises of different kinds. One or another kind of crisis hits the tourism sector often. Every year the growth of tourism is hampered by crises of various magnitudes and natures. Yet, the sector shows extreme resilience to bounce back to growth. Among the components of tourism, air transportation is one sector that faces regular crises. Terrorist attacks, bomb blasts, flight hijackings, fire, flight accidents, etc. become severe issues with wider impacts. Malfunctions or damage to key airport equipment and accidents cause a different type of crisis for air transportation. Natural disasters constitute other major issues. Terrorism often hits tourism hard in specific locations and can decimate industries, causing extreme socio-economic hardship. Similar issues can include demonstrations, strikes, war, violence, etc. The tourism industry can be faced with heavy storms, hurricanes, floods, bush fires, earthquakes, avalanches, tsunamis, etc. Communicable diseases that spread rapidly create panic among tourists, causing the destination's tourism industry to suffer severely due to the sudden decline in demand. Usually countries will have a broad crisis management framework, and based on the same, regions/states and other political divisions will have crisis management frameworks. At all these levels, there will be crisis management teams comprising all the relevant stakeholders and departments. Companies, airports, etc. also have crisis management teams. They undertake meetings to discuss possible crises and undertake mock drills to become trained and to ensure confidence among the stakeholders in handling emergencies. When a crisis occurs, the team will hold meetings immediately and actions will be quickly taken. The role and responsibilities of each of the divisions and members would have been specified and they have to perform their duties without delay. The crisis management communication team is also important. A spokesperson has to be officially appointed to communicate with the external world and assess the happenings, reduce the panic and prevent the wrong messages from being communicated. It would be ideal to establish notification and monitoring systems. A media and social media handling strategy has to be developed to minimize rumours. The crisis management team members need to act accordingly, quickly and with commitment. The efforts have to be monitored, reviewed and remedial actions need to be taken regularly. Furthermore, it is very important to conduct a post-crisis analysis with the objective to prevent such occurrences in the future.

Even if tourism is facing a range of challenges, it is poised for further growth. The advancements of tourism can be due to many factors. Some of the most important are listed here:

- Tremendous developments in information and communication technology
- Advancements in transport technology, particularly aviation-related
- Incredible dynamism and new product development in the niche tourism segment
- Emergence of new tourism markets
- Decreasing fuel prices and consequent reduction of travel costs
- Emergence of new destinations
- Progressing economic and social status of populations
- Emergence of new economic powers
- Increased urbanization
- Increasing affordability for air transport
- Enhancement in health status of people
- Growing awareness of travel opportunities
- Rising interest of governments in developing tourism
- Influence of social media and mobile applications in inducing travel propensity
- Globalization, privatization, liberalization, etc.

18.10 Summary

As carbon emissions and climate change loom large, urgent measures are warranted for mitigating such consequences of development. The leaders in aviation, like ICAO, have been urging stakeholders in the aviation sector to target carbon emissions reductions. Advancements in aircraft technology, operational improvements and the use of sustainable alternative fuels are the primary strategies being adopted by the industry at large. Research relating to pollution and carbon emissions reductions is ongoing. As the current and projected global economic, social and technological environments are favourable, tourism is poised for further remarkable growth. However, its impacts have been a matter of criticism for several years. A range of measures are being adopted to ameliorate the impacts of tourism. The concept of sustainable tourism is the most important among them. Sustainable tourism is aimed at the equitable development of tourism without harming nature, culture or society. Carrying capacity analysis, EIA and visitor management practices are popular among the sustainability measures for mitigating the impacts of tourism. Though tourism continues to progress, a range of issues threaten to halt its smooth run. As always, however, tourism is expected to demonstrate its resilience to various external forces. There are many reasons to facilitate the development of tourism to greater heights. Tourism has to progress and authorities have to develop it. However, it is necessary to develop tourism in a sustainable manner in order to minimize its impacts.

Review questions

Short/medium answer type questions

- Describe the carbon emissions reduction strategies in the aviation sector.
- Describe the concept of sustainable tourism development.
- What do we mean by carrying capacity?
- Discuss the application of environmental impact assessment (EIA) in tourism.
- What do we mean by environmental auditing?
- Define visitor management in tourism.
- What are the challenges faced by tourism currently?

Essay type questions

- Describe the strategies and measures used for mitigating the impacts of travel and tourism.

References

Clark, J. R. (1996) *Coastal Zone Management Handbook*. Boca Raton, FL: Lewis Publishers.

Cooper, C., Fletcher, J., Gilbert, D. and Wanhill, S. (1993) *Tourism Principles and Practices*. London: ELBS-Pitman Publishing.

FAA (2015) Aviation Emissions, Impacts & Mitigation: A Primer, available at https://www.faa.gov/regulations_policies/policy_guidance/envir_policy/media/primer_jan2015.pdf (accessed 24 May 2017).

Goeldner, R. C. and Ritchie, J. R. B. (2006) *Tourism Principles, Practices, Philosophies*. New Delhi: John Wiley & Sons.

Graefe, A. R., Kuss, F. R. and Vaske, J. J (1990) *Visitor Impact Management: The Planning Framework*. Washington, DC: National Parks and Conservation Association.

Green, H. and Hunter, C. (1992) The Environmental Impact Assessment of Tourism Development, in P. Johnson and B. Thomas (eds), *Perspectives in Tourism Policy*. London: Mansell.

Hall, C. M. and McArthur, S. (1998) *Integrated Heritage Management*. London: Stationery Office.

Holden, A. (2000) *Environment and Tourism*. London: Routledge.

IATA (2017) 2036 Forecast Reveals Air Passengers Will Nearly Double to 7.8 Billion, Press Release No.: 55, 24 October 2017.

IATA, Improving Environmental Performance, available at http://www.iata.org/whatwedo/environment/Pages/index.aspx (accessed 18 January 2018).

ICAO, Environmental Protection, available at https://www.icao.int/environmental-protection/Pages/default.aspx (accessed 14 January 2018).

ICAO, Sustainable Aviation Fuel User Group, available at https://www.icao.int/environmental-protection/GFAAF/Pages/Project.aspx?ProjectID=13.

ICAO (2016) Policies and Practices to Improve the Efficiency of International Aviation and Reduce CO_2 Emissions, available at https://unfccc.int/sites/default/files/07_icao_icao_secretariat.pdf.

Inskeep, E. (1991) *Tourism Planning: An Integrated and Sustainable Development Approach*. Toronto: John Wiley & Sons.

Khoshoo, T. N. (1991) *Environmental Concerns and Strategies*. New Delhi: Ashish Publishing House.

Koehler, T. (2008) Boeing Makes History with Flights of Fuel Cell Demonstrator Airplane, available at http://www.boeing.com/news/frontiers/archive/2008/may/ts_sf04.pdf (accessed 25 January 2018).

Middleton, V. T. C. and Hawkins, R. (1998) *Sustainable Tourism: A Marketing Perspective*, Oxford: Butterworth-Heinemann.

Mowforth, M. and Munt, I. (1998) *Tourism and Sustainability: A New Tourism in the Third World*. London: Routledge.

Nilsen, P. and Tayler, G. (1998) A Comparative Analysis of Protected Area Planning and Management Frameworks, pp. 49–57, in S. F. McCool and D. N. Cole (compilers), Limits of Acceptable Change and Related Processes: Programs and Future Directions. Proceedings of conference May 20–22 1997, Missoula, MN.

Page, S. (2007) *Tourism Management: Managing for Change*. Oxford: Butterworth-Heinemann.

Pearson, C. M. and Clair, J. A. (1998) Reframing Crisis Management, *Academy of Management Review* 23(1): 59–76.

Peiyi, D. (2000) Environmental Impact Assessment, in J. Jafari (ed.), *Encyclopaedia of Tourism*. London: Routledge, p. 299.

Stankey, G. H. (1984) Carrying Capacity in Recreational Settings: Evolution, Appraisal, and Application, *Leisure Science* 6(4): 453–473.

Swarbrooke, J. (2003) *The Development and Management of Visitor Attractions*. New Delhi: Butterworth-Heinemann.

UNWTO (1981) *Saturation of Tourist Destinations: Report of the Secretary General*. Madrid: United Nations World Tourism Organization.

UNWTO/UNEP (2005) *Making Tourism More Sustainable – A Guide for Policy Makers*. Madrid: UNWTO, pp. 11–12.

UNWTO (2011) Tourism Towards 2030: Global Overview. UNWTO General Assembly, 19th Session, Gyeongju, Republic of Korea, 10 October 2011, Madrid: UNWTO.

UNWTO (2018) International Tourism Results: The Highest in Seven Years, Press Release:18003, dated 15 January 2018, Madrid: UNWTO.

UNWTO, Sustainable Development of Tourism, available at http://sdt.unwto.org/content/about-us-5 (accessed 30 January 2018).

UNWTO–UNEP–WMO (2007) Climate Change and Tourism: Responding to Global Challenges, available at sdt.unwto.org/sites/all/files/docpdf/summarydavose.pdf (accessed 25 November 2016).

Veal, A. J. (2002) *Leisure and Tourism Policy and Planning*. Oxford: CABI International.

Wall, G. and Mathieson, A. (2005) *Tourism: Change, Impacts and Opportunities*. New York: Prentice Hall.

WCED (1987) *Our Common Future*. Oxford: Oxford University Press.

Index

Printed in the United States
by Baker & Taylor Publisher Services